RELIGION AND THE CONSTITUTION

Religion and the Constitution

VOLUME 1:
FREE EXERCISE AND FAIRNESS

Kent Greenawalt

PRINCETON UNIVERSITY PRESS

PRINCETON AND OXFORD

Library of Congress Cataloging-in-Publication Data

Greenawalt, Kent, 1936–
Religion and the constitution / Kent Greenawalt.
p. cm.
Includes bibliographical references and index.

Contents: Vol. 1. Free exercise and fairness

ISBN-13: 978-0-691-12582-4 (alk. paper)
ISBN-10: 0-691-12582-1 (alk. paper)

1. Freedom of religion—United States. 2. Church and state—United States. I. Title.
KF4783.G74 2006
342.7308'52—dc22   2005049522

British Library Cataloging-in-Publication Data is available

This book has been composed in Sabon and Helvetica Neue

Printed on acid-free paper. ∞

pup.princeton.edu

Printed in the United States of America

1 3 5 7 9 10 8 6 4 2

To Elaine, with love

CONTENTS

PREFACE

As I write this preface, the law of the religion clauses of the Constitution faces an uncertain future, with President George W. Bush appointing two new justices to a Supreme Court that has been sharply divided over the content of those clauses. Whatever the near-term effects of these appointments, we can expect debates about the meaning of religious liberty to persist, crucial as that liberty is to how we understand the society in which we live.

This volume, the first of two on the Free Exercise and Establishment clauses of the First Amendment and on the ideals of liberal democracy that those clauses represent, has been many years in the making, beginning back in 1994–95, when I was fortunate to be a Visiting Fellow at the Center for Human Values at Princeton University. Over that time, I have benefited enormously from the criticism of colleagues, discussions with students, some of whom have provided invaluable research help, and the help of assistants who have transformed my not so clear handwriting into readable drafts.

Among the academic institutions at which I have given presentations or attended conferences, and at which interchanges with colleagues have enriched my understanding, are the University of Illinois School of Law, University of Colorado, University of Notre Dame Law School, University of Texas Law School, University of Michigan School of Law, Loyola of Los Angeles School of Law, Loyola of Chicago School of Law, Villanova University School of Law, Fordham University School of Law, New York Law School, San Diego University School of Law, Harvard Center for Ethics and the Professions, Tulane Law School, Marshall-Whythe School of Law at William and Mary, Emory University School of Law, Catholic University, Marquette University, University of Pennsylvania School of Law, and my own institution, Columbia University. My greatest debt over the years has been to students in a seminar on the law of church and state, who have listened, mostly patiently, to my various ideas, and have responded with thoughtful suggestions of their own.

Among the colleagues who have contributed valuable criticisms and suggestions are Lawrence Alexander, Barbara Armacost, Vincent Blasi, Laura Brill, Michael Dorf, Harold Edgar, Melvin Eisenberg, Christopher Eisgruber, Stephen Ellmann, Cynthia Estlund, Richard Fallon, Jill Fisch, George Fletcher, Glenn George, Amy Gutmann, Alan Hyde, Jim Liebman, George

Kateb, Philip Kitcher, Stephen Macedo, David Mapel, Henry Monaghan, Gerald Neuman, James Nickel, Sachin Pandya, Andrzej Rapaczynski, Melissa Rogers, Lawrence Sager, Carol Sanger, Frederick Schauer, Stephen Smith, Geoffrey Stone, Peter Strauss, Jeremy Waldron, and Jay Wexler. Some of the persons who have provided superb research help are Rima Al-Mokarrab, Bethany Alsup, James Beattie, Edward Blatnik, Darrell Cafasso, Stephen Gale Dick, Michael Dowdle, Lisa Ells, Gregory Fayer, Michael Galligan, Paul Horwitz, Mark Hulbert, Adam Kolber, Daniel Krockmalnic, Young Lee, Kenneth Levy, Nancy Clare Morgan, Sachin Pandya, Thomas Rosen, Victoria Shin, Derrick Toddy, and Ken Ward.

Successive computer drafts of the chapters of this book were produced by Sally Wrigley (up to her death in 2001), Katherine Bobbitt, and Jinah Paek. They worked with great care, caught inaccuracies, and made editorial improvements. In addition to significant editorial assistance, Ms. Bobbitt also provided much nonlegal research help. Marc DeGirolami, Rachael Patterson, and Ms. Bobbitt prepared the index swiftly and with care.

As with my book *Does God Belong in Public Schools?* I have had the good fortune to work with Ian Malcolm, Richard Isomaki, Terri O'Prey, and Ellen Foos. In his substantive editing, Mr. Malcolm spotted many important issues that I had overlooked and many points in need of clarification, and he typically offered thoughtful suggestions for resolution that I was sensible enough to embrace. Mr. Isomaki scrutinized this long manuscript with great care, improving its language and greatly reducing its errors. Ms. Foos has seen the book through the publication process effectively and with good humor. Reviewing the manuscript for the press, Andrew Koppelman made many perceptive criticisms that led to improvements.

As throughout my academic career, my family—Elaine, Robert, Carla, Sasha, Claire, Andrei, Sarah, and David—have done much to sustain me and to give a sense of purpose to my life.

Some of the material in the chapters of this book has previously appeared in "All or Nothing at All: The Defeat of Selective Conscientious Objection," 1971 *Supreme Court Review* 31; "Religion as a Concept in Constitutional Law," 72 *California Law Review* 753 (1984); "Freedom of Association and Religious Association," in Amy Gutmann, ed., *Freedom of Association* 109–44 (Princeton: Princeton University Press, 1998); "Hands Off! Civil Court Involvement in Conflicts over Religious Property," 98 *Columbia Law Review* 1843 (1998); "Five Questions about Religion Judges Are Afraid to Ask," in Nancy L. Rosenblum, ed., *Obligations of Citizenship* 196–244 (Princeton: Princeton University Press, 2000); Title VII and Religious Liberty, 33 *Loyola University Chicago Law Journal* 1 (2001), "Teaching about Religion in Public Schools," 17 *Journal of Law and Politics* 329 (2002);

"Religion and the Rehnquist Court," 99 *Northwestern University Law Review* 145 (2004); *Does God Belong in Public Schools?* (Princeton: Princeton University Press, 2005); "Child Custody, Religious Practices, and Conscience," 76 *University of Colorado Law Review* 965 (2005).

In a work that will, I hope, be of value to both legal professionals and others who consider the religion clauses of the Constitution, I have adopted a system of citation that blends legal and humanities styles. The order of elements in a citation is generally that of legal style, while typefaces follow the conventions of the humanities.

RELIGION AND THE CONSTITUTION

Introduction

Americans should freely practice their religions, and government should not establish any religion: these are crucial principles of our liberal democracy. Although the principles themselves receive wide assent, people disagree intensely over what they signify and how they apply. Does treating religious individuals and organizations fairly mean regarding them like everyone else or giving them a mix of special benefits and disadvantages?

This book, volume 1 of *Religion and the Constitution*, concentrates on the free exercise of religion; a companion will focus on nonestablishment. These are of course the two main pillars in the Constitution's treatment of religion. Because issues about free exercise and nonestablishment intertwine, however, we need to examine various establishment concerns here, most notably problems raised by classifications along religious lines. Both volumes discuss the declaration in the Constitution's First Amendment that "Congress shall make no law respecting an establishment of religion, or prohibiting the free exercise thereof."[1] But in each volume we shall also consider legislative choices and claims of moral and political philosophy that reach beyond constitutional constraints.

My approach to the broad subject is grounded on three fundamental assumptions. First, ideas about free exercise and nonestablishment are not reducible to any single value; a number of values count. Second, sound approaches to the state's treatment of religion cannot be collapsed into any single formula or set of formulas. For example, one pervasive issue is whether religious claims may (or must) be treated differently from analogous nonreligious claims. Against those who assert that similar treatment should always or never be required, I resist any uniform answer, arguing that a great deal depends on what kind of claim is involved. Although no ready formula is available to resolve problems about government and religion, we can identify major considerations that legislators and judges need to take into account. I sketch the most important of these considerations in a later section of this introduction, as well as outline some of the most general values or principles that underlie or motivate this book on free exercise.

Third, we can best work toward sensible approaches by addressing many discrete issues. These reveal rich variations in the state's relations with reli-

---

[1] U.S. Const., amend. 1.

gion and show the complexity of arriving at satisfactory treatments of practical conflicts. This undertaking from the bottom up illuminates more than does a conceptual apparatus that works downward from a few abstract principles to particular applications. Thus, the strategy of both volumes is contextual, investigating the force of conflicting values over a range of legal and political issues.

This introductory chapter outlines a few free exercise problems and lays the conceptual framework for what follows.

TYPICAL FREE EXERCISE ISSUES

The most blatant affronts to people's free exercise of religion involve hardships they suffer just because of their religious beliefs and practices. Throughout history, public authorities have imposed a wide range of penalties and disabilities on dissenters from the dominant religious faith. In one modern American case, discussed in chapter 3, the City of Hialeah adopted ordinances to ban animal sacrifice.[2] Their undoubted target was the unpopular practice of animal sacrifice by adherents of the Santeria religion.

The Hialeah case is unusual for modern liberal democracies. Legislators rarely discriminate overtly among religions or target religious practices. Rather, they adopt laws that are uncontroversial in most of their applications; the crucial issue then becomes whether legislatures or courts should create privileged exceptions that are based directly on a person's religious convictions or rest on some other standard, such as "conscience," that includes religious convictions but does not distinguish between them and similar nonreligious convictions.

Here are some illustrations. Should the government excuse religious pacifists, all pacifists, or no pacifists from a military draft? Given a general requirement that children stay in school up to the age of sixteen, should officials allow a religious group to withdraw their children at an earlier age, so they may undertake vocational training for their communal life? Should a state that prohibits use of peyote allow members of a church to ingest that drug as the center of their worship services? Should a law that forbids gender discrimination in employment leave untouched religious groups that permit only men to be clergy?

Less stark conflicts between religious claims and standard legal duties also arise. Prisoners would like to wear religious jewelry despite a prison ban on jewelry. A church wants to use its community house for a school that is

---

[2] *Church of the Lukumi Babalu Aye, Inc. v. City of Hialeah*, 508 U.S. 520 (1993).

forbidden by zoning regulations. An Orthodox Jewish military officer wears his yarmulke in violation of a regulation that instructs personnel not to wear headgear indoors.

Conflicts between religious convictions and general laws may be indirect rather than direct. A Sabbatarian's religion requires him to close his store on Saturday. He *can* comply with that obligation *and* with a law that requires all stores to close on Sunday, but the law and his religion combine to create economic hardship, and a temptation to disregard his religious convictions.

Yet other free exercise problems arise because the law must settle disagreements between private persons. A couple divorces. The father wants to take his daughter to his church on Sunday; the mother wants to stop him, because they agreed when they married that their children would be raised as Jewish.

These and similar problems occupy this volume. Its companion analyzes establishment questions, such as these: should the government encourage or sponsor religious practice? should state schools teach about religion? should the government support religious hospitals and schools, and, if so, under what conditions? when do efforts to "accommodate" religious practices cross over the boundary to become impermissible establishments?

Basic Values and the Religion Clauses

Protecting free religious exercise is one undoubted and fundamental aim of the Constitution's religion clauses. Many people care deeply about their religious beliefs and practices, and they feel that their religious obligations supersede duties to the state if the two collide. These basic sentiments constitute a strong reason why governments should avoid interfering with religious participation insofar as they reasonably can. Another fundamental purpose of the religion clauses is to keep the enterprises of religion and government distinct. The state should not sponsor any particular religion; in turn, it should not be controlled by religious authorities.

I should perhaps say at the outset that I believe strongly in the major values that lie behind free exercise and nonestablishment. People should be free to adopt religious beliefs and engage in religious practices because that is one vital aspect of personal autonomy, and because recognition of that freedom is more conducive to social harmony in a modern society than any alternative. I believe, further, that most people experience some transcendent dimension in their lives and that, despite the unavailability of decisive evidence, that experience reflects some objective reality. Whether the government should involve itself in promoting religious values may be arguable, but my own view is that personal autonomy is most fully recognized and the flourishing of religion itself is best served if the government does not sponsor religious understandings and practices (this complex subject is mainly the concern of volume 2).

Many readers will disagree with some of these value judgments of mine. No doubt, what follows is influenced to some degree by my own fundamental understandings, but I am aiming to write in a way that does not depend directly on them. I will be making claims that rest on the country's political and legal traditions and on undeniable facts about its present condition, most particularly its religious diversity. No reader can dismiss claims about religious exercise with the observation that religious views are silly; no reader can dismiss claims about nonestablishment with the assertion that the true religious understanding is easily acquired. A serious person trying to grapple with the state's treatment of religion has to undertake a much more arduous effort to distill the nature of our country's traditions and of sound practice in modern political democracies.

These values of free exercise and disestablishment are broadly compatible, indeed reinforcing; and those who favored disestablishment at the country's founding believed that it promoted religious liberty.[3] A government that awards the high officials of one religion seats in the legislature, uses tax funds to pay its clergy, and teaches its doctrines in public schools impinges on the religious exercise of dissenters. Although nonestablishment still promotes free exercise across a wide span of subjects, modern social life also throws up situations in which values of free exercise and nonestablishment lie in tension or conflict. Should the government grant its workers who worship on Saturday that day off? Doing so would undoubtedly assist their exercise of religion; but the cost may be to "establish," or at least favor, their religious motivations in comparison with nonreligious reasons, such as time with family at home, that lead other workers to want free Saturdays.

Such conflicts of value illustrate how concerns about equality and fairness pervade religion cases. Are Saturday worshipers relevantly equal or unequal to workers who want to spend Saturdays with their families? Much turns on the respects in which people are significantly equal to each other, and on when they deserve the same treatment. Such inquiries, with their implication that unequal treatment is unfair, are a major aspect of problems about religion and the state. Because arguments about equality can confuse, a few clarifications are helpful.

A conclusion that people should get "equal treatment" may flow irresistibly from the application of an independent standard or reflect a more funda-

---

[3] The original clauses of the Bill of Rights applied only against the federal government. Some founders who wanted to prevent a federal establishment approved of degrees of state establishment of religion, and an important aspect of the Establishment Clause was keeping the federal govern-

mental notion about the equality of citizens.[4] If one aspect of the free exercise of religion is a principle that governments cannot compel individuals to attend church, all people will equally have the right not to be compelled; but their entitlement to equal treatment simply follows from the nature of the right against compelled religious exercise. Claims about individual *equality* are redundant here, doing "no work."

A more potent concept about equal treatment is that governments must recognize an equality of persons. Found in the Declaration of Independence, this ideal has grown in influence during the last two centuries. Although achievement has yet to match aspiration, political societies have rejected one barrier after another—class, race, ethnic origin, gender, sexual preference, physical disability—to the equal treatment of citizens. The question whether a law touching religious practice treats citizens as political equals may reach beyond the specific values of free exercise and nonestablishment.

Some equality claims about religion challenge specific lines of inclusion and exclusion that distinguish among categories of people. But other claims assert that a deep principle of equality demands differences in treatment that respond to variations in capacities, beliefs, or practices. (To take a noncontroversial, nonreligious, illustration, people now accept the deep principle that students suffering learning impairments should have opportunities equal to those of other students; this value is implemented by giving these students benefits, such as tutoring, not made available to all students.) One perspective on how equality should figure in respect to religion is that benefits for religious groups under the Free Exercise Clause should offset disadvantages under the Establishment Clause.[5] Very often, proponents of competing resolutions of political and legal problems enlist the value of equality in their behalf; we shall try to discern which particular kinds of equality are most salient for the fair treatment of religious individuals and groups.

MULTIPLE VALUE THEORIES AND THE PROBLEM OF COHERENCE

When theorists search for a single overarching value to explicate a legal subject, almost inevitably they omit too much or provide an overarching value that is so inclusive it yields little help in resolving practical problems.

---

ment out of state decisions about how to treat religion. The Supreme Court has resolved that most of the Bill of Rights was made applicable against the states by the Fourteenth Amendment.

[4] My views on the controversial subject of whether equality is an independent value are in "'Prescriptive Equality': Two Steps Forward," 110 *Harvard Law Review* 1265 (1997), and "How Empty Is the Idea of Equality?" 83 *Columbia Law Review* 1167 (1983).

[5] Abner S. Greene, "The Political Balance of the Religion Clauses," 102 *Yale Law Journal* 1611 (1993).

Within most legal domains, multiple values, which sometimes conflict with one another, are important. Even if we ignore the plurality of values that the concepts of free exercise, nonestablishment, and equality each embrace on their own, we see that none of these concepts can underlie a single value approach to the religion clauses. Nonestablishment cannot be the overarching value, because it is largely a means to serve free exercise. A thesis that every valid consideration reduces to free exercise is more plausible. But inquiring only whether a law threatens the religious liberty of citizens would neglect both *some* reasons for nonestablishment and the independent value of equality. A law might promote religious freedom at the expense of some unacceptable inequality among groups of citizens.[6] And one worry about establishment is that religious leaders will have too much political authority, a concern about political integrity that is not exclusively about the value of citizens' *religious* freedom.

One reason why equality cannot serve as the single overarching value is that we need to attend to the values underlying religious freedom and nonestablishment to determine which equalities matter most. A second reason is that some sacrifices in equality may be warranted to serve those other values.[7]

Many situations in which multiple values are at stake involve difficult trade-offs that are not resolvable by any higher metric that gives much practical assistance.[8] This truth has implications for the coherence we can expect in normative evaluation. Two people sharing the same theoretical approach may disagree about how to resolve a particular problem, and each may have difficulty explaining the exact weighting of relevant considerations that leads her to prefer the outcome she does. Someone who conceives such nuances of difference in normative appraisal will be modest about the opportunities for our practical reason to produce demonstrably correct conclusions for troublesome issues. Recognizing that the majority opinions of American courts often suffer the further liability of being produced by various compromises, such a person will hesitate to condemn judicial work as incoherent or

[6] One might or might not conclude that every instance of this sort amounted to an establishment of religion.

[7] A theorist might concede this much and respond that the aim, or consequence, of implementing religious liberty and nonestablishment may be to achieve an overall equal balance between religion and nonreligion. See note 5 supra. I am skeptical that the right balance of benefits and harms will produce such equality, but, in any event, such a broad aspiration to equality would not prove a handy guide for deciding how to treat individual problems.

[8] To say that trade-offs should be resolved to promote overall long-term happiness or autonomy is a formula too vague to provide such assistance. Robert Audi has written sensitively, and with a considerable degree of optimism, about how we can make choices involving conflicting prima facie ethical duties. *The Good in the Right* 81–202 (Princeton: Princeton University Press, 2004).

irrational, a charge frequently leveled against the Supreme Court's church-state jurisprudence.[9]

A person who believes that multiple values bear on the resolution of major social and legal issues will insist on contextual evaluation. He may feel confident about which features matter most and even about particular overall assessments, without being able to offer a set of abstract principles to demonstrate the correctness of his judgments. This book's emphasis on context allows the reader to understand troubling conflicts and undertake his own critical examination of them.

This is not to suggest that the book is rootless or that it takes a radically relativist stand on moral issues. Moreover, although no simple formulas are available to resolve difficult questions about free exercise, we shall find that a similar range of considerations or factors figures for many problems. In what we might call the standard situation, to which a number of chapters are devoted, the government imposes a general constraint, and the issue is whether an exception should be made for those who have an objection based on religious convictions or on broader grounds that include religious convictions. Chapter 4, on conscientious objection, chapter 5, on use of proscribed drugs in worship services, and chapter 6, on claims to withdraw children from school at the age of fourteen, discuss variations on this standard situation that the Supreme Court has addressed. In contrast to those illustrations, a government rule, as I have noted, may generate a less direct conflict with religious exercise. If a state requires that businesses close on Sunday, that requirement can penalize those whose religion requires that they not work on Saturday.

If one focuses on religious claims to be exempted from general requirements set by the government, two obvious, crucial, factors are the strength of the religious claim and the strength of the competing government interest (whether that interest is the government's own or that of a group or individual the government seeks to protect). The relevant government interest is not simply the benefits achieved by the general law, but the interest served by not creating an exemption for those who offer religious claims to be treated differently from others whom the law restricts. Another important consideration is the administrability of a possible exemption. Can administrative officials and judges or juries understand what they need to do and apply the necessary standards of judgment to the factual circumstances with reasonable assurance? Do those standards create opportunities for fraud, and, if so, are the risks tolerable? For exceptions based on religious claims, officials typically

---

[9] However, the work of courts is sometimes incoherent and irrational, even assessed generously.

must assess the sincerity of those who say they rely on their deep-seated convictions; officials must also be able to say if the claims qualify as religious.

Who is best suited to assess the strength of religious claims and government interests and to develop administrable standards? For this question of institutional competence, the basic value of free exercise and the history of adoption of the Free Exercise Clause are only of limited assistance. One may believe judges are not equipped to determine when religious claims should prevail, unless they are given highly specific guidance by legislatures, for example, by a law protecting use of peyote during worship services. Perhaps the most important chapter in the book is chapter 13, which analyzes how judges resolve issues when they have to work with a much more general standard that requires them to make the complex assessments that will determine whether to grant particular exemptions.

When legislators or judges ask whether people who do not claim religious grounds (however those are conceived) should be treated similarly to religious claimants, they must ask whether the nonreligious claims are likely to have a strength like the religious ones and whether expanding the category of those who benefit would seriously impair administration of an exemption or increase the risks of successful fraud. As we shall see, the answers to these questions differ radically for different subjects. What may be true for conscientious objections to military service may not be true for unwillingness to work on Saturday.

One overarching concern in a decision whether to limit favorable treatment to religious claimants is that the government should avoid promoting or endorsing particular religions or, more controversially, religion in general. That subject receives concentrated attention in the second volume.

As I have already noted, relatively few laws now target particular religions for unfavorable treatment or discriminate in favor of some religion as compared with others. Such laws are almost always inappropriate, and if a court is able to discern that a law is of this variety, it is almost certain to treat it as unconstitutional. The only complexity about such cases is in figuring out whether a law does target or discriminate in this way.

Most of the latter part of this volume is taken up with issues of a rather different sort. The law dictates how private enterprises and individuals treat each other. In the instance of laws that forbid discrimination on grounds of religion, the aim is both to protect workers (and others) from being discriminated against based on their religious identity and to protect their freedom to exercise their religion as they see fit. Protecting one worker's religious freedom can run up against claims of religious liberty advanced by an employer or by other workers. A grocery store owner may want to express his

Christian sentiments by having his cashiers say Merry Christmas as customers leave; an atheist or Jehovah's Witness cashier may object that uttering those words violates her religious conscience. The resolutions of these conflicts involves a comparison of conflicting interests, but one that differs somewhat from an analysis of what I have called the standard situation.

Yet another kind of issue we will examine is the resolution of disputes between private groups or individuals in which religious elements figure prominently. Two factions of a church assert a right to control a house of worship, or divorcing parties disagree about who will have custody of their children or about what religious services the children will attend. In these circumstances, a dominant consideration is that courts must avoid kinds of religious assessment that would favor some religions over others and would implicate judges in tasks for which they are ill qualified.

POLITICAL PHILOSOPHY AND DIMENSIONS OF LEGAL JUDGMENT

Resolutions and judgments about religion and the state can assume many forms. All governments implementing values of religious liberty, nonestablishment, and equality draw from moral and political principles. In most liberal democracies, governments must also respect the terms of a written constitution; in the United States, federal and state constitutions alike frame relations between religion and government,[10] restricting legislative choices.[11]

When legislators adopt statutes and judges develop constitutional rules, they aim, as I have said, to provide administrable standards of judgment. As a consequence, legislators and judges may reject an approach that, in a world of ideal knowledge and assessment, would best fulfill the values at stake, preferring instead a "second-best" approach that real human beings are better able to apply.

Judges also strive for something more, constitutional standards that relate coherently to other constitutional standards, and that flow from sound techniques of interpretation. Many disagreements among Supreme Court justices in church-state cases come down to disputes over how our federal Constitution should be interpreted. Some justices rely heavily on an "original understanding"; others (explicitly or implicitly) aim to be more responsive to mod-

---

[10] All states have their own free exercise clauses, and the great majority have nonestablishment provisions; but the language of these typically differs from that of the First Amendment. Thus, states are limited by a combination of federal and their own constitutional provisions.

[11] In between lies a kind of gray area, where a legislative choice may actually violate the Constitution, but not in a manner that courts will identify and prevent.

ern social conditions and values. Although disagreements about claims brought under the religion clauses inevitably connect to broad political ideas, distinctive features of the law should caution us not to suppose that the best answer to every constitutional question will necessarily track the most sound answer in the realm of political philosophy.

CHAPTER 2

History and Doctrine

Providing background for our study's contemporary, analytical perspective, this chapter sketches the original history of the Free Exercise Clause and its subsequent doctrinal development. It also relates enough about the Establishment Clause to show how the two religion clauses fit together.[1]

THE SIGNIFICANCE OF HISTORY AND DOCTRINE

History

That we can learn from history is a truism. Historical investigation rarely, if ever, tells us how to respond to modern problems, but it can teach us about our society's values and lines of division, and it can illumine pitfalls and possibilities.

Within constitutional law, history figures in two special ways. Anglo-American courts build approaches to legal issues over time, treating their predecessors' efforts as authoritative. According to the doctrine of precedent, judges follow the resolution of an earlier case, even if they would have decided that case differently. Although the United States Supreme Court overrules prior constitutional decisions it believes were seriously mistaken, nonetheless the doctrine of precedent produces substantial continuity over time.[2]

The precedential force of a case concerns both its specific outcome and the doctrines judges employ. Thus, in *Sherbert v. Verner*,[3] an important free exercise decision, the Supreme Court decided that a state could not deny a person unemployment compensation if her reason for refusing Saturday work was a religious conviction. As its doctrinal justification, the Court announced that a law that interferes with a person's exercise of religion can be enforced against her only if the state has a compelling interest in its application that cannot adequately be served by another, less restrictive, means. Thus, we can

---

[1] Volume 2 contains a fuller development of the history and doctrine of the Establishment Clause.

[2] Courts below the Supreme Court in the judicial hierarchy have much less discretion to disregard Supreme Court precedents than does that Court itself.

[3] 374 U.S. 398 (1963).

speak of the precedent of *Sherbert v. Verner* as it covers the application of unemployment laws and as it establishes a general approach for free exercise cases. Later courts usually feel freer to alter general approaches than to abandon the narrower outcomes of decided cases;[4] and as a guiding legal authority, *Sherbert v. Verner* suffered just this fate in the 1990 case that constitutes the controversial cornerstone of modern free exercise law.[5]

Another special way that history matters in constitutional law is that events that preceded the adoption of constitutional texts provide a source of the meaning of these texts. The basic idea is that judges determining what a legal text *means* now should discern what it *meant* when it was adopted. Almost everyone accepts the idea that original meaning carries significance, but judges and scholars divide sharply over how to determine that meaning and the weight to accord it. A modest grasp of the contending positions helps us understand fundamental disagreements among Supreme Court justices.

As a first approximation, "originalists" think a provision's initial meaning should determine modern understanding. When judges are able to ascertain an original meaning, they should follow it. "Nonoriginalists," including myself, believe the original meaning informs possible modern understandings and carries *some* independent weight; but the "meaning" of constitutional texts, which were adopted in open-ended natural language by people who realized how law develops over time, rightly evolves as social conditions and cultural values change.[6]

Two qualifications to the originalist position soften its dichotomy with the nonoriginalist one. Because even originalists believe that judges should give weight to prior decisions in constitutional cases, an originalist Supreme Court justice who is faced with precedents that contravene his opinion about what a provision originally meant may follow the precedents instead of his view about original understanding.

A second point is more subtle. Everyone agrees that constitutional protections, such as freedom of the press, apply to new technologies like television that the founders never foresaw. But what if changes are in social circumstances and public perceptions rather than technology? Suppose Americans in the late eighteenth century thought that all genuine religions recognize a Supreme Being, conceived in a manner that would not include the beliefs of

---

[4] However, if a general approach has become firmly settled, a court may be hesitant to scuttle it; and when courts occasionally say they are "limiting an earlier case to its facts," they may really mean the earlier case no longer has any precedential force.

[5] *Employment Division v. Smith*, 494 U.S. 872 (1990).

[6] That is, not only does meaning slowly evolve, judges should regard such evolution as appropriate.

most Buddhists.[7] In the twenty-first century, with many Buddhists living in their country, Americans widely regard Buddhism as a religion. An "originalist" might decide that according Buddhists protection of the Free Exercise Clause fits with the basic values underlying the text, even though the founders might have rejected this precise application. When originalists rely on abstract principles that lie behind provisions, the gap narrows between them and nonoriginalists, who typically believe that wise modern understandings of constitutional texts correspond with fundamental values they have always embodied. Although my own position about constitutional interpretation is nonoriginalist, readers attracted to originalism can filter the book's discussions through that approach.

The question of *whose* original understanding matters turns out to be of minor practical importance for interpreting the religion clauses. Competing positions focus on readers or on the officials who adopt constitutions. The notion that the understanding of a contemporaneous reader determines original meaning emphasizes that constitutions are instruments of government *for* citizens, that what their texts signify to these citizens is vitally important.[8] Judges trying to discern what citizens understood more than two centuries ago will rely partly on old dictionaries, on political and legal discourse of the times, on existing legal structures, and on the public statements of leaders about what constitutional provisions entailed.

An opposing position assumes that the intent of those whose votes adopted a provision is of great significance for its own sake (not just as a guide to what most ordinary citizens understood).[9] Although judicial opinions in religion cases have often quoted famous founders—most notably Madison, the main architect of the Bill of Rights, and Jefferson, who had spearheaded efforts to assure religious liberty in Virginia[10]—as if the constitutional text means just what its leading draftsmen believed, no one explicitly defends such a simplistic approach.[11] The opinions of drafters do not

---

[7] I express skepticism about such a narrow view below. See text accompanying notes 48 and 49, infra.

[8] Whether the crucial audience is ordinary citizens or lawyers may depend on whether a provision was designed to be understood broadly or deals with legal technicalities.

[9] Those who support this position do not deny that the reader's understanding is also significant.

[10] During the years of the adoption of the original Constitution and Bill of Rights, Jefferson was abroad, as ambassador to France.

[11] I do elsewhere suggest that because a strong reason to defer to original understanding is the wisdom of the founders, it makes sense, as a constitution ages, to give extra weight to the views of those who were responsible for the constitutional design. Kent Greenawalt, "Constitutional and Statutory Interpretation," in Jules L. Coleman and Scott Shapiro, eds., *The Oxford Handbook of Jurisprudence and the Philosophy of Law* 268 (Oxford: Oxford University Press, 2002).

stand alone; modern interpreters must take into account what other members of Congress (proposing the Bill of Rights) and members of state legislatures (ratifying the Bill of Rights) believed. The statements of prominent figures like Madison should count as authoritative only if they represented already existing opinion or influenced other legislators voting on the Bill of Rights. Anyone who was trying to assess what typical members of Congress and state legislatures believed about the content of the Bill of Rights would look to analogous legal standards and broader currents of political opinion, as well as to remarks by Madison and others responsible for the constitutional language. Thus, the sources we should now use to discern the understandings of the actual adopters do not differ very much from the sources we should consult to divine the understandings of readers of the time.

A further wrinkle about original understanding should carry more practical import, and it should be regarded more seriously than it usually has been. The Bill of Rights itself, apart from the vaguely worded Tenth Amendment, restricts only the federal government. According to modern Supreme Court doctrine, the Fourteenth Amendment made most of the Bill of Rights, including the religion clauses, applicable to the states. The original meaning of the Free Exercise Clause *as it restricts the states* depends on how legislators and citizens conceived of the clause in the years after the Civil War, not on the conceptions of their great-grandparents.[12]

Just what modern political significance a reader will find in this chapter will depend heavily on how she answers for herself the questions about the relevance of original understanding and precedents. For someone who believes that the original understanding, in one form or another, is determinative, this chapter will be the most important in the book as far as constitutional principles are concerned. The manner in which modern issues of federal constitutional law should be resolved will depend upon which resolutions conform to the relevant original understanding—an understanding about specific applications or an understanding about more general objectives. For someone who believes continuity of precedents is all-important, the Supreme Court cases I describe will largely dictate how future cases should be resolved.

My own sense of how this chapter fits is more complicated. In brief, if we can find, in the original understandings about the Free Exercise Clause and the Fourteenth Amendment, a decisive resolution of various problems, that will count in favor of a similar modern resolution but will not necessarily be determinative. If we find that we cannot discern a clear original understanding, that is a substantial reason to be guided by other considerations (rather

---

[12] The Fourteenth Amendment was proposed by Congress in 1866 and approved in 1868.

than to seek a resolution based on indecisive original sources). Something similar can be said about precedents. Continuity over time is an important objective, but existing precedents leave open many issues, and courts should abandon unwise precedents. As the following chapters will disclose, I believe the most important modern Supreme Court decision about free exercise is just such an unwise precedent.

Regardless of one's convictions about their direct legal relevance, having some understanding of original sources and decided cases helps one to place modern problems in historical context. That exercise can be valuable whatever weight one believes the original meaning and precedents should carry in the decision of legal cases.

Doctrine

Courts interpreting broad constitutional texts to decide specific disputes commonly develop intermediate principles or doctrines, such as the "compelling interest test" employed in *Sherbert v. Verner*, to guide their resolutions of cases. If we wish to understand the development of constitutional law, we must acquaint ourselves with the principles and doctrines courts have used to build bridges from very general constitutional texts to specific outcomes. Although these intermediate doctrines often do assist judges, sometimes they are so general and vague they create an illusion of coherence for decisions that are reached on other grounds and are not reconcilable with each other. Critics have often made this exact challenge to the Supreme Court's religion clause jurisprudence.

THE HISTORY BEHIND THE FREE EXERCISE CLAUSE

The First Amendment begins, "Congress shall make no law respecting an establishment of religion, or prohibiting the free exercise thereof."[13] The history leading up to that language helps inform a number of major issues about the Free Exercise Clause.

The most central debate about modern free exercise law concerns exemptions from laws of general application. A state forbids the use of peyote. Must it, may it, permit people to ingest peyote in religious ceremonies? More broadly, must, or may, governments exempt individuals from general laws that impinge on their religious practices. One understanding of the Free Exercise Clause, and analogous state provisions, is that they require at least some

---

[13] U.S. Const., amend. 1.

exemptions (and allow legislatures to grant other, further, exemptions).[14] A competing understanding denies that the constitutional provisions compel exemptions, though legislatures may choose to grant some. According to both understandings, if grants of exemptions become too generous, they cross over the constitutional line and "establish" the favored religions.

Four other issues arise from particular terms in the Free Exercise Clause. First, what sets of beliefs and practices constitute "religion" in the constitutional sense? Does the clause protect conscientious belief developed without respect to religion (in the usual sense), and, if not, is such conscientious belief protected under some other provision? Second, does the "exercise" of religion refer only to worship and expressions of religious convictions, or does it cover other actions strongly motivated by religious conviction, such as a refusal to perform military service? Third, how restrictive is the gerund "prohibiting," in the phrase "make no law . . . prohibiting the exercise . . ."? Is it only laws that forbid religious exercise, or coerce people in some way, that are unconstitutional, or can impairments without coercion as to religion, such as the development of federal lands used by Native Americans as natural sites of worship, violate the Free Exercise Clause? Fourth, and related to these other questions, when does the Free Exercise Clause require equal treatment, and what kind of equal treatment does it require? If all non-Christians earning fifty thousand dollars a year are taxed at a marginal rate of 35 percent, and Christians earning fifty thousand dollars are taxed at a marginal rate of 20 percent, are the free exercise rights of non-Christians infringed? May an exemption from military service be limited to members of "peace churches"?

Along with the issue of required exemptions, these are the main questions for which the history leading up to the adoption of the Bill of Rights might provide guidance. We now turn to a brief account of that history.

Emigrants to the American colonies wanted to worship according to their own convictions, but many of them were far from desiring religious liberty for everyone. Michael McConnell has described four different approaches in the colonies to church-state relations.[15] The Church of England was established in Virginia, with the government exercising close control over the church, and restricting other faiths.[16] New England, apart from Rhode Is-

---

[14] But see Ira C. Lupu, "The Trouble with Accommodation," 60 *George Washington Law Review* 743 (1992) (rejecting legislative discretion to grant exemptions).

[15] Michael McConnell, "The Origins and Historical Understanding of Free Exercise of Religion," 103 *Harvard Law Review* 1409, 1421–25 (1990).

[16] According to McConnell, during the eighteenth century "Virginia was the most intolerant of the colonies," id. at 1423; authorities tried to prevent preaching by Presbyterians and Baptists who entered the colony.

land, also had established churches, but of a different kind. Following congregational principles, each Puritan town selected its minister, and supported
him and the church by compulsory taxes. Ministers had substantial autonomy from government officials. In early Puritan communities, dissenters
lacked rights of participation, and in Massachusetts they were actively perse-
cuted. A third approach was de facto religious toleration. The Church of
England was established in the four counties of metropolitan New York, but
Protestants of various persuasions were generally free to worship as they
chose. Finally some colonies founded for religious dissenters did positively
embrace religious liberty, extending religious freedom to a wide variety of
groups.[17] Summarizing the early provisions governing religion in these latter
colonies, McConnell suggests that they expressly overrode contrary laws or
customs, that they reached all religious concerns, not just religious professions and acts of worship, and that they allowed the exercise of religion to
be restricted only to prevent licentiousness and disturbance of others.[18]

By the time of the Revolution, the religious establishments that remained
had become much milder, allowing worship by Christian dissenters at least
and often providing assistance to more than one religious denomination.

In a letter to the citizens of Quebec urging them to join the Americans
against the British, the Continental Congress said, "[W]e hold sacred the
rights of conscience and may promise . . . the free and undisturbed exercise
of . . . religion."[19] When the Articles of Confederation were in effect in the
years preceding adoption of the Constitution, Congress adopted treaties
with the Netherlands, Sweden, and Prussia that guaranteed liberty of conscience and worship.[20]

The most significant legal guide to what the Free Exercise Clause might
have meant is the content of state constitutions adopted after the outbreak
of the Revolutionary War and before the Bill of Rights was adopted.[21] Here
are three of those. The Maryland Declaration of Rights of 1776 said:

> [A]s it is the duty of every man to worship God in such manner as he thinks
> most acceptable to him; all persons, professing the Christian religion, are equally
> entitled to protection in their religious liberty; wherefore no person ought by
> any law to be molested in his person or estate on account of his religious persua-
> sion or profession, or for his religious practice; unless, under colour of religion,

---

[17] Maryland, Rhode Island, Pennsylvania, Delaware, and Carolina did so, although in 1689,
Maryland established the Church of England and became intolerant toward dissenters.

[18] Note 15 supra, at 1427.

[19] John Witte, Jr., *Religion and the American Constitutional Experiment* 59 (Boulder, Colo.:
Westview Press, 2000).

[20] Id. at 60.

[21] All these formulations are set out in McConnell, note 15 supra, at 1456–58.

any man shall disturb the good order, peace or safety of the state, or shall infringe the laws of morality, or injure others, in their natural, civil, or religious rights.[22]

The Massachusetts Constitution of 1780 provided:

It is the right as well as the duty of all men in society, publicly and at stated seasons, to worship the Supreme Being, the great Creator and Preserver of the universe. And no subject shall be hurt, molested, or restrained in his person, liberty or estate, for worshipping God in the manner and season most agreeable to the dictates of his own conscience, or for his religious profession or senti-ments, provided he doth not disturb the public peace or obstruct others in their religious worship.[23]

New York's Constitution of 1777 said:

The free exercise and enjoyment of religious profession and worship, without discrimination or preference, shall forever be allowed, within this State, to all mankind: *Provided*, That the liberty of conscience, hereby granted, shall not be so construed as to excuse acts of licentiousness, or to justify practices inconsis-tent with the peace or safety of this state.[24]

One obvious difference among these three state documents concerns the religious views they protect. Maryland appears to safeguard only persons professing the Christian religion;[25] the Massachusetts constitution is directed to the worship of God; New York's has no explicit limitation and thus may have protected people of all religious persuasion, including atheists.

For whatever persons are protected, the kind of tax discrimination I illus-trated with respect to non-Christians would be illegal; in the language of the Massachusetts constitution, for example, those paying higher taxes would be "molested" in their "estates" because of their religious "sentiments."[26]

Like many constitutions of the time, Massachusetts's focuses on worship. Maryland's refers to "religious persuasion or profession, or . . . practice"; New York's to "religious profession and worship" and then to "the liberty of conscience, hereby, granted." Language about profession and worship leaves unclear whether constitutional protection extends to acts of religious conscience such as refusing to take an oath or submit to military service.

On the significance of the phrase "prohibiting the free exercise" in the First Amendment, the word "prohibiting" sounds narrower in the kinds of impairments that it forbids than does a term such as "molested." The state

---

[22] Id. at 1457.

[23] Id.

[24] Id. at 1456.

[25] However, one might argue that language following the second semicolon is broader.

[26] New York's language barring discrimination would be to the same effect. Maryland pro-vided similar protection against uneven taxation, but probably did not aid non-Christians.

provisions themselves are not clear about the degrees of interference with religious exercise they may cover; and it is difficult to estimate just how far "prohibiting" might reduce the scope of protection.

On the crucial issue of exemptions, the language of the Maryland and Massachusetts constitutions is decidedly ambiguous. The Maryland Declaration says that "no person . . . ought . . . to be molested . . . on account of his religious profession or persuasion or for his religious practice." Suppose a congregant using peyote in a worship service is arrested. In one sense, his arrest is "on account of" his religious persuasion and "for" his religious practice; he would not find himself at odds with legal authorities except for his religious practice. But if he was breaking a general law against using peyote, officials might respond that the arrest had nothing to do with his religion. On this narrower view of "on account of" and of "for," the Maryland constitution protected only against laws directed at religious persuasions or practices. In decreeing that no one should be molested "for" his religious profession, the Massachusetts provision has the same ambiguity. With no such potentially limiting phraseology, the New York language leans more toward the creation of rights against the application of some laws that are not themselves directed at religious practices.

What are we to make of the common reservation, phrased in different ways, but well represented by New York's stipulation that protection does not extend to "acts of licentiousness . . . or practices inconsistent with the peace or safety of this state"? A straightforward reading suggests the following. Not all valid laws concern licentiousness or peace or safety, so religious claims have priority over some valid laws. Further, the very statement of these limits shows that constitutional protection extends to general laws as well as laws that are directed against religious practices. Thus, the constitution does establish *some* exemptions from valid laws. An opposed understanding of the New York language, defended by Philip Hamburger among others, is that, since all proper laws were then considered to promote morality, peace, and safety, the language does not accord protection against any ordinary laws. Rather, what it indicates are the circumstances in which laws could be directed against religious belief and practices themselves.[27]

A different source for understanding how state provisions, and the federal Free Exercise Clause, addressed conflicts between religious convictions and general legal requirements is how colonial and state governments had actu-

[27] Philip A. Hamburger, "A Constitutional Right of Religious Exemption: An Historical Perspective," 60 *George Washington Law Review* 915, 918–26 (1992). On this understanding, the language about "peace or safety" etc. is limiting, but not in respect to general laws not directed against religion. Professor Hamburger supports his understanding with an account of the process of enactment in New York. Id. at 924–26.

ally responded to such conflicts. McConnell discusses oath requirements, military conscription, and religious assessments.[28] Colonies had requirements to testify under oath, but most created an exception for those who objected to the oath for religious reasons.[29] In several colonies, Quakers and other groups were exempted from bearing arms, and the Continental Congress, recognizing that "some people, who, from religious principles, cannot bear arms in any case," said it intended "no violence to their consciences."[30] Finally, many of the colonies exempted members of dissenting groups from tax assessments to support the ministry of the dominant churches.

Legislators, thus, granted various exemptions, but did they believe these were required by provisions of colonial charters and state constitutions? McConnell understands the connection between charter protections and legislative grants as indicating a sense that the exemptions were required, but one might, instead, think that colonial officials who were sympathetic to the needs of religious dissenters did not suppose that the charter provisions themselves compelled exemptions.[31] Because legislators who grant exemptions rarely say whether they believe a constitution or charter requires them to do so, the exemptions are inconclusive evidence about constitutional understanding.

A more diffuse source for interpreting the Free Exercise Clause is the political culture of the times. How did people understand the free exercise of religion? John Witte has helpfully identified four important perspectives—two religious and two political—and six overarching principles.[32]

The Puritans believed in cooperation of church and state, but also a separation of political from clerical offices. Eighteenth-century Puritan leaders increasingly accepted a right to individual religious conscience,[33] but they continued to think that the state should support the dominant religion. The second religious perspective was that of Evangelicals, who emerged as a political force after the eighteenth century's Great Awakening and had suffered persecution or disadvantages under existing establishments. They supported religious liberty and disestablishment on principle, believing, unlike the Puri-

[28] McConnell, note 15 supra, at 1466–71.

[29] Id. at 1467. Given belief that oaths brought extratemporal consequences into play, people regarded them as a greater guarantor of truthfulness than we do today, so allowing an exception was not a trivial concession.

[30] Id. at 1469.

[31] Compare id. at 1466–71, with Hamburger, note 27 supra, at 929–31. McConnell says about exemptions from bearing arms, "It is presumably not coincidental that Rhode Island, North Carolina, and Maryland had explicit free exercise or liberty of conscience clauses in the seventeenth century, while New York [which refused an exemption] did not."

[32] See Witte, note 19 supra, at 23–55.

[33] Id. at 27. As Elisha Williams put it, "Every man has an equal right to follow the dictates of his own conscience in affairs of religion."

tans, that government should stay out of religion, partly because its involvement corrupts religion.

The two political standpoints were those of civic republicans and believers in Enlightenment ideas. Civic republicans accepted liberty of conscience, but they favored state support of religious groups and a public religion that would undergird civic virtue. As Nathan Strong said, "[R]eligion and its institutions are the best aid of government by strengthening the ruler's hand, and making the subject faithful in his place, and obedient to the general laws."[34]

In the colonies, the most influential Enlightenment writing on religion was John Locke's 1689 Letter Concerning Toleration.[35] For Locke, the concerns of government were clearly demarcated from religious conscience. Churches should be regarded as voluntary societies and people should be able to worship God as they choose.[36] Locke did not argue that religious convictions should confer immunity from laws serving legitimate government concerns.[37] In one example, he suggested that a government with good reason to ban the killing of cattle could apply the ban to religious sacrifices of cows. Jefferson was America's most important representative of the Enlightenment position in the late eighteenth century. Like Locke, he viewed religion as a private matter. Unlike Locke, he strongly opposed state support of religion. The famous Virginia Statute for Religious Freedom, drafted by Jefferson in 1779 and enacted in 1786, has the following language: "That it is time enough for the rightful purposes of civil government for its officers to interfere when principles break out into overt acts against peace and good order . . ."[38] This passage suggests obliquely what Locke's cattle example acknowledged more directly—that acts that are contrary to valid laws are not protected, even if they are motivated by religious conscience.

Although Enlightenment thinkers worried that a union of church and state could corrupt government, they, like dissenting Christians who were more concerned with government's corruption of religion, were strongly commit-

[34] Id. at 35. Noah Feldman argues that no significant group of civic republicans existed in the period Witte discusses, "The Intellectual Origins of the Establishment Clause," 77 *New York University Law Review* 346, 394 (2002).

[35] Reprinted in *John Locke, A Letter Concerning Toleration, in Focus,* John Horton and Susan Mendus, eds. (New York: Routledge, 1991). Noah Feldman claims a dominance during the late eighteenth century for a Lockean conception of liberty of conscience. Feldman, note 34 supra.

[36] Locke made exceptions for atheists and Roman Catholics; those limitations were based on the belief that atheists could not be trusted to keep promises and that Catholics had an allegiance to a foreign power.

[37] One might believe that arguing for much more basic rights of religious liberty, Locke did not worry much about exemptions.

[38] See Thomas Jefferson, Virginia Statute for Religious Freedom, reprinted in Philip B. Kurland and Ralph Lerner, eds., 5 *The Founders' Constitution* 77 (Chicago: University of Chicago Press, 1987).

ted to freedom of thought and conscience. Freedom of conscience was conceived mainly as the conscience of religious convictions; and religious ideas were so interwoven in discussions of politics, history, and morality, one could hardly imagine a freedom of thought and expression that did not include religious ideas.

Recognizing differences among proponents of his four positions, Witte discerns from late-eighteenth-century writings six fundamental principles regarding religious liberty.[39] *Liberty of conscience*, endorsed by almost everyone, included voluntarism, that is, private judgment about religion, a ban on religiously based discrimination, and, in the view of some founders, exemptions based on religious conscience. *Free exercise of religion* embodied the right to act publicly on one's religious conscience, by worship, speech, assembly, publication, and education, and by joining religious societies. *Religious pluralism* included both pluralism of different forms of religious expression and organization and the social pluralism of varieties of nongovernmental organizations (besides religious societies). *Religious equality* involved a principle of equal treatment of peaceable religious groups; few founders concerned themselves with equal treatment between religious endeavors and nonreligious ones or between positive religious views and atheism. *Separation of church and state* meant that civil and religious offices should be separate. *Disestablishment of religion* entailed that the government would not settle a religion for the community.[40] Those six widely accepted principles can help us to understand how people of the time would have understood language like that found in the religion clauses of the First Amendment.

Finally, we come to the history of the federal Constitution itself. The original Constitution established two important principles regarding religion. It forbade any religious test for holding federal office,[41] and provided that officials could be bound by "oath or affirmation," thus making unnecessary any legislative exception from a general oath requirement for people taking federal offices.[42]

States approved the Constitution on the understanding that a bill of rights would follow,[43] and the first Congress set about proposing one. James Madi-

---

[39] Witte, note 19 supra, at 37–55.

[40] Some founders, particularly Puritans, continued to support "mild and equitable" establishments. Those who favored disestablishment disagreed over whether modest, general supports of religion were acceptable.

[41] U.S. Const., art. 6.

[42] Id., art. 1, § 3, cl. 6; art. 2, § 1, cl. 8; art. 6, cl. 3.

[43] When objections were raised to the Constitution because it lacked a bill of rights, including a protection of religious liberty, one response was that no such protection was necessary because Congress lacked authority over religion. Since Congress had direct control over the territories (and later over the District of Columbia) and over some military forces, and it might have

son was the primary draftsman, but the final provision on religion varied significantly from his initial formulation: "[N]or shall the full and equal rights of conscience be in any manner, nor on any pretext, infringed."[44]

Although the historical record tells us what language was proposed and voted upon at various stages, the account of deliberations is sparse; for the most part we do not know if members of Congress rejected language because of its unacceptable implications or because it was redundant or inelegant. Because the religion clauses were mainly adopted to reassure the states that the federal government would not poach on their prerogatives with respect to religion, and no one thought much about what legislation Congress might adopt regarding religion, it is hardly surprising that so little consideration was directed at the implications of the constitutional language.[45]

We *can* reach three limited conclusions with confidence. "Free exercise of religion" included protection of religious conscience but not moral convictions unconnected to religion. Second, in its very generality, the phrase "free exercise" reached beyond belief, profession, and worship to other acts of religious conviction. Third, the word "prohibiting" did not mean "forbidding altogether." Madison later ridiculed that possibility,[46] which would have disappointed widely shared notions about what religious liberty entailed.

One point about the Establishment Clause that bears on understanding free exercise involves the word "respecting," in "Congress shall make no law respecting an establishment of religion." This language both forbids Congress from interfering with existing state establishments and controls what Congress may do in federal domains, such as federal territories.[47] The aspect that precludes federal interference with state establishments bears on how far Congress acting under its delegated powers could have promoted free exercise. For example, if a treaty adopted in order to assure religious exercise for Americans in a foreign country guaranteed similar rights for that

discriminated against some religions in favor of others in more general legislative enactments that taxed, spent money, and regulated commerce, any notion that the federal government could have nothing to do with religion was obviously misconceived.

[44] See McConnell, note 15 supra, at 1481. Madison also proposed an amendment that would have forbidden states from infringing "the equal rights of conscience," among other things; but the Senate rejected this idea.

[45] For two accounts, see id. at 1480–85; Witte, note 19 supra, at 64–85. See Steven D. Smith, *Foreordained Failure* 38–39 (New York: Oxford University Press, 1995), who doubts that the founders meant to enact any principle of free exercise.

[46] See McConnell, note 15 supra, at 1487–88.

[47] I defend this conclusion in Common Sense about Original and Modern Understandings of the Religion Clauses (to be published in the *University of Pennsylvania Journal of Constitutional Law*). For claims that the Establishment Clause was purely jurisdictional, leaving Congress free to establish religion in federal domains, see Akhil Reed Amar, *The Bill of Rights* 34 (Cambridge: Harvard University Press, 1998); Smith, note 45 supra, at 17.

country's nationals in the United States, the treaty *might have* interfered with religious establishments in some states.

"Respecting" sounds as if it precludes some laws within federal domains that are less than full-blown establishments, but it does not tell us just which supports of religion are "respecting" an establishment. Although the religion clauses have no specific language about equality, separately and together they foreclose many forms of favoritism for one or more religions over others.

Witte comments that the founders did not envision protecting African and Native American religions or nontheist Eastern religions.[48] I have already suggested that, according to some theory of evolving content, such protection should now extend in any event; but I do not think we should take Witte's comment about original meaning as conclusive. The Constitution and Bill of Rights provided very little (if any) protection for slaves and Native Americans, so most of the *people* who accepted African and Native American religions were not likely to benefit from the Free Exercise Clause; but that is not quite the same as saying that the religious views were not covered. The Free Exercise Clause is not explicitly limited to theists, and certainly not to Christians. Almost everyone in the founding generation was familiar with what Christians refer to as the Old Testament, which relates encounters of the Israelites with various people whose worship was not of a single God. The educated founders, through their study of Greek and Roman civilizations, were familiar with classical religions, and some were aware of Eastern religions. Even if the founders thought all such religions were foolish, and that very few modern persons would embrace anything like them, still constitutional protection would extend to a full, undoubted citizen who subscribed to one of these religions, or to an African or Native American religion.[49]

This leaves us with the crucial questions about exemptions. Given the historical pattern of exemptions, few people at the time could have supposed that disestablishment *barred* all religious exemptions from valid laws. Although Congress declined to include any constitutional right to exemption from military service,[50] everyone assumed that legislatures had authority to grant them.

The hard issue is required exemptions. Did people suppose that the Free Exercise Clause required some exemptions, and that courts would enforce them? As McConnell notes, the creation of judicial review was an important

---

[48] Witte, note 19 supra, at 83.

[49] One might resist this last conclusion on the basis that whatever the founders may have conceived about ancient religions, they would not have counted anything in the traditional beliefs and practices of Africans and Native Americans as religious. The scope of religion is one subject as to which the period of the Fourteenth Amendment is important. By 1868 many more educated citizens were aware of Eastern religions.

[50] McConnell, note 15 supra, at 1500–1503.

feature of the Constitution; some subjects previously left to legislative judgment were made enforceable constitutional rights. We have already seen that legislative grants of exemptions and the provisions of state constitutions are indecisive about whether exemptions are constitutionally required. McConnell's summarizing judgment is this: "It is . . . difficult to claim, on this evidence, that the framers and ratifiers specifically understood or expected that the free exercise clause would vest courts with authority to create exceptions from generally applicable laws on account of religious conscience . . . [H]owever, the modern doctrine of free exercise exemptions is more consistent with the original understanding than is a position that leads only to the facial neutrality of legislation."[51]

The evidence about any original understanding about compelled exemptions is sufficiently indecisive so that the issue is most sensibly resolved in terms of free exercise values and the appropriate functions of courts and legislatures. These are crucial components of this study.

DEVELOPMENTS PRIOR TO ADOPTION OF THE FOURTEENTH AMENDMENT

The meaning of the religion clauses cannot be determined exclusively by what people believed when the Bill of Rights was approved. Given the Supreme Court's assumption that the Fourteenth Amendment extended the religion clauses to the states,[52] that application should depend partly on how people conceived of the clauses' meaning when that amendment was adopted.[53]

Judicial opinions and scholars have paid relatively little attention to the understanding of free exercise up to and immediately after the Civil War. McConnell's article on the original understanding discusses a few early-nine-

[51] Id. at 1512. A contrasting view is taken by Hamburger, note 27 supra. Those who oppose constitutionally required exemptions do not, as McConnell's statement might imply, believe that *facial* neutrality is sufficient if it is an obvious cover for discrimination.

[52] Some, but not all, historians think this Supreme Court doctrine of incorporation fits the intentions of the adopters, or at least the amendment's major proponents in Congress.

The Supreme Court has relied primarily on the Due Process Clause (No state shall "deprive any person of life, liberty, or property, without due process of law") to reach this conclusion; proposers of the amendment intended that the Privileges and Immunities Clause ("No state shall make or enforce any law which shall abridge the privileges or immunities of citizen of the United States") would be the vehicle by which citizens were afforded protections of the Bill of Rights against state governments.

[53] If one concluded that meaning varied greatly from the time of the Bill of Rights to the time of the Fourteenth Amendment, one would face the interpretive problem whether actual protections should now differ significantly against the federal and state governments.

It is conceivable that the adopters of the Fourteenth Amendment had a specific intent to carry forward the original understanding, whatever that was, but this seems very unlikely.

teenth-century cases that provide some insight into judicial attitudes.[54] A New York court decided that the state constitution protected a Roman Catholic priest from having to testify about the identity of a man who had confessed to him that he had received stolen goods.[55] The Supreme Court of Pennsylvania, on the other hand, rejected arguments in favor of exemptions, including the claim of a Jewish litigant that he should not have to appear in court on Saturday;[56] and the Constitutional Court of South Carolina did not allow a member of a Christian sect to refuse service on a grand jury.[57]

In the period preceding 1868, most state provisions about religious liberty were much more detailed than the federal clause; most referred explicitly to liberty of conscience; many provided that no preference should be given for any religion over others; some exempted persons with religious scruples from bearing arms.[58] Most state constitutions had some ceremonial expression of gratitude to God, and many endorsed religion in other respects.[59]

Kurt Lash has undertaken the most systematic attempt to discern the understanding of free exercise at the time of the Fourteenth Amendment.[60] Lash suggests that, insofar as the original Free Exercise Clause reflected a norm of individual freedom (and was not just a concession to the authority of state governments), its scope appears limited to laws that "abridge religion *qua* religion."[61]

Lash concludes that in the early nineteenth century, when people assumed that Christianity was the national religion, that government could sponsor

---

[54] McConnell, note 15 supra, at 1503–11.

[55] *People v. Philips* (1812–13). An account of the unreported case is in William Sampson, *The Catholic Question in America* 8–9 (New York: Da Capo Press, 1974).

[56] *Simon's Executors v. Gratz*, 2 Pen. & W. 412 (Pa. 1831). In that case, state chief justice Gibson wrote, "That every other obligation shall yield to that of the laws, as to a superior moral force is a tacit condition of membership in every society." Id. at 417. McConnell, note 15 supra, at 1509–10, points out that Gibson was an opponent of judicial review.

[57] 13 S.C.L. (2 McCord) 393 (1823). It commented that indulging sincere objectors would open the gates for the "hipocritical" [sic] and "deceitful." Id. at 394.

[58] I am relying on John Witte's summary of state constitutional provisions on religion from 1787 to 1947. Note 19 supra, at 87–96. Witte does not distinguish pre-1868 from post-1868 provisions, but we have no reason to suppose there was any radical break in their content around that period.

[59] Witte notes that official discrimination against minority groups continued, and that "state and local governments patronized a 'public' religion that was generally Christian, if not Protestant, in character." Id. at 97. Subsidies were given to Christian groups, and public schools, as they developed, had a Protestant cast.

[60] Kurt T. Lash, "The Second Adoption of the Free Exercise Clause: Religious Exemptions Under the Fourteenth Amendment," 88 *Northwestern Law Review* 1106 (1994).

[61] Id. at 1113. According to Lash, this notion of the Free Exercise Clause fitted Jefferson's idea that religion and government should occupy separate spheres, that religion had no right to be free of "social duties." Id. at 1115. (Lash attributes the same view to Madison, but I am doubtful that the "Memorial and Remonstrance" should be so understood.) On this view of

religion in various ways, and that religion was a main support of public morality, religious exemptions from valid laws seemed "almost nonsensical."[62] But the rise of religiously inspired social activism, and most especially the abolitionist movement, brought a more individualist understanding of free exercise. Abolitionists contended that because slavery violated God's law, people had a religious duty to struggle against it. Southern states suppressed antislavery religious expressions and restricted religious meetings of slaves. "Neutral" laws against teaching slaves to read and write prevented slaves from reading the Bible, thus undermining their ability to exercise religious faith.[63]

Twenty of thirty-seven states in existence at the end of the Civil War had constitutions providing for religious exemptions from military service; during the Civil War, Congress had exempted members of denominations conscientiously opposed to military service, recognizing "rights of conscience."[64]

Leading proponents of the Fourteenth Amendment saw free exercise as a right of individual conscience—including not only worship but all duties to God and other people[65]—that "neutral" laws, such as those forbidding slaves to learn how to read, could violate.[66] By the time of the Fourteenth Amendment, Lash urges, the Free Exercise Clause was seen as an individual right that could require exemptions from valid general laws. Lash gives us good reason to suppose that in 1866 many people, including legislators, viewed the exemption issue differently than had their forebears of 1789, but I still do not think this later original understanding (i.e., the understanding that underlay the Fourteenth Amendment) is decisive enough to override other considerations of the kind we shall examine in succeeding chapters.

THE DEVELOPMENT OF SUPREME COURT DOCTRINE

In this section, we turn to the Supreme Court's development of free exercise doctrines, with a brief word about establishment principles. The account

---

separate spheres, the legitimate claims of government would rarely, if ever, clash with the legitimate claims of religion; there would be no occasion for exemptions.

[62] Id. at 1123.

[63] Lash says, "If the original Free Exercise Clause was intended to prohibit nothing more than laws that targeted religion qua religion, the abolitionists challenged the adequacy of that protection." Id. at 1137.

[64] Id. at 1143.

[65] Id. at 1151–52.

[66] Lash recognizes that other parts of the Fourteenth Amendment (and, one might add, the Thirteenth Amendment) would render such laws invalid; but the point is that the proponents of the Fourteenth Amendment regarded them as gross interferences with religious exercise. Id. at 1153–56.

here aims to be as doggedly descriptive as is possible. Later chapters undertake critical analysis of what the Court has done and offer suggestions about
directions for the future.

The Supreme Court's first major decision about the Free Exercise Clause,
Reynolds v. United States,[67] involved a challenge by a Mormon to his conviction under a territorial law that forbade polygamy. The Court left no doubt
that it regarded polygamy as a despicable practice condemned by all civilized
nations, but the opinion's main contribution to free exercise doctrine was a
sharp distinction between belief and action. Relying heavily on Jefferson,
the Court said, "Congress was deprived of all legislative power over mere
opinion, but was left free to reach actions which were in violation of social
duties or subversive of good order."[68]

Although *Reynolds* was the first case interpreting the Free Exercise Clause,
an earlier, common-law, decision relied heavily on concepts of religious liberty.[69] Considering a dispute that arose between proslavery and antislavery
factions of a Kentucky Presbyterian church, the state courts had declared
that church property was held in trust for the general church *if*, and *only if*,
it had not departed from basic church doctrines. The Supreme Court disagreed: for civil courts in the United States to decide when churches depart
too far from their prior doctrines would be at odds with American concepts
of freedom for religious organizations and of a division between church and
government authority. This understanding that courts cannot resolve disagreements about the content of a religion has subsequently become a part
of constitutional law.

In a series of cases in the 1920s and 1930s, the Supreme Court rejected
claims that conscientious objectors had a free exercise right to avoid military
service.

By 1940, the applicability of the Free Speech and Free Press clauses of the
First Amendment to the states was well settled; in that year, *Cantwell v.
Connecticut*[70] accorded the Free Exercise Clause similar treatment. Whatever
may be true of the Establishment Clause,[71] few doubt that the exercise of
religion is a basic liberty warranting treatment parallel to freedom of speech
and of the press. Reviewing Cantwell's conviction for engaging in religious

[67] *Reynolds v. United States*, 98 U.S. 145 (1878).
[68] Id. at 164.
[69] *Watson v. Jones*, 80 U.S. (13 Wall.) 679 (1871). Federal courts, during the nineteenth
century, issued rulings based on their interpretations of the common law. Present practice is to
the contrary; federal courts must follow state court rulings, no longer developing general common-law principles as they think best.
[70] 310 U.S. 296 (1940).
[71] Volume 2 considers arguments that the Court should not have applied it to the states.

solicitation without having obtained a certificate,[72] the Supreme Court said that designating an administrative official to determine if a cause was religious involved impermissible censorship of religious expression.

Cantwell represents a common circumstance when free exercise and free speech claims are closely linked. The right to engage in religious expression involves both free speech and free exercise. The *Cantwell* Court's treatment of the licensing scheme suggested that religious speech may be even more protected than other speech,[73] and in some later cases as well, the Court granted religious expression special constitutional protections. That approach has ended.[74]

Cantwell's significance for free exercise principle lies largely in its softening of the *Reynolds* belief-action dichotomy. Religious action could receive some protection, even against a general law. Here is what the Court said: "[T]he Amendment embraces two concepts,—freedom to believe and freedom to act. The first is absolute but, in the nature of things, the second cannot be. Conduct remains subject to regulation for the protection of society. . . . In every case the power to regulate must be so exercised as not . . . unduly to infringe the protected freedom."[75]

In 1940, the Supreme Court rejected the free exercise claims of Jehovah's Witnesses that their children be excused from a compulsory flag salute in school.[76] Three years later, the Court reversed itself in *West Virginia Board of Education v. Barnette*,[77] relying, however, on a general First Amendment right to freedom of conscience rather than the Free Exercise Clause alone. In one of our culture's most eloquent passages about liberty of conscience, Justice Jackson wrote, "If there is any fixed star in our constitutional constellation, it is that no official, high or petty, can prescribe what shall be orthodox in politics, nationalism, religion, or other matters of opinion or force citizens to confess by word or act their faith therein."[78]

A high-water mark for free exercise was reached in 1963. In *Sherbert v. Verner*,[79] a Seventh-day Adventist claimed that the state had violated her rights by denying her unemployment compensation because she refused to

---

[72] He was also convicted of breach of peace, in circumstances that violated the Free Speech Clause.

[73] The Court does not say in *Cantwell* that any solicitor with a noncommercial message could successfully challenge a requirement that he get a certificate in advance.

[74] Indeed, if a legislature now gives protection to religious speech or publications not granted to other speech or publications, that may be regarded as an establishment of religion.

[75] Note 70 supra, at 303–4.

[76] *Minersville School Dist. v. Gobitis*, 310 U.S. 586.

[77] 319 U.S. 624 (1943).

[78] Id. at 642.

[79] Note 3 supra.

work on Saturday, her Sabbath. The Court agreed. Justice Brennan's opinion indicated that states must sometimes create exceptions from valid general laws for claims of religious conscience. When a law infringes on a person's free exercise of religion, a state can apply it against that person only if it demonstrates a compelling governmental interest in doing so. The state had no such interest in denying unemployment compensation to Sherbert.

Given the history of the compelling interest test, the Court's use of it in *Sherbert* seemed to promise potent protection for free exercise claims, but the reality was bound to be more complicated. Under a well-settled constitutional doctrine, any statute can be challenged as failing to rest on a "rational basis." Showing that some rational basis supports a law proves a very low hurdle for the government to overcome, because courts accept, or make up, rational bases, however little connection they may have to the real reasons why laws are adopted. By contrast, when a statute engages in a "suspect classification," as between racial groups, or infringes upon a fundamental right, like free speech, a court will declare the law invalid unless it serves a compelling interest that cannot be achieved by less intrusive means. This is a very difficult constitutional test for the government; under it, few laws survive.[80]

The crucial point about *Sherbert* is that one could never have expected religious claimants seeking exemptions to have the rate of success of persons challenging racial classifications or laws infringing freedom of speech. Courts hesitate to exempt some individuals from laws that apply to everyone else. Unsurprisingly, the compelling interest test has never had the same force in religious exemption cases as when laws classify by race or infringe upon free speech. Courts have rejected most demands for exemptions. The other major Supreme Court case sustaining such a claim was *Wisconsin v. Yoder*,[81] allowing Amish parents to withdraw their children after the eighth grade to participate in the religious community's vocational education, despite a state law requiring children to remain in school until they are sixteen. More typical was *United States v. Lee*, in which the Supreme Court ruled that an Amish employer with a religious objection could not refuse to pay the Social Security tax, although the covered employees were Amish and the Amish consistently refuse to take advantage of Social Security.[82] According to the Court, the government has a compelling interest in not making exceptions to its standards of taxation.

---

[80] For some matters courts have used intermediate scrutiny, a test more difficult than rational basis but less so than compelling interest. A court may ask if the government has a substantial interest that is substantially served by the law in question.

[81] 406 U.S. 205 (1972).

[82] *United States v. Lee*, 455 U.S. 252 (1982).

In cases involving the military and prisons, the Court avoided the "compelling interest" test altogether, instead deferring to judgments of administrative officials. And, when Native Americans challenged development of federal land that would disturb sacred sites, the Court announced that it did not have to assess the government's interest because, absent coercion, direct or indirect, the government was not "prohibiting" the exercise of religion.[83]

Finally, in 1990, rejecting the claim by members of the Native American Church that they had a right to use peyote in their worship services, the Court in *Employment Division v. Smith*[84] explicitly abandoned the standard of *Sherbert v. Verner* (except for unemployment compensation cases).[85] It resolved that, if a law is generally valid, the government can apply it against religious claimants without having to surmount *any* hurdle beyond the minimal rational basis test. Returning to the belief-action distinction drawn in *Reynolds*, the Court relied little on original understanding. Its main thrust was that claimants for exemption should not win as a matter of course, and that courts could not manageably decide questions of sincerity, assess the strength of religious claims, and measure those against the importance of government interests. A strong believer in clear lines that reduce judicial discretion, Justice Scalia, the opinion's author, was unwilling to countenance the uncertainties and contextual judgments of any approach that required courts to weigh religious claims against state interests. Legislatures could choose to grant exemptions, but the constitution does not demand them.

Smith does not determine how states interpret their own free exercise provisions, and state courts have had to decide whether to follow *Smith*, adhere to the preceding approach of *Sherbert v. Verner*, or adopt yet another approach.

Although legislatures may grant exemptions, not any exemption will do. A legislature must classify properly; most obviously it must not favor some religions unfairly over others. It must also be careful not to grant too much by way of exemption, or it may run into Establishment Clause difficulties, as Connecticut found when the Supreme Court declared it could not give people an absolute right to avoid work on their Sabbath.[86]

A few years after *Smith*, the Supreme Court revealed much of what remains of judicially enforced free exercise rights. Hialeah ordinances were directed at animal sacrifice practiced by the Santeria religion, leaving un-

---

[83] *Lyng v. Northwest Indian Cemetery Protective Association*, 485 U.S. 439 (1988).

[84] Note 5 supra. The crucial issue at this stage of the case was the constitutional validity of applying the criminal prohibition against the claimants, although in fact they suffered dismissal from a job rather than criminal punishment.

[85] The Court also made an exception for "hybrid" cases involving two constitutional rights, a category into which it said *Wisconsin v. Yoder* fell.

[86] *Estate of Thornton v. Caldor, Inc.*, 472 U.S. 703 (1985).

touched numerous other ways of killing animals.[87] The ordinances were not a neutral law of general applicability. Because they targeted a religious practice, the ordinances were invalid unless they served a compelling interest. The state failed to make that showing, and the laws designed to prevent animal sacrifice, thus, violated the Free Exercise Clause and were invalid.

The most significant response to *Smith* was by Congress. Urged by a large number of religious groups, it passed the Religious Freedom Restoration Act (RFRA).[88] The act, applicable to all levels of government, readopted the compelling interest test of *Sherbert v. Verner*.[89] Because RFRA did not make any exceptions for the military and for prisons, it proposed to usher in a regime of free exercise rights more expansive than what had preceded *Smith*. But the Supreme Court had different ideas. It declared the act invalid as it applies to states and localities, because Congress had no authority acting to enforce the Fourteenth Amendment to redefine rights in a manner incompatible with the Court's approach.[90] The Court's opinion was murky about the status of the act as it applies against the federal government, but its theory of decision did not cover that; and the validity of that aspect of the law is now well established.[91] Since the Court's reaction to RFRA, Congress has adopted a law guaranteeing free exercise rights in a more limited category of circumstances involving prisons and land use.[92] For this law, which the court has upheld in its application to prisons,[93] Congress relied mainly on its spending power, a power more expansive than its authority under the Fourteenth Amendment.[94]

To summarize the law at this time, RFRA is apparently valid in its applications to the federal government. Congress may adopt some narrower protections against state laws and administrative practices. State legislatures may pass acts similar to RFRA to apply within their borders, and some states

---

[87] *Church of the Lukumi Babalu Aye, Inc. v. City of Hialeah*, 508 U. S. 520 (1993).

[88] Religious Freedom Restoration Act, 42 U.S.C. §§ 2000bb-1–2000bb-4 (2004).

[89] Its crucial language is this: "Government may not substantially burden a person's exercise of religion even if the burden results from a rule of general applicability . . . [unless] it demonstrates that application of the burden to the person (1) is in furtherance of a compelling governmental interest; and (2) is the least restrictive means of furthering that . . . interest."

[90] *City of Boerne v. Flores*, 521 U.S. 507 (1997).

[91] In February of 2006, a unanimous Court (Justice Alito not participating) relied on RFRA to hold invalid an application of the Controlled Substance Act to bar importation of a hallucinogenic tea used in religious services. *Gonzales v. O Centro Espírita Beneficente União Do Vegetal*, No. 04-1084. See also *Cutter v. Wilkinson*, 125 S. Ct. 2113, 2124–25 (2005) (upholding a subsequent statute, see note 92 infra, and assuming that the application of RFRA to federal prisons is uncontroversial.)

[92] The Religious Land Use and Institutionalized Persons Act, 42 U.S.C. § 2000cc (2004).

[93] *Cutter*, note 91 supra. The unanimous opinion, rejecting an Establishment Clause challenge, signals rather strongly the validity of RFRA as it applies to the federal government.

[94] Congress can place conditions on the receipt of federal money that could not be justified on the basis of any other enumerated power.

have done so. States may also avoid the restrictive approach of *Smith* if their courts declare that their own free exercise provisions confer more extensive rights than does the federal clause, as interpreted in *Smith*.

It remains to say a few words about the Establishment Clause, which is the subject of extended analysis in volume 2 of this work. From 1947 to 2002, the clause was interpreted to bar substantial direct aid to parochial schools and to prevent officially sponsored religious exercises in public schools. Over this period, the Court's approach was substantially separationist, opposed to mingling of the government and religious activities. In recent years, this opposition has softened when public assistance to private schools and other activities has been involved. The Court has given more attention to whether aid is available on a neutral basis to religious and nonreligious organizations,[95] and has been inclined to uphold such aid. In 2002, the Court sustained a voucher program under which money received as a consequence of parental choices afforded parochial schools substantial assistance.[96]

For much of the half century of the Supreme Court's active enforcement of the Establishment Clause, it has employed a threefold test of invalidity.[97] A law is invalid if it does not have a secular purpose, if its primary effect is to advance or inhibit religion, or if it creates an excessive government entanglement with religion. The use of this test, as such, has been waning, but its elements still help determine whether a state law will be rejected.

The intricacies of this test and alternatives are explored in volume 2, but we need to recognize two important points here. A majority of the Supreme Court has, over the past fifty years, consistently maintained the controversial position that the government cannot sponsor religion in general as compared with irreligion or nonreligious activities. A minority of Supreme Court justices and some scholars are firmly convinced that the government should be able to support religion, so long as it does not discriminate among religions. I directly address the principle of nonsponsorship of religion in the volume on nonestablishment. Here I take it as a background principle for the treatment of free exercise.

If government cannot support religion, how can it create exemptions for religious conscience from valid general laws? This question, which concerns legislative exemptions as well as ones judges might carve out as constitutional rights, is perhaps *the* most critical one about the relationship between the two religion clauses. It requires extensive analysis, but here are a few preliminary observations.

---

[95] In *Mitchell v. Helms*, 530 U.S. 793 (2000), four justices indicated that virtually any aid is permissible that meets this standard. (Plurality opinion of Thomas, J.)

[96] *Zelman v. Simmons-Harris*, 536 U.S. 639 (2002).

[97] *Lemon v. Kurtzman*, 403 U.S. 602 (1971).

First, not every exemption is support in the relevant sense. If a legislature or a court declares that a Sabbatarian, unwilling to work on Saturday, will be able to collect unemployment compensation, it does not really sponsor or endorse Saturday religions, in a country where Sunday is the day most people worship and do not work.

Second, the Supreme Court has never supposed that the threefold Establishment Clause test bars all exemptions. The language of the test creates the appearance of difficulty, because one might suppose that a religious exemption has a religious purpose and "advances" religion; but judges can respond either that a permissible exemption reflects a secular purpose and does not have a primary effect of advancing religion, or, more candidly, that the purpose and effect of an acceptable exemption may be religious but do not violate the Establishment Clause.

Third, it will sometimes be a delicate judgment whether an exemption is permissible or amounts to an establishment of religion.

Fourth, nonestablishment values bear heavily on how the beneficiaries of an exemption are cast. Most obviously, one religion cannot be favored over another religion that is similar in regard to the claim for exemption. More controversially, an exemption *may* amount to impermissible sponsorship of religion if similar nonreligious persons do not receive it. This question of classifications that distinguish between religious and nonreligious claims will occupy us in many of the following chapters.

CHAPTER 3

Freedom from Compelled Profession of Belief, Adverse Targeting, and Discrimination

Amidst modern controversies over what it protects, the Free Exercise Clause has a settled core, which overlaps what the Establishment Clause guarantees. The government cannot force people to profess religious beliefs, it cannot target religious practices for unfavorable treatment, and it cannot discriminate among religions. These basic, straightforward principles raise some intriguing questions about what constitutes discrimination, about the "freedom to believe," and about legislators' attitudes toward the value of religious activity.

FORCED PROFESSIONS OF BELIEF

The government cannot demand that anyone engage in religious practice or subscribe to a religious creed. Such compulsion both denies free exercise of religion and amounts to establishment of the favored practice or creed. Nor can the government make eligibility for civil benefits conditional on someone's having or expressing particular religious views.[1]

In the only modern case involving forced expression of a religious belief, a Maryland man was not allowed to become a notary public because he refused to declare his belief in God.[2] Although test oaths were common during the colonial period,[3] and they continued in the early republic, even in many states that had no establishment of religion as that concept was then understood, a religious test for office is indisputably unfair at this stage of history. A government that conditions public privileges on belief in God does not allow full free exercise of religion, and it establishes theism. And since

---

[1] I subsequently suggest that the government may withhold a public position from someone who expresses religious views that have disturbing implications for how he might perform his public duties.

[2] *Torcaso v. Watkins*, 367 U.S. 488, 489 (1960). The Maryland constitution declared that no religious test could be required for public office, except "a declaration of belief in the existence of God."

[3] Article 6 of the federal Constitution barred any religious test for federal officials, thus protecting this aspect of religious liberty prior to the Bill of Rights.

adherents of some religions, notably Buddhism, do not assert the existence of God, a test of belief in God also favors some religions over others.[4]

The Supreme Court had little trouble deciding that the Maryland test oath violated the First Amendment's religion clauses. Quoting comments from earlier cases that "freedom to believe" is absolute[5] and that government cannot force a person "to profess a belief . . . in any religion,"[6] Justice Black concluded that the test "unconstitutionally invades [Torcaso's] freedom of belief and religion."[7] Justice Black also said that the state cannot "aid those religions based on a belief in the existence of God as against those religions founded on different beliefs."[8]

TARGETING

When they adopted the Free Exercise Clause, the founders, recalling outright religious persecution of dissenters, undoubtedly aimed to prevent Congress from penalizing people because of their religious beliefs or practices. Under the First Amendment, the government cannot restrict practices, such as participation in a Roman Catholic Mass, because it regards their religious content as pernicious or misguided.[9] Modern American laws rarely target religions in this way. When the modern Supreme Court did address such a law, it struck it down. The Court earlier reached a similar conclusion about a law that aimed at religion in what was arguably a more benign manner.

Targeting Animal Sacrifice and Related Problems

In the more recent of the two cases, the Court considered ordinances aimed at animal sacrifice by members of the Santeria religion.[10] That religion, prac-

---

[4] A conceivable defense of such a test might be that many people who do not believe in God are unreliable, but this judgment is factually implausible and is not one a modern government should make, even were it otherwise plausible.

[5] *Torcaso*, supra note 2, at 492, quoting from *Cantwell v. Connecticut*, 310 U.S. 296, 304 (1940).

[6] Id. at 492, 495, quoting from *Everson v. Board of Education*, 330 U.S. 1, 15 (1947).

[7] Id. at 496.

[8] In response to the argument that no one need hold public office, Black said that government may not bar people from holding public office on the basis of constitutionally forbidden criteria.

[9] As Justice Scalia wrote in *Employment Division v. Smith*, 494 U.S. 872, 877 (1990), a state cannot ban "acts or abstentions only when they are engaged in for religious reasons, or only because of the religious belief that they display." By contrast, a law that forbids all use of alcoholic beverages, adopted because of a strong belief that drinking alcohol in every form creates an unacceptable danger of alcoholism, would not target Roman Catholic practices, even if the law were applied to prevent use of wine for the Mass.

[10] *Church of the Lukumi Babalu Aye, Inc. v. City of Hialeah*, 508 U.S. 520 (1993).

ticed by members of the Yoruba people from Cuba, fuses elements of traditional African religion and Roman Catholicism. Its rituals include sacrifices of chickens, pigeons, doves, ducks, guinea pigs, goats, sheep, and turtles, whose meat is typically eaten after a sacrifice. The City of Hialeah responded to plans to create a Santeria house of worship by adopting ordinances that prohibited animal sacrifice,[11] while continuing to allow kosher slaughtering, private slaughtering of a small number of hogs or cattle per week, hunting, and killing of animals not used for food.

According to Justice Kennedy for the Court, if a law's object is to "restrict practices because of their religious motivation, the law is not neutral . . . and it is invalid [under the Free Exercise Clause] unless it is justified by a compelling interest and is narrowly tailored to advance that interest."[12] Although noting that the words "ritual" and "sacrifice" now admit of a secular meaning, Justice Kennedy said that the choice of these words in an ordinance supports the conclusion that the legislative aim was to suppress the central element of Santeria worship. Virtually the only conduct the ordinances covered was the religious exercise of Santeria church members; killings no more necessary or humane went unpunished.[13] By devaluing religious reasons for killing, the city had singled out religious practice for discriminating treatment."[14] Applying the compelling interest test, the Court found the ordi-

---

[11] One of these made it unlawful to "sacrifice any animal," "sacrifice" being defined as "to unnecessarily kill, torment, torture, or mutilate an animal in a public or private ritual or ceremony not for the primary purpose of food consumption." Other ordinances prohibited owning animals intended to be used for food purposes and slaughtering of animals for food outside of areas zoned for slaughterhouse use. Id. at 527–28.

[12] Id. at 533.

[13] Id. at 536. In a part of the opinion joined only by Justice Stevens, Kennedy relied on the history of adoption of the ordinances to bolster the conclusion that they were designed to suppress Santeria practice because of its religious character. Justice Scalia, with Chief Justice Rehnquist, disagreed with Justice Kennedy's reference to the subjective motivations of lawmakers; he would have limited analysis to an objective evaluation of the laws. Id. at 58. This issue about subjective motivation is an important problem in Establishment Clause cases, and I consider it in more detail in the second volume.

[14] Id. at 537. A more general Florida statute prohibited "unnecessarily" killing any animal, but almost every other reason for killing animals, including using live rabbits to train greyhound racers, was regarded as necessary. Having determined that the ordinances were not neutral, Justice Kennedy further concluded that the laws were not of general applicability, because they did not treat similarly nonreligious conduct that endangers the interests in health and avoiding animal cruelty to the same degree. Id. at 543.

This point was developed further in Justice Scalia's opinion; he commented that the terms "neutrality" and "general applicability" substantially overlap. A defect in neutrality arises when laws by their terms impose disabilities on the basis of religion; lack of general applicability occurs when laws, though neutral in their terms, "through their design, construction, or enforcement target the practices of a particular religion for discriminatory treatment." Id. But laws that are nonneutral can be considered not to be of general applicability, and laws that are not of general applicability can be considered nonneutral.

nances invalid. The interests they served were not compelling, given the failure to prevent other extensive damage to those interests. And the ordinances were not drawn narrowly enough to achieve the objectives of protecting public health and preventing cruelty to animals; for those purposes, something less than a total ban on animal sacrifice would have sufficed.[15]

Justice Blackmun, concurring, picked up on the last point; a law "that targets religious practice for disfavored treatment" will "by definition" not be "precisely tailored to a compelling governmental interest."[16] For most conceivable laws, Blackmun's position is correct. If a law targets conduct *because* of its religious motivations or forbids conduct engaged in as a religious practice,[17] while leaving unregulated similar conduct engaged in for nonreligious reasons, the state will *never* be able to show that the law is narrowly tailored to serve a compelling interest. However, one can imagine a state defending a law that restricts only religious conduct on the ground that other conduct either does not present a similar threat or is justified by some strong necessity. These possibilities raise the perplexing questions just what it is to target conduct because it is religious and how religious activity should be valued by the state.

We might imagine that a religious group engages in a practice that involves dangers not presented by nonreligious activities. Suppose members of a church jump from the top of one-story buildings to demonstrate their faith in God.[18] Most jumpers emerge unscathed, but a few have broken bones, one has become paralyzed, and one has died. The city council passes an ordinance that forbids any jumping from buildings.[19] Is the religion being targeted? If the city council is concerned only about physical safety, and would have an equal concern if the dangerous activity did not involve religion, the religious practice is not being targeted in the sense that the Hialeah ordinances targeted animal sacrifice. Thus, the mere fact that only the adher-

---

[15] Id. at 538–39. Thus the Court did not need to decide whether the value of animal sacrifice outweighed concerns about human health and cruelty to animals. As the briefs of animal rights organizations showed, one could reasonably think that the harms the ordinance sought to prevent were sufficiently grave to warrant a prohibition. But even from the animal rights perspective, these ordinances were unfair to the practitioners of Santeria, because they left unregulated more popular, widespread activities that were at least as harmful.

[16] Id. at 579.

[17] This part of the sentence assumes that either this rationale is evident from the face of the law, as in a preamble, *or* that the ground of the law can be established by appropriate techniques of interpretation.

[18] Of course, people who jump from buildings to commit suicide endanger themselves, but jumping with an aim to harm oneself may be regarded as a different activity from jumping without such an aim.

[19] An exception is made for emergencies such as fires, when jumping may be necessary to save lives.

ents of one religion engage in a practice does not itself establish that a prohibition targets the religion.

A more troublesome question is posed if the city council allows some equally dangerous activity that people engage in because it is exciting and physically challenging—for example, bungee jumping. That this possibility is not wholly unrealistic is indicated by the government's allowing people who scale mountain peaks and engage in extreme sports to endanger themselves to a much greater degree than ordinary automobile drivers are allowed to endanger themselves.[20] If the council permits some other equally dangerous activity, its response to building jumping seems dictated partly by its sense that the religion is "crazy" or at least that such jumping is pointless and that the jumpers are deluded to think it has value.

To return to animal sacrifice, legislators might think that hunting is useful and enriching, but that killing healthy animals under one's control as part of a religious practice lacks value. How *should* a legislature regard the value of religious sacrifice? A legislator knows that the practitioners think the activity has significant religious value. He also knows that the vast majority of people in this society disagree; whatever their opinion about animal sacrifice as it is portrayed in the Old Testament, they do not believe animal sacrifice serves any genuine religious objective in modern life. If the legislature implicitly decides that religious killing of animals has no value and that virtually every other killing of animals has substantial value, that constitutes targeting, whether or not legislators positively abhor the religious practice and whether or not they fairly reflect general opinion about the merits of animal sacrifice. When people engage in an activity for religious reasons, perhaps legislators must count it as having *at least as much value* as similar activities people undertake for pleasure, ordinary recreational benefit, and simple usefulness.[21]

Although my hypothetical example about jumping from buildings is fanciful, the analogous problem of religious practitioners handling poisonous snakes and drinking strychnine is not. Within some charismatic Christian groups, dominantly in the southern United States, members handle poison-

---

[20] See, e.g., Timothy Egan, "Courting Disaster, in Search of Snowy Thrills," *New York Times*, February 14, 2003, A4 (people with skis, snowboards, and snowmobiles seeking untouched snow create risks of dying from avalanches). The acceptability of an activity depends partly on its harms and benefits. Suppose it is concluded that jumping fifty times from a one-story building is no more hazardous than attempting to climb Mount Everest. Climbing Mount Everest is regarded as heroic and ennobling; jumping from buildings as brash and foolish. One could reasonably allow climbing of high peaks and forbid jumping from buildings.

[21] I am putting aside here arguments that some dangerous activities, such as polar exploration and mountain climbing, have extraordinary value, and arguments that some equally dangerous activities need not be regulated because so few people want to undertake them.

ous snakes and drink poisons, following a passage in Mark that tells of Jesus'
appearance to the Apostles after his Resurrection, when he said that believers
"shall speak with new tongues; they shall take up serpents; and if they drink
any deadly thing, it shall not hurt them."[22] Those who handle poisonous
snakes during services feel they are moved by the Holy Spirit, and commonly
achieve a trancelike state of ecstasy.[23] Here is the way one reporter, who had
become closely connected with participants in the course of writing about
them, described his own experience:

> I felt no fear. The snake seemed to be an extension of myself. And suddenly there
> seemed to be nothing in the room but me and the snake. Everything else had
> disappeared. Carl, the congregation, Jim—all gone, all faded to white. And I
> could not hear the earsplitting music. The air was silent and still and filled with
> that strong, even light. And I realized that I, too, was fading into the white. I
> was losing myself by degrees, like the incredible shrinking man. The snake would
> be the last to go, and all I could see was the way its scales shimmered one last
> time in the light, and the way its head moved from side to side, searching for a
> way out. I knew then why the handlers took up serpents. There is power in the
> act of disappearing; there is victory in the loss of self. It must be close to our
> conception of paradise, what it's like before you're born or after you die.[24]

A number of states have laws against snake handling.[25] Kentucky's law,
which specifically covers handling "any kind of reptile in connection with
any religious service,"[26] plainly targets religious practice. That law cannot
be saved by the argument that few people are interested in handling snakes
outside of religious services. But what of the more typical approach of Tennessee, where it is unlawful to handle "a poisonous or dangerous snake or
reptile in such manner as to endanger the life or health of any person."[27]
Although religious ceremonies are not mentioned, we can be confident legis-

---

[22] Mark 16:17–18.

[23] A sympathetic and highly readable account is Dennis Covington, *Salvation on Sand Mountain* (New York: Penguin, 1995). See also Weston Labarre, *They Shall Take Up Serpents* (Min-
neapolis: University of Minnesota Press, 1962); Robert W. Pelton and Karen W. Carden, *Snake
Handlers: God-fearers? Or Fanatics?* (Nashville: T. Nelson, 1974).

[24] Covington, note 23 supra, at 169–70.

[25] In states without such statutes the activity may be regarded as a breach of peace.

[26] K.R.S. 437.060 (2002). The Kentucky law was upheld as a valid exercise of the state's
power to protect safety in *Lawson v. Kentucky*, 164 S.W.2d 972 (Ct. App. Ky. 1942). The court
wrote that a state may prohibit "the practice of a religious rite which endangers the lives, health
or safety of the participants, or other persons." It did not focus, as a modern court would, on
whether the prohibition may be explicitly cast in terms of a religious rite.

[27] Tenn. Code Ann. 39–17–101 (2002). See also 3 Del. C. § 7201 (2002); N.C. Gen. Stat.
14–418 (2003); Va. Code Ann. 18.2–313 (2003). For cases in two of these states sustaining
convictions for snake handling, see *State v. Pack*, 527 S.W.2d 99 (Sup. Ct. Tenn. 1975), cert.
denied, 424 U.S. 954 (1976) (handling snakes in public was a public nuisance); *State v. Massey*,
51 S.E.2d 179 (N. Car. 1949).

lators would not have bothered to adopt such a law were it not for concern over religiously motivated snake-handling.

The state undoubtedly has an interest in protecting the lives and health of its citizens. During services with snake handling, participants who have not voluntarily chosen to handle snakes may be in some danger, but the main risk is to adults who choose to expose themselves in that way. May the state decide to protect their life and health over their religious practice? Is its doing so a kind of targeting, involving a "discriminatory animus" that is unconstitutional?

We begin with the premise that if the state forbids an activity that is significantly dangerous and is engaged in for all sorts of reasons, including religious ones, it does not have to create an exception for the religious practitioners. Thus, a law requiring motorcyclists to wear helmets need not exempt riders whose religious convictions lead them to want to ride with heads uncovered. Under present Supreme Court doctrine, there are virtually *no* constitutional rights to exemptions; but even under the preceding more generous standard for free exercise rights (still used by many state courts) one who claimed a right to create a serious risk to his life would be likely to lose.[28] The state has a strong interest in preserving life.

But this analysis does not quite meet the targeting argument that a state allows equally dangerous activities and picks on snake handling and drinking poisons only because legislators, like most members of the society, regard the religious convictions that justify these as wildly irrational or incredibly silly. According to one set of figures, only a dozen of the eight thousand people in the United States bitten each year by poisonous snakes die. As of 1995, at least seventy-one people had been killed by poisonous snakes during religious services; the man who may have started snake handling was one of the seventy-one, but he may have been bitten more than four hundred previous times.[29] Undoubtedly, handling poisonous snakes is dangerous, but is it more dangerous than some extreme sports that legislators tolerate? Would legislators prohibit it if they accorded it a positive value anything like that the participants themselves give it?

Reflecting on snake handling and similar activities, Eugene Volokh has suggested that "courts ought to grant exemptions at least as long as the conduct is on average no riskier than dangerous behavior (perhaps such as

---

[28] The fact that most states do not now make suicide a crime is irrelevant. With the exception of an Oregon law limited to the terminally ill, states do not allow people to commit suicide, and encouraging or helping someone to commit suicide is generally a crime. The reason why suicide is not itself criminal has much more to do with the pointlessness of a criminal penalty than any judgment that people are free to take their lives.

[29] See Covington, note 23 supra, at 147–48.

skydiving) that the law does not forbid. If the law tolerates risking one's life to get an adrenaline rush, it seems appealing to carve out an exemption . . . for similarly risking one's life for spiritual reasons."[30] This comparison of degrees of danger, made with a respect for religious motivations, is one that legislators, at least, should undertake.

I am doubtful that such a comparison can usefully underlie a judicial approach to targeting, unless the activities are themselves closely analogous. The activities permitted by the Hialeah ordinances were virtually identical in terms of animal cruelty and risk to human health as those the ordinances prohibited. But essaying any precise estimation of the danger of snake handling that is the centerpiece of a religious service against the danger of skydiving is fraught with difficulty; and we cannot expect legislators to be exacting in that regard. They may prohibit activities brought to their attention, such as driving motorcycles without helmets, and leave unregulated more fringe activities (such as skydiving) that may be more dangerous. A court reviewing a law's constitutionality should not conclude that religion is targeted unless (1) religious activities are explicitly or implicitly singled out, as by the Hialeah ordinances, or (2) the prohibition of the activities would *obviously* not have been undertaken were the religious activities assigned a value approximating that of other permitted, yet equally dangerous activities.

Implicit in what I have said is that neither legislators nor judges should consider the truth or falsity of religious ideas in determining what activities may be prohibited. This general idea is explored, and qualified to a degree, in subsequent chapters of this book and in the volume on nonestablishment.

Clergy Disqualification

A case decided in 1978, prior to the Hialeah decision, involved a different kind of targeting. With the purpose of separating sacred and political functions, seven of the original thirteen states and six other states had laws excluding clergymen from some political offices.[31] After 1974, the only re-

---

[30] "Intermediate Questions of Religious Exemptions—A Research Agenda with Test Suites," 21 *Cardozo Law Review* 595, 626 (1999). (Interestingly, Dennis Covington describes being in a snake-handling service as feeling "an adrenaline rush," like one he had felt under fire in El Salvador. Note 23 supra, at 101.) Volokh acknowledges a possible counterargument that religious groups will put people under more pressure to engage in dangerous activities than they would be under to perform other dangerous activities. Id. at 627. On comparisons of dangerous activities, see also Robin Lovin, "Book Review: Rethinking the History of Church and State: The Believer and the Powers That Are; by John T. Noonan, Jr.," 76 *California Law Review* 1185, 1191 (1988).

[31] Anson Phelps Stokes, *Church and State in the United States*, vol. 1, 622 (New York: Harper, 1950). Philip Hamburger, *Separation of Church and State* 79–83 (Cambridge: Harvard

maining ban was Tennessee's prohibition against "ministers of the Gospel" serving in the state legislature or as delegates to a constitutional convention.[32] The Court held the prohibition invalid in *McDaniel v. Paty*.[33]

Among possible modern reasons for such restrictions are that religions should not have undue influence on government, that clerics may not be able fairly to perform their civil offices because of their sense of a higher obligation, and that citizens whose religious allegiance does not match that of an elected cleric may feel inadequately represented.[34] By imposing a negative consequence on clerics, and possibly exerting pressure on some of them to give up their clerical role, a law that restricts their ability to occupy offices in government interferes with their exercise of religion.[35] People may disagree about the desirability of active clergy holding important elective political offices,[36] but whatever may once have been true, a restrictive law now serves no significant public purpose. All the eight justices sitting on the case agreed that Tennessee's justifications were inadequate and that its clergy restrictions were unconstitutional.

Although Tennessee's disqualifications were not aimed at any particular religion, they did focus on religious status and practice, and perhaps belief. Regarding membership in the clergy as a status or practice, as did the plurality in *McDaniel*,[37] is most natural, but one could also see a disqualification as an inhibition on the expression of belief, Justice Brennan's position.[38] Because constitutional doctrine suggests that freedom of belief is more protected than freedom to practice one's religion, and opinions in *McDaniel* as

---

University Press, 2002) discusses the reasons for such laws and concludes that separation of church and state was not an objective.

[32] The state constitution barred service in the legislature; a statute extended that restriction to the constitutional convention.

[33] 435 U.S. 618 (1978).

[34] Some people also believe, as did many of the founders, that clerics should devote themselves to religious functions, not secular political ones. Members of various religions have different attitudes about clerical vocations. The government has no business deciding how clerics or ordinary citizens should conceive religious offices.

[35] That the law directly touches only the small number of clergy who would like to run is irrelevant.

[36] I have suggested that it is generally undesirable, in *Private Consciences and Public Reasons* 175 (New York: Oxford University Press, 1995). In the most thorough treatment of which I am aware, Paul Weithman reaches the opposite conclusion. "May Clergy Seek Elective Office?" 74 *Notre Dame Law Review* 1737 (1999). I respond briefly in "Religion and American Political Judgments," 36 *Wake Forest Law Review* 401, 417–21 (2001).

[37] The plurality opinion, written by Chief Justice Burger, treated ministerial status as "defined in terms of conduct and activity," not belief. Note 33 supra, at 627.

[38] Id. at 630–35 (arguing that freedom of belief includes freedom to profess that belief, and to do so to earn a livelihood). Justice White did not think the Tennessee law interfered with the exercise of religion; rather, the restriction violated a right to equal opportunity to hold elective office, guaranteed by the Equal Protection Clause.

well as earlier cases[39] suggest that freedom to believe is absolute, the exact characterization could matter.

The refrain that freedom to believe is absolute is almost certainly mistaken, *if* one takes that freedom to include expression *and* treats denial of office as a failure of protection—premises that both the plurality and Justice Brennan embrace in *McDaniel v. Paty*.[40] It is worth pausing to see why talk of absolute protection is an oversimplification.

Two examples help make the point. A mayor who is about to hire Hugh Barnett as police chief receives a recording of a sermon Barnett recently preached as an active lay member of a local church, in which he has urged that God intended a definite hierarchy of the races, that blacks are the condemned descendants of Ham, inferior and subordinate to whites, that members of all races should possess equal political rights, but that whites should never forget that they are superior in God's eyes. Barnett's sermon was an expression of religious belief, yet the mayor is doubly troubled about appointing him. Her first worry is that a person with these religious views may be unlikely to enforce policies of racial equality with appropriate sensitivity. Her second worry is that when nonwhites learn about the sermon, they will lose confidence in Barnett's fairness. As a sensible mayor, she looks for other candidates.

Second, consider a president's nominee for the head of the Environmental Protection Agency who has written in a church journal that a close comparison of the Book of Revelation against modern conditions shows that the world will end in twenty years. At confirmation hearings, she says this belief will have no effect on her performance in office, but senators are skeptical, apprehensive that a woman who is sure that our world will not survive beyond twenty years may have a limited concern with long-term environmental policies, and that she will fail to inspire confidence in the public that cares about the environment.

Is it unconstitutional, or inappropriate, for the mayor and the Senate to reject candidates because of religious expressions that bear on their performance of public duties in these ways?[41] I think not. No one should be refused

---

[39] See *Cantwell*, note 5 supra, at 304.

[40] I pass over the point that if religious expression directly includes speech that amounts to criminal solicitation or some other ordinary crime, or that gives rise to a civil action such as defamation, it is not absolutely protected. On the boundaries of constitutionally protected speech, see Kent Greenawalt, *Speech, Crime and the Uses of Language* (New York: Oxford University Press, 1989). For an argument that religious speech should receive extra protection against prosecution for sedition or conspiracy, see Joseph Grinstein, "Note, Jihad and the Constitution: The First Amendment Implications of Combating Religiously Motivated Terrorism," 105 *Yale Law Journal* 1347 (1996).

[41] The issue is not simply whether a court could overturn a rejection; it is also whether the mayor and Senate should regard themselves as constrained by the Constitution not to reject the candidates.

a nonreligious government position because they do not believe in the Trinity, but evaluators may use expressed religious views in judging a candidate's qualifications for a job, when those views connect directly to the performance of the job. I conclude that freedom to believe—understood to include any negative consequences because of religious expressions—is not absolute.[42]

DISCRIMINATION AMONG RELIGIONS

The Maryland oath case we reviewed earlier relied partly on a solidly entrenched principle, based on both religion clauses, that government may not favor one religion over another. Those favored are beneficiaries of an establishment; the losers suffer an impairment of free exercise. The hardest issue regarding claims of such discrimination is deciding exactly what amounts to discrimination among religions.[43] A differential impact on members of different religions, characteristic of many laws, does not alone constitute discrimination, but what more is needed?

The leading case involved a Minnesota law requiring extensive reporting requirements for most charities.[44] Religious organizations were exempted unless they received less than half of their contributions from members and affiliated organizations. Religious groups that raised more than half their funds by soliciting from the general public were treated like nonreligious charities. By strange coincidence, the Unification Church, colloquially known as the "Moonies," fit this category.

Was this law discriminatory,[45] and, if so, could it be justified? The law explicitly differentiated among religious organizations, and those with more

---

[42] Could one argue that these examples are irrelevant because no one has a right to an appointive position? Rejection of a candidate by those making the final decision might be analogized to rejection by voters. No one guarantees that voters will not take account of expressed religious views. Even if one concedes that voters may rely on whatever grounds they wish without acting unconstitutionally, the mayor and senators are government officials. Were freedom of expressed beliefs truly absolute, no government official should reach a negative conclusion about suitability for a government job because of a candidate's religious views. In *Hollon v. Pierce*, 64 Cal. Rptr. 808 (Ct. App. 3d Dist. 1967), the court upheld a school district's trustees' dismissal of a bus driver who had helped publish and distribute a religious tract that "express[ed] threats, violence, and retribution [and] had several specific references to the burning of schools and the death of school children." Id. at 815. The district's concern about the driver's mental stability was sufficient to justify its action, whose utility "outweighs its tendency to restrict the bus driver's freedom of belief and expression." Id. at 814.

[43] The clergy disqualification case sidestepped that issue. Justice Brennan noted the argument that a clergy disqualification favors religions that have no "counterparts" to clergy, but he did not pursue the point.

[44] *Larson v. Valente*, 456 U.S. 228 (1982).

[45] As a term, *discrimination* may mean simply differential treatment; it may mean worse treatment; it may mean worse treatment motivated by some antagonism or negative judgment; it may mean worse treatment that cannot be justified.

onerous reporting requirements received less favorable treatment. But from
the law's text, we cannot tell if legislators aimed at the Unification Church
(and perhaps other groups) because of a negative judgment about it and the
way it raises funds.

Comparatively unfavorable treatment is not enough alone to amount to
troubling discrimination. Suppose that charitable organizations raising more
than fifty thousand dollars a year must make more extensive reports than
those raising less than that amount. One would not think of this as discrimination against the larger charities in any strong sense; they are better able to
file more extensive reports, and the state's interest in oversight increases with
the amount of money a charity raises. Even if the fifty-thousand-dollar line
applied to religions, that would not reflect approval of one sort of religion
and disapproval of another.

Did the Minnesota law differ importantly from the fifty-thousand-dollar
line? Although its text did not reveal this clearly, the law probably reflected
the legislator's focused discontent with the Unification Church and its fund-
raising tactics. Legislators had carefully adjusted the language of earlier
drafts to avoid application to other religious groups, particularly the Roman
Catholic Church. The failure of the language to apply to any major religious
group in Minnesota should have warned the legislators to tread carefully
about making things hard just for a group that was widely disliked. That
disregarded counsel of restraint does not, however, tell us how a court should
have resolved the constitutional issue.

In *Larson v. Valente*, only seven justices considered the constitutional merits of the case.[46] Writing for the majority, Justice Brennan concluded that the
Minnesota scheme was a "suspect" denominational preference that called
for application of the compelling interest test. The state's reasons failed that
test, because it had no solid reason to suppose that the members will prevent
abusive public solicitations if their own contributions exceed 50 percent,
and because the need for disclosure does not rise with the percentage of
nonmember contributions (as contrasted with their total amount).[47]

---

[46] Two others did not, because they thought that it was insufficiently clear that members of
the Unification Church would get what they wanted even if the Supreme Court decided in
their favor. Federal courts will decide cases only if some practical consequence depends on the
outcome. They cannot render " advisory opinions." Minnesota had advanced the (ridiculous)
claim that the Unification Church is not a religion. If the church's members won the claim that
the exception to the religious exemption was invalid, they might still be subject to the reporting
requirements as a nonreligious charitable organization. This possibility was sufficient for four
justices to conclude that the Court should not have decided the case. See the dissent of Justice
Rehnquist, note 44 supra, at 264–72. Among this group of four, Justices White and Rehnquist
also disagreed with the majority on the merits. Id. at 258–63.

[47] Id. at 249–51.

Justice Brennan's opinion is unclear about which religion clause renders denominational preferences invalid[48] and, more crucially, about why this statute created a denominational preference.[49] One *should* straightforwardly say that a typical religious preference violates both clauses, although in various instances the aspect of establishment or inhibition of free exercise may loom as more prominent.[50]

The more important issue practically is what it takes to constitute a religious preference. According to Justice Brennan, the 50 percent rule "makes explicit and deliberate distinctions between different religious organizations"[51] and favors well-established denominations over new religious groups trying to raise money from the public.[52] Justice Brennan did not quite say that all categorizations of religious organizations involving advantage and disadvantage are discriminatory preferences,[53] and he did not quite say that any categorization that favors established religious groups over isolated newcomers is suspect.[54] Justice Brennan traded on the facts that the legislators were aiming to curb the Unification Church and designed the law not to cover established churches, but he did not root the holding in an explicit finding to that effect.

In sum, one is not quite sure just what the Court regards as establishing a discriminatory preference in the sense that triggers strict scrutiny. A sensible position would be that any classification among religious groups should be

[48] For the most part, Brennan treated the relevant clause as the Establishment Clause; "the clearest command of the Establishment Clause is that one religious denomination cannot be officially preferred over another." Id. at 244. But he wrote that the prohibition of denominational preferences is "inextricably connected with the continuing vitality of the Free Exercise Clause," id. at 245, and that the relationship between the Establishment Clause and the Free Exercise Clause achieves religious liberty by requiring that "government . . . effect no favoritism among sects." Id. at 246, quoting from an earlier opinion by Justice Goldberg.

[49] Had the Court not found a denominational preference, it would have applied the standard establishment test, one that presents an easier burden for the state to bear.

[50] One is tempted to say that if a constitution had only one clause and not the other, a religious preference would violate it; *but* the absence of an establishment clause might imply that the government can establish a religion, and that might imply that the right of free exercise does not include a right to be free of discriminatory preferences.

[51] Id. at 247.

[52] In response, Justice White pointed out that the rule names no churches or denominations and that eligibility for the exemption does not turn on the nature of a group's religious beliefs. Id. at 261.

[53] Were such a rule adopted, any distinction based on income, or size of membership, would be suspect. One *might* defend such an absolute rule as necessary to defend against unprovable legislative aims to prefer favored groups, but such a rule would sharply restrict a legislature's capacity to undertake reasonable classifications.

[54] Justice White wrote that the majority claimed that the "rule on its face represents an explicit and deliberate preference for some religious beliefs over others," id. at 261, but I do not find any such claim put forward clearly by Justice Brennan. The Court does say that "the provision was drafted with the explicit intention of including particular religious denominations and

treated as suspect unless it clearly does not involve discrimination based on judgments about the merits of various groups, a showing that would be difficult for a state to make if a law benefits established bodies in comparison with unpopular newcomers.[55]

DISCRIMINATION AND ORIGINALISM

The law about religious discrimination presents an interesting puzzle for originalist judges. In an opinion defending the proposition that the Establishment Clause allows preferences for religion over nonreligion, Justice Rehnquist relied on Joseph Story's claim that the original understanding allowed preferences for Christianity over other religions.[56] No Supreme Court justice or prominent legal scholar now defends *such* a preference, yet a justice purporting to be faithful to the original understanding in a simple sense should allow preferences for Christians, if he believes they were then assumed to be permissible. If a justice wants to rely on original intent to defend preferences in favor of religion generally but not in favor of Christianity, he needs to explain why the original understanding should carry weight for the first kind of preference but not the second.[57] It is just such difficulties that pose obstacles for those who would transform constitutional law by a strategy of interpretation that is rigorously originalist.

---

excluding others." Id. at 254. But intending exclusion and inclusion is not quite the same as preferring because of belief.

[55] For a recent case invalidating an exemption to immunization requirements limited to members of "a recognized church or religious denomination," because it discriminated against individuals with religious opposition who were not members of organized groups, see *Boone v. Boozman*, 217 F. Supp. 2d 938 (E.D. Ark. 2002).

[56] Justice Rehnquist dissenting in *Wallace v. Jaffree*, 472 U.S. 38, 104–5 (1985) .

[57] Justice Rehnquist neatly sidesteps, and obscures, the difficulty. Having quoted two paragraphs from Story's commentaries that clearly envision the possibility of favorable treatment for Christianity, Rehnquist says that "from the evidence," the well-accepted meaning of the Establishment Clause was that it "forbade establishment of a national religion, and forbade preferences among sects or denominations." Id. at 105. The problem is that the "evidence" from Story suggests that no preferences among Christian denominations were allowed but that Christian groups could be preferred to Jewish or Muslim ones. Rehnquist has subtly transformed this narrower restraint into a bar on both kinds of preferences.

One could *perhaps* rely on understandings when the Fourteenth Amendment was adopted to support preferences for religion, but not ones for Christianity.

CHAPTER 4

Conscientious Objection to Military Service

We can see crucial questions about free exercise exemptions and classifications in sharp outline by focusing on privileges for conscientious objectors to
avoid military service—an exemption from general legal requirements that
predates the Constitution itself and has had broad public support over the
years. Pacifists (and some others) cannot in good conscience engage in combat or in any military capacity. Most, but not all, pacifists base their objections on religious convictions of a traditional sort. Although the practical
importance of conscientious objection in the United States diminished when
a volunteer army replaced military conscription, excusing people from military service remains the quintessential exemption, against which we can
compare many other conflicts of legal duty and religious conscience.

The basic problem about conscientious objection is simple. The government requires persons to perform combatant military duty. Some individuals
believe that government should not engage in war, and feel deeply that they
cannot serve as combatants or cannot participate in the military at all.[1] If
forced to participate, they refuse, and end up in jail,[2] or they subordinate
their deep convictions and serve.

Should the government respond by granting objectors an exemption? If
so, should it define the exemption on the basis of religious convictions, group
membership, or pacifism, or grant it to all objectors? In the United States,
should these various decisions be left to Congress, or should judges resolve
some of them as matters of constitutional law?

Shared obligations of citizenship that contradict the deep moral sense of
many individuals pose powerful theoretical and practical challenges for a
liberal democratic society. Compulsory military service is at once the most
demanding of those obligations and the one that arouses the most intense
opposition. The convictions of conscientious objectors can affect not only
the parameters of conscription, but whether any draft is desirable.[3] And is-

---

[1] Some people may not object to the government's fighting wars, but their religious perspective precludes their participation.

[2] Of course, they do not end up in jail unless they are prosecuted and convicted.

[3] Given the tactical warfare the United States seems likely to engage in during the near future,
and the supply of young men and women who may be attracted to a volunteer army, a reinstated
draft does not seem probable, but conflicts like that begun in Iraq in 2003 may make military
service seem unappealing; we cannot be sure that the days of a draft are over. After the events

sues about conscientious objection do arise within a volunteer army, because volunteers are not free, as are civilians, to quit when they wish. Men and women who enter the military sign on for a term of years. Volunteers who leave when their company is assigned to Iraq or Kosovo are not resigning abruptly, they are committing the crime of desertion. And reservists who decline to leave civilian life when their unit is called up for a conflict also are committing crimes. Because some young soldiers and reservists have life-altering experiences and become pacifists, questions about conscientious objection have not disappeared with the end of conscription.[4]

LEGAL PROVISION FOR OBJECTORS

Throughout American history, conscientious objectors to military service have received exemptions of varying scope. Most colonies and early states, by legislation or constitutional right, exempted men who were scrupulously opposed to bearing arms. Some states limited the exemption to members of particular sects; some required men who were exempted to produce a substitute or pay a fee. James Madison's original proposal for the Bill of Rights included a clause that "no person religiously scrupulous of bearing arms shall be compelled to render military service in person," but that idea was dropped, in part because conscription was considered a state rather than federal function.[5] During the Civil War, the 1864 Draft Act, instituting national conscription, excused conscientious objectors who were forbidden by their denominations' articles of faith from bearing arms.[6] The Draft Act of 1917 exempted from combatant service only those who were members "of any well-recognized sect or organization at present organized and existing and whose existing creed or principles forbid its members to participate in war in any form."[7]

---

of September 11, 2001, one can also imagine a tremendous increase in personnel to protect internal security, some of whom might be conscripted.

[4] Department of Defense Regulation 1300.6 provides for discharge or transfer of those who object to participating "in war in any form." Discharge is "discretionary" but is granted if the applicant's views have altered since entering the service.

[5] See Brief for Petitioner at 61–68, *Gillette v. United States*, 401 U.S. 437 (1971); Kurt T. Lash, "Power and the Subject of Religion," 59 *Ohio State Law Journal* 1069, 1112–15 (1998).

[6] Federal adoption of state provisions for exemption preceded the act.

[7] 40 Stat. 76, 78 (1917). Executive practice ameliorated the membership requirement and the failure to exempt anyone from noncombatant military service. The War Department ordered that those with "personal scruples against war" be treated as conscientious objectors, and some conscientious objectors were furloughed for civilian service. See generally Mulford Q. Sibley and Philip E. Jacob, *Conscription of Conscience: The American State and the Conscientious Objector, 1940–1947*, 12–14 (Ithaca: Cornell University Press, 1952); Neil M. Wherry,

The 1940 Selective Service Act, whose essential provisions about conscientious objection remain intact, was more expansive than its 1917 predecessor. Largely through the legislative efforts of the "peace" churches, especially the Society of Friends (Quakers), Congress eliminated the requirement of membership in a pacifist sect, extending the exemption to anyone "who, by reason of religious training and belief, is conscientiously opposed to participation in war in any form."[8] And conscientious objectors to noncombatant service were allowed to perform alternative civilian service.[9] Because Congress did not set up a special register for conscientious objectors, men opposed to registering for the draft were prosecuted.[10]

The "religious training and belief" phrase first received variant interpretations within the Selective Service System,[11] and then provoked a sharp division between the Second and the Ninth Circuits. Judge Augustus Hand, in *United States v. Kauten*, construed the phrase broadly:

> Religious belief [finds] expression in a conscience which categorically requires the believer to disregard elementary self-interest and to accept martyrdom in preference to transgressing its tenets. . . . [A] conscientious objection to participation in any war under any circumstances . . . may justly be regarded as a response of the individual to an inward mentor, call it conscience or God, that is for many persons at the present time the equivalent of what has always been thought a religious impulse.[12]

In *Berman v. United States*, the Ninth Circuit declined to follow suit, concluding that Congress meant to limit the exemption to conscientious beliefs "based upon an individual's belief in his responsibility to an authority higher and beyond any worldly one."[13]

Conscientious Objection, Selective Service System Special Monograph No. 11, 49–59 (Washington, D.C.: Selective Service System, 1950).

[8] 54 Stat. 889 (1940).

[9] The 1940 statute was less liberal than the provisions operative in Great Britain throughout World War II, which exempted anyone who "conscientiously objects . . . to performing military service or to performing combatant duties." National Service (Armed Forces) Act, 1939, 2 & 3 Geo. 6, c. 25. The British law did not require a religious basis for one's objection or opposition to war in any form.

[10] See Fred C. Zacharias, "The Lawyer as Conscientious Objector," 54 *Rutgers Law Review* 191, 205, n. 62 (2001).

[11] Sibley and Jacob, note 7 supra, at 68. In 1940 a memorandum by the first director of Selective Service, Clarence A. Dykstra, stated: "Any and all influences which have contributed to the consistent endeavor to live the good life may be classed as 'religious training.' Belief signifies sincere conviction. Religious belief signifies sincere conviction as to the supreme worth of that to which one gives his supreme allegiance." But in 1942 a superseding instruction to the local boards by Dykstra's successor, General Hershey, indicated that the statute required recognition of a divine source of all existence.

[12] 133 F.2d 703, 708 (2d Cir. 1943).

[13] 156 F.2d 377, 380 (1946) (en banc).

In 1948, Congress apparently adopted the *Berman* interpretation by amending the statute to say: "Religious training and belief in this connection mean an individual's belief in relation to a Supreme Being involving duties superior to those arising from any human relation, but do not include essentially political, sociological, or philosophical views or a merely personal moral code."[14]

This is how things stood before three important Supreme Court cases, discussed below, were decided during the turmoil of the Vietnam War. And with one alteration, this is how the statute now stands.

BASIC ISSUES ABOUT CONSCIENTIOUS OBJECTION

Before we delve into the complexities of statutory and constitutional argument, we can ask what a just and desirable approach to conscientious objection would be.[15] There is a strong case for granting religious conscientious objectors an exemption and for including nonreligious objectors; but I shall argue that there is a preferable alternative that does not demand either difficult decisions about classification or delicate, uncertain administrative judgments.

However dotted by indefensible exceptions at various stages of the country's history,[16] a military draft exemplifies some idea of citizens as equals. All able-bodied men (or men and women)[17] are drafted or are subject to a lottery. Does an exemption create an unjustified inequality?

People are equal and unequal to each other in innumerable respects. One way of conceiving of a conscientious objector is as having moral convictions that make him like a man who is physically unable to serve. Given his feelings about fighting, he *cannot* serve in some crucial sense,[18] and thus is unequal

---

[14] Section 6(j) of the Selective Service Act of 1948, 62 Stat. 613, using language from a dissent by Chief Justice Hughes in *United States v. MacIntosh*, 283 U.S. 605, 633 (1931), that the court in *Berman* had noted.

[15] Most of the considerations that figure here also count for constitutional analysis; but one may think that the Constitution leaves Congress important choices about how to treat objectors.

[16] These created a serious problem of fairness during the Vietnam War. A range of exemptions, deferments, and special assignments made it possible for young men who were well educated and well-to-do to avoid ordinary combat duty. According to Katharine Q. Seelye, "Cheney's Five Draft Deferments During the Vietnam Era Emerge as a Campaign Issue," *New York Times*, May 1, 2004, A12, col. 1, about 60 percent of those eligible between 1964 and 1973 avoided the draft by legal means.

[17] Thus far, military drafts in the United States have included only men. Given broad perspectives about gender equality and the extensive tasks within the military now performed by women, any future draft, if there is one, should include women.

[18] Brian Barry, *Culture and Equality* 37 (Cambridge: Harvard University Press, 2001), is very critical of this comparison as "offensive to both parties"; but he is concentrating on situations

in a vital way to the able-bodied citizen who is willing to serve. But the fairness of granting an exemption depends on the basis for conscientious objection, the burden cast on those who are drafted, and the benefit that exempted objectors attain.

Consciences of pacifists are informed by values that are respected in American culture, not by perspectives that are evil or corrupt. Most Americans have ambivalent attitudes about war, as sometimes necessary, but always horrible and often unjust. Those who witness by their objection to the abhorrence of killing in war reinforce a crucial strand in our sentiments.

The extent to which those who are drafted suffer because others are exempted turns out to be debatable. In a symbolic sense, a burden is shifted from those who avoid conscription to those who submit. The practical effect is more doubtful. Objectors do not share any of the military burden if they sit in jail, and those who submit to the draft but refrain from fighting in combat conditions[19] may jeopardize their fellows and increase their actual burden.[20]

If the exempted objector is not to be relieved of all obligations in a way would be very unfair in comparison with conscripts, he must perform alternative civilian service. Typical forms of civilian service, such as work as a hospital orderly, do not present the risks to life and limb that go with combat service, but their unattractiveness to most young people renders any possible advantage in doing that work a slight one.

There is a way to reduce further any unfair advantage, a way that also ameliorates other difficulties with a system of exemptions. The government can grant everyone an option between a term of military service and *a longer term* of civilian service, or an option between a certainty of civilian service and a chance of military service. If everyone is free to choose as conscientious objectors will choose, no one can complain of unfair disadvantage.[21] A sys-

---

in which the objector can forego a benefit, not direct coercion to perform an unacceptable act. I think he is mistaken even for the examples he mainly discusses. Michael W. McConnell, in "Accommodation of Religion," 1985 *Supreme Court Review* 1, 26, has emphasized the difference between a religious sense of obligation and ordinary preferences and opinions; John H. Garvey, in "Free Exercise and the Values of Religious Liberty," 18 *Connecticut Law Review* 782, 798–801 (1989), draws a surprising parallel to insanity in claiming that religious people may sometimes feel they do not have a meaningful choice whether to obey the law.

[19] It is widely assumed that a significant percentage of infantry do not actually fire their guns in combat. See S.L.A. Marshall, *Men Under Fire: The Problem of Battle Command in Future War* (New York: William Morrow, 1947); Dave Grossman, *On Killing: The Psychological Cost of Learning to Kill in War and Society* (Boston: Little, Brown, 1996).

[20] A pacifist who does not receive an exemption will behave in one of four ways. He may stick with his convictions and go to jail. He may flee to another country. He may submit to the draft, but avoid fighting. He may submit and perform his military responsibilities.

[21] Objectors might complain that they should not have to perform service that is judged by most people to be more onerous than military duty, and that they should not have to submit to

tem of self-selecting alternative civilian service reduces to a minimum any possible unfairness, and is far preferable to administrative officials deciding who qualifies for an exemption.[22]

Because the reasons not to draft conscientious objectors are so powerful, Congress, if it does not institute such a system of self-selection, should maintain an exemption from future conscription for people who are conscientiously opposed to performing military service, and this should extend to men and women personnel who seek to resign from a volunteer army.

We now reach the difficult questions about how a legislature should cast an exemption. Should it be limited to members of pacifist religions, to believers in a Supreme Being, to religious individuals, or extended to all those whose opposition to military duty is genuinely conscientious? Whatever may once have been the case, many nonpacifists belong to "pacifist" religions and some pacifists belong to nonpacifist religions.[23] Conscientious objection is not a corporate religious activity; it is an individual moral choice.[24] If the

---

certain civilian service if others participate in a lottery that selects only a percentage for military service. But this is a small price to pay for a system that benefits the objectors by eliminating unreliable administrative decisions about eligibility and also eliminates the concern that those who face the prospect of death in war are being treated unfairly.

[22] Of course, the system makes sense only if it will yield adequate numbers to enter the military. With modern warfare, and the possibility of drafting women, the worry that such a system would yield inadequate military personnel seems remote for large industrial countries. I defend such a system in Kent Greenawalt, "Accommodation to Selective Conscientious Objection: How and Why," in Michael F. Noone, Jr., ed., *Selective Conscientious Objection* 7, 21–22 (1989). The system now in place in Germany is close to self-selection. Someone liable to the draft must state that he is a conscientious objector if he is to avoid service, but his statement to that effect is taken as nearly conclusive. According to the *New York Times*, "German Military Today; Job Grows, More Say No," A10, col. 1, July 5, 1996, a young man "by writing a form letter proclaiming reasons of conscience, may be exempted from the risks . . . of soldiering." An applicant must perform thirteen months of civilian service rather than ten months in the military. In 1995, 160,000 young Germans chose that course as compared with 135,000 draftees. On January 24, 2002, the Deutsche Presse-Agentur reported that in 2001 182,420 men applied for conscientious objector status.

[23] Although pacifism may be a required element of adherence to some religious denominations, that is not true of the most important pacifist group in American history, the Society of Friends. Many Quakers are not pacifists. Some pacifists belong to nonpacifist churches, such as the Roman Catholic Church. The standard Catholic doctrine about war is that countries may fight "just wars," so long as they observe standards of fairness for carrying out the war, e.g., not intentionally killing innocent civilians, and satisfy standards of proportionality. For a summary of the Catholic view, see *United States v. McFadden*, 309 F. Supp. 502, 504–5 (N.D. Cal. 1970), vacated and remanded, 401 U.S. 1006 (1971). Roman Catholic pacifists either disagree with the church's tradition about just war or they have concluded that no just war can be fought in modern conditions.

[24] I do not mean that the choice itself must necessarily involve individual moral reflection. Some pacifists may have belonged since childhood to authoritarian religions in which pacifism is a central element. If government is not to prefer some religions over others, it should be as accepting of the pacifist who follows standard denominational doctrine as of the pacifist who

government is to exempt pacifist Quakers, it should also exempt pacifists who happen to be Roman Catholics. Moreover, a law exempting only members of pacifist groups would push pacifists toward membership in those groups, an effect at odds with the principle that government should avoid influencing people to belong to one religion rather than another.

Depth of conviction and administrative arguments for tailoring an exemption to pacifist religions are not very persuasive. Regarding the former, being a member of a pacifist religious community could conceivably strengthen one's feeling that military service is wrong; but among longtime Quakers pacifism may have become the line of least resistance, whereas Roman Catholics may become pacifists only after struggling to decide that their church is mistaken about just wars. We cannot generalize about comparative depth of conviction.

The administrative argument is that draft boards, military review panels, juries, and judges have less difficulty telling if claims to be objectors are sincere if only members of pacifist groups qualify. If all pacifist groups were fringe religions removed from ordinary social life, limiting the exemption to those groups could reduce fraud. No one is going to join the Amish in order to avoid the draft. But people do freely switch denominations, and a person aiming to commit fraud could easily join a pacifist group such as the Society of Friends, which welcomes new members without imposing demands on their styles of life. Requiring membership in a pacifist group would not prevent enough fraud to justify excluding many deserving objectors.[25]

A similar analysis leads to the conclusion that any requirement of group membership is indefensible. Much of the challenge and solace of religion lies in religious community, but many Americans are highly individualistic about religion, and unattached individuals may develop pacifist beliefs. Ascertaining the sincerity of such claims may be difficult, but administrators must make similar assessments when individuals assert beliefs that do not fit standard doctrines of groups to which they belong, as when a member of a nonpacifist church claims pacifist convictions. In any event, someone bent on committing fraud can join a pacifist group.

What of requiring that a conscientious objector believe in God, or a Supreme Being? Chapter 8 deals with the "definition" of religion in depth. Here, it suffices to say that some major world religions, including branches of Buddhism, do not rest on belief in a Supreme Being, as God is familiarly

---

engages in deep soul-searching. But however it is arrived at, conscientious objection is individual in touching a person's life outside the religious community; it does not concern how the community carries on its activities.

[25] So long as nonpacifists belong to pacifist groups, the government would still need to screen applicants to determine which are pacifists.

conceived by Jews, Christians, and Muslims. Further, many practicing members of Christian churches and Jewish synagogues do not believe in a traditional God. Within Christian churches, that is particularly true for denominations with minimal doctrinal conditions of membership, including the Society of Friends, among whom belief ranges from fairly standard Christian doctrine to skepticism about the existence of God. People can be religious, and they can be conscientious objectors, without believing in a God.

An advocate of requiring belief in a Supreme Being might respond that the dilemma of conscience for believers in a God will be more acute than the dilemma for nontheist objectors. This claim may have a limited plausibility for people who believe God will damn them or severely punish them if they do what is wrong. However, many theists have faith that God forgives serious wrongs, or they think God is remote from human affairs, or they lack any clear sense of how God reacts to wrongdoing. Belief in a God may correlate to a degree with a belief in absolute moral standards and with intensity of conviction that one should not commit moral wrongs, but theism, by itself, is a poor marker of the intensity of someone's sense of obligation not to participate in war. The reasons for requiring a belief in God are much too weak to support categorization that distinguishes among religious objectors in this way.

Whether an exemption should be limited to religious believers (in any ordinary sense) is more troublesome. Some people can develop pacifist convictions without relying on religious beliefs or practices. Here is part of what Elliott Welsh, an applicant for conscientious objector status, said:

> I can only act according to what I am and what I see. And I see that the military complex wastes both human and material resources, that it fosters disregard for (what I consider a paramount concern) human needs and ends; I see that the means we employ to "defend" our "way of life" profoundly change that way of life. I see that in our failure to recognize the political, social, and economic realities of the world, we, *as a nation*, fail our responsibility *as a nation*.[26]

The Welshes of this world sharply delineate the matter of how to treat appropriately religious and nonreligious persons who are otherwise similarly situated. Both may become pacifist conscientious objectors, and both may have intense convictions that they should not fight. In a society that values equality of persons, making a privilege turn on a person's religious views is intrinsically unfair, when significant numbers of nonreligious persons have similar reasons to be accorded the privilege. Nor could preventing fraud justify excluding nonreligious pacifists, since an applicant aiming to deceive

---

[26] *Welsh v. United States*, 398 U.S. 333, 342 (1970).

could easily join a religious group insincerely[27] or merely claim a set of religious convictions.[28]

This leaves us with an issue of principle: is it appropriate to limit an exemption to religious objectors because of the intrinsic value of religion or the value citizens have ascribed to it, or because of relations between the state and religious organizations?

Before the country's founding, our culture, so far as one can speak broadly, treated religion as of central importance in a good human life.[29] Today's general culture—the culture of television, popular magazines and newspapers, and leading academic institutions—is largely secular; and the significance of religion in most people's lives may have diminished over time.[30] Still, a very high percentage of citizens acknowledge belief in God, and more than half participate frequently in organized worship,[31] and religiously informed "moral" views exerted a prominent influence in the 2004 presidential election. Religion remains a vital part of American life.

Avoiding conflicts between religious conscience and conscription is desirable, but, partly because the government should not declare the truth of religious views,[32] it should not restrict an exemption to believers on the basis

---

[27] Although young people would not need to join churches to receive exemptions, if the exemption extended to religious believers who were not members, applicants (sincere and insincere) who wanted to bolster their credentials might do so. This joining could occur to some degree even if nonreligious objectors were also eligible, since any applicant might suppose his claim would look strongest to a draft board member or army administrator if he were enrolled in a pacifist church. Douglas Laycock in "The Remnants of Free Exercise," 1990 *Supreme Court Review* 1, 16–17, suggesting that government should minimize its encouragements or discouragements of religious belief and practice, notes that exemptions from military service differ from most other exemptions in encouraging nonbelievers to join a faith.

[28] Insofar as limiting an exemption to religious objectors might incline people to join religious groups or form religious beliefs, these are not appropriate ambitions for the government. (A nonreligious objector would be much more likely to feign religious beliefs than acquire sincere religious beliefs; but the government's recognition of religious over nonreligious conviction would endorse religion and could conceivably influence someone's sense of acceptable belief at an earlier stage of life.)

[29] However William Lee Miller, in *The First Liberty: America's Foundation in Religious Freedom* 238 (expanded ed., Washington, D.C.: Georgetown University Press, 2003), says that religion was at a low ebb after the War of Independence.

[30] Alan Wolfe, *One Nation After All* 39–88 (New York: Viking, 1998), disputes the idea of a continuous decline in religion but suggests that most Americans practice religion quietly and with tolerance toward those of different faiths.

[31] According to a Gallup poll of May 2–5, 2005, 55 percent say religion is "very important" in their lives, 28 percent that it is "fairly important"; 65 percent are members of churches or synagogues. Gallup News Service 18–21 2005.

[32] This issue is explored more fully in the second volume. See also Kent Greenawalt, *Does God Belong in Public Schools?* (Princeton: Princeton University Press, 2005). Among these who have argued for equality of belief systems is William P. Marshall, "In Defense of Smith and Free Exercise Revisionism," 58 *University of Chicago Law Review* 308, 317–20 (1991),

of a judgment that religious views are true.[33] An exemption partly responds to the country's historic valuing of religious sentiment and to a recognition that religions often make absolute demands that can conflict with state law; but these bases to exempt religious objectors are not solid reasons to exclude nonreligious objectors. The intrinsic unfairness of treating nonreligious objectors differently from religious ones far outweighs any reasons for a restricted exemption. In framing an exemption, Congress should not restrict it to those with convictions that are religious in the ordinary sense.

American draft laws have consistently drawn yet another distinction: that between general objectors who believe they cannot participate in any war and selective objectors who cannot in conscience serve during a particular war. Selective objection lies much closer to ordinary dissent from the government's judgment in undertaking a particular war; and it may be based on debatable, or obviously mistaken, factual assumptions in a way that is not true of pacifism.[34] Further, in conditions of less than total war, a gap may arise between objections to a particular war and refusal of military service. The war to which someone objects may end quickly, and even if it continues, the objector may be assigned elsewhere.[35] A person's objection to troops being in Iraq should not necessarily exempt him from service in South Korea.

Yet the reasons to respect selective objectors are powerful. They may feel as intensely opposed to serving as do pacifists; and the just war tradition is strong among American religions. People who are fervently opposed to a military mission do not make ideal soldiers. Finally, as with pacifists, forcing people to choose between violating their most deeply felt conscientious convictions and going to jail (or leaving the country) is not wise. Selective objectors should not be drafted, and volunteer army personnel should be able to refuse to go to a theater of war where service would be repugnant to conscience.[36]

[33] Another reason why this would be inappropriate is that the government already implicitly rejects the soundness of pacifism, religious or not.

[34] No doubt, pacifists rely on factual premises about human behavior, especially judgments about how others will respond over time to the witness of nonviolent action. But those premises are not subject to a definitive judgment about their accuracy. Selective objection *may* be based on assumptions about the behavior of one's own country or its enemy that are demonstrably wrong. (I do not imply that this fairly characterizes most selective objections to the Vietnam War; many of the factual judgments that underlay such objections are now widely accepted to be true.)

[35] Most recent American wars have taken less than a few months, if one does not count peacekeeping, which itself can be very dangerous, that follows standard military conflict. Indeed, in the period after the overthrow of Saddam Hussein in Iraq, one can hardly say whether American troops are engaged in peacekeeping or a war against insurgents.

[36] I offer this comment without a sense of when the defection of a single individual will seriously impair the functioning of a larger unit. For such situations, exemption after assignment may be unacceptable. There may also be a special problem with reservists, most of whom

The radically different approach of a self-selecting alternative civilian service, which I have already proposed, is the best solution to selective objection, as well as other difficulties. For military personnel who wish to withdraw, the remainder of their period of service could be in less highly paid, less attractive (or longer) alternative civilian service.

CONSTITUTIONAL DIMENSIONS

Some of the Supreme Court's most interesting religion cases have involved conscientious objectors. During the 1920s and 1930s, the court indicated clearly in dicta that whether to grant any exemption to objectors was a matter of legislative judgment, that the Free Exercise Clause accords no right to an exemption.[37] During the Vietnam War, the Court rejected the argument that selective objectors, religious or not, had a constitutional right to an exemption, but it left open the issue whether pacifists had such a right.[38] Given the intrinsic significance of conscientious objection, and the granting of exemptions throughout the country's history, a strong argument can be made that at least religious pacifists have a constitutional right not to serve. International documents that have recognized conscientious objection as a human right[39] can bolster the claim about an American constitutional right. But, as we shall see in the next chapter, the Supreme Court's present interpretation of the Free Exercise Clause, as rarely requiring exemptions, leaves little room for any such argument.

Even if Congress is free to grant or withhold an exemption, it is not free to classify in any way it chooses. We can see that most easily if we focus on the classification Congress made during World War I, requiring objectors to be members of pacifist religions. Given the Court's present view that classifications that favor some religious groups over others are "suspect," the Court

---

have supposed they will never be called back to active duty. Distinguishing between those who genuinely object in conscience to service in a controversial war from those who strongly desire not to participate (but do not object in conscience) might be very difficult.

[37] E.g., *MacIntosh*, note 14 supra, at 623; *Hamilton v. Regents*, 293 U.S. 245, 264 (1934).

[38] *Gillette*, note 5 supra, at 461 n. 23.

[39] In 1967, the Parliamentary Assembly of the Council of Europe recognized conscientious objection as an individual right. Resolution 337, Eur. Parl. Ass. (1967). In a resolution of May 23, 2001, it recommended that the right be formally incorporated into the European Convention on Human Rights. Recommendation 1518, Eur. Parl. Ass. 2001 Sess., Doc. No. 8809 (1921). In 1998 the UN Commission on Human Rights issued a report treating conscientious objection as an aspect of freedom of thought, conscience, and religion as laid down in the Universal Declaration of Human Rights. Resolution on Conscientious Objection to Military Service, UN Commission on Human Rights, 54th Sess., Agenda Item 22, UN Doc. E/CN.4/1998/L.93 (1998).

would now decide that an exemption limited to members of pacifist religions is unconstitutional.[40]

Were Congress ever to adopt a law making an exemption conditional on membership in a religious group, pacifist or not, the classification would suffer a similar fate. For a subject as individual as conscientious objection, an exemption limited to members of religious bodies would impermissibly establish organized religious groups in comparison with individuals whose personal religious or moral development is apart from formally organized settings.[41]

The three criteria the Supreme Court actually addressed during the Vietnam War were the "Supreme Being" requirement, the "religious training and belief" requirement, and the requirement of opposition to all wars.

United States v. Seeger, combining three individual cases under one case name, presented the first issue.[42] The applicants' convictions varied significantly, but each was religious in a broad sense and none believed in a traditional God. Three sets of appellate judges had reached three different conclusions. The Ninth Circuit Court of Appeals said that its objector did not believe in a Supreme Being and that Congress was free to require that belief.[43] One panel of the Second Circuit read the statute in the same way, but held that Congress could not, constitutionally, favor believers in a Supreme Being over other religious objectors.[44] Another group of Second Circuit judges ruled that the statutory requirement should itself be understood very broadly, so broadly that the objector qualified.[45]

A unanimous Supreme Court adopted the third approach for all three applicants. The Court thus summarized its decision:

> We have concluded that Congress, in using the expression "Supreme Being" rather than the designation "God," was merely clarifying the meaning of religious training and belief so as to embrace all religions and to exclude essentially

[40] See *Larson v. Valente*, 456 U.S. 228 (1982).

[41] In *Levy v. Northport–East Northport Union Free School Dist.*, 672 F. Supp. 81, 97 (E.D.N.Y. 1987), the court declared that a right not to have children vaccinated could not be restricted to parents who are "members of a recognized religious organization whose teachings are contrary to the practices herein required." See also *Boone v. Boozman*, 217 F. Supp. 2d 938 (E.D. Ark. 2002) (holding invalid a state law exempting only members of "a recognized church or religious denomination" from immunization requirements).

[42] 380 U.S. 163 (1965). When individual cases are combined, as here, for Supreme Court consideration, the citation practice is to refer to one of the names.

[43] *Peter v. United States*, 324 F.2d 173 (1963).

[44] *United States v. Seeger*, 326 F.2d 846 (1964). (My father, Kenneth W. Greenawalt, was counsel for Seeger.)

[45] *United States v. Jakobson*, 325 F.2d 409 (1963). The court indicated that a narrower interpretation would create serious constitutional problems, particularly given the Supreme Court's invalidation of Maryland's test oath in part because it favored religions based on belief in God. *Torcaso v. Watkins*, 367 U.S. 488 (1961).

political, sociological, or philosophical views. We believe that under this con-struction, the test of belief "in a relation to a Supreme Being" is whether a given belief that is sincere and meaningful occupies a place in the life of its possessor parallel to that filled by the orthodox belief in God of one who clearly qualifies for the exemption. Where such beliefs have parallel positions in the lives of their respective holders we cannot say that one is "in a relation to a Supreme Being" and the other is not.[46]

Here is the Court's account of the views of one of the applicants:

[Seeger] declared that he was conscientiously opposed to participation in war in any form by reason of his "religious" belief; that he preferred to leave the ques-tion as to his belief in a Supreme Being open, "rather than answer 'yes' or 'no' "; that his "skepticism or disbelief in the existence of God" did "not necessarily mean lack of faith in anything whatsoever"; that his was a "belief in and devo-tion to goodness and virtue for their own sakes, and a religious faith in a purely ethical creed."[47]

Recall that Congress adopted the Supreme Being language to convey a narrow idea of eligible religious views. Yet, after *Seeger*, one can hardly imag-ine anyone who was a religious pacifist who would not also satisfy the Su-preme Being requirement.[48] By interpretation, the Supreme Court had elimi-nated the legal significance of the "Supreme Being" language.[49]

Why had the Court interpreted the statute as it had? Courts often interpret statutory language to avoid constitutional difficulties.[50] Everyone agrees that the Court strained the language considerably in *Seeger*. Scholars widely as-sumed that the justices did so because they would have regarded an explicit line between objectors who believe in a traditional God and other religious

[46] *Seeger*, note 42 supra, at 164–65.

[47] Id. at 166.

[48] *Seeger* was less than clear whether a qualifying belief had only to be as important psycho-logically for the claimant as belief in God for the traditional believer, or needed to have other "objective" characteristics. See John Mansfield, "Conscientious Objection—1964 Term," 1965 *Religion and the Public Order* 10. The typical religious pacifist affirms certain truths about God, the nature of human beings, and the relationship between God and people, from which his pacifist views follow. In referring to the dictionary's definition of a Supreme Being as "a power or being, or a faith, 'to which all else is subordinate or upon which all else is ultimately depen-dent,'" the *Seeger* Court gave modest support to the idea that, to qualify, conscientious objection must fit into a more encompassing set of beliefs that include notions of supremacy and ultimacy. But it is doubtful that such an approach would produce very different results from a more explicit and straightforward psychological test, since most conscientious objectors will have some system of beliefs about ultimate human reality that link to their objection. The imposition of such a test about general beliefs could serve primarily as a penalty for inarticulateness.

[49] Congress subsequently dropped its now ineffective reference to belief in relation to a Su-preme Being. 81 Stat. 104, 50 U.S.C. App. § 456 (j) (1967).

[50] Justices, and scholars, disagree about how far courts should stray from what would other-wise be the most plausible reading of statutory language.

objectors as unconstitutional. The Maryland test oath case we looked at in
the last chapter supports the view that favoring such believers violates the
Establishment Clause.[51] Congress cannot permissibly limit an exemption to
believers in a traditional God.

Welsh, whose beliefs, quoted earlier, were not religious in any ordinary
sense,[52] presented a more difficult issue than did *Seeger.* He had struck the
word *religious* from his application, referred to "reading in the fields of history and sociology," and based his opposition to participation in war in part
on his perception of world politics and the wastefulness of devoting human
resources to military endeavors.

The justices had three options, and various members of the Court adopted
each. It is worth examining each of these options, which have a broad significance for any examination of free exercise issues. Justice Black's plurality
opinion for himself and three other justices extended the approach of *Seeger.*
It declared that Welsh counted as "religious" within the meaning of the statute. The question

> is whether these beliefs play the role of a religion and function as a religion in
> the registrant's life. . . . If an individual deeply and sincerely holds beliefs which
> are purely ethical or moral in source and content but that nevertheless impose
> upon him a duty of conscience to refrain from participating in any war at any
> time, those beliefs certainly occupy in the life of that individual "a place parallel
> to that filled by . . . God" in traditionally religious persons. . . . Section 6(j) . . .
> exempts from military service all those whose consciences, spurred by deeply held
> moral, ethical, or religious beliefs, would give them no rest or peace if they al-
> lowed themselves to become a part of an instrument of war.[53]

If the *Seeger* Court had effectively written the Supreme Being clause out of
the statute, the *Welsh* plurality did the same to the requirement of "religious
training and belief." They indicated that almost any applicant who was a
genuine conscientious objector (and was found to be so) would succeed. If,
in the depth of one's being, one could not conceive of participating in war,
if one would rather go to jail or suffer other serious penalties than join the
military, one's beliefs would qualify as religious.[54]

---

[51] See note 45 supra.

[52] See text accompanying note 26 supra, quoting from *Welsh v. United States*, at 342.

[53] Id. at 339–40, 343–44. Douglas Laycock puts it this way: "The nontheist's belief in transcendent moral obligations . . . in obligations that transcend his self-interest and his personal
preferences and [with] which he has no choice but to comply . . . is analogous to the transcendent moral obligations that are part of the cluster of the beliefs that we recognize as religious."
"Religious Liberty as Liberty," 7 *Journal of Contemporary Legal Issues* 313, 336 (1996).

[54] This approach also answered the question whether qualifying beliefs had to meet some
test of covering the same subjects that ordinary religious beliefs address. See note 48 supra.
They did not. It was enough that a claimant have a deep objection to participation in war.

We shall examine in chapter 8 whether the plurality's construction of "religion" is a promising one for the Free Exercise Clause. In *Welsh*, the justices offered it as statutory interpretation. As with *Seeger*, powerful doubts among the justices about a line between religious and nonreligious objectors almost certainly explained why they so deftly dispatched Congress's attempt to draw just that line.

The other four justices took Congress at its word. Justice Harlan concluded that the line between religious and nonreligious objectors was unconstitutional.[55] If Congress chooses to excuse some objectors, it cannot exempt religious objectors and decline to exempt conscientious objectors with secular convictions.[56] Using an "equal protection mode of analysis" for the Establishment Clause, Harlan said that the "common denominator must be the intensity of moral conviction with which a belief is held."[57] Thus, he concluded that the Constitution requires categorization as inclusive as the plurality's reading of the statute itself.[58]

The other three justices agreed with Justice Harlan's statutory analysis but believed that Congress, when it responds to free exercise values and grants an exemption for religious claimants, need not extend the exemption to others like Welsh.[59]

The issue that separated Justice Harlan (and probably most members of the plurality) from the three dissenters puts in constitutional terms the question whether, in respect to conscientious objection, religious claimants may be treated better than nonreligious ones.

Justice White suggested that the Free Exercise Clause is a kind of authorization to legislators to make accommodations to religious convictions, even when it does not compel them to do so. No such provision exists for nonreligious objectors. Thus, Congress may choose to limit its exemption to those who are religious.

White's argument has some force,[60] but not enough. Once one realizes that nonreligious conscientious objectors can have convictions as deep as

[55] Id. at 344–54. He expressed regret about his acceptance of *Seeger*'s statutory construction, and argued that both the statutory text and legislative history indicated clearly that Congress wished to limit the exemption to theists.

[56] Id. at 356.

[57] Id. at 358.

[58] Believing that Congress would prefer an extension of the exemption to applicants like Welsh rather than total invalidation of the exemption, he made the fifth and decisive vote in Welsh's favor.

[59] Justice White initially supposed that exemptions were required by the Free Exercise Clause. About these he wrote, "Surely" they are not "invalid establishment[s] because they fail to include nonreligious believers as well." Id. at 370. He argued that the conclusion is the same if Congress chooses to accommodate free exercise, though it is not required to do so.

[60] One might object to White's position on the ground that the Free Exercise Clause concerns only interferences with religious practices, and does not authorize positive accommodations;

those of religious objectors, *and* one concludes that the extra administrative difficulties of including nonreligious objectors are modest, one should view an explicit line between the two groups as an impermissible establishment of religion. This conclusion is *not* at odds with thinking that the Free Exercise Clause helps to authorize the exemption of religious objectors. We may embrace that view *and* suppose that any exemption must be tailored to avoid a religious preference.[61]

It is the view of some scholars that *any* preferences formulated in terms of religion amount to an unconstitutional establishment of religion. As we shall see in subsequent chapters, that position is definitely not supported by the Supreme Court's decisions, taken as a group, and it is not an argument that Justice Harlan made in *Welsh*. My analysis in this book presupposes that preferences for religious claimants are not automatically ruled out in this way, but I do not evaluate that position in depth until the second volume, on establishment. And I also save for that volume many fundamental questions about when efforts to accommodate religious practices exceed proper boundaries and become impermissible establishments.

In *Gillette v. United States*,[62] the third important draft case arising out of the Vietnam War, the justices rejected both the argument that selective objectors had a basic constitutional right to an exemption, and the argument that they could not be treated worse than general objectors. The Court surveyed the various reasons not to exempt selective objectors, and concluded that they were powerful enough to support a refusal to exempt. It also concluded that a classification made in terms of convictions about war did not impermissibly favor some religions over others, although it was evident that members of pacifist groups would succeed much more often than members of "just war" religions.

These issues are troublesome, but the Court was right.[63] Focusing on attitudes about fighting in war does not constitute the kind of discrimination among religions that is unacceptable.[64]

---

but I believe White was right that the clause helps to support the judgment that Congress may tailor laws so they do not impinge on religious practice more than is necessary.

[61] But see Abner S. Greene's proposal in "The Political Balance of the Religion Clauses," 102 *Yale Law Journal* 1611 (1993), that free exercise exemptions are a kind of offset for the inappropriateness under the Establishment Clause of religious bases for laws, and that, therefore, exemptions need not extend to analogous nonreligious persons. I believe that the main ground for free exercise exemptions lies elsewhere, and that, in any event, the constitutional claims for equal treatment of religious and nonreligious objectors are very powerful.

[62] Note 5 supra.

[63] I explore these questions in much more depth in "All or Nothing At All: The Defeat of Selective Conscientious Objection," 1971 *Supreme Court Review* 31–94.

[64] The Court's recent disinclination, under the Free Speech Clause, to approve classifications that discriminate among different ideas should not alter this conclusion. *Any* conscientious

What Opposition Is "Conscientious"?

Apart from its requirement of a general objection, the crucial standard of the exemption provision is that of "conscientious opposition." The distinction between religious and nonreligious believers has disappeared, but the distinction survives between those whose desire not to serve is a "conscientious" objection and those whose desire is weaker or has another kind of basis. People have a solid intuitive sense of what being a conscientious objector to military service entails, but it is worth pausing over that subject because of questions about the quality and depth of religiously grounded reasons that might justify avoiding other legal demands.[65]

Though perhaps the word *conscientious* connotes a special degree of diligent reflection on,[66] and intensity of feeling about, an issue, *conscientious opposition* is virtually synonymous with "opposition based on conscience." Originally "conscience" was thought to designate a capacity for judgment about moral science, the principles of which were shared knowledge and the precise content of which was mediated by the church.[67] The modern notion of individual consciences with widely variant insights is in large part the product of the individualism of the Reformation. Now the dictates of conscience refer to moral claims strongly felt by individuals. Consciences are, at least in part, psychologically and sociologically conditioned, and conscientious judgments may be erroneous.[68]

---

objector provision relies on the content of ideas. A "conscientious objector" is exempted, but one who is unwilling to fight because it would not serve his self-interest or the interests of those he loves is not exempted. If this degree of classifying by the content of one's convictions is permissible, as everyone assumes it is, a distinction drawn on the basis of views about whether one must avoid fighting in all wars, or only some wars, is similarly acceptable.

[65] The issue here is *not* sincerity, it is what set of convictions, if candidly stated, amounts to a conscientious objection. My analysis is mainly in terms of the meaning of "conscientious" in general usage, but I assume here that the meaning reflects the quality and strength that the legal standard aims to capture.

[66] An Australian judge commented that "conscientious belief is an individual's inward conviction of what is morally right or morally wrong, and it is a conviction that is genuinely reached and held after some process of thinking about the subject." Quoted from an unreported case, *Grondal v. Minister of State for Labour and National Service* (Sup. Ct. West. Aust. 1953), in Norman Raeburn, "Conscientious Objection and the Particular War," 43 *Australian Law Journal* 317, 319 (1969).

[67] See Michael Walzer, *Obligations: Essays on Disobedience, War and Citizenship* 120–24 (Cambridge: Harvard University Press, 1970); see also the "note on etymology" on "conscience" in the *Oxford English Dictionary*, ed. J. A. Simpson and E.C.S. Weiner (2d ed., Oxford: Clarendon Press 1989).

[68] See, e.g., Richard J. Niebanck, *Conscience, War and the Selective Objector* 1–14 (New York: Board of Social Ministry, Lutheran Church in America, 1972). One who denies any objectivity to moral judgments might dispute the use of the term "erroneous."

Though some authors have emphasized the importance of discussion and mutual engagement with concerned fellows in the forming and correcting of individual consciences,[69] present use of the term does not imply such involvement. Nor does *conscientious* now imply an ability to articulate one's moral judgment within a rational structure of principles; a claim of conscience may be based on an intuition that may be very hard to articulate to others.[70]

One fairly simple aspect of delimiting the boundary of "conscientious opposition" is drawing the line between claims of moral duty and claims based on self-interest. A registrant who candidly states that fear or a desire for the easy life rather than moral duty undergirds his opposition to participation obviously does not qualify for an exemption.[71]

A far more difficult issue is the elucidation of the necessary degree of intensity and commitment for a belief to qualify as conscientious. In the closing sentence of his opinion in *Welsh*, Justice Black aptly expressed the necessary strength of feeling when he wrote of Section 6(j) as exempting "those whose consciences . . . would give them no rest or peace if they allowed themselves to become a part of an instrument of war."[72] People should not be exempted if their moral preference to avoid participation in war would give way easily in the face of personal inconvenience, or could be outweighed by conflicting moral considerations of moderate weight.

A person may *think* a course of action, such as military service, is morally wrong no matter what harmful consequences he, his family, and associates might suffer, but if he yields easily and without regret,[73] the moral views he takes on an intellectual plane are not accorded real significance in his life; he is not "conscientiously opposed" to the action he thinks immoral.

---

[69] See id.; Walzer, note 67 supra, at 130–45.

[70] While "conscientious belief" may require a process of continued reflection about a moral conclusion, it does not follow that the reflection must be rational thought, or that even if it includes rational thought, one must be able to defend one's judgment on rational grounds. Christopher L. Eisgruber and Lawrence G. Sager, "The Vulnerability of Conscience: The Constitutional Basis for Protecting Religious Conscience," 61 *University of Chicago Law Review* 1245, 1268, suggest that one's conscience may be felt "as raw impulse" or "as deep but unlocated conviction."

[71] A nice theoretical issue is posed by the individual who honestly believes his only moral duty is to pursue his self-interest. Probably "conscientiousness" can be taken to require a degree of disinterestedness in one's moral stance. In any event, in practice such a statement would probably not be believed, and someone who really adhered to that moral principle would fabricate a more appealing case.

[72] Note 26 supra, at 344.

[73] Plainly to be called "conscientious," a person need not actually be willing to undergo every conceivable form of suffering for his beliefs, for few individuals have that strength. Perhaps he can still be considered conscientious if he would give way under slight pressure, so long as he would suffer great remorse for doing so. Apart from the intrinsic meaning of the word "conscientious," the state may have an interest in not coercing such a person into a choice that will be painful for him and reduce his self-respect.

Although some persons believe that certain actions are absolutely wrong and that even if they could save the world by committing one sin, they should not do it, others take a more consequential view of morality, believing that what is a moral course of action depends heavily on likely results and alternative possibilities. A young teacher in an inner city school might believe that avoidance of military service is morally preferable to serving, since he believes he can contribute more constructively to the lives of others as a civilian than by risking his life in a foolish war. But if the alternative to military service is useless time in jail, he regards military service as morally preferable. Coercion changes his moral equation and renders service consistent with conscience. A person whose moral equation is changed by such weights on the other side would not be said to be "conscientiously opposed" to performing the military service he thinks morally wrong in the absence of such weights.[74]

Stating just how high on his moral scale a person's opposition to an act must be before it qualifies as "conscientious" is impossible; and the answer depends on the general importance assigned to the act to which the person is opposed. If a woman says she is conscientiously opposed to killing another human being in combat, we probably take that to imply that she believes she should suffer her own death rather than kill, but we might be willing to concede that she is "conscientiously opposed" to being vaccinated even if she thinks vaccination is morally preferable to a death sentence.

The question whether someone is a conscientious objector is not always straightforward. One consequence is that a legislative choice to exempt all conscientious objectors, rather than all those with religious reasons of conscience, does not necessarily simplify determinations about who qualifies.[75] And, as the next chapter shows, the reasons why it may be desirable to exempt religious claimants from a general rule do not always reduce to relief for objections in conscience.

---

[74] However, one who thinks his own military service is morally preferable to having every living relative killed would not thereby fail to be conscientiously opposed to service.

[75] Nor does that approach eliminate all questions about whether those who are excluded from an exemption are less deserving of it than those who are included. Eisgruber and Sager note, "We must still justify constitutionalizing sympathy for the strong pull of conscience over the pulls of love, passionately demanding life projects, and the infinitely creative demands of strong psychological compulsion." Note 70 supra, at 1269.

CHAPTER 5

Religious Exemptions and Drug Use

For many decades, harsh criminal laws against the sale and use of hallucinatory drugs—including LSD, marijuana, and peyote—have restricted the religious practices of some groups. The modern Supreme Court's most important free exercise decision involved use of peyote by members of the Native American Church.[1] How should the government respond to religious uses of these forbidden substances? As with conscientious objection, our inquiry about a possible exemption must encompass both wise policy and sound constitutional law. When we understand how factors about drug use differ from those regarding military service, we can see why contextual evaluation of particular problems is so essential, and we can reach conclusions that vary from those of the last chapter.

In this chapter, we shall also begin to examine the Supreme Court's reasons for sharply trimming free exercise law and the powerful objections to that step. The remainder of the book assesses those reasons in more detail.

PEYOTE AS AN ELEMENT OF WORSHIP SERVICES AND MARIJUANA FOR PRIVATE USE

Sixteenth-century Spanish sources in Mexico recorded religious use of peyote, a derivative from the cactus plant; and the practice was well established in the United States by the latter half of the nineteenth century. The Native American Church, a religious organization with a membership that was estimated at 250,000 in 1996,[2] uses peyote as the centerpiece of its ceremony and practice.[3] The church has no recorded theology, but members say that they accept certain Christian teachings, regard peyote as embodying the Holy Spirit, and believe that someone who partakes of peyote can enter into direct contact with God.

Here is what the California Supreme Court said in 1964 about the use of peyote in that church's services:

[1] *Employment Division v. Smith*, 494 U.S. 872 (1990).
[2] See Jay Fikes, "A Brief History of the Native American Church," in Huston Smith and Reuben Snake, eds., *One Nation Under God: The Triumph of the Native American Church* (Santa Fe: Clear Light, 1996).
[3] *People v. Woody*, 394 P.2d 813 (Sup. Ct. Cal. 1964).

The "meeting," a ceremony marked by the sacramental use of peyote, composes the cornerstone of the peyote religion.

A meeting connotes a solemn and special occasion. Whole families attend together, although children and young women participate only by their presence. At the meeting the members pray, sing, and make ritual use of drum, fan, eagle bone, whistle, rattle and prayer cigarette, the symbolic emblems of their faith. The central event, of course, consists of the use of peyote in quantities sufficient to produce an hallucinatory state.

Although peyote serves as a sacramental symbol similar to bread and wine in certain Christian churches, it is more than a sacrament. Peyote constitutes in itself an object of worship; prayers are directed to it much as prayers are devoted to the Holy Ghost. On the other hand, to use peyote for nonreligious purposes is sacrilegious. Members of the church regard peyote also as a "teacher" because it induces a feeling of brotherhood with other members; indeed, it enables the participant to experience the Deity.[4]

Not all religious use of drugs is in corporate worship services; some religions recommend personal use of marijuana or other drugs, as Timothy Leary once claimed about the branch of Hinduism to which he belonged.[5]

Should There Be an Exemption?

If we grant that prohibitions on the use of certain drugs, including peyote and marijuana, may represent sound policy,[6] we face the question of whether legislatures should exempt religious use.

An exemption for religious worship by members of the Native American Church would not be unfair to potential recreational users. As the California Supreme Court concluded, use of peyote is at the core of the worship of the Native American Church, more central than is wine in a Roman Catholic Mass; and for most members, use is a sincere act of devotion;[7] few, if any, people join the church to acquire an excuse for using peyote. Providing ex-

---

[4] Id. at 817–18.

[5] *Leary v. United States*, 383 F.2d 851 (5th Cir. 1967), rev'd on other grounds, 395 U.S. 6 (1969). Prosecuted for importation, Leary said that his religion encouraged use of marijuana to enhance meditation.

[6] Some observers believe that prohibitions on use of marijuana and peyote are a mistake, even if bans on heroin, cocaine, and LSD are desirable. If someone thinks that a prohibition is badly misguided, he may favor exemptions as a means to limit the law's effectiveness and hasten its demise. From this outlook, the possibility that an exemption will impede general enforcement is a positive virtue, not a drawback.

[7] The California court concluded that participation in the worship services does not have a tendency to increase a person's use of peyote on other occasions or to induce use of other drugs or alcohol, and no contrary evidence was put before the Supreme Court in 1990. (The California opinion suggests that corporate use of peyote in worship services may actually help curb

emptions for those who have the most powerful reasons of conscience and devotion to engage in the activity of ingesting peyote is not intrinsically unfair to others whose reasons to use are less compelling.[8]

The treatment of alcohol during Prohibition supports this conclusion. When legislatures forbade the use of alcohol, their exemption for sacramental use of wine[9] was not regarded as unfair to people who wanted to drink socially.[10] The analogy from alcohol to peyote, it must be acknowledged, is less than perfect in two respects. Moderate drinkers of alcoholic beverages tend to feel sensations of lightness, well-being, relaxation, and reduced inhibitions; heavy drinkers anesthetize emotions against painful memories and perceptions. Because a sip of wine at a Christian communion does not cause these sensations,[11] participants in communion do not really have the experiences denied to others by bans on alcohol. Members of the Native American Church *do* have the kinds of hallucinatory reactions recreational users seek.[12] Relatedly, because some recreational users claim that hallucinatory drugs illuminate fundamental aspects of existence and transform their lives,[13] the reasons for

---

alcohol and other drug consumption; but we need assume only that use in worship does not produce increased consumption of harmful substances outside worship.)

[8] One fairness concern about conscientious objection does not apply to use of peyote. Exemptions to military service create the possibility that some draftees—those who would not have been drafted but for the exemption given to objectors—will actually be made worse off. Nothing of this sort is relevant for drug use. People who are forbidden to use peyote for recreational purposes are no better or worse off if members of a church can use peyote for religious services.

[9] See, e.g., 27 U.S.C. § 12 (West, 1927) (repealed by 21st Amendment, Dec. 1933 (27 U.S.C.S., 2001)).

[10] Even now states that restrict use by minors of alcohol do not proceed against minors who participate in sacramental use or against their parents and other adults who allow such use.

[11] A Roman Catholic priest who has the responsibility of consuming leftover consecrated wine may drink a much larger amount than the average communicant.

[12] Jeremy Waldron, "One Law for All? The Logic of Cultural Accommodation," 59 *Washington and Lee Law Review* 3, 8 (2002).

[13] See, e.g., Timothy Leary et al., *The Psychedelic Experience: Manual Based on the Tibetan Book of the Dead* 11 (Carol Publishing Group ed., 1997) (1964) ("A psychedelic experience is a journey to new realms of consciousness. The scope and content of the experience is limitless, but its characteristic features are the transcendence of verbal concepts, of space-time dimensions, and of the ego or identity. Such experiences of enlarged consciousness can occur in a variety of ways: sensory deprivation, yoga exercises, disciplined meditation, religious or aesthetic desires, or spontaneously. Most recently, they have become available to anyone through ingestion of psychedelic drugs such as LSD, psilocybin, mescaline, DMT, etc. Of course, the drug dose does not produce the transcendent experience. It merely acts as a chemical key—it opens the mind, frees the nervous system of its ordinary patterns and structures") (footnote omitted); Aldous Huxley, *The Doors of Perception* 73 (New York: Harper and Brothers, 1954) ("I am not so foolish as to equate what happens under the influence of mescalin or of any other drug, prepared or in the future preparable, with the realization of the end and ultimate purpose of human life: Enlightenment, the Beatific Vision. All I am suggesting is that the mescalin experience is what Catholic theologians call 'a gratuitous grace,' not necessary to salvation but

religious use of peyote distinguish themselves less sharply from reasons for recreational use than do the religious reasons to use wine from reasons for social drinking. The absence of a sharp line dividing the experiences of worshipers from those of recreational users makes the fairness of exempting religious use of peyote more arguable than exempting typical sacramental use of wine. Nevertheless, the Prohibition experience confirms the obvious point that allowing people to participate in acts of worship that are at the center of their religious practice is a very strong reason to create an exemption.[14]

THE BOUNDARIES OF AN EXEMPTION

Difficulties in distinguishing among people's reasons for using peyote affect how legislators should formulate an exemption, rendering a requirement of group membership much more appealing than it is for conscientious objection.

Whether an exemption is to be administered by a licensing system or made a defense to criminal liability, excusing individuals who lack any institutional connection could be seriously impractical.[15] Determining the necessary mental attitude for an individual who wants to use drugs is much more elusive than figuring out who is a conscientious objector to military service.[16] Sup-

---

potentially helpful and to be accepted thankfully, if made available. To be shaken out of the ruts of ordinary perception, to be shown for a few timeless hours the outer and the inner world, not as they appear to an animal obsessed with survival or to a human being obsessed with words and notions, but as they are apprehended, directly and unconditionally, by Mind at Large—this is an experience of inestimable value to everyone and especially to the intellectual").

Drinking alcohol may bring pleasure and perhaps psychological and physical benefits; few assert that it transforms people's lives in a positive way. In this respect, I am focusing on the experience of drinking itself. Actions people allow themselves because their inhibitions are reduced could be life-transforming.

[14] One might, however, conclude that the lesson to be drawn is that all use of peyote should be allowed, especially if one believes that few people will be attracted to recreational use or that such use is not seriously harmful.

[15] The sentence in the text assumes that other prohibitions on the use of drugs are reasonably effective, and that a number of individuals would choose to use peyote on their own, were an exemption available. Peyote, because it tastes bitter, creates nausea, and is not widely accessible, has proved much less a drug of choice then marijuana, but were the laws against marijuana well enforced, more people would wish to use peyote.

Despite prohibitions in virtually all jurisdictions, marijuana is easy to purchase and possess and is used by people at all levels of society. So long as marijuana is available and many people are willing to break the law to use it, a broad exemption from a ban on peyote might have relatively little practical effect. People would prefer to continue using marijuana to taking advantage of a peyote exemption. But it is troublesome to consider an exemption from one prohibition in light of the practical futility of another prohibition.

[16] If the exemption were a defense to criminal liability, prosecutors would make initial decisions whom not to prosecute, and juries or judges would make final determinations about whether those prosecuted warranted an exemption.

pose someone says (sincerely) that use of peyote brings her in contact with the broad soul of the universe, or illuminates the nature of divine reality, or induces a worshipful attitude towards God's creation, or (moving to language that is not explicitly religious) shows her the unity of the universe. These formulations are not highly distinct from the meaning members of the Native American Church might ascribe to their use. Were an exemption to include individual use, many recreational users might begin to see peyote in such grand terms, and discerning whether someone who testified to that effect was lying would be very difficult. An exemption that depended only on individual conviction might swallow up the prohibition, leading law enforcement officials to give up prosecuting use.[17] For a drug prohibition to survive, an exemption must be limited to individuals who are part of an organized group.

Further, the connection should go beyond membership in a group that recommends beneficial individual use of a drug.[18] A state's strong policy against use of a drug should not give way simply because a group encourages individuals to use it. Overindulgence is a major concern about drug use; any exemption that covers all use at the place and time of an individual's choice is too broad.[19] An exempted individual should have to be participating within meetings of a group.

A harder question is whether only religious groups should qualify. A state prohibition of the central elements of worship services threatens the practice of a religion and, indeed, its existence. Given the intrinsic significance of religious practice, and the traditional value our country has accorded to religion and religious groups, we have strong reasons to protect practices of worship. Although a nonreligious organization—say a group devoted to human brotherhood whose members strongly experience the unity of humankind when they use peyote at their meetings—might present a similarly powerful claim to use a forbidden drug, nevertheless, for reasons of practical administration, limiting an exemption to religious groups makes sense. Few nonreligious groups would regard use of peyote as possessing the deep significance ascribed to it by members of the Native American Church. Moreover, were an exemption extended to them, the problem of fraud could be substantial. Since many people wish to use drugs, the step of creating a group of like-minded people, announcing a high-blown philosophy, and using the

---

[17] The exemption would presumably extend to sales to individuals for exempted use. Wholesalers could still be prosecuted for general distribution.

[18] Timothy Leary's claimed adherence to a branch of Hinduism that recommended the use of marijuana as spiritually beneficial is an example. *Leary,* note 5 supra.

[19] Compare *Commonwealth v. Nissenbaum,* 536 N.E.2d 592 (Mass. 1989), in which a church using marijuana and hashish had services three times a day.

drug within group meetings is far from fantastical.[20] Although someone might reasonably favor an exemption that could, in theory, cover a nonreligious group that meets demanding conditions, my own judgment is that clearly this is one of those subjects for which an exemption is better restricted to religious claimants.[21]

A restriction to meetings of religious groups will, of course, not make fraud disappear. People may "create" a supposed religion in order to use a drug. Officials or juries will have to estimate if a religion is genuine for those who happen to be prosecuted.[22] Legislators might respond to this worry by restricting an exemption to named groups that they are confident are sincere, or by requiring that any eligible group have existed for a substantial amount of time. Either of these strategies would have the unfortunate consequence of excluding potentially deserving members of groups formed recently. Because the precise effects of drug usage by members of any single group will often be arguable, a group's eligibility for an exemption should not turn upon a finding of how use affects its members; rather, legislators should ask whether the totality of effects among members of groups that would benefit from an exemption would be tolerable.[23] Because only a very small number of religious groups use peyote, and the history of the Native American

[20] If an individual says he subscribes to the group's philosophy that this drug is the key to understanding life, concluding that the individual, and other group members, are insincere will be hard, especially since the line between sincerity and insincerity about such amorphous concepts is not easy to trace. Were it proposed to limit a privilege to use to groups that genuinely accept a high-blown, nonreligious philosophy, the answer is that this inquiry would be too difficult for administrators and courts.

The comments in the text do not apply to claims to the use of marijuana and other drugs to relieve acute physical pain. Were such claims to be entertained, neither group membership nor religious practice should be crucial.

[21] Scholars, who believe that, as a general principle, government should never or rarely be able to favor religious beliefs and practices, will think that an exemption should be broad enough to permit possible application to nonreligious users. See, e.g., Christopher L. Eisgruber and Lawrence G. Sager, "The Vulnerability of Conscience: The Constitutional Basis for Protecting Religious Conduct," 61 *University of Chicago Law Review* 1245, 1306–8, 1999 (should not disfavor fundamental secular commitments); William P. Marshall, "In Defense of Smith and Free Exercise Revisionism," 58 *University of Chicago Law Review* 308, 310–11 (1991) (should not place imprimatur on certain types of belief systems).

[22] One can imagine a "religion" that is not believed by its leaders but is believed by followers. Some critics have asserted that L. Ron Hubbard, the creator of Scientology, did not regard it seriously, but without doubt many people believe in Scientology. *United States v. Kuch*, 288 F. Supp. 439 (D.D.C. 1968), was a rare instance in which a group's tenets showed its lack of seriousness. The "Catechism and Handbook" contained pronouncements of Chief Boo Hoo, and the group's official songs were "Puff, the Magic Dragon" and "Row, Row, Row Your Boat."

[23] If those effects are not acceptable, refusing to grant any exemption would make sense. This would be appropriate if legislators concluded that among the few religious groups for whom a drug is central, use in most of these is highly destructive, leading to abuse and addiction, although most members of one or two groups use without destructive effects.

Church reveals little abuse, legislatures should adopt an exemption broad enough to cover it.

One final point remains: should a religious group need to think use is vital or necessary, or is it enough that the group believes it to be beneficial? Within some Protestant religions, local churches decide whether to use wine or grape juice for communion, and they may switch from one to the other without believing much is at stake. Legislators should not exempt anyone from use of a substance unless some religious bodies consider use essential or very important. But officials and jurors should not have to engage the exact degree of importance for any particular religious group; the exemption should require only that use be a regular aspect of standard worship services.

CONSTITUTIONAL PRINCIPLES

For more than two decades, courts other than the Supreme Court rendered the only constitutional decisions about free exercise rights to use drugs. The leading case was the California Supreme Court's determination that members of the Native American Church had a free exercise right to use peyote in worship unless the state had a compelling interest in enforcing the law against its members.[24] "To forbid the use of peyote is to remove the theological heart of Peyotism."[25] Concluding that members did not suffer harmful effects from using peyote in worship, and finding no evidence that other enforcement efforts would be hampered by an exemption for the church,[26] the court dismissed assertions by the state about the need to prevent those consequences. Finally, addressing the argument that peyote could be regarded as a symbol that "shackles the Indian to primitive conditions,"[27] the court responded that a state cannot deny the practice of a religion on grounds that it is unenlightened.[28] Thus, members had a free exercise right to ingest peyote during worship services. With its focus on central corporate

[24] *Woody*, note 3 supra. The court drew its compelling interest approach mainly from the U.S. Supreme Court's *Sherbert v. Verner*, 374 U.S. 398 (1963).

[25] *Woody*, note 3 supra, at 818.

[26] On this point, the opinion relied partly on a case involving a conscientious refusal to submit to jury service. After a remand from the Supreme Court, the Minnesota Supreme Court sustained the free exercise claim, rejecting the state's unsubstantiated argument that an exemption would encourage fraud. *In re Jenison*, 125 N.W.2d 588 (1963). The opinion also noted that some other states had granted statutory exemptions for religious use of peyote.

[27] Id. at 818.

[28] In this comment, we can see the California court excluding one possible reason the City of Hialeah might have put forward to justify the banning of animal sacrifice. *Church of the Lukumi Babalu Aye, Inc. v. City of Hialeah*, 508 U.S. 520 (1993). That case is discussed in chapter 3.

practice within an undoubtedly genuine religious group, the court did not have to worry about the outer boundaries of a constitutional exemption.

A federal court of appeals reached a contrasting result when Timothy Leary, America's most famous proponent of psychedelic drugs, defended against a charge that he had illegally imported marijuana.[29] As a member of a Hindu sect that uses marijuana for religious illumination and meditation, Leary's claim of a right to use was not restricted to corporate worship.[30] The court decided that the government has a paramount interest in enforcing laws against marijuana. Were an exemption carved out for religious purposes, "For all practical purposes the anti-marijuana laws would be meaningless, and enforcement impossible."[31]

Cases after *Leary* also rejected claims of a religious right to use marijuana. In one of these, the Supreme Judicial Court of Massachusetts assumed that use of marijuana and hashish is at the center of religious services of the Ethiopian Zion Coptic Church.[32] At services conducted three times a day, marijuana was distributed to nonmembers and sometimes to children. The court held that neither the federal Free Exercise Clause nor the state constitution, which forbids restraint of subjects worshiping God according to their conscience, provided they do "not disturb the public peace,"[33] protects any religious use of marijuana or hashish. When the court balanced the value of religious exercise against the state's interest in enforcement, the latter prevailed, in part because an exemption for religious use would render the laws unenforceable.[34]

Not until 1990 did the Supreme Court of the United States squarely face religious use of drugs.[35] Two men had been dismissed from their jobs with a

[29] *Leary*, note 5 supra.

[30] Id. at 857. According to the court, "[Leary] draws no distinction between his religious beliefs and his scientific experimentation."

[31] Id. at 861. About the California peyote decision, the court, having noted that it was not bound by that court's rulings, emphasized peyote's central role in the ceremony of the Native American Church. Leary had made no such argument about his use.

[32] *Nissenbaum*, note 19 supra. See also, e.g., *People v. Trippet*, 66 Cal. Rptr. 2d 559 (Ct. App. 1st Dist. 1997); *Trujillo v. State*, 2 P.3d 567 (Sup. Ct. Wy. 2000); *Rhueark v. State*, 601 So. 2d 135 (Ct. Crim. App. Ala. 1992).

[33] Id. at 593.

[34] In this respect, it did not matter that the defendants' use was public, as in *Woody*, rather than private, as in *Leary*. A footnote about *Woody* remarked on the federal and state exemptions for religious use of peyote; nothing comparable existed for marijuana. Id. at 593. Against the argument that action without any victim does not "disturb the public peace" (language from the state constitution), the court responded that all criminal offenses are breaches of the peace in a sense. Id. at 596. The court did not take as conclusive the legislature's determination that even religious use of marijuana disturbs the public peace, but gave it "significant weight and deference." Id.

[35] *Smith*, note 1 supra.

private drug rehabilitation organization because they had used peyote in services of the Native American Church. The state refused them unemployment compensation on the ground that they had been discharged for misconduct; they claimed that treating their religious use of peyote in this way violated their free exercise rights. After a series of state decisions, an initial disposition by the Supreme Court, and a further decision by the state supreme court, the case returned to the U.S. Supreme Court with the simple central question whether members of the church had a free exercise right against criminal sanctions, the same issue that the California Supreme Court had decided a quarter of a century earlier.[36]

Three justices would have upheld the free exercise claim, on the basis that the state lacked a compelling interest in applying the law against members of the church.[37] Oregon had failed to enforce the criminal law against religious users of peyote, and the state had presented no evidence that peyote has harmful effects. Partly echoing the California court in *Woody*, Justice Blackmun's opinion suggested that the unpleasantness of eating peyote discourages recreational use, that the Native American Church has helped combat alcoholism, and that any illegal traffic in peyote is slight.[38]

Disagreeing with the dissenters about the strength of the state's interest, Justice O'Connor urged that the criminal law represents the "State's judgment that possession and use of controlled substances, even by one person, is inherently harmful and dangerous,"[39] and that even religious use violates the purpose of the law.

The issue that divides Justice O'Connor from the dissenters raises sharply what kind of state interest counts as compelling, a subject to which we shall return at many points in this book. Justice O'Connor did not rely on the possibility of diminished enforcement against nonreligious users, which Justice Blackmun effectively argued will be nonexistent or slight. So the question came down to use by religious participants in worship ceremonies. On

---

[36] The Supreme Court's first decision established that Oregon could count religious use of peyote as misconduct if it constituted a criminal act. The state supreme court then said that Oregon law provided no exemption but that punishment would violate the federal Free Exercise Clause. The U.S. Supreme Court then addressed that issue.

[37] Id. at 907–21 (Blackmun, J., dissenting).

[38] Any worry that exempting religious use of peyote will produce a flood of other religious claims was largely met by the fact that no court had sustained a free exercise right to use any drug other than peyote. The opinion explicitly contrasted claims of members of the Ethiopian Zion Coptic Church, which does not restrict use of marijuana to a "limited ceremonial context" but asserts that marijuana is properly smoked all day. Further, the substantial illegal traffic in marijuana and heroin means that "it would be difficult to grant a religious exemption without seriously compromising law enforcement efforts." Id. at 918.

[39] Id. at 905 (concurring opinion of O'Connor, J.). She took the state's policy at face value, not considering the absence of enforcement against religious users of peyote.

the one hand, that use is crucial for the religion of the Native American Church. What is the harm? O'Connor relied on no findings about the physical harm of using peyote or about any connection between group members using peyote and using other drugs or alcohol. A legislative judgment that hallucinatory states are potentially harmful in themselves is a sufficient basis for a law against the use of peyote *in general*. Remember, the only standard most laws must pass is that they rest on a rational basis. But, absent a concrete analysis of harmful effects, a legislative judgment about harm hardly establishes a significant interest in stopping this religious use, much less a compelling interest. The state's consistent nonenforcement against religious users belied its claim that preventing use in isolated religious ceremonies amounts to a strong state interest.[40]

What is crucial about the *Smith* decision is not this intriguing division between Justice O'Connor and the three dissenters, but the majority's repudiation of the whole mode of analysis they employed. The Court held that people with religious convictions that they should engage in forbidden acts have no constitutional claim to an exemption—none. An "individual's religious beliefs [do not] excuse him from compliance with an otherwise valid law prohibiting conduct that the State is free to regulate."[41] If a reasonable law is neither directed against a religious practice nor discriminates among religious groups, it may be validly applied against people with religious objections, however powerful. The state need not satisfy *any* test beyond the easy task of showing that the law is otherwise valid. The claimants in *Smith*, therefore, lost, without any evaluation of the strength of their religions claim as opposed to the state's interest in prohibiting their acts.

The Court, strikingly, abandoned the free exercise doctrine that prevailed during the previous quarter century, according to which the state had to show a compelling interest in applying a law against people whose religious exercise is burdened.

Justice Scalia's opinion struggled mightily to make the decision appear consonant with prior cases. Remarking that few religious claimants had actually won in the Supreme Court, Justice Scalia did not survey how other courts around the country had applied the compelling interest test, and he did not ask the crucial question how the presence of that test probably affected bargains struck, between those asserting and resisting claims of free exercise, in disputes that never reached court.[42] He referred to older cases,

[40] The interest in preventing physical harm and the use of other drugs cannot be compelling in the absence of some evidence of those effects.
[41] Id. at 878–79.
[42] See Ira C. Lupu, "*Employment Division v. Smith* and the Decline of Supreme Court Centrism," 1993 *Brigham Young University Law Review* 259, 262. In fact, claims for constitu-

including notably *Reynolds v. United States*, the polygamy decision.[43] Although the opinion reads as if it marks no significant change, it fooled no one familiar with free exercise law.

One would have expected the Court to support such a radical departure by claims of an obligation to be faithful to the constitutional text; but, about that, the Court wrote, "As a textual matter, we do not think the words must be given" the meaning that a general law (not aimed at religion) can prohibit free exercise.[44] "It is a permissible reading of the text . . . to say that if prohibiting the exercise of religion . . . is not the object . . . but merely the incidental effect of a generally applicable and otherwise valid provision, the First Amendment has not been offended."[45] These references to the import of the textual language, asserting only that the Court's reading is "permissible," are surprisingly modest.

The heart of Justice Scalia's opinion is that courts should not have to decide when religious claims of variant strength should triumph over state interests of variant strength. If the state really had to show a "compelling interest" in order to apply a law against religiously motivated conduct, that "would be courting anarchy."[46] Against the possibility that courts should invoke the compelling interest test only when the conduct prohibited is central to a religion, Scalia responded that judges cannot appropriately determine the importance of religious ideas.[47]

---

tional exemptions on religious grounds had not fared well in lower courts. Eisgruber and Sager, note 21 supra, at 1260; Frederick Mark Gedicks, "The Normalized Free Exercise Clause: Three Abnormalities," 75 *Indiana Law Journal* 77, 84 (2000). Among lower-court cases decided in favor of a claimant was *Quaring v. Peterson*, 728 F.2d 1121 (8th Cir. 1984), in which the court held that a state could not require someone with a religious objection to have a photo on her driver's license. The decision was affirmed by an equally divided Supreme Court, *Jensen v. Quaring*, 472 U.S. 478 (1985) (Such affirmances have no weight as precedents.)

[43] *Smith*, note 1 supra, at 879, referring to *Reynolds* at 98 U.S. 145 (1879). That case is described in chapter 2.

[44] Id. at 878. As Ira C. Lupu has written, note 42 supra, at 260, although "Justice Scalia claims to be an originalist, . . . the Court's opinion totally ignores both the text and the history of the Free Exercise Clause." Justice Scalia claimed that his approach was more decisively supported by the historical understanding in a concurring opinion in *City of Boerne v. Flores*, 521 U.S. 507, 537 (1997). He there responded to Justice O'Connor's arguments in dissent. Id. at 544. Both opinions concentrated on understanding when the Bill of Rights was adopted, not on conceptions of free exercise at the time of the Fourteenth Amendment.

[45] Id. I have deleted the words "of the tax" after "object." In many contexts, such an omission would unacceptably change the meaning of a sentence (in the manner in which advertisements for movies sometimes distort reviews), but Justice Scalia's point here is just to generalize from his tax illustration to other kinds of provisions.

[46] Id. at 888. Especially a society as diverse religiously as ours "cannot afford the luxury of deeming *presumptively invalid*, as applied to the religious objector, every regulation of conduct that does not protect an interest of the highest order." Id.

[47] Interestingly, neither Justice O'Connor nor Justice Blackmun actually defended an inquiry into centrality, although Justice O'Connor would have required a claimant to show a "constitu-

Justice Scalia did not address the possibility that free exercise rights against neutral laws might extend only to worship (and perhaps other core activities of typical religious bodies), but not to various claims of conscience of a broader sort. To employ such an approach, a court would not have to evaluate what is central for any particular religion; it would need a sense of what is central for most religions. This version of a centrality approach would fail to protect many important aspects of religious exercise, and it would apply a Procrustean one-size-fits-all to the bewildering richness of religious practice and convictions. But, in contrast to *Smith*, it would protect a modicum of religious exercise against the force of general laws.

Justice Scalia expected legislatures to be responsive to religious values to a degree that goes beyond what the Constitution requires, but he was aware that his approach could render smaller religious groups vulnerable to legislative indifference. "It may fairly be said that leaving accommodation to the political process will place at a relative disadvantage those religious practices that are not widely engaged in; but that unavoidable consequence of democratic government must be preferred to a system in which each conscience is a law unto itself or in which judges weigh the social importance of all laws against the centrality of all religious beliefs."[48] This candid acknowledgment sums up what many find distressing about *Smith*: because of concerns about judicial propriety, the Court has simply given up on protecting a wide range of free exercise rights for religious minorities.

---

tionally significant" burden on the exercise of religion, id. at 899, and Justice Blackmun said that courts need not "turn a blind eye to the severe impact of a State's restrictions on the adherents of a minority religion." Id. at 919. Justice Scalia argued that these inquiries are ones into centrality, by another name. Id. at 887–88 n. 4. Chapter 13 takes up this complex and subtle issue in more depth.

Michael W. McConnell, a strong opponent of the *Smith* ruling, has acknowledged that the doctrine it replaces was "poorly developed and unacceptably subjective." "Free Exercise Revisionism and the *Smith* Decision," 57 *University of Chicago Law Review* 1109, 1199 (1990).

[48] Id. at 890. In a lengthy opinion in the Santeria case, which we considered in chapter 3, Justice Souter criticized the Court's ruling in *Smith* that persons with religious reasons to disobey have no free exercise claim against general laws. Souter argued that a law can fail substantive neutrality if it imposes on religious believers much more heavily than on others. *Hialeah*, note 28 supra, at 568. Souter made his point in terms of a law's effects, but one might adopt a similar approach about legislators' attitudes, viewing failures to respond to strong religious claims as themselves a kind of discrimination. The concern that *Smith* is insufficiently protective of minority religions is pervasive of among critics of the decision. See e.g., McConnell, note 47 supra, at 1147; Jesse H. Choper, "Separation of Church and State: 'New' Directions by the 'New' Supreme Court," 34 *Journal of Church and State* 363, 365–66 (1992); Kathleen M. Sullivan, "Religion and Liberal Democracy," 59 *University of Chicago Law Review* 195 (1992).

For the view that legislative accommodations that are not themselves constitutionally required are impermissible establishments of religion, see Ira C. Lupu, "Reconstructing the Establishment Clause: The Case Against Discretionary Accommodations of Religion," 140 *Univer-*

Largely to accommodate precedents that flew in the face of his general approach, Justice Scalia elaborated two exceptions to his dominant principle. One exception is for denial of unemployment compensation because an applicant has refused to work on Saturday or has declined war-related work. The Court, thus, accepted these specific free exercise rights earlier cases had created; it left unresolved whether the approach of those cases might be extended to other situations when eligibility for benefits depends on a system of individual exemptions.[49]

Another exception is more puzzling. Justice Scalia argued that in most decisions sustaining free exercise claims, these had been linked to other constitutional claims. *Smith* does not preclude success for such "hybrid" claims.

For one kind of hybrid, this conclusion is easy to reach. When the issue concerns treatment of religious expression, free exercise claims may be unnecessary or redundant, because free speech claims warrant success. Cases of this variety are untouched by *Smith*'s narrowing of free exercise doctrine. But the opinion suggests another, stranger, sort of hybrid. Neither the free exercise claim nor the other constitutional claim would be sufficient alone for success, but together they are adequate. Justice Scalia implies that the proper analysis of the right of Amish to withdraw children from school, discussed in the next chapter, relies in this way on two relevant constitutional rights, free exercise and parental liberty.

Three aspects of this hybrid analysis are anomalous. Saying that two different constitutional claims might combine in strength to generate an actual specific right, although neither claim alone would be powerful enough to sustain the right, is perfectly sensible. But if the two kinds of claims in combination can generate practical rights, how can we be sure that one of the kinds will *never* be strong enough by itself? Without surveying the wide domain of possible claims, a project beyond Scalia's ambitions, one cannot reasonably conclude that a single claim will never do the work by itself. Yet that is what Scalia asserted about free exercise claims.

The second anomaly is the arbitrariness of deciding when another constitutional claim is in play. *Smith* itself could easily have been viewed as a hybrid involving free exercise and free association (to worship). Justice Scalia says *Smith* is not a hybrid, but he doesn't go very far to explain how courts are to decide that preliminary issue.

The third anomaly is that if free exercise claims are to carry genuine weight in hybrid cases when someone challenging a law relies on two claims, judges will presumably have to evaluate the strength of the free exercise claims in

---

sity of Pennsylvania Law Review 555 (1991), and "The Trouble with Accommodation," 60 *George Washington Law Review* 743, 771–72 (1992).

[49] *Smith*, note 1 supra, at 884.

just the manner to which Justice Scalia objects when free exercise claims stand alone. All these problems suggest that the Court probably does not regard this second sort of hybrid situation seriously; rather the concept is jerry-built to cover the Amish decision.[50]

Employment Division v. Smith marks a crucial divide in free exercise law. Final evaluation of the line that distinguishes the majority from the other four justices must await a more detailed evaluation in subsequent chapters of various difficulties courts face when they adjudicate free exercise claims. But I offer some initial comments here.

To limit free exercise rights to laws that target religion or classify according to religion is sharply to restrict the scope of the Free Exercise Clause.[51] This position fails to safeguard even acts of worship central to a faith. It does not protect Roman Catholic use of wine in Mass, any more than it protects use of peyote, so long as the law that forbids drinking of wine is aimed at drinking of alcoholic substances (or wine)[52] in general. This particular failing of constitutional protection has little practical significance, because use of wine in the Mass will never be forbidden. (Were a locality with few Catholics to adopt such a law, a state government would step in and override it.) But to focus on the actual danger to Catholics is to miss the point. It is just because Roman Catholicism is now solidly established as a major American faith that such a law is unthinkable. Small minorities do

[50] Although a number of lower federal courts have assumed that certain cases fall within the relevant category of hybrids, they have been hesitant to make decisions turn on that basis and have (understandably) developed no clear principles to demarcate the category. The Second Circuit Court of Appeals, as well as the Sixth Circuit, has treated Smith's "hybrid" language as dictum. See *Leebaert v. Harrington*, 332 F.3d 134 (2d Cir. 2003), which contains a summary of developments in other circuits.

[51] The clause also protects religious belief and speech, but in this respect it is entirely redundant or almost so, since the Free Speech Clause provides the same protection. (A possible exception is that in the absence of a Free Exercise Clause, perhaps the government could rely on someone's religious belief to make a negative judgment about a matter such as employment to a greater extent than would now be permitted.) The Court's approach is defended in William P. Marshall, note 21 supra; and in Suzanna Sherry, "Enlightening the Religion Clauses," 7 *Journal of Contemporary Legal Issues* 473, 493 (1996). Among critical treatments are Douglas Laycock, "The Remnants of Free Exercise," 1990 *Supreme Court Review* 1; Michael M. McConnell, "Accommodation of Religion: An Update and a Response to Critics," 60 *George Washington Law Review* 685 (1992); David E. Steinberg, "Rejecting the Case Against the Free Exercise Exemption: A Critical Assessment," 75 *Boston University Law Review* 241 (1995). Steven D. Smith has made the interesting point that the doctrine of *Sherbert v. Verner* encourages courts to consider what can be tolerated in religious practice. The combination of *Smith* and the Santeria decision shape a discourse of disrespect, of asserting that legislatures had malign purposes. "Free Exercise Doctrine and the Discourse of Disrespect," 65 *Colorado Law Review* 519, 532–75 (1999).

[52] A law that forbids drinking wine but not other alcoholic beverages might be regarded as aimed at religious use, because it is hard to imagine what reason one could have to allow drinking of scotch, bourbon, gin, beer etc., but not wine.

not have that comfort. If the majority of the population is unsympathetic, a legislature may pass an ostensibly neutral law largely in order to discourage the exercise of that religion.

The more pervasive concerns are relative indifference to minorities and easy condemnation of what seems odd. The dangers of using alcohol are far better documented than the dangers of using peyote; many millions of American lives have been stunted by alcoholism, and drinking continues to figure in many traffic deaths. Although a sip of wine does not cause these harms, sips during services might help tempt a small number of individuals to wider, irresponsible, use. We can be sure that if members of an important church used peyote, legislatures would not forbid religious use. The rule of *Smith* risks legislative unconcern with the plight of unfamiliar minority religions. We should accept that approach only if the administrative problems with a more protective standard are truly overwhelming.

State courts interpreting their own constitutional provisions, most of which have language that is more elaborate than the federal Free Exercise Clause, are free to follow *Smith* or employ a form of weighing that resembles pre-*Smith* constitutional law. Many have wisely chosen the latter course.[53]

Smith concerns the allocation of responsibility between courts and legislatures for creating exemptions from general laws. It does not undercut the appropriateness of particularized legislative exemptions, address the fairness of various kinds of categorizations, or settle whether legislatures may choose to enact more general exemptions that require courts to perform the tasks that the Court has determined are not imposed by the Free Exercise Clause itself.

The *Smith* opinion makes clear that a legislature not only may exempt members of the Native American Church from a ban on using peyote, it may create similar free exercise exemptions from other valid laws. Nothing in the opinion is at odds with my analysis of a desirable exemption for religious use of drugs, but it decisively leaves to legislatures the choice whether to exempt. Many state legislatures have adopted such exemptions, and the Oregon legislature created one following *Smith*.

---

[53] See, e.g., *Rupert v. City of Portland*, 605 A.2d 63, 65–66 (Sup. Jud. Ct. Mass. 1992); *State v. Balzer*, 954 P.2d 935–36 (Ct. App. Wash. Div. 2 1998). In "Comment: A Decade After *Smith*: An Examination of the New York Court of Appeals' Stance on the Free Exercise of Religion in Relation to Minnesota, Washington, and California," 63 *Albany Law Review* 1305 (2000), So Chun is sharply critical of New York's failure to rely on its constitutional language (closely similar to that we reviewed in chapter 2) to protect free exercise; other states with similar language have been more protective. David H. E. Beaker, "Free Exercise of Religion Under the New York Constitution," 84 *Cornell Law Review* 1088 (1999), suggests that the state constitution imposes a compelling interest test. *People ex rel. DeMauro v. Gavin*, 92 N.Y.2d 963 (1998) suggests that courts should balance claims of religious worship against state interests.

Although a legislature can create *an* exemption, that does not mean it can create *any* exemption. The seriously doubtful questions are whether it can limit an exemption to religious groups or to named religious groups.

A legislature can definitely distinguish among drugs, deciding that religious use of peyote will not undermine general enforcement but that a similar exemption for marijuana would do so. Almost certainly, a legislature may require corporate membership (of some sort) and use within the group, not opening the exemption to anyone who believes individual use has religious significance.

We can be reasonably confident that the present Court would not require that an exemption be extended to nonreligious groups. This conclusion would be sound.[54] I have argued that sometimes the government must accommodate those who are nonreligious if it chooses to accommodate similarly situated religious persons; but for use of peyote, members of nonreligious groups, though they may find deep understanding in their hallucinatory experiences, will rarely, if ever, have reasons to use peyote—reasons according to their own scale of values—that are *as powerful* as those of religious groups like the Native American Church. And an extension to nonreligious groups would increase dangers of fraud. These factors justify limiting an exemption to religious bodies.

An exemption, like the present federal one,[55] that is explicitly restricted to members of the Native American Church is more troublesome. Affording an exemption to members of one church and not to members of other similar religious groups would ordinarily be an unconstitutional establishment of religion.[56] Against a conceivable response that no other similar group now exists, the answer is that one might arise. An exemption should not be limited to groups that exist at a particular point in time.

---

[54] But see note 21 supra.

[55] 2 C.F.R. § 1307.31 (West 2003). See also Iowa: I.C.A. § 124.204; Kansas: K.S.A. § 65–4116(c); Tex. H & S. C. Ann. § 481.111(a); Wisconsin: W.S.A. § 961.115. Colorado grants an exemption for use "in religious ceremonies of any bona fide religious organization." C.R.S.A. § 12–22–317(3), § 18–18–418(3). Idaho limits its exemption to persons of Native American descent on an Indian reservation. I.C. § 37–2732A. In *Employment Division v. Smith*, Justice Blackmun bolstered his argument that the state lacked a compelling interest in applying its criminal law against ceremonial use of members of the Native American Church by referring to the American Indian Religious Freedom Act, which establishes a policy of protecting the religious ceremonies of American Indians. Although the act does not create enforceable legal rights, he took it to suggest that courts must "scrupulously apply [their] free exercise analysis to the religious claims of Native Americans." Note 1 supra, at 921.

[56] However, given differences between use of marijuana and peyote, courts have rightly rejected the argument that a peyote exemption discriminates unconstitutionally against religious groups using marijuana. *People v. Peck*, 61 Cal. Rptr. 2d 1, 5 (Ct. App. 4th Dist. 1996); *State v. McBride*, 955 P.2d 133, 138–39 (Ct. Apps. Kan. 1998); *State v. Matteson*, 530 N.W.2d 69 (Ct. Apps. Wisc. 1995).

The restrictive exemptions of federal and Texas law were actually challenged by a group called the Peyote Way Church of God, made up mostly of persons who were not of Native American descent.[57] The Fifth Circuit Court of Appeals upheld the classification that denied to this church the privilege given to the Native American Church. Its basis for avoiding the force of the church's establishment and equal protection arguments was that the federal government has a special relationship with the quasi-sovereign Native American tribes, that the Native American Church allows as members only those who are at least 25 percent of Native American descent, and that a special privilege for a Native American religious group was therefore constitutionally acceptable. Whether the special relationship of the federal government with Native American tribes is a sufficient justification for this unmistakable religious differentiation strikes me as highly doubtful,[58] but in any event the principle of the decision has no relevance for religious classifications of other kinds.

Since the Native American Church is apparently the dominant group using peyote in worship, were an exemption for it by name to be regarded as overly narrow, the proper relief would be to extend the exemption to any otherwise similar unnamed group.[59]

The Court's decision in *Smith* led directly to Congress's enacting a different kind of exemption—one cast in terms of religious claims generally. By its near-unanimous adoption of the Religious Freedom Restoration Act, Congress reinstituted the compelling interest language of *Sherbert v. Verner.*[60] Under the act, when someone suffers a substantial interference with his exercise of religion, the government cannot apply a law against him unless it shows that doing so serves a compelling interest that cannot be achieved by less intrusive means. As chapter 2 recounts, the Supreme Court responded by declaring RFRA unconstitutional as it restricts states and local-

---

[57] *Peyote Way Church of God, Inc. v. Thornburgh,* 922 F.2d 1210 (5th Cir. 1991).

[58] One of the three judges in the case dissented. Id. at 1220 (Clark, J., dissenting). See also Francis X. Santangelo, "Proposal for the Equal Protection of Non-Indians Practicing Native American Religions: Can the Religious Freedom Restoration Act Finally Remove the Existing Deference Without a Difference?" 69 *St. John's Law Review* 255 (1995).

[59] Employing the sort of analysis Justice Harlan uses in his concurring opinion in *Welsh v. United States*, which we reviewed in chapter 4, one can conclude that a legislature, having chosen to exempt the dominant group using peyote in worship, would choose a broader exemption over no exemption at all.

The sentence in text leaves open whether any group must endure and establish a "track record" before it can receive an exemption. A statute might limit an exemption, for example, to groups that have existed for half a century. I think such a restriction should also be unconstitutional, unless the state can demonstrate that there are very serious dangers that only existence over time can show to be ill founded.

[60] Religious Freedom Restoration Act §§ 2000bb-1–2000bb-4 (2004).

ities;[61] but this decision does not undercut the validity of RFRA as it relates to the federal government, or of similar laws, adopted by at least thirteen states,[62] or of a more recent federal act, the Religious Land Use and Institutionalized Persons Act of 2000.[63]

Can legislatures favor religious claims in this general way? Can they impose on courts the very endeavor Justice Scalia regarded as so distasteful in *Smith*? In February of 2006, a unanimous Supreme Court answered these questions in the affirmative; under RFRA, the federal government, failing to show a compelling interest, could not apply the Controlled Substance Act to bar the importation of a hallucinogenic tea used in religious ceremonies.[64]

If legislatures are constitutionally permitted to adopt this approach to religious claims, are they wise to do so? Subsequent chapters address issues about constitutionality and wisdom, and chapter 13 is devoted to the central concern whether the standards these laws adopt are administrable and effective. That chapter also considers various techniques for expanding free exercise protection without justices or legislators overturning the approach of *Smith*. These techniques include vigorous review of claims of unequal treatment, adaptation of free speech doctrines to free exercise claims, and expansive interpretation of the circumstances in which individualized exemptions of other sorts require exemptions for religious claims.

[61] *Boerne*, note 44 supra.

[62] The language of these state provisions varies somewhat. Some of the differences are explained in chapter 8 (on prisons) and chapter 13 (on burden and government interest).

[63] Pub. L. No. 106–274, 114 stat. 803. Because this act rests partly on the spending and commerce powers of Congress, its validity does not depend entirely on the limited authority of Congress to enforce the Fourteenth Amendment, the source of difficulty with the Religious Freedom Restoration Act as it applied to states and localities. Congress may attach conditions on its expenditures of funds, even if those conditions do not serve any independent delegated power. In the 2004 term, the Supreme Court rejected an Establishment Clause challenge to the part of RLUIPA that applies to prisoners. *Cutter v. Wilkinson*, 125 S. Ct. 2113 (2005).

[64] *Gonzales v. O Centro Espírita Beneficente União Do Vegetal*, No. 04–1084 (Justice Alito not participating).

CHAPTER 6

Free Exercise Objections
to Educational Requirements

When parents insist that what or how schools teach is at odds with their family's religious beliefs and practices, should the state grant exceptions from its normal demands and, if so, in what form?

The underlying concerns in educational conflicts involve children's development, as well as what they are required to do in the present. The state aims to educate children to make autonomous choices and to participate in democratic government. Parents who want their children to avoid teaching that will erode religious faith, may object to "mere exposure" in the form of reading or listening to objectionable ideas, as well as more active affirmations or behavior, such as dancing or swearing allegiance to the flag.

Both in respect to the parties concerned and possible remedies, conflicts over education are more complex than those about conscientious objection and religious use of drugs. Instead of a relatively simple opposition between the government and an adult, we have parents, children, and the government. With younger children, parents and educational authorities divide responsibility; but as the children grow older, their own convictions should count.

Whereas the basic remedy for anyone receiving an exemption from a law requiring military service or forbidding drug use is that he need not comply, when parents object to an aspect of a public school curriculum, education of some sort may need to continue. Does the school have to provide a suitable alternative, or is that up to the parents? And what counts as a suitable alternative? Worries about appropriate remedies can affect judgments about what educators and courts should do.

Two cases provide helpful prisms for examining conflicts over education. One involved Amish parents who sought to withdraw their children from ordinary education after eighth grade.[1] The other concerned Fundamentalist Christians whose children were enrolled in public elementary school; objecting on religious grounds to its collection of diverse stories, they did not want the children to use the Holt, Rinehart and Winston series of readers.[2]

---

[1] *Wisconsin v. Yoder*, 406 U.S. 205 (1972).

[2] *Mozert v. Hawkins County Board of Educ.*, 827 F.2d 1058 (6th Cir. 1987), cert. denied, 484 U.S. 1066 (1988). My discussion of this case draws substantially from Kent Greenawalt, *Does God Belong in Public Schools?* (Princeton: Princeton University Press, 2005). That book

The Basic Conflicts

Amish Education and Ordinary High School

The Old Order Amish represent a long-standing radical Protestant tradition loosely called Anabaptist.[3] The Amish, as well as other Anabaptists, suffered severe persecution in Europe, and some emigrated to America to escape. About 130,000 Amish now live in the United States and Ontario, Canada; the largest group is the Old Order Amish.[4]

The Amish believe that members of a true Christian community should live devoutly and simply with religion pervading all aspects of daily life. They live mainly by farming in relative isolation from the larger society. They eschew most modern technology, declining to use conventional electric appliances and to own television sets, radios, computers, or automobiles. They live by an *Ordnung*, an unwritten code of conduct. Authority is patriarchal and hierarchical.[5] Amish practice involves submission to an authority, self-denial, lack of individuality, and rejection of intellectual attainment.[6] The rules of the Amish lead them to "lives that are starkly different from the lives of the members of mainstream society."[7]

In Amish governance, few matters are considered a person's private business. Members may be punished for purchasing a radio as well as for wronging a fellow member. For serious offenses, the community may expel members and shun them in their personal and business lives.[8] Amish children are not baptized until about the age of eighteen;[9] if a young man or woman then chooses not to be baptized, he or she does not suffer the shunning meted out to expelled members.

The Amish believe in a radical division of the sacred and secular kingdoms that involves their substantial withdrawal from the wider political commu-

---

also contains treatments of students' and teachers' free exercise rights within public schools, topics not considered here.

[3] The Amish developed as a separate group in the 1690s when Joseph Ammann maintained, among other things, that expelled members should be shunned in ordinary social relations. Jeff Spinner, *The Boundaries of Citizenship* 88–89 (Baltimore: Johns Hopkins University Press, 1994).

[4] Brian Barry, *Culture and Equality* 178 (Cambridge: Harvard University Press, 2001).

[5] Women cannot be among the church leaders; they are expected to be their husbands' helpers. Spinner, note 3 supra, at 91.

[6] Id. at 91.

[7] Id. at 90. Barry asserts that, in contrast with the popular image, the Amish are not ascetics. Note 4 supra, at 181.

[8] Spinner, note 3 supra, at 90. Legal regulation of shunning is discussed in chapter 17.

[9] Id. at 91.

nity.[10] Amish pay taxes, but they do not serve in official positions or perform jury duty or military service, and they do not accept public welfare. Most do not vote. Disputes among members are resolved internally, rather than by civil litigation. Although the Amish are not active participants in the democratic process,[11] sympathetic outsiders have helped them gain concessions from legislators[12] and a few significant victories in courts, including the Supreme Court decision granting their right to withdraw fourteen-year-olds from school,[13] and a state court ruling that a small subgroup of Amish need not display orange triangles on their horse-drawn vehicles.[14]

Because Amish children need to read and write and do arithmetic, the Amish have no objection to ordinary schooling up to eighth grade; at that stage, they want their children to move to community vocational education. Wisconsin, among other states, required that children receive regular schooling until the age of sixteen. Virtually all states now permit home schooling, and when the Amish case arose, Wisconsin did permit a substitute for school attendance; but the Amish vocational education did not qualify as "substantially equivalent" to that given in school.[15] Failing an accommodation of the sort reached in many school districts with a substantial Amish population, the state arrested Amish parents who kept their children away from school.[16]

The Amish parents believed that allowing their children further ordinary education would endanger their own salvation and that of their children. High school teaches values that conflict with those of the Amish, and can interfere with an Amish child's integration into the religious community. By contrast, Amish development of vocational skills by learning through doing fitted Amish convictions about how to live. According to one expert, high school could greatly harm Amish children psychologically; and requiring all Amish children to attend high school could eventually destroy the Old Order Amish community as it now exists.[17]

Parents' Complaints about the Holt Reading Series

The Fundamentalist Christian parents who wanted their children excused from the Holt reading series were, like the Amish, fearful that exposure to

---

[10] Barry, note 4 supra, at 177–179.

[11] See Spinner, note 3 supra, at 93.

[12] Barry, note 4 supra, at 179–80.

[13] *Yoder*, note 1 supra.

[14] *State v. Hershberger*, 444 N.W.2d 282 (Minn. 1989); *State v. Hershberger*, 462 N.W.2d 393 (Minn. 1990).

[15] *Yoder*, note 1 supra, at 208.

[16] Spinner, note 3 supra, at 87.

[17] *Yoder*, note 1 supra, at 212.

the standard education would undermine their children's religious beliefs.[18] The exact parameters of their complaint were more elusive than that of the Amish. The controversy began when Vicki Frost discovered a story involving mental telepathy in her daughter's sixth-grade reader.[19] She and some like-minded neighbors then found other objectionable material, which according to their understanding, promoted such ideas as "one-world government," evolution, and a skeptical view of religion. The Holt series, with stories from different traditions, was designed, among other things, to stimulate imagination, critical understanding, and tolerance for diversity. Two excerpts to which the parents objected were a version of Goldilocks in which her misbehavior remained unpunished,[20] and a passage from the *Diary of Anne Frank* in which Anne remarks to her friend Peter, "I wish you had a religion. . . . it doesn't matter what. Just believe in something."[21] That comment was sacrilege to parents who believed that faith in Jesus is necessary for salvation.[22] The parents also objected to scant attention the Holt series gave to Protestant Christianity.[23]

One way in which the protesters conceived the Holt readers was as promoting secular humanism, which they understood to encourage sexual permissiveness, gender equality, and a decline in biblical morality.[24] The protesters wanted their children excused from using the books. Various schools in the county responded differently,[25] but the school board's resolution that the county schools would use only the Holt readers[26] led to the parents' free exercise claim that their children should be excused from using those readers.

[18] Fundamentalism, developed as a reaction to modernism in religion (including acceptance of evolution and "higher criticism" of the Bible), drew its name from a group of tracts published early in the twentieth century called *The Fundamentals: A Testimony to the Truth*. Stephen Bates, *Battleground: One Mother's Crusade, the Religious Right, and the Struggle for Control of Our Classrooms* 44 (New York: Poseidon Press, 1993); see Nomi Maya Stolzenberg, "He Drew a Circle That Shut Me Out: Assimilation, Indoctrination, and the Paradox of a Liberal Education," 106 *Harvard Law Review* 581, 614–23 (1993). Although *Fundamentalists* is now often used by critics to label a group of Christians whose members themselves would be more likely to use a term such as *Evangelical Christians*, the latter phrase is broader and includes many Christians whose beliefs vary from those of the parents in this case. Thus, I adhere to the more precise characterization of *Fundamentalist*.

[19] Bates, note 18 supra, at 19.

[20] Id. at 82.

[21] Id. at 206–7. (The ellipsis in the text omits Peter's response to Anne's initial comment, as well as some of what Anne said.) The reader also contains the fable of the blind man and the elephant, suggesting that all religions have some part, but not all of the truth.

[22] Id. at 207.

[23] Id. Paul Vitz, a New York University professor of psychology, testified at the trial that none of the six hundred stories and poems in the readers depicted biblical Protestantism, whereas many stories presented non-Christian religions favorably.

[24] Id. at 54.

[25] Id. at 71–77.

[26] Id. at 86–90.

In a perceptive article, Nomi Stolzenberg has suggested that the parents' general allegations included claims that the books teach false beliefs, that they are pervasively biased against the parents' religion, that they "pressure children to accept the view that all religions lead to God and are equally valid," that they cause "the children to become more rebellious, to believe that they are their own authority," and that permitting their children to read the books would violate the parents' own religious duty to protect them from evil influences that could lead them from God's way.[27]

The appellate judges in the case disagreed over just what changes would have satisfied the complaining parents. Some of their objections would have applied to other English readers; but the specific relief the parents sought was that their children not study from the Holt series.

Competing State Interests

Among the reasons why Wisconsin and Hawkins County refused to bend to satisfy parents, some are easy to grasp; others are less obvious and more controversial.

States have a stake in their children being educated, as their compulsory attendance laws reflect. Although people can disagree about the age at which education should no longer be compulsory, Wisconsin sensibly mandated standard education up to the age of sixteen. Remaining in school promotes the welfare of most children; and the state's interest in this good is sufficient to override the ordinary wishes and opinions of children and their parents who would end schooling earlier.[28]

Education beyond eighth grade serves at least five distinct purposes. It increases the skills a child needs for a career.[29] It also enhances an individual's ability to choose how to live. Youngsters leaving school at fourteen to be integrated into the Amish community may forfeit the values of a more independent existence without ever acquiring an adequate basis for choice.[30] And

---

[27] Stolzenberg, note 18 supra, at 596–97.

[28] Although some few children do not actually profit from education after the eighth grade, no one can identify them in advance. The state rightly educates all, because the vast majority will benefit. The instruction need not be provided directly by the government; it may take place in a private school or at home, but the state reasonably insists that children make progress according to ordinary educational criteria.

[29] For some jobs, it may not matter much whether an individual leaves school after eighth grade, but many jobs demand a higher level of skill, and the percentage of these has increased since 1972, as more and more workers use computers.

[30] Stephen Macedo had written that "allowing Amish parents to withdraw their children from high school could thwart the children's ability to make informed decisions about their own futures. All children should have an education that provides them with the ability to make *informed* and *independent* decisions about how they want to lead their lives in the modern

adults who subsequently leave the Amish community may be poorly prepared for life in the wider society.[31] A young woman of twenty-five who has
participated exclusively in Amish vocational tasks is a long way from being
prepared to be a teacher, a banker, or a doctor.[32] True it is that had she left
school at sixteen, she would not have been much better prepared; but two
extra years in school might have led her to choose to get further education.

Education assists people to enjoy forms of culture; cutting their education
short restricts development of that capacity in students. The most obvious
ability that will not be developed is that of reading serious works of literature
and nonfiction. A person whose education has stopped at eighth grade is
very unlikely ever to read *Moby Dick*, *War and Peace*, a serious biography
of Abraham Lincoln, or works of philosophy.

Education beyond eighth grade helps students understand principles of
American government and learn to participate actively in democratic institutions; education also assists moral development beyond those aspects of morality that concern citizenship. The years between fourteen and sixteen can
be particularly important in the teaching of tolerance, respect for others,
critical thinking, and self-expression.

Two simple grounds not to accommodate the Fundamentalists of Hawkins
County involve the locus of educational decisions and the value of uniformity. Educators, not ad hoc collections of parents, should choose texts;
teachers should not have to concern themselves with using alternative texts
for a few children and with students' leaving the room when the class gets
to controversial material. In lower grades at least, teachers should be able
to bridge various subjects by references to what they have taught previously;
they can do this effectively only if everyone in class is studying the same
materials.

Use of the Holt readers also touched the values of choice and democratic
participation. The superintendent of schools testified that the readers were
selected because they "expose the student to varying values and religious
backgrounds [without] promoting any particular value or religion."[33] The
readers were designed to teach tolerance and respect for many religions and
ways of life; children who were excused would miss not only the readings

---

world." Stephen Macedo, *Diversity and Distrust: Civic Education in a Multicultural Democracy* 207 (Cambridge: Harvard University Press, 2000).

[31] Roughly 20 percent of Amish teenagers decide not to be baptized and leave the community
around the age of eighteen, see Barry, note 4 supra, at 178; and some of those who are baptized
leave or are expelled later in life.

[32] She may pick up further education, but starting over will not be easy. She may lack the
resources to pursue much further education, and years of housework may have reduced her
motivation or ability to study.

[33] *Mozert*, note 2 supra, at 1063.

themselves but the give-and-take in class that is part of an education in critical thinking and respect for others.

What Accommodations Should Be Made?

The conflicts between parents' religious claims and standard education pose
difficult issues about how the government should respond. At the center of
the problem are (1) the respective authority of parents and the state, and of
older children, and (2) the reasonable aspirations of the state to educate
children to think for themselves and participate in democratic government.

Some Preliminaries

The serious question about excusing children arises only if the education the
state is providing does not itself impermissibly endorse a particular religious
view or discriminate among religions, a subject explored in the second volume.[34] We will assume here that what the state is teaching is itself constitutionally acceptable, and that the crucial issue is not discontinuing the use of
materials for all students but accommodating objecting parents. All states
allow parents to enroll children in private schools, including religious
schools, and this right is constitutionally protected.[35] All states also allow
home schooling if the parents choose it and are willing to comply with whatever regulations their state imposes.[36] Parents who pursue either of these
options enjoy wide latitude to provide the kind of religious instruction they

---

[34] Two ways in which materials could fail these standards would be to present a particular
religious view as the correct one or to condemn some religious views, but the unfairness could
be more subtle, as by presenting stories in which the villains are Roman Catholics, Jews, or
Muslims.

The Hawkins County parents did suggest that the Holt readers established the religion of
secular humanism and discriminated against Protestant Christianity, especially conservative
Protestant Christianity. Had these complaints been valid, the proper response would have been
to substitute different reading materials for everyone.

[35] In *Pierce v. Society of Sisters*, 268 U.S. 510 (1925), the Court found such a right as a
matter of substantive due process. More recently, many have assumed that the Free Exercise
Clause is what mainly supports the right. On that understanding, the constitutional right might
not extend to nonreligious private schools.

[36] For a summary of the regulations in each state, see Home School Legal Defense Association at http://www.hslda.org/laws/default.asp. See, e.g., Ira C. Lupu, "Home Education, Religious Liberty and the Separation of Powers," 67 *Boston University Law Review* 971 (1987);
Barbara Kantrowitz and Pat Wingert, "Learning at Home: Does It Pass the Test?" *Newsweek*,
October 5, 1998, 64; June Gross, "Unhappy in Class, More Are Learning at Home," *New York
Times*, November 10, 2003, A1, col. 2. For a case rejecting parental claims to be free of state
regulations, see *State v. DelaBruere*, 577 A.2d 254 (Vt. 1990).

want. Further, in their regulation of private schools and home schooling, states concentrate on basic competence, not values education, tolerance, and critical thinking.[37] Thus parents are now able to avoid having their children exposed to many of the nonreligious perspectives that the Amish and Hawkins County parents found so troubling.

Should Children of the Amish Be Excused from Two Years of Compulsory School, and If So, What Should Be the Content of an Exemption?

In considering the basic conflict of Amish religious practice and state interest, I assume that the children share their parents' religious outlook and agree with them about withdrawing from school. Parents should not be able to force a child to withdraw from school, if he or she wants to fulfill the amount of schooling that the state prescribes.[38]

Believing in a simple life, the Amish do not think their members should pursue intellectual and cultural ambitions, or participate in complex modern forms of work. Advanced education is triply harmful. It draws children away from the community at a stage vital for their integration into Amish society; it involves activity directly opposed to the simplicity of Amish life, at-tracting—tempting one might say—young people to alternative styles of liv-ing; and it may make more difficult someone's faithful adherence to the Amish community. A student who is broadly educated may not be able to accept a simple life in quite the same way as those who have been nurtured in it from childhood, without great exposure to other forms of life.[39]

As we have seen, the state has an interest in a child's education, whatever life choices she finally makes. For the state, unlike the Amish, opening up a range of choice is a positive attribute of education. This conflict in perspec-tives is irreconcilable. The state cannot maximize conditions of choice for all its children and defer to the Amish wish to take over the education of teenagers.

The argument for resolution in favor of the Amish is straightforward. When the teenagers agree, parental judgments about the kind of education their children need should have priority over ordinary state requirements.

[37] See the summary of regulations, note 36 supra.

[38] Indeed, a child should be able to receive education until the age of eighteen if he or she wants it and the parents do not.

[39] Of course, in the modern United States, all Amish know that their way of life is extraordi-nary, and teenagers are exposed enough to the wider society to have some sense of life within it, but that is not the same as participating in alternative forms of living directly, or vicariously through advanced education. Simple acceptance of a simple life becomes harder the greater the exposure to other possibilities.

The Amish have consistently believed that the life they practice accords with God's plan. If their children are baptized into the Amish community, they will lead productive lives that do not disturb others or require welfare benefits from the larger society. When the Amish came to these shores, it was to maintain their strict religious way of life; that should not now be made difficult or impossible because the government adopts invasive laws about the education of teenagers.

The grounds for denying an exemption are also straightforward. The basic good of education extends at least to the age of sixteen. The reason why the state generally accords parents a wide range of choice about how to raise their children is that parents are better able to raise children than the state, *not* that parents have a right to fly in the face of fundamental social judgments about children's welfare.[40] Parents cannot deny children medical help; they cannot put them to work at young ages; and they should not be able to deny them the benefit of two years of education. Fourteen-year-olds are too young to make an informed decision about further education.

To assess the strength of these competing positions, we need to consider the authority of parents, and the state's aims to develop students' competence, autonomous choice, and democratic participation.

Children are not the property of parents. Although parents have wide freedom to determine their children's religious upbringing, they cannot rely on religious grounds to deprive their children of what the state deems vital benefits, such as literacy. The religiously based wish of Amish parents to withdraw their children from school is *a* reason to accommodate, but it is not by itself conclusive.

Competence is a matter of degree; students remaining in ordinary school are prepared to perform a wider variety of tasks than those who withdraw to receive Amish vocational education.[41] This extra competence would not aid those who stay within the Amish community, but 20 percent of teenagers refuse baptism and leave the Amish community,[42] and a smaller number later depart. We might try to calculate the loss in "wasted education" were an exemption denied, for those who are forced to stay in school and remain

[40] Amy Gutmann, in *Democratic Education* 32 (Princeton: Princeton University Press, 1987), speaks of "the value of parental freedom at least to the extent that such freedom does not interfere with the interests of children in becoming mutually respectful citizens of a society that sustains family life."

[41] It might be argued that the teenagers who leave school after eighth grade will have a gain in competence to carry out the vocations of the Amish, but insofar as one refers to the ordinary work of the Amish, this seems implausible. This work could be learned as well at the age of sixteen as at the age of fourteen; and indeed nothing would prevent ninth and tenth graders doing part-time work within the community.

[42] See Barry, note 4 supra, at 178.

Amish, *against* what the loss in competence would be, were an exemption granted, for those who stop schooling at fourteen but later leave the Amish community. The latter loss depends heavily on the skill sets of various jobs in society.[43]

On this balance, and taking into account both effects on individuals and society, the overall loss of competence because of two lost years of school for roughly one-fifth of those who leave school when they are fourteen is probably not too great a sacrifice to avoid wasted education of the other four-fifths. However, one cannot fairly rely on such a calculation without reflecting on the voluntariness of teenagers' choices to leave school and on reasons why the rate of departure from the Amish community is what it is. As Brian Barry has strongly urged, a rate of departure from the community tells us very little by itself, because it does not reveal the strength of desires to leave against the pressures to stay.[44] If many youngsters accept baptism at the age of eighteen because they feel unable to function in jobs in the wider society, then their very removal from school helps explain why they remain within the Amish community. However, it seems unlikely that a sense of vocational incompetence is a primary explanation of the choices of most eighteen-year-olds. Over the years, many Amish have remained in the community despite having skills that would serve them well in outside jobs.

A more troubling question is whether fourteen-year-olds can make an intelligent choice to cut off their acquisition of general skills. Even if most Amish children would never use these skills, perhaps they should not lose their opportunity to develop them before they can make a rational judgment about that choice. The question of voluntariness of choice is more a matter of contestable evaluation than fact. If a fourteen-year-old, supported by parents, wants to live his life in the Amish community, and would be able, with effort, to acquire further education at a later stage, I would take the choice

---

[43] For shifts in kinds of jobs since 1994, see W. Michael Cox, Richard Alm, and Nigel Holmes, "Where the Jobs Are," *New York Times*, May 13, 2004, A25, col. 1. The loss in competence also depends on how many children allowed to leave at age fourteen would have continued in school beyond age sixteen if forced to stay in school at fourteen, and on how many are able later to acquire competence they would have gained in ninth and tenth grades, and beyond. Legislators and educational authorities should judge what skills may be acquired in ninth and tenth grades, how critical they are for a range of jobs, and how easy it would be for those who are eighteen or older to acquire these skills if they have initially left school after eighth grade.

[44] Id. at 187–93. Stephen Macedo, note 30 supra, at 208 writes, "How high would the number [of Amish children leaving the community] be if Amish children had a fuller knowledge of the ways of life available to them in the modern world? The answer to this question is precisely what worried the Amish parents who sued the state of Wisconsin to have their children removed from high school."

to leave school as *voluntary enough*—if all that were at stake was the level of vocational skill.[45]

One reason to keep children in school is to enable them to participate actively in the political institutions of liberal democracy. A crucial aim of public education should be to help develop ideals of equality, mutual respect, and critical thinking.[46] Amy Gutmann has urged that "a society that supports conscious social reproduction must educate all educable children to be capable of participating in collectively shaping their society."[47] Stephen Macedo suggests, "Liberal political institutions and public policies should be concerned to promote . . . the capacities and dispositions conducive to thoughtful participation in the activities of modern politics and civil society."[48]

The step from the positions of Gutmann and Macedo to requiring schooling for everyone up to sixteen may seem a short one, but we need a more discriminating analysis. Some people believe that democratic participation is a crucial aspect of a fulfilling life. However, many well-educated people choose to devote themselves to science, art, or business with very little attention to politics, and a few enter monastic orders, choosing a mode of living far removed from politics. Such choices cannot be dismissed as undesirable because they exclude political participation. When a conference speaker once urged that a citizen could not be a good Christian if he did not know the names of his federal senators and representative and state senator and assemblyman, I inquired how Jesus would have fared had he been given an analogous test. The mistaken idea that participation in politics is a good in which everyone should participate is not a sufficient basis to force two further years of unwanted education on Amish children.[49]

If one asks what is good for society, the extra two years of education seem of marginal benefit. Most Amish will not participate in politics, whatever they learn in ninth and tenth grades. Because the Amish are withdrawn as far as they are from normal civic life, they are not a serious drag on the

[45] I am not addressing a plausible argument that the whole structure of the Amish community makes it particularly difficult for fourteen-year-olds to exercise choices in opposition to parental wishes—choices often seen in the wider community.

[46] See, however, Michael McConnell, "Education Disestablishment: Why Democratic Values Are Ill-Served by Democratic Control of Schooling," in Stephen Macedo and Yael Tamir, eds., *Moral and Political Education* (Nomos XLIII) 87 (New York: New York University Press, 2002), urging that the genius of American democracy is to leave development of civic virtue to the private sector.

[47] Gutmann, note 40 supra, at 39.

[48] Macedo, note 30 supra, at 10.

[49] Despite Gutmann's remark about "all educable children," neither she nor Macedo actually claims that participation in politics is part of the good life for everyone.

political process.[50] Allowing Amish children to leave after eighth grade will not seriously interfere with the civic aims of education. This conclusion is supported to a degree by the state's allowing parents to provide their children with private or home schooling that contains scant civic education. Although one may regard that concession to parental choice as a regrettable sacrifice in likely civic benefit, still the value of civic education is not itself a strong enough reason to bar parents withdrawing children after eighth grade.[51]

This leaves us with the irreconcilable conflict between maximum autonomy of choice for teenagers when they reach sixteen and full participation in the life of their religious community. Against the argument that the state should ensure the long-term autonomy of children by educating them at least until they are sixteen is the concern that such education may make it difficult for them to participate in Amish life with the same attitude and emotional involvement they might have if they started that life at an earlier age. Education opens up choices; but it forecloses the very choice that the teenager and his parents want when they seek withdrawal from school.

How free are the decisions of Amish children? Those of us in a vastly different society, puzzled about the degree of freedom of our own choices and those of our children at the age of fourteen, can hardly begin to estimate the quality of the choices of Amish children at that age.[52] But Amish youngsters at eighteen, even if they are not *very* free, have a sense of what life is like in the larger society.[53] They realize that baptism will lock them into community life unless they are later expelled or leave the community in a manner that severs all social and business relations. I am doubtful that many youngsters would self-consciously be driven by fear of life in the outside world to undertake the momentous commitment of baptism.[54] The opportu-

---

[50] Jeff Spinner, note 3 supra, at 95–99, refers to them as "partial citizens." They are both inside and outside the political community; they are not inept participants, because they are hardly participants at all.

[51] A counter to this argument is that the state should curb parental choice more broadly, assuring that children do receive this kind of civic education in private as well as public schools. See Gutmann, note 40 supra, at 117; Macedo, note 30 supra, at 202–3.

[52] Stephen Macedo has suggested that *Wisconsin v. Yoder* should be overruled "unless it can be shown that Amish children are not significantly impeded in making their own choices by ignorance and communal pressure." Id. at 208. Since one can hardly imagine that anyone could *show* this about the Amish or about any other set of children, I think we can take Macedo's comment as close to a conclusion that the choices are not free. Macedo writes more generally, id. at 236–37, "Public schools seem well designed to make effective the child's right to separate from the moral ideals and religious convictions of his or her parents."

[53] Spinner, note 3 supra, at 10.

[54] Who can say what the complex springs of psychological motivation yield at the nonconscious level?

nity of eighteen-year-olds to avoid a permanent commitment moderates concern that fourteen-year-olds are not making a free choice.[55]

Given the significant value of religious communities being able to practice their forms of life, I believe the reasons in favor of an exemption for the Amish outweigh the reasons against.[56] Any exemption for the Amish from schooling raises fewer concerns about fairness than similar issues about military service and drug use. Schooling benefits most children; they do not suffer by comparison with the Amish children who are allowed out of school.[57]

If Amish and similar religious communities are to be allowed to withdraw children from ordinary education after eighth grade, how should a state frame an exemption? Should it require religious belief, or participation in a group, or both?

Group membership connects much more significantly to withdrawal from school than it does to conscientious objection to military service. One reason to support their choice to withdraw is that the Amish have sustained the members of their own community remarkably well; they do not become burdens on the state. Barring great wealth, individual parents cannot offer such a guarantee for their children's lives, and, without participation in a group, children are much less likely to continue in a simple life their parents might select.[58] Fraud is yet another reason not to allow detached parents to withdraw children from school. No one joins the Amish to get work out of their teenage children, but a detached parent who is a small farmer or craftsman and covets nonpaid help might be willing to express a religious view that education past eighth grade is evil. Officials could be hard put to sort honest expressions from dishonest ones. Thus, strong reasons support limiting an exemption to parents who are attached to groups carrying on forms of life into which the children fit.

[55] Of course, it does so only if one thinks that the young adults of eighteen are capable of making a free enough choice.

[56] One other factor is that if the Amish are adamant about avoiding further education, any one community or state may perceive that the realistic choice is between accommodating or having the Amish move to a more sympathetic environment. As with conscientious objection and military service, the benefits of further education for Amish children may seem an abstract consideration if the Amish would leave rather than submit to compulsory schooling.

[57] Only if the few children who do not actually benefit from education after eighth grade were identifiable in advance would an issue of unfairness arise.

Another conceivable fairness argument might concern parents put at an economic disadvantage vis-à-vis the Amish parents of the exempted children. "The Amish farm undersells us because their fourteen- and fifteen-year-olds are working, while ours are in school." Such an argument could have force if it reflected economic reality, but no one has suggested it does.

[58] Young people withdraw from the Amish and other religious communities, but the chances that a child will continue on a path the parents select—say of an agricultural life—are radically lessened without a community connection.

Should an exemption be limited to members of religious groups? Belief that further education will contribute to damnation constitutes a powerful reason for an exemption that is unlikely to be matched by nonreligious groups.[59] A further argument for not exempting members of secular groups relies on history. Insular religious communities have often shown staying power; few, if any, small nonreligious communities have survived in isolated form over time in Western countries. If her community will probably disintegrate, the less well educated child will predictably lack community support as she matures. Because many religious communities also fail to survive, a legislature wisely restricts an exemption to groups that have survived over a specified time.[60] A statute might declare that certain named communities qualify, so long as it does not preclude the possibility that other religious groups could also qualify.[61]

A separate argument for limiting the classification to religious groups rests directly on the Free Exercise Clause and its tradition of respecting religion. Amish vocational life is a central aspect of the Amish community, just as use of peyote is a central aspect of the practice of the Native American Church. The idea that government should respect the exercise of religion affects not only individuals but also religious institutions. The government, so the argument goes, does not owe the same degree of respect to the corporate life of nonreligious groups.

One might respond (as I did to similar arguments about conscientious objection) that the desirability of exempting religious persons is not a solid basis to refuse to exempt nonreligious ones. But the government has powerful reasons to require children to be educated to the age of sixteen. If the reasons *for* exemption are much weaker for secular groups, and the reasons not to grant an exception are strong, restricting the exemption to members of religious groups makes sense.[62]

---

[59] I am not supposing that *no* prospective consequence for a nonreligious person could be as bad as damnation would appear for a religious one: death, extreme physical hardship, and the complete ruin of a life might qualify as secular analogues. I am, rather, suggesting that members of a nonreligious group will be very unlikely to think these terrible consequences would attach to two further years of education.

[60] If local educational authorities are deciding on an exemption on an ad hoc basis, they should consider the solidity of the group.

[61] The Court in *Wisconsin v. Yoder* cited to a provision allowing exemption from payment of Social Security taxes for members of a "a recognized religious sect" opposed to receipt of Social Security benefits if "the Secretary finds that the sect makes reasonable provision for its dependent members." Note 1 supra, at 204–5, citing 26 U.S.C. § 1402(h).

[62] A law might leave open the possibility that members of a secular group *could* qualify if their reasons for an exemption were very strong; but if a survey of past and present secular groups indicates that none would qualify, explicitly limiting the exemption to religious groups is preferable. This basis for judgment could shift over time. If a number of secular groups devel-

My conclusions, then, are that states should grant an exemption from schooling after eighth grade for Amish children, that they should limit the exemption to members of groups that (1) are religious, (2) provide an alternative form of social life into which the teenagers training outside school will fit, (3) and have maintained themselves over time *and* retained within their ranks a high percentage of their young people. In contrast to issues about drug use and conscientious objection, these concerns about classification here have more theoretical than practical significance, because few groups are seriously opposed to the education of teenagers.

Should the Children of Christian Fundamentalists Be Excused from Using English Readers to Which Their Parents Object?

Hawkins County parents wanted their children to remain in public school but to be excused from using the Holt, Rinehart and Winston readers for their English classes. Should the schools have afforded them an accommodation and, if so, what form should it have taken?[63]

We may begin with the proposition that state schools should make some accommodations to parents who object to certain aspects of the curriculum; whatever they should insist upon in relation to the core curriculum, schools should not require children to engage in military training or dancing if their parents strongly object. The reality that religious views of parents influence the curricular decisions of some schools can affect one's judgment about accommodations even in academic subjects. Many textbooks are designed to avoid offense—biology texts that downplay evolution are a prime example—and educational authorities aim to minimize antagonism toward their curriculum and texts. If the majority (or a vocal minority) is able to achieve

---

oped powerful philosophies of withdrawal from modern economic life and culture, and many of these groups survived for generations and maintained the attachments of the great majority of children raised within them, the reasons to refuse an exception would diminish greatly. Of course, if one thinks the law should never explicitly favor religious claims over analogous nonreligious ones, one will believe that any formulation in a statute must allow the possibility of qualifying nonreligious groups. Although they do not take such an absolute position, Christopher L. Eisgruber and Lawrence G. Sager, in "The Vulnerability of Conscience: The Constitutional Basis for Protecting Religious Conduct," 61 *University of Chicago Law Review* 1245, 1259 (1999), suggest the fundamental bases for equal treatment of nonreligious claims.

[63] For elementary school children, any conflict is between parents and the state. The attitudes of the children themselves should not count, except insofar as they may make it difficult to carry out what parents or educational authorities want. The fact that the children are too young to make judgments themselves may strengthen the state's authority, as contrasted with the situation when the state lines up against parents and older children who agree with their parents.

education that does not offend it religiously, accommodating smaller minorities who are out of step is not in principle misguided.[64]

Because statewide legislation cannot deal with critical matters of degree, including the expense, inconvenience, and potential disruption of having some students pursue an alternative course of study, local educational officials, aware of precise parental claims and potential remedies, should make most decisions whether to excuse children from aspects of the curriculum. Judicial review stands in the wings.

Educators should not grant exemptions from ordinary curricular demands unless parental objections are intense. Schools should yield to a few nonreligious objections—such as a pacifist objection to military training—but religiously based objections will often be more intense than nonreligious ones, and it is doubtful whether any secular objection would be powerful enough to justify excusing children[65] from a reading series, not itself constitutionally flawed in its treatment of religion.

The strength of the reasons against an accommodation depends on three factors. The first is the degree to which the curriculum would be disrupted by adverse effects, such as the inability of a third-grade teacher to refer to stories in the standard reader throughout the day. The second is the time, effort, and money a school would need to expend to reach a satisfactory accommodation. For example, is space available for excused students to study alternative materials, and would the school have to use personnel to supervise that study? The third factor is the magnitude of educational loss—viewed from the state's point of view—for excused students. (Students who miss history or science, without an adequate substitute, will suffer more than those who miss square dancing.)

The weight of the considerations bearing on the Hawkins County conflict differed from those in the Amish case. The Fundamentalist parents' greatest concern was about the overall effect of the readings, which they saw as teaching that various religious beliefs are equal, that people should choose their morality, and that unfettered imagination is good. The parents were not in a bind as acute as that of the Amish, since they could withdraw their children from public school, enrolling their children in congenial Christian schools (though at considerable financial cost).

---

[64] Whether educators *should* take the religious views of parents into account in designing a curriculum raises more subtle questions regarding the reach of the Establishment Clause. See Greenawalt, note 2 supra, at 120–21, 139–40.

[65] Secular objections might be very powerful if a reading series declared that Christianity is the true faith or that evolution did not occur; but a school could not use such a set of readings consistent with the Establishment Clause. See id. The proper remedy would be to stop using these readings, not to excuse children of objecting parents.

The five state interests we identified for the Amish case were student competence, independence of choice, openness to cultural enrichment, potential for democratic participation, and moral development. The concerns about the competence and openness to culture of the Hawkins County children were much less stark than for the Amish. Students using some alternative to the Holt readers could learn English well enough to manage a job and engage in social activities. An alternative could also provide a platform for reading works of literature and nonfiction.

The state could reasonably protest that *if* the parents' objection was to opening up areas of personal choice for students, that is precisely an objective of the Holt series. But so long as a state permits parents to give their children private or home schooling that need not include perspectives that differ from the parents' own, the argument that preserving the students' freedom of choice justifies public schools in overriding parental objections to materials they believe threaten religious well-being has diminished force.[66]

The state's aims to promote tolerance, equality, and participation in democratic institutions raise more troubling issues. Unlike the Amish, Fundamentalist Christians are active in the political process. If parental objections to diverse perspectives are validated, children may become more rigid and doctrinaire and less suited for civic life in a liberal democracy.[67] This argument against exemptions, like the argument about independent choice, runs up against the parents' ability to choose narrow private education, a choice that some parents will make if their objections are not met. Thus, denying an accommodation in order to promote democratic education becomes doubtful as a matter of principle[68] and possibly counterproductive in its likely consequences.[69]

If the parents could have assured that excused children would maintain an adequate level of competence, and the schools would have suffered nei-

[66] To be clear, the argument about free choice may still have some force, because the state's acceptance of private and home schooling may be a concession to parental decision-making, not a judgment about effective education. See note 51 and accompanying text, supra. In any event, a public school student excused from one course is likely to be exposed to a wider range of choice than a child schooled at home or at a doctrinaire religious school.

[67] See Macedo, note 30 supra, at 202. Of course, people *can* be doctrinaire about religion and flexible and tolerant in politics.

[68] The state might respond: Insofar as the state can control education, we think it is in the public interest the use the system to encourage acceptance of diverse perspectives. We recognize, however, that we do not have the right to control the system so thoroughly that private education along different lines is out of the question. See note 66 supra, for a similar point about free choice. These matters are also discussed in Greenawalt, note 2 supra.

[69] Macedo, note 30 supra, at 205–6, suggests that as a matter of strategy and procedure, the *Mozert* families should have been accommodated if this would have helped keep the children in public school. This inquiry about what frustrated parents are likely to do is not one in which courts should engage in setting constitutional rights.

ther serious disruption of their standard program nor substantial expense to develop alternatives, educators should have excused the Hawkins County children from the Holt series. This overall evaluation, however, assumes that parental objections did not reach most of the public school program (parents should not be allowed to selectively pick and choose what subjects their children will take) and that other similar parental objections would not have overwhelmed the schools, making it unduly cumbersome to satisfy them all.

CONSTITUTIONAL PRINCIPLE

Withdrawal of Amish Children from School

We now turn from discussion of what accommodations might be made in these circumstances to a discussion of the underlying constitutional principles. In *Wisconsin v. Yoder*,[70] the Supreme Court decided that the Amish had a constitutional right to withdraw their children from school after eighth grade. Having summarized the place of home vocational education in Amish belief and practice, the Court easily concluded that the compulsory education law "carries with it precisely the kind of objective danger to the free exercise of religion that the First Amendment was designed to prevent."[71] Turning to evaluate whether the state had "interests of the highest order" in keeping children in school after eighth grade,[72] the Court acknowledged two strong state interests: educating children "to participate as citizens" "effectively and intelligently in our open political system" and preparing them to be "self-reliant and self-sufficient."[73] Exempting the Amish would not seriously affect those interests.

About economic self-sufficiency, the Court noted the absence of evidence that Amish who left the community, with "their valuable vocational skills and habits,"[74] would become burdens on society.[75] The Court did not face candidly the likelihood that a mature adult leaving the community would find his or her work opportunities to be severely circumscribed, but it suggested that an extra year or two of schooling would not make a great differ-

---

[70] Note 1 supra.

[71] Id. at 218.

[72] Id. at 215.

[73] Id. at 221.

[74] Id. at 225.

[75] One suspects that the difficulty of finding a suitable job may be greater now than it was three decades ago, given the decline of work that does not depend on machines, especially computers. See Cox et. al., note 43 supra.

ence.[76] This judgment may have been roughly accurate, except for students who, after tenth grade, would have chosen further education.

Chief Justice Burger's opinion conveniently glossed over the reality that the Amish do not participate as citizens in any ordinary sense. The Court remarked on their law-abidingness and capability to "fulfill the social and political responsibilities of citizenship";[77] but not engaging in criminal activity or falling into dependency is hardly the equivalent of actively involving oneself in the political life of one's locality and country. By conviction, the Amish refrain from doing that.

The Court was very clear that the constitutional right does not extend to nonreligious groups, specifically referring to people like Henry David Thoreau. Here is what it said:

> Although a determination of what is a "religious" belief or practice entitled to constitutional protection may present a most delicate question, the very concept of ordered liberty precludes allowing every person to make his own standards on matters of conduct in which society as a whole has important interests. Thus, if the Amish asserted their claims because of their subjective evaluation and rejection of the contemporary secular values accepted by the majority, much as Thoreau rejected the social values of his time and isolated himself at Walden Pond, their claims would not rest on a religious basis. Thoreau's choice was philosophical and personal rather than religious, and such belief does not rise to the demands of the Religion Clauses.[78]

Emphasizing the continuity of the Amish, their valuable vocational education, and tradition of community support, the Court did not explicate which features of the Amish other religious groups would need to replicate to be treated similarly, but it did say that the Amish had made "a showing . . . that probably few other religious groups could make."[79]

The Court did not explicitly exclude the possibility of successful claims by unassociated parents, but both its emphasis on the qualities of the Amish community and its assumption that some religious groups would fail to gain an exemption, strongly indicate that detached parents would not enjoy a free exercise right to withdraw children from school.

In its idea of what counts as religious and its emphasis on the history and practice of a particular religious group, the Court's approach in *Yoder* was far different from what it had been in the conscientious objector cases. The main explanation lies in the difference between the two subjects.

[76] Id. at 225.
[77] Id. at 225. It also suggested that the gain of further education was speculative. Id. at 227.
[78] Id. at 215–16.
[79] Id. at 235–36.

Given the country's history and the language of the Free Exercise Clause, *Yoder*'s basic approach was sound. Although its conclusion that the state did not have a compelling interest in requiring Amish children to go to school was debatable, the Court was true to a tradition of respect for religious practice and conviction in deciding that Amish parents should be able to provide the vocational education called for by their religious way of life.[80] *Yoder* allows a state to make a still broader exemption, but it does not require one.

The precise constitutional basis for *Yoder* seems less clear now than when the case was decided. Recall that the Court in *Employment Division v. Smith*[81] treated *Yoder* as a hybrid case, in which two constitutional claims joined to sustain the result. This account was necessary because *Yoder* misfits the *Smith* Court's guiding principle that religious claimants have no special privileges against neutral laws of general application. Indeed the *Yoder* opinion strikingly exemplifies aspects of adjudication that Justice Scalia found intolerable in *Smith*, most notably a close examination of a religion to determine the importance of a practice. Although it relied to an extent on the right of parents to control the education of their children,[82] a right that had justified two decisions about education in the 1920s,[83] the *Yoder* Court overwhelmingly stressed the free exercise of religion. Justice Scalia's treating of *Yoder* as a hybrid resting on two separate legs was not quite creation *ex nihilo*, but it came close; it is the kind of imaginative reclassification that later courts occasionally perform on earlier cases whose approach does not appeal to them. Although the general category of hybrids in which Justice Scalia placed *Yoder* may not have a long shelf life, nonetheless the *Smith*

---

[80] Compare Macedo, note 30 supra, at 208, taking a highly critical view of *Yoder*; and Marci A. Hamilton, *God vs. the Gavel: Religion and the Rule of Law* 131 (New York: Cambridge University Press, 2005), characterizing *Yoder* as a "love letter to the Amish" that is "the worst religion clause case in the United States." That the Court appeared to make the constitutional right of the Amish partly depend on their continuity and cohesiveness may seem troubling, but I believe it is defensible. See text accompanying notes 41–45 and 60–61 supra, discussing these features in connection with wise legislation.

[81] 494 U.S. 872 (1990).

[82] *Yoder*, note 1 supra, at 232.

[83] In *Meyer v. Nebraska*, 262 U.S. 390 (1923), the Court had said that a state may not prevent education in the German language. In *Pierce v. Society of Sisters*, note 35 supra, it had held that the state may not require children to attend public, rather than parochial or other private schools. At that stage of constitutional doctrine, the Supreme Court had not decided that the religion clauses were applicable against the states, and it maintained that requirements of "substantive" due process (i.e., substantive justice) set significant limits on state regulation. By the time of *Yoder*, substantive due process had receded into insignificance; scholars assumed that under modern doctrine the right of parents to send children to parochial schools should be viewed as a matter of free exercise, not as a general parental right to control their children's education.

Court treated *Yoder* as correctly decided. That determination seems to resolve that courts should treat other cases involving parental claims regarding
their children's education similarly.

Children Using the Holt Readers

In the most important constitutional case on the topic of exemptions for
public school students from parts of the curriculum, the Sixth Circuit Court
of Appeals, in *Mozert v. Hawkins County Board of Education*, rejected the
claim of Fundamentalist parents to have their children excused from using
the Holt, Rinehart and Winston basic reading series.[84] Acting prior to *Employment Division v. Smith*, the judges assumed a state could burden the
exercise of religion only if it had a compelling reason to do so. Given *Smith*'s
comments about hybrid cases, that approach probably remains valid for cases
like *Mozert*.[85] Although all three judges agreed that the parents had failed to
state a relevant burden on free exercise, they offered different reasons.

Doubting that the parents' objections could be satisfied by any alternative
that did not teach that religious views opposed to their own were in error,[86]
Judge Lively in his majority opinion concluded that exposure to offensive
materials did not create a burden on free exercise.[87] Referring to an earlier
Roman Catholic view that one could commit a mortal sin by reading books
on an Index, Judge Boggs responded that forced exposure of children to
materials that parents think might cause their damnation or lead them seriously astray could impose a burden on their religious exercise.[88] In any ordinary sense, Judge Boggs is certainly right,[89] as we can imagine if adults were
forced to witness religious ceremonies they abhor.

---

[84] *Mozert*, note 2 supra.

[85] Since *Mozert*, like *Yoder*, involved free exercise and parental rights, it must also be classed
as a hybrid case. However, because the court in *Smith* was unsympathetic to the actual inquiries
necessary to resolve *Yoder*, one cannot predict what it will do about hybrids in the future.

[86] He apparently believed that the only way to satisfy the *Mozert* parents was to violate the
Establishment Clause.

[87] Id. at 1069. He relied on the famous decision in *West Virginia Board of Education v.
Barnette*, 319 U.S. 624 (1943), discussed id. at 1066, that students could not be compelled to
profess beliefs they did not hold, and he cited a court of appeals case involving conscientious
objection to military training in school as suggesting that students could not be forced to commit acts they found objectionable. Id. at 1063, discussing *Spence v. Bailey*, 465 F.2d 797 (6th
Cir. 1972).

[88] Id. at 1079. As Judge Boggs explained, a crucial aspect of the parents' complaint was that
their own religious convictions forbade exposing their children to the readers.

[89] The court recognized that *Wisconsin v. Yoder* was a case involving undesired exposure,
but the opinion said it rested on a singular set of facts, involving a wish to be free of the entire
high school curriculum. Id. at 1067.

Judge Kennedy joined the opinion of Judge Lively, but she also contended that the state had a compelling interest that would justify burdening parents' rights of free exercise. Requiring students to participate in a reading program was the least restrictive means of helping them develop critical reading skills and the ability to discuss social and moral issues.[90] Allowing children to opt out from aspects of the core curriculum would disrupt the classroom and cause religious divisiveness.[91] Kennedy's conclusion about the state's strong interest in critical discussion lies in some tension with the state's allowance of private and home schooling, and the degree of disruption and divisiveness will vary with circumstance.[92]

The *Mozert* parents did suffer a burden on their exercise of religion, and constitutional relief from some burdens of that kind is appropriate. Courts should often sustain objections when students are forced to declare beliefs or engage in activities abhorrent to them, or are forbidden to refer to their religious beliefs when they respond to questions about how they would handle social problems. But objections to parts of the core curriculum may be too complex for courts to evaluate in light of available alternatives, especially given the difficulty of reviewing what teachers say about materials in individual classes.[93] The conclusion of the *Mozert* court is reasonable;[94] but I believe the judges should have recognized that parents might have free exercise rights to have their children excused even from parts of the core curriculum.

When school authorities or courts extend an exemption to religious claimants, they may treat nonreligious claimants less favorably in most instances, for the same reasons that apply to claims to be excused from school altogether.[95] Authorities should not insist on formal attachment to a religious group, but numbers may be important. If parents are unable on their own

[90] Id. at 1071.

[91] Id. at 1071–72.

[92] Judge Boggs thought that school authorities can often accommodate parents with religious objections to the curriculum, but he voted with his colleagues because the Supreme Court had not used free exercise grounds to interfere with the prerogatives of school boards. Id. at 1079–81. It is not clear why Boggs did not regard *Yoder* as having established a principle of accommodation of the sort he seemed to favor.

[93] See Christopher L. Eisgruber, "How Do Liberal Democracies Teach Values," in Macedo and Tamir, note 46 supra, at 58–86; Ira C. Lupu, "Where Rights Begin: The Problem of Burdens of the Free Exercise of Religion," 102 *Harvard Law Review* 933, 950–52 (1989).

[94] Amy Gutmann contends, in "Civic Minimalism, Cosmopolitanism and Patriotism: Where Does Democratic Education Stand in Relation to Each?" in Macedo and Tamir, note 46 supra, at 23, 38, that, based on principles of democratic education, "courts should not overturn the decisions of public school boards on matters of reasonable curriculum requirements."

[95] However, conscientious objection to military training should be treated like conscientious objection to actual military service. That is, religious and nonreligious pacifists should be treated similarly.

to provide a satisfactory alternative to the study they find objectionable, educators cannot be expected to finance parallel instruction unless many children are involved.[96]

With this examination of conflicts between religious convictions and the educational policy of states, we are ready to turn from specific kinds of free exercise problems to two more general topics: assessing sincerity and determining what counts as religious. Each of these subjects touches most constitutional and statutory standards that are cast in terms of religion. Thus, sincerity and the boundaries of religion concern not only the problems we have already examined, but the great majority of chapters that follow. Another subject that is similarly pervasive is how courts assess the degrees of burden on religion and the strength of competing state interests. That difficult subject is reserved for chapter 13; it follows the treatment of other free exercise issues for which administrators and courts may have to make these delicate judgments.

---

[96] In this respect, at least, a religious objection to study does not warrant the treatment given to disabilities.

CHAPTER 7

Sincerity

This chapter and the next involve a shift in focus. Having reviewed a number of discrete topics concerning the law's treatment of religious claims, we turn now to questions that cut across a wide range of subjects. How far can officials or juries decide whether people making claims of free exercise are sincere? And, if judgments about sincerity are needed, just *how* should they be made? The next chapter takes up the complicated issue to which we were introduced by the conscientious objector cases: how should courts decide what is religious? These chapters constitute two of a trilogy of general questions about assessing free exercise claims. The third question is the one that mainly troubled Justice Scalia in *Employment Division v. Smith*: can courts reasonably assess the force of religious claims against the strength of asserted state interests? I have postponed that discussion until we have under our belts four chapters that further illustrate the kinds of conflicts between free exercise and state interests with which courts have grappled.

When an exemption from ordinary legal requirements depends on people's beliefs, a critical question arises: are they telling the truth? For conscientious objection, for drug use, for withdrawing children from school, and for problems we will consider in later chapters, administrators, and juries or judges, must apply a standard of sincerity. Administrators may not have to ask exactly whether a particular individual claimant is probably telling the truth or probably lying, but they must employ some method to distinguish genuine from fraudulent claims. Even if every constitutional right to exemptions disappeared, the need to distinguish between such claims would remain as long as legislature or executives granted exemptions to persons with particular beliefs or attitudes.

The complexities of determining sincerity provide one reason why people may choose "second-best" legal standards, rather than different standards that they would choose as better if all relevant facts were easily knowable. One reason not to grant an exemption is that administering it would become too complicated, and assessing sincerity is one complicating factor.[1]

---

[1] Problems of administration largely determined the result in *Employment Division v. Smith*, 494 U.S. 872 (1990), but the Court's main focus in that case was on the impossibility of evaluating degrees of burden on religious exercise against state interests. Chapter 13 takes up that topic.

Inquiries into sincerity do not require anyone to determine the intrinsic *truth* of religious claims—deciding, for example, whether God exists or Jesus was a pacifist—but if an exemption is limited to religious claimants, officials do have to determine whether a claim is religious (the subject of the following chapter), and they must also determine if a claim is sincere. Even if nonreligious claimants may also qualify, officials will often have to pass on the honesty of asserted religious views. For example, if an applicant for conscientious objector status says that when Jesus encouraged us to "turn the other cheek,"[2] he enjoined Christians to be pacifists, a draft board or military officers will have to judge whether the applicant honestly states what he believes.

Any system that requires some people to determine the honesty of others risks arbitrary decisions and the favoring of the familiar over the unfamiliar, even by evaluators who try to be fair. The difficulty of assessing sincerity is one reason for the law to avoid exemptions that depend on individualized judgments, but that reason (along with others that are similar) must be measured against the positive reasons to grant such exemptions.

UNITED STATES V. BALLARD AND THE PROBLEM OF FRAUDULENT SOLICITATION

Basic problems about judging sincerity are set well by a confusing sixty-year-old case in which Supreme Court justices said more about sincerity than they had before or have since. That case provides a perspective from which to assess more typical exemption claims.

In *United States v. Ballard*,[3] leaders of the I Am movement, a popular religious movement influenced by spiritualism and theosophy, were prosecuted for mail fraud, a federal crime that generally requires proof that one has knowingly misrepresented a fact in order to obtain money or property.[4] According to the indictment, the Ballards claimed that Guy Ballard had been visited by Jesus and by Saint Germain, and had been designated as a divine messenger; the Ballards also claimed that Guy[5] and his wife and son had

---

[2] Matt. 5:39.

[3] 322 U.S. 78 (1944).

[4] The modern statute is at 18 U.S.C. § 134. The elements of common-law fraud are summarized in *Miller v. Premier Corp.*, 608 F.2d 973, 980 (4th Cir. 1979). It can be sufficient for fraud that one is "recklessly indifferent" to truth or falsity. See *United States v. Mackay*, 491 F.2d 616, 623 (10th Cir. 1973). A person would rarely, if ever, be recklessly indifferent about whether she had a spiritual experience herself, but one person might be recklessly indifferent about whether a colleague had a spiritual experience she was claiming to have had.

[5] By the time the Ballards were indicted, Guy had died. John Noonan, in *The Lustre of Our Country: The American Experience of Religious Freedom* 141–76 (Berkeley and Los Angeles:

cured hundreds of people of diseases. The indictment charged that the Ballards knew that these representations were false. The Ballards argued the Constitution did not allow a jury to decide either whether their religious representations were true or whether they sincerely believed them. Were the Ballards' position fully accepted, people could not be prosecuted for fraud in their religious representations.[6]

The trial court permitted the jury to pass on the Ballards' sincerity, but not on the truth of what they believed. It advised the jury, "The issue is: Did these defendants honestly and in good faith believe those things? If they did, they should be acquitted."[7] Given the indictment, the court of appeals decided that the government had to prove that representations were actually false; therefore, the trial judge should not have restricted the jury's decision to the Ballards' good faith.

No one suggested before the Supreme Court that juries should decide directly whether spiritual events had actually taken place. The principle that government should not determine what is truth in matters of religion precludes jurors from directly determining that spiritual events had or had not occurred. If prosecutions for mail fraud depended on such judgments, they would be unconstitutional. But a conclusion that neither officials nor juries can rely on their own judgments about religious truth leaves open three other avenues for determining that claims are false: inferring falsehood from insincerity, treating the crucial falsehood as about a defendant's state of mind, and distinguishing intrinsically spiritual claims from claims about practical effects.

One can construct an argument that juries should be able to determine the falsity of spiritual claims in the narrow instances when falsity is closely linked to insincerity. If a person who asserts that she had a personal spiritual experience does not believe it happened, the experience, almost certainly, did not happen. If a woman claims that Jesus (the historical figure) spoke to her and she has no belief that he did, it is very unlikely that Jesus did speak to her. Perhaps for such claims, juries, ordinarily disqualified from judgments about religious truth, can first find insincerity and then move on to inferring falseness about a person's claimed experience.

This is a subtle argument. Ordinarily, truth is distinguishable from belief. I claim that Thomas, whom I hate and wish to discredit, is a thief, though I believe he is completely honest; Thomas turns out to be a thief. My claim

University of California Press, 1998), provides a very interesting account of the case and of the damage the government inflicted on the I Am movement.

[6] Legislators might find the position to be persuasive, even if it is not constitutionally required.

[7] *Ballard*, note 3 supra, at 81.

was true enough though I was not sincere. The special wrinkle about the Ballards' asserted spiritual occurrences is that they involved their own direct perceptions.[8] If the Ballards lied about perceiving such extra-natural events, the occurrence of the events was highly improbable.[9]

Two obstacles stand in the way of allowing juries to infer falsehood from insincerity for this special class of claims. First, developing a special doctrine that untruth can be inferred from insincerity for one limited kind of claim would be awkward.[10] Second, it is logically possible that someone witnessed an event, has forgotten that fact or been persuaded he suffered a bad dream, and now dishonestly claims to have had an experience that, in fact, did occur. Although common sense usually warrants the negative inference, jurors should not infer the falsity of even claimed spiritual experiences from a claimant's insincerity.[11]

A different argument for allowing fraud prosecutions for spiritual claims concedes that their truth cannot be determined, and concentrates instead on states of mind. When I say an event occurred, I implicitly assert my belief in its occurrence. If I say Jesus rose from the dead, I assert my belief in his Resurrection. A dishonest person is representing his state of mind falsely. In *Ballard*, Chief Justice Stone urged that misrepresentations about one's state of mind are adequate to sustain a prosecution for mail fraud.[12]

[8] I pass over the further complexity that if Edna Ballard believed that Guy Ballard had the experience Guy insincerely claimed, Edna would not be guilty of fraud although Guy had lied and the spiritual event had not occurred.

[9] People frequently do believe that others are making sincere but mistaken claims of spiritual events.

[10] A further difficulty of this approach as applied to the *Ballard* case is that it does not cover all of the claims involved. The Ballards might successfully have cured some people of illness, even though they did not believe that they had done so, attributing apparent successes to confusion and deception. As to such matters, falsity would need to be independently established.

[11] I need to be clear that I reach this conclusion only because of the awkwardness of carving out a special category of claims for which falsity is inferred from insincerity and because of the special sensitivity of religious claims. If all that were involved were the "beyond the reasonable doubt" standard for criminal conviction, one could usually move from patent insincerity about spiritual experiences to falsity beyond a reasonable doubt.

[12] *Ballard,* note 3 supra, at 91. There is no doubt that misrepresentations about one's state of mind can sometimes be the basis for fraud. See Restatement (Second) of Torts § 525 comment c (1997). Suppose A, B's financial advisor, says that, in his expert opinion, the best investment B can make is to buy land from C, and B does so. In fact, A tenders this advice because he has received five thousand dollars from C. He has misrepresented his state of mind and has acted fraudulently toward B, even if a reasonable person could believe that buying the land from C was an excellent investment. However, a nettlesome aspect of the *Ballard* case for this approach is that the indictment apparently required proof of falseness, not just insincerity.

One question that has arisen under the federal statute is how far it protects "intangible rights" to honest services. The Supreme Court interpreted 18 U.S.C. § 1341 narrowly in *McNally v. United States*, 483 U.S. 350, 355 (1987), and it also construed a 1988 inclusion of an "intangible right of honest services" not to cover diverse forms of public corruption. *Cleve-*

Someone might respond that "consumers" do not care about states of mind, only the truth of the spiritual claims; but that view would be artificial. People rarely pay positive attention to spiritual claims of those they think are lying.[13] An implicit misrepresentation of one's state of mind is often very important. If juries properly determine sincerity about claimed spiritual experiences, insincerity should be sufficient to convict for fraud.

The government pressed yet a third argument most strongly. It urged that the jury had found some of the Ballards' claims to be false: namely, that the Ballards had cured hundreds of persons, that they had particular religious experiences, and that phonograph records would contribute to salvation.[14] We can quickly see that a claim that a man has cured hundreds of people is not quite like a claim that a spiritual being has talked to him. He should have supporting evidence—if not medical testimony, at least the witness of individuals who think they were cured. The Supreme Court rejected the government's effort to distinguish among the Ballards' representations, finding that since the trial judge had withdrawn the issue of falsity for all the Ballard's claims, one could not understand the jury determination to represent a judgment that some claims were actually false.

In a striking opinion, Justice Jackson argued that juries should decide *neither* falsity nor insincerity, because they cannot separate the two inquiries. "The most convincing proof that one believes his statements is to show that they have been true in his experience. Likewise, that one knowingly falsified is best proved by showing that what he said happened never did happen. . . . If we try religious sincerity severed from religious verity, we isolate the dis-

---

land v. United States, 531 U.S. 12 (2000). Were intangible rights understood very broadly, they could include a right to honest spiritual guidance, in which event a leader's misrepresentation of his state of mind would be sufficient for fraud. But when money is involved, when people donate in response to religious appeals, one would not need an intangible rights approach. Those who commit fraud in making these religious appeals are acquiring money under false pretenses.

[13] A recipient of a Ballard mailing would not seriously consider the possible truth of what they claimed if she thought they were lying. Matters are more complicated if one has been raised in a religious faith, or practiced it a long time, and comes to believe that some deceit was involved at the founding. In conversation, a distinguished Protestant scholar told me of a serious Mormon who believes that Joseph Smith wrote the Book of Mormon, rather than discovering tablets that contained it. Since Smith explicitly claimed to have discovered the book, he must have lied if he wrote the book, unless some complex psychological explanation accounts for the difference between reality and Smith's perception. Yet the modern Mormon to whom my friend referred adheres to the faith despite, apparently, assuming that the founder lied about this vital fact.

[14] Ballard, note 3 supra, at 83–84. If one were to distinguish claims of religious beliefs from claims of a more objective sort, it is arguable on which side the "experience" and "phonograph record" claims should fall. Since these claims are not susceptible of independent proof in the manner of claimed cures, they fall on the religious belief side.

pute from the very considerations which in common experience provide its most reliable answer."[15] He went on to say that juries could not "separate fancied religious experiences from real ones, dreams from happenings, and hallucinations from true clairvoyance. . . . When one comes to trial which turns on any aspect of religious belief or representation, unbelievers among his judges are likely not to understand and are almost certain not to believe him."[16] Jackson is certainly right that jurors who are asked to review the sincerity of spiritual claims will inevitably rely on their own sense of what is plausible.

Drawing from William James, Jackson made a more subtle point that faith often involves a degree of disbelief, and that people often use religious symbolism with mental reservations. To take a familiar example he does not employ, the Apostles' Creed, one of the most basic formulations of Christian faith, includes affirmations that Jesus "was born of the Virgin Mary" and that on the third day after he was crucified "he rose." To most worshipers, those phrases literally mean that Jesus was not conceived by ordinary sexual intercourse and that his physical body came to life again after it was entombed. Many Christian ministers do not believe these propositions. If these ministers repeat the Apostles' Creed Sunday after Sunday without explaining that they take these phrases in a nonliteral way, thus leaving many parishioners with the impression that they do accept them literally, are they misrepresenting their beliefs to their congregants? Jackson's observation raises this delicate question.

Concluding that prosecution for fraud about religious claims "easily could degenerate into religious persecution,"[17] Jackson would have dismissed the indictment. For crimes of fraud, his position is attractive. If people are aware that the state does not involve itself in prosecutions for spiritual fraud, they will be on notice that they must rely on themselves for protection. Almost certainly, most recipients of spiritual literature now do assume that, and their suppositions correlate with a dearth of actual prosecutions.[18] They do not reflect: "As sellers of food fear prosecution if they make bogus claims, sellers of spiritual claims are similarly deterred from lying." A clear legal rule

[15] Id. at 92–93.

[16] Id. at 93.

[17] Id. at 95. He would have allowed prosecutions for fraud only "for false representations on matters other than faith or experience," as when someone claims that funds actually being spent for personal use are being employed to build a church. Jackson does not say how claims about physical cures would fit in this dichotomy, but he seems to suppose they typically fall on the side of unprosecutable claims of faith and experience.

[18] See Stephen Senn, "The Prosecution of Religious Fraud," 17 *Florida State University Law Review* 325, 326–27 (1990). But see *United States v. Rasheed*, 663 F.2d 843 (9th Cir. 1981), cert. denied, 454 U.S. 1157 (1982); *Jeffers v. United States*, 392 F.2d 749 (9th Cir. 1968).

against enforcement for fraud might reinforce most people's reliance on their own judgment about essentially religious claims.[19]

Justice Douglas's opinion for the Court in *Ballard* is both eloquent and mystifying. It said that "the First Amendment precludes determination of the truth or verity of respondents' religious doctrines or beliefs." It continued, "Heresy trials are foreign to our Constitution. Men may believe what they cannot prove. They may not be put to the proof of their religious doctrines or beliefs. . . . The Fathers of the Constitution . . . fashioned a charter of government which envisaged the widest possible toleration of conflicting views. Man's relation to his God was made no concern of the State."[20] The district court had properly withheld all questions about the truth of religious beliefs from the jury.[21]

What is confusing is that, without explicitly saying so,[22] the opinion implies, as the district court had held, that a fraud conviction may be based on insincerity;[23] if so, it evokes a tradition of religious liberty reaching the most unorthodox views, but formally gives the unorthodox *less* protection than had the court of appeals, which had required the government to establish both insincerity *and* falsity. Justice Douglas might have judged that, were falsity introduced into the mix, jurors would be more likely to find insincerity, making the court of appeals' approach worse for defendants in practice than a direction that jurors must consider only sincerity. But the opinion provides no such explanation.[24]

Like a number of other commentators, I think the wisest course is not to have prosecutions for fraud about spiritual matters,[25] although I do not think

[19] Such a rule would require courts to distinguish essentially spiritual claims from more ordinary ones. What was patently a pyramid scheme that people were encouraged to join in order to become rich would fall on the ordinary side despite the use of religious language. See *Rasheed*, note 18 supra.

[20] Id. at 86–87.

[21] Douglas expressed uncertainty whether the court of appeals had believed the indictment could be construed only as charging fraud by misrepresentation of religious doctrines or beliefs, or had concluded that the withdrawal of the truth of representations "resulted in a substantial change in the character of the crime charged."

[22] It does not expressly resolve whether the *Ballard* indictment, or the mail fraud statute more generally, permits conviction based on insincerity about spiritual claims.

[23] On remand, the court of appeals so understood the opinion, *Ballard v. United States*, 152 F.2d 941, 943 (9th Cir.), reversed on the ground that women had been excluded from the jury pool, 329 U.S. 187 (1946).

[24] Why was the Supreme Court not more precise about its view of the district court's disposition? Possibly Justice Douglas had to cobble together an opinion that would satisfy the five justices necessary to make a majority, and these justices may have diverged on crucial questions.

[25] E.g., Marjorie Heins, "Other People's Faiths: The Scientology Litigation and the Justiciability of Religious Fraud," 9 *Hastings Constitutional Law Quarterly* 153, 165 (1981); Ira Lupu, "Where Rights Begin: The Problem of Burdens on the Free Exercise of Religion," 102 *Harvard Law Review* 933, 953–55 (1989).

the Free Exercise Clause should be taken to require an absolute rule to that effect. No doubt, immunity from prosecution, and presumably from tort liability as well, will protect some clever charlatans preying on the vulnerable who seek spiritual comfort and respond to requests for donations. One reasonable alternative to what I have suggested is to allow prosecutions for spiritual fraud under conditions that minimize the chance that convictions will occur because juries, or judges, are unsympathetic with the defendant's religion.[26]

To consider this problem carefully, we need to have a more precise sense of what count as "spiritual claims." The category includes assertions about religious truth and about religious experiences. "God wants us to care for the poor" and "God wants you to support my ministry" are assertions about religious truth. "Jesus has appeared to me in a dream and told me that God wants everyone to support my ministry" is an assertion about religious experience. The claimed experience falls closer to the realm of ordinary truth and falsity than the straightforward religious assertion,[27] but the dangers of jurors passing on the sincerity of claims of personal religious experience are severe enough to treat these as protected spiritual claims.

Definitely *not* in the category of the spiritual are claims about how money has been or will be spent. If money that donors have been told will be used to build a hospital instead finances the leader's personal yacht, that is fraud[28] that can be prosecuted; the highly publicized prosecution of Jim Bakker and his aides for just such fraud is uncontroversial.[29]

We should also place outside of the spiritual category claims that are objective, undeniable falsehoods that are connected to what are otherwise spiritual claims. Suppose a religious evangelist says to a television audience, "You can be sure that Jesus talked to me on October 3 in Green Bay because I gave a prayer before the Packers' football game and a stadium full of people saw Jesus appear next to me." In fact, the Packers did not play at home that day, and the evangelist had never given the prayer before a Packers game. When such "objective" facts are demonstrably inaccurate, and they could

[26] See Senn, note 18 supra.

[27] That is, the claimed experience is about a particular event that may not have happened and about which the speaker may entertain no belief that it did happen.

[28] Although there is some language in cases saying that a promise of future events cannot be the basis for a fraud prosecution, a specific promise about how one will spend money if donated, certainly qualifies if it is false when made.

[29] Jim Bakker, the founder of a religious ministry called PTL ("Praise the Lord," and "People that Love"), was convicted for selling more lifetime partnerships, including annual lodging, in vacation park facilities than could possibly be accommodated, and for using partnership funds to pay operating expenses of PTL and to support his lavish lifestyle. *United States v. Bakker*, 925 F.2d 728, 731–32 (4th Cir. 1991). See Senn, note 18 supra, at 327.

have substantial persuasive power with an audience, they are appropriately the basis for a fraud prosecution.

A more troublesome, intermediate category includes claimed cures or other physical benefits of spiritual interventions.[30] Here, perhaps the approach should be that minimal support is sufficient to render a claim immune from a fraud prosecution. As long as there are people who believe they have been cured, or people who believe they have witnessed cures (that prosecutors cannot show to have been faked), that should be sufficient. No one should be passing on whether immediate improvements in physical conditions are cures or are believed to be so by the person who "performs" them. But if the religious leader can produce no beneficiaries or witnesses, a claim of cures can be treated as fraudulent.

Another category of claims that should not count as spiritual are schemes cloaked in religious language in which the incentive to participate is financial self-interest, not spiritual development.[31]

In an illuminating article, Paul Horwitz suggests an alternative to my position,[32] arguing for a very limited range of prosecutions for religious fraud. Individuals could be punished if they fraudulently invented and benefited from a religion (or insincerely deviated from standard church doctrine to their benefit) *and* their insincerity was evidenced by their own admissions (as, say, in letters to friends), the commission of secular fraud, or activity attempting to cover up fraud.[33] This approach provides significant safeguards against prosecutorial abuse or misjudgment; however, I prefer the more straightforward line of no prosecution whatsoever for spiritual claims.

Although the wisest course is not to have prosecutions for fraud about spiritual matters, I do not think the Free Exercise Clause requires such an absolute rule—to this extent I agree with Horwitz. The Free Exercise Clause does not directly protect outright lies about spiritual experiences and beliefs that are designed to elicit money. But the clause should be taken to protect

[30] A borderline case involved the claimed benefits of Scientologists using E-meters to help remove engrams. The United States Court of Appeals for the District of Columbia held that the claims were essentially spiritual. *Founding Church of Scientology v. United States*, 409 F.2d 1146 (D.C. Cir. 1969).

[31] See *United States v. Rasheed*, 663 F.2d 843 (9th Cir. 1981), cert. denied, 454 U.S. 1157 (1982).

[32] Horwitz, "Scientology in Court: A Comparative Analysis and Some Thoughts on Selected Issues in Law and Religion," 47 *DePaul Law Review* 85 (1997).

[33] Senn, note 18 supra, at 342–43, writes that a finding of insincerity can be made if "defendant's behavior is substantially inconsistent with the requirements of the faith." This makes sense so long as it does not cover "ordinary sin." It is an aspect of traditional Christian doctrine that everyone falls into sin; religious leaders are not exempted. Thus, to draw on an actual example, visits to prostitutes by an evangelist should not count as behavior that is relevantly inconsistent with the requirements of the faith.

against any prosecution that raises the risk that disbelief of religious claims by jurors will lead to their finding insincerity in the manner that worried Justice Jackson. Under such an approach, prosecution should be permitted only when unmistakable independent proof is made of fraud. This could occur, for example, if the government offers ample evidence that a group of individuals has deliberately formulated spiritual claims in order to deceive the gullible, or the government can show that claims about visible effects in the physical world, such as apparent cures, have no evidential support.[34] However, for claims like the central ones in *Ballard*, the Free Exercise Clause should bar prosecution.

A reader of *Employment Division v. Smith*,[35] which eliminates any free exercise right to violate general, neutral laws, might wonder whether that case ends all free exercise protection against religious fraud prosecutions. The law against committing fraud is general; does it follow that religious claims have no exemption? *Smith* cannot reasonably be understood to have this breadth. *Smith* is founded substantially on the undesirability of judges examining religious convictions and practices. In fraud prosecutions, the treating of spiritual claims *like* other claims demands examination of religious convictions and practices. For ordinary fraud, the prosecution must show that a claim is false and insincerely made; were spiritual claims treated similarly, prosecutors would need to prove both insincerity and falsity. But everyone agrees that a core element of the Free Exercise Clause is that courts and jurors should not pass on the truth of religious claims. Thus, one element of a typical fraud prosecution is undoubtedly barred by the Free Exercise Clause. *Smith* presumably does not affect this conclusion, and it yields no automatic conclusion about appraisals of sincerity under the Free Exercise Clause. At the most, it supports the judgment that prosecutions are permissible, so long as neither juries nor judges need make evaluations that contravene the Free Exercise Clause.

SINCERITY AND OTHER RELIGIOUS CLAIMS

Unfortunately, when the state offers exemptions based on people's convictions, it cannot avoid all inquiry into sincerity. As I have said, the exact inquiry need not be whether an individual is probably sincere or not. Judges, or legislators, may adjust the precise question or the standard of probability, or both.

---

[34] See note 14 and following text, supra.
[35] *Smith*, note 1 supra.

Were all legal distinctions based on religion abolished, officials would *still* have to assess religious sincerity, so long as the government offered exemptions based on conscience. If a member of a volunteer army claims he has become a conscientious objector, officers must evaluate his sincerity.[36] The alternative of excusing all those willing to lie would be dispiriting for those who also want to leave military service but not at the price of lying.[37] As chapter 4 explains, the Supreme Court has interpreted the controlling federal statute so that a person need not have traditional religious beliefs to qualify as a conscientious objector. But most men and women who seek that status do assert a traditional religious belief in God, and liars, trying to make their beliefs as appealing as possible, will be likely to do so. Thus, officials continue to judge the sincerity of claimed religious beliefs. In doing so, they should give due regard to the uncertainty of many religious convictions and to the possibility of a kind of cognitive dissonance that allows people to embrace propositions that are in tension with each other.

The critical inquiry about sincerity need not be whether an individual claimant has probably told the truth. The law on judicial review of denials of exemptions changed drastically during the Vietnam War, in a way that profoundly affected draft boards. Congress had provided that courts should sustain draft board decisions if they had "a basis in fact."[38] This standard was initially conceived as providing very limited judicial review of administrative action. If draft board members, finding an applicant's presentation unconvincing, concluded that he was lying, courts let the determination stand. As the law evolved, courts construed "a basis in fact" to mean an objective basis in fact, something other than mere disbelief of a claimant.[39]

---

[36] The standards and procedures for claiming conscientious objector status are in 32 CFR 75.1–75.11. When military personnel claim they are conscientious objectors, initial hearings and evaluations (including ones by a psychiatrist and a chaplain) are made by officers not in the chain of command of the applicants. Final decision is by the headquarters of the military service concerned. 32 CFR 75.6(f). Although administrative discharge is discretionary, and conscientious objectors are not provided an absolute right to discharge (or relief from combat duty, if one is willing to serve as a noncombatant), the relevant provision indicates that relief should ordinarily be given. 32 CFR 75.4(a).

[37] A test of sincerity could be avoided by a shift to a system in which anyone could be excused from military service by accepting a longer term of civilian service, discussed in chapter 4. For how such a system could work in the context of conscription, see Kent Greenawalt, *Conflicts of Law and Morality* 327–28 (New York: Oxford University Press, 1987), and "Accommodation to Selective Conscientious Objection: How and Why," in Michael F. Noone, Jr., ed., *Selective Conscientious Objection: Accommodating Conscience and Security* 7 (Boulder, Colo.: Westview Press, 1989).

[38] 50 U.S.C. App. § 460(b)(3).

[39] See *United States v. Owen*, 415 F.2d 383, 389 (8th Cir. 1969); Kent Greenawalt, "All or Nothing at All: The Defeat of Selective Conscientious Objection," 1971 *Supreme Court Review* 31, 45–46 (1972). Development of the "basis in fact" test is described in detail in Donald L.

At that point, shrewd draft boards did not deny relief without objective evidence that a claimant was lying, for example, blatant contradictions or false claims of church membership. Such objective proof was not usually at hand; and draft boards upheld some claims they disbelieved, or they were overturned by judges who were unable to discern any objective basis to deny the exemption.[40] Neither draft boards nor courts were determining whether it was more likely than not that a claimant was lying.

When exemptions are restricted to those with religious grounds, individuals seeking them must be sincere not only in their opposition to conforming with the standard requirements, but also in their assertion that their reasons rest on religious grounds. In two cases involving mandatory immunizations, district court judges did not doubt that the parents' sincerely opposed their children being inoculated, but the judges did not believe the parents' stated religious grounds were honestly held.[41]

When officials pass on the sincerity of particular individuals, they must remember Justice Jackson's point that religious sincerity is not always as straightforward as whether one is telling the truth about a simple factual matter. Winnifred Fallers Sullivan discusses a deposition by Walter Dickey, a prison administrator, that may provide an example.[42]

> [A] guy . . . who said he was Jewish . . . wanted to have a Jewish dinner . . . at Rosh Hashanah or whatever it was. . . . I had to decide whether he was really Jewish, and I decided he was. . . . I figured the guy had five life sentences, we

---

Doernberg, "Pass in Review: Due Process and Judicial Scrutiny of Classification Decisions of the Selective Service System," 33 *Hastings Law Journal* 871 (1982).

[40] I reviewed such cases as deputy solicitor general from 1971 to 1972. Rarely, if ever, did claimants then lose in the courts when the basis for denying them the exemption was disbelief of their asserted convictions. My impression is that only a relatively small percentage of reservists who have claimed to be conscientious objectors after being ordered to service in Iraq have succeeded. I am not sure whether a stricter standard is being applied to them or whether one might say that someone's remaining in the reserve, a status chosen by the applicant, fairly constitutes a kind of objective evidence that one is not opposed to participating in all wars.

[41] See *Sherr v. Northport–East Northport Union Free School Distr.*, 672 F. Supp. 81 (E.D.N.Y. 1987) (one couple had sincere religious beliefs, another couple did not); *Faring v. Board of Educ. of City of New York*, 116 F. Supp. 2d 503, 508 (S.D.N.Y. 2000). In *Doswell v. Smith*, 139 F.3d 888 (4th Cir. 1998), the court found itself unable to tell whether the district court judge had determined that a prisoner's wish for a kosher diet was purely secular (and his religious claim was insincere) or the judge had misunderstood what beliefs would qualify as religious. See Caroline L. Kraus, "Religious Exemptions—Applicability to Vegetarian Beliefs," 30 *Hofstra Law Review* 197, 215–17 (2001), suggesting that among kinds of relevant evidence of sincerity are (1) whether a person acted inconsistently with his claimed belief, (2) gained materially by masking a secular belief, (3) asserted beliefs connected to a religion of some size and historical existence.

[42] Sullivan, "Judging Religion," 81 *Marquette Law Review* 441, 453 (1998). Dickey's account is taking from *Sasnett v. Sullivan*, 908 F. Supp. 1429 (W.D. Wis. 1995), aff'd, 91 F.3d 1018 (7th Cir. 1996).

could cut him a little slack, since he obviously wasn't Jewish or if he was, he was a very recent convert. He just wanted to have his own dinner.

One way to take Dickey's response is that, although he thought the prisoner was probably not Jewish, he figured a Jewish dinner wouldn't hurt. But we might understand the story differently. Although the prisoner may have had some sense of Jewish identity—perhaps his father was Jewish but he was raised as a Christian by his mother—whether he deeply regarded himself as Jewish was doubtful. This apparently is how Professor Sullivan, who writes of religious and cultural indeterminacy,[43] takes Dickey's story. She speaks of "the occasional lifer who needs to have a Seder. This flexibility . . . comes out of a real respect for the individual and for cultural difference: an acknowledgment of an American cultural style in the case of cultural conflict."[44] Officials may need to recognize that people can have multiple and shifting religious identities, that "sincerity" need not lock them into one religious affiliation and set of doctrinal propositions.

A sensitive evaluator of individual sincerity needs to recognize three related truths. First, as James Boyd White has emphasized, people may be attached to rituals and other practices more than to doctrines.[45] Sincerity could mean attachment to practice rather than propositions. Second, as Justice Jackson indicated, sincerity admits of doubt and stumbling.[46] Officials should not require certain conviction or unwavering practice. Third, an individual's convictions need not correspond with the dominant beliefs of his religious group. It may even be that an individual is not recognized by others as a member of a group, though he genuinely considers himself a member.[47]

Amish claims to withdraw children from school[48] raise yet other issues about sincerity. Courts have assumed that Amish claimants are sincere. Probably the definitive question should not concern a parent's exact views about further school education. No one doubts that groups of Amish, in general, believe that their children should not receive ordinary education beyond the

---

[43] She refers to Lawrence Rosen, "The Integrity of Cultures," 34 *American Behavioral Scientist* 594 (1991).

[44] Sullivan, note 42 supra, at 457.

[45] White, "Talking about Religion in the Language of the Law: Impossible But Necessary," 81 *Marquette Law Review* 177, 187 (1998).

[46] *Ballard*, note 3 supra, at 93–95 (dissenting opinion).

[47] In *Jackson v. Mann*, 196 F.3d 316 (2d Cir. 1999), the court said that an inmate requesting a kosher diet might consider himself to be Jewish, although the Jewish chaplain said he was not, because he had not been born Jewish or gone through a conversion process. What counted were Jackson's own beliefs. In this instance, the court correctly looked to the individual's sense of identity; were the crucial right that was being asserted a right to participate *as* a member of a group (say the Native American Church), the group's criteria of membership might be more controlling.

[48] See *Wisconsin v. Yoder*, 406 U.S. 25 (1972).

eighth grade. Individual parents should succeed in a claim to withdraw their child once they show they are practicing members of an Amish group that undertakes community vocational education after that grade, even if they happen to doubt the wisdom of withdrawing children at exactly that stage. If all Amish children in a locality are expected to participate in vocational education beyond eighth grade, individual children should be able to do so even if their own parents personally could accept further ordinary education.[49] The close relation of the Amish claim to corporate religious practice affects the precise inquiry about sincerity.[50]

For people who seek an exemption from a law against substance abuse, the inquiry about sincerity should be similar to that for Amish education. Is the individual a sincere member of a group that meets the requisites for the exemption?[51] Each individual need not think use of the substance is extremely important. Imagine a Protestant church in which 80 percent of the members strongly believe wine should be used for communion. The other 20 percent believe grape juice is preferable. If only wine *is used* for communion, a member who thinks grape juice is preferable should have the same legal right to use wine as the 80 percent.

For use of drugs like peyote, the inquiry about sincere membership may be somewhat more troubling than inquiries about the Amish and our hypothetical Protestants. No one joins the Amish in order to withdraw children from school; no one joins a church to receive a minuscule amount of wine in communion; but someone might join a church in order to use a hallucinogenic drug. Perhaps a jury could consider evidence that a claimant had no interest whatsoever in the church, that he joined only to use a drug of choice. But if he is a sincere member of the church, he should be able to engage in its practices of worship, whatever his particular opinions about drug use.

Although some inquiry into sincerity is often essential, both the best inquiry, and the range of constitutionally permissible inquiries, vary according to the subject. Two final points warrant emphasis. A finding that a claimant is sincere should be easy if one cannot discern any secular advantage from a

[49] The situation would be different in a community in which the Amish were divided on this issue, and many Amish children attended ordinary school beyond eighth grade.

[50] The differences between such claims and those to be conscientious objectors are explored in chapters 4 and 6.

[51] See *United States v. Meyers*, 906 F. Supp. 1494 (D. Wyo. 1995), determining that the "Church of Marijuana" was not a bona fide religion; the court doubted Meyers's sincerity but did not rest its determination on that.

I assume, for reasons explored in chapter 5, that individual convictions not connected to group practice are not a sufficient basis for an exemption. That chapter also explains the connection that is needed. I do not mean to preclude the possibility that the relevant group could be a subgroup of a larger organization, most of whose members do not use the drug in question.

person's engaging in the behavior she asserts is part of her religious exercise. In any context, searching inquiries into sincerity of religious belief are troubling, for just the reasons Justice Jackson offered.[52] Alternative approaches are preferable if they are feasible. This is why allowing anyone to opt out of military service by undertaking alternative service that most people would consider more onerous is preferable to screening people's beliefs. The undesirability of inquiries into sincerity, and especially the risk of discriminatory disbelief of the unorthodox, count against introducing a scheme of legal regulation in which officials must evaluate people's honesty; but not all schemes in which officials make that inquiry are invalid or unwise. Tests of sincerity are frequently a necessary price to attain objectives that the Constitution requires or permits.[53]

---

[52] The Second Circuit Court of Appeals called the analysis of sincerity "exceedingly amorphous," requiring "the fact finder to delve into the claimant's most veiled motivations." *Patrick v. Lefevre*, 745 F.2d 153, 157 (2d Cir. 1984). See also *Selah v. Goord*, No. 00-cv-0644, 2002 WL 73231 (N.D.N.Y. Jan. 2, 2002) (passing on sincerity of claim to avoid test for tuberculosis).

[53] See David E. Steinberg, "Rejecting the Case Against the Free Exercise Exemption: A Critical Assessment," 75 *Boston University Law Review* 241, 278–86 (1995). Brian Freeman, in "Expiating the Sins of Yoder and Smith: Toward a Unified Theory of First Amendment Exemptions from Neutral Laws of General Applicability," 66 *Missouri Law Review* 9, 37–41 (2001), offers a contrary appraisal.

CHAPTER 8

Saying What Counts as Religious

When statutes and constitutional principles give special treatment to a religious action or organization, courts must be able to say what is religious. Usually something clearly is or is not religious, but religion is hardly a straightforward concept. In this chapter, we shall ask how courts should proceed when they consider phenomena on the edge of what qualifies as religious.

The simplest context in which the question about "religion" can arise is when someone seeks a privilege granted only to those with religious grounds. For example, a person who invokes the Religious Freedom Restoration Act (RFRA) protection against substantial burdens on the "exercise of religion"[1] must establish that his claim concerns religion.[2] In free exercise cases, courts may, as we have seen, need to determine sincerity, and they may also analyze the relative strength of religious claims and government interests, matters taken up chapter 13.

A different context in which courts must say whether a practice is religious is when opponents try to stop the practice as establishing religion. In a notable case, the issue was whether a course in Transcendental Meditation, offered in public schools, was religious. Courts may also need to determine whether a classification among different groups, such as the favoring of "general" objectors over "selective" objectors in the law granting an exemption from military service, is religious,[3] and whether discrimination is in relation to religion, not always an easy inquiry, as we shall find in chapters 18 and 19.

The subject of how to define religion is complex. We shall look at what the major cases have said and explore various alternatives, trying to settle on an approach that is sound. Six preliminary points help focus the discus-

---

[1] 107 Stat. 144 (codified principally at 42 U.S.C. 2000bb (Supp. V 1993)). In June 1997, the Supreme Court held the act invalid as it applies to state and local laws. *City of Boerne v. Flores*, 521 U.S. 507 (1997).

[2] A particular claim by an undoubted religious group need not necessarily be religious; were a church falsely to advertise that food it sells contains Vitamin C, that assertion would not be religious. In *Founding Church of Scientology v. United States*, 409 F.2d 1146 (D.C. Cir. 1964), the court held that claims by the Church of Scientology about the health benefits of using E-meters were religious.

[3] A classification that favors some religious views or practices over others is presumptively invalid. The issue about conscientious objection is discussed in chapter 4. Even if a classification itself were not regarded as religious, some impermissible religious objective might underlie it.

sion. (1) Any judicial test of what counts as "religious" is worrisome; it is intrinsically difficult to apply and creates the danger that judges will favor the familiar over the unorthodox. (2) A test of what counts as religious is nevertheless unavoidable for certain cases. If, as almost everyone agrees, religious discrimination is unacceptable, officials must be able to say whether unfavorable treatment relates to religion. (3) How often the law requires courts to determine whether something is religious depends on substantive principles of constitutional and statutory law. For example, by announcing that people with religious reasons have no claim under the Free Exercise Clause to violate criminal laws, *Employment Division v. Smith*[4] eliminated a need to decide whether some claims are religious that the preexisting constitutional standard required.[5] (4) It counts in favor of an approach to "defining religion" that it is easily comprehensible and consonant with the values underlying the religion clauses. (5) An approach should fit well with existing or desirable standards of rights and duties. (6) Only a small percentage of actual claims about religion raise a serious question of whether something is religious or not;[6] the need to determine what is religion is more tolerable if that determination is usually uncontroversial.

Major Cases

Given the intricacies of defining a concept as complex as religion, the Supreme Court understandably has remained relatively silent. It did offer a constitutional definition of religion in 1890,[7] speaking of "one's views of his relations to his Creator, and to the obligations they impose of reverence for his being and character, and of obedience to his will." In a 1931 dissent,[8]

---

[4] 494 U.S. 872 (1990).

[5] Congress responded to *Smith* with the Religious Freedom Restoration Act (RFRA), which reintroduced the need to determine what is religious for many circumstances. The Court then declared in *City of Boerne v. Flores* that Congress lacked power under the Fourteenth Amendment to create a broad exemption for religious exercise from state and local laws. That decision drastically reduced the occasions when courts will need to determine whether practices people want to protect are really religious.

[6] If individual claims counted as religious only when individual claimants reflected the dominant view in their group, the definitional problem would arise more frequently. The Supreme Court rightly dismissed such an approach in *Thomas v. Review Bd.*, 450 U.S. 707 (1981), a case in which the state supreme court had called Thomas's objection to working on tank turrets "nonreligious," apparently because the objection was idiosyncratic and uncertain. See also *Love v. Reed*, 216 F.3d 682 (8th Cir. 2000) (prisoner had religious belief he should adhere to Jewish dietary practices although he did not consider himself to be Jewish and would not be considered to be Jewish by standard criteria).

[7] *Davis v. Beason*, 133 U.S. 333, 342 (1890).

[8] *United States v. McIntosh*, 283 U.S. 605, 633–34.

Chief Justice Hughes similarly referred to "belief in a relation to God involving duties superior to those arising from any human relation." The Court adopted a much more inclusive concept of religion in 1961 in *Torcaso v. Watkins*.[9] Invalidating a state law that required officeholders to declare a belief in God, because it preferred theistic religions, Justice Black's opinion for the Court indicated that Buddhism, Taoism, secular humanism (at least in the organized form of the Fellowship of Humanity), and ethical culture (Justice Black had in mind the Ethical Culture Society), and similar groups were religions.

In conscientious objector cases during the Vietnam War, which we examined in chapter 4, the Supreme Court gave its fullest exposition of religion. Despite the draft act's evident endorsement of a traditional theistic idea of religion,[10] the Supreme Court interpreted the statute more broadly, to cover applicants like Daniel Seeger, who rejected dependence on a Creator for a guide to morality and had a "belief in and devotion to goodness and virtue for their own sakes, and a religious faith in a purely ethical creed."[11] After considering modern conceptions of religion, the Court concluded that "[a] sincere and meaningful belief which occupies in the life of its possessor a place parallel to that filled by the God of those admittedly qualifying for the exemption comes within the statutory definition."

A plurality of four justices went even further in *Welsh v. United States*,[12] in which the objector had struck the word "religious" from his application, and based his objection to military service on his perception of world politics and the wastefulness of devoting human resources to military endeavors. According to Justice Black, Welsh's beliefs "play the role of a religion and function as a religion in [his] life"; the statutory exemption covered "those whose consciences, spurred by deeply held moral, ethical, or religious beliefs, would give them no rest or peace if they allowed themselves to become part of an instrument of war."

In light of the extremely awkward fit of congressional language and the plurality's construction, commentators believed that the justices' interpretation was based on constitutional doubts about the line Congress had tried

[9] 367 U.S. 488 (1961).

[10] Section 6(j) of the Universal Military Training and Service Act required that conscientious objection be based on "religious training and belief." Congress provided a further definition that drew from the language of Chief Justice Hughes; religious belief was "an individual's belief in a relation to a Supreme Being involving duties superior to those arising from any human relation, but [not including] essentially political, sociological, or philosophical views or a merely personal moral code." Congress had adopted this definition after a disagreement among the courts of appeals over how broadly religion should be understood.

[11] *United States v. Seeger*, 380 U.S. 163, 166 (1965).

[12] 398 U.S. 333 (1970).

to draw.[13] The Supreme Court's broad statutory construction of religion, as well as its decision in *Torcaso*, has led other courts and scholars to assume that the constitutional definition of religion is now highly inclusive.

Applications by the Washington Ethical Society and a California Fellowship of Humanity for tax exemptions available to churches yielded important judicial opinions about the boundaries of religion. In the former case, the United States Court of Appeals for the District of Columbia held that the Ethical Society, although it propounded no theist beliefs, was a religious corporation or society within the meaning of the District's tax code.[14] Traditional religious practices and aims strongly resembled those of the society. The society focused on spiritual values and guidance and the need for inward peace; it held Sunday services with Bible readings, sermons, singing, and meditation, as well as Sunday school classes; and it used "leaders," trained graduates of established theological institutions who preached and ministered and conducted services for naming, marrying, and burying. Emphasizing the broad purposes of the tax exemption statute, the court adopted a wide notion of religion without attempting a definition. A California court of appeal took a similar approach to the nontheist Fellowship of Humanity.[15] It said that religion includes, among other things, "a belief, not necessarily referring to supernatural powers" and moral practice that results from adhering to the belief.[16]

Various courts have considered whether Scientology and its practices are religious. In one case, decided by the United States Court of Appeals for the District of Columbia, the government had proceeded against Hubbard "E-meters" on grounds of misleading labeling.[17] The crucial question was whether claims about the physical benefits of a process using the E-meters were essentially spiritual or nonreligious. Since the movement's leader had developed a theory of mind similar to the ideas of some Eastern religions, and ministers performed functions like those of traditional ministers, the court regarded Scientology as a religion. The process of auditing with E-meters, which was designed to enable people to work clear of "engrams"

[13] This judgment drew support from the Court's declared aim to avoid imputing an intent by Congress to exempt some religious beliefs and not others. *Seeger*, note 11 supra, at 176.

Justice Harlan, who also voted to exempt Welsh, said that Congress had impermissibly differentiated between religious conscientious objectors and nonreligious objectors. *Welsh*, note 12 supra, at 344–67.

[14] *Washington Ethical Soc'y v. District of Columbia*, 249 F.2d 127 (D.C. Cir. 1957).

[15] *Fellowship of Humanity v. County of Alameda*, 153 Cal. App. 2d 673, 315 P.2d 394 (1957). See *Kalka v. Hawk*, 215 F.3d 90 (D.C. Cir. 2000), for the suggestion that the Court's inclusion of secular humanism as a religion in *Torcaso v. Watkins*, note 9 supra, was limited to this particular organized group in California.

[16] Id. at 693, 315 P.2d at 406.

[17] *Founding Church of Scientology*, note 2 supra.

that allegedly cause mental disorder, was substantially religious; many claims on its behalf were essentially spiritual, and they could not be challenged on any ordinary theory of misleading labeling.[18]

Two opinions by Judge Arlin Adams of the Third Circuit are the most careful and sophisticated about the concept of religion. In *Malnak v. Yogi*, an establishment case,[19] his court upheld a challenge to a course titled Creative Intelligence—Transcendental Meditation that was offered as an option in the New Jersey public schools. Contrary to what teachers of the course claimed, the court determined that it was religious, largely because students received individual mantras at a *puja* where the students heard teachers chant and make offerings to a deified "Guru Dev." Concurring, Judge Adams concluded that cases had established a "new definition" that could be described as one by analogy.[20] In determining the criteria from which courts should draw analogically, Judge Adams emphasized that religions concern themselves with "fundamental problems of human existence"[21] and lay claim to a "comprehensive 'truth.' "[22] A third element was the presence of formal or surface signs similar to those of accepted religions. Adams was clear that external signs need not always be present, but he seemed to suggest that the other two criteria embody necessary conditions of religion. Yet he subsequently cautioned that the three indicia "should not be thought of as a final 'test' for religion."[23]

---

[18] Subsequently, however, the district court determined that some claims made were scientific and could be distinguished from religious propositions. It restricted assertions that could be made on behalf of E-meters in order to ensure that their use was only in religious counseling. *United States v. Article or Device*, 333 F. Supp. 357 (D.D.C. 1971). For an account of Germany's more restrictive view of whether Scientology qualifies as a religion, see Emily A. Mosely, "Defining Religious Tolerance: German Policy Toward the Church of Scientology," 30 *Vanderbilt Transnational Law Review* 1129 (1997); Paul Horwitz, "Scientology in Court: A Comparative Analysis and Some Thoughts on Selected Issues in Law and Religion," 47 *DePaul Law Review* 85, 118–27 (1997).

[19] 592 F.2d 197 (3d Cir. 1979) (per curiam).

[20] Id. at 207 (Adams, J., concurring). In a case sustaining a claimed exemption from payroll taxes for the Church of Scientology, the opinions of the High Court of Australia discussed the American cases and Judge Adams's *Malnak* opinion at some length. *Church of the New Faith v. Commissioner of Pay-roll Tax* (Vict.) 154 CLR 120 (1983). Justice Murphy wrote, "There is no single acceptable criterion, no essence of religion," and the opinion of Justices Wilson and Deane also evidenced sympathy with the analogical approach. Justices Mason and Brennan proposed a twofold standard of religion for legal purposes: belief in something supernatural and acceptance of canons of conduct to give effect to that belief. Their assumption is that any religion must display both characteristics, though the degree of emphasis might vary.

[21] Id. at 208.

[22] Id. at 209.

[23] Id. at 210. Adams regarded the challenged course as religious, partly because its teachers were associated with an organization devoted to the Science of Creative Intelligence, whose doctrines concerned a pervasive and fundamental life force. Id. at 213–14. The organization possessed only some of the surface aspects of traditional religious groups.

In *Africa v. Commonwealth*,[24] Judge Adams, for a unanimous panel, employed the same basic approach to determine whether a state prisoner was entitled on free exercise grounds to a "religious" diet of raw food based on his membership in MOVE, a "'revolutionary' organization absolutely opposed to all that is wrong,"[25] with organizational tenets about peace, nonviolence, purity, and harmony with the natural. The court determined that MOVE lacked the structural characteristics of religion and had an ideology that was not sufficiently comprehensive and focused on fundamental questions.[26]

Approaches to "Defining" Religion

With a modest review of possible approaches, we can identify a number of discrete ways in which courts might decide whether something is religious. For borderline instances of religion, different approaches can yield different conclusions. Courts have not always said how they decide what counts as religious, but they must use some approach, whether or not they make it explicit.[27]

Single-Factor Approaches

The most straightforward way to define religion for legal purposes is according to a single factor, which is taken to be crucial.

---

[24] 662 F.2d 1025 (3d Cir. 1981).

[25] Id. at 1026.

[26] The opinion bears the signs of some agonizing, for it concedes that whether MOVE deals with ultimate ideas is "not wholly free from doubt," id. at 1033, and that the conclusion about comprehensiveness "is not unassailable." Id. at 1035. Further, the court acknowledges that other members of MOVE might be able to establish free exercise rights, id. at 1036 n. 22, and it strongly intimates that prison officials should exercise their discretion to give Africa his diet of raw food. Id. at 1037. For criticism that the result in *Africa* was connected to starting points biased in favor of traditional Western religions, see Eduardo Peñalver, "Note: The Concept of Religion," 107 *Yale Law Journal* 791, 818–20 (1997).

Among significant cases employing approaches like that of Judge Adams, see *United States v. DeWitt*, 95 F.3d 1374 (8th Cir. 1996); *DeHart v. Horn*, 227 F.3d 47, 52 (3d Cir. 2000); *United States v. Meyers*, 906 F. Supp. 1494 (D. Wy. 1995), aff'd, 95 F.3d 1475 (10th Cir. 1996).

[27] Since courts generally should indicate reasons for conclusions, I assume they should explain how they determine what is religious; but even if judicial silence in the face of this complex problem is a part of wisdom, courts need to have some approach to use. A court might (implicitly at least) decide that something would be religious under any plausible approach, and thereby avoid determining which of the plausible approaches is most sound. For a suggestion that courts have managed, and may manage, without a coherent conceptual approach, but with a commonsensical approach that implicitly relies on various models of religion, see Rebecca Redwood French, "From Yoder to Yoda: Models of Traditional, Modern, and Postmodern Religion in U.S. Constitutional Law," 41 *Arizona Law Review* 49 (1999).

Supreme Being

Courts might define religion in terms of belief in a Supreme Being, but this approach restricts the legal concept of religion artificially. If free exercise protections extended only to those who believe in a single Lord of the universe, traditional Western religions would be strongly favored.[28] The Supreme Court clearly rejected the Supreme Being approach for constitutional purposes in *Torcaso v. Watkins*;[29] and in *United States v. Seeger*, it interpreted the statutory reference to belief in a Supreme Being as being much broader than its language suggested.

Extratemporal Consequences

Jesse Choper, a leading expert on the religion clauses, has urged that an appropriate constitutional test of a religious claim is belief in extratemporal consequences.[30] He defends this conception of religion on the ground that

---

[28] That approach *might* be defended on the basis of "framers' intent," the idea that those who adopted the First and Fourteenth Amendments conceived of religion in relation to a Supreme Being. See, e.g., George C. Freeman III, "The Misguided Search for the Constitutional Definition of 'Religion,'" 71 *Georgetown Law Journal* 1519, 1520–24 (1983); Lee J. Strang, "The Meaning of 'Religion' in the First Amendment," 40 *Duquesne Law Review* 181, 183 (2001–2). Although citizens of the founding generation were theists, I am hesitant to conclude that their concept of religion, had they been asked to give one, would have included only theists. My doubts center on their acquaintance with the Old Testament and with ancient Greek and Roman beliefs and on their possible sense of the beliefs and practices of Native Americans and of Africans brought to these shores as slaves. Americans had wide exposure to biblical stories in which the ancient Hebrews contested with various cultures that worshipped idols. Advanced education included study of Greek and Roman civilizations. What did teachers and students make of idol worship and the Greek myths about assemblies of gods headed by Zeus (Jupiter) and about the power of oracles? Did they think no one then really believed in those ideas, that such beliefs were "not religious," that these beliefs were religious but no modern human being could hold anything like them? In the instance of practices and beliefs of Native Americans and Africans that we might now regard as pantheist, did members of the white establishment comprehend these to any significant degree, and, if so, did they consider them to be religious? Would they have classified all these "retrograde" forms of belief as nonreligious, or as somehow excluded from the protection of the religion clauses despite being religions, if some undoubted full citizen happened to embrace one of them? I do not think we can have a well-formed opinion about the founders' view of the full ambit of religion without answers to these questions. Thomas Jefferson did explicitly state that the Virginia statute Establishing Religious Freedom protected the "Mahometan, the Hindoo, and infidel of every denomination." Sherryl E. Michaelson, "Note, Religion and Morality Legislation: A Reexamination of Establishment Clause Analysis," 59 *New York University Law Review* 301, 317 (1984).

A further wrinkle is that the Fourteenth Amendment is what makes the religion clauses applicable to the states and localities. By the time it was adopted, many people had a sense of nontheistic or polytheistic Eastern religions. *Their* concept of religion may have embraced these.

[29] Note 9 supra, at 495.

[30] Choper, "Defining 'Religion' in the First Amendment," 1982 *University of Illinois Law Review* 579. More recently Choper has maintained his position against criticisms, including

people have distinctively strong feelings about performing acts when they believe powerful extratemporal consequences are involved: "[I]ntuition and experience affirm that the degree of internal trauma on earth for those who have put their souls in jeopardy for eternity can be expected to be markedly greater than for those who have only violated a moral scruple."[31] This passage indicates that a person who asserts a free exercise right to perform an act should, to be successful, have to believe that significant extratemporal consequences would flow from his failing to perform that particular act.

This test is very restrictive. Traditional Christians who believe use of wine for communion is highly important, without supposing damnation, or something similar, will follow if the practice is abandoned, would have no claim to maintain this practice during the central moment of worship services.

Reflection on the varieties of Christian belief about extratemporal consequences reveals deeper difficulties with Choper's standard. Many Christians believe that God forgives the sins of the contrite, thus removing potential extratemporal consequences for those who repent. Many suppose that sins bring definite negative consequences, such as time in purgatory, but that these consequences may not be eternal. Others who believe in extratemporal consequences do not suppose that they follow from particular sinful acts. Still others believe in divine love and an afterlife, but not in extratemporal divine punishment. Many Christians are uncertain what happens after death, while retaining faith in the continuing power of God's love. Many are deeply unsure about the precise relation of sins in this life to the nature of existence in a possible afterlife. Given this wide range of views among Christians who believe in some life beyond this one, we cannot generalize confidently about whether they suffer more torment from violating their consciences than do nonbelievers who contravene their deepest convictions in the only life they expect to live.

Choper's position does not provide a viable approach to the free exercise of religion. If claimants had to believe in a tight connection between nonperformance of an act and severe extratemporal consequences, protection for religious practices would be much too narrow. Moreover, courts would have to investigate specific beliefs about life after death carefully; and the uncertainty many people feel about the precise nature of extratemporal consequences would severely complicate issues of sincerity. Under a broader con-

---

my own. Jesse H. Choper, *Securing Religious Liberty: Principles for Judicial Interpretation of the Religion Clauses* 77 (Chicago: University of Chicago Press, 1995). Paul Horwitz gives a broad reading of Choper's standard in "The Sources and Limits of Freedom of Religion in a Liberal Democracy: Section 2(a) and Beyond," 54 *University of Toronto Faculty of Law Review* 1, 11 (1996).

[31] 1982 *University of Illinois Law Review* at 598.

struction, virtually any belief in extratemporal consequences would suffice; but the result would be the protection of many claims that lack the underlying rationale of special psychological pain that supports Choper's proposal.

The inaptness of Choper's test for Establishment Clause cases is obvious. States cannot teach in public schools that religions that do not refer to extratemporal consequences are true, nor may they financially support activities of prayer and worship by persons who do not believe in life after death.[32]

Ultimate Concern

The idea that the central feature of a religious claim is "ultimate concern" gained currency after *United States v. Seeger*,[33] in which the Supreme Court drew from Paul Tillich's writings the suggestion that an individual's ultimate concern is his God.[34] In *Welsh v. United States*,[35] a plurality interpreted the statutory exemption requiring "religious training and belief" to cover avowedly nonreligious persons. Courts using "ultimate concern" as their standard of religion could avoid parochial and narrow understandings of religion. But ultimate concern is not sustainable as a single criterion for religiousness.[36]

As a concept for legal use, ultimate concern is ambiguous and vague. The standard focuses on what matters in someone's life, not just the grandness of questions answered by a system of belief; but beyond this solid ground, one faces perplexing uncertainties. Are a person's cognitive beliefs or her psychological attitudes central? The intensity with which people care about aspects of their lives often does not fit their intellectual beliefs. A man believes that salvation matters more than earthly happiness and also believes that remarriage will forfeit his hope of salvation, yet he remarries. His intellectual priorities are reversed in his feelings.

If we think abstractly about "ultimate concern," we are likely to equate absolute mandates of conscience with people's most powerful concerns, but

[32] Choper is able to employ his approach for establishment cases only by giving a very broad reading of the Free Speech clause. See Choper, "Defining 'Religion,'" supra note 30, at 610–12.

[33] *Seeger*, note 11 supra, at 187.

[34] Id. at 187.

[35] Note 12 supra.

[36] "Ultimate concern" receives careful articulation and a spirited defense in "Note, Toward a Constitutional Definition of Religion," 91 *Harvard Law Review* 1056 (1978), written by John Sexton, later dean of the New York University Law School and now president of that university. In Greenawalt, "Religion as a Concept in Constitutional Law," 72 *California Law Review* 753, 806–11 (1984), my discussion of ultimate concern focuses on that note. For references to "ultimate concern" in cases brought by parents opposed to immunization of their children, see *Mason v. General Brown Central School Distr.*, 851 F.2d 47 (2d Cir. 1988); *Lewis v. Sobol*, 710 F. Supp. 506 (S.D.N.Y. 1989).

these do not always match. Addicts may center their lives around using a drug, doing almost anything to avoid being deprived of it. Yet their obsession does not concern conscience.[37] On the other hand, people suppose they have absolute duties, such as never worshiping an idol, to which they rarely give a thought.

The example of idol worship might suggest that any beliefs that flow from an ultimate concern of living according to God's will should qualify. But this reasonable construction of ultimate concern has sweeping implications. For people devoted to doing God's will, *any* judgment about right and wrong may *connect* to their ultimate concern. This would include such nonabsolute judgments as "it is preferable to use wine rather than grape juice for communion unless members of the congregation who are alcoholics suffer too much." Once "ultimate concern" is opened up in this way, it no longer demarcates strong claims deserving protection from weaker ones.[38]

Any apparent simplicity of ultimate concern is dispelled further when one recognizes that many people care a great deal about a number of things— their own happiness, their family's welfare, their country, their religion— without any clear ordering among these *and* without any single ordering principle for clashes between them.[39] Unless one says that such a person lacks any ultimate concern, one must understand the concern as an amalgam of the things about which he cares deeply and the ad hoc resolutions he makes among them.

If ultimate concern *were* to be used as the free exercise test of religion, it should be understood as requiring a claimant to be moved by a powerful claim of conscience. Conscience, in this sense, would include a very powerful feeling that performance of an act or ritual, such as use of peyote in worship, represents the best way to act.[40]

An ultimate concern approach to defining religion for constitutional purposes is misconceived. Some claims should count as religious even though they do not satisfy a standard of ultimate concern or overarching conscience. Although most modern religions answer major questions about human exis-

[37] Further, some addicts who have what may be termed a first-order desire to use a drug also have a second-order desire to stop wanting to use the drug (see Harry Frankfurt's "Freedom of the Will and the Concept of a Person," lxviii *Journal of Philosophy* 5–20 [1971], reprinted in *The Importance of What We Care About* [New York: Cambridge University Press, 1988]). One would strongly hesitate to call a very powerful desire an ultimate concern if the person with the desire actually wants to stop having that desire.

[38] If someone's ultimate concern was the welfare of her children, then any honest assertion relating to their welfare, say to have a particular third-grade teacher, would become religious.

[39] Most people with traditional religious beliefs accept intellectually that religious concerns are ultimate, but their feelings and behavior often do not accord with that premise.

[40] That is, one would not *necessarily* need to think one was committing a moral wrong if one refrained from the act.

tence and offer a comprehensive focus for people's lives, some belief systems, commonly regarded as religious, have not made such claims. Worship has been to placate the gods and enlist their help for one's own projects. People with these views should have rights to religious exercise, yet their religious activities (in the ordinary sense) would not involve ultimate concern. If the test demanded a close connection between particular claims and overarching feelings of conscience, it would also unduly restrict rights of members of more traditional religions. For example, members of Protestant churches would have no religious claim to use wine during communion if they believed wine to be preferable to grape juice, but not required. Another drawback of a restrictive ultimate concern test would be the inquiry into sincerity it would require. In order to decide whether claims were religious, courts would have to assess whether people accurately described their intensity of commitment and unwillingness to compromise.

An ultimate concern approach is plainly inadequate for establishment cases. Consider again people who enlist the help of gods but do not develop ultimate concerns in response to them. The state should not be able to give such a group direct financial assistance to carry out its activities of prayer and sacrifice, nor could it teach the group's doctrines as true in the public schools. Yet the state, by its own teaching or by grants to private groups, may promote ethical principles, such as caring for fellow human beings, that represent the ultimate concerns of some persons. Ultimate concern is not, finally, a defensible approach for either free exercise or establishment problems.

Although the exact analysis differs, other approaches that focus dominantly on how beliefs and practices function in a person's life are subject to similar objections.[41]

Higher Reality

The most plausible single-factor approach to religion is "higher reality," in some suitably broad sense. Under this approach, the essential feature of religion is faith in something beyond the mundane observable world—faith in some higher or deeper reality than exists on the surface of everyday life or can be established by scientific inquiry. The phrase "higher reality" includes

---

[41] See, e.g., Ben Clements, "Note, Defining 'Religion' in the First Amendment: A Functional Approach," 74 *Cornell Law Review* 532, 558 (1989) (religious function in an individual's life is "addressing the fundamental questions of human existence and providing a guide for how to conduct one's life"); James M. Donovan, "God Is as God Does: Law, Anthropology, and the Definition of 'Religion,'" 6 *Seton Hall Constitutional Law Journal* 25, 95 (1995) (proposes as a "candidate definition" of religion "any belief system which serves the psychological function of alleviating death anxiety").

both belief in a "transcendent" reality, and belief that the deepest truths are "immanent," found within oneself once layers of illusion are peeled away. Stanley Ingber, for example, refers to Émile Durkheim's view of religion as a "unified system of beliefs and practices relative to sacred things," and urges that it "is the role played by the sacred or divine that separates religions from other belief systems . . . for legal purposes."[42]

Since the edges of natural and social science, and of rational philosophy, are hardly sharp, and some overarching perspectives about life make claims to scientific support that outsiders view as ill-founded, the proper application of a "higher reality" approach is not always evident; but its main outlines are clear. It treats as religions the vast majority of groups, practices, and beliefs now thought of as such. It does not treat as religious the activities or groups, such as Ethical Culture, that engage in practices closely resembling those of traditional religions but that do not assert a realm of meaning inaccessible to ordinary observation.[43] The exclusion of such groups is, indeed, the main difficulty with this approach. It downgrades the significance of profound forms of social practice that closely replicate those of undoubted religions.

Strategies of Avoidance

Our survey of single-factor approaches suggests tentatively that none is acceptable. Before we turn to more complex approaches we need to see why courts cannot employ a strategy to avoid or sharply limit inquiries about the boundaries of religion.

[42] Ingber, "Religion or Ideology: A Needed Clarification of the Religion Clauses," 41 *Stanford Law Review* 233, 285 (1989); the Durkheim quote is from *The Elementary Forms of the Religious Life* 62 (J. Swain trans., New York: Free Press, 1965). Ingber's discussion, especially at 286 n. 326, makes clear that he sees his proposal as one specification of what I term a "higher reality" approach. Paul Horwitz suggests a criterion of "a belief that is spiritual, supernatural or transcendent in nature." Horwitz, note 30 supra, at 10. (Horwitz has two other criteria, but these concern what he regards as necessary for a claim in Canada to fall under the constitutional guarantee of freedom of religion; they are not requisites of religion itself.) See also Richard O. Frame, "Note, Belief in a Nonmaterial Reality—A Proposed First Amendment Definition of Religion," 1992 *University of Illinois Law Review* 819, 837.

For approaches that put more emphasis on experience and on faith than on the substance of what is taken to be beyond ordinary understanding, see *United States v. Sun Myung Moon*, 718 F.2d 1210, 1227 (2d Cir. 1983), relying on the understanding of religion employed by William James in *The Varieties of Religious Experience* (set forth on p. 31 of the Penguin Classics edition [New York: Penguin Books, 1985]); Dmitry N. Feofanov, "Defining Religion: An Immodest Proposal," 23 *Hofstra Law Review* 309, 386 (1994) (religions as "non-rational (i.e., faith-based belief concerning the alleged nature of the universe)").

[43] Ingber, note 42 supra, at 286 n. 326, is explicit that he so understands his proposed standard. Criticizing my "a priori" assumption of the accuracy of decisions such as that awarding the Ethical Society a tax exemption available to churches or religious societies, he says his "position is that these cases were decided wrongly."

Strict Neutrality

One enduring worry about courts "defining" religion is that they will inevitably favor some religious views over others. This worry is one basis for proposals that the First Amendment should always be read to forbid government action favoring (or disfavoring) particular religions or religion in general. If a principle of strict neutrality were followed, the Constitution would be understood not to permit any accommodations specifically to religious practices. That would greatly reduce the number of occasions when courts would decide what is religious;[44] but they would still need to determine when legislative classifications among various groups are religious and when public and private discrimination is religious.

Self-Definition

Another way courts could minimize their involvement would be to accept as dispositive, or give great weight to, an individual's own honest determination whether her practice is religious or not.[45] But protection of religious exercise should not depend on idiosyncratic views of what constitutes religion. If two members of a group that takes a forbidden drug share opinions about ultimate reality and the place of drugs in human life, but, having taken different college courses about religion, disagree over whether their use is religious, the amount of legal protection they receive should not vary.

A more moderate reliance on self-definition would require that some minimum objective requisites of religion be met, and that the individual regard his claim as religious. The moderate version avoids locking courts into highly unusual personal opinions about religion, but it suffers from the same basic problem as its more extreme sibling. The Free Exercise Clause (and relevant statutes) protect beliefs and practices, however hard these may be to categorize; protections should not depend on an individual's notions about the edges of the concept of religion.

Self-definition is even more obviously ill suited for establishment cases, for which the perspectives of outsiders are very important. Whether a government can provide financial support for an activity, for example, should

[44] If legislative accommodation is allowed but not required, courts infrequently have to decide what is religious for *constitutional* free exercise purposes. This is the present posture of federal constitutional law under *Smith*, note 4 supra.

[45] In *Mason*, note 36 supra, the court refused to accept the claimant's characterization as dispositive. Gail Merel, "The Protection of Individual Choice: A Consistent Understanding of Religion Under the First Amendment," 45 *University of Chicago Law Review* 805 (1978), recommends reliance on an individual's sense of what is religious, so long as minimum requisites are satisfied.

not depend exclusively on whether those engaged in it, or those challenging its support, conceive of it as religious. The opinions of others in society should count as much as those of members and challengers.

Multifactor Approaches

It is time to pause over what we have learned. Courts cannot avoid determining what amounts to religion in some cases. Certain approaches to the substantive law of the religion clauses, most particularly the strict neutrality approach, could greatly reduce the number of occasions when determinations of religion would be necessary. Such a reduction does count in favor of an approach, but that is much less important than its ability to serve the purposes of the religion clauses. Very briefly, the strict neutrality approach restricts statutory accommodations and constitutional privileges too severely,[46] and it may allow some assistance to religious groups that should be impermissible.[47]

If single-factor approaches to religion and self-definition are too crude in their application to the range of phenomena that should count as religious for legal purposes, perhaps a multifactor approach will work better. Three points of difference highlight varieties among these approaches. (1) Courts might require that each factor be present to some degree; or they might allow satisfaction of some factors to make up for a failure to satisfy others.[48] (2) For any important factor, courts might insist that it be satisfied to a particular degree (if it is to count at all); or they might allow strength in respect to one factor to compensate for weakness in another.[49] (3) Courts might decide that what is religious for one purpose is religious for all purposes or make determinations that are sensitive to the legal issue involved. One version of the latter approach is to distinguish free exercise "religion" from establishment "religion."

In the approach I defend, no single factor is essential, strength in some factors can make up for weakness in others, and what counts as religion may vary with legal issues but not along the lines of a simple free exercise–establishment split.

---

[46] Other chapters in this volume supply the basis for this judgment.

[47] This subject is covered in the volume on establishment.

[48] Or they might make one or more factors necessary, while leaving others as relevant but not necessary.

[49] As a college might require that applicants have high school grades of at least B and test scores of at least 600, or instead evaluate applicants by grades and test scores, with high performance in one making up for weak performance in the other.

Required Conditions

The most straightforward multifactor approach posits a number of neces-sary conditions that together are sufficient to constitute religion. In granting a tax exemption to the nontheist Fellowship of Humanity, the California court of appeal said that religion includes "(1) a belief, not necessarily refer-ring to supernatural powers; (2) a cult, involving a gregarious association openly expressing the belief; (3) a system of moral practice directly resulting from an adherence to the belief; and (4) an organization within the cult designed to observe the tenets of belief."[50] The opinion implies that each standard must be satisfied. This particular specification is both too narrow and too broad. An exemption should not be denied to a theistic group with otherwise traditional religious practices that takes no position on moral questions. Yet the third criterion makes such a group nonreligious. By con-trast, some fraternal orders and professional associations that should not count as religious are covered by the criteria. They have a belief, gregarious association, moral practice, and organization. Of course, one court's failure to elaborate generally adequate criteria does not prove that no effort will succeed, but it should make us cautious about whether this is the best way to proceed.

Crucial Conditions That May Not Be Absolutely Necessary

The approach that Judge Adams takes in his opinions on Transcendental Meditation in public schools[51] and on whether a member of MOVE is enti-tled to a special prison diet[52] is more flexible. He cautiously avoids a rigid commitment to the status of his three fundamental criteria—concern with fundamental problems, claim to comprehensive truth, and formal signs—but they clearly will have overarching importance for evaluation.[53] Under his approach, a court looks to see how closely a practice resembles what is undoubtedly religious; if it exhibits some "religion-making" characteristics with great strength, that can make up for weakness in respect to some other characteristics.

---

[50] *Fellowship of Humanity v. County of Alameda*, 315 P.2d 394, 406 (Cal. Ct. App. 1957). A somewhat similar four-factor approach is proposed in Steven D. Collier, "Comment: Beyond Seeger/Welsh: Redefining Religion under the Constitution," 31 *Emory Law Journal* 973, 998 (1982).

[51] *Malnak*, supra note 19, at 200–215 (Adams, J., concurring).

[52] *Africa*, note 24 supra.

[53] See text accompanying notes 19–26 supra.

A More Flexible Analogical Approach

An approach somewhat more open-ended than that of Judge Adams is to inquire how closely the practice in question resembles undoubted religious practices, without prejudging whether some conditions are absolutely necessary or usually crucial. This kind of multifactor approach assumes that religion is a highly complex concept, and that all that may connect some examples of religion may be what Wittgenstein calls "family resemblance."[54] The reason why agreement on defining religion has proved so elusive may be that any definition by "necessary and sufficient conditions" is inadequate.

Courts may best decide what constitutes religion by seeing when the concept of religion indisputably applies, and asking how closely analogous the doubtful instances are to the indisputable instances.[55] What is distinctive about this "definition by analogy" is not the reasoning by analogy. Commonly, when people apply concepts to borderline instances, they consider how closely those instances resemble instances clearly within the concept; that is, they reason by analogy. To do so, they need a sense of the aspects, the important factors, of the clear instances that are relevant. Definition by analogy also looks to important factors, but declines to say that any precise set of these is essential. Indeed, one feature of this approach is that it can yield applications of a concept to instances that share no common feature. If skepticism about a search for essential conditions of religion is warranted, analogical reasoning has a kind of exclusivity here that it lacks when people reason analogically to discern the presence of necessary and sufficient conditions.

To determine the boundaries of religion, one begins with what is indisputably religious. Agreement about clear instances of religion does not require a consensus about all the concept of religion signifies. No one in our society doubts that Roman Catholicism, Greek Orthodoxy, Lutheranism, Orthodox Judaism, Islam, Hinduism, and Buddhism (at least in many forms) are religions. We identify what is indisputably religious largely by reference to their beliefs, practices, and organizations. These may include a belief in God or gods; belief in a spiritual domain that transcends everyday life; a comprehensive view of the world and human purposes; a belief in some form of afterlife; communication with God or gods through ritual acts of worship and through corporate and individual prayer; a particular perspective on moral

[54] Ludwig Wittgenstein, *Philosophical Investigations* §§ 66–67 (G.E.M. Anscombe trans., 3d ed., New York: Macmillan, 1958). Wittgenstein famously uses the example of games. We have a sense of what count as games, but games do not share any single feature or set of features.

[55] I proposed this approach in Greenawalt, note 36 supra. Shortly before my article appeared, George C. Freeman III, note 28 supra, proposed a similar approach in an article that was oriented more philosophically than mine.

obligations that is derived from a moral code or from a conception of a
divine nature; practices involving repentance and forgiveness of sins; "religious" feelings of awe, guilt, and adoration; the use of sacred texts; and
organization to facilitate the corporate aspects of religious practice and to
promote and perpetuate beliefs and practices.[56] One could alter details in
this list, but the critical point is that a number of these specific elements, if
not all, are found in what we take to be religions.

One's exact starting point may matter. If one concentrates on religions
most familiar in the United States, this might slant conclusions undesirably
by introducing a bias toward features of Western religions.[57] Starting with
major world religions would at least moderate the tendency. As more Hindus
and Buddhists immigrate to the United States, the difference between these
two beginning points lessens.

The next step in discerning the boundaries of religion is to see how closely
disputed beliefs and practices resemble the clear instances. The absence of a
single element does not render a group or practice nonreligious. A set of
practices could be religious if participants were not theists, or if they saw no
connection between transcendental reality and moral practices. No single
feature is indispensable for religion;[58] and two things might be religious without sharing any common features.[59]

Whether any feature by itself is sufficient to make a practice religious is
more complicated. Many features common to religious practices and organizations are also found in nonreligious settings. Professional organizations
have nonreligious rituals and ethical codes. Marxism has a comprehensive

---

[56] See William Alston, "Religion," in P. Edwards, ed., *Encyclopedia of Philosophy* 140 (New
York: Macmillan, Free Press, 1967). Alston's catalog of features is somewhat tilted toward
Western religions.

[57] Eduardo Peñalver, note 26 supra, at 815–16, fairly criticizes my original article for beginning
with religions most familiar to Americans, and thus introducing a pro-Western bias in application
of the analogical approach. One corrective he suggests is that features such as a concept of God
(or gods) can count positively toward classifying something as religious but cannot count negatively against something qualifying. Id. at 818–19. I agree with him that the absence of this feature
and of certain institutional aspects should not disqualify a set of practices and beliefs from being
religious, or create a strong presumption against its qualifying. But the line between counting
positively and negatively is not magical. If two sets of beliefs and practices are otherwise similar
and lack enough other features to make them religious, the one with a concept of God (counting
positively) may make it, while the one without such a concept may not.

[58] Someone might resist the claim that no feature of religion is indispensable with the assertion that a deep characteristic such as "faith" or the "transcending of ordinary experience"
unites all instances of religion. Were a feature cast at a high enough degree of generality and
vagueness, it might, indeed, unite all instances of religion; but such a feature would be too
amorphous to greatly assist someone classifying beliefs and practices as religious. Judges in
legal cases need features specific enough to employ usefully. With this understanding, we can
conclude that no feature is indispensable for religion.

[59] See Greenawalt, note 36 supra, at 768.

view about human existence, but is not (usually) considered religious. Ordinary nonreligious psychotherapy helps people assuage their feelings of guilt. Belief in God may always be religious, but a simple requirement that all members have that belief would not, alone, make an organization religious, nor does an initial prayer make a meeting religious. One categorizes an organization or set of practices in light of its combination of characteristics, and how these compare with paradigm instances of religion.

Although no single feature makes an organization or set of practices religious, a single feature could be sufficient to make a particular act religious. Suppose a person says honestly, "God has ordered me to refuse jury service." Assuming that her sense of "God" is not highly unusual, her claim is religious. But for most assertions, more than a single feature is needed.[60]

Judges could apply an analogical method in a relatively context-free or context-sensitive way. A context-free approach would ask whether a practice or organization is religious *in general*. An inquiry would be context-sensitive if it focused on the particular legal issue; under that approach, what is religious for one purpose might not be for all others. Given the wide range of legal issues regarding religion, we should not assume that the borders of religion will be exactly the same for every purpose. Inquiry should be sensitive to context.

Some suggestions about line-drawing in this regard mark a basic distinction between free exercise and establishment cases. Lawrence Tribe, for example, once proposed that everything "arguably religious" should count as religious for free exercise purposes, and everything "arguably nonreligious" should count as nonreligious for establishment purposes.[61] No neat separation of free exercise from establishment issues supports this position.

The "arguably" standards are highly amorphous, and the unclear boundaries of religion make many practices arguably religious and arguably nonreligious. Not every "arguably religious" practice should be treated as religious for free exercise purposes. Perhaps any use of psychedelic drugs is "arguably religious" but not every use should count as religious. Not every "arguably nonreligious"

---

[60] As I indicate below, I disagree with Douglas Laycock's suggestion that atheism and agnosticism count as religious under the Free Exercise Clause. Laycock, "Religious Liberty as Liberty," 7 *Journal of Contemporary Legal Issues* 313, 326–37 (1996). Insofar as Laycock's proposal is based on concerns about unequal treatment of convictions that should be treated similarly, my response is that these concerns can be met by direct reliance on constitutional doctrines of equality.

[61] In the first edition of *American Constitutional Law* § 14–6, at 828 (Mineola, N.Y.: Foundation Press, 1978) Lawrence Tribe supported this dual standard in terms of promoting voluntarism, which can be achieved by broad free exercise and narrow establishment concepts of religion. He abandoned this proposal in his second edition. *American Constitutional Law*, § 14–6, at 1186 n. 53 (2d ed. 1988).

practice should be treated as not religious for establishment purposes. Transcendental Meditation may be arguably nonreligious, but the Third Circuit rightly concluded that it should not be taught in public schools. The standards of arguably religious and arguably nonreligious yield a crucial intermediate category that is too large for wise interpretation of the religion clauses.[62]

An illustration helps show why any bright-line distinction between free exercise and establishment issues is likely to be misguided. An organization that is only arguably religious sponsors meditation that is arguably religious for members of the general public and students in the public schools. Under Tribe's approach, the organization would have a free exercise right to be treated by taxing authorities like religious groups, but it could overcome the establishment argument that its school activities involve forbidden state sponsorship of religion. The organization, thus, would be more favored than explicitly religious and plainly nonreligious organizations. The free exercise and establishment issues here are not sufficiently different to warrant this paradoxical result. What counts as religious should be sensitive to context; but no rigid categorization in terms of free exercise and establishment issues makes sense.

STANDARDS FOR A SOUND APPROACH, AND HOW WELL A FLEXIBLE ANALOGICAL APPROACH MEETS THEM

Competing approaches to "defining" religion have different strengths and weaknesses. Six criteria relevant for a sound approach are comprehensiveness, correspondence to concepts of religion in ordinary language, unity of approach, fit with Supreme Court jurisprudence, a capacity (when linked to other standards of evaluation) to yield sensible resolutions of legal problems, and compatibility with adequate tests of sincerity.[63] Let us examine how the analogical approach does against these six criteria, drawing occasional comparisons to alternative approaches.

Coverage of All Cases in Which Threshold Characterizations May Be Needed

An adequate approach has to work whenever courts must decide whether something is religious.[64] An approach that looks good for one problem may

---

[62] In *Malnak*, supra note 19, at 212–13 (concurring), Judge Adams makes a similar criticism.

[63] The best approach overall might not satisfy each standard well; but satisfying a standard counts in favor of an approach.

[64] Of course, an overall approach might consist of different approaches to different kinds of issues. Such an approach would meet the criteria of covering all cases if the overall approach contained standards for when each of the more particular approaches would be used.

not work for others, and some proposals fail precisely because they do not relate well enough to a wide range of religious claims. The second, corollary, truth is that one must attend to issues that arise under statutes and other constitutional provisions, as well as the religion clauses.[65] The analogical approach I have outlined applies smoothly to relevant constitutional provisions and related statutory protections.

Linkage to Modern Nonlegal Concepts of Religion

Since the term *religion* is one of ordinary language that refers to a deep and important social phenomenon, it would be unfortunate if the law's idea of religion differed greatly from ideas of religion outside the law. Although legal applications of a concept need not correspond precisely with how people use the concept in other contexts, it counts in favor of an approach to a basic constitutional concept that it ties to more general understandings. An analogical approach fits our culture's ideas of what counts as religious better than approaches depending on necessary and sufficient conditions, and it remains open to changing understandings about which elements are of greater or lesser importance in deciding whether something is religion.[66]

A Unitary Approach

The First Amendment proscribes any law "respecting an establishment of religion, or prohibiting the free exercise thereof." The single appearance of the word "religion" and the place of the word "thereof" strongly point toward a concept of religion that applies to both clauses. Although this implication of the language of the religion clauses might be overcome by powerful reasons to use different concepts of religion for the two clauses, a "unitary" approach is more natural. As I have explained, the analogical approach should not be unitary in the sense that whatever amounts to religion in one context automatically amounts to religion in another. But the approach is unitary in the more subtle sense that courts employ a uniform strategy to

---

[65] Courts must decide what makes a classification religious under the Equal Protection Clause; that determination involves a judgment deeply informed by the values underlying the religion clauses.

[66] See Peñalver, note 26 supra, at 811–12. One possible argument that a legal approach need not correspond to modern ideas about religion rests on a "framer's intent" position about constitutional interpretation. See note 28 supra. Were a drafter's intent approach applied to statutes as well, what counted as religion in modern statutes would be discerned according to notions of modern legislators. The result might be that the statutory range of religion would differ significantly from religion according to constitutional law. I agree with the assumption of virtually all modern courts and commentators that courts have a scope for interpretation that encompasses changing concepts of religion.

make determinations about religion. This strategy allows the sensitivity to context that has led scholars to propose different ideas of religion for free exercise and establishment cases, but without the awkwardness that a dual approach involves.

Consonancy with Supreme Court Jurisprudence

If an approach to determining what is religion is to be applicable by courts here and now, it must fit reasonably well with what the Supreme Court has said about "defining" religion and with the substantive principles the Court has employed to decide cases involving religion. The analogical approach is compatible with most cases that deal with definition, and is flexible enough to correspond with a variety of substantive approaches to free exercise and establishment rights, including those the Supreme Court has used during the last five decades.

Consonancy with Sensible Results

An approach to defining religion within law is not ultimately descriptive; it is one element in a conceptual structure for normative evaluation. When combined with appropriate legal principles governing rights and duties, an approach to the concept of religion should not generate unsound results. One requisite is that an approach be workable; another is that it fit existing or desirable substantive principles.

A major challenge to a flexible analogical approach is that its application is uncertain. This is a serious worry. The worry is reduced, but not eliminated, by recognition that issues of definition arise infrequently because the presence of religion is usually not in doubt. Nevertheless, when the issues do arise, courts need a workable approach.

The fundamental answer to the worry about uncertainty is that the analogical approach is not much less determinate than other plausible positions. Even apparently hard-edged standards like "extratemporal consequences" or "ultimate concern" are extremely vague in their actual application. A "higher reality" standard is still more vague. Indeed, since an analogical approach focuses partly on manifested practices and institutions, it has more solid reference points than "higher reality." Focusing on a handful of crucial factors, as Judge Adams has done in his insightful opinions, reduces the vagueness of the analogical approach *somewhat*. But insisting that satisfaction of any particular factor is always required would be a mistake. Such an insistence might yield a slight gain in determinacy, but it would sacrifice the greater sensitivity to the values of the religion clauses that a more flexible approach allows.

The connection between an analogical approach and existing and desirable substantive standards of decision is a crucial inquiry. Here I settle for a few general observations. An unduly restrictive approach to threshold definition may foreclose appropriate relief; an unduly generous approach may compel legal relief that is unwarranted.[67]

If applied with relative generosity for cases under the religion clauses and important statutes, the analogical approach will not foreclose consideration of anything that should matter. The approach does not artificially restrict what counts as religion and, thus, prematurely bar examination of a legal claim.

What of the potential difficulty that designation of something as religious may propel a court to apply a doctrine derived from the religion clauses or a statute when the outcome dictated by the doctrine is inapt? The compelling interest test for free exercise claims may seem particularly troublesome in this respect.[68] Although the Supreme Court now infrequently uses that test for *constitutional* claims of free exercise, legislatures remain free to adopt that standard. In other domains, the Supreme Court has said that to satisfy the compelling interest test, the government must establish that restricting an activity is required to satisfy an interest of major importance. On that understanding, the government would face a very heavy burden whenever a forbidden activity was labeled religious. However, as I have explained in earlier chapters and explore more fully in chapter 13, courts have hesitated to impose such a heavy burden on the government whenever a genuinely religious claim appears. So long as courts recognize that they need not employ a highly stringent compelling interest test for all free exercise claims, the analogical approach to definition does not promise undue validation of such claims.

Religion and Sincerity

As we have seen in the last chapter, for a broad range of free exercise cases, officials have to determine whether claimants sincerely believe the ideas they espouse. The analogical approach to religion adequately fits with appropriate tests of sincerity. In many instances, courts will need implicitly to decide whether claims are religious and whether they are sincerely believed.

---

[67] In ordinary establishment cases, a generous approach to what counts as religion favors those challenging the practice, not the practitioners; thus for both free exercise and establishment claims a generous definition favors those who seek legal redress.

[68] The Supreme Court's treatment of Establishment Clause problems has avoided this difficulty. Even when activities or organizations receiving some form of aid are identified as religious, invalidity has not followed when effects of aiding religion are remote, indirect, and slight. Thus, categorization of things as religious does not push courts to invalidate when that would be inappropriate.

The approach to religion I have suggested draws a clear distinction between the nature of a claim and the honesty of the person making the claim. It desirably avoids judicial determinations about a person's belief concerning subtle nuances of faith, such as the force of extratemporal consequences for the commission of sins.

ATHEISM, AGNOSTICISM, AND SECULAR CONSCIENCE UNDER THE RELIGION CLAUSES

This final section of the chapter illustrates in more detail how approaches to what counts as "religion" interrelate with substantive constitutional and statutory principles. More specifically it focuses on secular conscience, atheism, and agnosticism. A desire to accomplish a certain kind of equality can generate a very broad definition of religion. But equality, to the degree that it is desirable, can be better achieved in an alternative way, as we can see from considering the classification of atheism and agnosticism and the status of conscience that is motivated by other than traditional religious beliefs. Taking a constrained view of what counts as religious, but arguing that constitutional norms of equality should often require similar treatment of religious and nonreligious assertions, I offer these specific claims: "Religion" under the religion clauses does not cover all assertions about religious truth. However, the "free exercise of religion" includes significant freedoms for nonreligious people. Further, about many subjects, the two religion clauses together, reinforced by the Equal Protection Clause, call for equal treatment of all assertions of religious truth and falsity. Thus, government speech supporting negative assertions about religion is more restricted than government speech about nonreligious subjects. Finally, for some claims of liberty, as earlier chapters suggest, the religion clauses should be taken to require equal treatment of those with religious grounds and those whose grounds do not rest on answers to religious questions.

My treatment responds particularly to an article by Douglas Laycock that attempts to offer decisive answers to these problems of constitutional classification.[69] Although Laycock's "bottom line" on most questions of equal treatment is appealing, he has oversimplified the conceptual possibilities. By treating atheism, agnosticism, and claims of conscience not based on religion in the ordinary sense, as religious, he fails to leave open interpretive distinctions that courts should be able to make.

[69] Laycock, note 60 supra, at 316–24.

Atheism, Agnosticism, and the Religion Clauses

Distinguishing Atheist and Agnostic Beliefs and Reasons
for Action from Most Nonreligious Reasons for Action

Atheism and agnosticism are negative answers to religious questions. In standard usage, atheism is disbelief in the existence of God; agnosticism is strong doubt about the existence of God. An atheist or agnostic may belong to a religious group that does not assert the existence of God[70] or may even participate actively in some theist religion. (Numbers of atheists and agnostics occupy pews of traditional Christian churches and Jewish synagogues.) When I talk, without qualification, about atheists, I mean people who do not believe in God or gods *and* who reject all common forms of religion. When I talk, without qualification, about agnostics, I mean people who are skeptical about all claims of religious truth and about the value of religious exercise and who do not participate in any common form of religion.[71]

Typical nonreligious reasons for action are reasons that are not significantly connected to religious beliefs and practices. Among such reasons, I am interested primarily in motivations that do not flow from answers to religious questions, whether these answers are positive or negative.[72] To take a trivial example, few people in modern societies would say that their choice of a house, restaurant, or spouse is determined by their religion. Of course, someone's religion may restrict alternatives or influence choice without becoming the main determinant of his or her actions. Orthodox Jews may limit themselves to kosher restaurants, but their religion may not help them choose among kosher restaurants.[73] Religious influence is often less clear cut. Many young people prefer to marry persons with religious views similar to theirs; but they will choose partners with dissimilar views if other attractions are very powerful. A woman's religious perspective may inform the personal

---

[70] Michael Perry, "Religion, Politics, and the Constitution," 7 *Journal of Contemporary Legal Issues* 407 (1996), says, "Although some Buddhist sects are theistic, Buddhism . . . is predominantly nontheistic, in the sense that Buddhism does not affirm the meaningfulness of 'God'-talk." See Walpola Sri Rahula, *What the Buddha Taught* (New York: Grove, 1959).

[71] Douglas Laycock, note 60 supra, at 353, describes himself as "agnostic about matters of religion" and says, "None of the claims of the world's religions seem to me either plausible or falsifiable." I do not doubt that Professor Laycock is an agnostic; but someone is also an agnostic who says: "Some religious claims are moderately plausible but not persuasive; some crucial religious claims are falsifiable but our evidence for and against them is radically inconclusive."

[72] If atheists and agnostics do not count as religious, then motivations that flow from their atheism or agnosticism will be nonreligious, but they will differ from most nonreligious reasons in deriving from answers to religious questions.

[73] The choice to marry could be similar if someone would not consider anyone outside the faith, but did not aim for particular compatibility in religious outlook among those inside the faith.

qualities she seeks in a husband or the time she spends with family, although she does not consider those choices to be religious. When I say that reasons for action are not religious, I mean that the reasons do not connect to religion or that the person making the choice perceives the connection as weak.

Negative Answers to Religious Questions—the Extreme Alternatives

How should "negative answers" be regarded under the religion clauses? A dichotomy that makes everything turn on whether negative answers are "religious" has some initial appeal, but the reasons to reject this dichotomy are stronger than the arguments in its favor.

Douglas Laycock suggests, "The only way to avoid [preferring one set of answers to religious questions over other answers to the same questions] is to recognize that for constitutional purposes, any answer to religious questions is religion."[74] If atheism and agnosticism are not religions, the argument goes, the exercise of atheism is not protected as the free exercise of religion, and atheists have no rights under statutes framed in terms of religious exercise.[75] Further, a comparison of religious clause law with free speech law reveals a startling conclusion about government communication.[76] The religion clauses bar the government from sponsoring religious views and from preferring one set of religious views to another. The rules are different for other domains of human understanding. In many forums, government officials can present ethical, political, and historical ideas as valid and true; they can reject other views. In public schools and elsewhere, people on government payrolls tell citizens that racial equality is good, that Nazism and Communism are bad, and that certain accounts of history are accurate.[77] If atheism and agnosticism are not religions, then they fall into the category of nonreligious views the government can promote. If atheism and agnosticism are religions, they are subject to the same rules as other

[74] Laycock, note 60 supra, at 329.

[75] See id. at 330–31. It is logically possible for Congress to adopt, and for the courts to acknowledge its adopting, a narrower or broader concept of religion than is attributed to the constitutional clauses. I assume here that the sense of religion in most relevant legislation is the same as under the religion clauses.

[76] See id. at 330.

[77] Some scholars argue that the government should be neutral between ideas of the good life, but this view goes far beyond existing constitutional principle, and even it would not bar teaching about matters of justice. For suggestions that the Free Speech and Free Press clauses may place limits on government speech, see Mark Yudof, *When Government Speaks: Politics, Law and Government Expression in America* (Berkeley and Los Angeles: University of California Press, 1985); Robert Kamenshine, "The First Amendment's Implicit Political Establishment," 67 *California Law Review* 1104 (1979); Steven Shiffrin, "Government Speech," 27 *UCLA Law Review* 565 (1980).

religious views and sources of motivation. They have equal status as the basis for exemptions, and they cannot be taught by the government.

If interpretive options were limited to the stark alternatives Laycock offers, the choice would be difficult. The idea that, in a country in which religious believers have always predominated heavily over unbelievers, public schools can teach atheism but not theism is bizarre. The idea that atheists and agnostics have no rights of religious exercise available to believers is deeply disturbing. On the other hand, the claim that atheists and agnostics have every privilege of religious believers fits uncomfortably with an approach to interpretation that gives much weight to original understanding;[78] it strains the textual language;[79] and is at odds with much of the Court's opinion in *Wisconsin v. Yoder*,[80] which strongly indicates that a free exercise claim of the Amish to be exempt from school attendance requirements works only for religious believers in the ordinary sense.

A More Satisfactory Approach

The interpretive options are richer than these stark alternatives, and the most desirable approach differs from each of them.

We may start with the uncontroversial point that atheists have free exercise rights, whether or not atheism is a religion. The free exercise of religion includes refusing to perform religious acts. Were a state to require that people, whatever other worship services they attend, spend one hour each week participating in a Roman Catholic Mass, its rule would deny the free exercise of religion, as well as violate the Establishment Clause. Neither an Orthodox Jew nor an atheist is allowed the free exercise of religion if she is compelled to go to Mass.[81] Part of a right to free exercise is a right not to participate in religion in a way to which one objects, whether or not one is religious.[82]

---

[78] Laycock suggests that although the founders may not have considered atheism a religion, they were aware that the "principal antagonists in religious conflict varied from time to time and place to place." Note 60 supra, at 383. Laycock urges that the term *religion* should be read to cover the major modern conflict between believers and unbelievers.

[79] Laycock, id. at 328–30, has an interesting discussion of the linguistic problem, including the characterization of humanism as religious in the first Humanist Manifesto (1933), a characterization dropped in Humanist Manifesto II (1973).

[80] 406 U.S. 205 (1972).

[81] Many countries and international human rights documents, as well as the constitutions of some of our states, protect religious exercise without guaranteeing nonestablishment. Coerced participation in an alien religion would violate those guarantees, whether or not the person coerced has any religious convictions of her own.

[82] Therefore, it cannot be argued that the atheist (lacking religious convictions) has only an Establishment Clause objection to forced participation in a Mass, whereas the religious Jew has *both* a free exercise and establishment objection to her participation.

If atheists have a right not to be coerced into religious participation, does it follow that atheists have free exercise rights to exemptions for behavior that flows from atheism that parallel the rights of traditional believers to exemptions? For reasons I shall explain, this question has virtually no practical consequences, but the answer to the question is "Not necessarily." Consider again the claim in *Wisconsin v. Yoder.* Compulsory school was at odds with the religious beliefs and practices of the Amish parents; they were entitled to an exemption for their children. Suppose compulsory school beyond a certain age was at odds with someone's atheism. Since compulsory school is itself not a religious practice or religious principle, forcing atheist children to go to school would not interfere with religious liberty, if atheism were not a religion. Unless atheism is a religion, atheists do not have free exercise rights that are equal in all respects with those of religious believers. The key to the issue of exemptions for atheists lies in considerations of equality. We can understand these most clearly if we first take a minor detour and examine the parallel "establishment" problem of official instruction.

Would official teaching of atheism (or agnosticism) constitute an establishment of religion? If atheism does not count as a religion, perhaps the Establishment Clause does not bar its being taught. But a sensible view of the whole Constitution renders the status of atheism different from that of typical nonreligious topics of discourse. The questions that atheism answers concern religion. If the government cannot make positive assertions about religious truth, it would be unfair to allow it to make negative assertions. Of course, unfairness does not always entail unconstitutionality; but three convenient avenues can lead to a conclusion that the state may not teach atheism. The simplest approach is to say that teaching the truth of atheism denies the free exercise of religion of believers by discriminating against them. A second approach is to conceive the religion clauses together (or the Establishment Clause)[83] as barring the government from taking positions on religious questions. The third, closely related, approach focuses on equal protection as requiring that negative assertions about religion be treated like positive ones.

Conceptually, the latter two approaches are preferable to the first. The reason is that not every government sponsorship of one religion violates the free exercise of members of other religions.[84] If this much is granted, not

---

[83] Various formulations of the threefold establishment test of *Lemon v. Kurtzman* suggest that aiding *or inhibiting* religion may constitute an establishment. Teaching atheism would inhibit religion. In *Linnemeir v. Board of Trustees*, 260 F.3d 757 (7th Cir. 2001), Judge Richard Posner wrote that a state university could not have a *policy* of promoting atheism.

[84] I assume here that countries with weak establishments of religion could provide full free exercise rights to citizens. That proposition may be disputed; that is, someone might argue that a weak establishment itself involves a mild violation of free exercise.

every sponsorship of atheism constitutes a denial of free exercise of believers. An "equality" approach, one that is based on the original religion clauses together or the Equal Protection Clause, or both, does not raise this difficulty. Every government sponsorship of the truth of atheism, like every sponsorship of positive religious views,[85] can be treated as forbidden. It should be so treated.

Once we recognize the equality approach as an answer to government sponsorship of atheism, we can easily understand how that approach applies to exemptions. The problem can be formulated as follows: "Would granting an exemption for action derived from religious belief and refusing the exemption for action derived from atheist belief deny the atheist equal protection (or a right to equal treatment gleaned from the religion clauses together)?" When the issue is so formulated, we can see that the best answer is not necessarily always yes or always no; perhaps not all kinds of exemptions should be treated in the same way,[86] a position for which I have argued in earlier chapters.

Close examination of reasons for action that do not derive from ordinary religious beliefs reveals that very few claims to perform acts actually *derive* from atheism or agnosticism, skeptical positions that rarely supply positive grounds to behave in a certain way.[87] An atheist or agnostic will exclude all positive religious reasons for his acts, but that does not make all his reasons atheist or agnostic. This conclusion is clearest for the agnostic, who says, in essence, "I am uncertain whether God exists or religion has any intrinsic value, so I am going to live without answers to these questions." A typical claim for exemption involves belief that a legally required or encouraged act is forbidden (or that a legally forbidden or discouraged act is required).[88] The Amish claimants in *Yoder* believed that their children should stay away from school; in a case we will examine in chapter 10, Ms. Sherbert believed

[85] I here pass over the problem that various practices in the United States, e.g., "In God We Trust" on coins, "under God" in the Pledge of Allegiance, do involve mild endorsement of positive religious views. These are discussed in volume 2. The modern Supreme Court has never acknowledged that something is both a serious sponsorship and is constitutionally permitted. Although the government cannot sponsor atheism or positive religious views, it may undertake actions (such as fighting wars) and teach scientific principles (such as evolution) and moral ideas (such as racial and gender quality) that conflict with some religious views.

[86] By contrast, an approach under which atheism and agnosticism are religions requires equal treatment automatically.

[87] As Michael McConnell, "Accommodation of Religion," 1985 *Supreme Court Review* 1, 10, has written, "[U]nbelief entails no obligations and no observances. Unbelief may be coupled with various sorts of moral conviction. . . . But these convictions must necessarily be derived from some source other than unbelief itself."

[88] The claim might be instead that an act is religiously favored or disfavored (rather than required or forbidden).

she should not work on Saturday.[89] Agnosticism, by itself, could not lead to beliefs like those of the Amish and Sherbert;[90] agnostics will need beliefs other than skepticism about answers to religious questions to generate grounds to be exempted.[91]

Although an atheist's disbelief in God could conceivably lead him to a claim to engage in particular action, coming up with a realistic modern example of an atheistic claim for exemption is not easy. If the law prohibited an action that involved an offense to religion, such as blasphemy, the atheist might have a conviction, based on his atheism, that he should engage in the act. But this kind of law, is, by modern lights, violative of the Establishment Clause and the Free Speech Clause, and perhaps the Free Exercise Clause; therefore, atheists do not need an exemption.

In our pluralistic religious society, in which nonreligious values are a central aspect of public culture, most ordinary laws (such as compulsory school attendance laws) are justified on grounds that unite people of a wide range of religious beliefs. Nothing about atheism per se is at odds with such laws. Perhaps an atheist might make a complicated argument that his atheism leads him to insist on a day off other than Sunday, because of the religious origin of laws and customary practices of closing on Sunday. Such an atheist would be an antireligious analogue of Sherbert, whose religion forbade Saturday work.

Apart from the highly unusual case in which atheist belief would directly underlie a strong claim for exemption from a valid secular law, atheism might connect to a claim for exemption in a different way. Atheism might be a component of some overarching view of life that leads to a claim of conscience. Atheism is a central feature of Marxist Communism. Marx and his orthodox followers have believed that atheism was significantly tied to other aspects of his philosophy. A communist who thought all wars were between competing capitalists might base a claim to be a conscientious objec-

[89] *Sherbert v. Verner,* 374 U.S. 398 (1963).

[90] What I have said is not accurate about claiming a privilege to declare agnostic beliefs and read agnostic (and other) literature. Agnosticism could provide a reason for these acts; but any law forbidding those acts would directly violate the Free Speech Clause and perhaps the religion clauses. Agnostics would not need an exemption.

[91] I put aside here the possibility that some overall philosophy includes agnosticism along with other elements. Such a philosophy might be a cohesive whole with agnosticism as a central element. This would be an analogue for agnosticism of how Marxism relates to atheism. What I say about that would be relevant if such an agnostic philosophy existed; but I am not aware of any such approach. One might think of some Unitarian-Universalist groups as a kind of religion for agnostics. When I speak of agnostics here, I mean individual, detached agnostics. For them, it is hard to see how agnosticism could provide a reason for an exemption from a valid secular law.

tor on Marxism. Thus, atheism could function as a component in a philosophy of life that might lead to claims of exemption like those that religious believers could make. But most claims for exemptions by atheists will lack this strong a connection to atheism. Thus, very few claims by nonbelievers for the same treatment given to traditionally religious persons will rest on their atheism or agnosticism.

A constitutional principle of nonsponsorship of religion, discussed in volume 2, should require that moral convictions closely connected to atheism (or agnosticism) be treated like moral convictions similarly related to religious beliefs. But this conclusion has little practical bite, because so few claims to exemption from valid laws will possess the required connection.

Nonreligious Reasons for Action as a Basis of Exemptions

What is the constitutional status of nonreligious reasons that do not arise from answers to religious questions or from participation in a religion?[92]

The constitutional place of nonreligious ideas is straightforward. Claims of truth that do not concern religious subjects are in the domain of the First Amendment outside the religion clauses. Officials of the government may take positions on many political, moral, economic, historical, scientific, and other questions. Any treatment of these subjects without reference to religion risks conflict with the way some religious believers conceive the subjects— they see religious understanding as affecting the whole range of human concerns. For these believers, nonreligious (secular) treatment of moral and other issues may implicitly diminish the significance of religion, but this diminishment by disregard is the unavoidable, acceptable consequence of the government's not taking positions about religious questions.

Analysis of bases for exemption is more complicated. Positions on political, moral, and historical questions might underlie claims to be exempted from ordinary laws. How do these claims compare with claims based on religion? I shall mention two examples. A young man, without reference to religious questions, concludes that all wars are wrongful and that it would be gravely immoral for him to fight in them. Should he be given an exemption from military service afforded religious pacifists? My second example is imaginary. A mother places great value on family life, and feels that she "cannot" work on Saturday, the main day for shared family activities.[93]

---

[92] One might conceivably have a religious claim based on religious activity that did not depend on one's answers to religious questions.

[93] Notice that the mother might be a religious person who remarks, "I care a lot about my family. Parents need to be with children if children are to feel loved and to develop in a healthy

Should the mother be treated like those who believe God commands that they not work on the Sabbath?

Two different grounds might be offered why some reasons that are nonreligious according to ordinary usage should qualify for the same treatment as typical religious reasons. One is that their place in the lives of claimants makes the reasons religious; another is that, although not religious, these reasons should be treated equally with religious ones.

Without doubt, a legislature may choose to exempt claims that are not based on answers to religious questions; it may accord equal treatment to religious and nonreligious claimants. The plurality in *Welsh v. United States* read the Selective Service Act to have this effect.[94] Even had the three dissenters in *Welsh* won the day, limiting the statute to its straightforward linguistic coverage of ordinary religious believers, Congress could have chosen to extend the exemption to nonreligious claimants like Welsh. The crucial issues are whether (1) for legislatively created exemptions, legislatures *must*, constitutionally, treat nonreligious claimants as they treat religious claimants; and (2) for exemptions by constitutional right, nonreligious claimants must be given privileges equal to those of believers.

Using a "borders of religion" approach, some scholars have concluded that any claim of sufficient power qualifies as religious because of its importance to the claimant. All such claims have to be treated like claims derived from traditional religion; otherwise there would be impermissible discrimination among religious approaches. The "ultimate concern" standard of religion we have already examined exemplifies this approach; it could be constitutionalized across the board.[95] The consequence of this approach would be that what counts as religious for the purpose of free exercise exemptions would depend on conscientious belief or strength of feeling. An atheist's "family life" objection to work on Saturday would be religious if her feelings about such work were as strong and unshakeable as that of a religious believer who thought God does not want persons to work on the Sabbath.[96]

---

way. This is not really a religious matter. I just feel it is extremely important to be with my children." If pressed hard enough, she might see that her religious values connect somehow to her concern for family, but she does not perceive the connection as strong.

[94] Note 12 supra.

[95] See, e.g., Laycock, note 60 supra, at 336. Laycock talks of the "nontheist's belief in transcendent moral obligations" that serve "the same functions in his life" as "moral beliefs drawn from religious views." See also Laura Underkuffler-Freund, "The Separation of the Religious and the Secular: A Foundational Challenge to First Amendment Theory," 1995 *William & Mary Law Review* 837; David A. J. Richards, *Toleration and the Constitution* (New York: Oxford University Press 1986).

[96] It is an interesting question whether a religious believer (in the ordinary sense) could have a claim strong enough to qualify as religious, even if the claim did not connect significantly to

We should not suppose that treating deep claims of conscience as religious will eliminate all problems of defining religiousness. Saying what amounts to a conscientious objection to military service is not too difficult; it is much harder to say what constitutes a compelling enough belief to qualify for other sorts of exemptions.

An approach that focuses on the power and quality of moral conviction to determine whether it is religious treats traditionally religious and other analogous objections with formal equality, but it leaves open the possibility that for some matters only traditional religious believers will have claims that are strong enough to receive an exemption. As I will suggest in chapter 10, it is hard to imagine nontheists having objections to Saturday work as unconditional as those who believe God has set Saturday apart as a day of rest.

A better conceptual approach assumes that conscientious claims that are not based on religious reasons do not qualify *as religious*, leaving open the question whether distinctions between religious claims and otherwise similar nonreligious claims are acceptable. As earlier chapters suggest, analysis does not yield an identical conclusion for all kinds of exemptions. The argument for equal treatment is very strong for conscientious objection to military service; I urged in chapter 4 that a preference for religious claimants should be regarded as an establishment of religion or denial of equal protection. On the other hand, conceptualizing a nonreligious objection to schooling beyond a certain age or to Saturday work that is like one that might be based on religious understanding is not easy. A law may appropriately require that religious belief or practice be a condition for a valid claim to exemption from such rules.

---

his religious beliefs. The "ultimate concern" argument, as typically put, usually compares the moral convictions of the nontheist to the central concerns of the religious believer. The implicit assumption is that the crucial convictions of the believer will be tied to his religion; for him there will be no ultimate concern not related to his religion. But actual people care deeply about many different things. Some religions may have relatively little bearing on some aspects of moral life. Some adherents of more comprehensive religions do not actually make the connections between religious view and moral choice that one might expect. (For example, many people in the United States who are believing Christians treat most family responsibilities as a separate moral domain, not closely related to their religious belief and practice, although ministers and others who think deeply about Christianity believe it bears significantly on how we should treat members of our families.) In a society in which so much moral discourse is not religious, we must acknowledge that some believers will have moral convictions they perceive as separate from their religion that will be as strong as the deep moral convictions of nonbelievers. The logic of the position that the deepest moral convictions of nonbelievers can qualify as religious leads to the conclusion that some moral convictions of believers that are not connected to their religious beliefs might also qualify as religious.

An approach that refuses to conflate religion and conscience is not only the most sound in terms of constitutional language, it also allows a nuanced evaluation of constitutional claims for equality. Concerns about equality that have led some scholars to a very broad constitutional definition of religion can be better handled by more discrete inquiries about equal treatment.[97]

---

[97] In *Wells v. City and County of Denver*, 257 F.3d 1132, 1152 (2001), the Tenth Circuit Court of Appeals assumed, without deciding, that atheism is a religion for First Amendment purposes. No court should actually resolve this issue without carefully exploring the implications of competing alternatives.

CHAPTER 9

Controlled Environments:
Military and Prison Life

We have considered three fundamental conflicts between religious conscience or practice and secular laws—objections to military service and educational materials and claims to use forbidden drugs in worship—and we have viewed general concerns about sincerity and what counts as religious. We now turn to the kinds of clashes between general regulations and the religious needs of individuals that arise with regularity in military bases and prisons, restricted environments in which the government controls people's lives to a degree unthinkable for adult civilians, who choose what to eat and wear and schedule their own activities, subject only to the demands of employers and families. The government determines what soldiers and convicts eat, makes them wear uniforms, and plans their activities in detail. This pervasive oversight can run afoul of religious imperatives if, for example, an Orthodox Jew requires kosher food, a Sikh needs to wear a turban, or a Muslim feels he must pray when his companions are working.

An individual's tenure in prison or the military is not the product of unconstrained choice. The state forces convicted criminals to reside in prison. Military draftees are also subjects of compulsion, and even volunteers differ from ordinary employees. Once they sign on for a term of service, they cannot leave; serious refusals to perform their duties are criminal acts. If a soldier develops religious convictions that are at odds with her military duties, she is not free to resign when she pleases.[1]

Neither soldiers nor prisoners enjoy all the civil liberties of ordinary citizens. The military inculcates a sense of regularity and discipline, on the view that sloppiness and lack of rigor interfere with military effectiveness, risking soldiers' lives and the attainment of wartime objectives. Among other restraints of military discipline, personnel on duty lack the complete freedom to speak their minds.

Discipline also figures strongly in prison; here it is often accompanied by the view that simply by committing a serious crime, a person forfeits certain of the rights of law-abiding citizens. The general sense is that convicted crimi-

---

[1] Even were resignation always an option, it would be regrettable if the circumstances of military life were so inflexible they effectively foreclosed participation by members of particular religions.

nals should not live in comfort. Beyond assuring at a minimum that prisoners and guards are safe and that prison life runs smoothly and at reasonable expense, the state, at least in the ideal, takes a kind of paternal responsibility for prisoners' lives, its officials aiming to rehabilitate convicts and to prepare them to function lawfully in the broader society when they complete their sentences.

Not only do military and prison officials have good reasons for restraining liberty, outsiders—judges and other civilians—may worry that they cannot fairly evaluate military and prison needs. Recognizing that they are not expert, these civilians may defer to professional judgments about these matters.[2] These considerations are the context for the more specific subjects of this chapter: an illustration of constraint drawn from the military and a review of some analogous issues within prisons.[3]

MILITARY RESTRICTIONS ON WEARING HEADGEAR: THE PLIGHT OF THE ORTHODOX JEW

In the most famous free exercise case about military demands, Simcha Goldman, an Orthodox Jewish rabbi serving as a psychologist at a mental health clinic who felt a religious obligation to wear a yarmulke, covering his head before God, challenged an air force regulation that forbade the wearing of headgear indoors.[4] The case record suggests a retaliatory motive for the sweeping order that Goldman not wear the yarmulke any place indoors;[5] but, as the Supreme Court did, we shall consider the regulation at face value, asking whether it was justified and whether people like Goldman should have received exemptions.

The military, uncontroversially, imposes uniform dress requirements that reinforce the sense that its personnel belong to a united force, subject to strict discipline. Dress standards also assure that styles and quality of clothing do

[2] For courts, this deference may extend to judgments made by Congress, partly on the basis of expert evaluation, about military matters. See *Rostker v. Goldberg*, 453 U.S. 57 (1981).

[3] Military and prison life also raise a rather different kind of problem. Government authorities may provide clergy or encourage religious practice in various ways. These supports to religion, which raise establishment problems, are discussed in volume 2.

[4] *Goldman v. Weinberger*, 475 U.S. 503 (1986). This regulation was replicated in the other branches.

[5] For a long time Goldman was permitted to wear his yarmulke while performing hospital duties; after he wore it when testifying for a court-martialled defendant, he was told not to violate the regulation outside the hospital; after his attorney protested, he was ordered not to wear the yarmulke even in the hospital. On appeal, Goldman did not pursue the claim that application of the regulation was unjustified in this instance even if the regulation itself was valid.

not highlight divergent social backgrounds. Were nothing else involved, a requirement that headgear be worn outdoors but not indoors would be perfectly reasonable. The crucial questions are whether the religious reasons that some personnel have to wear a form of headgear indoors render any general rule against that unwise, or call for an exception.

About other aspects of personal dress, the rules were more flexible. Service personnel could wear up to three rings and an identification bracelet; these could be of individual design, and might include emblems of religious or ethnic identity.[6] The image of a "disciplined service member," according to the regulation, "excludes the extreme, the unusual, and the fad." Personnel could also wear religious symbols underneath ordinary uniforms. The allowance of rings, bracelets, and concealed items left ample latitude for Christians to wear articles with religious significance.

Should the regulations have adopted a similarly flexible approach to headgear? Perhaps not. Soldiers wear their military headgear outdoors; few will strongly want to supplement their military caps or helmets with embellishments.[7] And few will regard the indoor rule of no headgear as frustrating their ambitions to maintain a desirable personal appearance. If the rule is to accommodate personnel who wish to cover their heads for religious or cultural reasons, the better approach may be to create a specific exception to the "no headgear" rule, rather than to allow any head covering that is not "extreme" or "faddish."

Should there be any exception and, if so, how should it be formulated? If we focus on Dr. Goldman's narrow circumstances, we might ask whether allowing clinical psychologists (and others with similar jobs)[8] to wear yarmulkes indoors would interfere with military discipline. To most civilians, "no" seems the obvious the answer, though some students with military service have urged that, even in such circumstances, enforcing standard dress requirements is important.

Perhaps focusing on so narrow a set of circumstances is a mistake. Drawing a line among classes of military personnel could be difficult, and one might believe that granting psychologists a privilege to wear yarmulkes that is denied ordinary soldiers would produce resentment and be unfair. We might formulate the crucial question as whether Orthodox servicemen, in general, should be forbidden to wear yarmulkes indoors. Many civilians would still answer "no," that the occasional sight of yarmulkes indoors could hardly disrupt discipline.

[6] *Goldman*, note 4 supra, at 517–18 (Brennan, J., dissenting).

[7] One can certainly imagine soldiers who would like to have some accessory on their caps or helmets, but such wishes reasonably yield to the desirability of uniform appearance.

[8] Here, one major feature of a similar job might be distance from fighting units.

More serious doubts arise if we draw other analogous claims into the circle. Sikhs believe they should wear turbans both indoors and outdoors; an exception broad enough to satisfy Sikhs would demand relief from the rule requiring personnel to wear military caps. In our culture, a turban is much more distracting than a yarmulke, partly because it is more noticeable but mostly because it is more exotic. One might think that allowing turbans would be undesirable, and that allowing yarmulkes but not turbans would be unfair.

This concern is troubling. Few Sikhs are now in the American armed forces, but, given the long history of military service by Sikhs within India,[9] that may be largely because the modern United States military has not accommodated to their religious sense of appropriate dress. An exception for Orthodox Jews would not make Sikhs worse off practically. They are unable to wear their turbans, whether or not the headgear rule has a limited exception for someone else. Largely because turbans are an impediment to safety and yarmulkes are not, fairness to Sikhs is not a particularly powerful basis to deny a privilege to Jews. But it is also important that the primary unfairness in the regulations was in favoring the majority religion: by allowing rings, bracelets, and symbols underneath uniforms, they effectively allowed the expressions of religious identity most Christians would want. An exception for Orthodox Jews would have increased fairness overall, not diminished it.[10] And, indeed, after the Supreme Court rejected Goldman's claim, Congress responded that members of the armed forces should be permitted to wear pieces of religious apparel that are "neat and conservative" and

---

[9] According to one author, Sikhs once constituted almost a quarter of the British Indian army and now compose about 10 percent of the Indian military. Khushwant Singh, *The Sikhs* 11 (Sigra, Varanasi: Lustre Press 1989).

Orthodox Sikhs believe they are required to wear their hair and beards unshorn; this practice would also conflict with standard military requirements. Interestingly, from 1958 to 1974 the army specifically exempted conscripted Sikhs from regulations about hair and headgear; in 1974 the exemption was extended to cover enlisted Sikhs; the exemption was eliminated in 1981, because other groups sought similar exemptions, and because long hair and beards were deemed to impair the effectiveness of using gas masks against chemical attack. See *Khalsa v. Weinberger*, 779 F.2d 1393, 1395 (9th Cir. 1985), which also indicates that the elimination of the exemption did not apply to the approximately fifteen Sikhs on active duty. Under a doctrine of limited review of military regulations, that court rejected the claim of a Sikh that the army's refusal to process his enlistment because he could not comply with hair and dress regulations violated his free exercise rights. The same court earlier reached the same conclusion about a navy rule requiring standard uniforms, on the basis that helmets (incompatible with Sikh turbans) were crucial to safety aboard ships. *Sherwood v. Brown*, 619 F.2d 47 (9th Cir. 1980).

[10] I am assuming here that the "favoring" of Christian practices counts as unfair to a degree even if it is not explicit or self-conscious. Were most citizens Jewish, the regulations certainly have looked different; if those making the regulations had been as concerned with Jewish symbols as Christian ones, yarmulkes would have been allowed.

would not interfere with military performance.[11] Implementation was left to the Department of Defense, which in turn give unit commanders substantial discretion to address a range of claims for religious accommodation; but the aim of Congress to permit Jews to wear yarmulkes was plain.

For these various reasons, the government should provide an exception that specifically refers to yarmulkes, or is cast in general terms that would apply to them and to other modest headgear worn for religious reasons.

CONSTITUTIONAL PRINCIPLE

When Dr. Goldman's claim arrived at the Supreme Court,[12] many scholars thought that he would win easily. According to the prevailing constitutional standard, a regulation could interfere with a religious practice only if its application served a compelling interest that could not be otherwise accomplished. Even those who realized that a "compelling interest" did not have to be of overwhelming strength to defeat claims for exemption, could hardly imagine that a court exercising its own judgment would find that the government had demonstrated a compelling interest in applying the "no headgear" rule to Goldman and others like him, whether "others like him" included only Orthodox Jews holding similar positions or all Orthodox Jewish men in the armed forces. Nonetheless, the Supreme Court decided in favor of the air force.

The majority, puzzlingly, failed to enunciate a standard of review. In retrospect, we can see that most of its members were marching down the road toward outright rejection of the compelling interest standard, in favor of the minimal level of review espoused in *Employment Division v. Smith*.[13] If *Smith* was rightly decided, then Goldman properly lost.

We still initially take the Supreme Court opinions at face value, against a background in which the compelling interest approach applied to most restrictions on the exercise of religion. Despite *Smith*, this analysis remains relevant because the Religious Freedom Restoration Act of 1993 (RFRA),[14] adopted by Congress after *Smith*, includes compelling interest language and makes no exception for military or prison situations.[15] Goldman's claim that

---

[11] 10 U.S.C. § 774; see Michael J. Benjamin, "Justice Shall You Pursue: Legal Analysis of Religious Issues in the Army," *Army Lawyer*, November 1998, 1, at 10–13.

[12] *Goldman*, note 4 supra.

[13] 494 U.S. 872 (1990).

[14] 42 U.S.C. § 2000bb.

[15] The theory the Supreme Court relied on to rule that Congress lacked authority to apply the statute against the states, *City of Boerne v. Flores*, 521 U.S. 507 (1997), does not touch the act's continued application against the federal government. See, e.g., Kent Greenawalt, "Why

the military had failed to accommodate free exercise rights would now arise under RFRA.[16]

No justice doubted that Goldman's claim was based on a sincere religious conviction involving a matter of importance; Goldman easily cleared whatever threshold was needed to invoke constitutional review. For the Court, Justice Rehnquist wrote that "courts must give great deference to the professional judgment of military authorities."[17] In light of the professional judgment that standardized uniforms encourage service members to subordinate personal preferences and identities to the group mission, Rehnquist concluded that the First Amendment does not require the air force to accommodate practices that would detract from uniformity. In failing to indicate how courts should review military assertions of need, the Rehnquist opinion provides woeful guidance for other judges.

The other opinions in the case are important not only because of the manner in which they resolve Goldman's claims, but because their perspectives on judicial deference and on the relevance of potential requests by others for similar treatment bear more broadly on how courts should approach problems under the religion clauses. Justice Stevens, with two colleagues, relied in his concurrence mainly on a comparative analysis,[18] testing the rule's validity in relation to various potential conflicts.[19] Referring to Sikh turbans, the saffron robes of Satchidananda Ashram-Integral Yogis, and the dreadlocks of Rastafarians, Stevens emphasized the importance of similar treatment for members of all faiths, and the impropriety of making an exception that depends on most people's reactions to a particular form of dress.[20]

Justice O'Connor's dissenting opinion is mainly interesting because of her unusual rendering of a compelling interest test. She would have found in Goldman's favor because the government's claimed need to restrict him was contradicted by other existing exceptions to absolute uniformity and by the fact that his superiors had allowed him to wear his yarmulke for years. She

---

Now Is Not the Time for Constitutional Amendment: The Limited Reach of *City of Boerne v. Flores*," 39 *William & Mary Law Review* 689, 696 (1998).

[16] If more precise statutory language applied, that would take precedence. Congress effectively created an exemption from the headgear regulation for people like Goldman, after his case was decided. See note 10 supra.

[17] *Goldman*, note 4 supra, at 507. Only Chief Justice Burger joined Justice Rehnquist's opinion without subscribing to another.

[18] Id. at 510–11. He acknowledged that Goldman's wearing of a yarmulke would create little danger of impairing military discipline.

[19] Id. at 512.

[20] Justice Blackmun, in dissent, agreed with Justice Stevens that the air force could justifiably consider the costs of accommodating exemptions similar to the one Goldman sought, but found that the air force had failed to establish it would receive requests for such exemptions from members of less established groups. Id. at 524–27.

urged use of the compelling interest standard of review, favorable to religious claimants,[21] but what she gave with one hand, she took back with the other. Because the "unique fragility of military discipline" often necessitates rigidity,[22] a claimant will win only "[i]n the rare instances where the military has not consistently or plausibly justified its asserted need for rigidity of enforcement, and where the individual seeking the exemption establishes that the assertion by the military of a threat to discipline or esprit de corps is in his or her case completely unfounded."[23] Under this formulation, religious claims would not often succeed.

Justice Brennan criticized the majority for giving uncritical deference to military judgment.[24] Addressing the concern about turbans, saffron robes, and dreadlocks, Justice Brennan said each would have to be evaluated against the reasons for prohibiting them.[25] A reviewing court could defer to rules that have "a reasoned basis in, for example, functional utility, health and safety considerations, and the goal of a polished, professional appearance."[26]

Goldman thus raises two important general questions: (1) What is an appropriate standard of review for military cases? (2) How does the possibility of hypothetical claims by members of other groups figure in a free exercise analysis?

The dissents reveal a kind of trade-off between a formal standard of review and the degree of judicial deference. Everyone agrees that rights of military personnel may be restricted more than those of civilians, and everyone agrees that courts should afford some deference to military judgment. But how do these understandings translate into an appropriate "test"? Courts could use a "rational basis" test, tipping the scales strongly toward the government. If they instead use a compelling interest test, like that specified by RFRA, the degree of deference becomes crucial. If courts required the government to establish a compelling interest and afforded administrative authorities only moderate deference, religious claimants would acquire significant pro-

[21] Id. at 530.

[22] Id. at 531.

[23] Id. at 532.

[24] Id. at 515. Noting in a footnote that he continued to think the compelling interest test is applicable, Brennan asserted that the government could not succeed even under a much more deferential standard. Id. at 516. In his dissent, Justice Blackmun said that the case did not require a determination of how far the ordinary free exercise test should be modified for the military context, because the air force had failed to provide even a minimally credible explanation for its policy. Id. at 526.

[25] Brennan rejected the argument that disparate treatment of Sikhs and Orthodox Jews might be unacceptably unfair, because the existing "neutral" rules resulted in treatment of Christians different from that given both Orthodox Jews and Sikhs.

[26] A footnote suggests that the air force would have no trouble justifying rules forbidding flowing robes and requiring short hair. Id. at 519.

tection, certainly adequate for Goldman to win. Combining a compelling interest test with great deference, as Justice O'Connor does, yields markedly less protection.

The most appropriate standard for reviewing religious claims to be exempt from military rules is an intermediate one, such as the court of appeals used in *Goldman*,[27] a standard that requires the government to show more than a mere rational basis for its regulation but does not insist that it establish a compelling interest that it cannot achieve by alternative means. The government should have to show a substantial reason why an exception is undesirable; judges should make their own independent evaluation, extending only moderate deference to professional military judgment.[28]

The Religious Freedom Restoration Act contains a compelling interest test.[29] Once it has found a substantial burden on religious exercise (obviously met in *Goldman*), a court applying the statute must use that test. The statute does not explicitly address the question of deference. Although courts should not defer as much to military judgment as Justice O'Connor proposes,[30] judges have reasonably concluded that they should afford a measure of deference to military judgment. When the compelling interest test is applied in this manner, its practical effect does not differ much from the intermediate test that is best suited for these problems.

The potential claims of members of other groups complicate any constitutional judgment and the application of RFRA. It is fine if distinctions are based on whether dress is suitable for combat or protecting health. If yarmulkes are allowed indoors, but Sikhs are not permitted to wear turbans on board ships because helmets are necessary for safety, the differentiation is not unfair. But the standard of a "polished" appearance is disquieting, because its application depends partly on social acceptance, that is, on what ordinary people take for granted or find bizarre.

Nevertheless, the use by three justices of possible unfairness to Sikhs and other groups as a basis to reject Goldman's claim was unjustified for three reasons. First, Sikhs were not competing directly with Orthodox Jews. Although some Sikhs might have felt that an exception limited to yarmulkes was unfair and would reinforce attitudes that Jews are within the main-

[27] That court asked if the regulation sought to achieve "legitimate military ends" and was "designed to accommodate the individual right to an appropriate degree." Id. at 506.
[28] An unusual case in which military regulations were not accepted involved a bar against on-base child care providers (not themselves military personnel) having any religious activities during day care in their homes. *Hartmann v. Stone*, 68 F.3d 973 (6th Cir. 1995).
[29] 42 U.S.C. § 2000bb.
[30] It is seriously misleading to combine extreme deference, which is very favorable to the government, with a compelling interest approach, which favors claimants. For the analogous degree of deference to prison officials, see *Cutter v. Wilkinson*, 125 S.Ct. 2113 (2005).

stream of American culture and Sikhs are not, Sikhs were no better off because Jews were forbidden to wear yarmulkes. Second, the accommodation
for items Christians were likely to wear contrasted disturbingly with the
rigidity of the rule that disfavored Orthodox Jews and other minorities.
Third, the military presented no evidence that other groups would advance
similar claims,[31] and the claims that one can easily imagine could be accepted
or could be rejected on uncontroversial grounds such as safety. The mere
possibility that troublesome cases might arise when someone seeking an exemption adopts a form of dress that is compatible with performing military
duties but subjectively distracts others because it is "strange" or "unfamiliar" was an insufficient basis to reject Goldman's constitutional claim, and
it would be an insufficient basis to reject any analogous claims made under
RFRA . However, the potential unfairness to other groups if an exemption
excludes them could be one aspect of a legitimate government interest in
denying the exemption.[32]

The government has more latitude in dealing with military personnel than
in its regulation of ordinary civilians, but neither the special requisites of the
military nor hypothetical scenarios of comparative unfairness should preclude serious judicial review of interferences with religious exercise. The other
major locus of diminished privileges is prison life, to which we now turn.

FREE EXERCISE IN PRISON

Although penal authorities have long assumed that religious practice among
inmates reduces disciplinary problems and the likelihood of recidivism, and
some empirical research supports this view,[33] pervasive prison regulations

[31] However, the Ninth Circuit did report that the army withdrew an exemption previously
given Sikhs, in part because other groups requested similar exemptions. *Khalsa*, note 9 supra,
at 1395. Sikhs themselves have recently made claims to wear turbans as members of police
forces, mainly in Canada but also in the United States. See James Barron, "Two Sikhs Win Back
Jobs Lost by Wearing Turbans," *New York Times*, July 29, 2004, at B3 ("Two Sikhs who were
told they could not wear turbans on the job as traffic enforcement agents will be reinstated and
allowed to wear their turbans, their advisers said yesterday. The two unrelated cases followed
different routes through the legal system but essentially involved similar allegations: both men
said they were denied exemptions from police uniform rules for their turbans, a central element
of daily religious practice for Sikh men"). The military could probably reject on grounds of
safety any form of dress that interfered with wearing a helmet.

[32] If a limited exemption would actually violate the religion clauses, or the Equal Protection
Clause, that would be a decisive reason for no such exemption to be given. If a limited exemption would be somewhat unfair but constitutionally permissible, the government's reason to
avoid it would be less strong.

[33] See, e.g., Todd R. Clear and Melvina T. Sumter, "Prisoners, Prison, and Religion: Religion
and Adjustment to Prison," in Thomas P. O'Connor and Nathaniel J. Pallone, eds., *Religion,*

generate conflicts with various religious practices, including participation in
worship, celebration of special religious holidays, diet, grooming, and the
possession of sacred objects.[34] All American penal systems make concessions
to the religious inclinations of inmates. Reading the relevant cases gives one
the sense that prison officials often are less flexible than they should be, but
reported cases do not reveal all the accommodations officials do grant without being forced to by litigation. According to a study based on extensive
interviews with prison chaplains, these voluntary accommodations are quite
common in many systems.[35] The study classes three basic approaches as
"neutral-restrictive," "neutral-accommodating," and "targeted accommodations." The neutral-restrictive approach is to treat everyone equally by
refusing to accommodate all religious practices that conflict with regulations. Targeted accommodations involve exemptions for those who want to
engage in religious activities that do not threaten prison security or involve
undue cost. What the study calls "neutral-accommodation" is a tactic by
which the religious needs of some prisoners are accommodated by creating
a generic option available to all prisoners. The simplest illustration is diet.
Recognizing that some prisoners, mainly Muslims and Jews, object on religious grounds to eating pork and that other prisoners are vegetarians, a
prison will offer pork-free and vegetarian alternatives for any prisoner who
chooses. The study reports that this approach, similar to that I have recommended for conscientious objection, is employed frequently because it eliminates the resource-intensive screening of claims by individual prisoners and
the resentment that may arise if a few individuals receive the benefit of a
targeted accommodation.[36] That approach is also a convenient way to reduce
the possibility of lawsuits against prison practices.

A typical example of what seems to be unwarranted hostility or insensitivity to a religious claim is provided by *Friedman v. Arizona*, in which two
Jewish prisoners said that shaving their beards would transgress their religious beliefs.[37] Their claim was supported at trial by a rabbi who testified

---

the Community, and the Rehabilitation of Criminal Offenders 125–56 (New York: Haworth
Press, 2002).

[34] See "Developments in the Law, IV. In the Belly of the Whale: Religious Practice in Prison,"
115 Harvard Law Review 1891, 1904–14 (2002); G. De Groot, ed., Religion Behind Bars,
Corrections Compendium 23(4), 8, 17–19 (April 1998). Marci A. Hamilton, in God vs. The
Gavel: Religion and the Rule of Law 156–62 (New York: Cambridge University Press, 2005),
emphasizes the cumulative effect on prison officials of having to respond to a multiplicity of
claims for special treatment.

[35] See "Developments," note 34 supra.

[36] Id. at 1899–1900.

[37] 912 F.2d 328 (9th Cir. 1990). See generally, Abraham Abramovsky, "First Amendment
Rights of Jewish Prisoners: Kosher Food, Skullcaps, and Beards," 21 American Journal of Criminal Law 241 (1994).

that some segments of the Jewish community regard wearing a beard as fundamentally important. Although the prison permitted one-quarter-inch beards for medical reasons, no exception was made for religious reasons.

According to the state's witness, the rule forbidding beards aided in rapid and accurate identification, which was needed for conducting prisoners' day-to-day activities (such as going to meals and the inmates' store), for controlling disturbances, and for catching escapees. Prisoners with beards could change their appearance quickly by trimming them differently or shaving them off. And a religious exemption for two Jewish prisoners would lead others to claim to be Jewish or to want a similar exemption by virtue of belonging to other groups, such as Sikhs or Muslims. Outsiders may be ill-equipped to evaluate claims related to prison order, but let us try. Insofar as people without beards are simply easier to identify individually than those with beards, the wearing of beards by a small percentage of a group should not make the individuals in the group much harder to identify. (One can quickly tell that those with beards are not any of the individuals without beards, and vice-versa.) For day-to-day activities, such as going to the inmate store and meals, the risk of prisoners' changing appearance should not be a significant impediment. Were prisoners told that they could not alter their facial hair without informing the warden, that should largely take care of the problem. No one is going to alter his appearance drastically to get to a meal sooner; and an occasional extra few seconds for identification by guards should be tolerable.

This leaves the risk of a prisoner altering his appearance prior to a disturbance or an escape.[38] This risk's gravity would depend on the size of the facility, the dangerousness of the inmates, and the exact methods of control and identification. That eighteen of twenty-nine states surveyed allow beards suggests that the risks are not severe.[39] Refusal to grant a claim to wear a beard represents a strong priority for considerations of order against perceived religious needs.

Constitutional claims by prisoners have generally failed, in large part because courts, hesitant to second-guess the judgments of prison officials about what security requires within their institutions, have employed standards of review that are highly favorable to prison authorities.[40] As far as the formali-

[38] The witness did not mention it, but if some prisoners have beards, a clean-shaven inmate might feign a beard in order to pass as one of the prisoners with a beard. Other concerns about beards and long hair are that they may be a hiding place for contraband, signal a gang affiliation, or pose a health risk. "Developments," note 34 supra, at 1909.

[39] Id. at 1910. That conclusion is bolstered by the fact that medical exceptions have not generated any serious problems.

[40] On deference to prison authorities, see *Jolly v. Coughlin*, 76 F.3d 468, 475–76 (2d Cir. 1996); *Hamilton v. Schriro*, 74 F.3d 1545, 1554 (8th Cir. 1996). A range of cases is reviewed

ties are concerned, the exact standards of federal constitutional law and related federal enactments have shifted over the years, but the practical results for prisoners have not changed radically. In rough outline, the formal standards have been these: (1) prior to 1990, courts reviewed free exercise claims under a standard that was highly deferential to prison authorities; (2) in 1990, *Employment Division v. Smith* indicated that no accommodations had to be made to religious claims to be free of burdens resulting from general regulations;[41] (3) the Religious Freedom Restoration Act of 1993 established a compelling interest test for free exercise claims, creating no exceptions for military and prison claims—thus, apparently, establishing a more favorable standard for prisoners than had existed before *Smith*;[42] (4) the Supreme Court held the act invalid as it applied to states and localities, leaving its status for the federal government uncertain—for federal free exercise claims against states, the standard of *Smith* once again dominated; (5) Congress in 2000 adopted the Religious Land Use and Institutionalized Persons Act, which reinstated the compelling interest standard of review for prisoners in programs or activities that receive federal financial aid or affect interstate commerce;[43] (6) after circuit courts of appeals divided over whether the accommodations to religion that RLUIPA requires are permissible or unacceptably favor claims of free exercise over other claims of fundamental rights, thus violating the Establishment Clause,[44] the Supreme Court unanimously held that granting exemptions based on the religious claims of prisoners was appropriate.

---

in John W. Palmer and Stephen E. Palmer, *Constitutional Rights of Prisoners* 91–122 (6th ed., Cincinnati: Anderson, 1999); Barbara B. Knight and Stephen T. Early, Jr., *Prisoner's Rights in America* 187–213 (Chicago: Nelson-Hall, 1986).

[41] *Smith* left some room for argument that if some individual exceptions were granted, religious claims also needed to be considered.

[42] The Senate narrowly defeated an amendment that would have excluded prisoners from the law's protections. See Ira C. Lupu, "The Failure of RFRA," 20 *University of Arkansas at Little Rock Law Journal* 575, 583 (1998); Douglas Laycock and Oliver S. Thomas, "Interpreting the Religious Freedom Restoration Act," 73 *Texas Law Review,* 209, 239–43 (1994).

[43] 42 U.S.C. § 2000c-1(b)(1), (2). (The language of RLUIPA covers only state and local prisons, it being assumed that RFRA applies to federal prisons.) It has been suggested that the new act is more generous to religious claims than was RFRA because it specifically says that covered "religious exercise" need not be compelled by or be central to a system of religious belief. § 2000cc-5(7)(A). See "Developments," note 34 supra, at 1895. I believe that what the new act provides in its definitional section is nothing more than the best understanding of RFRA. See chapter 13, infra.

[44] *Cutter v. Wilkinson,* 125 S. Ct. 2113 (2005). The constitutionality of the prison provisions of the act had been upheld in *Charles v. Verhagen,* 348 F.3d 601 (7th Cir. 2003), and in *Mayweathers v. Newland,* 314 F.3d 1062 (9th Cir. 2002). The act has been struck down as to prisoners in *Cutter v. United States,* 349 F.3d 257 (6th Cir. 2003). Among other reasons offered by the court was the suggestion that whether a prisoner had a right to receive racist literature should not depend on whether the literature was religious (thus bringing RLUIPA into play) or nonreligious (thus leaving only a weaker free speech standard of review).

We need not trace all the nuances in these different approaches. Two points are salient. If one looks at formal standards, federal claims of state prisoners should have flourished most after RFRA was adopted and before it was declared unconstitutional in its coverage of states and localities, and again after RLUIPA was adopted. Even then, and most definitely in other periods, a prisoner's prospects for relief have never been promising. One study showed that in reported cases under RFRA, prisoners succeeded in only nine of ninety-nine of the cases that reached trial.[45]

In theory, prisoners might fare better in states that have adopted their own Religious Freedom Restoration Acts, but the slender evidence thus far suggests that that is not likely to happen. A few states actually have statutory language that explicitly treats prisoners' claims less favorably than others. Pennsylvania has adopted a reasonableness test to measure the legitimacy of a restriction;[46] Texas shifts the burden of proof and presumes the validity of prison regulations;[47] Oklahoma prescribes that if an activity directly threatens health, safety, or security, within the prison, the state has a compelling interest in stopping it;[48] Missouri provides a generous version of the relevant circumstances that justify imposing restrictive regulations on incarcerated religious claimants.[49] The few state courts that have decided cases under state RFRA's have not been more enthusiastic about upholding prisoners' claims than their federal brethren.[50]

The beard case whose facts we have examined well represents the sentiments of most federal and state judges. Although the decision was handed down two months after *Smith* was decided, the court applied pre-*Smith* standards:[51] "[W]hen a prison regulation impinges on inmates' constitutional rights, the regulation is valid if it is reasonably related to legitimate penological interests."[52] Under this test, a court considers the impact that accommodation of an asserted right would have, the other means prisoners enjoy

---

[45] Ira C. Lupu, "Why the Congress Was Wrong and the Court Was Right—Reflections on *City of Boerne v. Flores*," 39 *William & Mary Law Review* 793, 802–3 (1998). Sixteen out of sixty-nine nonprison claimants were successful.

[46] Penn. Stat. Ann. tit. 71 § 2405 (g).

[47] Tex. Loc. Gov't Code Ann. § 361.101 (Vernon 1999).

[48] Okla. Stat. Ann. tit. 51, § 254.

[49] Mo. Rev. Stat. § 1.302 (1)(2), 1.307 (4). See James A. Hanson, "Missouri's Religious Freedom Restoration Act: A New Approach to the Cause of Conscience," 69 *Missouri Law Review* 853, 872–74 (2004).

[50] See, e.g., *Steele v. Guilfoyle*, 76 P.3d 99 (Okla. Civ. App. 2003); *Diggs v. Snyder*, 775 N.E.2d 40 (Ill. App. Ct. 2002); *Yasir v. Singletary*, 766 So. 2d 1197 (Fla. App. 2000).

[51] *Friedman*, note 37 supra, at 331. In its first footnote, the court indicates that it did not need to consider *Smith*, since the prisoners lost anyway.

[52] The Supreme Court first employed the approach in a free speech case, *Turner v. Safley*, 482 U.S. 78 (1987), and used it eight days later to a demand for religious accommodation. *O'Lone v. Estate of Shabazz*, 482 U.S. 342 (1987).

to exercise the right, and the availability of a ready alternative that would accommodate the right "at de minimis cost to valid penological interests." These criteria of decision are far more favorable to the government than any moderately serious version of a compelling interest test.

The court had no difficulty deciding that the rule against facial hair served a penological interest.[53] The prisoners could express their religion in other ways, an accommodation would increase difficulties of identification, and no ready alternative was available.[54] Thus, authorities did not have to make an accommodation.[55]

In a more recent case, the Fifth Circuit Court of Appeals reached a similar conclusion, although it remanded to the district court to consider whether it was a violation of equal protection rights to maintain a medical exception to the rule against facial hair without having a religious exception.[56]

As a class, prisoners with free exercise claims have fared poorly in courts. One wonders whether part of the reason is skepticism about the sincerity of some claims that prisoners make and a concern that they are aiming to flout prison rules, as well as a broader lack of sympathy for a situation they have brought on themselves by antisocial behavior. Many rejected claims are asserted by members of the Nation of Islam, hardly a favored group among the American establishment.

Whether courts should accord prison officials the degree of deference they give military officials is doubtful. With adequate information, a judge should be able to comprehend the basic considerations of order and security within prisons more easily than the subtle aspects of military discipline, and none of the realistic prison risks, serious though they are, seems comparable to a concern that military personnel who are not strictly disciplined will fail to perform well in combat. At the least, courts that are in theory applying some version of a compelling interest standard should review failures to accommodate with more rigor than has been typical.[57]

A dissent in a 1985 case, *Hill v. Blackwell*,[58] suggests what more serious review looks like. A Muslim prisoner in the Missouri prison system made a

---

[53] Id. at 331.

[54] Photographing prisoners twice, with and without beards, would not prevent them from altering their facial hair so they would be hard to identify.

[55] See also *Hill v. Blackwell*, 774 F.2d 338, 343 (8th Cir. 1985) (rejecting prisoner's claim to grow facial hair despite district court's judgment that the prison's security rationale was exaggerated).

[56] *Taylor v. Johnson*, 257 F.3d 470 (5th Cir. 2001). The court did not consider whether the grooming policy violated the Religious Land Use and Institutionalized Persons Act, because that claim had not been raised in a timely manner in the district court.

[57] See *Hicks v. Garner*, 69 F.3d 22 (5th Cir. 1995) (vacating dismissal of RFRA challenge to grooming regulations).

[58] *Hill*, note 55 supra, at 348.

claim to grow a beard. Missouri allowed no prisoners to grow beards, except in minimum security facilities. Acting before the Supreme Court had established a standard that was highly deferential to the judgments of prison authorities, the district court had enjoined enforcement of the antibeard regulation on grounds that security concerns were exaggerated. The court of appeals reversed, ruling that although federal institutions and roughly half the states did not have rules against wearing beards, it did not follow that Missouri's need for a strict rule was insubstantial.

Judge Arnold believed that prison officials had not shown a need for such a strict approach, and he pointed to obvious exaggerations and flippant remarks by the only defense witness, the warden of the Missouri State Penitentiary, as suggesting that officials had not made a serious attempt to balance prisoners' religious needs against security concerns.

In upholding the part of RLUIPA that concerns prisons, Justice Ginsburg's opinion for the Supreme Court cited legislative history suggesting that Congress intended continued deference to the judgments of correctional officials;[59] but under federal acts that are designed to protect their religious rights, prisoners deserve at least the degree of judicial testing of security rationales that Judge Arnold essayed.[60] We shall return to the standards of review for a number of prisoners' cases in chapter 13, which deals generally with burdens on religious exercise and the weight of government interests.

---

[59] *Cutter*, note 44 supra, at 2115.

[60] For a contrasting view, see Hamilton, note 34 supra, at 150–65. A recent case that takes RLUIPA as affording significant protection and does not give prison officials exaggerated deference is *Warsoldier v. Woodford*, 418 F.3d 989 (9th Cir. 2005).

CHAPTER 10

Indirect Impingements:
Unemployment Compensation

Oppositions between religious practice and government regulations do not always involve direct conflicts between what the government requires and what a person feels constrained to do for religious reasons. The government may set conditions for the receipt of benefits, such as unemployment compensation, or it may establish rules of behavior, such as Sunday closing for stores, that allow someone to exercise his religious convictions but make it costly.[1] This chapter and the next deal with these topics.

In all states, laid-off workers receive unemployment compensation for some months.[2] To be eligible, workers must be available for work and not have been discharged "for cause."[3] Statutes or administrative standards typically require that someone who seeks unemployment benefits should not refuse an offer of suitable work. Suitable work may include jobs with work on Saturday. This condition creates difficulties for religious Jews and those relatively few Christians who believe that Saturday is a day of worship on which no work should be performed. The leading Supreme Court case involved a Seventh-day Adventist who believed she should not work on Saturday.[4]

In a different kind of case, which this chapter will also discuss, a Jehovah's Witness, unwilling to help make weapons, resigned after being moved to a department that made turrets for tanks.[5]

---

[1] One might view the armed services rule requiring that no headgear be worn indoors in this way, if one focuses on the point of time when someone who wears a yarmulke chooses whether to join a volunteer army. In effect, the government says, "You do not need to join the military, but if you want to have that benefit, you must submit to this condition that is at odds with your religious preferences."

[2] This compensation is temporary, not the final residual form of support for those unable to work. All states have a form of welfare that is less generous than unemployment compensation for people without other sources of income.

[3] *Sherbert v. Verner*, 374 U.S. 398, 401 (1963).

[4] Id.

[5] *Thomas v. Review Board*, 450 U.S. 707 (1981).

Should Any Exemptions from Normal Requirements Be Granted and, If So, How Should They Be Cast?

When the state establishes eligibility standards for unemployment compensation, to what extent should it grant exemptions responsive to claims of religious conscience? If it grants exemptions, how broad should they be?[6]

No state can explicitly prefer Sunday worship over Saturday worship or endorse the idea that religious reasons call on people to rest from work on Sunday rather than Saturday.[7] The issue of accommodation to Sabbatarians becomes more complicated if the reason why a state requires availability for work on Saturday, but not Sunday, is that Sunday is a general day of rest and many businesses are then closed.

Sabbatarians who are unwilling to work on Saturday because of their deep religious convictions should receive unemployment compensation. The ordinary worker who must be available for Saturday work and who gets a job suffers no unfairness;[8] as with conscientious objectors who refuse combat, one might think of the Sabbatarians as, in a significant sense, unable to work on Saturday. Saturday workers suffer no practical disadvantage if the Sabbatarians receive unemployment benefits without being willing to work on that day.[9] The conditions for benefits remain roughly the same for those who do not object to Saturday work, whether or not the law creates a limited exception.[10]

---

[6] More precisely, as far as "just cause" discharge is concerned, the issue may be one of interpretation of what constitutes just cause rather than exemption from a requirement that discharge not be for just cause.

[7] A direct state preference for those who wish to worship and rest on Sunday over those who wish to worship and rest on Saturday would be indefensible discrimination. The greater the erosion of Sunday closing laws and the more extensive the amount of Sunday work, the more a requirement that workers be available for Saturday but not Sunday work begins to look like such discrimination. Were a court to conclude that such discrimination was present, it would apply the principles discussed in chapter 3.

Insofar as people are now required to work to receive welfare, and the government employs those unable to find other work, the government risks such discrimination as an employer if it demands Saturday work of everyone and demands Sunday work from no one.

[8] Most workers prefer a job that includes Saturday work to receiving unemployment benefits. A very few workers may prefer getting unemployment compensation to having a job with Saturday work, but it is not treating equals unequally, it is not unfair, to exempt only those with strong reasons of conscience. A worker who is available for Saturday work but finds no job is given the same compensation as Sherbert, so he suffers no comparative disadvantage.

[9] Matters are quite different if some workers have to work on Saturday because other employees are excused from Saturday work. This problem is discussed in chapter 18.

[10] This generalization is subject to two conceivable qualifications. Payments from the unemployment compensation fund would be reduced if none went to Sabbatarians who refused Saturday work. Over time, were a fund to benefit fewer persons, individual awards might be greater. However, benefits are not calibrated precisely to the number of recipients, and Sabbatarians are such a small slice of the total population that their ineligibility could produce only

No doubt, employers pay more into the fund if more people collect,[11] but this disadvantage is not unfair if all who collect deserve to do so.

A further consideration is raised if a state that insists that applicants for unemployment compensation be willing to accept a job that includes work on Saturday do not have a similar stance about Sunday work.[12] Even granting that the state's reasons for distinguishing between Saturday and Sunday concern a general day of rest, and do not involve intentional religious discrimination, still, the effective privilege for Sunday worshipers is a strong reason to treat Saturday worshipers similarly.

Finally, most people prefer working, even including Saturday work, to receiving unemployment compensation; they do not want to lose their jobs. This general preference for work sharply reduces worries about fraud.[13]

This conclusion that a state should not deny unemployment compensation to Sabbatarians raises questions about classification we have looked at in other contexts. Should the exemption be limited to religious claimants? To members of groups? To those who feel they cannot in principle work on Saturday?

The exemption should not be restricted to those who reject Saturday work in principle;[14] it should include those whose Saturday religious services occur

---

negligible gains for other recipients.

Denial of an exemption for Sabbatarians could actually disadvantage some other workers. If a Sabbatarian needed unemployment compensation so badly he compromised his principles and made himself available for Saturday work, he might end up taking a job that would otherwise have gone to another worker, who would be worse off as a consequence.

[11] Programs are financed mainly by state and federal taxes levied on employers; a few states collect contributions from workers as well.

[12] See, e.g., *Sherbert*, note 3 supra, at 406 (textile workers could not be ordered to work on Sunday in national emergencies). Christopher L. Eisgruber and Lawrence G. Sager, "The Vulnerability of Conscience: The Constitutional Basis for Protecting Religions Conduct," 61 *University of Chicago Law Review* 1245, 1277–79 (1994) regard the granting of unemployment benefits to Sabbatarians as a matter of avoiding discrimination.

[13] Some people do prefer receiving unemployment compensation on a periodic basis, working for a while, receiving compensation, then working again. These people could have an incentive to feign religious reasons for being unavailable for Saturday work, if that would benefit them financially. But lying about unavailability for Saturday work is an unlikely strategy for the periodic worker. If he has previously worked on Saturday, or interviewed for jobs that required Saturday work, he may have a hard time explaining why religion convictions now preclude that work. One can usually avoid getting a job by making a bad impression on prospective employers. For the person who wants to avoid work, that approach seems more promising than declaring unavailability for Saturday work, especially since the latter tactic leaves him vulnerable to getting a job that does not demand such work.

[14] Many Sabbatarians accept an absolute (or nearly absolute) rule against doing work on the Sabbath. The rule is nearly absolute if it allows "work" necessary to save a life or for some other dire emergency. Taking an ordinary job with Saturday work because one otherwise would not qualify for unemployment compensation would definitely not qualify as such an emergency.

during working time, but who would be willing to work at other times on that day.[15] If a central part of a person's religious practice is attending Saturday services, and doing so precludes Saturday work, he has a powerful religious reason not to work on that day. The added opportunity for deceit if such people are allowed to receive compensation is minimal; anyone bent on committing fraud could lie that he was unwilling in principle to work on Saturday.

For those who do object to Saturday work in principle, group membership should not be a condition of qualifying for an exemption. A person whose individual reading of the Bible and personal reflection convinces him that Saturday work violates God's injunctions should receive an exemption available to those whose religious group rejects Saturday work.[16]

An exemption should be limited to religious claimants. Although a person may be convinced she should not work on Saturday without being connected to institutionalized religion, a nonreligious person is extremely unlikely to conclude that Saturday work is wrong in principle. From an ordinary secular point of view, one day is like another; the seven-day week is an arbitrary designation. The human mind is fertile; but a nonreligious person's claim that, in conscience, he cannot work on Saturday because that day of the week is intrinsically special is so improbable the state may disregard it.

The comparison of nonreligious with religious claims becomes more troubling when the reason to avoid work on Saturday is a conflict in available time. Someone might care deeply about a nonreligious meeting that is held only on Saturday, or feel an obligation to spend Saturday with his family.[17] However, a sense of obligation to attend meetings is a matter of degree. Although *some* people feel a heavier obligation to go to nonreligious meetings than do many churchgoers to attend weekly worship, few feel an obligation to attend secular meetings that is at the highest range of the scale. Officials should not have to figure out just how intensely an individual feels she should go to a Saturday meeting and whether non-Saturday meetings of a related kind are available.

Something closely similar is true about family time. Most people prefer not to work on Saturday, partly because Saturday activities involve family.

---

[15] This is the attitude many Christians have about Sunday work.

[16] Similarly, a nonaffiliated individual who concludes that he must engage in a religious activity on Saturday, such as extensive prayer at certain times, that cannot be fitted around a work schedule should be exempted. I do not know if anyone falls into this category.

[17] Interestingly, someone might conceive a responsibility to spend lots of time with children, including the weekend, based on a traditional religion. William P. Marshall, "In Defense of *Smith* and Free Exercise Revisionism," 58 *University of Chicago Law Review* 308, 320 (1991), has argued that "religious belief cannot be qualitatively distinguished from other belief systems in a way that justifies special constitutional consideration."

For parents, being with their children is not just a question of having a good time; it is an important responsibility.[18] Were assertions about family time a basis to be exempted from the state's demand that one be available for Saturday work, the requirement would be effectively undone.[19]

A requirement of availability for Saturday work may well be misconceived in a culture that stresses family values. Perhaps no one with minor children should be compelled to be willing to accept Saturday work as a condition of getting unemployment benefits. The dilemma of whether to work on Saturday can be acute for parents who cannot find adequate child care;[20] and officials should not be deciding whether a particular parent can or cannot get adequate child care at a reasonable price. Many jobs do not require work on Saturday, and the state should not insist that parents of minors who spend weekdays in school hold themselves available for jobs that include work on Saturday.

Nonetheless, *if* availability for Saturday work is imposed as a condition for unemployment benefits, officials should not have to decide whether a parent who wants to spend time with family feels *enough obligation* to qualify for an exemption. Barring an exemption cast in terms of children's ages, potential "family time" claimants should lose, whether their wish for "family time" is related to their religious understanding or is nonreligious.[21]

In summary, only religious claims should qualify for exemption, and these should be restricted to "in principle" objections to Saturday work and to irreconcilable conflicts between such work and participation in worship services and other similar religious activities.

The treatment of Saturday work should extend to other days of the week. A person unavailable for work on a weekday will find it harder to fit religious obligation with ordinary work than someone who cannot work on Saturday, but fairness calls for similar treatment of those whose religious day is neither Sunday nor Saturday.[22]

An unemployed person should not be considered unavailable for work if she declines to take a job that offends her religious conscience—if she is a pacifist unwilling to make arms or a Muslim unwilling to raise pigs for

[18] Many people have a similar attitude about time with elderly parents, but the elderly parents are more likely than young children to be available on weekdays.

[19] Of course, many of those who are unemployed would continue to be willing to take Saturday work, but such a willingness would cease to be an effective condition of receiving unemployment benefits.

[20] The problem may be especially severe for single parents.

[21] Note that a religious person could have a nonreligious desire for family time, that is, a desire to be with family not tightly connected to religious convictions.

[22] However, should a person have religious requirements such as praying all day, that preclude availability for all standard jobs, he should not receive unemployment benefits, which are reserved for people willing to enter the workforce.

slaughter. And a worker who faces a conflict because his work has altered or he has developed new religious convictions should be able to refuse an abhorrent task without losing the chance to get unemployment compensation.[23] For this purpose, he should not have to belong to a religious group, or conform with dominant views of a group to which he does belong.

The claims of nonreligious conscience in respect to *kinds* of work are greater than those concerning days of work. A nonreligious pacifist might be unwilling to make weapons, a strong nonreligious proponent of animal rights might refuse to work on a factory farm, a nonreligious environmentalist might find strip mining unconscionable. As with military service, people with nonreligious objections of conscience to kinds of work should receive an exemption.

A person's objection to a particular form of work will not typically be an obstacle to his finding a job. He can be practically "available for work" even if he has ruled out a few jobs on grounds of conscience.[24] Including nonreligious objections to particular kinds of work in an exemption from rules for unemployment compensation will not significantly increase the dangers of fraud.[25]

Our review suggests an important theoretical lesson. Objections to Saturday work and objections to the nature of a job are highly similar in many respects, yet the former exemption should be limited to religious grounds, the latter not. The crucial inquiries that produce this discrepancy are whether nonreligious claims are likely to have a strength similar to religious ones and whether the inclusion of nonreligious claims will substantially increase difficulties of official evaluation and dangers of fraud.

Constitutional Principles

In 1963, in *Sherbert v. Verner,* the Supreme Court upheld a worker's right to receive unemployment benefits despite her unavailability for Saturday

---

[23] If what produces the loss of work is a refusal to perform a task he regards as unacceptable, it should not matter if he ultimately is discharged or resigns. The discharge should not be treated as "for cause" in a sense that would bar unemployment benefits; the resigning should not be treated as quitting with that consequence.

[24] This could be more troublesome if he has spent most of his life developing expertness in just the sort of work to which he now objects, say experimental work with animals.

[25] With nonreligious claims of conscience about work, the line between "I really do not like this work" and "I object to doing this work as a matter of conscience" may be less sharp than the line between extreme dislike and feelings of religious conscience; but one is talking of relatively few instances.

I want to distinguish here possible "claims of conscience" not to work with particular kinds of fellow employees. Were such reasons admitted as exceptions from ordinary conditions, the

work.[26] When she was originally hired, her textile mill operated only five days a week; but in 1959 all shifts were required to work Saturday as well. As a Seventh-day Adventist, Sherbert was unwilling to work on Saturday, and was discharged. To receive unemployment benefits in South Carolina, a person had to be "available for work."[27] An administrative commission found that Sherbert's unwillingness to work on Saturday constituted a failure to accept suitable work; state courts rejected her claim that the commission's ruling violated her free exercise of religion.

The Supreme Court reversed, setting the basic framework of free exercise law for the next quarter century. Justice Brennan for the Court determined initially that the disqualification burdened Sherbert's exercise of religion. Although the law had not actually prohibited her from living according to her religious beliefs, a law may be invalid "even though the burden may be characterized as indirect."[28]

Referring to a provision dealing with national emergencies during which mills might be open on Sunday, Brennan wrote that its guarantee that workers who were conscientiously opposed could not be compelled to work on that day effected a religious discrimination.[29] But Brennan did not place much weight on the discriminatory aspect of South Carolina's overall approach. Instead, he asked whether South Carolina had a compelling interest to justify the substantial infringement of Sherbert's free exercise; he found no such interest. The argument that allowing an exemption might facilitate fraud had not been made in the lower courts and was not sustained by the record. In any event, the state could succeed only if it demonstrated that alternative forms of regulation could not combat that danger.[30] Justice Brennan concluded that an exemption would not "establish" Seventh-day Adventism but represented neutrality in the face of religious differences.[31] Justice Harlan, dissenting, thought the state could choose to regard religious reasons like other personal reasons, such as the inability to get a babysitter,

---

difficulties of deciding whether intense antipathy had become a genuine claim of conscience would be extremely difficult.

[26] *Sherbert*, note 3 supra.

[27] If someone "failed, without good cause . . . to accept suitable work" offered by the employment office or an employer, the Employment Security Commission determined that the person was ineligible for benefits. Id. at 400.

[28] Id. at 404. Here Justice Brennan relied upon language from a Sunday closing law case discussed in the next chapter.

[29] Id. at 406. See Eisgruber and Sager, note 12 supra.

[30] In a footnote, Justice Brennan remarked that other state supreme courts had treated a conscientious objection to Saturday work as making Saturday employment unsuitable, thereby treating people like Sherbert as available for suitable work. Id. at 407–8.

[31] He also remarked that Sherbert's religious convictions did not render her an unproductive member of society.

that would not relieve someone of the standard requirement to be available for Saturday work.[32]

Sherbert v. Verner raises four basic questions about free exercise law. Does an indirect impingement on religion raise a free exercise problem? Does neutral application of a law not directed against religion raise a free exercise problem? What standard is appropriate for reviewing such interferences with the exercise of religion? With what stringency should that standard be applied?

Sherbert takes an expansive view of "prohibit" in the Free Exercise Clause. A state action can "prohibit" free exercise if its rule penalizes and discourages religious practice, even if it does not forbid it. This position both fits the original understanding of the Free Exercise Clause and, in a society in which government parcels out many conditional benefits, represents a sound modern approach. Because it did not rely heavily on any discrimination between Sunday and Saturday worshipers, the Court plainly decided that neutral applications of valid laws can generate free exercise violations. If *Employment Division v. Smith* was incorrectly decided, as I have claimed, this basic resolution of the *Sherbert* Court was appropriate. Even under the rule of *Smith*, there may be room for constitutional exemptions from unemployment compensation standards, or, more generally, from standards with a range of individualized exceptions.

Sherbert was the first case that explicitly adopted a compelling interest approach for free exercise claims. The test had previously been used for equal protection cases involving suspect classifications, such as racial classifications,[33] and for review of laws infringing free speech rights.[34] In both kinds

---

[32] Justice Harlan assumed that the Court's decision would come out the same way if Tuesday rather than Saturday was involved, and commented that it would be inappropriate for a court to decide if a particular person's religious convictions prevent him from being "productive." Id. at 420 n. 2.

Justice Stewart, concurring, pointed out that South Carolina would deny benefits to a mother unable to get a babysitter on Saturday, but regarded the positive protection of a religious freedom for people like Sherbert as entirely appropriate. Id. at 416.

[33] *See Korematsu v. United States*, 323 U.S. 214, 215 (1944) ("[A]ll legal restrictions which curtail the civil rights of a single racial group are immediately suspect. That is not to say that all such restrictions are unconstitutional. It is to say that courts must subject them to the most rigid scrutiny. Pressing public necessity may sometimes justify the existence of such restrictions; racial antagonism never can"); cf. *Bolling v. Sharpe*, 347 U.S. 497, 499 (1954) ("Classifications based solely upon race must be scrutinized with particular care, since they are contrary to our traditions and hence constitutionally suspect") (footnote omitted) (citing *Korematsu*).

[34] *See NAACP v. Button*, 371 U.S. 415, 438 (1963) ("The decisions of this Court have consistently held that only a compelling state interest in the regulation of a subject within the State's constitutional power to regulate can justify limiting First Amendment freedoms"); *Gibson v. Florida Legislative Investigation Committee*, 372 U.S. 539, 546 (1963) ("[I]t it is an essential prerequisite to the validity of an investigation which intrudes into the area of constitutionally protected rights of speech, press, association and petition that the State convincingly show a

of cases, a court asks whether a law or government practice is valid, not whether an exception should be carved out. In these cases, the government so rarely succeeded in demonstrating a compelling interest that could not be served by less restrictive means that one distinguished scholar called the test "fatal in fact."[35] If *Sherbert* was fundamentally an instance of state discrimination between Sunday worshipers and Saturday worshipers, use of this demanding compelling interest approach would have been entirely unsurprising; religious *discrimination* is no more acceptable constitutionally than is racial discrimination.

Whether the compelling interest test is apt for claims to exemption from nondiscriminatory, generally valid rules—as the Court ruled in *Sherbert*—is much more doubtful. *If* such a test applies at all to such exemption claims, the state should not have to meet *as heavy a burden* as it carries in discrimination cases. Because the Court treated the state's interests as very weak in *Sherbert*, we have little indication just what showing would have enabled the state to succeed.

When one views the circumstances of *Sherbert*, it is hard to argue against the result. The state's interest in denying benefits to Sherbert was indeed weak, and even if one disregards its treatment of Sunday work, South Carolina's regulatory scheme showed an unconcern, an insensitivity, toward Saturday worshipers that one would not have expected had many of its citizenry worshiped on Saturday.[36]

What of the other possibilities, the variations on Sherbert's situation, I discussed as matters of legislative wisdom? A worker facing an unavoidable clash of Saturday worship services and Saturday work would receive the same treatment as Sherbert, whether or not he objected in principle to Saturday work.[37] In contrast to the *Yoder* opinion, the Court in *Sherbet* does not emphasize institutional religion. An unaffiliated individual with a religious belief that work on Saturday is forbidden by God would presumably have

---

substantial relation between the information sought and a subject of overriding and compelling state interest").

[35] Gerald Gunther, "Foreword: In Search of Evolving Doctrine on a Changing Court: A Model for a Newer Equal Protection," 86 *Harvard Law Review* 1, 8 (1972).

[36] A later case, *Hobbie v. Unemployment Appeals Commission*, 480 U.S. 136 (1987), involved a worker who had become a Seventh-day Adventist after she began her employment in a jewelry store that was open on Friday evening and Saturday. Justice Brennan rejected the argument that converts should be treated less favorably than those whose work has shifted.

In separate concurring opinions, Justices Powell and Stevens suggested that the root of the decisions in *Sherbert* and *Hobbie* was discriminatory treatment. If the state sets up a system of individualized exemptions and refuses to exempt religious claimants, it is discriminating against those claims.

[37] Perhaps the necessity of attending services would count as a conscientious opposition to conflicting work on Saturday.

received similar treatment, a consequence confirmed by a decision a quarter of a century later.[38] Justice Brennan's opinion assumes that those with strong nonreligious reasons to avoid Saturday work have no constitutional right to an exemption.

Nearly two decades after *Sherbert*, the Court reviewed a Jehovah's Witness's objection to helping make turrets for tanks.[39] When he realized that all departments were then engaged directly in the making of weapons, Thomas asked for a layoff, which was denied. His subsequent resignation was regarded by the courts[40] as equivalent to his being fired. Thomas claimed that treating his termination as based on "good cause"[41] amounted to an unconstitutional burden on his exercise of religion.

Chief Justice Burger's opinion for the Court initially rejected the state court's conclusion that Thomas had made a personal philosophical choice rather than a religious one; it was irrelevant that other Jehovah's Witnesses thought work on armaments was acceptable, that Thomas may have been struggling with his beliefs, and that he could not articulate them precisely. "[R]eligious beliefs need not be acceptable, logical, consistent, or comprehensible to others in order to merit First Amendment protection."[42] A court's narrow function was to examine an individual's own convictions to decide if he terminates work because he believes his religion forbids it.[43] Absent evidence that giving benefits to people like Thomas would burden the unemployment fund or necessitate detailed inquiry into religious beliefs, the state's claimed interests in denying benefits were insufficiently compelling.[44]

Thomas, like *Sherbert*, seems to make success turn on having a religious basis for refusing to work.[45] But should that matter? If religious pacifists cannot be barred from unemployment benefits if they refuse to make arms, why should not the same be true of nonreligious pacifists? This equality is, I have argued, constitutionally required for conscientious objection to mili-

---

[38] See *Frazee v. Illinois Employment Security Dept.*, 489 U.S. 829 (1989) (unwillingness to work on Sunday based on Christian belief but not institutional membership).

[39] *Thomas*, note 5 supra.

[40] Thomas might have presented himself at the factory, refused to work, and been dismissed. The resignation did not make a legal difference.

[41] One was ineligible for compensation under the statute if his employment was terminated upon a "good cause [arising] in connection with [his] work."

[42] Id. at 714.

[43] Id. at 718–19. John H. Garvey, "Freedom and Equality in the Religion Clauses," 1981 *Supreme Court Review* 193, challenges the notion that the government restricted Thomas's choice by withholding benefits: he regards the real issue in the case as one of equality, not freedom.

[44] Id. at 718–19.

[45] The Supreme Court explicitly rejected the state court's bizarre conclusion that Thomas's reasons were not religious.

tary service. The result should be the same here. Because few people accept jobs whose tasks they find abhorrent,[46] most will object strongly to their duties only if they undergo a marked shift in their beliefs or their employers alter work demands. Although such instances of nonreligious conscientious refusals to do work must be rare, a court should nevertheless inquire whether a particular kind of objection to work is likely to arise on nonreligious grounds, treating nonreligious and religious claims similarly when claims of comparable intensity are easily imaginable and nonreligious claims present no special dangers of fraud.

In *Employment Division v. Smith*,[47] the Court explicitly accepted the *Sherbert* line of cases. Thus, the compelling interest test (in some form) still applies to unemployment compensation claims. The *Smith* Court hesitated to overrule a well-established line of decisions, but the opinion suggests two other bases for treating *Smith* differently from *Sherbert*.

Passages in the opinion read as if, whatever else may be true, the Free Exercise Clause never authorizes disobedience of criminal prohibitions. Does this mean *Smith* does not apply when crimes are not concerned? The state's interest in enforcing its criminal law is greater than its interest in maintaining conditions for benefits, but the impairment of religious exercise is also greater when someone is absolutely forbidden to engage in a religious practice than when he "merely" sacrifices benefits. Any suggestion that *in general* people should have more vital free exercise rights against inconvenient conditions than against outright prohibitions is wholly unpersuasive.[48]

The second possible ground of distinction between *Smith* and *Sherbert* has more appeal: if a state creates a variety of exceptions to some standard requirement, it must allow those with strong religious claims to qualify for an exception. Thus, if people may be excused from jury service for a number of reasons, perhaps a state must excuse those who are conscientiously opposed on religious grounds to such service.[49] The *Smith* opinion is unrevealing about just what schemes the Court might treat in this way.

The *Smith* Court does not acknowledge the obvious point that the most basic grounds for its decision can apply when a legal scheme incorporates

---

[46] A refusal to take a job because one strongly objects to its particular duties would not render one unwilling to take suitable work.

[47] *Employment Division v. Smith*, 494 U.S. 872 (1990).

[48] Various Supreme Court opinions dealing with indirect interferences support this conclusion by assuming that a free exercise argument would be even stronger if a claimant faced a direct prohibition.

[49] After *Sherbert*, the Supreme Court remanded a jury case and the Minnesota Supreme Court held that an objector to jury service had a free exercise right not to serve. *In re Jenison*, 125 N.W.2d 588 (1963). Of course, that case does not tell what the result should be after *Smith*.

various exceptions.[50] The difficulties of courts passing on sincerity, religious importance, and compelling interest can arise in circumstances like *Sherbert* every bit as much as in cases involving direct prohibitions. These truths create doubt that the present Court will expand on the *Sherbert* class of free exercise rights to most other areas in which administrators make individualized evaluations whether persons or organizations will gain privileges or enjoy benefits.

---

[50] The condition-prohibition line is not the same as the absolute rule–other exemptions line. For example, jury service, like military service is mandatory, but people with pressing reasons can be excused. A condition, without exceptions, of holding some jobs is being an American citizen.

CHAPTER 11

Sunday Closing Laws and Sabbatarian Business Owners

Since the country's founding, state laws have required businesses to close on Sunday. A combination of legislative reform and judicial limitation has attenuated these laws, but many states still retain various Sunday restrictions.[1] What exceptions, if any, should a state grant if it chooses to have Sunday closing laws? Of course, such laws create exceptions for emergency needs—at least one pharmacy in a broad geographical area will open so that people can get medicines—and for public pleasure and convenience—buses run on Sunday and people attend professional sports events, concerts, and movies. But these exceptions do not tell us whether store owners should be allowed to stay open on Sunday because their religion requires them to close on Saturday.

To evaluate claims for exemptions, we need to focus briefly on why Sunday closing laws are adopted (a subject that falls within the broad compass of volume 2). In their origins, these laws were designed to induce and enable Christian worship, and they reflected dominant Christian ideas about how people should spend their Sundays. As time passed, a nonreligious rationale emerged: the desirability of a uniform day of rest. As with the ban on peyote and the condition that people be available for Saturday work if they are to receive unemployment compensation, one may question the value of a uniform day of rest. As long as activities are not noisy and do not directly disturb other people, why not let anyone do what he wants on Sunday? Part of the answer is that activities inevitably do affect others. Most directly, a store owner may want to open on Sunday, but his employees may wish to stay home.

A state that selects Sunday as the day of rest is not necessarily pursuing a religious purpose. States must take citizens as they find them. Most people do not want to work on Sunday. *Their* basis may be religious, but the legislature reasonably begins with that preference, whatever its source, and picks Sunday as the uniform day of rest.[2] Its aims need not be religious, any more than

---

[1] Every state but Alaska has some restrictions on Sunday activities. Forty-six restrict the sale of alcohol; more than twenty restrict some other form of business. http://www.libertymagazine.org/article/article view/397/1/71 (published Nov.–Dec. 2003).

[2] It could be argued that the state should disregard any preference that itself is based on religious reasons. But it would not make sense for the government to declare some other day

when it recognizes Christmas as a holiday. To examine the issue of exceptions, we need to assume that the state's underlying aim in picking Sunday is not now religious, whatever the origins of these laws.[3]

Those who seek an exemption from Sunday closing laws do not object in principle to closing on Sunday.[4] Rather, they wish to open on Sunday to compensate for closing on another day. The Sabbatarian store owner—unlike Sherbert—does face a prohibition, but the choice he faces is like hers. Both can follow their religious convictions and suffer financial loss, or they can avoid that loss by foregoing their religious demands and behaving in the way government regulations induce them to behave—opening on Saturday or becoming available for Saturday work.

SHOULD THERE BE AN EXCEPTION, AND IF SO, HOW BROAD?

An exception for Sabbatarians to Sunday closing laws is not unfair to store owners who would like to remain open every day or who have a mundane reason for preferring a day off other than Sunday. Unlike owners who want to stay open every day, the Sabbatarian is willing to close his store one day a week; and unlike those who have ordinary reasons to close on a day other than Sunday, the Sabbatarian has a claim of conscience. Treating the person who is moved by conscience differently from someone who acts out of self-interest or a complex calculation of what is desirable is not unfair.

But in three respects, two directly involving fairness, exceptions to Sunday closing laws prove more complicated than allowing unemployment benefits to Sabbatarians. One concern is interference with the uniform day of rest. As it is usually conceived, the uniformity argument is weak, and it grows weaker still as more and more events take place on Sunday. The basic idea is that the peace and quiet of those taking Sunday off will be disturbed if others work; but given all the activities that are now permitted on Sundays, the opening of a few extra stores will not much affect any general atmo-

---

as the uniform day of rest if the vast majority of its citizens strongly wish not to work on Sunday.

[3] If we thought of Sunday closing laws as fulfilling religious purposes, Saturday worshipers would have a very powerful claim to be exempted. Their religion requires closing on Saturday; forbidding them to open on Sunday would constitute a form of religious discrimination. Indeed, from the standpoint of nonestablishment of religion, states should not be able to choose Sunday as the uniform day of rest if the object is to promote Sunday religious practice.

[4] We could imagine such a person. An atheist, or a religious person, committed to combating Christian notions of rest on Sunday, might positively believe he should do business on Sunday to express his beliefs. For such a person, the laws would directly prohibit activity his convictions move him to undertake.

sphere of peace and quiet. An aspect of the "uniformity" argument with more bite concentrates on families and friends. When businesses operate every day of the week, close family members may have schedules that leave them without any common day off. This reason has more force as it relates to large businesses than to small ones with only one or two employees.

Two other concerns are yet more troubling. The Sabbatarian open on Sunday could have a competitive advantage. Imagine that ten small grocery stores in a neighborhood are all open from Monday through Friday. Nine are open on Saturday and closed on Sunday. One is open on Sunday and closed on Saturday. The store open on Sunday will do more business on that day than any one store open on Saturday, *and* the weekly revenues of each of those other stores will be less than if all stores closed on Sunday, in which event customers would buy products on a different day. This disadvantage of other store owners vis-à-vis the Sabbatarian will not always occur, but its potentiality generates genuine worries about fraud and unfairness. Store owners could have an incentive to feign Sabbatarian convictions, even to join a religious group that worships on Saturday. Minor losses for other businesses are a tolerable consequence of accommodating Sabbatarians, but were the business losses to be very great (because many people prefer Sunday shopping), they would be as regrettable as the plight of Sabbatarians who are hard pressed to survive financially if they close two days a week.

The employees of a Sabbatarian store-owner who is allowed to open on Sunday raise a further dilemma. The owner may need most of his workers on Sunday for work, yet some may believe that worshiping on Sunday is very important. The store owner may end up hiring workers who want Saturday off and do not mind working on Sunday—and many of these will turn out to be his co-religionists.[5]

Were the distribution of various religious persuasions among workers and store owners roughly the same, the upshot of an exception for Sabbatarian store-owners might be equal opportunity for potential workers. But the cost of store owners' hiring co-religionists is not an optimal result in a society that forbids conscious religious discrimination. And, of course, owners and employees may not have the same distribution of religious persuasions.[6]

Whether the government grants store owners a right to remain open on Sunday should rest on a judgment about conditions in general; it should

---

[5] In many communities, people who neither attend worship services nor are disinclined to work on Sunday, along with active churchgoers able to coordinate their schedules to include both worship and work on Sunday, can fill some of these jobs. And one might welcome the opportunities for Sabbatarian workers that an exception for store owners could create.

[6] If a higher percentage of store owners are Sabbatarian, for example, Sunday-worshiping potential employees may suffer a disadvantage.

not depend on an administrator's individualized assessment of employment opportunities and competitive relations for a particular enterprise. My own evaluation is that Sabbatarian owners of small enterprises with few employees should be able to open on Sunday, unless someone offers a convincing showing that, in general, their remaining open will generate a serious competitive advantage. I doubt that such a showing can be made in many parts of the country.

Just who should receive the privilege to be open and work on Sunday? (1) Should the exemption be limited to religious claims? (2) Should a claimant have to participate in a religious (or other) group on Saturday? (3) Should the objection to Saturday work have to be in principle? (4) Should a claimant have to work himself on Sunday? (5) Should a size limit be set for eligible businesses?

Imagining principled nonreligious objections to Saturday work (by people wishing to work on Sunday) is difficult. The claim of the Sabbatarian is sui generis; an exception should be limited to religious claims.

The issue of group membership and participation is harder. Suppose an individual who is not a member of any religious group and does not attend services develops the conviction that God does not want Saturday work. An administrator passing on routine applications of store owners to remain open on Sunday will not know if an individual owner is sincere, and the owner could certainly have an incentive to lie. To guard against insincere claims, a state might reasonably insist that an applicant belong to a religious body with other members who believe that working on Saturday violates God's will. A law might name such religious groups, but should not bar unnamed groups from qualifying as well.

Should the state be in the business of assessing the degree of conviction of someone who belongs to a Sabbatarian religious group? We cannot expect a searching investigation of a store owner's status and beliefs; administrators should not attempt refined evaluations of Orthodox Jews who attend services irregularly and fail to observe some Orthodox Jewish practices. The limited possibility of fraud this introduces is tolerable, *so long as the state can check*, with help from complaining competitors, that a qualifying business does close on Saturday.

The store owner's crucial belief must be that it is wrong in principle to work on Saturday. If his only conflict is between the time of worship services and business hours, he should be able to close his store or have someone else run it while he attends services.[7]

---

[7] If the applicant has an independent craft, like being a carpenter, he can work during Saturday hours other than those in which his religious services take place.

An exception should probably be granted only to owners who work regularly in their businesses,[8] and a limit should be set according to the size of an enterprise. The competitive concerns and worries about indirect discrimination in employment increase tremendously if a Sabbatarian employer has a chain of stores that hires hundreds of employees. The owner's personal convictions should not determine whether so many workers and customers will be drawn away from the uniform day of rest.

CONSTITUTIONAL PRINCIPLES

Two years before the Supreme Court sustained a Sabbatarian's claim to receive unemployment compensation in *Sherbert v. Verner*—which we examined in the previous chapter—it rejected claims that Sunday closing laws established religion and denied equal protection of the laws.[9] In reviewing statutes from Massachusetts, Maryland, and Pennsylvania, the Court acknowledged that the laws' origins lay in protection of Christian worship and Christian ideas about Sunday activities,[10] but it determined that the modern laws were based on the secular rationale of a uniform day of rest.[11] Against the equal protection claims, the Court found that each statutory scheme satisfied minimal requirements of rational classification.

In the central case for this chapter, *Braunfeld v. Brown*,[12] an Orthodox Jew argued unsuccessfully that he should be able to keep his retail clothing store open on Sunday. Chief Justice Warren wrote for himself and three other justices. Having struck the theme that freedom of religious belief is absolute but freedom to act "is not totally free from legislative restrictions,"[13] he noted that the conflict facing Braunfeld was less sharp than when an individ-

---

[8] Many Orthodox Jews believe it is all right to have non-Jewish partners who keep businesses open on Saturday. See Isaac Klein, *A Guide to Jewish Religious Practice* 90–91 (New York: The Jewish Theological Seminary of America, 1979).

[9] *McGowan v. Maryland*, 366 U.S. 420 (1961).

[10] It assumed that were the laws now designed to reinforce Christian practice, they would impermissibly establish religion. Justice Douglas dissented in all the cases, on the ground that the laws prohibited others from working because of the majority's views about Sunday. Id. at 573. (Douglas, J., dissenting in *McGowan v. Maryland*).

[11] The Court relied on changes in the activities the laws curtail and on reasons offered for the laws. A reader of *McGowan v. Maryland*, in which this issue is most fully discussed, is left with the sense that the motivation behind Sunday closing laws remained partly, and significantly, religious. The Court's opinion may reflect the view that courts should assume permissible purposes, rather than impermissible ones, when the two are intertwined, a matter discussed more fully in volume 2.

[12] 366 U.S. 599 (1961).

[13] Id. at 603.

ual must abandon his religious principles or be prosecuted.[14] Although some of Warren's language sounds as if the legislature has free rein when laws merely impose an indirect burden on religious exercise, the crucial passage envisions a more active judicial role. "If the purpose or effect of a law is to impede the observance of one or all religions . . . that law is constitutionally invalid even though the burden may be characterized as being only indirect." But if a law's "purpose and effect . . . is to advance the State's secular goals, the statute is valid despite its indirect burden on religious observance unless the State may accomplish its purpose by means which do not impose such a burden."[15]

Since the effect of a Sunday closing law *is* to "impede the observance" of religions that forbid Saturday work, such a law might be invalid if the state could accomplish its objectives without imposing such a burden. The opinion's subsequent examination of alternatives was, thus, essential to the decision.

Recognizing that a number of states provide exemptions, Chief Justice Warren said "this may well be the wiser solution to the problem."[16] But allowing exemptions might undermine the goal of providing a day free of commercial noise and activity, increase enforcement problems, produce an economic advantage for stores open on Sunday, create a temptation to fraud that would necessitate an inquiry into sincerity, and, finally, induce Sabbatarian store-owners to hire employees who would qualify for an exemption to work on Sunday, a consequence at odds with the state's policy against religious discrimination in hiring. For all these reasons, state legislatures could decide whether to create exemptions; they were not constitutionally compelled to do so.[17]

---

[14] Id. at 605.

[15] Id. at 607.

[16] Id. at 608.

[17] Justice Frankfurter, writing for himself and Justice Harlan for all four Sunday closing law cases, covered much of the same ground in more detail. *McGowan*, note 9, supra, at 514 (concurring opinion). According to him, of thirty-four jurisdictions with statutes banning labor or the selling of goods on Sunday, twenty-one states had some exception for Sabbatarians, but only about nine of these exempted Sabbatarians who sold goods. Id. at 514–15. (I include the "about" because Justice Frankfurter treats a few statutes as not clear on the point. Two states with an exemption forbade an exempted person from employing persons not of his belief on Sunday.) Exactly what the state exemptions required varied. Ten demanded that a person claiming an exemption "conscientiously" believe in the sanctity, or "conscientiously" observe as the Sabbath, a day other than Sunday. Five required that someone keep a day other than Sunday as holy time. Four extended the exemption only to members of a religious society observing another day. (Thus, we see that most exemptions covered both those who had a conscientious belief that they should not work on Saturday [or some weekday] and those who worshiped on a day other than Sunday.)

Discussing the possibility of a competitive advantage, Frankfurter wrote that a legislature might worry that someone would pick the slowest day of the week and claim that as his day

In a dissenting opinion, Justice Brennan wrote that the issue was whether a law may put to an individual the choice between his business and his religion. According to Brennan, the Court assumes that "any substantial state interest will justify encroachments on religious practice"; but this "clog" on religious practice could be justified only by a "compelling interest."[18] An inquiry into the good faith of a religious claim is perfectly acceptable and the worry about religious hiring is "almost chimerical," since most state statutes allow hiring on a religious basis if religion is a bona fide occupational qualification.[19] In Brennan's view, the Court should have been more responsive to rights of conscience.[20]

No opinions in the case address how states should classify those eligible for exemptions, if they choose to grant them. But all of the opinions seem to assume that an exemption may be limited to those with religious reasons or even to those with a religious affiliation.

Two comments are in order about how *Braunfeld* relates to *Sherbert*. As Justice Stewart, concurring, points out in *Sherbert*, the economic harm that Braunfeld may suffer, if the combination of state law and religious conviction allow him to be open only five days a week, may be as great as Sherbert's loss if she cannot get unemployment benefits. Adopting a compelling interest standard that the majority in *Braunfeld* rejected two years earlier, *Sherbert* may seem a hardly explicable sea change in the law of free exercise.

The law of Supreme Court decisions is determined by majorities. Most members of the Court who sat on the two cases actually believed that both Braunfeld and Sherbert should have won, or that both should have lost.[21] Even if most voting justices viewed the cases similarly, did those who did not have a defensible position? We have seen fairly powerful reasons why exceptions to Sunday closing laws should be left to legislative choice, even

---

off. Frankfurter referred to the British experience as indicating the complexity of enforcement problems, noting that under Britain's 1950 act, if local authorities believed someone who registered for an exemption did not qualify, a London Committee of Deputies of British Jews had to decide whether the shop occupier was Jewish and held a conscientious objection to trade on the Jewish Sabbath. Id. at 519.

Frankfurter concluded that exempting Sabbatarians might itself entail "a not inconsiderable intrusion into matters of religious faith." Id. at 520. Given the importance of a uniform day of rest, as evidenced by the existence of closing laws over the centuries and in three-quarters of the states, the burdens on Sabbatarian shop owners and consumers were a permissible imposition on their religious freedom.

[18] *Braunfeld*, note 12 supra, at 614.

[19] Id. at 615. Justice Brennan does not explain why a willingness to work on Sunday should be regarded as making religion a bona fide qualification.

[20] Id. at 616.

[21] Only Chief Justice Warren, Justice Black, and Justice Clark were in both majorities, Justices White and Goldberg (who voted for Sherbert) having replaced Justices Whitaker and Frankfurter (who voted against Braunfeld) in the interim.

if a free exercise exemption is granted from the condition of being available for Saturday work. These reasons include enforcement problems and potential for fraud, the possibility that a privilege to remain open on Sunday should depend on economic conditions that vary in different parts of the country, a concern that Sabbatarians with a privilege will hire co-believers, and the desirability of lines of distinction, as between small and large businesses, that statutes or regulations can manage better than can constitutional standards.

Nevertheless, assuming that the compelling interest test represents a sound approach, people like Braunfeld should be granted a free exercise right, absent a state's showing that competitive and employment difficulties are grave.[22] Few states could make such a showing.

---

[22] Even someone who thinks *Braunfeld* should have been decided differently needs to recognize that this judgment is much closer than approval of the result in *Sherbert*.

CHAPTER 12

Government Development of Sacred Property

How far should the government restrict activities of its own, such as land development, because they impinge on religious beliefs and practices? The government decides to construct a dam, build a road, allow timbering, or make an area accessible for recreational use. A group of Native Americans objects that the land is sacred, and that development would destroy the undisturbed natural setting essential for worship at sacred sites. Should the government forego its proposed development? Issues like these differ from any we have yet considered. The government does not demand or forbid actions by citizens; it does not set conditions for receiving benefits. Rather, it behaves in a manner that diminishes opportunities for some people to exercise their religion or that offends their religious convictions.

We can sharpen the central question about land development. When, in a liberal democracy, citizens come forward with reasons why the government should not develop land in a certain way, the government should listen. Thus, if people who want to keep a forest unspoiled oppose building a ski resort in a national park, that sentiment is a reason not to build the resort.[1]

Suppose people oppose development because of their religious beliefs and practices. I assume that, so long as it is responding to the public opinion and not to the intrinsic merit of the religious assertion, the government can count religiously based sentiment at least to the degree that it counts other sentiment.[2]

Should the government give claims about religious use of land some special weight, more than it gives to other intrinsically sound secular sentiments against development, such as environmental protection? To translate this question into institutional terms, should a statute or regulation require that officials consider religious objections, and should judges review such objections as aspects of free exercise law?

We can see the dimensions of this issue best with a sense of the religion of Native Americans. A leading historian of American religious history writes:

---

[1] The citizen sentiment alone counts for something; it should count for more if officials believe the sentiment reflects an independently sound reason.

[2] One might take the contrary view that for government to pay attention to religious reasons offends separation of church and state, in which event citizen sentiment based on religion should carry less weight than nonreligious sentiment. (Although giving religious reasons at least equal weight seems to me the right approach for land development, it may not be right for

With regard to the Indian's religion, the modern American imagination falters. The Christian has considerable difficulty understanding the piety of the Jew (and vice versa), but the spiritual life of the pre-Columbian Indian is removed at another order of magnitude. Beyond this fact is the sheer diversity of cultures. . . . [W]ith distinguished anthropologists disagreeing on the interpretation of individual tribes, generalizations about *all* of the tribes must be of the simplest sort. . . . One can say perhaps that the American Indian, like other peoples, stood in awe and relative helplessness in the face of the mysteries of nature and life. . . . His beliefs were animistic—the world of multifarious forces and things was animated or controlled by a hierarchy of spirits whose acts and intentions could in some degree be interpreted or conditioned through shamans and by appropriate ceremonies and rituals. . . . [M]ost tribes tended to read the earth and its powers with greater veneration and respect than the Europeans who would cut down the trees and plough up the prairies. It seems clear, too, that the Indian's way of life contrasted sharply with the Puritan view of work and individual advancement. Western acquisitive society with its notions of fee simple land tenure mystified and outraged him. . . . Indians of the Taos Reservation who in 1970 had 48,000 acres of land returned to them made their plea on religious grounds—this land was sacred to them, nature is their church, Blue Lake their *sanctum sanctorum*. Essential to our understanding, however, is the fact that the religion of each of the many tribes and nations upon which the white man intruded was a functional element of its culture. The sanctions and consolations of religion were and are intricately related to a whole way of life.[3]

We can conceive of groups of Christians or Jews objecting to land development as violating a kind of sacred location. If Christians believed Jesus was crucified in South Dakota rather than Jerusalem, on land now owned by the government, Christians would be shocked if the government proposed to build a gambling casino on the site. But even this extreme hypothetical does not capture the claim of the Native Americans, because Christians do not believe particular geographical locations are sacred in the way that Native Americans do.

Should the Government Accommodate Religious Claims and, If So, Who Should Benefit?

The government should show respect for all kinds of religions, foregoing some activities that would severely impair religious practices.[4] The history

---

choices of public school textbooks. Declining to develop land does not impose opinions on others in quite the same way as choosing texts.)

[3] Sydney E. Ahlstrom, *A Religious History of the American People*, vol. 1, 144–45 (Garden City, N.Y.: Doubleday, 1975).

[4] Australia has legislation to protect sites that are of special importance for Aborigine religion and culture. For federal legislation, see Aboriginal and Torres Strait Islander Heritage Protection Act 1984 and Australian Heritage Council Act 2003.

of Indian tribes in the United States bears on why the government owes special sensitivity to Native American religious concerns. Most federal land was once the domain of groups of Indians, and much of its transference into the hands of settlers of European origin was gravely unjust. Moreover, the federal government long aimed to suppress "primitive" Native American religions in favor of Christianity. The tie between Native Americans and areas of land, the history of unjust transfers, and the outright suppression of their religions combine to give Native Americans a powerful claim to have the government protect their religious practices.

Officials need to strike a balance between a project's importance and its interference with religious exercise, reaching resolutions on a case-by-case basis. Because isolated individuals with religious views should rarely be able to block land development the government deems desirable, officials usually need to give serious consideration only to objections that groups make. The more people whose religious practice will be impaired, the weightier their claim to have the government desist.

Should the claim have to be religious? Citizens might well have a nonreligious attachment to a site of land; descendants of immigrants processed at Ellis Island might be deeply offended if the government constructed a resort hotel on the island.[5] But such objections belong in the ordinary mix of views officials take into account; they need no special formal status. A formal requirement of accommodation can reasonably be limited to religious claims.[6]

This leaves the question of whether a law or regulation requiring accommodation should name religions. Among religions now practiced in the United States, apparently only Native American religions treat as sacred tracts of land owned by government. But it would be a mistake to limit claims warranting special consideration to those made by organized groups of Native Americans; a law should not foreclose the possibility that another religious group might unexpectedly make a similar claim.

---

[5] See Robert Hanley, "Park Service Backs Demolition on Ellis Island," *New York Times*, November 23, 1991, at 25 ("After fighting for years to save all 32 historic buildings on Ellis Island, the National Park Service has endorsed a plan to demolish 12 small, crumbling structures to provide room for a $140 million conference center with 325 hotel rooms, a restaurant and shops").

[6] Objections to development might be raised by distinctive cultural groups, but any cultural claims that rose to the intensity of religious claims about sacred sites would themselves probably be partly religious.

Of course, accommodations may also be accorded on grounds that public policy supports, but which may be presented by private groups, such as environmental harm. Religious grounds are different in that the government does not endorse the validity of the religious viewpoint involved.

CONSTITUTIONAL PRINCIPLES

Discerning sound constitutional principles for land development is much more complex than ascertaining desirable policy. Perhaps the most fundamental question is whether courts are equipped to render the necessary evaluations; but there is also a conceptual issue whether the government's land development can constitute a "prohibition" of religion. The Supreme Court considered these issues in 1988 in *Lyng v. Northwest Indian Cemetery Protective Association*,[7] when Native Americans objected to a timber road project in a national forest. To put that case in context, we need to step back to the Court's rejection two years previously of a Native American complaint about government activities.

In *Bowen v. Roy*, parents objected to government use of the Social Security number of their daughter, Little Bird of the Snow,[8] and to their having to supply that number when they applied for benefits. According to the parents' Native American beliefs, a person needs control over his life for spiritual purity; modern technology is "robbing the spirit of man," and uses of the Social Security number will "rob the spirit" of their daughter.[9]

Eight justices agreed that the government could use the number for its own purposes.[10] In the key sentence of the Court's opinion, Chief Justice Burger wrote, "The Free Exercise Clause simply cannot be understood to require the Government to conduct its own internal affairs in ways that comport with the religious views of particular citizens."[11] Because the government's use of a Social Security number does not impair anyone's freedom to exercise his religion, the Court had no occasion to balance the government's need against a possible religious detriment.

The Court's treatment of the parents' claim that they should not be required to supply the Social Security number was more complicated, but a majority of five justices actually voted to sustain the claim.[12] They regarded the standard free exercise compelling interest test as applicable, and concluded that the government's ability to combat welfare fraud would not be

[7] 485 U.S. 439 (1988).

[8] 476 U.S. 693 (1986). Initially, the parents objected to obtaining a number for their daughter, but on the last day of the trial it was discovered that the government had already assigned a Social Security number to Little Bird of the Snow.

[9] Id. at 696.

[10] Justice White thought that *Thomas v. Review Bd.* and *Sherbert v. Verner* were controlling and that the parents should succeed. 476 U.S. at 699.

[11] 476 U.S. at 699.

[12] Some justices doubted that the Court should have resolved that issue, because it was not clear that the parents would ever have to supply the number.

much compromised if those with religious objections did not have to supply Social Security numbers.[13]

In *Lyng v. Northwest Indian Cemetery Protective Association*,[14] the Supreme Court tackled the more troublesome matter of objections to land development. Courts of appeals had already resolved a number of these cases, and in *Lyng* the Court of Appeals for the Ninth Circuit had sustained the religiously based objection to the Forest Service's completing a road in the Chimney Rock area of the Six Rivers National Forest. The Service had commissioned a study that recommended that the road not be built, because successful religious use of the area by three tribes depended on "privacy, silence, and an undisturbed natural setting."[15] The court of appeals ruled that the government had failed to show a compelling need to build the road.

The Supreme Court, by a five-to-three margin, rejected the Native Americans' free exercise claim. Justice O'Connor, for the Court, relied first on a conceptual argument that the government practice did not "prohibit" the free exercise of religion; she also offered a more complex argument about the difficulties courts would face in such cases.

O'Connor's conceptual argument conceded that the road might severely affect the claimants' religious practice.[16] Although it was uncertain whether the road would be "so disruptive that it will doom their religion," the claimants should lose even if the road would "virtually destroy the . . . Indians' ability to practice their religion."[17] This ambivalence about the road's likely damage reflects a common perplexity when people consider religions that differ radically from their own. An outsider is inclined to say, "Look, the road may make the high places used for religious rituals a little less private, quiet, and serene, and that may disturb participants at first; but everyone will adjust and things won't change very much." But an outsider is poorly placed to evaluate just how severely religious exercise is impaired when a

---

[13] 476 U.S. at 724 (opinion of O'Connor, J.); id. at 712 (opinion of Blackmun, J.); id. at 733 (opinion of White, J.).

Chief Justice Burger wrote for three justices that parents could be required to furnish the number as a condition of receiving AFDC benefits. For a law administering benefits for millions of people that is facially neutral and uniformly applied, it is enough that it "is a reasonable means of promoting a legitimate public interest." Id. at 708. The Burger opinion indicated that a free exercise claim against an outright prohibition would have more strength than one made against a condition imposed for securing benefits. Id. at 706.

[14] *Lyng*, note 7 supra.

[15] Id. at 442. The Forest Service rejected this recommendation, but it did select a route as far removed from the sacred sites as possible. It also adopted a proposal to allow timber harvesting in the area. Subsequently Congress designated the location as a wilderness area, which meant that timber harvesting was forbidden.

[16] Id. at 447.

[17] Id. at 451.

site's quality is somewhat diminished. A Protestant can understand the views of a Roman Catholic who recognizes the authority of the pope, or of a Jew who does not regard Jesus as divine; but grasping the belief that the welfare of tribes, or even of mankind, depends on ceremonies being performed at specific undisturbed sites is much harder.[18]

In any event, O'Connor's conceptual argument does not turn on the likely effect of the road. The constitutional word "prohibit" is critical; the Free Exercise Clause is not implicated if incidental effects of government programs make the practice of religion more difficult but "have no tendency to coerce individuals into acting contrary to their religious beliefs."[19] According to this conceptual argument, *Lyng*'s result would be the same if the government used the area for a helicopter base or bombing range. These activities might destroy the area for religious ritual, but they would not tend to coerce anyone to behave contrary to his beliefs.

Justice Brennan, in dissent, objected strenuously to the majority's conceptual approach. If a government action restrains people from practicing their religion, that is enough to raise a constitutional question.[20] The government's proposed activities here would restrain religious practice to a "far greater degree" than the conditions on unemployment benefits.[21]

Justice Brennan wins this conceptual argument. To say that a moderate discouragement of religious practice, such as the denial of unemployment benefits, counts as "prohibiting" the exercise of religion but that total destruction of a sacred site does not is strained, even artificial.

How could five justices have accepted O'Connor's conceptual argument? The four justices who joined her were in the majority in *Employment Division v. Smith*, decided two years later. Unlike Justice O'Connor,[22] these justices were poised to abandon all free exercise protection against ordinary laws that are not themselves directed at religion—laws that are general and neutral in the Court's words. These justices cared less about whether a law exerted any coercion than she did.

Justice O'Connor did not rest on the conceptual argument alone; she also emphasized the inability of courts to evaluate the degree of incidental interference with an individual's spiritual activities. "[C]ourts cannot offer to

[18] See id. at 460–61 (Brennan, J. dissenting).

[19] Id. at 450. Land development was not relevantly distinguishable from the government's own use of Social Security numbers. Cases like *Sherbert v. Verner* differed because conditions for benefits encourage individuals to violate their religious convictions.

[20] Id. at 465–66.

[21] Id. at 467. Land development, Brennan wrote, involves substantial external effects, unlike the government conduct of its internal affairs involved in *Bowen v. Roy*. Id. at 467–68.

[22] She showed in *Goldman v. Weinberger* and in *Smith* that she is a strong believer in free exercise protection.

reconcile the various competing demands on government, many of them
rooted in sincere religious belief, that inevitably arise in so diverse a society
as ours."[23]

Justice Brennan's dissent, recognizing the difficulties if all government programs were subject to religious objections of various sorts, referred to two
courts of appeals decisions that indicated that Native Americans must initially demonstrate that the lands are "'central' or 'indispensable' to their
religious practices."[24] A showing of "centrality" should precede the government's having to establish a compelling interest, but "'centrality' should not
be equated with the survival or extinction of the religion itself."[25] At another
point, Brennan phrased his approach somewhat differently: "[A]dherents
challenging a proposed use of federal land should be required to show that
the decision poses a substantial and realistic threat of frustrating their religious practices."[26]

Justice O'Connor objected that this approach would require courts to
"weigh the value of every religious belief and practice that is said to be threatened by any government program."[27] She worried that courts having to decide if beliefs or practices are central would end up saying that some religious
claimants misunderstand their own beliefs. Justice Brennan denied this implication. Religious adherents would be arbiters of which practices are central,
subject only to requirements of genuineness and sincerity.[28]

Justice Brennan's threshold requirement does not, in form, necessitate
courts making their own evaluations of the importance of religious practices;
but the problems are more complicated than he acknowledges. If a test required "centrality" in some form, claimants, with lawyers' assistance, would
say that the practice threatened is "central"; who is to say how "central" is
"central"? Asserting that the eighth most important practice is central is not
to be insincere in any simple sense. And if one grants that religious rituals
in the high places of Chimney Rock are central practices, does the proposed
road pose a substantial and realistic threat to them? The Native Americans
urged that any interference with the undisturbed environment would significantly undermine their rituals, but if the rituals will continue, how severely

[23] Lyng, note 7 supra, at 452.
[24] Id. at 473 (citing courts of appeals cases).
[25] Id. at 474.
[26] Id. at 475.
[27] Id. Ira Lupu criticizes centrality as a standard for judging burdens on free exercise in
"Where Rights Begin: The Problem of Burdens on the Free Exercise of Religion," 102 *Harvard
Law Review* 933, 959 (1989).
[28] The issue, thus, would not be whether claimants understood their religion, but whether
they have demonstrated, as did the claimants in *Wisconsin v. Yoder*, a substantial or realistic
threat of undermining or frustrating their religious practice. Id. at 475.

will a modest interference with the setting affect them? Is an honest assertion that the road will undermine the practices "very greatly" sufficient to show a substantial and realistic threat? Courts would have to choose whether to take such claims at face value, to themselves evaluate the practices of the religion, or to inquire more deeply into the perceptions of practitioners about the road's effects.

Another difficult aspect of evaluation is estimating the government's interest in developing its land, and, if comparison is relevant, comparing that interest to the interference with religious practices. In this respect, *Lyng* is easy; the government's interest in building the road was slight. But courts could well find that government interests of greater strength were supporting activities, such as the building of a major highway through a mountain pass that constituted by far the most economical route, that inflict serious interference with religious practices.

Perhaps courts can deal with all these complexities, but they do give one pause whether judges should be dealing with objections to government development of federal lands as constitutional free exercise cases. Indeed, we have seen that the Court in *Employment Division v. Smith* thought these complexities were disturbing enough to justify general rejection of constitutional claims for exemption from neutral laws. We shall explore these delicate issues in the next chapter.

NONCONSTITUTIONAL LEGAL PROTECTION

The decision in *Lyng* leaves the protection of religious practices on federal lands up to the political branches. In *Lyng*, both Justice O'Connor and Justice Brennan discussed the American Indian Religious Freedom Act (AIRFA),[29] enacted in 1978. That act did not create legally enforceable rights, but it did provide a formal statement of a policy to preserve the exercise of traditional religious practices, including access to sites.[30]

Various efforts to strengthen AIRFA to create legally enforceable rights have not succeeded.[31] Congress has, however, adopted protective legislation dealing with particular lands. For example, in the El Malpais National Monument and Recreation Area, Congress has authorized the secretary of the interior to close entry to the general public to one or more specific areas "in

[29] Pub. L. No. 95–341, 92 Stat. 469 (sec. 1 codified in 42 U.S.C. § 1996).

[30] Justice Brennan believed the act showed that land practices were not regarded as "internal" government procedures and should be subject to constitutional challenges.

[31] The Religious Land Use and Institutionalized Persons Act of 2000 apparently does not apply to government development of its own land.

order to protect the privacy of religious activities . . . by Indian people."[32] And the National Park Service adopted a plan for the Devil's Tower National Monument in Wyoming that asked rock climbers voluntarily to refrain from climbing Devil's Tower during June when Native Americans engage in traditional ceremonies.[33] More broadly, President Clinton issued an executive order instructing federal administrative agencies to, among other things, "accommodate access to and ceremonial use of Indian sacred sites by Indian religious practitioners and avoid adversely affecting the physical integrity of such sacred sites."[34]

The Religious Freedom Restoration Act, which apparently remains valid in its application to federal activities, might conceivably be relevant. The act itself does not specify whether the kind of interference with religious practice involved in *Lyng* counts as a burden on religious exercise. However, legislative history suggests that the act did not broaden the Supreme Court's approach to what constitutes a burden.[35] Claimants opposing land development could succeed under the act only by persuading a court that the act's concept of burden on religious exercise is more generous than was the Supreme Court's constitutional approach in *Lyng*.[36]

---

[32] 16 U.S.C. § 460 uu-47(c)(199). See Mindy Sink, "Religion and Recreation Clash at Park," *New York Times*, July 1, 1996, at A8.

[33] See *Bear Lodge Multiple Use Assn. v. Babbitt*, 175 F.3d 814 (10th Cir. 1999). A challenge to the plan as impermissibly establishing religion failed in the district court. The court of appeals ruled that the plaintiffs lacked standing. See generally Joel Brady, " 'Land Is Itself a Sacred Living Being': Native American Sacred Site Protection on Federal Public Lands Amidst the Shadows of Bear Lodge," 24 *American Indian Law Review* 153 (2003).

[34] Executive Order No. 13007, 61 Fed. Reg. 26771, § 1 (1996).

[35] See 106 *Cong. Rec.* S7776 (July 27, 2000) (Joint statement of Senators Hatch and Kennedy) ("The Act does not include a definition of the term 'substantial burden' because it is not the intent of this Act to create a new standard for the definition of 'substantial burden' on religious exercise. Instead, that term as used in the Act should be interpreted by reference to Supreme Court jurisprudence. Nothing in this Act, including the requirement in Section 5(g) that its terms be broadly construed, is intended to change that principle. The term 'substantial burden' as used in this Act is not intended to be given any broader interpretation than the Supreme Court's articulation of the concept of substantial burden on religious exercise").

[36] The claimants would then have to establish a substantial interference with religious exercise that is not supported by a compelling government interest.

CHAPTER 13

Difficult Determinations:
Burden and Government Interest

When legal standards cast only in general terms tell officials what religious claims to accommodate, administrators and courts must evaluate burdens on religious exercise and the strength of competing government interests. Under the constitutional free exercise standard that predated the 1990 ruling in *Employment Division v. Smith*, and that continues in some states, and under various statutes, including the Religious Freedom Restoration Act,[1] thirteen similar state statutes, and the Religious Land Use and Institutionalized Persons Act of 2000,[2] a claimant succeeds only if he is sincere, suffers a significant enough burden on his religious exercise, and could be exempted from general requirements without impairing a compelling governmental interest. These inquiries—which risk arbitrary decision and unjustified favoritism—are undeniably difficult; their very difficulty was a major reason *Smith* was decided as it was. Perhaps the practical problems of administering these standards are so great that a simpler approach is preferable. If no one provides religious exemptions, no one need worry about sincerity, burden, and government interest. A legislature can also avoid imposing these inquiries on administrators and judges by creating highly specific exemptions, say for use of peyote in worship services, in which event officials need only determine if easily identifiable narrow conditions are met.

Much of this chapter is an exploration of whether judges are capable of fairly applying standards that call for assessments of burden and government interest. The last section examines some alternative constitutional approaches to protecting free exercise, ones that better fit the framework of First Amendment law that *Employment Division v. Smith* creates.

In struggling with the difficulties of evaluating burden and government interest in various contexts, this chapter faces the largest obstacle to conferring exemptions in terms that are general. It may well be the most important chapter in the book.

[1] 42 U.S.C. § 2000bb.
[2] 42 U.S.C. § 2000cc et seq.

Formulations about Burden

When legislators or courts grant broadly phrased religious exemptions from standard legal requirements, a claimant should succeed only if she suffers a nontrivial burden on her religious exercise, and the government's interest in denying her an exemption is not strong. In previous chapters we have considered various standards to evaluate burdens on religious practice and degrees of government interest; here we look more carefully at how these standards might be formulated, and how these formulations should be understood.

The fundamental idea behind a test of burden is that the government should not have to demonstrate a powerful public need if its actions interfere only slightly with religious practice. The Religious Freedom Restoration Act and the Religious Land Use and Institutionalized Persons Act both require that someone seeking an exemption have suffered a "substantial burden" on the exercise of her religion.[3] States that have interpreted their constitutions to be more generous toward free exercise than is *Employment Division v. Smith*, or that have passed their own RFRAs, have generally adopted similar language.[4] Because they involve delving into religious perspectives, assessments about degrees of burden on religion are even more unsettling than inquiries into sincerity or religiousness, but they are needed to strike an appropriate balance between public interests and religious freedom.

Even when a burden is substantial, a claim will not succeed if the government has a strong interest in denying an exemption; a claim that human sacrifice is the center of one's religious practice will not provide a defense to murder. In typical formulations, examination of the burden on religious practice is formally distinct from assessment of government interest; a court proceeds by two independent steps. In reality, courts consider burden in light of government interest and government interest in light of burden, striking a kind of balance.

The first Supreme Court case that sharply posed the problem about judicial assessments of burden was *Lyng v. Northwest Indian Cemetery Protec-*

---

[3] The word "substantial" was added by the Senate to the Religious Freedom Restoration Act after the House had passed the bill without that language. See W. Cole Durham, Jr., "State RFRAs and the Scope of Free Exercise Protection," 32 *UC Davis Law Review* 665, 697–98 (1999).

[4] On state constitutional interpretation, see Angela Carmella, "State Constitutional Protection of Religious Exercise: An Emerging Post-Smith Jurisprudence," 1993 *Brigham Young University Law Review* 275; Ira C. Lupu, "*Employment Division v. Smith* and the Decline of Supreme Court Centrism," 1993 *Brigham Young University Law Review* 259; Tracey Levy, "Rediscovering Rights: State Courts Reconsider the Free Exercise Clauses of Their Own Constitutions in the Wake of *Employment Division v. Smith*," 67 *Temple Law Review* 1017 (1994). Among thirteen states with religious freedom legislation, Alabama, Connecticut, Missouri, New Mexico, and Rhode Island do not require a "substantial burden."

tive Association.[5] Justice Brennan dissented from the Court's declaration that, because no coercion was involved, Native Americans lacked a free exercise right to block a proposed road on federal land. He acknowledged that the government's development of land should not be constrained if it affects religious activities only marginally; he suggested that claimants must initially make a showing of the "centrality" of affected practices,[6] demonstrating that the government's activity "poses a substantial and realistic threat of frustrating their religious practice."[7]

Although *Smith* eliminated most investigations into "centrality" or "burden" as aspects of federal constitutional law, it left standing the line of cases from *Sherbert v. Verner,*[8] under which people who are unemployed and are unwilling to work on Saturday for religious reasons are entitled to unemployment compensation, despite a state law that conditions benefits on availability for Saturday work. If someone refuses Saturday work for reasons in which religion figures tangentially—"My faith tells me family time is important and Saturday is an opportunity to be with my children"—a court might still have to decide whether the interference with religious exercise is great enough to sustain a constitutional claim.[9]

Whether cast in a statute or as a feature of constitutional free exercise, how should the inquiry about burden be formulated, and how should that formulation be understood and applied? A formulation must be coherent and sensible, and capable of assisting judges in resolving actual cases. To undertake a complete analysis of alternative approaches, we would have to make an exhaustive survey of litigated cases, and of administrative decisions, correlating results to various formulations. Judicial opinions in litigated cases are likely to deal with the most difficult issues. A standard might work reasonably well for situations that do not get to courts or produce judicial opinions, even though applications that we read about in case reports strike us as highly arguable. We would need to be attentive to the possibility that the exact language of the test may not matter very much; we would also want to be alert to the concern that no formulation works very well, that all

[5] 485 U.S. 439 (1988).

[6] Id. at 473–74. Language about centrality is also found in *Hernandez v. Commissioner,* 490 U.S. 680, 699 (1989).

[7] *Lyng,* note 5 supra, at 475.

[8] 374 U.S. 398 (1963).

[9] The same basic issue could be differently formulated as whether the claim to spend time with children is "really" religious, in which event the question would become one concerning the borderlines of what counts as religious. If a parent said, "My church has services every day, and attendance on Sunday is not necessary, but this is the most convenient day for attending with my family," there would be no doubt that religious exercise was involved, but the burden might not be great enough for a successful claim.

of them leave too much unguided discretion to judges. My more modest effort is to make sense of subtle differences among abstract formulations, and then to review some representative cases to ascertain if inquiries into burden and compelling interest are workable.

One specific question about "substantial burden" language, such as that of the Religious Freedom Restoration Act, is whether it differs from a requirement that a religious practice that is interfered with be mandatory or be "central" or "important"? As John Garvey has noted, free exercise can involve an infinite variety of acts: "Belief or conduct may be commanded, recommended, rewarded, encouraged, desired, permitted, discouraged, forbidden, or punished within a claimant's belief system."[10] Often, a requirement of a substantial burden on religious exercise will lead to the same result as a requirement that a practice be mandatory or central. A person's religious exercise is not substantially burdened if a law interferes only with a trivial, nonmandatory aspect of his religion (as he understands it). The various requirements will also have the same application if a central, mandatory practice is forbidden outright. But if one carefully parses the crucial terms, the standards could yield different results on occasion.

One could have a "substantial burden" if a forbidden practice is "moderately significant" but not "central" or mandatory, and a *slight* impairment of a central and mandatory practice could impose a burden that is less than substantial. For example, members of a particular church might regard communion as mandatory and central and hymn singing as neither mandatory nor central. Yet a ban on all singing might constitute a substantial burden, whereas a ban on all use of wine might not, if the members believed they could use grape juice for communion without loss of religious effect.

Although focus on the importance or obligatoriness of an affected practice is not exactly the same as inquiry about a substantial burden, judges are unlikely to slice these distinctions too finely for practical legal purposes. Justice Brennan's opinion in *Lyng* shifts from "centrality" to "substantial threat" without a sense that the two inquiries might vary in consequence. Moreover, a number of courts applying the "substantial burden" language of the Religious Freedom Restoration Act have asked whether practices that are impaired are mandatory or optional, or are central or not central. For example, Chief Judge Posner, whose court was reviewing a claim by Muslim prisoners to have conditions suitable for observance of Ramadan, wrote, "We hold . . . . that a substantial burden . . . . is one that forces adherents of a religion to refrain from religiously motivated conduct, inhibits or constrains

---

[10] John H. Garvey, "Free Exercise and the Value of Religious Liberty," 18 *Connecticut Law Review* 779, 785 (1986).

conduct or expression that manifests a central tenet of a person's religious beliefs, or compels conduct or expression that is contrary to these beliefs."[11] Whatever its exact phrasing, a test of "substantial burden" turns on the importance of the burdened practice and the extent to which it is burdened.[12]

How can judges possibly determine the substantiality of a burden to religious practice?[13] A court must avoid deciding what is *really* important religiously; it cannot tell Roman Catholics that, after all, grape juice is just fine for communion, if they believe wine is essential. In line with the general approach to disputes over the requirements of religious traditions, a problem we shall examine in chapter 16, a court must also avoid deciding which among competing versions of a practice represents a correct understanding of a religious tradition. Courts must take claims as they are sincerely presented by those who seek an exemption.

Federal courts struggling with the question of substantial burden under the Religious Freedom Restoration Act have come up with different abstract formulations. Although these formulations may have varied more than results of cases, they retain importance because they direct judicial inquiries. The two vital aspects of any formulation are whose perspective is to count and how stringent is the legal test.[14]

---

[11] *Mack v. O'Leary*, 80 F.3d 1175 (7th Cir. 1996), vacated and remanded, 522 U.S. 801 (1997). See, e.g., *Bryant v. Gomez*, 46 F.3d 948 (9th Cir. 1995), cert. denied sub nom. *Thomas v. McCotter*, 515 U.S. 1166 (1995).

[12] For example a curfew during all hours of darkness would constitute a complete impairment of nighttime worship services; the scheduling of a public fireworks display on July 4 (a Sunday that year) at 9:00 p.m. (the usual hour of church services) on a lot next to a church would constitute only a modest interference with nighttime services. For some churches, having services at night would be important; for others it would not. As this example also illustrates, different ways of phrasing what is essentially the same issue will affect perceptions of importance and extent of burden. If one asks about *worship services*, in general, the practice is immensely important, but a curfew's preclusion of nighttime services may or may not constitute a large burden. If one asks about nighttime worship, a general curfew imposes a severe burden, but the importance of having nighttime services may or may not be great. The more narrowly one construes the relevant practice, the more the burden on *that practice* will be great and the crucial issue will become the importance of the practice.

[13] The difficulties of such an endeavor are emphasized in a case in which debtors in bankruptcy claimed a religious obligation to donate one hundred dollars monthly to their church. *In re Tessier*, 190 B.R. 396, 403–4 (D. Mont. 1995), appeal dismissed as moot, 127 F.3d 1106 (9th Cir. 1997). In another case, in which a trustee in bankruptcy sought to recover money given as tithing to a church while debtors were insolvent, the Court of Appeals for the Eighth Circuit ruled that the bankruptcy code, under which the trustee would have succeeded, imposed a substantial burden on the exercise of religion and that the government lacked a compelling interest in recovering the money. *United States v. Crystal Evangelical Free Church (In re Young)*, 82 F.3d 1407 (8th Cir. 1996), vacated and remanded, 521 U.S. 1114 (1997), decision reinstated on ground that RFRA is constitutional as applied to federal government, 141 F.3d 854, 856 (1998).

[14] Some courts seem mistakenly to have supposed that focus on "the religion," as contrasted with focus on the individual's perspective, goes naturally with a stringent standard—what is

In principle, the appropriate perspective to adopt is *usually* that of individual claimants. How do they understand their own religious beliefs and practices? The individuals are the ones seeking to act in certain ways, for example, to wear crosses or to have a special diet. One aspect of focusing on the individual's perspective is recognizing that for some people, doctrinal belief figures less importantly than liturgies and other practices. Attention to individual understandings does not favor more Protestant views over those in which individual perspectives largely reflect those of a corporate leadership; the free exercise rights of members of cohesive religious groups in which all accept the views of powerful leaders will depend on these shared conceptions. The law is not taking a stand for or against hierarchical authority.[15]

Some arguments for focusing on religious entities rather than individuals are that most administrators have neither the talent nor the time to scrutinize individual religious sentiments and that individuals may be less than candid or genuinely uncertain about what they believe. The possible gains in relying on the standard doctrines of groups do not override the powerful reasons in favor of concentrating on the individual rather than on official versions of various religious faiths (if they exist). Administrators and judges may look to standard doctrines in order to understand individual claims or to test their sincerity, but the claimants' own honest perceptions should usually be the final determinant.

Existing law, especially the Supreme Court cases on conscientious objection and unemployment compensation,[16] strongly supports a focus on the beliefs, feelings, and practices of individuals who assert free exercise claims.

---

religiously *required* for the claimants. See, e.g., *Sasnett v. Sullivan*, 908 F. Supp. 1429, 1440 (W.D. Wis. 1995), aff'd, 91 F.3d 1018 (7th Cir. 1996), vacated and remanded, 521 U.S. 1114 (1997). As this opinion reflects, one reason for the linkage is that the government argues for a stringent test focusing on "the religion," whereas claimants argue for a relaxed test focusing on the individuals. Perspective and stringency are separate issues, however; there is no obvious linkage of either perspective with any particular degree of stringency. If a prisoner makes a claim to wear religious jewelry, despite a ban on all jewelry, a court might ask whether his religion treats jewelry as one appropriate form of devotion, not whether it insists that adherents must wear jewelry. That inquiry would combine focus on "the religion" with a standard that does not insist that a practice be required. For someone's status as a conscientious objector, the focus of inquiry is definitely on the individual, but the test is stringent—does he feel religiously compelled not to participate in war?

[15] For the view that a test focusing on the individual's subjective understanding does have a Protestant basis, see Winnifred Fallers Sullivan, 81 *Marquette Law Review* 441, 448–49 (1998). Even were it true that focusing on individual claimants has some slight effect of encouraging individuality in religion, the law has little choice. Free exercise rights are mainly individual; legal rules should not insist that members see things according to prevailing views within a denomination.

[16] In *Thomas v. Review Bd.*, 450 U.S. 767 (1981), a Jehovah's Witness said he could not engage in the production of materials to make arms; the Supreme Court held that as long as

This conclusion does not apply when claimants ask for an action that would be reasonable only if it affects a larger group. For example, one would not expect the government to forego road building in a national forest if a single individual regarded the area as a sacred site and honestly claimed that his worship would be severely disturbed. The claim in *Lyng*[17] was appealing because it represented the religious sentiments of a large number of Native Americans. In cases of this sort, a court must investigate the views of a larger group (though such a group need not necessarily be the authoritative representative of a tradition).[18]

How stringent, or difficult to satisfy, should the requirement of a burden be? We can mark out three rough possibilities for laws that forbid (or compel) behavior. Courts might demand that a claimant feel that a legally forbidden act is religiously compelled,[19] a test of absolute conflict. Courts might, instead, find that any act motivated by a sincere religious conviction satisfies a burden test. Or they might use a test that is intermediate between these two.[20]

One of these three possibilities is eliminated when a law inhibits or discourages a religious act without prohibiting it, as with laws that sought to condition unemployment compensation on availability for work on Saturday.[21] For these situations, no absolute conflict arises, because, at some cost, a person can comply with the law and satisfy his religious obligations. Claimants suffering such indirect burdens would never succeed under an absolute conflict approach. Under a sincere motivation standard or an intermediate approach, claimants could sometimes win.

Chief Judge Posner's language in *Mack v. O'Leary* contains different elements for prohibitions and indirect impairments. He says, to repeat, that a substantial burden "forces adherents to refrain from religiously motivated conduct, inhibits or constrains conduct or expression that manifests a central

---

his views were sincere, it did not matter whether other Witnesses agreed, or even whether Thomas's views were comprehensible.

[17] *Lyng*, note 5 supra.

[18] A similarly broad inquiry is necessary for most Establishment Clause issues that depend on perceptions. If, for example, a court asks if the government has endorsed a religion, the perceptions that count are not those of particular individuals. As the endorsement test has developed, Justice O'Connor has emphasized that the test involves a reasonable observer, not any actual persons. But judges who ask how a reasonable (informed) observer would react must have some sense of how most actual people would react if they were suitably informed.

[19] A similar approach would be employed to see if a claimant felt that a legally required act was religiously forbidden.

[20] Courts might adopt somewhat variant standards depending on the sort of claim involved.

[21] The analysis is similar here for laws that forbid or compel behavior that itself has no religious significance for the claimant, when observance of the law (e.g. closing on Sunday) might indirectly affect religious practice (closing on Saturday).

tenet of a person's religious beliefs, or compels conduct or expression that is contrary to those beliefs."[22] The language does not demand that the religious practice be mandatory. It also does not demand "centrality" if adherents are forced to refrain from religiously motivated conduct (or compelled to engage in conduct that offends religious convictions). But it does require conduct manifesting a central tenet if a law only "inhibits or constrains."[23] However the exact distinction should be drawn, Posner makes sense in demanding that a more important practice or belief be involved when behavior is discouraged rather than forbidden outright.[24]

Apart from difficulties of administration, an intermediate approach is definitely preferable to each of the other major alternatives. Although a few courts of appeals have spoken as if an absolute conflict between legal requirement and religious obligation is necessary to establish a substantial burden,[25] that approach is unfaithful to the Religious Freedom Restoration Act and to similar laws. The two major Supreme Court cases sustaining claims of free exercise are *Sherbert v. Verner* and *Wisconsin v. Yoder.* Since Sherbert's refusal to work on Saturday entailed (only) losing unemployment compensation, she did not claim an absolute conflict. Even in *Yoder,* it was doubtful whether the Amish felt compelled to remove their children from school after the eighth grade.[26] In its abstract formulation and its endorsement of those cases, the Religious Freedom Restoration Act treats claimants more generously than does a requirement of absolute conflict.[27] That conclusion is strongly confirmed by language of the Religious Land Use and Institutionalized Persons Act. Written after courts had interpreted RFRA in different

[22] Note 11 supra, at 1179. In one respect, Posner's language seems too generous to claimants forced to refrain from religiously motivated conduct. Conduct could be religiously motivated but understood to be of slight significance. Forbidding that conduct would not impose a substantial burden.

[23] An initial reading of the opinion's language might suggest that when conduct is compelled, the claimant can succeed only if the religious belief that forbids the legally compelled conduct is central. But, "those beliefs" in Posner's formulation does not include the element of centrality explicitly; and it would be illogical to treat compelled behavior differently from forbidden behavior (as to which centrality is not required).

[24] In *Sasnett v. Sullivan,* 91 F.3d 1018, 1022 (7th Cir. 1996), involving a prohibition on wearing jewelry, Posner referred to religious motivation without mentioning centrality.

[25] Requiring absolute conflict are *Goodall v. Stafford County School Bd.,* 60 F.3d 168, 172–73 (4th Cir. 1995), cert. denied, 516 U.S. 1046 (1996); *Cheffer v. Reno,* 55 F.3d 1517, 1522 (11th Cir. 1995); *Bryant,* note 11 supra. Various approaches of counts of appeal are reviewed in *Mack,* note 11 supra, at 1178. For an earlier suggestion that constitutional free exercise exemptions should be limited to conflicts between laws and religious *duty,* see Geoffrey R. Stone, "Constitutionally Compelled Exemptions and the Free Exercise Clause," 27 *William & Mary Law Review* 985, 993 (1986).

[26] See Ira C. Lupu, "Of Time and the RFRA: A Lawyer's Guide to the Religious Freedom Restoration Act," 56 *Montana Law Review* 171, 203 (1995).

[27] On relevant legislative history, see *Sasnett,* note 14 supra, at 1441–44.

ways, its language explicitly says that "religious exercise" need not be "compelled by, or central to, a system of religious belief."[28]

On the other hand, to require only a simple religious motivation would protect too much. Although some constitutional cases decided before *Smith* did not specifically require that a burden on free exercise be of a particular weight, all successful claims involved serious burdens, and no one supposed that a slight effect was sufficient to qualify for an exemption. Not every interference with a sincere religious motivation constitutes a significant burden, and we cannot rest comfortably in the assurance that no one will bother to sue over peripheral religious concerns. People care a great deal about some matters, such as spending time with family on Saturday, even when they think the religious implications of the behavior are minor. More importantly, administrative officials, not courts, are typically the first recipients of individuals' free exercise claims. Were it once established that every sincere religious motivation could be sufficient to sustain a right, people who would not bother to expend the time and money to litigate about minor concerns might be prepared to make demands over them to administrators, such as school principals and housing officials.

We could expect offsetting developments if legislators or courts made sincere religious motivation the exclusive standard of a required burden. When the religious component of a claim was not predominant, as perhaps in the family time illustration, a court would say the motivation was nonreligious. Judges would also disqualify various categories of claims as not touching the free exercise of religion, as the Supreme Court did in *Lyng* when it said that land development did not involve coercion; and judges would be likely to consider government interests to be compelling when they regarded religious claims as trivial.

What is called for is an intermediate test, less demanding than absolute conflict and more demanding than sincere motivation. The only ground for preferring a simpler test is doubt that judges can formulate a standard that is both sensitive to individual perspectives and allows nonarbitrary decision of cases. The underlying task for courts is developing a standard that satisfies these two objectives reasonably well.

A crucial question about any intermediate standard is whether it should require that a belief or practice be central or mandatory. It should not. Within many religions, practices may be less than mandatory but still very important. If "centrality" were taken seriously and restricted to a handful of beliefs and practices, and if a tight connection had to exist between what

---

[28] 42 U.S.C. 2000cc-5(7)(A). At least six state RFRAs are similar in this respect, and the language of the federal RFRA has been reformed accordingly. See Durham, note 3 supra, at 708, suggesting that verbal formulae can affect the level of protection.

is central and the behavior in which the claimant sought to engage, the requirement would be too strict. Prisoner A might not consider wearing a cross to be a central practice or to follow closely from a central belief, and yet he could regard wearing the cross as an important symbol of witness and commitment, and a great aid to devotion. Were a prison to forbid all wearing of jewelry (including crosses), A's convictions should be enough for him to get over the threshold of "substantial burden," although he would fail a strict centrality test. If a centrality approach treated central aspects of religions expansively *or* allowed the connection between these aspects and the behavior at issue to be highly attenuated, the centrality test might preclude few claims. For example, consider prisoner B, who is used to wearing a cross but has ceased to think of that as having much religious significance. Still B does understand that the cross represents the Crucifixion and Resurrection of Jesus in Christian belief, central aspects of the faith. A centrality test so attenuated that B would succeed would be too generous. In contrast to A's situation, a prison rule forbidding B from wearing jewelry would not constitute a substantial burden on his religious exercise.

In some inexact way, a requirement of centrality of practice or belief may possibly help courts to be realistic about the magnitude of burden, but the assistance is more likely illusive than actual. Judges follow a cleaner, more coherent approach if they rely exclusively on the language of "substantial burden," recognizing that other, more complicated formulations do not aid in resolving the crucial question about the weight of interference with religious exercise.[29]

Once judges reasonably comprehend a person's religious beliefs and practices (and thus have surmounted all the obstacles to perceiving fairly what are that person's religious perspectives),[30] they will be able to identify some interferences as very great and others as trivial. The difficulties arise "in between," yet a standard requiring some debatable classifications is preferable to one that fails to do justice to what is involved.[31]

---

[29] For authors objecting to use of "centrality" by courts applying RFRA, see Durham, note 3 supra; James A. Hanson, "Missouri's Religious Freedom Restoration Act: A New Approach to the Cause of Conscience," 69 *Missouri Law Review* 853, 858 n. 30 (2004); David J. Solove, "Note: Faith Profaned: The Religious Freedom Restoration Act and Religion in Prisons," 106 *Yale Law Journal* 459, 476–77 (1996).

[30] The risk of inconsistent treatment among claimants is undoubtedly heightened because judges may not well understand the religious lives they evaluate. See generally Sullivan, note 15 supra. It may be that there are serious intrinsic limits on our capability to understand the religious lives of others, and even our own religious lives. Here I refer mainly to avoidable failures to understand.

[31] On why people should have constitutional protection against indirect burdens on rights, see Michael Dorf, "Incidental Burdens on Fundamental Rights," 109 *Harvard Law Review*

We will discover no magical word or phrase for how the necessary magnitude of burden should be formulated. My own sense is that "substantial" is about right for this purpose, demanding a burden that is more than trivial, but not huge or intolerable. However, some authors have expressed concern that judges have been much too ready to throw claims under RFRA out on the basis that the burden is not substantial enough.[32] Among the cases I discuss in the latter part of this chapter, and in the rest of the book, are some in which courts demand too much in the way of burden; but one would need to look at the cases more exhaustively to reach a firm conclusion whether judges pervasively misapply substantial burden requirements. If so, it would make sense to drop "substantial" from legislative formulations.

Whatever exact formulation may be best, a somewhat amorphous intermediate standard of burden is preferable to each alternative; providing no protection for religious claims (the Supreme Court's present free exercise approach); requiring an absolute conflict[33] between law and religious duty; or sustaining any claim based on a sincere religious motivation.

The principle that courts should adopt the claimants' perspectives and use a standard that measures magnitude of burden needs to be understood in a fairly precise way. A court (or jury) may say that a claim is not sincere. It might conceivably conclude that a claimant honestly asserts that the state is interfering with a religious practice, but is not entirely sincere in his statement about the practice's importance or the degree of interference with it.[34]

Once judges accept a claimant's sincerity, ultimate categorization of the burden as substantial or not is their responsibility. Although courts must accept sincere claims about the structure of religious practices, attachments

---

1176 (1996); on burdens on free exercise, see Ira C. Lupu, "Where Rights Begin: The Problem of Burdens on the Free Exercise of Religion," 102 *Harvard Law Review* 933 (1989).

[32] See, e.g., Ira C. Lupu, "The Failure of RFRA," 20 *University of Arkansas at Little Rock Law Journal* 575, 594 (1998). One problem is lack of sympathy with prisoner claims in particular. Cole Durham, note 3 supra, at 698, recommends that states not include "substantial" in their own RFRAs.

[33] Chief Judge Posner's opinion in *Mack v. O'Leary* suggests, interestingly, that courts can better administer a test that asks about religious motivation and centrality of religious belief than they can determine absolute conflicts. Note 11 supra, at 1179. See also *In re Young*, 83 F.3d 1407 (8th Cir. 1996). His point is that courts cannot easily determine whether, according to the religion to which the claimant belongs, a direct conflict is created. Once we focus on the individual, no such straightforward conclusion about comparative administrability is warranted. When it is reasonably arguable that a direct conflict may exist, an intermediate standard of burden will be easier to apply, because it will almost certainly be satisfied. For less pressing claims, such as a claim by Christians to wear jewelry, an intermediate standard will be less certain, because most claimants would definitely lose under a direct conflict requirement.

[34] However, anyone would be hard put to make such a refined judgment about sincerity without impermissibly invoking his own view of comparative importance.

to practices, and feelings about impairments,[35] the final labeling of a burden as substantial is judicial. A conclusory allegation on this score is not dispositive. Suppose, for example, a minister representing a congregation in the United Church of Christ said: "We decide whether to use wine or grape juice by a congregational vote. Either substance is acceptable for the fundamental purpose of commemorating the last supper and Christ's life and death, but various people think that one or the other substance is preferable. We recently decided to use wine by a vote of one hundred to ninety-three. Therefore, using wine is important, even central to us, and any interference substantially burdens our religious exercise." If it became relevant whether an interference with this church's use of wine constituted a substantial burden, a court might decide that the minister's comments reveal that the burden is less than substantial, despite her own honest conclusion to the contrary.[36] While accepting the religious understanding that claimants provide, courts must determine what interferences satisfy the prevailing legal standard.[37]

Understanding just what is involved, we need to ask whether difficult judgments about substantial burden should be avoided.[38] One strategy of avoidance, of course, is for courts not to reply on any general standard to delineate free exercise exemptions against the application of general, valid, statutes—an approach Marci Hamilton has strongly defended.[39] A second way to avoid judgments about burden is to categorize in terms of different kinds of government acts, as the majority of the Supreme Court did in *Lyng* and in the earlier case of *Bowen v. Roy*,[40] and refuse to entertain religious complaints about internal processes, noncoercive land development, and other subjects. This strategy, standing alone, has two serious drawbacks. The first is that if religious practice suffers as much as the Native Americans claimed in *Lyng*, and the government's interest is as slight as it was there, those affected should obtain relief. The second drawback is that this strategy can-

[35] For example, courts cannot say that wine does not really matter for communion if Catholics sincerely assert that wine is essential.

[36] Her conclusion, of course, may have been responsive to a lawyer's encouragement.

[37] See, e.g., *Thiry v. Carlson*, 78 F.3d 1491 (10th Cir. 1996), cert. denied, 519 U.S. 821 (1996) (holding that parents would not suffer substantial burden if land containing gravesite of stillborn child was condemned and gravesite relocated).

[38] One constitutional argument against the Religious Freedom Restoration Act, not (yet) relied upon by the Supreme Court, has been that these judgments are *so difficult* that courts cannot be required to make them consistent with the Establishment Clause and with separation of powers.

[39] Marci A. Hamilton, *God vs. The Gavel: Religion and the Rule of Law* 295–98 (New York: Cambridge University Press, 2005). Under this approach, legislatures would limit any free exercise exemptions to very specific terms, such as use of peyote in worship services, that do not demand that courts assess the burden.

[40] 476 U.S. 693 (1986). See also *In re Tessier*, note 13 supra.

not solve the entire problem of determining importance. Many government rules of the types that could generate free exercise claims would have effects too slight to require the government to show a strong interest in its restrictions. Some inquiry about burden would still be needed to filter out those instances.

A third strategy would be to determine the importance of a practice in light of general characteristics of religious believers and religious institutions.[41] For example, a burden on corporate worship would be regarded as more substantial than a burden on providing social services to nonmembers. Courts would be required to make judgments of degree under this approach, but the judgments would be about general categories and their applications, not about burdens felt by particular claimants. In simplifying judicial assessments and in curbing judicial discretion, as well as discouraging insincere claims, this approach has something to recommend it; but it is too insensitive to the needs of particular groups and individuals. The Salvation Army should not be treated like a typical church, for which aid to the poor is not a central activity, if leaders say that serving the poor is the center of their mission. Further, this "sociological approach" to importance reinforces the outlook of dominant religions. Perhaps in otherwise doubtful cases, courts appropriately look to religious practices in general, but these should not be the over-riding guide to the degree of burden.

Although I have suggested that categorization of kinds of government acts cannot eliminate delicate judgments about substantial burdens, some specific inquiries can help courts resolve cases. Ira Lupu has suggested that courts ask whether an action by a private party similar to what the government has done would violate a common-law right.[42] Claimants threatened by imprisonment would satisfy this test, and Native Americans whose sites of worship are endangered could claim a kind of easement for peaceful use of the land. Michael Dorf has proposed that courts consider what alternatives may be available to religious claimants and whether they suffer more from a challenged regulation than others who are affected.[43] These inquiries can assist courts, but neither singly nor in combination should they eliminate all matters of judgment about degrees of burden.

[41] See Marc Galanter, "Religious Freedom in the United States: A Turning Point?" 1996 *Wisconsin Law Review* 217.

[42] Lupu, note 32 supra, at 966–77. Lupu's first approximation of a rule of this sort is this: "Whenever religious activity is met by intentional government action analogous to that which if committed by a private party would be actionable under general principles of law, a legally cognizable burden on religion is present." Id. at 966. Lupu supplements this approach by attention to entitlements, such as unemployment compensation, id. at 977–82; and he assumes that a burden resulting from discrimination is unconstitutional, id. at 982–87.

[43] Dorf, note 31 supra, at 1217–18.

Although engaging in such an exercise is indeed troublesome for courts, it remains preferable to each of the three main alternatives. This is one of those domains of law in which messiness at the edges, and uneven application, are the regrettable costs of a legal standard that is minimally responsive to the underlying values that matter.

COMPELLING INTEREST

Earlier chapters have analyzed the strength of government interests in considerable detail. Here I offer a few general remarks by way of recapitulation, and note what some scholars have suggested about how courts should evaluate government interests.

First, it should matter less than may appear whether a standard requires that a government not only possess a compelling interest in achieving an objective, but also lack less restrictive means for attaining it. RFRA, RLUIPA, and nearly all the state RFRAs, unlike some constitutional cases prior to *Smith*, include an explicit least restrictive means component. But the purpose of this component is achieved implicitly through the compelling interest question itself, which is properly seen as whether the government has a compelling interest in applying a law against the claimant and people like him. The government will lack a compelling interest *of this kind* if it has an alternative, less restrictive means available to achieve its purpose. "Least restrictive means" clearly puts the emphasis on how the government deals with the claimant and those like him, and it focuses attention on other possible alternative approaches to a problem.[44] Nevertheless, the application of a compelling interest test should not depend crucially on whether the test includes an explicit reference to alternative means.

Second, the strength of the government's interest is not viewed in isolation from the substantiality of burden. Judges assess one with an eye toward the other. To be more precise, a burden is likely to be judged less substantial if the government's reason to restrict is strong, and when a burden on religious exercise is heavy, the government's interest will seem weaker than it might otherwise.

Third, to repeat a point from earlier chapters, the compelling interest test in exemption cases has never been quite what it seems. The "compelling interest" formulation is mainly familiar from challenges that laws violate

---

[44] Lupu, note 31 supra, at 949–50, regards the weight of government interests as less significant than the possibility of less restrictive means. See also Jesse H. Choper, "The Rise and Decline of the Constitutional Protection of Religious Liberty," 70 *University of Nebraska Law Review* 651, 680 (1991).

equal protection or free speech. In such cases, governments have had a hard time satisfying the test, and the nearly universal result has been invalidation of the laws. Within this broad category fall instances of discrimination among different religions; once a court decides that a law does discriminate among religions, its condemnation is virtually automatic. Free exercise exemption cases typically do not involve such discrimination; the religious claim is to be exempt from the operation of a law that itself is valid and will continue to apply to everyone else. These cases raise issues of unfair advantage (for those to be exempted) and of possible fraud that do not exist for laws that discriminate among religions or along racial lines (where sincerity is not an issue). Referring to Gerald Gunther's comment that in equal protection and free speech cases, the compelling interest test is "strict in theory, but fatal in fact," Ira Lupu has written that the test for exemptions deriving from *Sherbert v. Verner* has been "strict in theory, but ever-so-gentle in fact."[45] Courts are understandably hesitant to grant exemptions freely, and religious claimants, whether under a constitutional or general statutory standard like RFRA, have usually lost. Perhaps the courts have not been generous enough; but we need frank recognition that a compelling interest test for exemption cases neither has been, nor should be, *as stringent* as the test is in other contexts. Absent such candor, judges appear dishonest, and observers are confused why claimants so rarely win under a standard of review that sounds so favorable to them.

It would be an advance in clarity if some weaker term (such as *significant*) were substituted for "compelling," and if courts also used a standard more permissive to the government than demanding that the challenged law be the "least restrictive means," perhaps requiring only that some other less restrictive means not be obviously workable.[46] But the terminology of legal tests does not shift easily, and indeed judges cannot alter the language of standards legislators create in statutes. If judges and legislators continue to use the language of compelling interest, everyone should be clear that its force for standard equal protection and free speech contexts differs from its force for free exercise exemptions.

Just what makes an interest compelling is hard to say. Among negative proposals are suggestions that an interest is *not* compelling (1) simply be-

---

[45] Ira C. Lupu, "The Trouble with Accommodation," 60 *George Washington Law Review* 743, 756 (1992).

[46] If a less restrictive means is obviously workable, the government should exempt religious claimants. If an alternative means would be more costly, courts would need to decide when that cost should be borne by the government; but they must make the same decision under the "least restrictive means" formulation if the means chosen is less expensive than an alternative. Under either formulation, it is a modest problem that precise costs and the ability of government to bear them can shift over time.

cause the government says it is,[47] (2) if the interest is slight,[48] (3) if it involves only modest expense or administrative inconvenience,[49] (4) if the government has not protected the interest in other contexts,[50] (5) if claims of harm are highly speculative.[51] Although each of these suggestions seems innocuous, some court decisions are hard to square with them.

The government *does* have a compelling interest in avoiding constitutional violations; thus, it need not, indeed cannot, create an exemption that would violate the Establishment Clause. And the government also has a compelling interest in avoiding exemptions, as from tax burdens, that would create strong incentives for people to advance spurious, self-interested claims.[52] Stephen Pepper has put the test of compelling interest in this form: "[I]s there a real, tangible (palpable, concrete, measurable) non-speculative, non-trivial injury to a legitimate, substantial state interest[?]"[53] Whatever their exact formulation, we may doubt that courts will do better than this relatively vague language.[54] What is critical is that judges both recognize that the free exercise exemption test is sui generis, and take "compelling interest" and "least restrictive means" as serious hurdles.

SOME APPLICATIONS

A look at a sample of cases can give us an idea how the courts are handling formulations that call on them to assess interferences with religious exercise

[47] Michael Stokes Paulsen, "A RFRA Runs Through It: Religious Freedom and the U.S. Code," 56 *Montana Law Review* 249, 254 (1995).

[48] Douglas Laycock and Oliver S. Thomas, "Interpreting the Religious Freedom Restoration Act," 73 *Texas Law Review* 209, 222–23 (1994).

[49] Paulsen, note 47 supra, at 255.

[50] Laycock and Thomas, note 48 supra, at 224.

[51] Thomas C. Berg, "What Hath Congress Wrought? An Interpretative Guide to the Religious Freedom Restoration Act," 39 *Villanova Law Review* 21, 34 (1994).

[52] See Douglas Laycock, "RFRA, Congress, and the Ratchet," 56 *Montana Law Review* 145, 199; Berg, note 51 supra, at 41–43.

[53] Stephen L. Pepper, "The Conundrum of the Free Exercise Clause—Some Reflections on Recent Cases," 9 *Northern Kentucky Law Review* 265, 289 (1982). This formulation may be regarded as the flip side of negative standards for what do not count as compelling interests. In February of 2006, a unanimous Supreme Court had little difficulty deciding that the government did not have a compelling interest in barring importation of a hallucinogenic tea used in worship by a small religious group. *Gonzales v. O Centro Espírita Beneficente União Do Vegetal*, No. 04–1084.

[54] Michael W. McConnell, "Taking Religion Seriously," *First Things*, May 1990, 30, 34, has proposed a less vague test that would sustain a law's application to religious practices only if it protects the private rights of others or ensures "that the benefits and burdens of public life are equitably shared." Since this approach would not allow government ever to protect adults from their own dangerous religious choices and would downgrade public interests, other than rights protection and equitable sharing, we should not expect courts to adopt it.

against degrees of government need. We are interested in (1) whether individual results make good sense, and (2) whether the whole endeavor is one that courts should be required to undertake. The cases we shall consider are ones decided under RFRA and RLUIPA, federal statutes, but the fundamental issues are the same when courts apply state statutes or constitutional standards with a similar scope. The cases involve significantly different topics: worship and celebration in prisons, prisoners' appearance, property regulation, control and protection of wild animals, compelled testimony, and bankruptcy.

Worship and Celebration in Prisons

We may begin with *Mack v. O'Leary*,[55] resolved with an opinion by Chief Judge Posner, which, as we have seen, allows a claim of burden to succeed even when a religious practice is not compulsory, if the government forbids the practice outright or requires actions at odds with it. The opinion covers two independent claims by prisoners to engage in religious practices. One plaintiff, a member of the Moorish Science Temple of America, wanted to have a banquet on January 8, the founder's birthday. State prison authorities had classed the three hundred denominations at the prison under four major groupings, allowing members of each group one or two picnic days per year, which they could use for sacred feasts. The authorities did not make an exception to allow the Moors to banquet on the day they wanted. Posner said that the plaintiff had gotten over the threshold of a substantial burden, though having the banquet on this particular day was a nonmandatory observance. But, given the difficulties of scheduling many separate feast days for individual groups, the state had established "both a compelling governmental interest in imposing the modest burden and the absence of any less restrictive alternative."[56] Posner's linking of the phrase "modest burden" with evaluation of the government's interest certainly intimates that the strength of the state's interest is being compared directly with the degree of burden on the claimant, which the court does not regard as great.

This reality is stated more explicitly in connection with the other complaint, that in various respects prison officials had not accommodated the needs of Muslim prisoners to have their ritual dinners after sunset during Ramadan (for example, the floor was in such a mess after the regular prison dinner that participants were unable to prostrate themselves for prayers). The court determined that the prisoners suffered a substantial burden, and remanded the case for a determination of the government's interest, ruling that prison order is a compelling interest and that by adopting the Religious

[55] Note 11 supra.
[56] Id. at 1180.

Freedom Restoration Act, Congress did not mean to undermine the policy of judicial deference to prison authorities on issues of discipline.[57] After indicating that some of the prisoners' complaints were probably ill-founded—tables had to be belted to the floors, and alternative eating places might not be available—Posner remarked, "The prison officials do not have to do handsprings to accommodate the religious needs of inmates, and the less central an observance is to the religion in question the less the officials must do."[58] This comparative language explicitly conveys that the less important a religious practice, the more easily the state will establish a compelling interest.

One powerful illustration of how much difference a court's formulation of its standard of review can make is found in *Bryant v. Gomez*.[59] An inmate sought "full Pentecostal services," in which participants could use the "traditional instruments" of their faith, including "speaking in tongues" and "laying hands on each other." His prison, rather than permitting such services, merely had "inter-faith" Christian services, though it did provide Pentecostal literature and a Pentecostal volunteer for Bible study classes. The court held that Bryant failed to establish a substantial burden on his religious exercise because he did not show that the relevant "practices and instruments" were mandated by his faith. Anyone who has witnessed (or even read about) the differences between an ordinary Protestant service and a Pentecostal service should quickly realize that being able to sit through ordinary services will hardly satisfy a Pentecostal's sensibilities about worship.[60] Given the centrality of group worship services for religious practice, and particularly, perhaps, the practice of Pentecostals, being denied a Pentecostal service is certainly a substantial burden on religious practice, on any fair understanding of "substantial burden." Being afforded Pentecostal literature and a volunteer advisor is a pathetic substitute. The facts of the *Bryant* case demonstrate how misguided is the court's demand for absolute conflict.[61]

Prisoners' Appearance and Physical Integrity

Some cases have involved prisoners' claims about their appearance or physical integrity—claims to wear a beard, long hair, or external adornments or

[57] Id. at 1180. See also *Jolly v. Coughlin*, 76 F.3d 468, 475–76 (2d Cir. 1996); *Hamilton v. Schriro*, 74 F.3d 1545, 1548 (8th Cir. 1996) (relying on legislative history of RFRA to conclude that deference appropriate).

[58] Id.

[59] Note 11 supra.

[60] Further, in a typical Protestant service, no small subgroup would be encouraged to begin speaking in tongues and laying on hands.

[61] Because the court did not find a substantial burden, it did not have to pass on the assertion of prison authorities that they had a compelling interest in preventing "speaking in tongues" and "laying hands on each other," because these would create a danger of assaults.

not to be strip-searched by a female guard. In one case involving an issue we examined in chapter 9, a prisoner forbidden to wear any beard succeeded in establishing a substantial burden by showing that he believed Muslim traditions required that he wear a beard.[62] He was willing to restrict his beard to one-quarter inch, the size allowed to prisoners with medical reasons not to shave. The magistrate had granted the inmate's motion for a preliminary injunction, because prison officials had not shown it was necessary for identification purposes to forbid all beards.

In a decision under RLUIPA, the court granted a permanent injunction for Muslim inmates against a prison policy that provided for discipline of prisoners wearing one-half-inch beards; the government had no compelling interest in grooming regulations that did not allow prisoners with religious reasons to wear such beards.[63] In another RLUIPA case, the court granted a preliminary injunction that prevented correctional authorities from cutting the hair of a Native American inmate who grew hair long as "an essential part of his Native American beliefs and practices."[64] Although the state might well have a compelling interest in its grooming regulations, it probably could not show it needed to apply the regulations to an inmate whose religious belief was that he should wear long hair and who was not a significant security risk.

In other cases, claims have involved items prisoners wanted to wear that did not conform to strict regulations. In *Sasnett v. Sullivan*, one issue was whether prisoners had a right to wear crosses in violation of regulations.[65] The district court and the Seventh Circuit Court of Appeals decided that their strong religious motivation to carry these representations of their faith was sufficient to establish a substantial burden on the prisoners, and, further, that claimed interests in avoiding theft and use of crosses as weapons or symbols of gang identification were not sufficiently compelling to justify the application of new regulations banning religious jewelry.

Somewhat more complicated legal issues were posed by *Lemay v. Dubois*,[66] a claim by a prisoner, as part of his Native American religion, to be able to wear a "spiritual necklace" and medallion made of leather, bone, whale teeth, and porcupine teeth; he also wanted to possess a deer tail tie and sage, cedar, and feathers that had been taken from him. The ground on which the district court based its finding about the necklace did not actually

---

[62] *Triplett v. Commissioner*, 1996 U.S. Dist. Lexis 21821 (D.N.H. 1996).

[63] *Mayweathers v. Terhune*, 328 F. Supp. 2d 1086 (E.D. Cal. 2004).

[64] *Hoevenaar v. Lazaroff*, 276 F. Supp. 2d 811 (S.D. Ohio 2003). A preliminary injunction is based on a court's estimate of how a case that is not yet resolved will probably be decided. See also *Collins-Bey v. Thomas*, 2004 U.S. Dist. Lexis 21348 (N.D. Ill. 2004).

[65] *Sasnett*, note 14 supra. Excerpts from the statements of prisoners are in Sullivan, note 15 supra, at 450–51.

[66] *Lemay v. Dubois*, 1996 U.S. Dist. Lexis 11645 (D. Mass. 1996).

require it to find a substantial burden, though the rest of its opinion suggests that it did believe Lemay had established such a burden. Although ostensibly neutral, prison rules about what medals and chains could be worn effectively discriminated in favor of Christian medals and against the no more dangerous necklace Lemay wished to wear. If one is suffering religious discrimination, one's free exercise rights are being violated, whether or not one's exercise is substantially burdened. The state lacked any compelling interest to support this discrimination.[67] In respect to the other items Lemay wished to possess, the court concluded he could probably show that permanent confiscation would constitute a substantial burden on his religious exercise, but the Department of Correction had indicated he could use those items in a room designated for that purpose. Lemay had not (yet) shown that restricted use, prior to and during prayer, in a special room would, in comparison with possession in his cell, constitute a substantial burden for him.

A decision by the Court of Appeals for the Seventh Circuit rejecting a prisoner's claim to wear a religious pin on the outside of his clothing, rather than on the inside as regulations required, may show the virtues, or pitfalls, of the modern practice of having unpublished opinions that do not carry the authority of published opinions.[68] Although the court reasonably decided that plaintiff McNair-Bey had not shown that wearing the pin inside his clothing would constitute a substantial burden, the court stumbled to this result by a confusion or sleight of hand that is astonishing. Partly by omitting crucial language from the controlling standard of *Mack v. O'Leary*,[69] the court turned that standard into what it exactly is not, a requirement that a person show that his faith *mandates* a prohibited practice. The case shows that busy courts unsympathetic to religious claims may not be overly careful about the standards they apply, especially when they need not defend their result in published opinions.

In a much more troubling case, *Collins v. Scott,* a district court held that a Muslim prisoner had failed to show that a strip search by a female guard

---

[67] It also lacked any basis to insist that those wishing to practice Native American religions must prove Native American ancestry. A Hindu prisoner seeking a diet free of meat and dairy products without verification from a member of the clergy of his adherence to Hinduism succeeded in his argument that the state did not establish a compelling interest, on the ground that the prison offered vegan meals to Hebrew Israelites without such a requirement. *Agrawal v. Briley*, 2004 U.S. Dist. Lexis 16997 (N.D. Ill. 2004). However, courts sometimes have allowed forms of differential treatment defended on the basis of efficiency and cost. See, e.g., *Williams v. Morton*, 343 F.3d 212 (3d Cir. 2004) (prison that provided kosher meals not required to provide Halal meals for Muslim inmates).

[68] *McNair-Bey v. Bledsoe*, 1998 U.S. App. Lexis 31162 (7th Cir. 1998) (unpublished).

[69] I assume that the Lexis report accurately describes the court's mangled quote from *Mack*. Even taking the test it makes up from *Mack*, the court interprets it inaccurately.

would substantially burden the exercise of his beliefs.[70] The court reached this conclusion on the basis of Collins's having submitted to such searches by male guards, even though his religious belief was that no one should see him naked. As stated, this rationale is unconvincing. Perhaps Collins regarded being strip-searched by a male guard as a substantial burden, but saw little hope of a successful complaint.[71] Perhaps from his religious perspective, Collins regarded being seen naked by a woman as much worse than being seen naked by a man. His submission to searches by male guards does not itself tell us whether the strip search by a female imposed a substantial burden. The court also said that despite a general policy of searches by guards of the same gender and the presence of male guards when Collins was searched, strip searches not only satisfied a compelling need to maintain security but searching by a female guard was the least restrictive means. Both the "substantial burden" and "compelling interest" aspects of the court's conclusion are hard to explain, except as manifesting a distaste for vindicating prisoners who refuse to submit to prescribed discipline.

Property Regulations

Zoning laws and other regulations of property can conflict with forms of religious exercise. In *Murphy v. Zoning Commission*,[72] a town zoning commission had a cease and desist order issued to prevent the Murphys from hosting in their home weekly prayer meetings that exceeded twenty-five persons. The Murphys claimed that these meetings, which had been taking place for seven years, should not be limited to a specific number of persons, because the meetings were meant to help persons in need of the prayer group's support, and the Murphys did not want to turn people away. Resolving the case under the Religious Land Use and Institutionalized Persons Act,[73] which contains "substantial burden" and "compelling interest" language and explicitly states that an "exercise of religion" need not be "compelled by, or central to, a system of religious belief," the court concluded that the commission's order imposed a substantial burden on the religious exercise of those who attended the prayer meetings. Turning to the town's interest, the court determined that limiting the number of people in attendance was not the least restrictive means of protecting the health and safety of neighbors, which could have been accomplished by regulating the increased volume of traffic.

---

[70] *Collins v. Scott*, 961 F. Supp. 1009 (E.D. Tex. 1997).

[71] He might have realized that in circumstances in which strip searches were generally practiced, he would not be able to at avoid them altogether.

[72] 148 F. Supp. 2d 173 (D. Conn. 2001).

[73] 42 U.S.C. § 2000cc et seq.

When a Christian college relied on the same federal act to compel a city to rezone and permit it to operate its campus on a piece of property zoned for hospital use, the court doubted that an "exercise of religion" was at issue and said the college had not shown that a denial of rezoning imposed a substantial burden on its religious exercise.[74]

In a different kind of case, the Second Circuit considered a claim by a New York church, located in a wealthy section of Manhattan, that its provision of outdoor sleeping space to the homeless effectuated a religious belief, and that removal of the homeless by the police was a substantial burden on its religious exercise under RLUIPA.[75] The court did not need to decide whether the city's actions imposed a substantial burden on the church's religious exercise, because the city did not contest the point. Having determined that the city had failed to demonstrate any neutral law of general applicability that warranted its dispersing the homeless from the church's landing and steps, the court decided that the city had not established that its action was the least restrictive means of serving a compelling interest.[76]

Two cases decided prior to the adoption of RLUIPA involved historic preservation. In one, the city of Cumberland, Maryland, relied on a historic preservation ordinance to refuse the Catholic Church permission to demolish an old monastery and replace it with other church facilities.[77] In the other, New York City's Landmark Commission refused a church permission to demolish its Community House to build an office tower.[78] In the first case, the district court said the historic preservation ordinance was not a neutral, generally applicable law, that the city therefore could restrict the church only if it had a compelling interest, and that historic preservation was not a compelling interest. In the New York City case, the court said the Landmarks Law *was* a neutral regulation of general applicability, providing adequate criteria for what buildings are to be designated landmarks. The two decisions form an odd couple. When a whole district is declared to be historic, as in Cumberland, that seems more neutral and general as to particular structures than when individual buildings are singled out for their special historic or architectural value, as in New York.[79] Perhaps part of the explanation for

[74] *San Jose Christian College v. City of Morgan Hill*, 2001 U.S. Dist. Lexis 23162 (N.D. Cal. 2001).

[75] *Fifth Ave. Presbyterian Church v. City of New York*, 293 F.3d 570 (2d Cir. 2002).

[76] Because the court discerned no relevant neutral law of general applicability, it treated the city's action as unconstitutional, falling outside the circumstances covered by *Employment Division v. Smith*, 494 U.S. 872 (1990).

[77] *Keeler v. Mayor and City Council of Cumberland*, 940 F. Supp. 879 (D. Md. 1996).

[78] *Rector of St. Bartholomew's Church v. City of New York*, 914 F.2d 348 (2d Cir. 1990).

[79] My judgment about this may be affected by the fact that both my father and I were involved in the losing effort for St. Bartholomew's.

the contrasting results is that the wish to replace unusable facilities with more practical structures for religious purposes seemed more appealing, closer to the heart of religious exercise, than the wish to raise money from an office tower to expend for religious endeavors.

An interesting conflict over property regulation is posed when landlords do not want to comply with antidiscrimination laws for religious reasons. In one California case in which the landlord said she would not rent to an unmarried couple, the Supreme Court of California held that the California law forbidding such discrimination did not substantially burden her religious exercise, because her religion did not require her to rent apartments.[80] Although the court noted that the law did not threaten her livelihood,[81] it is not clear that this landlord differs significantly from Sabbatarian store owners or even Sherbert. The store owners could be closed two days or sell their businesses, and Sherbert might have managed on the form of welfare she could have received if she were ineligible for unemployment compensation. If the objecting landlord is in the business of renting apartments, an antidiscrimination law does require her to perform acts at odds with her religious convictions. That the court discerned no substantial burden on her exercise of religion may be largely explained by its hesitancy to undercut laws against discrimination.[82]

Animals with Spiritual Significance

When Native Americans made claims about animals with special spiritual meaning, two courts decided that they had shown a substantial burden on free exercise; the courts then proceeded to reach differing assessments of government interest.

One plaintiff, a holy man who used two bears he had raised from infancy in religious ceremonies, faced the prospect that one of the bears, who had bitten two people after her pen had been vandalized and she escaped, would be destroyed by the game commission for a rabies investigation.[83] Finding

[80] *Smith v. Fair Employment & Housing Comm'n*, 913 P.2d 909 (Cal. 1996).

[81] The court suggests that the landlord can sell properties that she rents and redeploy her capital in other investments. Id. at 925.

[82] Indeed, the court emphasized the rights and interests of third parties. Id. Interestingly, Justice Thomas dissented from a denial of certiorari, in a case in which the Alaska Supreme Court had held that the government has a compelling interest in ending discrimination against unmarried couples, and did not need to create an exemption. *Swanner v. Anchorage Equal Rights Comm'n*, 513 U.S. 979 (1994).

[83] *Black Hawk v. Pennsylvania*, 114 F. Supp. 2d 327 (M.D. Pa. 2000). Subsequently, Black Hawk succeeded in a claim to be free of permit fee requirements. *Black Hawk v. Pennsylvania*, 381 F.3d 202 (3rd Cir. 2004). Because other exemptions were given on a discretionary basis, the rule of *Employment Division v. Smith* did not apply. For cases dealing with federal regulation of

that the two men suffering bites were already receiving treatment to avoid getting rabies, that rabies was rare among bears, and that keeping the bear in her pen would prevent a danger to anyone else, the court decided that the state failed to show that killing the bear was the least restrictive alternative to protect the public welfare. In the other case, the defendant Jim had killed bald and golden eagles in response to a request of his religious elders. He claimed that killing the eagles for feathers and other parts of their bodies was a religious act.[84] The court acknowledged that legal means to acquire parts of eagles would not satisfy Jim's religious needs; nonetheless, the government had a compelling interest in protecting the eagles and a general prohibition was the least restrictive means of satisfying it, because allowing exceptions would significantly undercut the effectiveness of enforcement.

Compelled Testimony by Children

In a case in which a grand jury was investigating whether a parent was conducting illegal business activities, three Orthodox Jewish children who were also employees were subpoenaed to testify; they said that to testify would violate teachings of their religion.[85] The court refused to bend. Exhibiting some skepticism about the sincerity of the children's claim, the court resolved the case on the ground that the state's compelling interest in criminal investigations and prosecution outweighed any incidental burden on the children's religion. Although it is doubtful whether children should be required to testify against their parents, a court, not surprisingly, does not want to get into the business of deciding exactly *how* compelling is the interest in testimony of particular persons who are within the general categories of those who can be forced to testify.

Bankruptcy

A number of cases applying RFRA have involved bankruptcy. Since bankruptcy proceeds under federal law, RFRA's application to it is not directly affected by the Supreme Court's determination that the law is unconstitutional as it applies to the states. The issue about religious exercise and bankruptcy can arise in two contexts. In the more straightforward, the person applying for bankruptcy has a plan for personal expenses, which she will

---

eagle feathers, which favors distribution to members of Native American tribes over other Native Americans and those who are not Native American, and for discussion of the delicate constitutional issues, see Kevin J. Worthen, "Eagle Feathers and Equality: Insights on Religious Exemptions from Native American Experience," 76 *University of Colorado Law Review* 989 (2005).

[84] *United States v. Jim*, 888 F. Supp. 1058 (D. Ore. 1995).

[85] *In re Three Children*, 24 F. Supp. 2d 389 (D.N.J. 1998).

continue to spend while turning over other assets for creditors. She seeks to reserve a substantial amount, typically 10 percent of her income, to tithe to her church. In the second context, the trustee in bankruptcy seeks to recover money already donated to a religious group within the year before someone files for bankruptcy, on the theory that the money was given at a time when doing so was an evasion of obligations to creditors.

In two cases arising in the second context, that is, involving attempts to recover money that had already been donated to churches while the debtors were insolvent but had not filed for bankruptcy, courts ruled that recovering the money would impose a substantial burden on the debtor's religious exercise and that the government presented no compelling interest that could not be achieved by a less restrictive means.[86] In one of these decisions, rendered by the Eighth Circuit Court of Appeals, one judge dissented vigorously as to both substantial burden and compelling interest.[87]

One bankruptcy judge declined to find a substantial burden on the insolvent debtors' exercise of religion when the trustee sought to recover money tithed to their church.[88] The judge employed a standard that was demanding, if of uncertain scope, first referring to conduct "the faith mandates" and shortly thereafter retreating to a criterion of significant inhibitions on conduct that manifests a central tenet of one's beliefs.[89] He also disagreed with the Eighth Circuit about compelling interest; the government does have a compelling interest in giving debtors a fresh start and treating creditors fairly, and the rules allowing recovery are narrowly drawn to achieve that purpose.

Two cases specifically address the feature of RFRA that, if it protects donations to religious organizations, does so without protecting donations to other charities. One judge straightforwardly ruled that insofar as RFRA pro-

---

[86] *Crystal Evangelical Free Church*, note 13 supra (allowing debtors a fresh start and protecting interests of creditors not compelling interests); *Magic Valley Evangelical Free Church v. Fitzgerald (In re Hodge)*, 220 B.R. 386 (D. Idaho 1998) (no compelling interest in maintaining current balance between debtors and creditors; for prevention of actual fraud, less restrictive means available).

In a case involving a trustee's rejection of a plan by debtors to contribute one hundred dollars a month to their church, the bankruptcy court declared that the debtors would suffer a substantial burden under the Religious Freedom Restoration Act and that the government's interest in the Bankruptcy Code "is not compelling when weighed against" the religious exercise. *In re Tessier*, note 13 supra, at 398. But these conclusions proved of no moment, because the court proceeded to hold that RFRA was unconstitutional, and that under *Employment Division v. Smith* and standard bankruptcy rules, the debtors had no right to have their plan confirmed.

[87] See *Crystal Evangelical Free Church*, note 13 supra. In *Waguespack v. Rodriguez*, 220 B.R. 31 (W.D. La. 1998), a court, treating RFRA as unconstitutional, said that a bankruptcy plan could include some donation to a church, but that giving $267.58 to the church and reserving $213.00 for the general creditors was unreasonable.

[88] *In re Newman*, 183 B.R. 239 (D. Kan. 1995).

[89] Id. at 251. One could have an inhibition of conduct manifesting a central tenet *without* being prevented from doing what the faith mandates.

tects tithing to churches, it favors religion over nonreligion and is therefore unconstitutional under the Free Exercise Clause.[90] Another judge was more ingenious, indeed too ingenious. Addressing the question of substantial burden under RFRA, he wrote, "Surely, the Religious Freedom Restoration Act would not allow a debtor who pledges to tithe to receive a chapter 7 discharge when another similarly situated debtor who does not tithe would not receive such a discharge."[91] Of course, what RFRA does is precisely to protect actions connected to religious faith without protecting analogous actions not connected to religion. If such issues of fairness are to figure at all *in the application* of RFRA and similar laws, as contrasted with posing a question about the constitutionality of these laws, compelling interest is a more logical category than substantial burden. The "burden" on religious exercise suffered by a religious person has little to do with how others are affected; but arguably part of the government's interest in administering the bankruptcy laws, tax laws, and so forth, is in treating religious and nonreligious people equally.[92]

In the face of disagreement over whether trustees in bankruptcy could recover generous donations to churches, Congress took the sensible course of adopting specific legislation. The 1998 Religious Liberty and Charitable Donation Protection Act established that, in the year prior to a debtor's filing for bankruptcy, donations up to 15 percent of his gross annual income were protected if the debtor did not aim to defraud creditors and the donations were consistent with his prior practice.[93] Congress wisely deflected any concern about inequality by treating all charitable donations equally.

These bankruptcy cases pose difficult questions. One way of looking at bankruptcy law is that it relieves debtors, by their own choice, from obligations they would otherwise have. If creditors would otherwise be entitled to a debtor's assets (though it might take cumbersome legal processes to get at them), the fact that bankruptcy proceedings don't leave the debtors all they would like for church donations does not really seem to be imposing a burden, in comparison with the alternative. Donations already made may be different in this respect. Perhaps creditors could not get at those were it not

---

[90] *In re Saunders*, 215 B.R. 800, 803–4 (D. Mass. 1997).

[91] *In re Faulkner*, 165 B.R. 644, 648 (W.D. Mo. 1994). In a case involving the somewhat related issue of "undue hardship" discharge of student loan obligations, a court reached the dubious conclusion that the debtor had failed to show that her decision not to work outside an "apostolic" community had a religious basis. *In re Belcher*, 287 B.R. 839, 847 (B.R.N.D. Ga. 2001). That others did work outside the community may have suggested that the debtor did not perceive an obligation to refuse such work, but it hardly undermined her assertion that her motivation was religious.

[92] Of course, the issue of equality raises again concerns that have been a consistent theme in this volume. One can reasonably argue that people making secular charitable contributions rarely feel the sense of obligation of those who feel that tithing is a religious mandate.

[93] See *In re Witt*, 231 B.R. 92 (Bankr. N.D. Okla. 1999).

for the filing for bankruptcy; but the step of filing is still one the debtor has chosen to take in order to lighten her burden.[94]

Even on this modest sample of a variety of cases, we can see that what amounts to a substantial burden and what is a compelling interest that cannot be satisfied by less restrictive means is not always easy to say, and very often people can reasonably react differently. I have suggested that some conclusions that courts have reached are not persuasive and that others are debatable; yet in most of these instances courts have arrived at sensible results that fit the abstract formulations they have used. I do not think these cases are noticeably more difficult than some others that courts have to resolve, and I see little evidence of arbitrary favoritism toward some particular religious perspectives,[95] though we can see a hesitancy to uphold inmates who rock the boat for prison authorities. Even if judges display some comparative lack of empathy for novel and nontraditional perspectives, their adherents are not worse off than they are under the rule of *Smith*, which provides no scope for special treatment based on religious conviction. My conclusion is that the substantial burden–compelling interest approach, somewhat awkward though it may be, is reasonably manageable by administrators and courts, and that it far better reflects free exercise values than the harsh religion-blind principle of *Smith*.

This conclusion does not itself answer a rather different challenge to the flexible standard we have considered: namely that because courts *will* usually not protect religious exercise, the standard gives an assurance that is illusory. At one time, the number of successful claimants under RFRA was 15 percent.[96] Although statistics like these may well suggest that judges, in general, are giving insufficient weight to religious claims, nonetheless 15 percent is more than zero, and courts have established some significant precedents protecting religious exercise.[97] Perhaps more importantly, the existence

---

[94] There is, however, a special wrinkle about those cases. If money is retrieved from the church, has the debtor actually failed in her religious obligation or was that satisfied by her donating the money in the first place? That obviously depends on her religious understanding, but most people with a responsibility to tithe will presumably regard their own religious exercise as frustrated if the government snatches back money they donate.

[95] Gregory C. Sisk, "How Traditional and Minority Religions Fare in the Courts: Empirical Evidence from Religious Liberty Cases," 76 *University of Colorado Law Review* 1021 (2005), concludes on the basis of a study of decisions from 1985 to 1994 that members of outsider faiths have not fared worse in the courts than members of traditional Christian groups.

[96] Lupu, note 32 supra, at 590. The rate of success in cases other than those involving prisoners was 23 percent (sixteen out of sixty-nine). In a study involving a much broader range of kinds of cases, Gregory Sisk, note 95 supra, at 1028, found that individual federal judges reached resolutions favorable to free exercise claimants 35.6 percent of the time. (This calculation treated dissenting judges according to the resolutions their votes would have reached.)

[97] See, e.g., Thomas Berg, "State and Federal Religious Liberty Legislation: Is It Necessary? Is It Constitutional? Is It Good Policy? The New Attacks on Religious Freedom Legislation, and Why They Are Wrong," 21 *Cardozo Law Review* 415, 419–21 (1999).

of statutory or constitutional protection can affect how administrators treat claimants in the large class of situations that never reach judicial decision; and it constitutes a symbolical affirmation of the need to safeguard religious belief and practice against government interference. These consequences matter, even if judges find it hard to apply the relevant standards and religious claimants do not usually succeed in court.

ALTERNATIVE PROTECTIONS OF FREE EXERCISE

This chapter, and the book up to this point, has concentrated mainly on determinations of free exercise rights that depend on assessments of burden and government interest. Are there approaches that could protect forms of free exercise but not demand such difficult evaluations by administrators and judges? The answer to this question could matter both because various alternative approaches might be intrinsically preferable and because, given the discouraging rate of success for religious claimants under the compelling interest test and the total rejection of most exemption claims under *Employment Division v. Smith*, these alternatives might promise greater protection in the future.[98] The main alternatives, which could supplement or supplant the substantial burden–compelling interest test, and their inclusion in RLUIPA, are discussed in the chapter on land regulation that follows; but some initial comments here fill out the subject of this chapter.

One important approach, which could be expanded from its present scope, concentrates on equality. We saw in *Church of the Lukumi Babalu Aye, Inc. v. City of Hialeah*, in chapter 3, that if the legislature singles out a particular religious activity for treatment worse than is given other similar activities, that is unconstitutional discrimination.[99] So also is discriminating in favor of some religions over others.[100] The focus of these cases is on self-conscious targeting and discrimination. One respect in which equality rights could be enhanced would be to treat legislative classifications that peculiarly disadvantage members of particular religions as potentially unconstitutional if they are based on ignorance about, or indifference toward, those religions. Thus, one might argue that the military services would never have forbidden personnel wearing yarmulkes indoors,[101] and that the state legislature would not have failed to create an exemption for sacramental use of peyote,[102] if dominant Christian

---

[98] See generally Frederick Mark Gedicks, "Toward a Defensible Free Exercise Doctrine," 68 *George Washington Law Review* 925 (2000).

[99] 508 U.S. 520 (1993).

[100] *Larson v. Valente*, 456 U.S. 228 (1982).

[101] See *Goldman v. Weinberger*, 475 U.S. 503 (1986).

[102] *Smith*, note 76 supra.

groups had engaged in those practices; the prohibitions reflected an insensitivity to the needs of Orthodox Jews and the Native American Church. Remarking that "oppressive laws may be enacted through hostility, sheer indifference, or ignorance of minority faiths," Douglas Laycock has proposed that "[a] serious requirement of formal neutrality must consider legislative motive, religious gerrymanders, exceptions, defenses, gaps in coverage, actual or potential bias in enforcement, and whether the state regulates comparable secular conduct or pursues its alleged interests in secular contexts."[103] Arguing that the constitutional protection of religious exercise should be based not on a theory of privilege but on a theory of protection against discrimination, Christopher Eisgruber and Lawrence Sager suggest that courts seeking to assure equal regard for religious exercise should condemn "behavior that lies in a middle ground between purposeful discrimination and unintended disparate harm."[104] Presented with a claim by a minority religious group, such as the Native American Church in *Smith*, a court could ask the counterfactual question whether Oregon would have granted an exception allowing use of peyote if it had been required by strong secular needs (such as medical uses) or mainstream religious needs.[105] Were notions of equality developed in such a fashion, they could provide religious claims a great deal of protection.

One aspect of a robust equality approach could build on what the Supreme Court said in *Smith* about schemes in which other individualized exemptions are given but none is available for religious claimants.[106] In part, the concern here is that if decision is left to individual decision-makers under vague standards, they may act in an arbitrary and unfair manner.[107] In part, the concern is that if rule makers create a set of exemptions and do not include religious claims, they may be undervaluing those claims in comparison with others.[108] An illustration of this approach is the ruling of some courts about prison rules against wearing beards: if the rules make an exception for medical needs, they may also have to make an exception for religious needs.[109]

I will not here try to connect these various claims of equality to other branches of constitutional law, but they receive some support in standards

---

[103] Douglas Laycock, "The Remnants of Free Exercise," 1990 *Supreme Court Review* 4, 43. "Formal neutrality" is not commonly taken to involve such a searching examination.

[104] Christopher L. Eisgruber and Lawrence G. Sager, "The Vulnerability of Conscience: The Constitutional Basis for Protecting Religious Conduct," 61 *University of Chicago Law Review* 1245, 1297 (1994).

[105] Id. at 1289.

[106] *Smith*, note 76 supra, at 884.

[107] See Gedicks, note 98 supra, at 938–40.

[108] Frederick Mark Gedicks, "The Normalized Free Exercise Clause: Three Abnormalities," 75 *Indiana Law Journal* 77, 103–14 (2000).

[109] See, e.g., *Taylor v. Johnson*, 257 F.3d 470 (5th Cir. 2001). See also the opinion by Judge Samuel Alito in *Fraternal Order of Police Newark Lodge No. 12 v. City of Newark*, 170 F.3d 359 (3rd Cir. 1999) (police officers).

under the Equal Protection Clause dealing with suspect classifications—such as racial classifications—and with fundamental rights—such as free speech and the right to travel. Of more direct interest to us here is whether these approaches can get courts out of the business of weighing burdens on religion versus government needs. Yes and no. These approaches do not demand the direct comparison that the compelling interest standard, on which we have focused, requires. But one makes a judgment about insensitive indifference of legislators and about whether religious claims should be treated like other claims partly on the basis of the strength of the religious claims and the inconvenience for the government of accommodating them. Thus, to stick with the beard example, if the medical reasons not to shave were very powerful (some prisoners became susceptible to a fatal skin disease if they shaved) and the religious reasons were comparatively trivial (a beard was one of many nonmandatory ways to show respect), granting a medical exception but not a religious one could make perfect sense. Thus, judges do need to develop some sense of the comparative strength of the medical and religious claims. Further, in equality cases the government can still defend a classification that would otherwise be unacceptable if it has a compelling interest, as it might if many of the inmates presenting religious claim to wear beards were highly dangerous terrorists whose escape might be aided by beards. In summary, although equality approaches do not call for direct comparisons of burden and government need, they cannot be applied without some attention to those factors.

Other approaches draw from free speech law. They might be applied to religious claims on a theory that many, or all, religious activities are a form of expression[110] or that even religious activities that do not amount to expression should be treated as favorably as expression.[111] In *United States v. O'Brien*,[112] a prosecution of a young man who had burned his draft card during the Vietnam War, the Supreme Court, with a disarming professional naïveté, declared that Congress had adopted the law against destroying draft cards to protect the physical draft cards, not to thwart powerful antiwar expression. But the Court went on to say that when such a law incidentally interferes with free expression, it can be applied against expression only if it furthers an important government interest and the incidental restriction of expression is no greater than is needed to further that interest.[113] The *O'Brien*

[110] See generally William P. Marshall, "Religion as Ideas: Religion as Identity," 7 *Journal of Law and Contemporary Issues*, 385, 392–401 (1996) (suggesting that protection should be limited to ideas).
[111] Gedicks, note 98 supra, at 930–32.
[112] 391 U.S. 367 (1968).
[113] Id. at 377.

test sounds as if it gives significant protection to speech, but its application has not borne this out.[114] I need say little about this approach because it is a fairly straightforward "intermediate" standard that demands less of the government than does the compelling interest test but could provide more protection of religious claims than does the total disregard of those claims made under the standard of *Smith*. Indeed, one anomaly created by *Smith* is that core activities of religious worship get no protection against incidental restriction, whereas speech and writing presumably continue to get the modest protection of *O'Brien*.[115]

Another kind of protection given to expression is review of regulations about time, place, and manner. If, for example, the city will not allow a demonstration in New York's Central Park, a court will consider whether that restraint is reasonable. Two aspects of that review are whether the government's regulation is content neutral—not aimed at messages it does not like—and whether those who wish to demonstrate will have other means available to convey their message. This approach has obvious appeal when a court reviews a determination that is directly about the location or time of religious activities—as when a zoning board decides whether a church may be built in a residential district, or prison officials set the hours of worship services. With many religious claims—for example, to worship on Saturday—it may be hard for the government to establish that an alternative is a fair substitute from the perspective of those who worship.[116] Time, place, and manner review seems less apt when the state has decided that the very activity in which the religious claimants want to engage is always harmful or dangerous, as with a uniform ban on the use of peyote or marijuana. The religious claimants might argue they should have a reasonable opportunity to worship according to their convictions; the state's answer is that it wants to prevent this kind of worship.

Does a review of time, place, and manner involve courts in weighing burden and government need? In the instance where the government seeks to prevent the activity altogether, this form of review could require judges directly to assess the government interest and the burden on religion. It would be distinctive only in leading judges to focus heavily on alternative possibilities for religious exercise when they evaluate burdens on religion. When the government is regulating only place and time, the direct weighing that has proved so troublesome is not required. But judges deciding on the reason-

[114] Ira C. Lupu, "To Control Faction and Protect Liberty: A General Theory of the Religion Clauses," 7 *Journal of Contemporary Legal Issues*, 357, 378 (1996), suggests that, despite *O'Brien*, the Court has not developed a "viable doctrine" about free speech exemptions.
[115] See Gedicks, note 108 supra, at 85–94.
[116] Id. at 93.

ableness of regulation and on the availability of alternatives will still end up
having to develop a sense of the strength of the government's interest and
the degree to which a restriction burdens religion.[117]

Although none of these various approaches wholly avoids troublesome
assessments of burden and government interest, some do mute the direct
comparison that so troubled the *Smith* Court. They deserve attention both
(1) because the law should move towards more robust equality protection
for religious minorities and a protection of free religious exercise that is as
strong as its protection of free speech; and (2) because courts sympathetic
to religious claims can profitably use techniques that are not explicitly
blocked by the ruling in *Smith*. In the following chapter, we shall see how
these alternative approaches to protecting free exercise can function in one
particular context.

[117] See Gedicks, note 98 supra, at 947–48.

CHAPTER 14

Land Development and Regulation

Legal regulation of land development by private parties has long been a fertile source of conflict between the free exercise of religion and restraints that the government imposes, ostensibly at least, for the common good. This kind of regulation differs from the laws we have reviewed in previous chapters in mainly affecting religious organizations, rather than individuals. The regulation is typically local and is often focused on particular properties, with administrative boards of municipalities deciding for or against a proposed religious use. What was once a question of common-law nuisance— did a church interfere with its neighbors to such a degree that it had become a nuisance?—has become almost entirely a matter of zoning regulation, regulation that involves much more pervasive control of uses of property. The typical question now is whether a zoning board should grant or deny a religious use. In answering this question, administrators and judges have been influenced by respect for the exercise of religion, drawn from federal and state constitutions and our country's traditions. Since 1993, judicial engagements with regulations of religious usage have also been affected by federal legislation—the Religious Freedom Restoration Act[1] and more recently the Religious Land Use and Institutionalized Persons Act of 2000, adopted unanimously by Congress.[2] The general theoretical question that has drawn our continuing interest—should religion enjoy a special place of privilege or be treated according to a principle of equality with other pursuits?—has played itself out in debate over the most promising judicial approaches to land use regulation. In contrast with its ruling on the development of government land,[3] discussed in chapter 12, the Supreme Court has said very little about the complexities surrounding typical land use regulation as it affects religious institutions.

VARIETIES OF DISPUTES OVER LAND USE BY RELIGIOUS GROUPS

Untangling the various complaints that religious bodies may have about land use regulation is our initial task.[4] Zoning is designed to protect property own-

---

[1] 42 U.S.C. §§ 2000bb-1–2000bb-4 (1994).
[2] 42 U.S.C. § 2000cc.
[3] *Lyng v. Northwest Indian Cemetery Protective Assoc.*, 485 U.S. 439 (1988).
[4] See generally Kenneth A. Young, *Anderson's American Law of Zoning* §§ 12.21–12.31 (4th ed., Deerfield, Ill.: Clark Boardman Callaghan, 1996).

ers and to support rational land development. A city will not allow someone to construct a factory in the middle of a residential area or to sell parcels of one-tenth acre in an area zoned for two-acre lots. Zoning laws involve a mix of categorical exclusions and discretionary judgments. A religious group might find itself frustrated because a municipality excludes houses of worship absolutely from an area. Or a zoning board might refuse a special use permit or variance that would allow the group to construct a building on a site. Or a board might set conditions, such as a limit to the capacity of the sanctuary, that the group is unwilling to satisfy. Not all controversies involve churches or similar structures; some individual claimants want to use their homes for group worship, despite the complaints of neighbors.

Other disputes arise over ancillary uses. A church's right to exist and to hold worship services may not be in doubt, but can it run a shelter for the homeless or operate a school?

Crosscutting these various subjects of dispute are a range of grounds on which groups or individuals may object to a municipality's requirements. A religious group may contend that it is suffering discrimination in comparison with other religious groups, or that the zoning board is giving inadequate consideration to the value of religious use, or that the law, or the board in its decisions, treats religious uses unfairly in comparison with other analogous uses, or that, given the expressive aspects of religious practice, a board's grounds to exclude religious use do not meet the standards required when free speech is at issue. It is a fair indication of the nuances in theories of how religious groups can be unfairly treated that RLUIPA itself contains five separate standards for wrongful land use regulation.[5] Section 2(a) forbids government from imposing a substantial burden on free exercise unless it is furthering a compelling interest by the least restrictive means. This is the familiar formulation from *Sherbert v. Verner* and from the Religious Freedom Restoration Act.[6] Section 2(b) contains four distinct criteria for impermissible government action. It provides that religious institutions cannot be treated worse than nonreligious ones and that no institution can be discriminated against on the basis of its religion; it also precludes a total exclusion of religious assemblies from a jurisdiction and unreasonable limits on religious assemblies and structures.

---

[5] 42 U.S.C. § 2000cc.

[6] However, the statute specifically protects exercises of religion that are not compelled by or central to systems of religious belief—perhaps a precaution against the overly narrow views of some courts applying RFRA—and it states that using or building religious structures for religious exercise counts as religious exercise. In *Civil Liberties for Urban Believers v. City of Chicago*, 342 F.3d 752, 760 (7th Cir. 2003), the court talked of a congressional intent to expand the concept of earlier decisions. The statute's exact language might allow a court to say that its

Although issues about land use regulation usually concern zoning, historic preservation laws can also generate conflicts. A church is designated a historic landmark (or is within a historic preservation area); it wishes to do something with its property that would be permitted to ordinary landowners, but the board protecting historic buildings denies its application.

DISCRIMINATION AGAINST PARTICULAR RELIGIONS

The most straightforward violation of religious exercise occurs when those who administer the law favor some religious denominations over others. As we have seen in chapter 3, the federal Free Exercise Clause is now understood to protect against instances of conscious discrimination and targeting, of the sort that occurred in *Church of the Lukumi Babalu Aye, Inc. v. City of Hialeah*.[7] These days, few, if any, laws about land use will explicitly differentiate among religious groups according to the content of their beliefs and practices, but the discretionary aspects of zoning regulation supply ample opportunity for zoning boards to discriminate in practice. Often such discrimination will be hard to prove, and we should be surprised neither that minority religions are involved in a disproportionate percentage of land use cases[8] nor that courts usually proceed without assuming that outright discrimination has occurred. When such discrimination does indisputably surface, courts treat it as unconstitutional.[9]

Islamic Center of Mississippi, Inc. v. City of Starkville[10] was an unusual case of this sort. Faculty and students at the University of Mississippi sought

---

generous concept of "religious exercise" does not entail a generous understanding of "substantial burden," but such a reading would be at odds with the law's evident purpose.

[7] 508 U.S. 520 (1993).

[8] Apparently, of twenty-five land use cases decided under RLUIPA up to 2005, fifteen involved religious groups represented by 4 percent or fewer adults in the state. (Unpublished manuscript of Heather Takahashi.) A possible "innocent" explanation for this phenomenon is that minority groups disproportionately want to disturb historically established arrangements. A church that existed in a residential district long before churches had to comply with zoning rules will not need relief; a group that wants to build a new structure will have to pass the hurdles of modern land law. However, the Joint Statement of Senators Hatch and Kennedy (sponsors in the senate) of RLUIPA, 146 *Cong. Rec.* S. 7774, at 7774 (2000), claimed "massive evidence" of discrimination against religious exercise in land use regulation. Marci A. Hamilton, *God vs. The Gavel: Religion and the Rule of Law* 87–88 (New York: Cambridge University Press, 2005) disputes that claim.

[9] It would now also violate the terms of Section 2(b) of RLUIPA.

[10] 840 F.2d 293 (5th Cir. 1988). This case bears strong resemblance to the old equal protection decision in *Yick Wo v. Hopkins*, 118 U.S. 356 (1886), as Robert W. Tuttle points out, "How Firm a Foundation? Protecting Religious Land Uses after *Boerne*," 68 *George Washington Law Review* 861, 883 (2000).

to build a Muslim house of worship. For areas near the university, a special
use permit was required for religious uses. Nine Christian churches had presented the only other applications for places of worship, each of which had
been granted. The board of aldermen repeatedly denied applications by the
Muslims based on concerns about traffic congestion, parking, and neighborhood opposition. A Christian facility that had never applied for a permit,
had provided no off-street parking, and had services with twice as many
congregants as those of the Islamic Center functioned next to the Muslims'
site; and the city defended this use. The Fifth Circuit Court of Appeals easily
concluded that the city was not applying its permit process neutrally and
that no legitimate zoning interest was being served by the least restrictive
means. More difficult cases arise when such discrimination is not established
by the evidence. In a challenge to Chicago's zoning restrictions applicable to
churches in commercial districts, Chief Judge Posner suggested that the city
plan favored established traditional religions over new groups that might
thrive in storefront churches and that the plan lacked a sufficient basis under
the Equal Protection Clause, but he was unable to persuade his colleagues
that the plan was unconstitutional.[11]

PRIVILEGED TREATMENT FOR RELIGIOUS USES

The simplest kind of claim that religious groups can make is that municipal
governments are giving insufficient weight to the value of religious facilities
in comparison with the reasons that lead to restrictions. It is difficult to gauge
the present status and future of such claims. An important article by Robert
Tuttle provides a prognosis that is discouraging for religious groups.[12] His
evidence is this: from 1963 to 1990, the prevailing rule of *Sherbert v. Verner*
required states to show that regulations were serving a compelling interest
that could not be satisfied by less restrictive means, if they were to impose a
substantial burden on the exercise of religion. From 1993 until 1997, when
the statute was declared unconstitutional in its application to state and local
governments,[13] RFRA imposed the same standard. Yet in all those years,
federal courts avoided holding zoning decisions invalid; they denied that
interferences with religious exercise were substantial, or they treated government interests that did not seem particularly urgent as compelling, and they
did not carefully examine alternative means. Given this historical record,

---

[11] See *Civil Liberties for Urban Believers*, note 6 supra. The Court also rejected various challenges under RLUIPA. Chief Judge Posner's dissent is at 768–73.
[12] Note 10 supra.
[13] *City of Boerne v. Flores*, 521 U.S. 507 (1997).

Tuttle says, we should not expect reintroduction of the compelling interest test in RLUIPA, even if the act is sustained in this application to land use,[14] to be of much assistance to religious groups. These prospects are especially bleak because the Supreme Court's recently has emphasized equality between religious and other activities, and because it is hard to defend special privileges for religion in a liberal democracy within which theological reasons seem inappropriate for political life.[15] It is too early to judge the accuracy of Tuttle's prediction, but as of the end of 2004, nine of twenty-five cases decided under RLUIPA had been won by plaintiffs, most on the basis that they had suffered a substantial burden not justified by a compelling government interest.[16] These results are somewhat more favorable than Tuttle would have predicted.

Before we tackle the underlying premises of Tuttle's appraisal, and some actual decisions under RLUIPA, we need to describe the background of state law against which the federal law operates. Over the years, many state courts have overturned decisions of zoning boards that were unfavorable to religious groups. Employing an analysis that often rested primarily on substantive due process standards of reasonableness, but was influenced by a sense of the importance of religious exercise, judges determined that standard considerations regarding property values and traffic congestion should give way to the value of having houses of worship within communities.[17] Not all states have followed this pattern; California courts, notably, have required only equal treatment of religious uses.[18] And changes in patterns of worship[19]— with new churches often drawing many congregants from outside communities instead of mainly benefiting local residents—as well as changes in the particular religious usages that are restricted, may well affect judicial attitudes toward zoning decisions. Still, one cannot acquire an accurate sense of the law about religious uses without understanding how those uses are regarded by state courts and, indeed, by the municipal legislatures that establish basic laws about zoning and by the zoning boards that administer these laws.

It is too soon, as much of this volume argues, to dismiss all special privileges for religious groups as inappropriate in light of some general move toward equality of religion and nonreligion. The Supreme Court has not

---

[14] The Supreme Court in *Cutter v. Wilkinson*, 125 S. Ct. 2113 (2005) has upheld the act in respect to prisoners, against the challenge that it favors religious rights over other fundamental rights, such as free speech, and that it encourages prisoners to become religious or feign religious beliefs.

[15] See Tuttle, note 10 supra, at 922–23.

[16] See Takahashi, note 8 supra.

[17] See Young, note 4 supra, at § 12.21, pp. 562–65; Tuttle, note 10 supra, at 877.

[18] Young, note 4 supra, at § 12.21A, pp. 579–80.

[19] See Marci A. Hamilton, "Freedom and the Public Good: The True Story Behind the Religious Land Use and Institutionalized Persons Act," 78 *Indiana Law Journal* 311, 340 (2003).

come close to saying that legislative decisions to confer such privileges necessarily violate the Establishment Clause or the Equal Protection Clause. And
one does not need a "theological" argument to justify such privileges. A
rational constitution-maker or legislator, herself agnostic about fundamental
issues regarding religious truth, might reason as follows: "Most people in
this country believe in transcendental sources of truth. They will understand
their religious beliefs, practices, and obligations as even more important than
their political connections and duties. Because of the value they place on
their religion, the state should make strenuous efforts to avoid frustrating
their religious exercise. Further, viewing the recent span of history, in particular the secular totalitarian political movements of the twentieth century, we
can see that it is healthy for many members of a society to regard their political responsibilities as penultimate, subject to evaluation by other criteria,
even if this attitude occasionally proves inconvenient for government." In
respect to a topic we shall take up in the next chapter, Jeremy Bentham, a
famous disbeliever, offered a spirited argument on behalf of the priest-penitent privilege, which he regarded as following from a principle of toleration
of religion. We need not rely on a theological argument to defend some special privileges for religious groups. But whether such a privilege is workable,
and makes sense, for land use depends on whether administrators and courts
can apply it and on how religious uses relate to other uses.

We can begin by asking if the law can coherently give some kind of privileged treatment to religious uses. Can legislators and judges elaborate standards that both are comprehensible and give adequate guidance to administrators and courts? For the moment, I shall put aside special features and
difficulties of the compelling interest test and focus on the kind of general
favoritism toward religious uses that has long existed in New York and the
majority of states that have adopted a similar stance. Under New York's
approach, municipalities cannot exclude religious uses totally, exclude them
from residential districts, exclude them from 90 percent of the community,
or require that 75 percent of the community agree to them.[20] Further, when
zoning boards make individualized decisions to exclude religious uses, say
forbidding the building of a church because of a concern about property
values and traffic, courts will give those decisions less deference than they
would decisions about most other uses. That such an approach is feasible is
partly evidenced by its continuing dominance in a majority of states. For
virtually all religions, corporate worship is a vital activity; courts, without
entering into a detailed understanding of particular religious faiths, can say
that building places of worship has a high value if religious practice is as-

---

[20] Young, note 4 supra, at 575–77, has a discussion and citations.

signed, a high value. Municipal interests that might be sufficient to block many other uses may not be sufficient to block the construction of houses of worship.

Is this approach unfair to other uses that receive less favorable treatment? If we think of the core religious use as worship, it is hard to see what competing use suffers. Of course, the surrounding landowners who would like to keep a church out suffer, but they could not complain if the law generally gave less weight to their interests in favor of a broad range of nonresidential uses of property—such as are made by libraries, hospitals, social clubs, and halfway houses—or indeed provided them with no zoning protection whatsoever.

So long as we understand any benefit to religious uses to include benefits to groups, such as the Ethical Culture Society, that lack transcendental beliefs but carry on practices that parallel those of typical religious groups,[21] it is hard to see that any of these other uses are in competition with religious worship. (An exception would be a group that propounds atheism without any of the paraphernalia of religious services; perhaps such a group would have to be treated equally with religious ones.) Of course, nonreligious groups might benefit if legislatures had to treat them no worse than religious organizations, and legislators wanted to treat religious organizations well; but these other groups do not suffer directly if houses of worship can be built where they may not build their own structures.[22]

The same cannot be said about certain ancillary uses. If religious groups run schools or day care centers as adjuncts to their houses of worship, their ability to build in residential neighborhoods may prove a disadvantage to competing schools and day care centers. (One might also say that if churches shelter and feed the homeless, in locations close to where the homeless stay, they will have an edge over other groups seeking to benefit the homeless; but it is hard to think of competition in this respect.)[23] The concern about fairness seems mainly concentrated on accessory uses as to which other groups might be in competition with religious ones; it follows that states that do favor religious accessory uses need to be sensitive to the risks of unfair advantage.

The substantial burden–compelling interest formulation, the standard used in RFRA and RLUIPA, by most state RFRAs, and by some state courts

---

[21] I concluded in chapter 8, supra, that such groups are religious.

[22] This conclusion is subject to a modest qualification. Virtually all uses might be seen as in *some* competition with each other. Whether I play tennis or go to church on Sunday morning *might* depend on whether a tennis club or a church is next door or ten miles away. Other uses could suffer to the degree that the closer proximity of churches leads people to spend more time at church and less time engaging in the nonreligious use. But this degree of "competition" seems too remote to be significant.

[23] Conceivably, a nonreligious group with a less desirable location than a religious one might lose public funds, which could pay salaries, because it shelters and feeds fewer homeless people.

interpreting the free exercise clauses in their own constitutions, introduces a number of complications. In the last chapter, we reviewed difficulties that courts face in deciding what amounts to a substantial burden on religious exercise and whether a state has a compelling interest that cannot be served by a less restrictive means. Here we shall look at some special problems with land use cases and evaluate judicial responses.

How is a court to evaluate substantial burden in these cases? When an individual such as Sherbert claims a privilege, judges must focus on her sense of religious obligation; if the question is building a church or providing shelter for the homeless, a court must address the group's sense of its religious priorities. For either endeavor, judges may be hard put to say that what people claim is a substantial interference really is not, but when judges focus on a group, they face the added difficulty of evaluating the dominant convictions and attitudes within a group that may not be of one mind.

Assessing "compelling interest" presents equal difficulties. Opposed to desired religious uses are community interests such as property values, traffic control, and neighborhood quiet. These do not seem to be interests of "the highest order," particularly when one considers the limited degree to which any particular religious use, or a combination of all likely religious uses, is likely to interfere with these interests. Unless proposed religious uses that manage to get over the substantial burden hurdle are to win as a matter of course, courts need to find some way of evaluating state interests that does not treat all plausible interests as compelling and yet does not effectively treat as irrelevant most interests that are actually at stake. Because courts sensibly evaluate burdens and state interests in relation to each other, they need an approach that is not arbitrary and can yield sensible resolutions to the conflicts they face.

In some cases, courts have managed to decide in favor of municipalities by adopting an unduly restrictive approach to substantial burden. A striking illustration is *Lakewood Congregation of Jehovah's Witnesses, Inc. v. City of Lakewood*,[24] in which the Board of Zoning Appeals had denied the group's application for an exemption so that it could build a Kingdom Hall in an area zoned for residential use. The court declared that "building and owning a church is a desirable accessory of worship, not a fundamental tenet of the Congregation's religious beliefs"[25] and that it need not construct a church in a residential district.[26] Religious groups generally regard having

[24] 699 F.2d 303 (6th Cir. 1983).

[25] Id. at 307. See also *Messiah Baptist Church v. County of Jefferson*, 859 F.2d 820 (10th Cir. 1988).

[26] See id. at 306.

formal houses of worship as very important aids to religious practice; an outright bar on construction of houses of worship should certainly qualify as a substantial burden, even if possessing such a building is not itself a central element of the faith.[27]

The issue about location in a residential area is less clear-cut. One question concerns the status of financial considerations. If a church can spend less money by acquiring a site in a residential neighborhood, it will have more money left to construct a building and to expend for other religious purposes. Any financial disadvantage constitutes some burden in carrying forward its projects. But it cannot be that a church establishes a *substantial burden* whenever it shows that any alternative site would be somewhat more expensive. And courts are in a poor position to say when a merely financial disadvantage crosses over the line to being substantial. Courts have sensibly concluded that neither mere inconvenience nor scarcity of property and high price are sufficient to constitute a substantial burden.[28]

Ordinarily, however, a congregation's reasons to build in a residential area go beyond cost. The location may be closer to members than locations in commercial districts, and the members may regard it as more congenial for a place of worship. If a congregation puts forward plausible reasons related to accessibility and atmosphere, that should be sufficient to get over the hurdle of substantial burden, and to trigger a comparison of the municipality's interest in foreclosing that location. In this respect, the *Lakewood* court took too narrow an approach to substantial burden.[29] By its broad definition of religious exercise, RLUIPA implicitly rejects any narrow approach to substantial burden.[30] Courts that have ruled that a religious group does not suffer a substantial burden unless regulation restricts its current practices or

---

[27] Robert Tuttle, note 10 supra, at 872, suggests that Kingdom Halls do have special theological significance for Jehovah's Witnesses. At id. 872–73, Tuttle strongly criticizes the court's approach to substantial burden in this case.

[28] See, e.g., *Guru Nanak Sikh Soc'y v. County of Sutter*, 326 F. Supp. 1140, 1152 (E.D. Cal. 2003) (mere inconvenience insufficient); *Midrash Sephardi, Inc v. Town of Surfside*, 366 F.3d 1214, 1227 (11th Cir. 2004) (on scarcity and high price of land). Perhaps the greater expense of a permitted alternative site could constitute a substantial burden if the cost differential for purchasing a site and building a church is very great. One example of a very great financial sacrifice in a historic preservation case was *Rector of St. Bartholomew's Church v. City of New York*, 914 F.2d 348 (2d Cir. 1990), cert. denied, 499 U.S. 905(1991). The church's inability to destroy its Community House and build a tall office building cost it many millions of dollars. It is at least arguable that a church may have to suffer such a sacrifice in lost opportunities without sustaining a "substantial burden," though it would sustain a substantial burden if the only available property on which it could build a house of worship was that much more expensive than the site on which it wished to build.

[29] See Tuttle, note 10 supra, at 872–73.

[30] 42 U.S.C. § 2000cc-5(7)(A)&(B). See text accompanying note 6, supra.

keeps it from a location that is necessary or makes its exercise of religion "effectively impracticable" have failed to be faithful to the spirit of the federal statute.[31]

In land use cases, some courts have been very undemanding in what they require in terms of a compelling interest that cannot be served by less restrictive means. It has been enough that the municipality have a rational zoning scheme that could be undermined by too many exceptions. In *Messiah Baptist Church v. County of Jefferson*,[32] the church was denied a special use permit to build on property zoned for agricultural use. Although the permit procedure contemplated the granting of some exceptions, the court held that the county had a compelling interest in accomplishing its plan of "true differentiation." A more appropriate approach would have been to inquire whether granting this application and other likely applications from religious, and perhaps other nonprofit, groups would significantly undermine the effort to create an agricultural district. Courts rightly do not ask whether a single exception would impair a zoning plan; but they should ask whether foreseeable requests for exceptions of the same kind are likely to do so. If the answer to this question is "no," they should not decide that a plan permits no exceptions.

In *Grosz v. City of Miami Beach*,[33] the court used an explicit balancing approach to evaluate a claim by a rabbi to use his garage for religious services in an area zoned for single-family homes. Minimizing Grosz's interest in holding the services, which would have been permitted had he resided in an area within four blocks of where he then lived, the court declared that the city had a compelling interest in not making exceptions to its zoning plan. As in *Messiah Baptist Church*, the court too quickly reached the conclusion that a municipality need not make exceptions to its zoning plan. By contrast, a district court engaged in a more nuanced inquiry in a decision under RLUIPA when a town tried to restrict weekly prayer meetings at a home in an area zoned for single-family residences.[34] The zoning commission had declared that no more than twenty-five persons could be present. The court determined that less restrictive means were available to meet the safety concern arising from increased traffic.

Issues about substantial burden and compelling interest also arise over ancillary uses. One district court, doubtful that a church had a religious

---

[31] See *Vineyard Christian Fellowship of Evanston, Inc. v. City of Evanston*, 250 F. Supp. 961, 986, 990–93 (N.D. Ill. 2003) (group has failed to show that its worship must be at that location); *Civil Liberties for Urban Believers*, note 6 supra, at 761 (religious exercise not rendered "effectively impracticable").

[32] 859 F.2d 820 (10th Cir. 1988).

[33] 721 F.2d 729 (11th Cir. 1983).

[34] *Murphy v. Zoning Comm'n of New Milford*, 148 F. Supp. 2d 173 (D. Conn. 2001).

interest in running a food bank and homeless shelter, upheld a denial of a special use permit to engage in those activities.[35] Another district court decided that a church's feeding the hungry was a "form of worship akin to prayer."[36] Since the city did not assert that it had a compelling interest in stopping the program, it could not justify the substantial burden on religious exercise that its application of zoning regulations entailed. Yet another district court held that a county could not deny a special use permit for a church to operate a religious school on its premises.[37] In respect to the burdens of denials of ancillary uses, courts permissibly give some weight to traditional religious practices; but they should remain open to claims that a particular use has an importance for a group that exceeds that within most religions. The municipality's interest should be judged both in terms of the degree of disturbance the use creates and the degree of disadvantage of accommodating similar uses by other groups. If nonreligious uses are closely similar to the particular use that a church seeks, a locality has a strong interest in avoiding the possibly unconstitutional favoring of the religious use over the nonreligious one.

APPROACHES THAT RELY ON FUNDAMENTAL RIGHTS BUT DO NOT BALANCE THE BURDEN ON RELIGION DIRECTLY AGAINST THE STATE'S INTEREST

Both because success in land use cases, as in other areas, has been limited under the substantial burden–compelling interest standard and because that standard calls upon courts to engage in very difficult—some say impossible—inquiries, scholars have proposed that courts rely primarily on other approaches, and, as we have seen, RLUIPA explicitly includes other approaches. The final section of the previous chapter discusses such approaches in general. As we saw there, the substitution of these other approaches is especially attractive for those who believe that, in principle, religion does not warrant special privileges; but it may also have the appeal of practical feasibility for those who do not think special privileges for religion are inher-

---

[35] *Daytona Rescue Mission, Inc. v. City of Daytona Beach*, 885 F. Supp. 1554 (M.D. Fla. 1995).

[36] *Western Presbyterian Church v. Board of Zoning Adjustment*, 862 F. Supp. 538 (D.D.C. 1994). See also *Stuart Circle Parish v. Board of Zoning Appeals*, 946 F. Supp. 1225 (E.D. Va. 1996).

[37] *Alpine Christian Fellowship v. County Commissioners of Pitkin County*, 870 F. Supp. 991 (D. Colo. 1994). For a similar decision under RLUIPA, see *Westchester Day School v. Village of Mamaroneck*, 280 F. Supp. 230 (S.D.N.Y. 2003).

ently wrong.[38] In this chapter, we have already looked at one alternative approach, a claim that a particular religion suffers discrimination in comparison with other religions. If it can be proven, such a claim will lead to victory for the religious group, but such claims are hard to prove. Protection against such unfair treatment would be significantly enhanced if courts were to consider indifference and inattention, as well as self-conscious discrimination, as possible bases for redress.

Another kind of claim is also explicitly comparative. Based on the status of religion as a fundamental right, a religious group can raise an equal protection argument that it cannot be treated worse than analogous nonreligious activities, and, as we have seen, Section 2(b) of RLUIPA contains an explicit provision to this effect. Of course, it is not easy to say what activities are relevantly comparable, but in one case a church had been denied permission to build in a commercial zone, because it would not stimulate economic development. The Eighth Circuit was unwilling to accept this justification without a satisfactory explanation why churches were excluded when other noncommercial uses were allowed.[39] In this context, the city's reason for not allowing a religious use helped to define other noncommercial uses as the relevant class for comparison.

Other approaches look to standards of judgment in free speech cases. One might say that free exercise resembles free speech and thus warrants similar treatment, but it is more straightforward simply to conclude that RLUIPA implicitly invokes standards like those governing free speech or that basic forms of religious practice are themselves one kind of speech.[40] When government regulations impinge on speech but are not directed against speech, they must not foreclose all opportunities to communicate, they must be reasonable in their constraint of the time, place, and manner of speech, and they must provide administrative officials sufficient direction to prevent arbitrary exercises of discretion. These various principles, as Robert Tuttle contends, can provide courts with significant review of zoning regulations and of administrative decisions to deny special use permits.[41] The time, place, and manner inquiry allows courts to review the reasonableness of a board's denial of a religious use without having to grant great deference to the board's judgment or trying directly to balance religious burden against state's inter-

---

[38] Robert W. Tuttle, note 10 supra, develops a powerful argument along these lines.

[39] *Cornerstone Bible Church v. City of Hastings*, 948 F.2d 464, 471 (8th Cir. 1991).

[40] The latter conclusion will not work for forms of religious practice that are not speech in any sense that is ordinary or is embraced by First Amendment notions of free speech. Sheltering the homeless would be one example.

[41] See *Vineyard Christian Fellowship*, note 31 supra, at 979–89.

est.[42] And courts focusing on the standards of judgment that boards are directed to use in reviewing claims for exemptions can limit themselves to an inquiry whether regulations provide guidance that is sufficiently definite.

A somewhat related question is whether a scheme of regulation is sufficiently general and neutral to be controlled by *Employment Division v. Smith*. Some courts have held that schemes for historic preservation, based on individualized judgments, do not qualify, and they have sustained claims of churches to be free of constraints imposed on them.[43] Similar challenges have been made to special permit processes.[44] Of course, even if a scheme is not neutral and general, a municipality may succeed in arguing that it serves a compelling interest; but a court that decides to class regulations as other than neutral and general is also likely to look favorably on claims for relief from application of the regulations.

It may well be that other approaches are now more promising ways to protect religious uses of land, and perhaps a broader range of religious claims, than is the more direct, and seemingly generous, standard of substantial burden–compelling interest.[45] Despite the modest results for churches when courts have employed the latter approach to review challenges to land use regulation, I am not ready to see the approach thrown overboard in those cases (or more generally); but it does need to be applied with a realistic eye to what is in contention in controversies between religious groups and municipalities over land use.

---

[42] A persuasive argument for such an approach was developed by Judge McKay, dissenting in *Messiah Baptist Church*, note 32 supra, at 832–33. Of course, as we found in chapter 13, deciding if restraints are reasonable does implicitly involve *some* assessment of a church's and a city's interests.

[43] See *First Covenant Church of Seattle v. City of Seattle*, 840 F.2d 174 (Wash. 1992); *Maryland, Keeler v. Mayor of City Council of Cumberland*, 940 F. Supp. 879 (D. Md. 1996). But see *St. Bartholomew's Church*, note 28 supra. It may or may not be relevant that in *First Covenant Church* the group sought to alter its building's exterior in a way that had religious significance. In *St. Bartholomew's Church* (only) money was involved. Ira C. Lupu and Robert W. Tuttle, in "Historic Preservation Grants to Houses of Worship: A Case Study in the Survival of Separationism," 43 *Boston College Law Review* 1130 (2002), compare various approaches to government regulation and government funding. They conclude that church interiors, but not exteriors, should be free of regulation and not proper subjects of funding for historical preservation.

[44] See *Cottonwood Christian Center v. Cypress Redevelopment Agency*, 218 F. Supp. 2d 1203, 1222–24 (C.D. Cal. 2002). Such a challenge was rejected in *Ehlers-Renzi v. Connelly School of the Holy Child, Inc.*, 224 F.3d 283 (4th Cir.), cert. denied, 531 U.S. 1192 (2001). And in *Mount Elliott Cemetery Ass'n v. City of Troy*, 171 F.3d 398 (6th Cir. 1999), the court held that ordinances under which the city denied the application of a Catholic church to build a cemetery were neutral laws of general applicability.

[45] See Tuttle, note 10 supra.

CHAPTER 15

Confidential Communications with Clergy

People often speak to clergy as pastors of the soul. They expect what they say to them to be kept in confidence. How far should the laws protect this secrecy (1) by relieving clergy from obligations to disclose that are imposed upon other members of society and (2) by rewarding lawsuits against clergy who have chosen to disclose what they have learned? In this chapter, we shall look at the issues these questions pose about the exercise of religion and about acceptable classification, considering the legal privileges of clergy not to reveal confidences, as well as what legal obligations they may have to remain silent. Although a state's regulation of privileges and disclosure is not always regarded as within the boundaries of what constitutional provisions protecting free exercise may cover, it decidedly concerns the range of religious practice the law as a whole will safeguard.

THE PRIEST-PENITENT PRIVILEGE AND OTHER PROTECTIONS AGAINST DISCLOSURE

All jurisdictions in the United States have some form of priest-penitent privilege that protects clergy from having to testify about what they have learned in their professional roles. We shall shortly turn to some of the more specific controversies about this privilege, but it helps to see at the outset what are the overriding concerns of policy and constitutional law. For the major part of its history the Roman Catholic Church has required its members to confess their sins to individual priests if they are to receive the sacrament of Holy Communion. At least since 1215, the church has imposed an absolute duty on priests not to break the seal of confession;[1] violators may be excommunicated.[2] If a priest were required to testify about what someone told him in confession, he would face a stark conflict between his religious and secular duties. Given the importance of the sacrament of confession for Roman Catholics and the conviction of priests that they may not disclose what they have heard, strong free exercise reasons support not requiring testimony

[1] Fourth Lateran Council, Canon 21.
[2] See John C. Bush and William Harold Tiemann, *The Right to Silence* 27 (3d ed., Nashville: Abingdon Press, 1989), quoting and summarizing modern canons.

about the confessional; and those who are aware that Jeremy Bentham was both an unbeliever and a powerful opponent of most testimonial privileges may be surprised to learn that he claimed that the priest-penitent privilege was required by religious toleration.[3]

Some other branches of Christianity retain the practice of individual confessions to priests or ministers, but none make such confessions a requisite for receiving communion or assert that church members should make such confessions, rather than general confessions during worship services and individual confessions directly to God.[4] "Free church" Protestants do not have any practice of individual confessions to clerics.[5]

In all Christian denominations, and indeed in virtually every religion that has clerics,[6] members consult with them about spiritual anxieties and personal problems, including marital problems. In the course of such conversations, members may disclose actions that are criminal or that would, if revealed, hurt their positions if their spouses sought divorces and the custody of children. In some other branches of Christianity as well as Roman Catholicism, a cleric is thought to have an absolute duty not to disclose what he has heard; in yet other Christian denominations, however, and among Jews and Muslims, duties of confidentiality may be overridden by other considerations. These differences are revealed by responses from the perspectives of various faiths about what a cleric should do if a confession reveals that an innocent man is about to be executed for a crime he did not commit.[7]

For religious groups that do not perceive the cleric as under an absolute religious duty to keep silence, the free exercise argument that the law should confer an absolute privilege is considerably less powerful than it is for Roman Catholics. At a minimum, clerics who counsel church members should receive the less than absolute privilege given secular psychotherapists. If an absolute privilege is granted only to Roman Catholics (and those groups with similar views of confession), that may appear to be unacceptable favoritism. If a privilege is calibrated to views of confidentiality within any particular group, judges would need to investigate the precise tenets and practices of various groups. A concern with any privilege is whether it can fairly be limited to people who are clerics within recognized religious groups. All these questions raise doubts whether legislatures and judges can craft a privi-

---

[3] Charles Alan Wright and Kenneth W. Graham, Jr., 26 *Federal Practice and Procedure* § 5612, pp. 55–56 (St. Paul: West, 1992).

[4] See Bush and Tiemann, note 2 supra, at 55–75.

[5] Id. at 77–84.

[6] See id. at 85–90 on the Jewish tradition.

[7] See the essays responding to this hypothetical in 29 *Loyola of Los Angeles Law Review* 1717–84 (1996).

lege that avoids serious unfairness and does not trespass on one constitutional principle or another.

Historically, the priest-penitent privilege has concerned testimony at trials and other formal proceedings. The law now also imposes various obligations to report information outside the trial process. For example, various people aware that parents are physically abusing their children have a responsibility to report to authorities. From a cleric's point of view, it will rarely matter whether a legal duty that he disclose confidential information concerns compelled testimony or a separate responsibility; but those determining the scope of privileges need to consider both kinds of obligations.

Whether the common law recognized a priest-penitent privilege after Henry VIII's break with the Roman Catholic Church is a matter of some uncertainty.[8] What is sure is that every American state now has a statutory privilege and that the Supreme Court has indicated that federal law also includes such a privilege.[9] Because Congress refused to approve various formulations of privileges proposed by an advisory committee and submitted to it in 1972, federal privileges are developed by the federal courts "in the light of reason and experience";[10] the courts assume that this vague direction includes a priest-penitent privilege. Because many of the states have drawn upon the language of the privilege that was drafted for, but not adopted by, Congress, I shall have occasion to refer to terms of the rejected Rule 506[11] proposed by the federal advisory committee.

For Penitents or for Others as Well?

Taken most narrowly, the privilege might cover only those who are engaged in a penitent's act of confession. For Roman Catholics, confession to a priest is a specific action that is considered a sacrament; the priest alone prescribes penance and plays a crucial role in absolution for the sin the penitent confesses. Within some other Christian denominations, members may also decide less formally to confess sins to members of the clergy.

When church members and others are counseled by clergy, the main object of the interchanges is not confession, although the person in need may admit to wrongs he has committed, some of which may carry legal consequences. We can see this easily if we think of marriage counseling, when the cleric meets with one or both spouses. To oversimplify, a minister asks the hus-

---

[8] See Wright and Graham, note 3 supra, § 5612, at 28–54. There are relatively few reported instances of priests being penalized for refusing to break the confessional seal.

[9] See, e.g., *Trammel v. United States*, 445 U.S. 40, 51 (1980).

[10] Wright and Graham, note 3 supra, § 5611, at 14.

[11] See generally id. at 8–14, 18.

band, "Well, just what is going wrong between you and Janis." He responds, "She got very mad and slapped me when she found out I was having an affair with our next-door neighbor. The slap made me furious and I knocked her down. She's barely spoken to me since."

Some modern statutes clearly cover communications that are not dominantly confessional in their nature. For example, rejected Rule 506, followed in a number of states, privileges "a confidential communication by the person to a clergyman in his professional character as spiritual advisor."[12] Other states retain statutory language that appears to be narrower. Arizona's law, for example, refers to "any confession made to [a clergyman] in his character as clergyman or priest in the course of discipline enjoined by the church to which he belongs."[13] Such language *could* be taken to require that the communication must be dominantly a confession, that the person talking to the cleric must be a member of the cleric's church, and that the confession must be enjoined by the discipline of the church.[14] Were the language so understood, the provision would be narrow in its scope. However, in accord with a modern trend toward liberalization of the privilege, the language could be construed to reach any admissions of wrong, given according to a practice that the church encourages, such as marital counseling.

When we focus on confessions of sin that are believed to carry important spiritual significance, made to clergy who regard themselves as under a religious obligation not to disclose what they have learned, the justifications for a legal privilege vary from the secular reasons that support the lawyer-client and doctor-patient privileges. The ability of lawyers and doctors to keep confidences is regarded as socially desirable. For the priest-penitent privilege, desirability must be evaluated differently. In accord with the fundamental principle of this book that the government of a modern liberal democracy should not determine what *really* is spiritually efficacious, a justification cannot rest on any notion that God welcomes confessions to priests. But the government may decide that as long as many people regard confession as crucial to their religious practice, the state should not interfere. It may also decide that trying to compel testimony is not only futile because priests will not break the seal of confession, but will generate pointless conflicts that bring the law into disrepute.

We can discern a rather different justification for a privilege that reaches the broader range of conversations between church members and clergy.[15]

[12] Id. at 8.
[13] Id. at 21, n. 3.
[14] Bush and Tiemann, note 2 supra, at 89–90, comment that some courts interpret these laws narrowly; the authors assert that this raises serious First Amendment issues.
[15] This justification can also cover many instances of the narrower practice of confession.

These can help people attain psychological balance and resolve practical problems in much the same manner as consultations with secular counselors. Of course, exchanges with family members, friends, and even strangers at a bar can yield similar benefits, and no one suggests granting a privilege for anyone who happens to be sought out for advice; but in most modern religions in the United States, clergy see themselves as having a professional counseling role that is not unlike that of licensed secular therapists.

A Privilege for Clergy

The cleric's privilege not to testify applies to confidential communications with clergy in their profession as clergy.[16] This simple proposition conceals a number of issues. We shall concentrate on the one that matters most for our overall study, after noting some of the others.

The communication must be to the member of the clergy in her professional role as pastor. If I disclose a criminal act to my sister Ann or my friend Bruce in an ordinary conversation, the fact that they happen to be members of the clergy does not give rise to the privilege. And if a minister investigating missing church funds asks the treasurer, "What do you think happened to the five thousand dollars?" and the treasurer responds, "I took a short-term loan to pay my gambling debts, but I'll repay the money soon," his admission is not protected. Needless to say, if confidential communications are to plan a scheme of embezzlement *with* a minister, that communication is not protected under the priest-penitent privilege.[17]

The communication must be intended to be confidential. If I intend, or understand, that a minister will relate what I say to someone else, I cannot claim that he must remain silent if the government tells him to speak. If I communicate to a minister in a group setting in which others will hear as well as he, I cannot treat the conversation as confidential.[18]

Unanticipated overhearing is different.[19] Suppose, for example, that the person next in line hears a crucial admission a confessant makes to a priest, or prison authorities record a conversation between a prisoner and a minister.[20] Clearly this overhearing does not affect whatever privilege attaches to the cleric. The question is whether the third party who overhears can disclose

---

[16] See Wright and Graham, note 3 supra, at §§ 5613–19, pp. 93–199.

[17] Each person might, however, plead the privilege against self-incrimination.

[18] The presence of a nonclergy assistant or of one's own spouse, as in marriage counseling, would typically not undermine the privilege.

[19] For this purpose, unanticipated overhearing would cover hearing that the parties to the conversation think is fairly likely, so long as they are aiming to preserve secrecy.

[20] See, e.g., *Mockaitis v. Harcleroad*, 104 F.3d 1522 (9th Cir. 1997).

what he has heard. If the government itself has intentionally overheard, it should not be able to profit from its interference with a protected relationship. Matters are more doubtful if the overhearing is fortuitous or occurs by the design of a private person. In favor of allowing eavesdroppers to testify and in favor of having their testimony compelled, one might argue that what matters from a religious point of view are the actions of clerics, and what parishioners are willing to say will be little affected by occasional revelations by eavesdroppers. However, the better approach is to subject the eavesdroppers to the restriction of the privilege, in order to protect the communications themselves and to discourage intentional interferences with them.[21]

What if the person speaking believes he is communicating to a member of the clergy, but he is not? If his assumption is reasonable and, according to his understanding of the facts, the person to whom he speaks would be recognized by the law as a member of the clergy, he should be able to rely on the privilege.[22]

This question of "mistake" slides into the status of persons who are "quasi-clergy."[23] Various people, including nuns, seminary students, and church elders, perform functions of clergy without being ordained. Should the privilege extend to them? Even if these individuals cannot perform the formal rite of confession, they may be encouraged to provide the kind of consultation and advice offered by priests or ministers. Some religious groups have no clergy, but they have leaders. A court might avoid deciding if one of these people really counts as clergy by saying that a person communicating to her may consider her to be clergy, and thus can benefit from her mistake.[24] But the less disingenuous, more straightforward approach is to acknowledge that persons can count as clergy for this purpose, even if they are not formally ordained and are distinctive from designated clergy within a religious denomination, so long as they occupy positions of leadership and perform the kinds of clergy functions that give rise to the privilege.

This raises the most fundamental question about the limits of the privilege. Whatever its extension to quasi-clergy, the privilege reaches only persons who are treated as clergy within recognized religious groups. Someone who has divulged personal information cannot invoke the privilege by claiming that he treats the woman to whom he has communicated as clergy, although

---

[21] This result is unambiguously provided in rejected Rule 506, Wright and Graham, note 3 supra, at 8.

[22] Wright and Graham, note 3 supra, § 5614, at 128.

[23] Id. at 128–34.

[24] If this is genuinely a "mistake," it is more precisely a mistake about the content of the law than one of fact. People must usually, but not always, bear the consequences of their legal mistakes.

she does not occupy any formal position of leadership in a group.[25] And, typically, one cannot invoke the privilege if everyone in one's religious group is considered clergy and one has "confessed" to another ordinary member. However broadened the category of clergy, the privilege still depends on someone occupying a position of leadership within a religious group.[26] Is this approach defensible, in light of the general tendency to rely on the individual religious convictions of the persons making claims of free exercise?

We can certainly see the logic. The law of compelled testimony is harsh; it requires many family members and close friends to testify in a way that can be highly damaging to those they love. A person who belongs to a religious group that regards all members as clergy might be fortunate enough to have most family members and friends as "clergy." Or someone might say he regards a particular close friend as a "minister" to him. If courts had to recognize all such honestly held claims, they would significantly extend privileges against compelled testimony. And judges would face thorny factual determinations when those called to testify offered such claims of privilege. Restricting the category of clergy avoids this inconvenience. But the consequence may be a kind of favoritism of groups with formal clergy, or with leaders whose functions approximate those of clergy, and favoritism for institutional "churches" over private convictions and arrangements. Whether such favoritism creates problems under the Establishment Clause and the Free Exercise Clause is a subject to which we shall return.

A Privilege Held by the Cleric or the Person Who Communicates with Him or Her?

Who exactly should hold the clerical privilege not to testify?[27] Usually it will not matter. Someone will admit wrongdoing to a minister. That person will not want the minister to testify and the minister will not want to testify. But attitudes will not always correspond. The person who has spoken to the priest may have said things that are actually exculpatory; he may want the priest to testify, but the priest may believe he should not break the seal of the confession. Or a minister may believe that according to a balance of values he should testify. Suppose a defendant has admitted to her that he has

[25] In modern formulations, one need not be a member of the particular religious group the cleric represents.

[26] Wright and Graham are sharply critical of this approach as it might apply to Jehovah's Witnesses, where a member might confess to the whole group. Note 3 supra, at 109–11. What Wright and Graham miss is the anomaly that would be created if someone could confess to all his close acquaintances, with none being eligible to testify to the fact.

[27] See Michael J. Mazza, "Should Clergy Hold the Priest-Penitent Privilege," 82 *Marquette Law Review* 171 (1998).

already killed six children; the minister may fear that if he is not convicted he will kill more, and the prosecutor may have persuaded the minister that an acquittal is likely unless the minister can testify to admissions the defendant may have made. The minister, putting the saving of lives ahead of maintaining confidentiality, desires to testify; the defendant wants her to remain silent. In such situations, it matters who holds the privilege.

The fundamental rationale of the privilege is to protect statements made in confidence to clerics. The power to invoke the privilege should rest with the person who has made the statements, relying on the confidentiality of the conversation.[28] However, at least for those clerics who believe they would commit a serious wrong by testifying, perhaps they should not be required to do so, even if the persons who have spoken to them consent or have died.

Possible Qualifications and Ranges of Coverage

The traditional priest-penitent privilege covers formal testimony and is absolute. Given modern reporting requirements for certain professionals—of plans to commit crimes, of gunshot wounds, of abuse of children—questions arise about what range of coverage the priest-penitent privilege should have and whether it should be absolute.

We may begin with the proposition that from a religious point of view, the locus of required disclosure is not crucial. Protecting against compelled testimony is no more important than protecting against compelled disclosure to the police or to welfare officials. A modern privilege to remain silent should not be restricted to formal testimony; it should cover all kinds of disclosure that might otherwise be compelled. But for clergy whose role is primarily that of counselor, justifying a privilege against disclosure that is more absolute than the privileges of psychiatrists and of other secular therapists is not simple. If clergy providing counsel learn that children are suffering physical abuse, why should they be allowed to keep that secret if secular professionals are not?

There are some reasons to provide a privilege for clergy that is absolute or more nearly so. (1) The privilege covers, with other conversations, formal acts of confession for which a more absolute privilege is warranted. (2) Even "ordinary" counseling by clergy contains a perceived spiritual component that may warrant a privilege that is more extensive. (3) Clergy, unlike secular counselors, will not comply with limits on the privilege, and their refusal

---

[28] One might defend placing the privilege exclusively with the cleric on the following basis. The cleric will ordinarily protect the interests of someone who has revealed confidences to her. If she is willing to testify, that is probably an indication that the interest in testimony outweighs that in silence.

will be based on a strong sense of religious duty. Thus, qualifying the privilege will invite undesirable conflicts of law and religious duties. On this last point, much depends on the precise attitudes of clergy who counsel parishioners. Within many religious groups, clergy do not regard themselves as under an absolute duty to remain silent; if the consequences of silence are grave enough, they will speak out. For such clerics, legal requirements to disclose could affect the balance of considerations, even if they were not taken as conclusive;[29] and qualifying the privilege could therefore help produce disclosures in some circumstances.

The possibility remains that if clergy were to divulge under legal compulsion, people would be more guarded in their conversations with clergy, declining to reveal secrets they would not want disclosed. However, the same possibility occurs with respect to qualifications on lawyer-client, doctor-patient, and therapist-patient privileges, and we have no reason to suppose that any qualifications in the priest-penitent privilege will be particularly liable to dry up constructive interchanges, even those involving admissions of criminal activities.[30]

Ordinarily, the person who admits child abuse to a member of the clergy should have no greater claims to secrecy than one who admits abuse to a secular therapist; but legislators and judges must be wary of demanding that clergy disclose what they feel bound not to disclose. Perhaps the best resolution is to carve out exceptions for which only the cleric, not the communicant, has a privilege to avoid disclosure. In that event, the person who has admitted abusing a child could not prevent a cleric from speaking, *if* the cleric believed he should.

How to Frame a Privilege

In light of the various concerns we have examined, the following solution is tempting: create a basic privilege that covers clergy in general, that reaches disclosures other than formal testimony, that is held by the person who communicates with the clergy,[31] and that is qualified in accord with qualifications that apply to secular professionals; create, for those clerics who assert a religious obligation not to disclose, an extra privilege that is as absolute as their

[29] Probably few clergy would take a legal requirement to disclose as decisive, given their sense that whether to disclose or not is ultimately a matter of religious responsibility.

[30] From a religious point of view, the refusal of someone to confess to a priest might be regarded as particularly harmful, risking the welfare of the soul, but that is not a standpoint the government of a liberal democracy should adopt, especially in a country where most citizens do not believe that individual confession to a priest is a religious necessity.

[31] However, one might place the privilege with that person only for testimony, leaving it with the cleric to decide whether to disclose to police and welfare officials.

perceived religious obligation.[32] By this twofold approach, one could pre-serve the seal of the confessional without having a privilege that is closer to absolute than would otherwise be desirable for the many other communica-tions to clergy that deserve only more limited protection.[33]

Constitutional Considerations

The law regarding clergy privilege is rife with substantial constitutional is-sues, none of which have been directly addressed by the Supreme Court. Because these issues resemble nonconstitutional choices we have just exam-ined, our treatment can be relatively brief.

Is there a free exercise *right* to a privilege not to testify or to disclose information? Probably courts would decide against a constitutional privi-lege. They have consistently said that the government has a compelling inter-est in requiring testimony. Under *Employment Division v. Smith*, the law is not required to give conversations with clergy any special status,[34] but even in states with RFRAs or with a constitutional standard of compelling interest for free exercise claims, legislatures could probably decide to abolish any priest-penitent privilege. Although one could argue that the history of the privilege demonstrates that the law can carve out this limited exception to compulsory testimony without undue effect, and that the government, thus, has less restrictive means to accomplish the objectives served by compulsory testimony, courts have hesitated to rule that various kinds of testimony are really not necessary, and they would probably not override legislative judg-ments that the priest-penitent privilege should give way. My own view, how-ever, is that at least basic aspects of the priest-penitent privilege should be protected by constitutional free exercise standards.

In all probability, a court would decide that religious counselors must have privileges as great as those of secular counselors who are not doctors. Al-though state licensing of secular counselors *might* be thought to justify their receiving special privileges, the absence of governmental licensing for clerics reflects the powerful rationale that religious counselors should not bear the

---

[32] One could place this privilege in the hands of the person making a disclosure to a cleric within a system in which confidences are absolutely respected; but I think it is sufficient to rely on the cleric. That avoids delicate inquiry into the exact practice of a religious group and the expectations of the person making a disclosure.

[33] Margaret Battin, in *Ethics in the Sanctuary*, 42–53 (New Haven: Yale University Press, 1990), challenges the absoluteness of the Roman Catholic rule of nondisclosure under a struc-ture that accepts for ethical analysis 0-level, fundamental, principles of religions and allows evaluation of less basic principles, into which the doctrines about confessing fall.

[34] However, it can be argued that other testimonial privileges introduce a kind of individual-ization that cannot exclude religious considerations.

imprimatur of the state. To treat confidential conversations with these counselors less favorably than those with secular counselors would be to discriminate unconstitutionally against religious practices.

Because the priest-penitent privilege is so solidly entrenched, the constitutional issues of practical importance do not concern potential elimination,
or even disadvantage vis-à-vis secular counselors, but the acceptability of
various protective approaches. We need to view these issues about establishment and equal treatment in light of the reasons of religious exercise for
offering a privilege. We can break down these issues into ones about (1)
favoritism toward religion, (2) preference for institutional forms of religion,
and (3) denominational preference.[35]

In a sense, any privilege for conversations with clerics that is more expansive than a privilege for conversations with analogous secular professionals
does favor religious interchanges. But, because clerics and those who speak
with them have a sense of confidentiality that has transcendent dimensions,
bolstering a privilege to accommodate these conversations is acceptable. A
two-pronged approach that reserves an absolute privilege only for those clerics who have a sense of religious obligation not to speak is more circumspect
in this regard—creating less of break between conversations with clerics and
those with other professionals—than a privilege that is absolute in respect
to all clerics in all circumstances.

Any privilege that relies on the institutional position of the cleric does
relegate to a secondary position the particular understandings of individuals
(other than factual mistakes about whether someone is a cleric to whom the
privilege would definitely apply), *and* it does require courts to identify who
count as clerics. For most issues in this volume, I have agreed with courts
that have placed primary emphasis on individual understandings; but here,
as with the claims to withdraw children from school after eighth grade and to
use peyote in worship, there are powerful reasons to include an institutional
requirement. These reasons are strong enough to support any implicit "discrimination" against peculiar private understandings and whatever modest
difficulties courts may have in deciding who count as clerics. This conclusion
illustrates one of the important aspects of the entire book. Precisely what
categorization is appropriate, or best, for one subject within the general
realm of free exercise may not be appropriate for another. Across-the-board
simple principles are bound to founder when one tries to apply them to a
complex and diverse set of problems.

A privilege that relies on the institutional position of clerics may also be
defended against the argument that it implicitly favors some denominations

---

[35] Wright and Graham, note 3 supra, at 66–78, regard these issues as very troubling.

over others. The Supreme Court has a strict rule against denominational preferences.[36] But refusing to treat as clergy all members of groups that regard all their members as clergy is a reasonable attempt to keep the privilege within bounds, and should not be understood as a denominational preference.[37] And I think the same is true about my proposed two-pronged privilege. The "preference" argument against it is that it explicitly gives a broader privilege to those groups that have a more absolute privilege internally. But in this respect it is a little like the conscientious objector law that favors pacifists over nonpacifists. The "extra" privilege goes to those who need this accommodation to their beliefs and practice. Any worries about favoritism to particular groups and about judicial investigations of the precise views of various groups are softened by making the "extra" privilege depend on the cleric's sense of his religious obligation. This makes his sincerity the key legal issue; group practices are relevant only as background to assess whether he honestly states what his sense of religious duty requires.

Recovery for Disclosure

In some instances, people who have committed secrets to clerics sue to recover damages because the clerics, though not legally compelled, have chosen to disclose the secrets.[38] A person may reveal intimate details of her life to a member of the clergy; when the cleric discloses those details more widely, the person may sue for invasion of privacy or intentional inflictions of emotional distress. (These are common-law theories of recovery for damages developed by courts: chapter 17 discusses them in more detail.)

A cleric's possible liability for disclosing embarrassing facts should depend on understandings within his particular religion, on information he has provided to the member who has revealed the facts to him, and on broader understandings within society about how people in similar circumstances should behave.

That recovery when clergy reveal secrets is *sometimes* appropriate is clear. The disclosure may lack any supporting reason and violate both specific understandings within the religion and general expectations about those who occupy similar roles. Mrs. A, a woman in a small town, reveals in con-

---

[36] *Larson v. Valente*, 456 U.S. 228 (1982), discussed in chapter 3, supra. Such a preference may be sustained if it is supported by a compelling interest, but in this context a compelling interest must be of the kind required to support a disadvantageous classification by race.

[37] In *Larson*, the Court assumed that requiring extra reporting of religious groups that raised more money would not be a denominational preference.

[38] See, e.g., Nadine Brozan, "Women Allege Betrayal by Rabbis' Talk," *New York Times*, December 14, 1998, B1, col. 3.

fession that she was once a prostitute. Her priest, having had too much to drink, tells his buddies in a poker game that they will be surprised to learn that respectable Mrs. A was a prostitute. The news spreads around town. This gross violation of expectations of confidentiality lacks any justification. Recovery would be appropriate against a secular counselor, and it is appropriate against the priest.

The right approach becomes more debatable if either (1) the cleric advances a justification for his respecting confidences to a lesser degree than would an analogous secular counselor; or (2) the person suing claims a degree of protection beyond that generally accorded communications to members of the clergy and analogous secular counselors.

The responsibilities of clergy to their own church members may be more intense than what secular counselors owe to society at large. These responsibilities might include making disclosures a secular counselor would not make. Suppose a man reveals that he has had sexual relations with children in the distant past. A psychotherapist, at least if he does not think repetition is likely, would feel no duty to disclose this information. But a minister *might* understandably feel he needs to tell others in the church in order to protect the children in his parish. Or, within an extremely close-knit religious community that believes knowledge of sinful actions should be shared, a minister might reveal that a member is having an extramarital affair, even though the affair poses no threat (by ordinary standards) to others.

When particular clerics are less respecting of confidences than most clergy and secular counselors, the key to their potential liability should be whether the persons who disclose intimate details to them would reasonably have been aware of their sense of role. This condition is satisfied if the person belongs to a religious group and should be aware of its practices of sharing intimate information[39] *or* the cleric reveals at the outset just how far he will respect confidences. If the cleric doubts whether a client knows how far he will respect confidences, he should say something like, "You know, before we start talking in earnest, I should let you know that if you reveal anything to me that I think is of concern to the broader church membership, including any crimes you have committed or any sexual relations outside of marriage, I will tell other members about it." If a "warned" person then reveals intimate details, he cannot complain if they are disclosed. A person who is *not* reasonably warned in either of these ways should be able to rely on general assumptions about how clergy and people in similar positions behave.

The right standard for clergy who do not offer any *special* understanding related particularly to their religious groups is more troublesome. A cleric

---

[39] Whether someone should be able to limit disclosure by resigning from the group is a question that chapter 17 discusses.

says, " I faced a difficult choice, but I believed I had an overriding obligation to protect my congregation." People who reveal secrets to lawyers, doctors, and psychotherapists do not have unqualified assurances of confidentiality, since all these professionals have legal duties to reveal certain kinds of information in order to protect others from serious harm. Generally, clerics able to prevent similar harms should be free of liability on the same basis as secular counselors. More controversially, clerics should have a privilege to reveal that is somewhat more extensive than that of secular counselors, because of their special responsibilities to their own group members. Courts should not tell clerics the precise limits of this range of responsibilities, granting them a defense if their sense of pastoral responsibilities and that of clergy in general would call for disclosure. Thus, a person who revealed facts that a cleric subsequently disclosed to members of his congregation could typically recover only if the disclosure would be definitely unreasonable (and not justified by a special religious understanding of which the counseled person should reasonably have been aware). Although this standard is modestly unfavorable to recovery, it serves to preserve the liberty of ministers who act according to their reasonable understandings of what their religious responsibilities require.[40]

What of the claimant who acknowledges that disclosure might appropriately have been made by an ordinary minister or secular counselor, but who claims that her cleric violated more stringent obligations of confidentiality imposed by his religion? Thus, a Roman Catholic might urge that her priest has an absolute duty of secrecy, and should have remained silent, even if other clergy would have disclosed what she told him. Briefly, the law should not be in the business of *enforcing* standards of silence that exceed those generally accepted for clergy.[41] Otherwise, people could recover damages for disclosures that most members of society would feel are wholly appropriate.[42]

I shall not retrace the various reasons for and against allowing disclosure as they bear on constitutional law. In brief, I think that in circumstances in which I have argued that a cleric should have a right to disclose information he has learned because of his religious responsibilities, he should be regarded as having a free exercise right to do so. My suggestions about protecting clergy disclosures that serve more general public objectives, such as pre-

[40] This approach unfortunately requires courts to evaluate *to some degree* the typical responsibilities of clergy, but I now see no way around this.

[41] The question of enforcement differs from the question whether the law should accommodate those stringent standards by not forcing disclosure.

[42] It is, of course, possible that a non-Catholic, informed of the Catholic Church's rule of absolute secrecy, might conclude that a priest should not have disclosed information that another cleric should have disclosed; but I am doubtful most people would be persuaded by this subtle analysis.

venting crimes, and my suggestions about when disclosure should be penalized are not constitutionally required, but they are permissible under the religion clauses.

RECOVERY FOR NONDISCLOSURE

In certain circumstances, a person may contend that a cleric caused harm by remaining silent rather than disclosing. In these instances, the people complaining are third parties, not involved in the initial interchange, who object that clergy have failed adequately to protect their interests. Suppose someone has told a minister in confidence that he hates B so much he is planning to burn down his house. The minister fails to tell B or anyone else, and the speaker sets fire to B's house. B, having learned of the confession from someone in whom the arsonist confided, sues the minister for remaining silent.[43]

The analysis of nondisclosure is similar to that of disclosure up to a point. Unless statutory standards require disclosure, the cleric who acts upon a reasonable understanding of clergy responsibilities should not be liable. A cleric who remains silent and lacks any justification related to his responsibilities or who offers a justification that strays beyond the bounds of reasonable clergy behavior may be liable.

When the injured person is a third party, it is more debatable whether special understandings within a religious group, conveyed to the person who discloses secrets, should matter. If B's protection is at stake, he may argue that he should not suffer because of the understandings of a cleric and his penitent. One possible reason to protect these understandings is that penitents would not reveal their plans if they did not feel assured of secrecy, but another reason is more fundamental. If, as I have argued, the law should not *compel* disclosure of confidential communications when clerics perceive religious obligations not to disclose, the law should not indirectly force disclosure, or penalize failures to disclose, by allowing judgments in damages after the fact.

The constitutional analysis in respect to private suits for nondisclosure largely tracks that for the basic clerical privilege not to be compelled by law to reveal confidences.

---

[43] In some cases the initial harm may be to the person counseled, if disclosure would have allowed others to help protect him (as when someone has suicidal tendencies).

CHAPTER 16

Settling Disputes over Church Property

In this chapter, we turn to judicial resolutions of disputes among factions of religious groups. For the most part, this subject has not involved legislatures;[1] rather, judicial approaches developed as aspects of state common law have been measured against what the religion clauses together require.

When members of a religious group cannot resolve internal disputes about the use of property, they may turn to civil courts. The law's involvement in these instances is more constrained than it would be if courts were ruling about secular associations. But is this fair? Other questions of equality, and fairness arise between members of different kinds of religious bodies, between different members of the same religious bodies, and between those who donate property and those who later use it. This subject, initially developed as part of the common law, is now overlain with constitutional doctrine. Reviewing actual cases with complex factual situations, we shall ask which judicial approaches are desirable and which should be constitutionally acceptable when a religious group splits—each faction claiming to represent the true faith.

Religious organizations, like other groups in society, regulate themselves. The principles of internal governance they have chosen are diverse and relate closely to their religious visions; a Quaker meeting, with its insistence on unanimity, differs greatly from the hierarchy of the Roman Catholic Church. When internal disagreements over who controls religious property have become so intractable that one side goes to civil court,[2] judges must resolve cases, but are they fit to decide issues that divide members of religious associations?

The Supreme Court's constitutional approach, established between 1969 and 1979,[3] is that, under the Free Exercise and Establishment clauses, secular courts must not determine questions of religious doctrine and practice. Not

---

[1] Within the range of acceptable approaches, a state legislature could choose to establish one approach rather than another; but I am assuming that, in the main, legislatures will leave this particular subject to the courts.

[2] The dispute may be between local and national organizations, or between local factions, one of which may be allied to a national group.

[3] *Presbyterian Church in the United States v. Mary Elizabeth Blue Hull Memorial Presbyterian Church*, 393 U.S. 440 (1969); *Serbian Eastern Orthodox Diocese v. Milivojevich*, 429 U.S. 873 (1976); *Jones v. Wolf*, 443 U.S. 595 (1979).

only must they refrain from deciding what doctrines and practices are correct or wise, they must also avoid deciding which are faithful to a group's traditions. Rather, courts must choose between deferring to a group's hierarchy or using neutral principles of law, that is, relying on documents that do not require choosing between controverted interpretations of doctrines or practices. The basic stance is one of noninvolvement: government may not resolve internal problems by criteria that have a religious character. This basic stance reflects the limited competence of secular courts, and it serves the autonomy of religious organizations. Although the courts' approach to property disputes differs from standard free exercise and establishment tests,[4] it reflects modern attention to equality in constitutional law and the dominant theme of religion-clause adjudication, that too much intertwining of government and religion is unhealthy.

After exploring justifications for various approaches, the elements of fairness and unfairness that each exhibits, and practical barriers they may pose for religious bodies wishing to order their affairs, I conclude that the Supreme Court's "hands off" approach to governance of church property is fundamentally sound, but that aspects of the Court's two major alternatives to assure that judicial hands are off raise serious problems. Most notably, a rule to defer totally to decisions within church hierarchies is too rigid, whereas certain understandings of "neutral principles" block out too much information that is relevant to the lives of religious groups. In light of these problems, I offer recommendations for choices that state courts should make under the prevailing constitutional regime and for certain revisions of that regime by the Supreme Court. These revisions, or modifications, would allow greater sensitivity to the concerns of religious groups and their members, while compromising only slightly, if at all, the sound aspiration to keep civil courts out of religious affairs.

All the important cases involve Christian organizations, but whatever standards apply to churches also apply to all analogous religious groups—Jewish, Muslim, Buddhist, Hindu, and so on. The concern here is not *just* one of terminology. As the variety of religious practices within the country continues to increase, so also will the number of cases involving non-Christian groups, and judges will be forced to apply legal standards to religious groups with which they are unfamiliar.

---

[4] The approach did not follow directly from the free exercise "compelling interest test" the Court employed from 1963 to 1990, nor does it follow from the free exercise principle of *Employment Division v. Smith*, 494 U.S. 872 (1990), that religious claimants should be treated like all others. The Court has not derived the approach from the standard establishment test discussed in volume 2. See the brief discussion in the conclusion (chapter 23) and in note 74, infra.

The Lessons of History: The Inappropriateness of Civil Courts Resolving Religious Issues

Present principles governing property disputes originated well over a century ago. Following a number of state cases, the Supreme Court dealt extensively with the problem of church property disputes in 1872, in *Watson v. Jones*.[5] That case reveals important issues and persistent difficulties.

Watson involved a division of the Presbyterian Church that occurred as a consequence of the Civil War. From the beginning of the war, the General Assembly, the highest body of the national Presbyterian Church in the United States of America, had urged that citizens support the federal government, and it favored the Emancipation Proclamation. In May 1865 (just after the end of the war), the General Assembly instructed church organizations that applicants for membership from Southern states who had supported the Confederacy or had accepted the doctrine that Negro slavery is a divine institution should be required to repent and forsake these sins before being received.

In Kentucky, a slave state that had remained within the Union, church bodies at all levels divided between groups aligning themselves with the General Assembly and those asserting that the assembly's stances on slavery and the war were erroneous and heretical. Within the state synod (the statewide organization), the Louisville Presbytery (the local regional organization), and the Walnut Street Church, proslavery and antislavery factions each claimed to be the true representatives of the Presbyterian Church.

The conflict in *Watson v. Jones* turned on the use of local church property. Members of the antislavery group claimed that the proslavery elders had effectively seceded from the national church, leaving an antislavery member as the sole lawful elder. The Supreme Court agreed.

The crucial question, which fell within the general common law developed by federal courts,[6] was whether the national church could forfeit a control it would otherwise have because it had failed to adhere to the religion's basic principles. In England courts made such judgments about dissenting churches as well as the established Anglican Church; but in the United States, with its freedom to practice all religions, "The law knows no heresy and is committed to the support of no dogma, the establishment of no sect."[7] Here,

---

[5] 80 U.S. (13 Wall.) 679.

[6] Under then prevailing doctrine, established in *Swift v. Tyson*, 41 U.S. 1 (1842), federal courts could use their own best judgment about most common-law issues, rather than following state court decisions.

[7] *Watson*, note 5 supra, at 728. H. M. Ogilvie, in "Church Property Disputes: Some Organizing Principles," 42 *University of Toronto Law Journal* 377, 381–92 (1992), describes the devel-

courts should not make any "implied trust" in favor of a general church depend upon its faithfulness to preexisting doctrines and practices. People who organize voluntary religious associations give "implied consent" to their governments. Allowing aggrieved members to have recourse to civil courts, whose judges are much less competent to determine ecclesiastical law and religious faith, would subvert the religious bodies.

In propounding its understanding of freedom of religion and nonestablishment, the court divided questions concerning rights to church property into three categories, two of which still guide courts. A case falls within the first category when a deed or will respecting the property provides "by the express terms" that it is to be "devoted to the teaching, support, or spread of some specific form of religious doctrine or belief."[8] Such terms could be enforced; for example, were property given for "exclusive use of those who believe in the doctrine of the Holy Trinity," courts could prevent the property from being used to disseminate Unitarian doctrine.[9]

The second category includes property held by a religious congregation that "is strictly independent of other ecclesiastic associations" and owes no "obligation to any higher authority." For such congregational churches, absent an express trust, "rights must be determined by the ordinary principles of governance for voluntary associations."[10] If the ordinary standard for making decisions is majority rule, courts should accept judgments made in that way, not expelling a majority that "may have changed . . . their views of religious truth."[11]

In the third category are congregations subordinate to "some general church organization in which there are superior ecclesiastical tribunals with a general and ultimate power of control . . . over the whole membership." The appropriate rule, then, is that "legal tribunals must accept the decisions of the highest of these church judicatories as final."[12] Applying this rule, the Court accorded the General Assembly the final say about Presbyterian doctrine and practice; consequently the antislavery group succeeded in *Watson v. Jones.*

The Court's reasoning is straightforward. Civil courts are woefully ill-suited to judge "departures from doctrine," and their doing so would frustrate changes in religious understandings; nevertheless, the Court's opinion

---

opment of English doctrine and Canadian approaches. An example of the willingness of modern courts in Canada to entertain inquiries that would be foreclosed in the United States is *Lakeside Colony of Hutterian Brethren v. Hofer* (1992) 3 S.C.R. 165.

[8] *Watson*, note 5 supra, at 722–23.
[9] Id. at 723.
[10] Id. at 725.
[11] Id.
[12] Id. at 727.

raises troubling questions. Why is ultimate decision ceded to superior church bodies? The Court disregards the import of substantive provisions in church constitutions and the possibility of a mix of authority (not unlike a federal system) in which neither a local nor a central body is the final authority on all questions. According to ordinary social contract theory, citizen consent is given to governments, *so long as* they act within appropriate limits. Why should "implied consent" to authoritative church bodies be absolute? And why should civil courts not investigate to see how, for each religious association, authority is actually allocated?

How the Court treats express deeds and wills is curiously dissonant with its general resolutions for hierarchical and congregational churches. If courts may not competently resolve matters of doctrine and practice, even if these are parts of a church constitution, why are they competent to enforce express trusts that prescribe the same doctrinal conditions? The *Watson* Court failed to explain why courts should fully enforce express trusts and not require governing bodies in hierarchical churches to comply with their documents of church governance.

The Modern Framework

In three cases decided between 1969 and 1979, the Supreme Court built on *Watson v. Jones* to develop comprehensive constitutional restrictions on civil court involvement over church property disputes. Embracing *Watson*'s underlying "hands off" understanding, the first of these cases indicates that courts must not decide which doctrines and practices are faithful to a tradition.[13] The second establishes that this restriction applies to actions that arguably violate church rules of governance.[14] The third settles that the courts of states may choose between the alternative approaches of deferring to the highest authorities of hierarchical churches or applying neutral principles of law.[15]

The Supreme Court evidenced unusual unanimity for a religion case when in 1969 it decided a Presbyterian Church conflict that resembled *Watson v. Jones*. In *Presbyterian Church in the United States v. Mary Elizabeth Blue Hull Memorial Presbyterian Church*,[16] local Georgia churches that had withdrawn from the national organization claimed they should retain local church property, because the general church had departed from its doctrines and practices. The range of objections included predominantly doctrinal

---

[13] *Presbyterian Church*, note 3 supra.
[14] *Serbian Orthodox Diocese*, note 3 supra.
[15] *Jones*, note 3 supra.
[16] Note 3 supra.

matters, such as the teaching of "neo-orthodoxy alien to the Confession of Faith and Catechisms"; church practices, such as the ordaining of women as ministers and elders; and political and social stances, such as support for removing prayers from public schools and acceptance of the leadership of the National Council of Churches, which had advocated civil disobedience.

The Georgia trial court submitted the case to the jury on the theory that local church property is held in an implied trust for the general church unless its actions "amount to a fundamental or substantial abandonment of the [church's] original tenets and doctrine."

Overturning a judgment for the local church, Justice Brennan's opinion for the Supreme Court quoted passages from *Watson v. Jones*: "The logic of this language leaves the civil courts *no* role in determining ecclesiastical questions in the process of resolving property disputes."[17] Under the religion clauses, courts must not "resolve underlying controversies over religious doctrine."[18]

Within the next decade, the Court clarified just how civil courts may resolve church property disputes. *Serbian Eastern Orthodox Diocese v. Milivojevich*[19] involved a hierarchical church with its highest authority in a Communist country, Yugoslavia. The primary dispute was whether Milivojevich, who had been elected bishop of the American-Canadian Diocese by the Holy Assembly of Bishops in 1939 (when Yugoslavia was a monarchy), or a bishop appointed in his stead by the same body in 1963, had authority to control properties in Illinois. The Illinois Supreme Court agreed with Milivo-

---

[17] Id. at 447. The opinion also talked of "the hazards . . . of inhibiting the free development of religious doctrine." Id. at 449. John Garvey has understood this language as suggesting that the First Amendment was designed to promote the free development of doctrine. "Loosely translated, it means that heresy is a good thing." Garvey, "Churches and the Free Exercise of Religion," 4 *Notre Dame Journal of Law, Ethics and Public Policy* 567, 577 (1990).

[18] Id. at 449. The opinion left a question about *Watson v. Jones*'s first category, the express trust. Much of Justice Brennan's language is absolute, apparently precluding enforcement relating to specific doctrines and practices, even when these are embodied in express trusts; and one can easily see the pitfalls of civil judges or juries deciding about the status of "neo-orthodoxy," whatever the context. Justice Harlan joined the Court's opinion on the understanding that it did not forbid "civilian courts from enforcing a deed or will which expressly and clearly lays down conditions limiting a religious organization's use of the property which is granted." Id. at 452 (Harlan, J., concurring). Since Justice Harlan's examples were conditions that women not be ordained and that specified articles of the Confession of Faith not be amended, he required that an outsider be able easily to understand the nature of the condition and to identify a breach. Anyone, for example, can conclude that most Protestant churches now allow women to be ordained. What did the other justices think about Justice Harlan's reservation and examples? One cannot say. They did not dispute his reservation, but neither did they incorporate it. Justices in the majority probably disagreed among themselves or did not want to think hard about the question, or both. No subsequent Supreme Court decision directly discusses the possible validity of enforcing some express trusts.

[19] Note 3 supra.

jevich, and the Diocesan National Assembly, that his removal as bishop violated the constitution of the mother church.[20]

The United States Supreme Court declared that state courts may not make a detailed assessment of relevant church rules and adjudicate between disputed understandings.[21] Courts cannot inquire whether the highest ecclesiastical tribunal of a hierarchical church has complied with its own law. Justice Rehnquist, in a dissent with Justice Stevens, urged that religious organizations should be treated like other private voluntary associations, that civil courts should not "rubber-stamp ecclesiastical decisions of hierarchical religious associations."[22]

In *Jones v. Wolf*,[23] another Presbyterian Church case, the Court indicated that civil courts need not defer to higher church authorities if they instead rely on authoritative documents that can be interpreted without invoking religious understandings. Most of a local congregation had voted to withdraw from the general church. Applying "neutral principles of law," the Georgia courts had determined that the property belonged to the local church, represented by the majority. The deeds conveyed property to it; neither state statutes nor the local church charter conferred a property interest on the general church; and the national's Book of Church Order did not have language creating a trust in its favor. Since Georgia's courts had required no resolution of issues of doctrine and church polity, their approach was constitutionally permissible, ruled five of nine Supreme Court justices.[24]

---

[20] It relied on a trial court determination based on the testimony of experts for each side.

[21] Id. at 709. "Where resolution of the disputes cannot be made without extensive inquiry by civil courts into religious law and polity, the First and Fourteenth Amendments mandate that civil courts shall not disturb the decisions of the highest ecclesiastical tribunal within a church of hierarchical polity, but must accept such decisions as binding on them." In *O'Connor v. Diocese of Hawaii*, 885 P.2d 361 (Haw. 1994), the court relied substantially on *Serbian Orthodox Diocese* as the basis for an ecclesiastical abstention doctrine that precluded civil court review of claims of wrongful excommunication that could not be resolved without any examination of church doctrine or governance.

[22] Id. at 734 (Rehnquist, J., dissenting).

[23] Note 3 supra.

[24] Having determined the local church's right to the property, the state courts awarded it to the local majority. The Supreme Court found the basis for this last step to be unclear. Had the courts merely adopted an ordinary, acceptable, legal presumption that, absent a contrary indication, a majority represents a voluntary religious association; or had the courts relied on laws and regulations of the Presbyterian Church to determine who represents the local church? The latter reliance could involve civil courts in resolving debatable matters of church polity— the very difficulty that doomed the efforts of the Illinois courts in *Serbian Orthodox Diocese*. An ordinary presumption of majority rule, however, would be entirely appropriate. The Supreme Court said that a presumptive rule of majority representation could be overcome by provisions in the corporate charter or constitution of the general church that show that the identity of the local church is to be established differently, but what courts could not do is rely on "considerations of religious doctrine and polity." It is not easy to mark the distinction be-

Justice Powell's dissent objected that the Court's opinion endorsed greater involvement of civil courts in church controversies than had earlier decisions.[25] Because the "neutral principles" approach will yield results at odds with the doctrines and polities chosen by churches, states should be required to defer to the decisions of the highest bodies within hierarchical churches. Justice Blackmun's opinion for the Court responded that parties can assure the results they want by expressing their understandings in formal documents. Many religious organizations have put their property affairs in order, but limited foresight, ambiguities of language, and uncertainties about how courts will decide render this opportunity less than a perfect guarantee that aspirations will be fulfilled.

With *Serbian Orthodox Diocese*, *Jones v. Wolf* leaves state courts a choice between "neutral principles" and deference to hierarchical decisions; but an examination of the opinions in the two cases shows that only three justices actually favored that course. The four dissenters in *Jones v. Wolf* rejected the neutral principles approach in favor of deference to hierarchical authorities, and Justices Rehnquist and Stevens indicated in *Serbian Orthodox Diocese* that courts should use principles like those for other voluntary organizations, an approach less "hands off" than what the Court endorsed in *Jones v. Wolf*. Should the present justices believe that the principles governing church property cases inadequately serve values of free exercise and nonestablishment, they will not cling tenaciously to what was said a quarter of a century ago.

SURVEYING THE LANDSCAPE OF DOCTRINAL POSSIBILITIES

If we are to inquire what approaches are preferable and which should be constitutionally required, it helps to clarify the major alternatives the Supreme Court has provided, to highlight crucial problems, and to suggest criteria for evaluating competing approaches.

The Supreme Court has accepted two basic approaches, "deference" and "neutral principles." The "deference" approach is, more precisely, the most important component of a "polity" approach. A court initially decides what kind of government a church has. Legal tradition, from which some courts have begun to deviate, acknowledges only two tracks, congregational (in

---

tween inquiries the Court allows and those it does not, but apparently courts cannot make determinations about religious polity *unless* those are clearly established by documents that can be interpreted apart from any religious understanding.

[25] "[T]he First Amendment's Religion Clauses . . . are meant to protect churches and their members from civil law interference, not to protect the courts from having to decide difficult evidentiary questions." *Jones*, note 3 supra, at 613 n. 2.

which a local church controls its own destiny) and hierarchical (in which authority is ranged in an ascending hierarchy). But this convenient dichotomy may not fit when a self-standing local church has chosen to govern itself by undemocratic rules. More important, the dichotomy does not attend to possible differences in ways the superior church authorities are constituted (from the top down or by some form of representational government) and to nuances in balances of authority between higher authorities and local churches. This Procrustean attitude risks giving central bodies more power than members of some churches have assigned them.

Under the polity approach, if a church organization is congregational, courts assume that it governs itself like an ordinary voluntary association. If the church is hierarchical, courts treat the decisions of the highest church adjudicators as binding[26] with the predictable consequence that local church property is held for the general church.[27]

Crucial questions about the "polity approach" include these: How does a court decide what is a church's polity if its members dispute that? How much review is warranted if a church is congregational? May a church be hierarchical for some purposes but not others? Is deference appropriate for "ecclesiastical issues" even if not for "secular" issues? Can deference to high church authorities be defended as the best way to give effect to the intent of relevant people or must it be justified in other terms?

The neutral principles approach (which should not be confused with the idea of laws that are neutral and of general application) calls on courts to use secular neutral, not religious or ecclesiastical, principles when they resolve church disputes. The following issues are crucial to how neutral principles are applied. What kinds of documents may courts examine? How stringently must courts avoid determination of disputed matters of church government and practice? How specific must indications be that crucial property interests lie in hands other than those of the formal title holder, usually the local church? How is the neutral principles approach to be justified?

In considering various doctrinal possibilities, we can conceive an ideal set of standards for church disputes over property, standards derived from the values of religious freedom, equality, nonestablishment, and fulfillment of the intent of affected persons. Such standards would (1) accord churches

---

[26] The highest judicial authority in a church *could* award property to a local church against the national legislature and executive.

[27] As the Pennsylvania Supreme Court once put the rule, "When a local church . . . subscribes to the doctrine and control of a hierarchically governed denomination, it cannot sever itself from such religious denomination without forfeiting its property to the parent denomination." *Western Pennsylvania Conference of the United Methodist Church v. Everson Evangelical Church of North America*, 454 Pa. 434, 437, 312 A.2d 35, 37 (1973).

significant autonomy of governance; (2) afford individuals freedom of religious worship; (3) give effect to the intent of people who donate money for the purchase of church property *and* who pay for its upkeep; (4) treat different religious groups in an evenhanded way, without favoring any particular doctrine or form of organization; (5) replicate the standards used in respect to other charitable and nonprofit organizations; (6) keep courts out of determining ecclesiastical matters for which they are ill suited. One needs only to state these criteria to recognize that accomplishing some as fully as possible means sacrificing others. It follows that no simple formula can tell us which approaches are best overall.

The "Polity-Deference" Approach

The "polity-deference" approach has substantial defects. As we shall see, its sharp difference in treatment between hierarchical and congregational churches cannot be justified. It produces treatment of religious groups that differs from that of nonreligious voluntary associations. Its extreme deference to high church bodies does not follow from any plan to fulfill the expectations of members and donors and may not, consistent with the religion clauses, be based on any policy of preferring the unity of general churches over separation. It raises serious problems about how judges determine a church's polity.

Comparative Treatment of Congregational and Hierarchical Churches

The traditional polity approach accords strikingly different treatment to congregational and hierarchical churches, an anomaly impossible to justify. In *Serbian Orthodox Diocese*, Justice Brennan wrote, "[I]t is the essence of religious faith that ecclesiastical decisions . . . are to be accepted as matters of faith whether or not rational. . . . Constitutional concerns of due process . . . are therefore hardly relevant to such matters of ecclesiastical cognizance."[28] A large gap separates this language from how courts have regarded congregational churches, which, like other voluntary associations, have been held to conform to their bylaws and to fundamental principles of fair process.

To an extent, greater review of congregational church decisions than of hierarchical ones is inevitable.[29] Imagine that a minister has strong minority support but realizes that a majority of the congregation will dismiss him at

---

[28] Note 3 supra, at 714–15.
[29] See *Bouldin v. Alexander*, 82 U.S. (15 Wall.) 140 (1872).

the next regular meeting. He schedules a worship service for Wednesday, and privately urges his supporters to attend. At the service, he announces that a congregational meeting will follow. A majority of attendees vote to terminate the membership of everyone not present. At the "ordinary" regular Sunday meeting, a majority of those present vote to dismiss the minister. A civil court resolving which group controls church property would have to determine the effect of the Wednesday meeting. Having recourse to church bylaws or ordinary democratic principles, a court would conclude that a minority faction could not terminate their opponents' membership at what was virtually a secret meeting. This problem of identifying an authoritative body does not often arise for the adjudicatories of hierarchical churches. One knows who they are and when they have acted.

What is nettlesome about the hierarchical-congregational divide is that for congregational churches, courts have enforced church rules *and* democratic principles of governance that go beyond ascertaining a valid majority. If the bylaws require notice and a hearing, a court will invalidate a dismissal done without notice or hearing; and it may require those even if the church rules are silent,[30] affording protections the Supreme Court has said civil courts cannot insist upon with hierarchical tribunals, even if church rules provide them. This sharp difference between the degree of procedural protection courts afford members of congregational churches and hierarchical ones favors institutional authorities of hierarchical bodies over their members who may rely on procedures found in their governing documents. Although the parallel development of secular democratic governance with democratic church governance may provide some historical justification for the radical distinction in treatment between hierarchical and congregational churches,[31] many modern American adherents of hierarchical churches are as attached to procedural justice as are members of congregational churches. One might defend greater scrutiny of congregational decisions on the practical grounds that abuse and unfairness are more likely in small, local bodies, and that hierarchical governance is often complex and intertwined with religious his-

---

[30] In 1985, the Supreme Court of Virginia said that for congregational churches, "the analogy to hierarchical churches breaks down because there is no body of ecclesiastical law to invoke, no internal tribunal to appeal to. A member of a congregational church, seeking the aid of the court in protecting his civil and property rights, may appeal only to the simple and fundamental principles of democratic governance which are universally accepted in our society. These principles include the right to reasonable notice, the right to attend and advocate one's views, and the right to an honest count of the votes." *Reid v. Gholson*, 229 Va. 179, 189, 327 S.E.2d 107, 113 (1985).

[31] Members of congregational churches may have expected internal procedures they would judge fair for secular government. The certainty of faith in decisions of religious officials, however rendered, may have been more apposite for hierarchical, nondemocratic, churches.

tory and doctrine; but differences in risks of abuse and complexities of review do not warrant such a stark dichotomy in how hierarchical and congregational churches are treated.[32]

Comparison with Nonreligious Associations

Some value inheres in courts' treating church disputes as they treat disputes
that arise within secular associations.[33] Varying treatment according to an
organization's underlying purpose is not necessarily unconstitutional, but
special distinctions between religious and nonreligious groups stand in need
of justification.[34]

In comparing the treatment of religious and secular organizations, we have
to imagine a dispute in which those in control have a vision of the aims of
the secular association that differs sharply from the vision of those who sue.[35]
If the controlling members deviated far enough from the terms under which
an association was founded (or under which major assets were given), a court
would find that to be a breach of fiduciary duty. A court "would resolve the
conflicts by interpreting the relevant rules, agreements and conduct of the
parties," inquiring about reasonable expectations.[36] To take an extreme example, if a large grant were given to an association to finance the work of
needy artists, the managers could not spend the money to assist needy scholars, even if they honestly believed that scholarship was a form of art.

[32] Michael Galligan, "Note, Judicial Resolution of Intrachurch Disputes," 83 *Columbia Law
Review* 2007, 2023, 2025 (1983), has argued that a rigid rule of deference frustrates free exer-
cise, and has objected to the Court's observation that "concepts of fundamental fairness are
secular and irrelevant to church affairs." See also Arlin M. Adams and William R. Hanlon,
"*Jones v. Wolf*: Church Autonomy and the Religion Clauses of the First Amendment," 128
University of Pennsylvania Law Review 1291, 1294–95 (1980).

[33] If participants in religious organizations lack various rights that attach to membership in
secular organizations, one could argue that this denies their free exercise of religion. And if
religious organizations have powers not granted to secular groups, one could argue that this
establishes religion. Needless to say, an approach that gives ordinary members less protection
may also enhance the power of hierarchical authorities.

[34] The significance of achieving equal treatment of religious and secular organizations may
seem greater now than it has in our earlier history. As I have mentioned in earlier chapters, the
Supreme Court has constructed a principle barring discrimination by content as the centerpiece
of free speech analysis, and it is moving toward a view of both the Free Exercise and Establishment clauses under which a government acts constitutionally if it treats religious claimants and
organizations like nonreligious ones.

[35] Members of nonprofit corporations or the government often bring suit claiming that those
controlling assets of the corporation either are incompetent or are diverting assets for personal
use. Such claims of incompetence or corruption are not closely analogous to the church cases
we are addressing.

[36] See Louis J. Sirico, Jr., "Church Property Disputes: Churches as Secular and Alien Institutions," 56 *Fordham Law Review* 335, 338 (1986).

In a more complicated actual case, New York's highest court reviewed the plan of the Multiple Sclerosis Service Organization of New York, Inc. to distribute its assets.[37] The Appellate Division assumed that the controlling statute adopted the traditional *cy pres* standard, under which assets must be distributed to organizations performing activities "as near as possible" to those of the dissolving charitable corporation.[38] The Court of Appeals interpreted the phrase "engaged in activities substantially similar to" to allow somewhat more latitude of choice.[39] Under both the common law *cy pres* standard and New York's less restrictive approach, courts compare the purposes of various charitable organizations to see how closely they resemble each other, an inquiry they would not undertake about religious purposes. For *both* hierarchical and congregational churches, the polity approach differs from how secular associations are treated, in that courts will not say when a shift in dominant understanding of purpose has become too great.[40] And the absolute deference courts afford to the highest judicatories of hierarchical religions is unparalleled for secular groups.[41]

Although courts are more willing to consider the procedures of internal governance of nonreligious organizations than of religious ones, perhaps we can imagine a secular analogue to judicial withdrawal from issues of religious doctrine. Courts have rarely, if ever, dealt with splits in ideological or expressive secular organizations, whose main purpose is to promulgate ideas. Sup-

[37] *In the Matter of Multiple Sclerosis Service Organization of New York, Inc.*, 68 N.Y.2d 32, 496 N.E.2d 861, 505 N.Y.S.2d 841 (1986). MSSO had withdrawn from the National Multiple Sclerosis society in 1965 because it wished to concentrate on rehabilitation, whereas the National Society focused mainly on research. When MSSO could no longer continue its major activities because of "dwindling finances and the advancing age of its members," a committee proposed to donate its remaining assets to other organizations. These organizations provided service to clients with irreversible and chronic medical conditions other than MS. The New York City Chapter of the National MS Society claimed that assets built on donations to help sufferers of MS should go to it. See also *New Jersey Assoc. for Children with Learning Disabilities v. Burlington County Assoc. for Children with Learning Disabilities*, 174 N.J. Sup. 149, 415 A.2d 1196 (1980), in which the Superior Court of New Jersey, Appellate Division, looked at relevant documents to conclude that property was held by the local section. It explicitly rejected the trial court's view that the case was governed by the principles applicable to hierarchical religious organizations.

[38] Since most donations had come from victims of MS and their relatives and friends, that court concluded that the assets should go to an organization helping those afflicted with MS.

[39] The statutory provisions were also designed to confer a substantial role on the board of the dissolving corporation in making the choice of beneficiaries.

[40] However, the courts would presumably not accept a decision by the highest authorities to abandon religion altogether and convert efforts to another sphere of activity.

[41] One writer has commented that the deference component of the polity approach treats churches as alien; its assumptions "about the nature of church organization and about judicial competence describe an extremely autonomous organization that courts treat as more immune from judicial review than any other organization in American Society." Sirico, note 36 supra, at 351, 353.

pose that a national organization whose charter provides that its aim is to "protect freedom of speech" shifts from earlier libertarian positions and now supports stringent restrictions on sexually explicit and hate speech, on the grounds that these interfere with the free speech of those who are adversely affected. A local chapter, faithful to the old views, withdraws from the national and claims that it should keep property donated to it. Suppose, further, that a court would be inclined to find that property was given in trust for the national, absent any deviation from the organization's basic purposes.

The Supreme Court has strongly emphasized that the First Amendment often bars government from making content distinctions among speech, favoring one position over another. Of course, the local's claim is only that its positions fit the understandings of those who donated property to it. But, a court (or jury) reaching a judgment about faithfulness will find it hard to avoid considering the merits of the national's shift. A judge persuaded by the feminist argument that pornography oppresses women might reason that a donor would have regarded a shift on sexually explicit speech as desirable, if she had been aware of that argument.[42]

A court might take the view that it should avoid deciding which stances on particular issues fit with overall political purposes, because that would be too close to deciding which stances are sound. In that event, we would have a secular parallel to the courts' incapacity to assess controversial claims about religious doctrines and practices.

A Contractual Approach?

The *Watson* and *Serbian Orthodox Diocese* courts cast the deference approach as one based on contractual principles, but the idea that members give implied consent to the hierarchy, whatever it does, is often not sustainable. Many members may have consented, instead, that the hierarchy make decisions, so long as it observes the rules of the church and does not change radically.[43] Much may depend on the particular denomination. Roman Catholics continue to have a sense that their main attachment is to an interna-

---

[42] On the other hand, a judge who regards the feminist argument as weak might decide that the national organization must have given way to political pressure or been captured by people who no longer sympathize with its basic purposes. Steffan N. Johnson, "Expressive Organizations and Organizational Autonomy," 85 *Minnesota Law Review* 1639, 1652 (2001), has argued that courts should not decide if a secular association has forsaken its "true" mission.

[43] Even without violating its own rules, the hierarchy may shift radically in some respect. It may admit women as priests for the first time, or fall under the control of an atheist government. Do local church members mean to accept hierarchical decisions in such altered conditions, rather than principles prevailing when they joined or the authority of beloved local clerics who refuse to follow the hierarchy? One cannot say in general what local members have in mind.

tional church, but many American Protestants now join a local church that seems suitable, switching denominations freely and considering the government of their local church as most important.[44] Where I went to school, the "community" church happened to be Dutch Reformed. Most teenagers who were confirmed, and many adult members, had little special feeling for the Dutch Reformed Church, as compared with the Presbyterian, Methodist, or Congregational denominations, which they might have joined just as comfortably had the local church been attached to one of those. Donors of property or large sums of money may be more attached to a central denomination than the average parishioner, but one can hardly assume that loyalty is to the general denomination, regardless of how doctrines shift, procedures are observed, or foreign political influences are brought to bear. Any notion that loyalty would be to the general church in all circumstances is a fiction.

Favoring Unity of the General Church?

Another conceivable reason for favoring the general church as much as the deference approach does is to promote unity or centralized government. *Watson v. Jones* may evidence a distaste for secession. Whatever view the Supreme Court may have been taken after the Civil War, a general opposition to separation could not now be defended. Legal rules of the state should be as neutral as possible about forms of church governance.[45]

Avoiding Ecclesiastical Questions: Determining the Form of Polity

As it has developed, the polity approach allows civil courts to avoid most ecclesiastical questions; but it does require an initial decision about the nature of a church's government. Although forms of religious organization

---

[44] See Roger Bennett, "Church Property Disputes in the Age of 'Common-Core Protestantism': A Legislative Facts Rationale for Neutral Principles of Law," 57 *Indiana Law Review* 163, 171–72 (1982). John Garvey, note 17 supra, at 586–87, who is a Roman Catholic, suggests that the general church prevails under a rule of deference because that is the choice the formerly united group made for its own self-government.

[45] Were there to be *any* favoring, it should be for local participation and fair procedures. If one focused on desirable involvement of citizens in political life and recognized churches as one of the main sources of civic participation, one might favor participatory forms of church organization over forms in which decisions are made by "professionals" from the top down. This would generate a preference for congregational and presbyterial governance over more strictly hierarchical forms; and it would suggest a degree of scrutiny of procedures of the highest judicatories of general churches. The model of extreme deference is hardly a democratic one. Both the dominant norm that the state should not favor any form of church government and a conceivable norm that the state should favor participatory forms of church government condemn notions of extreme deference.

relate to doctrine—the Reformation tenet of the "priesthood of all believers" partly explains why Protestant denominations have more representative forms of church government than the Roman Catholic Church—civil courts usually can identify principles of governance without inquiring into connected doctrines.

However, some decisions about polity are more intractable. I was once consulted in a case involving a split among a group of Plymouth Brethren who did not believe in formal rules of organization. Part of what divided the local members was their degree of loyalty to a leader in England. For the group treating that loyalty as a paramount aspect of their faith, the church was genuinely hierarchical; for the other group, it was congregational. A court could reach a definitive resolution of church's government only by delving into the group's understood faith at some point in time, or by accepting the majority's view in conditions of disagreement and uncertainty.[46]

One reason why courts following the standard polity approach have no problem classifying most churches is the crudeness of the two categories. Any church whose central body has significant power is treated as hierarchical; Baptist and Congregational churches are congregational.[47] The more

---

[46] See *Clough v. Wilson*, 170 Conn. 548, 368 A.2d 231 (1976). Some other cases have caused difficulty in classification, as when two merged local churches of different denominations established contact with one of the denominations, but were not completely absorbed by it. *Master v. Second Parish of Portland*, 124 F.2d 622 (1st Cir. 1941), discussed in "Judicial Intervention in Church Property Disputes—Some Constitutional Considerations," 74 *Yale Law Journal* 1113, 1121–22 (1965). In another case, the Pennsylvania Supreme Court, considering a "Greek Catholic Church" that had accepted Roman Catholic priests, concluded that the local church had never rendered itself subject to the authority of the Roman Catholic Church. *Malanchuk v. Saint Mary's Greek Catholic Church*, 336 Pa. 385, 9 A.2d 350 (1939). See generally Robert C. Casad, "The Establishment Clause and the Ecumenical Movement," 62 *Michigan Law Review* 419, 440 n. 69 (1969) (discussing cases where congregational local affiliated with hierarchical denomination and later withdrew). One writer has suggested that the governance of an autocratic minister of a storefront church may be hard to classify—a single local church hardly constitutes a hierarchy, but the church lacks the democratic form of a congregational church. Ira Mark Ellman, "Driven from the Tribunal: Judicial Resolution of Internal Church Disputes," 69 *California Law Review* 1378, 1404 (1981). He notes one instance in which a Baptist church was considered hierarchical. Id. at 1384. In *Antioch Temple, Inc. v. Parekh*, 442 N.E.2d 1337, 1343, 383 Mass. 854, 862 (1981), the Supreme Judicial Court of Massachusetts indicated that the determination of church structure is a fact. Although courts must eschew inquiry into religious doctrine and usage, they may look at ecclesiastical documents. An Ohio appellate court noted in dictum that certain Ohio cases had used a "living relationship" test that "looks beyond ordinary indicia of property expressed in deeds, articles of incorporation, and like documents, and examines the rituals and practices of the churches in dispute to determine the governmental relationship or polity prevailing." *Southern Ohio State Executive Offices of Church of God v. Fairborn Church of God*, 61 Ohio App. 3d 526, 543, 573 N.E.2d 172, 182–83 (Ct. Apps. Greene County 1989).

[47] For this purpose, the merger into the United Church of Christ has not altered the status of Congregational churches; see, e.g., *St. John's–St. Luke's Evangelical Church v. National Bank of Detroit*, 283 N.W.2d 852 (Ct. App. Mich. 1979).

courts attempt to refine distinctions, asking whether hierarchical bodies have authority over particular subjects, the more their classifications in individual cases may turn on disputable ecclesiastical matters. Some modern courts have suggested that a denomination may be hierarchical for matters of doctrine and practice, but not for control of local church property. We can imagine that a local church might affiliate with a general church and adhere to its doctrines and practices, without wishing to surrender control over its property. Were a dispute to arise between the general and local churches, the general church could expel the local church, but the local church would keep its property.[48]

A court inclined to find that a church is hierarchical only in some respects must be very careful how it slices the pie. In some churches, a regional or national organization has final say over who are the church members and the trustees (whose responsibility it is to control property). If the general church can expel local members and replace wayward trustees, assigning local churches (final) power over property may be ineffective, since the general church can designate which individuals in the local church will be in crucial positions.

One can also see how this combination of authority could dismally affect relations of local and national. When the local, by majority vote, chooses to withdraw before the national expels members or replaces trustees, it may succeed in keeping its property. Knowledge of this fact might lead local members to reason: "We had better withdraw before the national learns of our serious disaffection. If they find out, they'll expel members or replace trustees, and we may forfeit our property." A national, learning of serious disaffection, may reflect: "We had better ensure that the membership and trustees are loyal or we may lose this church property." The dynamics of local church control of property and central church control of membership and trustees could encourage preemptive strikes rather than efforts to settle differences. Any court should strain to allocate responsibilities in a manner that is not potentially destructive in this way.

We have seen that the standard polity approach has some manifest virtues and some grave defects. Most important among the defects are (1) the extreme deference to higher church authorities, even when they have violated their own rules, and (2) the indefensible differentiation between congregational and hierarchical churches in respect to requirements of fair process.

[48] The Minnesota Supreme Court treated a local church of the Serbian Orthodox Church in this way, holding that the general church could not dictate how an intracongregational dispute about membership and property should be resolved. See *Piletich v. Deretich*, 328 N.W.2d 696 (Minn. 1982).

Neutral Principles of Law

Under the neutral principles approach, courts employ ordinary secular principles to resolve disputes involving church government, drawing no sharp distinction between congregational and hierarchical churches. Courts do not defer to church authorities more than to authorities of secular associations, but the restriction on religious evaluation precludes them from investigating organizational purposes and internal relations as fully as they can for most nonreligious associations. Although neutral principles afford religious groups more ability to carry out their exact intentions than the extreme deference of the polity approach, results still may fail to match intentions. Courts employing neutral principles have reached variable results in similar cases. The approach needs to be refined according to which documents courts may examine and what kind of inquiry they may undertake. We shall look at some important comparisons and a possible contractual basis for "neutral principles" before turning to some nuances in the application of that approach.

Comparative Treatment of Congregational and Hierarchical Churches

One advantage of a neutral principles can be briefly stated: courts need not place religious bodies into one of two arbitrary boxes, congregational or hierarchical,[49] with very significant differences in treatment depending on the classification. Courts can be more responsive to the range of actual polities of religious organizations.

Comparison with Nonreligious Associations

Although neutral principles of law may also appear to have a distinct advantage over deference to hierarchical authorities in treating churches more nearly like nonreligious trusts and associations, that approach limits inquiries into purpose. With ordinary secular associations, courts may examine relevant documents and extrinsic evidence to discern whether activities fit underlying purposes, and to gauge whether primary attachment is to a local or general organization. With churches, because courts cannot examine significant indicia of purpose and attachment,[50] churches receive treatment un-

---

[49] Perhaps, at the end of the day, they may treat decisions of hierarchical bodies as more final than votes of congregational bodies, but that will be because of powers granted within religious organizations, not because of an initial categorization by civil courts.

[50] I have previously suggested that courts might entertain similar limits for organizations mainly engaged in ideological advocacy. The free speech principle of "no content restriction"

equal to that of secular associations. The degree of inequality depends on how much is put aside as impermissible inquiry. As to which documents and practices they will investigate and the tools of interpretation they use, state courts diverge.

Neutral principles differentiate churches from secular associations in an indirect, often unrecognized, way, which involves the operation of the principles against the preexisting legal background. Courts have consistently been hesitant to create trusts in favor of parties who do not hold property, deciding that express trusts exist only if the language creating them is explicit, and deciding that implied trusts exist only when the considerations favoring them are strong. Founders of secular associations have been (or could have been) aware of what they needed to do if they wanted to create trusts for general organizations. For some modern cases involving religious bodies, crucial transactions took place years ago under a legal regime in which statutes required that property be held by local churches, with a decisional law that adopted implied trusts in favor of general churches. General churches could understandably have taken the view that express trust language in their favor was unnecessary. Given this striking difference in legal background, when courts afford similar effect to old documents for religious and secular associations that look about the same, the result may be far from equal treatment.

Of course, once *Jones v. Wolf* was decided, churches could put their affairs in order, but people may disagree about what should be done and be unwilling to undertake the required formalities. Many clerics and members feel that churches should handle their own affairs, without relying on civil courts, and, for reasons similar to those that disincline engaged couples from facing how they will distribute property if they get divorced, church members may resist detailing the consequences of a split in their spiritual community. If the general church thinks that property should be held for it, but some disaffected local churches disagree, the general church may wish not to exacerbate existing tensions by forcing a definitive decision. Thus, the power of churches now to "set their affairs in order" does not eliminate entirely the significance of the legal background of times past.

Yet another aspect in which treatment of religious associations may differ from that of most secular associations is the absence of external state policies to resolve difficult disputes. Because states should not prefer some forms of church government over others,[51] courts relying on "neutral principles" must

---

might entail limits on judicial inquiry similar to those that apply for religious associations. But no cases establish such a limit, and none exists for most secular associations.

[51] This comment does not apply to some preference for fair procedures, including notice and hearing, for example, over unfair procedures.

steer clear of external policies they might otherwise use, such as ones favoring democratic governance or local control.

A Contractual Approach?

Insofar as the law should carry out the understandings of those who have agreed to governing documents or made donations, a neutral principles approach for churches is superior to extreme deference, because church organizations and members can model relations as they want, so long as they make their choices clear. However, judicial reliance on neutral principles can frustrate the fulfillment of intentions in other ways. Because courts may not inquire into some matters about which the parties care a great deal, namely religious doctrines and practices, results may diverge from the actual understandings of those concerned. To be sure, church organizations can ensure that appropriate secular documents embody shared intents, but they may face unexpected contingencies for which they have failed to make explicit provision. We have already seen the complications caused by transactions that were undertaken against an older legal background, and by the hesitancy of those setting out on a journey of faith to concentrate too hard on who will control property in the event of an unanticipated disaffection. Another difficulty concerns small, relatively informal churches, who regard delineating precise legal relations as antithetical to religious faith or who may lack funds to pay lawyers to formalize desired relations.

People often may have no exact understanding of who should control property after an unforeseen bitter split, or they may disagree. A court seriously trying to give effect to their intentions might have to ask what people dominantly would have wanted, based on their primary loyalties, if they had been confronted with a split they did not foresee. As the examination allowed under neutral principles becomes more restrictive, a court's actual inquiry will diverge further from a full inquiry about intent.

Avoiding Ecclesiastical Questions:
Which Documents and What Kind of Inquiry

What Documents May Be Examined?

Like the polity approach, "neutral principles" is designed to keep civil courts out of the business of resolving disputed ecclesiastical questions. A court employing neutral principles must initially determine whether it may examine, and rely upon, any relevant documents, or secular documents and those sections of church constitutions and bylaws that are secular in their import, or only secular documents. Another issue is whether the court may consider practices not reflected in the relevant documents, in order either to give meaning to vague or ambiguous passages in documents or to indicate that the church's real practices do not correspond with the formal documents.

The most restrictive proposal is that courts look *only* at secular documents, such as deeds and instruments of trust.[52] The proposal's claimed merit is that courts could then manage church disputes over property; but, because understandings may diverge or be uncertain and because many churches do not line up their secular legal affairs with great care, we cannot suppose that churches, like most major corporations, will formulate their understandings precisely in secular documents.[53]

Few courts have adopted a stringent secular documents test, and the Supreme Court certainly has not suggested one.[54] Occasionally, courts have indicated that passages should not be considered because they are parts of essentially religious documents; but if language in an internal church document is designed for civil enforcement and does not demand a special religious understanding, civil courts should give it effect.[55] Most courts, sensibly,

[52] Sirico, note 36 supra, at 357–58. The author is clear that this approach may not capture the expectations of parties, but he regards an approach that candidly is not designed for this purpose as preferable to one that purports to reflect expectations and fails to do so.

[53] Further, the stringency of this approach's restrictions could produce very unfair results when the crucial transactions had occurred prior to its adoption.

[54] In *Jones v. Wolf*, on the issue of identifying the "true congregation" within the local church, the Court indicated that Georgia might have a presumption of majority rule, but that a court was *required* to look in the corporate charter or constitution of the general church to see if that presumption should give way.

When it decided *Presbyterian Church v. Mary Elizabeth Blue Hull Presbyterian Church*, the Supreme Court remanded to the state courts a pending Maryland case in which two local churches had separated from the Church of God. On remand, the Maryland Court of Appeals determined that it had properly applied a neutral principles approach. After examining state statutes governing the holding of church property, the terms of the instruments deeding the property to the local churches, and provisions of the constitution of the general church and of the local church charters, the state court had concluded that the majorities within the local churches could withdraw from the general church and retain their properties. The Supreme Court dismissed an appeal, a decision on the merits, in *Maryland and Virginia Eldership v. Church of God at Sharpsburg*, 396 U.S. 367 (1970). Its per curiam opinion said that "the Maryland court's resolution of the dispute involved no inquiry into religious doctrine."

[55] In *Presbytery of Beaver v. Middlesex Presbyterian Church*, 489 A.2d 1317, 1325 (1985), the Pennsylvania Supreme Court said, "The . . . reliance on selected passages from the Book of Order was misplaced in that the court ignored the overall intent of that book as a means of overseeing the *spiritual* development of member churches." However the court's language is interpreted, its argument fails. The court might have believed that what was mainly a religious document was not intended to have secular legal significance. It is as if two friends exchanged promises with the clear understanding that they would not be enforceable at law. Although churches might want provisions to be nonenforceable, most church constitutions and similar legal standards are designed to have relevance for disputes civil courts must resolve. A second reading of the opinion is that the religious significance of the entire document renders interpretation of apparently secular passages impossible. Again, one can imagine that ordinary sounding terms would take on specific significance in a doctrinal setting, but ordinary provisions

have not construed neutral principles to restrict the kinds of documents that can be examined.

The Nature of the Inquiry

Deciding *what* documents may be examined is simpler than determining *how* they may be examined and what else may be considered. Language in documents with secular importance may be examined for its ordinary (nonreligious) implications, but may courts go beyond this? To understand the possibilities, it helps to distinguish doctrines, practices, and church government. Doctrines include belief in the Trinity, the significance of communion, the authority of the Bible. Practices are such matters as an all-male priesthood (or a priesthood open to women), worship on Sunday (or Saturday), and use of wine for communion. Government includes procedures and structures of authority, including, crucially, relations between a denomination's general church and its locals. The results of state cases vary as much as they do partly because opinions reflect confusion over what should be taken into account, and whether it matters that a doctrine, practice, or institution of government is undisputed.

Courts typically go beyond express documentary language at least to consider *undisputed matters of church government*; they will look at the basic authority regional and national bodies have over local churches. No court takes into account contested claims about doctrine, whose consideration the Supreme Court has declared unconstitutional. Some courts talk as if even *undisputed matters of doctrine* are beyond their inquiry, and, indeed, civil courts probably should not try to draw conclusions about property relations from a group's doctrines, however well settled are the doctrines and however apparently evident are their relations to claims about property.

What of *disputed matters of governance*? Given the connections of doctrine to governance, a court employing neutral principles should try to avoid disputed questions of governance that cannot be resolved by examining documents with secular import.[56]

---

about control of property should not be so understood. The third understanding of what the Pennsylvania court said is that judges should simply not be interpreting documents whose main significance is religious. But this position makes little sense when particular passages bear on a civil dispute and do not themselves require an inappropriate form of interpretation.

[56] Some courts, however, have seemed willing to resolve disputed questions of governance as an aid to interpreting otherwise vague language, as is suggested by a "living relationship" test mentioned in *Southern Ohio State Church of God v. Fairborn Church of God*, 573 N.E.2d 172, 182–83 (1989). In determining the power of the diocese of a Bulgarian Orthodox Church over a local congregation, an Illinois appellate court suggested that "the court should weigh the conflicting testimony regarding the alleged oral subordination agreement between the local church and regional diocese." *Aglikin v. Kovacheff*, 163 Ill. App. 3d 426, 516 N.E.2d 704, 114

Some practices appear substantially more straightforward than doctrines, but in few cases after *Mary Elizabeth Blue Hull Presbyterian Church* have courts relied on practices (as distinct from governance) to help settle disputes about control of property. It is a difficult question whether a religious body should have to maintain at least certain of its basic practices if it is to continue to hold property that was given when those practices were in effect.

Shifts to mixed seating from the traditional separate seating of men and women in Orthodox Jewish synagogues raise the relevance of an undisputed prior practice that is altered. In two cases that preceded *Mary Elizabeth Blue Hull Presbyterian Church*, synagogues held their property under trusts limiting use to Orthodox Jewish services. A majority of each congregation voted to allow men and women to sit together. The Michigan Supreme Court sustained the argument by a minority faction that this violated the trust,[57] a result that would be mistaken under prevailing constitutional standards. The Louisiana Supreme Court decided that Orthodox principles did not bar mixed seating, even though that trust had specified Orthodox services as conducted in Poland.[58]

In a more recent version of the problem that did not involve control of property, a new Orthodox congregation, with members from congregations that had merged, allowed women only limited participation in services; but in 1983 a majority voted to grant them full participation, and subsequently amended the bylaws so that members had to commit themselves to this equality. After the trial judge concluded that the bylaws interfered with the rights of those who were opposed to mixed seating to continue as members,[59] New York's Appellate Division declared that "membership requirements are strictly an ecclesiastical matter and decisions of the church or synagogue are binding on the courts."[60]

Since religious practices often evolve with religious doctrines, courts, in general, should avoid decisions based on faithfulness to traditional practices, as they avoid decisions about faithfulness to traditional doctrines. This principle

---

Ill. Dec. 549 (1987). Unfortunately, witnesses' accounts of oral agreements may be colored by their understandings of doctrines and practices. Use of such sources is appropriate only if a court does not try to resolve serious factual disputes about agreements that have not been reduced to writing. This condition was met in a recent New Jersey case in which the court gave some weight to audiotaped assurances a Methodist bishop gave about the continuing control of local church trustees over property. *Scotts African Methodist Protestant Church v. Conference of African Union First Colored Methodist Protestant Church*, 98 F.3d 78 (3d Cir. 1996).

[57] *Davis v. Scher*, 356 Mich. 291, 97 N.W.2d 137 (1959).

[58] *Katz v. Singerman*, 241 La. 103, 127 So. 2d 515, appeal dismissed and cert. denied, 368 U.S. 15 (1961).

[59] The rights were evidenced by an earlier court-ordered stipulation.

[60] *Park Slope Jewish Center v. Stern*, 128 A.D.2d 847, 848, 513 N.Y.S.2d 767, 769 (2d Dept. 1987).

may leave some room for express trusts conditioned on traditional practices, but courts must be circumspect. Courts are hard put to judge "the essence of the grantor's intent" if she donated property before a sweeping change in conceptions of roles of men and women.[61] Courts should not assume that a grantor intended continuation of any specific practices,[62] unless the grant explicitly covers those practices, and the shift away from them is undeniable.[63]

To summarize this section, courts adhering to neutral principles determine issues of church governance mainly by attending to the ordinary secular implications of documents, like church constitutions, that are intended to have civil law effect; they may use undisputed principles of governance to interpret the significance of documents; they should not rely upon a prior practice (such as segregated seating) to assert that the conditions of a trust have not been kept, unless the grantor has explicitly insisted upon continuation of that particular practice.

Judicial Variations: Episcopalian Cases

Because courts apply neutral principles in various ways, cases with similar facts end up being decided differently. Some judges are very hesitant to conclude that the national church holds a trust when property is formally in the name of the local court. Others are more "liberal" about using church

---

[61] A judge deciding the importance of separate seating and limited participation of women in services is bound to be affected by how most Orthodox Jews now regard these practices, and by his deeper assumptions about changes in religions.

Matters are simpler when virtually no time has elapsed between an original understanding and a shift in seating arrangements. In *Fisher v. Congregation B'nai Yitzhok*, 177 Pa. Super. Ct. 359, 364–65, 110 A.2d 881, 883 (1955), a rabbi had agreed to sing the chants at High Holiday services for twelve hundred dollars. He had been assured that traditional Orthodox principles, including separate seating, would be observed. On the eve of the services, the congregation voted to have mixed seating. The rabbi felt he could not attend; unable to find alternative work at the same fee, he sued in contract for the difference. The court held in his favor though nothing relevant appeared in the written contract, on the basis that a custom or usage may be considered part of the contract. Since the court needed only to decide what was a reasonable understanding between a rabbi and a congregation at a particular point in time, it could appropriately conclude that if many Orthodox rabbis will not sing at mixed services and the rabbi had been assured seating would not be mixed, the congregation had broken the contract.

[62] An exception to this general principle would cover new practices (ones that have not evolved strongly over time) that, according to an overwhelmingly dominant understanding, make the group a different kind of religious body. What I have in mind by this latter condition are such instances as a majority of an Orthodox Jewish congregation accepting Christianity or Islam, and adopting practices that go with that religion. In that event, a court could reject the congregation's claim that it continues to be Orthodox Jewish.

[63] If the grantor has explicitly conditioned a trust on separate seating, one could still argue that this no longer has the significance it had at that time. In order to protect express conditions, courts should rarely accept such arguments.

constitutions and bylaws, and the history of relations between national and local, to draw conclusions favorable to the general church.

A major California case was very stingy about finding a trust for the national Episcopal Church. In *Protestant Episcopal Church v. Barker*,[64] the court considered whether four Los Angeles churches that had seceded from the national church had lost title to property held in their names. According to the court, the crucial inquiry was whether an express trust had been created. The court looked to "four general sets of facts: (1) the deeds to the property, (2) the articles of incorporation of the local church, (3) the constitution, canons, and rules of the general church, and (4) relevant state statutes."[65] Until 1958, the constitution, canons, and rules of the general church did not mention any express trust; in 1958, Canon 10.06 made property distributable to the diocese when a parish dissolved. An express trust, thus, existed for the property of a local church incorporated in 1963 as a subordinate body of the general church and the diocese. The other churches, incorporated before 1958, did not implicitly accept the principles adopted by Canon 10.06. Although these parishes had agreed to be bound by the authority of the bishop and the general church and to accede to their constitution, canons, doctrine, and worship, the court called these "nothing more than expressions of present intention," as with the marriage vow, not precluding "a change in heart."[66] No express trust was impressed on these three churches.

The Supreme Court of Colorado, in *Bishop and Diocese v. Mote*,[67] adopted a much less restrictive approach to what courts might infer. Because the local parish had acceded in governance to the diocese and general church, and, in particular, to precise provisions in the general church canons that gave forms of control over local church property, no particular language was required to create what amounted to "an express trust created by implication in fact."[68]

---

[64] 115 Cal. App. 3d 599, 171 Cal. Rptr. 541 (1981).

[65] 115 Cal. App. 3d at 620, 171 Cal. Rptr. at 553.

[66] 115 Cal. App. 3d at 623; 171 Cal. Rptr. at 555. The court's analogy is itself disconcerting. Legal permission to divorce should be viewed as allowing people to withdraw from promises, not as an indication that marriage vows are merely "statements of present intention." "It is my present intention—I don't promise" is language better suited to parents planning to take children to movies on the weekend.

[67] 716 P.2d 85 (Colo. 1986).

[68] Id. at 100–101, 103. The court treated the provision in the local church's corporate bylaws that accepted the constitution and canons of the general church as much more significant than had the *Barker* majority. Various canons that specify forms of control over local property by the general church were sufficient to establish that a trust has been imposed for use of the general church. Id. at 101. The court said that it need not shy away from "documents or provisions in documents, that intertwine religious concepts with matters otherwise relevant to the issue of who controls the property."

POLITY VERSUS NEUTRAL PRINCIPLES:
PREFERABLE APPROACHES AND CONSTITUTIONAL REQUIREMENTS

Our examination has shown three serious defects in the standard polity approach. The extreme deference to the highest adjudicatories in all hierarchical churches is far out of line with treatment of nonreligious associations and fails to reflect the expectations of many church members. The stark variation in treatment of hierarchical and congregational churches is unwarranted. Finally, drawing the line between hierarchical and congregational churches can sometimes be troublesome. These problems can be partially met by regarding church organizations as hierarchical in some respects but congregational in others; but such a division may introduce other difficulties.

In sum, the polity approach in its pure form has serious flaws, despite its endorsement in *Serbian Orthodox Diocese*. These flaws are sufficient to make a neutral principles approach preferable.[69] The difficult question is how neutral principles should be applied. Here, appellate courts face a general jurisprudential problem. What would be the best standard for sensitive, fair-minded, able, intelligent judges may not be the best standard for most actual judges. If one believes that cases involving religious organizations often trigger prejudices or are beyond the range of judicial competence, one might favor sharper, more rigid rules than one would want for the best judges.

A sound doctrinal standard should be attuned to the competence and likely prejudice of judges; but it should not bar judges from examining factors that are obviously relevant to how a church is organized and to its members' expectations. Ignoring provisions regarding property because they happen to be in a church constitution that covers matters of faith is, for example, quite unjustified. Demanding explicit trust language for transactions that occurred at a time when general churches reasonably expected to succeed without such language is also unjustified. Courts should not determine the centrality of altered doctrines or practices *or* the correct answer to

---

See also *Bennison v. Sharp*, 121 Mich. App. 705, 329 N.W.2d 466 (1982), indicating that the general church would win under either the deference approach or neutral principles approach; *Protestant Episcopal Church v. Graves*, 83 N.J. 572, 417 A.2d 19 (1980), cert. denied, 449 U.S. 1131 (1981) (similar). See generally William Ross, "The Need for an Exclusive and Uniform Application of 'Neutral Principles' in the Adjudication of Church Property Disputes," 23 *St. Louis University Law Journal* 263 (1987); Robert Bohner, "Note, Religious Property Disputes and Intrinsically Religious Evidence: Towards a Narrow Application of the Neutral Principles Approach," 35 *Villanova Law Review* 949 (1990).

[69] Of course, neutral principles analysis *may* yield the conclusion that a church is organized to give absolute authority to its highest bodies. And, for issues that are so inextricably religious that secular neutral principles will not help, a court may reasonably adopt a deference approach for hierarchical churches.

genuine and substantial disagreements over practices and church government; but they should interpret church documents in a manner that does not
require such judgments, paying attention to clear, established practices and
understandings about organizational authority.

It might be said that giving courts this degree of latitude will produce
uncertainty, but the present situation, in which many courts sound more
restrictive about what they may consider, is hardly better in this regard. The
law now is highly unpredictable in its application for religious groups that
are neither as rigorously hierarchical as the Roman Catholic Church nor as
straightforwardly congregational as the old Congregational churches, that
is, for a vast range of religious organizations in the country.[70]

The uncertainties of decision under neutral principles may make unques-
tioned deference to hierarchical bodies more attractive than I have thus far
portrayed it. Here is a possible defense of deference:

> However a higher court formulates standards under neutral principles, judges
> of trial courts will bend the principles to yield outcomes that strike them as fair
> in the circumstances. They will, for example, be very hesitant to take a church
> building away from a local membership that overwhelmingly wants to secede.
> Local memberships rarely decide to leave on their own; they follow ministers or
> priests who have fallen out with the national. "Neutral principles" makes it
> difficult for national churches to maintain the degree of discipline called for by
> their fundamental principles. Most major national churches in the United States
> have well developed internal judicial systems. Under a polity-deference ap-
> proach, the highest church courts can be much better trusted to deal with com-
> peting claims of locals and the national than can civil courts, especially since the
> church courts need not wear blinders about religious understandings. Therefore,
> deference is preferable to civil courts struggling with neutral principles.[71]

This argument shows that a defense of absolute deference need not rest
on confusion or outdated conceptions of the attitudes of typical church members. Nonetheless, its most powerful aspects should be incorporated within
a framework based on neutral principles. National churches should specify
the range of authority of their highest courts in documents clearly designed
for recognition under civil law. If that authority is inclusive, civil courts
should treat disputants as having agreed to decision by that (religious) court

---

[70] States with rather different approaches can each have a settled law within its own borders.
But the higher courts in some states have yet to give authoritative guidance. In other states, the
language of opinions is too vague or confused to give clear direction. In still other states, appellate
courts of equal status have reached different results. Thus, uncertainty about how courts will deal
with actual disputes between general and local churches exists within many individual states.

[71] Something like this argument was made to me by a close friend who long served as the
chief executive of a regional church organization.

system. Barring extreme delay, civil courts should await determinations by those religious courts, and they should then accept them, unless the determinations are infected by a gross defect.

What I have said thus far does not settle how far the preferable approaches should be constitutionally required by the Supreme Court.[72] It should require some form of "neutral principles" approach, allowing courts to consider a broad range of documents and also settled principles and practices of church authority that bear clearly on matters of governance and control of property. It should declare the rigid deference component of the polity approach to be unconstitutional, as insensitive to the diversity of American religions.[73]

Conclusion

A few concluding observations about how the constitutional law of church property disputes relates to major directions in free exercise law may be illuminating.[74] The dominant recent trend in free exercise law has been to withdraw special constitutional protection for religious claimants in favor of a view that people with religious reasons to violate laws should be treated like all other violators *unless* a legislature grants them an exemption. But,

[72] State courts may well decide that state constitutional limits reach further than what the federal Supreme Court has said or implied about the national Constitution.

[73] However, when church documents intended for civil enforcement grant wide authority to church courts to resolve disputes, civil courts must give effect to decisions of church courts rendered according to the authority conferred.

[74] The connection of church property principles to major threads of Establishment Clause law is also important. I do not include that discussion in the text, because establishment doctrines are treated in volume 2. Here, however is a summary.

For a substantial time the Supreme Court employed a threefold test drawn from *Lemon v. Kurtzman* as its overarching standard for establishment cases. The two relevant prongs of that standard, now folded into one, are that the government may not have the effect of advancing or inhibiting religion and that the government may not become excessively entangled with religion. The Supreme Court sometimes has relied on a complementary principle that the government may not discriminate among religions. The Supreme Court has not abandoned the major elements of *Lemon*, though recent cases have emphasized the acceptability of treating religious and nonreligious groups similarly. The entanglement worry fits very well with a strong "hands-off" approach; courts should not become the adjudicators of religious matters. The nonadvancement prong of *Lemon* and the "neutrality" approach of allowing similar treatment of religious and nonreligious groups may point mildly against the strong deference for hierarchy in the polity approach. Within a religious denomination, the latter approach seems to "advance" higher bodies whose behavior is challenged; and it affords those higher bodies a degree of deference that analogous bodies in nonreligious associations would not receive. The "neutral principles" approach does not match perfectly the treatment of nonreligious associations either, because it withdraws so much from consideration; but its emphasis on formalities and on language in church documents understandable by those outside the faith does not on its face favor one level of church authority over another.

as we have noted, *Employment Division v. Smith* rests heavily on the idea that courts should not have to assess religious understandings and the strength of religious feelings. The inquiry that the *Smith* Court is unwilling to make about what an individual claimant, or group such as the Amish, believes is not nearly as difficult as an inquiry about which of *competing assertions* from within a group is more true to a religious tradition. That is the inquiry that the modern church property cases say courts cannot undertake. Thus, we might view *Smith* as a kind of extension from the underlying premises of *Watson* and modern church property cases. Although both polity-deference and neutral principles largely avoid judicial assessment of religious matters, the neutral principles approach fits somewhat better with the *Smith* Court's proclivity not to have special constitutional rights for religious claimants. The Supreme Court should move to requiring a neutral principles approach, one that includes significant (though not absolute) deference to what church *judicial* bodies have concluded and that allows sensitive consideration of virtually all documents designed (at least partly) for civil enforcement, including whatever natural inferences an outsider might draw without getting into debatable matters of doctrine, practice, and polity.

CHAPTER 17

Wrongs and Rights of Religious Association: The Limits of Tort Liability for Religious Groups and Their Leaders

With this chapter we return to the fundamental question whether people with religious reasons to act should be free of liability imposed on others. Here we will focus on whether religious practices should be protected against claims that religious groups and leaders have inflicted injuries and should pay damages under the law of torts.

A tort is a civil wrong. It typically gives rise to a claim for monetary damages by the victim, and may also be the basis for an injunction to stop the offending behavior. Aspects of the law of torts generate issues about the balance of religious exercise and social protection that differ from any we have yet considered.

Although legislatures often adopt statutes that provide recovery for wrongful behavior, the main standards regarding civil wrongs have been developed over time by judges. The substance of many grounds for recovery in tort overlap significantly with bases for criminal liability. If I don't like a stranger's looks and punch him in the face, I have committed the crime of assault and the tort of battery. I am subject to the state's penalties and to paying damages to my victim.[1] Other standards for liability in tort extend beyond criminal sanctions[2] and may be highly flexible or open-ended in their content. A person may be liable for *unreasonably* intruding on the privacy of another or engaging in *outrageous* conduct that inflicts emotional distress. Standards like these, ordinarily applied by juries in cases that go to trial, would probably be regarded as unconstitutionally vague if they were embodied in criminal statutes, but they are accepted aspects of tort law. The combination of judicially developed standards and jury applications possesses the

---

[1] In legal systems in the civil-law, continental tradition, criminal prosecutions often combine with claims for damages, but the two kinds of proceedings are almost always separate in common-law countries.

[2] The tort standards for battery are not exactly the same as the criminal law. Some incidences of offensive touching may amount to batteries even though they would not give rise to criminal liability.

virtue of keeping the law of torts abreast of social mores.[3] If people regard behavior as seriously wrongful, judges can adjust legal standards to encompass it and juries can assess liability.

Jurors not only have discretion to determine if conduct is unreasonable or outrageous, they set damages. If the wrong is an invasion of privacy or an infliction of emotional distress, the measure of what a victim has suffered will hardly be objective; and juries may in addition impose punitive damages that penalize the wrongdoer in excess of what the victim has suffered. This ability to set damages affords juries a very wide range in deciding how to respond to what they perceive as wrongdoing.

One can easily see how this regime of tort law may threaten religious liberty. Most simply, religious groups may engage in behavior—such as shunning of former members who have fallen into serious sin or apostasy—that would be tortious in a nonreligious setting. The groups may claim that their conduct should not be considered wrongful, because they act from a sense of religious obligation. With recovery for the infliction of emotional distress, further issues arise. Jurors who are considering high-pressure tactics to obtain converts, by a group whose religious perspectives they regard as abhorrent, may decide that the group's behavior has been outrageous, meriting a huge award of damages. The law has reason not to render religious groups, and especially untraditional, fringe religious groups, highly vulnerable to negative reactions by jurors.

One obvious way to protect religious groups is to give them a special defense based on their religious motivation. After *Employment Division v. Smith*,[4] it is doubtful whether the federal Free Exercise Clause will be interpreted to require such a defense, but state courts may grant one under their own state constitutions, and state legislatures may indirectly create a defense by adopting local Religious Freedom Restoration Acts. Short of providing an explicit constitutional defense, courts may develop common-law standards in a manner that protects religious activities.[5] They may say, for example, that proselytizing tactics also used by traditional religions cannot be regarded as outrageous. Courts may also insist, as a matter of constitutional or common-law interpretation, that jurors making decisions about liability must avoid any judgments about the merits of a group's underlying religious

---

[3] See, e.g., Paul T. Hayden, "Religiously Motivated 'Outrageous' Conduct: Intentional Infliction of Emotional Distress as a Weapon Against 'Other People's Faiths,'" 34 *William & Mary Law Review* 579, 580 (1993).

[4] 494 U.S. 872 (1990).

[5] The practical significance of courts developing common-law standards in light of constitutional values rather than relying directly on a constitution is that a legislature could alter the standards if it chose.

vision. (Some commentators have suggested that jurors should never be able to judge the soundness of religious perspectives,[6] but I shall show why that is an oversimplification.) Beyond the question of whether *any* special protection of religious activities is warranted are inquiries whether the nature of such protection should vary with either the kind of intrusive behavior or the particular theory of recovery. A common concern about freedom for religious groups is that their freedom can often stand in opposition to maximum religious liberty for individuals against whom the groups act. We can best understand these issues by focusing on three major categories of behavior: internal church discipline, tactics of conversion, and pastoral counseling.

DISCIPLINE FOR THOSE WHO HAVE FALLEN AWAY

Religious groups have long practiced forms of internal discipline for members who have strayed. Within the early Christian tradition, discipline could involve public abasement or exclusion from the Christian community.[7] Relying in part on biblical passages,[8] a few groups continue to practice particularly rigorous forms of discipline and exclusion, revealing wrongs publicly and avoiding excommunicated former members to a much greater degree than they avoid other nonmembers. As Carl Esbeck summarizes the view of Menno Simons, "[T]hose who are excommunicated are to be avoided completely, not merely treated as strangers."[9]

Shunning of Insiders

When members of a religious group together avoid contacts with a member or former member, the practice is usually called *shunning*. Even though any individual is free legally to avoid contacts with another individual, people who organize together to refrain from contact may commit a civil wrong. In many states, organizing a boycott of a business is a tort. In regard to marriage, even one person's urging another to avoid contact with his spouse may

---

[6] See Hayden, note 3 supra.

[7] See Carl H. Esbeck, "Tort Claims Against Churches and Ecclesiastical Officers: The First Amendment Considerations," 89 *West Virginia Law Review* 1, 40–53 (1986). Esbeck also outlines developments in the Middle Ages and Reformation era, id. at 53–62.

[8] In Matt. 18:15–17, Jesus says, "If your brother sins against you, go and tell him his fault. . . . But if he does not listen, take one or two others with you, that every word may be confirmed by the evidence of two or three witnesses. If he refuses to listen to them, tell it to the church; and if he refuses to listen even to the church, let him be to you as a Gentile and a tax collector." Revised Standard Version (2d ed. 1971).

[9] Esbeck, note 7 supra, at 61.

constitute a civil wrong.[10] And whether or not shunning amounts to a more specific tort, a shunned person may claim he has suffered the intentional or reckless infliction of emotional distress.

For the churches that isolate members who stray, including groups in the Mennonite tradition and Jehovah's Witnesses, shunning aims at repentance and restoration, increasing the offender's shame and preventing the faithful from becoming contaminated.[11] In some modern churches, all members shun their former associates in business and social affairs, and married partners avoid both physical and social contact with wayward spouses. Those joining churches whose discipline includes shunning usually are aware of the practice from the outset.

Courts considering complaints that religious shunning is wrongful may adopt one of three broad approaches. They may treat religious motivation as irrelevant, as did *Employment Division v. Smith*; they may turn religious practice into a virtually absolute defense; or they may somehow weigh religious practice against public need. Whatever the precise import of *Smith* in respect to religious shunning,[12] common-law doctrines that forbid it can burden corporate religious life. For this reason, state courts, by common-law or constitutional interpretation, should impede shunning of members and former members by religious groups only if the government establishes a strong interest in doing so.

Various state decisions support this conclusion, but reach divergent practical results. In 1975, the Supreme Court of Pennsylvania, although using compelling interest language then embodied in the federal constitutional standard, took a view favorable to the shunned former member.[13] Church officials argued that even if Mr. Bear's claims that he was shunned by church

---

[10] According to Esbeck, id. at 88, only a minority of states in 1986 retained a specific tort (alienation of affections) of encouraging a wife or husband to avoid spousal relations, and only seven states retained the tort as of late 2005. See http://en.wikipedia.org.wiki/alienation_of_affections.

[11] This is a paraphrase of Esbeck's summary, id. at 61.

[12] One might consider tort doctrines as neutral rules of general application; according to *Smith*, religious motivation would be no defense. The religion clauses continue to protect aspects of internal church organization, and one might argue that shunning, which has to do with the organization of membership, is a protected internal church affair. However, it is hard to see why a church should have more latitude in dealing with excommunicated members than determining its basic worship service, the issue presented in *Smith*. Another possible argument for avoiding *Smith* is that shunning involves religious exercise *and* expression, making the claim to shun a combination, or hybrid, claim somewhat like that involved in *Yoder*.

Even if *Smith* is taken to render religious motivation no defense, that does not solve the problem of how courts should treat religious reasons to engage in behavior when a tort is defined in terms of unreasonable or outrageous behavior. Such assessments ordinarily take into account the reasons for actions as well as their risks.

[13] *Bear v. Reformed Mennonite Church*, 462 Pa. 330, 341 A.2d 105 (1975).

members, including his wife, were all true, the Free Exercise Clause provided a complete defense. The court responded that "the shunning may be an excessive interference within areas of 'paramount' state concern, i.e. the maintenance of marriage and family relationship, alienation of affection, and the tortious interference with a business relationship." The court's opinion implied that the state's interests against shunning were powerful enough to allow Bear to recover if he could show at trial that church officials had acted as he asserted.[14]

In 1987, the Court of Appeals for the Ninth Circuit also used compelling interest language but reached substantively different conclusions.[15] Paul, who had been "disfellowshipped" [*sic*] from the Jehovah's Witnesses, claimed he had suffered emotional disturbance, alienation of affections, and harm to reputation. The Ninth Circuit said, "We find the practice of shunning not to constitute a sufficient threat to the peace, safety, or morality of the community as to warrant state intervention."[16] It continued, "Intangible or emotional harms cannot ordinarily serve as a basis for maintaining a tort cause of action against a church for its practices—or against its members."[17] The Alaska Supreme Court, in 2001, quoted from *Paul* and determined that the emotional harm to an individual from shunning "as such is not a threat to the public."[18]

The *Bear* and *Paul* courts diverged over a fundamental issue: Does the state have a compelling interest in the quality of life of a few individual adult members of society, when any impairment will have only a slight influence on the larger culture? Without doubt, protecting a few individuals *can* constitute a compelling interest, in American legal understanding. When the

---

[14] The court did not quite *decide* that the state's interests were strong enough for Bear to succeed, but a trial could establish little more about the strength of state interests. Thus, the determination that Bear's action should not have been dismissed prior to trial indicated a substantial likelihood of success.

For other cases suggesting possible recovery, see *Snyder v. Evangelical Orthodox Church*, 264 Cal. Rptr. 640 (Cal. App. 1989); *Hester v. Barnett*, 723 S.W.2d 544, 555 (Mo. Ct. App. 1987) (if interference goes beyond mere advocacy of faith without improper motive); *O'Neil v. Schuckardt*, 733 P.2d 693 (Idaho 1986) (abolishing tort of alienation of affections but allowing recovery for invasion of privacy); *Carrieri v. Bush*, 419 P.2d 132 (Wash. 1966) (on alienation of affections).

[15] *Paul v. Watchtower Bible and Tract Society of New York*, 819 F.2d 875 (9th Cir. 1987). *Snyder v. Evangelical Orthodox Church*, note 14 supra, purports to follow *Paul*, but is more favorable to the possibility of recovery.

[16] The court drew from language of *Sherbert v. Verner*, 374 U.S. 398 (1963), the case holding that unemployment compensation could not be denied for an unwillingness to work on Saturday, if the unwillingness was based on religious convictions.

[17] *Paul*, note 15 supra, at 883.

[18] *Sands v. Living Word Fellowship*, 34 P.3d 955, 959 (Alaska 2001) (shunning directed at members of another religious group).

lives of children are at stake, courts may require medical procedures their parents do not want, a topic we take up in chapter 21. And *Yoder* assumes that educational impoverishment of even a few children is something the state can avoid.[19] But what about *adults* who suffer harms less severe than death or bodily injury?

That shunning can be truly devastating for the individuals who suffer it is a reason for the state to intervene.[20] But the fact that individuals separately are undoubtedly free to do what their leaders encourage them to do together casts doubt on whether the encouragement should lead to liability. Shunning differs from physical assault, slander, and other torts that are wrong even if committed by an isolated individual. That the wrongs committed by shunning do not impinge on vital state interests is shown by the infrequency of recovery for group boycotts that are not motivated by economic gain, and by the widespread abolition of recovery for alienation of a spouse's affections.[21]

At least when adults have voluntarily become members of a religious group that they know engages in shunning, the state lacks a compelling state interest in protecting them from the financial and emotional consequences of that practice. It is not that their joining the group binds them legally to accept any penalties the group may inflict, or eliminates the state's interest in their welfare vis-à-vis that of the group. Rather, their voluntary acceptance of membership reduces the urgency of the state's interest, so that it does not override the group's fundamental freedom to exercise a form of religious practice whose historical pedigree is extensive, however unpalatable it may be to modern sensibilities.[22]

Of course, shunning does reduce the freedom of individuals who face that sanction to practice religion as they see fit. A man aware that his family will shun him if he rejects the church has a powerful incentive to remain faithful, at least in outward appearance. Although this inhibiting effect is disturbing, most of a group should not have to forego what it believes is vital religious practice so that individual dissidents will have maximum freedom of choice at a particular moment. We need to remember that deciding what maximizes freedom over time is no simple exercise. Individuals may wish to join reli-

---

[19] The court sustained the claim of the Amish parents only upon determining that children withdrawn from school after eighth grade will not be seriously disadvantaged in life.

[20] See "Shunning Called Devastating," *Oregonian*, March 21, 2002, A1, reporting on a man who had been shunned by the Jehovah's Witnesses before killing his family and himself.

[21] See note 7 supra.

[22] See Esbeck, note 7 supra, at 103–4. We may note that degrees of voluntariness in joining religious groups differ. A woman who joins to satisfy her husband and keep her family together may later be shunned for her deviations from correct belief or practice. Nonetheless, the law reasonably considers ordinary choices to become members of religious groups as adequately voluntary.

gious groups with strong cohesiveness and discipline. If the law undermines forms of discipline, as by forbidding shunning, it eliminates or erodes the liberty of individuals to join groups whose cohesiveness rests partly on stringent discipline.[23] Within a liberal democracy, the government's aim, as I have argued in the last chapter, should be to allow freedom of religious practice, not to encourage the religions that most recognize individual autonomy in the realm of religion.[24] The law should not be designed to favor religious groups with little discipline over those with strong discipline.

Should a privilege to shun be limited to religious groups or extended to other groups? We could imagine that an organization devoted to political and social principles might feel so betrayed by a member that expulsion and shunning would seem an appropriate response. A group advocating animal rights might learn that a member continues to participate in fox hunting or to model fur clothing, for example. Although it may have more difficulty than a religious group in showing that shunning is related in some crucial way to its associational identity and purposes, a nonreligious expressive group[25] should have the same privilege, if it can make this showing.[26] That result could be achieved under the common law or as an aspect of free speech.[27]

One argument for a privilege for expressive associations is that their internal discipline should itself count as an expressive activity. The religious message that a church projects to nonmembers is affected by the behavior of its members and by its disciplinary practices, and the same might be true about the nonreligious message of an organization for racial justice or environmental quality. However, forms of discipline, especially those otherwise amounting to civil wrongs, should not generate privileges unless an extra ingredient is present, a way in which a particular form of discipline carries forward the group's self-understanding.

---

[23] I do not want to overstate this point. A ban on slavery eliminates the freedom to choose to be a slave, but we do not doubt that the ban serves liberty.

[24] See Esbeck, note 7 supra, 10–11, who comments, "A purely individualistic conception of liberty denies associations the very characteristics that enable them to offset government power." Id. at 11.

[25] I assume that groups without expressive aspects would not have a strong reason to shun; however, a trade association might regard that as an appropriate penalty for dishonest dealing.

[26] As with other topics we have examined, one might defend a privilege limited only to religious groups, on the basis that religion deserves special protection and that similar intense desires to exclude will be rare among nonreligious groups. Except for groups concerning themselves with relations among spouses (e.g., against domestic violence), I cannot think of strong reasons for nonreligious groups to encourage spousal shunning.

[27] Other legal pegs are the Establishment Clause and the Equal Protection Clause, either of which could underlie an argument that religious groups should not be preferred to nonreligious expressive groups.

Any privilege to shun should probably be limited to groups. Isolated individuals who act on their own to insist that others avoid contact with someone should not be given a defense to a civil suit, even if their motivation is religious and the victim is a former associate. Allowing such a defense would place some individuals too much at the mercy of others who have idiosyncratic religious missions or use religion as a cover to conceal more malign motives.

Boycotting of Outsiders

Not all refusals to relate to people are intended to preserve a group's purity and to encourage reformation. Groups that boycott outsiders are not aiming to keep wayward members within the fold, and they cannot rely on any prior consent by their victims. A group may believe that an outsider is acting harmfully or unjustly and want to alter his behavior. Victims and boycotters typically have opposing economic interests, and the boycott is designed to wring concessions from the victim. If such behavior is reasonably treated as tortious, should a group be in a more favorable position if its interest is religious or expressive?

The Supreme Court has established that expressive groups have First Amendment rights to boycott outsiders. Most notably, in *NAACP v. Claiborne Hardware Co.*,[28] the Court indicated that the ordinary civil law regarding business boycotts could not be applied when boycotters were engaged in a political protest.[29] A church wishing to publicize its religious objections to a business, say, one that sells pornography, presumably enjoys the same freedom to boycott.

What purposes suffice to make objectives relevantly political or religious? If a boycotting group has no complaint about how a merchant runs his store but objects to his adulterous affair or his vote at a school board meeting, their aims should not count as protected political expression. The connection of political or religious principle to the store's operation must be closer if boycotters are to be exempt from ordinary civil liabilities.

The privilege to boycott should be broader if a group's aim is to avoid corrupting influences, not inflict economic damage, and its encouragements to avoid contact are directed only at its own members. In an Alaska case, members of one religious community were urged to shun members of an-

---

[28] 458 U.S. 886 (1982).

[29] Although sympathy with the boycotting civil rights advocates may have influenced the Court, the opinion's logic protects boycotters with other political objectives. In *Federal Trade Commission v. Superior Court Trial Lawyers Association*, 483 U.S. 411 (1990), the Supreme Court declined to protect boycotters whose immediate objective was their own economic advantage.

other religious community.[30] The state supreme court rightly held that emotional harm was not a sufficient basis to override a privilege for sincere religious conduct.

Penalizing Former Insiders

Our examination of refusals to associate with insiders and outsiders sets the stage for considering tactics that go beyond shunning and aim directly to injure former insiders. In various cases, people have complained that the Church of Scientology has a policy of "fair game" toward persons who have left the movement.[31] According to this policy, set out in a letter of L. Ron Hubbard, the founder of Scientology, "suppressive persons" may "be deprived of property or injured by any means, by any Scientologist. . . . May be tricked, sued, lied to, or destroyed."[32] Although the church has said that this policy has been cancelled,[33] former members have asserted that they have suffered vicious attacks for leaving the movement. Larry Wollersheim provided evidence that the church had deliberately set out to ruin his photography business, telling Scientologist employees to resign and Scientologist customers to cease doing business with him and to refuse to pay him money they already owed.[34] In characterizing the "fair game" policy as designed to strip the "heretic" of economic, political, and psychological power, the California court cited an instance in which a former church member was falsely accused of grand theft.[35]

In *Wollersheim*, the court concluded that the Scientologists had gone far beyond social shunning, that leaders had "made the deliberate decision to ruin Wollersheim economically and possibly psychologically."[36] Uncertain whether a deliberate campaign to ruin someone by telling people to dishonor legally owed debts to him could qualify as a "religious practice," the court found no case protecting such action and concluded that the state has a compelling interest in discouraging it.[37]

The comparison between ordinary shunning and a "fair game" policy raises a more general issue of how courts should determine what religious

---

[30] *Sands*, note 18 supra.

[31] *Van Schaick v. Church of Scientology of California, Inc.*, 535 F. Supp. 1125 (D. Mass. 1982); *Wollersheim v. Church of Scientology of California*, 66 Cal. Rptr. 2d 1 (Ct. App. 2d. Dist. 1989); *Christofferson v. Church of Scientology of Portland*, 644 P.2d 577 (Or. Ct. App. 1982).

[32] See *Christofferson*, note 31 supra, at 590.

[33] Id. at n. 13.

[34] *Wollersheim*, note 31 supra, at 342.

[35] Id. at 341–42 (citing *Allard v. Church of Scientology*, 129 Cal. Rptr. 797 (1976)).

[36] Id. at 342.

[37] Id. at 343

claims deserve protection. If group members believe that ruining former members is called for on religious grounds, why should their motivation be treated less favorably than the aim to engage in more traditional shunning?

Among possible approaches are these: jurors should never be allowed to pass on the truth of religion; religious motivation should always be protected against a decision that conduct is outrageous; actions directed at a former member should be protected only if the main object is to benefit her; malicious acts should be distinguished from nonmalicious ones; a flexible compelling interest standard should be used to distinguish among instances of behavior.

Focusing on the tort of intentional infliction of emotional distress, Paul Hayden argues that jurors should not be allowed to determine if religious beliefs are "fundamentally flawed."[38] When jurors determine that religiously motivated actions are "outrageous," they implicitly decide that the belief systems are fundamentally flawed.[39] Courts, according to Hayden, should insulate from such an attack any disciplinary action that is motivated by religious belief.[40]

In considering Hayden's proposal, we need to distinguish between what we can expect from the government writ large and what may be sound for jury trials of the tort of infliction of emotional distress (and similar bases of tort liability).

The idea that jurors should not pass on the truth of religious beliefs is appealing. As Hayden puts it, "If we truly believed in a religion that used 'deception' or 'coercion' as part of its indoctrination methods, would we ever conclude that such methods are intolerable in a civilized society?"[41] But a moment's reflection shows why this cannot be the crucial inquiry for every standard of criminal and civil law. If *we* (the society as a whole) truly believed in a religion that demands human sacrifice, the law would make an exception from the crime of murder for human sacrifice.[42] What this illustration reveals is that it is only in a sense that the state can avoid judging the truth of religious views. The government cannot teach the truth of any particular religions or antireligious position; it cannot, according to *United States v. Ballard*,[43] ground criminal liability on the untruth of representations about religious experiences. It cannot, according to cases we considered in chapter 16, determine what doctrines and practices accord with the traditions of a particular religious faith. But much the government does teaches implicitly

---

[38] See Hayden, note 3 supra.
[39] Id. at 638.
[40] Id. at 653.
[41] Id. at 637.
[42] More precisely, the exception would reach at least some human sacrifices.
[43] 322 U.S. 78 (1944).

that certain religious views are unsound. By fighting wars, the national government implies that religious pacifism is misguided; by integrating schools, the courts imply that God does not insist on racial segregation; by not exempting human sacrifice from statutory prohibitions on murder, legislatures imply that God does not want human sacrifices.[44] The law in many ways indicates that particular religious views are unsound, though without endorsing any particular positions as true or sound.[45]

Hayden's stricture against passing on the truth of religious views and his suggestion that all religiously motivated conduct should be protected could not serve as a guide for all government action, but his actual claim about a particular tort might still be sound. Although the tort is often denominated "intentional infliction of emotional distress," in fact a person may be liable for acting recklessly, in disregard of an unjustified risk that his behavior will cause severe emotional distress.[46] Put more simply, without trying to distress someone, I may commit the tort, so long as I realize my actions may well have that consequence.[47] The key to recovery is whether the behavior is outrageous; only the outrageous causing of emotional distress is wrongful.[48] Because emotional distress is so hard to assess, a jury that thinks behavior is truly outrageous is likely believe it has caused distress; and such a jury is also likely to tack on substantial punitive damages. Hayden's essential point is that it is unacceptable to allow jurors to assess the "outrageousness" of religiously motivated behavior, because they will inevitably be judging the persuasiveness of religious reasons to engage in the behavior.

Hayden has identified a genuine problem, but his remedy is too drastic. If we can be confident that behavior would be viewed as "outrageous" whatever group engaged in it, that is a safeguard against unfair treatment of unpopular religious groups. To revert to *Wollersheim*, in few, if any, circumstances would such harsh efforts to undermine someone be other than outrageous. One possible approach would be to say that religiously motivated behavior could be labeled as "outrageous" only if it violates (or urges violation of) a more spe-

---

[44] It might be said that the government relies exclusively on secular reasons, without addressing religious considerations, but no democratic society will punish as murder actions that most citizens believe are religiously required.

[45] For example, a law requiring racial integration does not imply a judgment about whether any particular religious views in support of such a law are correct. These questions are treated at greater length in Kent Greenawalt, *Does God Belong in Public Schools?* chap. 5 (Princeton: Princeton University Press, 2005).

[46] See Restatement (Second) of Torts, § 46.

[47] Some state courts even impose liability for negligent infliction of emotional distress, distress a reasonable person would have foreseen but which the actor may not have foreseen.

[48] See Hayden, note 3 supra, at 589–90.

cific legal norm.[49] In *Wollersheim*, it was enough that the church instructed members to violate their legal obligations toward the victim.

An alternative suggestion is that disciplinary conduct should be unprotected only if it is malicious, in the sense of not being motivated largely by an effort to benefit the person who is disciplined.[50] This proposal is promising. It distinguishes *Wollersheim* from the basic shunning situation;[51] but this exact line gives insufficient regard to the religious interest a group has in its own purity. If a member has done such horrible things that the group regards him as beyond redemption (at least in this life and as recognized by the religious group itself),[52] leaders may still recommend nonassociation to protect other members from a corrupting influence.

Michael J. Broyde, writing from the Jewish tradition, would allow shunning based on the need of a faith community to exclude, but would leave unprotected "claims based . . . on [the] need to convince the 'unfaithful' to return or to punish them."[53] Of the two grounds Professor Broyde would not protect, discipline aimed at encouraging a former member to repent and rejoin the community seems a more legitimate concern for a religious group than pure punishment. In any event, Broyde's particular differentiation between the aim to exclude and the aim to encourage repentance has limited practical effect, since the aim to preserve group purity usually accompanies aspirations to encourage a repentant return to the fold.

The most appropriate division is to treat individual redemption and "group purity" as provisionally protected, and efforts to destroy the individual and to preserve the group against criticism as unprotected. The "fair game" tactics of Scientologists had little to do with either redeeming the victim or preserving the group's purity. Rather they were designed to protect the group from criticism and to punish any member bold enough to reject the group.

---

[49] I think Hayden's position about this is that recovery under another tort standard that precisely defines wrongful behavior is acceptable, but that infliction of emotional distress should not be drawn in. That position strikes me as too restrictive for behavior that constitutes another tort *and* is outrageous in its risk of emotional distress, and for circumstances in which a violation of legal obligations will not fit another standard tort theory.

[50] See Daryl L. Wiesen, "Note, Following the Lead of Defamation: A Definitional Balancing Approach to Religious Torts," 105 *Yale Law Journal* 291, 318 (1995).

[51] Id. at 321–24.

[52] Esbeck, note 7 supra, at 45–46, notes that Tertullian and other early church fathers regarded some sins as irremissible by the church; but Augustine was careful to leave open the possibility that God will forgive what the church does not.

[53] Michael J. Broyde, "Forming Religious Communities and Respecting Dissenter's [sic] Rights: A Jewish Tradition Model for a Modern Society," in John Witte, Jr. and Johan D. van der Vyver, eds., *Religious Human Rights in Global Perspective: Religious Perspectives* 203, 227 (The Hague: Martinus Nijhoof, 1996).

My suggested division falls close to the more general line proposed by Carl Esbeck: a privilege for religiously motivated discipline could be overcome only by "clear and convincing proof of either fraud motivated by a secular purpose or malicious acts that cause injury beyond the reasonable bounds of any religious interest of the church in relationship to its members."[54]

Both my suggested line and Esbeck's are open to two serious criticisms— namely, that such distinctions are too difficult to draw and that they favor more conventional religious views over unconventional ones. On the first point, distinguishing the preservation of group purity from efforts to hurt an apostate may not be easy. The "fair game" policy of the Scientologists seems squarely to fall into the latter category, but leaders might argue that the threat of such harsh retribution for former members helps to preserve the group's coherence.[55] Perhaps a judge should have to make the determination that the group's purity is not a dominant objective before allowing a claim of infliction of emotional distress to go the jury. A further protection might be to insist that, in order to be liable, the leaders of a group must recognize that extreme emotional distress is a highly likely result of their tactics.[56]

The point about discrimination among religions is more troubling. Both my specific division and Esbeck's (more implicitly) favor traditional ideas about the legitimate interests of religious groups. Suppose that Scientologists believe the power and truth of their ideas is partly demonstrated by their ability to crush dissidents—a religious version of "might shows right." Why should that "group interest" have less force than more traditional ideas of avoiding group corruption? The answer is twofold. We cannot completely avoid judging the interests of religious groups by a historically developed sense of where those interests lie. And we cannot avoid regarding tactics that are positively aimed at destroying people's welfare as seriously antisocial.[57] To this extent, standards of distinction should reflect some judgment about reasonably defensible interests of religious groups.

Once a court employs principles of exclusion and inclusion to determine that a group presents religious motivations to which the law should give

---

[54] Esbeck, note 7 supra, at 102.

[55] Familiar notions of general deterrence suggest that the threat of punitive treatment may accomplish goods that the actual infliction of a penalty does not; but in our society no group should be able to achieve coherence by threatening to commit acts that violate legal obligations and are specifically designed to hurt their victim in other than a spiritual way.

[56] One might go even further and require that the infliction of emotional distress be a specific objective; but that would leave uncovered a situation where a group aims to ruin someone, but does not care if the victim receives his ruin with equanimity.

[57] The idea of "double effect" is relevant here. Being aware that social and financial harm will follow from a group's refusal to associate is different from acting specifically in order to harm.

weight, it should then use some version of a compelling interest standard to determine when those motivations should take priority over state interests. The issue of priority may be played out either in a nonconstitutional judicial determination of what can amount to outrageous conduct or in a specific "free exercise" defense of what would otherwise be wrongful behavior. The standard of judgment, as the court in *Wollersheim* recognizes,[58] should demand a more powerful government interest when the religious claim is more substantial.

The Disclosure of Highly Embarrassing Facts

In a highly publicized case,[59] elders of a local Church of Christ had informed the congregation and four surrounding churches that Ms. Guinn, a member who had resigned shortly before, had been engaging in fornication. She claimed the elders had committed the civil wrongs of invasion of privacy and the intentional infliction of emotional distress. The elders explained that "this process . . . causes the transgressor to feel lonely and thus to desire repentance and a return to fellowship with the other members, and . . . it ensures that the church and its remaining members continue to be pure and free from sin."[60] The competing claims and interests resemble those of the shunning cases. A church disciplines according to its religious understanding; the victim is harmed, and her religious liberty is inhibited. A similar resolution is appropriate.

The Oklahoma Supreme Court distinguished between members and nonmembers, determining that the church elders had no right to commit torts against nonmembers. The court emphasized that if a church treats harshly those who have fallen away, the religious exercise of individuals no longer convinced by a church's values will be constrained.[61] The victim's religious liberty thus was treated as an important state interest justifying the legal restriction on the church.

In a case decided three years later, *Hadnot v. Shaw*, the same court explained that, under *Guinn*, "The church privilege extends in this case to

---

[58] Note 31 supra, at 339–41. This question has been discussed in more detail in chapter 13, supra.

[59] *Guinn v. Church of Christ*, 775 P.2d 766 (Okla. 1989).

[60] Id. at 768.

[61] As the court put it, "No real freedom to choose religion would exist in this land if under the shield of the First Amendment religious institutions could impose their will on the unwilling and claim immunity from secular judicature for their tortious acts." Id. at 779. Judge Wilson, in a separate opinion, also emphasized the claimant's religious freedom and suggested that if she were not protected, the court would be aiding the church in violation of the Establishment Clause. Id. at 790.

activities or communications which occurred *after excommunication* if these
may be termed as mere implementation of previously pronounced ecclesiastical sanction which was valid when exercised."[62] Together *Guinn* and *Hadnot*
seem to create a thin, not easily defensible, line. If the elders excommunicate
a wayward member and one consequence is disclosure of her sins, they can
go ahead even if, between her excommunication and any disclosure, she
forswears all association with the church. If the elders warn her that if she
does not repent and change her ways she will be excommunicated, with
disclosure as a consequence, she can, like Guinn, quickly resign and turn
disclosure into a tort.

The court's disposition in *Guinn*, though qualified in *Hadnot*, slights the
church's concerns for recent former members and for continuing members
who have ties with them.[63] Churches typically do not conceive of relations
with members as just like any voluntary club; they have a special interest in
those who have belonged and fallen away.[64] Although a liberal democratic
government regards religious groups as voluntary associations, it should not
insist that the groups themselves employ a voluntaristic conception that
leaves them comparatively indifferent to the fate of former members.

Apart from their regard for former members, churches may conceive a
responsibility to inform present members that a recent communicant lacks
the character they would expect.[65] In this day and age, most of us blanch at
the thought of church officials disclosing the sexual behavior of nonmembers
to their congregations and sister churches; but if members of the Church of
Christ regard nonmarital sexual relations as deeply sinful, they will care
whether a former member has simply shifted membership to another church
or has continued an affair even after being privately chastised by the elders. If
an usher had consistently stolen money from the collection plate or a Sunday
school teacher had sexually abused a member of his class, church leaders
could surely inform their members, even if the offender resigned as soon as
anyone suspected his misbehavior. Of course, these crimes directly against

---

[62] *Hadnot v. Shaw*, 826 P.2d 978, 987 (1992). See *Smith v. Calvary Christian Church*, 462
Mich. 679, 614 N.W.2d 590 (2000), in which plaintiff's active involvement with the church
indicated his continuing consent to its disciplinary practices.

[63] See Esbeck, note 7 supra, at 98–103, who also discusses older cases.

[64] This differentiation is acute in at least in some understandings of Islam, which acknowledge much greater religious freedom in those who have never been Muslims than in those who
have once adhered to the faith. Some Islamic states forbid apostasy from Islam. See Abdullahi
An-Na'im, "The Islamic Law of Apostasy and Its Modern Applicability: The Case from the
Sudan," 16 *Religion* 197 (1986).

[65] In *Ventimiglia v. Sycamore View Church of Christ*, 1988 Tenn. App. Lexis 710, the Court
of Appeals of Tennessee (Western Section) said that actions motivated by the utmost sincerity
and best of intentions did not amount to the outrageous conduct required for the tort of in-
flicting emotional disturbance.

church members are a far cry from nonmarital sexual relations, but some churches consider the latter to be a very serious wrong. Leaders should also be able to caution continuing members about such relations, however much it goes against the grain of modern culture that the behavior is "private."

Although allowing leaders to disclose the behavior of members may inhibit the free exercise of religion of those who would like to continue to engage in "forbidden" behavior and resign, the free exercise concerns of a former member are diminished if she has chosen to join a church that she knew engaged in such disclosures.[66] Indeed, as we have seen in respect to shunning, if secular law penalizes such disclosures, people may forfeit the opportunity to choose a group that practices this form of self-protection.[67] Suppose, however, that when Guinn joined the church she was neither aware, nor should have been aware, of how the church might treat members who resigned, and that she would not reasonably have learned about these disclosure practices during her membership; in that event, a court should regard her like a full outsider after she resigns, someone who could not be the target of damaging revelations about her sexual life.[68]

Nonreligious expressive associations have much less reason to disclose the personal behavior of members and former members. Few, if any, claim the command over the whole lives of their members that is characteristic of many churches. The sexual relations of an active member of an environmental organization or rifle association are hardly relevant. We can, however, imagine personal behavior that is taken as a betrayal of a secular group's ideals. For fervent advocates of vegetarianism, a member's eating of meat might call for disclosure. Closer to *Guinn*, leaders of a nonreligious group devoted to sexual fidelity might feel impelled to reveal failures. Once one recognizes that plausible claims to disclose personal information will be much less frequent for nonreligious than for religious groups, one might choose to allow those organizations try to establish a privilege in individual instances or limit any privilege to religious bodies. As with shunning, I am inclined toward the former alternative.

---

[66] Of course, as I indicate in note 22, supra, people may join religious groups with varying degrees of voluntariness. Further, people often make choices without full understanding and without knowing the future. A legal rule of "no divorce" restrains liberty even if it applies only to people who have married with full awareness of the rule. Original awareness of constraining practices does not eliminate concern about their effect on an individual's religious freedom, but it does diminish the force of that concern.

[67] I say "may forfeit" because a group may continue practices despite the threat of legal liability.

[68] I assume here that religious groups should not be able to disclose to all members details of the private lives of nonmembers. "Church purity" should not a basis to allow a church to become a censor of everyone's personal life.

In broad summary of these shunning and privacy cases, we may say that a church's claim of religious liberty is important, and that a court should use something like the compelling interest test to measure whether ordinary civil remedies will be available to the injured target. My own view is that the state lacks a sufficient compelling interest when a church seeking repentance and group purity engages in isolation and accurate disclosure against recent former members who were aware of those practices. Although instances will be rare, secular expressive associations should have a similar privilege if shunning or disclosure connects powerfully to the group's self-understanding.

Defamation

In contrast to Guinn, who did not deny the facts that church leaders had publicized, some victims claim that damaging statements about them are untrue. Should church leaders and ordinary members ever be able to publish damaging falsehoods about others? No one suggests that church members should be able to commit battery or fraud on those who have fallen away. By the same token, church officials should not be allowed to spread what they know are lies. The question is whether religious groups should have a special qualified privilege to make mistakes.

Highly damaging comments may be made during an internal process of decision or to a wider audience, in fulfillment of some religious purpose. Suppose a church is considering hiring a minister, whom the deacons have recommended. At a general meeting, a member repeats his sister's report that the candidate had extramarital affairs in his previous parish. The church decides not to hire the candidate, and he learns why. He sues the accusing member, asserting that he had no such affairs. Under the ordinary law of defamation, which covers writing (libel) and speaking (slander), one who damages the reputation of another by a false statement can be liable even if he believes what he has said; but persons who have a responsibility to evaluate the qualifications of candidates for a job have a privilege to say what they believe is true, so long as the "information" is relevant to the position.[69] Within many churches, all members have a responsibility to choose their minister. As part of this process, each member should have a qualified privilege; each who believes she is speaking truth that is relevant should be pro-

---

[69] Rodney A. Smolla, *Law of Defamation*, vol. 2, 8:47, 8:53 (2d ed., St. Paul: West, 1999). They have no privilege to say what they suppose is false in order to injure someone, what is sometimes referred to as actual malice in the common law.

tected.[70] For these circumstances, the traditional common-law privilege probably offers an adequate safeguard.

In the second kind of situation, a church leader discloses untrue facts that he believes merit the attention of his congregation. In one modern case, the plaintiff was the ex-wife of a minister of the Worldwide Church of God who had remarried.[71] The church accepted divorce and remarriage only in certain circumstances. In a speech to the annual meeting of ministers and in a pastoral publication, the director of pastoral administration offered a doctrinal explanation of when divorce was permissible and explained why the behavior of the former Mrs. McNair justified her husband's divorce. She claimed that she had been defamed. Insofar as what the administrator asserted was that she had been fighting against the church, that was a matter of opinion about which a church official could offer a judgment. (Defamation covers only facts, not expressions of opinion.) But the administrator also accused her of cursing at her husband and spitting in his face. The court's resolution was that she could succeed only if she proved constitutional malice, that is, that the administrator knew the facts were untrue or acted with reckless disregard of the truth.

In the famous case of *New York Times v. Sullivan,*[72] the Supreme Court developed this standard of constitutional malice under the Free Speech and Free Press clauses to protect criticism of public officials. Speakers generally have less protection if they defame ordinary citizens. What the *McNair* court does is to extend *New York Times* to exercises of religion, even if the person defamed is an ordinary citizen.[73]

That extension makes sense. It may also be appropriate in cases of religious exercise to impose on the plaintiff the burden of proving falsehood (in standard defamation law, the defendant must prove truth) and to limit damages, all part of the constitutional law of libel relating to public officials.[74]

---

[70] Even within a hierarchical church in which ordinary members have no formal say in choosing a cleric, they have enough stake in the matter to warrant a privilege for communications that could affect choice.

[71] *McNair v. Worldwide Church of God*, 242 Cal. Rptr. 823 (Cal. App. 2d Dist. 1987).

[72] 376 U.S. 254 (1964). The state courts of Alabama had sustained an extremely high award of damages for an advertisement about official's reactions to the activities of Martin Luther King, Jr.; the advertisement contained minor errors.

[73] "Constitutional malice" is not exactly the same as "actual malice" under the common law, see note 69 supra, but if one believes there is a high risk that what one says is untrue, one will ordinarily not have a legitimate basis to put it forward. However, someone who believes there is one chance in ten that a prospective minister engages in sexual abuse of children might regard that as a sufficient reason not to hire him, yet the victim might recover under the *New York Times* standard if that statement was made about him. (But perhaps he could not if the low probability was honestly expressed.) Here the speaker might have a greater privilege under the common-law actual malice standard than a standard of constitutional malice.

[74] See Smolla, supra note 69, vol. 1, at 5:12.

When religious leaders have no religious reason to harm someone's reputation, they should have no special privileges.[75] Courts should resolve doubts in favor of the conclusion that claimed religious reasons are genuine; but, as with other tactics aimed specifically to hurt persons, they should not count among legitimate religious reasons an aim to do damage. Thus, if religious leaders spread to a broad public the message that a former member has embezzled bank money, they should, under the ordinary defamation standard, be liable if their accusation is false, even if they believe it is true. Whatever justification they may have to address their own members, the broad accusation serves no religious purpose. If the leaders claim that it does serve a purpose that is within their religious understanding, it should still not carry force in our legal system. In considering fair game, we saw why a purely punitive objective should not be given weight. If the leader's objective is not to punish but to do good for the general community, religious reasons to pursue that good should not count more than analogous nonreligious reasons that could be invoked in other instances of defamation. Although the point is arguable, the law rightly does not create a "do good" privilege to defame, and religious groups should not have a distinctive "do good" privilege of their own.

The Internal Life of Religious Groups

Former members sometimes claim they have been severely damaged by aspects of life within religious groups. These complaints are usually that fringe groups, often called "cults" by their detractors, have inflicted extreme emotional distress. Subsequently we will inquire whether the term *cult* has a meaning that goes beyond condemnation; suffice it here to say that some of these groups make very strenuous demands on adherents, which those who leave may view as unjustifiably harsh.

Perhaps the major problems for any tort liability are that groups within traditional religions have imposed similar demands on those who choose to participate, and that testing and emotional stress have often been regarded as necessary steps for spiritual growth. One who reads about the rule St. Francis established for his brethren in Assisi[76] or what is expected of modern monks and nuns finds rigorous constraint.[77] A Trappist monk leaving his order might

---

[75] See *Madsen v. Erwin*, 395 Mass. 715 (1985).

[76] See, e.g., Frank Pakenham, Earl of Longford, *Francis of Assisi: A Life for All Seasons* (London: Weidenfeld and Nicolson, 1978).

[77] See, e.g., Monica Baldwin, *I Leapt Over the Wall* (London: Hamilton, 1949).

believe that adhering to a vow of silence for twenty years[78] has harmed him emotionally, and that the order should have foreseen that risk. Not surprisingly, we do not see lawsuits by former Trappist monks. No one doubts that the modern choice to enter such a demanding life is voluntary, and many people have a vague sense that such a life can be spiritually uplifting.

Popular attitudes are quite different about many of the cults. People are suspicious of their practices and doubt that choices to enter are truly voluntary. Hostility toward cults, however, cannot by itself be a basis to treat them less favorably than traditional religions. If differential treatment is to be justified, it must be because a cult exhibits objective features that are less acceptable.

One possible complaint about a religious group is that its very teachings predictably cause emotional distress. In *Murphy v. I.S.K. Con. of New England*, a woman claimed that she was caused distress by the Krishna Consciousness teachings that "women are inferior to men" and that "the female form is the form of evil."[79] Absent a genuinely malicious motive to harm, a group's teachings themselves should never be the basis for a tort action. Listening to disturbing doctrines can be distressing, but principles of free speech, as well as free exercise, preclude treating the exposition of ideas as outrageous behavior. Whether or not a person asserts other causes of emotional distress, a judge must not to allow a jury to decide that a church's behavior has been outrageous based on its presentation of basic doctrines.[80]

At the other end of the spectrum from protected to obviously unprotected are outright coercion and other physical harms. A religious group has no privilege to inflict physical injury or restrain a member physically from leaving. Such actions could underlie recovery for battery or false imprisonment, and they could make up part of an emotional distress claim.[81] At least one court has considered the Scientologists' policy of "freeloader debt" as coercive.[82] Staff members receive courses, training, and auditing (a process to work clear of negative "engrams") at reduced rates. However, if they leave the movement, they must pay the difference between what they have been charged and what a member of the public would pay for the same services. A religious group might defend such a practice on the basis that the reduced rates are designed to confer a benefit on the group, one that is lost when

[78] On Trappist practices, see Thomas Merton, *The Seven Storey Mountain* (New York : Harcourt Brace, 1998).

[79] 409 Mass. 842, 851–52 (1991).

[80] Id. at 855–59. However, evidence of a church's teaching can be presented to support a claim that it has engaged in actions that can underlie recovery in damages. Thus, evidence that a church teaches that former members should be attacked physically could be presented to support a plaintiff's assertion that she was attacked physically.

[81] See *Wollersheim*, note 31 supra, at 15–16.

[82] Id. at 14.

someone drops out. But the court writes that L. Ron Hubbard devised "free-loader debt" as a "means of punishing members who, inter alia, chose to leave the Church or refused to disconnect from a suppressive person."[83] Given this evidence, the court fairly treated "freeloader debt" as a form of economic coercion.

Courts have resisted claims that urging adherents to sever family ties can be tortious;[84] disengaging from ordinary family life has been a common practice of many religious and other ideological movements. Former members have also failed to recover damages because they have been exposed to various deprivations in communal life and have been required to work long hours performing charitable services.[85]

Courts have been more receptive to assertions that a religious group has promised secular benefits, such as lodging, food, and a job, which it did not provide and had no intention of providing.[86] Given sufficiently specific allegations, false representations of this sort could amount to fraud.

One court has suggested that even if services for which someone pays are offered ostensibly to induce that person to join and participate in a religion (Scientology), a jury might determine that the services are really offered for the wholly secular purpose of obtaining their money, a form of fraud.[87] Barring overwhelming evidence that those who provide the services have no genuine religious motivation, a court should not allow such a question to go to a jury. The risk is too high that jurors disaffected with a church's philosophy will conclude that its only aim is to make money.

METHODS OF RECRUITMENT

Some of the most intense controversy about "cults" has centered on recruiting tactics; this has played itself out in claims by former adherents that they have been "brainwashed" and in criminal and civil cases against deprogrammers who have employed indisputably coercive tactics to reverse the allegiances of cult members. Here is a sketch of two stories that state opposing positions in a highly simplified form.

---

[83] Id.

[84] See, e.g., *Van Schaick v. Church of Scientology of California, Inc.*, 535 F. Supp. 1125, 1139 (D. Mass. 1982).

[85] See, e.g., *George v. International Society for Krishna Consciousness of California*, 4 Cal. Rptr. 2d 473, 494–95 (Ct. App. 4th Dist. 1992); *Turner v. Unification Church*, 473 F. Supp. 367, 377 (D.R.I. 1978).

[86] *Van Schaick*, note 84 supra, at 1140–41.

[87] *Christofferson*, note 31 supra, at 604–5.

Story 1. Although the religious groups that we call cults do not usually engage in physical restraint of their targets, they often conceal their true purposes and employ tactics such as deprivation of food and sleep and insistent breaking down of psychological defenses that amount to a "coercive persuasion" resembling the "brainwashing" of some American soldiers captured during the Korean War. The "conversions" these tactics produce are not truly voluntary; the persons on whom they succeed have ceased to act as rational agents, as we can see by their flat, uncommunicative affect when they meet family members and friends to whom they have been close. Because the cult adherents have been coerced into accepting one set of beliefs and practices, and because they have been incapacitated to alter their acceptance, loved ones are justified in taking drastic steps to reverse their thinking, including taking them by force and restraining them while expert deprogrammers force them to listen to countervailing messages.

Story 2. The proselytizing of new religious groups does not differ fundamentally from that of many Christian groups over the centuries. Whether people's fundamental outlooks can be altered by outright coercion is doubtful; so-called coercive persuasion is a misnomer. New adherents join cults because they are attracted by the spiritual messages and the presence of close-knit loving communities. Their choices are every bit as voluntary as those of typical converts to Christianity, and their continuance within their religious communities remains voluntary. If they fail to engage lovingly with their parents, the usual reason is that the parents are extremely hostile to their new religion and insist that they abandon it to fulfill the parents' expectations about what their lives should be. Coercive deprogramming is no more justified for young adult members of cults than it would be for young Catholic women who have chosen the life of a nun against their parents' wishes.

Trying to sort out the truth between these two competing accounts is complicated; but, for purposes of assessing civil wrongs, courts should regard the tactics of most new religious groups as within acceptable bounds and should accept most conversions as sufficiently voluntary.

A 1988 California case provides a helpful entry point.[88] According to his complaint, David Molko, who had graduated from law school and passed the Pennsylvania bar examination, came to San Francisco to visit and perhaps find a job.[89] While he was waiting at a bus stop, two men approached him and said they lived in an "international community" of socially conscious people. Molko accepted their invitation to join the group for dinner, after they responded negatively to his question as to whether they had a

---

[88] *Molko v. Holy Spirit Association for the Unification of World Christianity,* 252 Cal. Rptr. 122 (Sup. Ct.).

[89] Id. at 125. I omit the similar account of a co-plaintiff.

"religious connection." When a dinner at which he was held in constant conversation was over, Molko agreed to visit a farm depicted as a rural getaway. At the farm, he was exposed to a constant schedule of lectures, discussions, and exercises. He again asked about a religious connection, and was told that the group had no association with a religious organization. Only on his twelfth day of continuous group activity was he told that the group was part of the Unification Church. Two months later, he joined the church.[90]

The theory of Molko's claim for fraud and infliction of emotional distress was that he had been induced by false representations into subjecting himself to techniques of brainwashing. Two experts on coercive persuasion who had examined Molko stated "that they believed the Unification Church's sophisticated indoctrination techniques had rendered [him] . . . incapable of exercising his own will and judgment, or of responding independently upon learning of [his] deceptive recruitment."[91] The California Supreme Court decided that a summary judgment granted to the church had been in error. Because of controversy over the concept of brainwashing, the question whether Molko was brainwashed was a factual question that a jury should resolve.[92]

In analyzing the issue of coercive persuasion, we may begin by noting that the word *cult* has no precise definition and is commonly employed in a pejorative way. According to one account, groups commonly labeled as cults are "1) authoritarian; 2) communal and totalistic; 3) aggressive in their proselytizing; 4) systematic in their programs of indoctrination; 5) relatively new in the United States; 6) middle-class in their clientele."[93] Because no one would self-consciously say that a group that was otherwise identical to a cult would fail to be one because its main clientele was lower class or because the group had been in the United States a long time, the first four attributes would appear to be the crucial ones. We probably do better to avoid the term and use an alternative such as "new religious movements" that may be equally indeterminate but less value laden.

The theory of coercive persuasion is that by an arsenal of psychological techniques, new religious groups are able to direct people's minds without the physical coercion that helped accomplish brainwashing during the Korean War.[94] Among the elements are isolation of a recruit and manipulation

[90] Id. at 127.

[91] Id. at 131.

[92] Id.

[93] Dena S. Davis, "Joining a Cult: Religious Choice or Psychological Aberration?" 11 *Journal of Law and Health* 145, 147–48 (1996–97), summarizing attributes included in Thomas Robbins and Dick Anthony, "Deprogramming, Brainwashing, and the Medicalization of Deviant Religious Groups," 29 *Social Problems* 284 (February 1982).

[94] On brainwashing involving physical coercion, see Robert J. Lifton, *Thought Reform and the Psychology of Totalism* (New York: Norton, 1961).

of his environment, control over communication, inadequate diet and fatigue, degradation of his self, peer pressure, the generation of guilt and open confessions, assignment of monotonous tasks, the inducement of acts of symbolic betrayal of previously held values.[95] If someone were converted on the basis of tactics that left her unfree, the conversion would not itself constitute a tortious wrong, but she might be able to recover for emotional distress and other negative consequences that ensued, such as the donation of money to the group.

This theory of coercive persuasion faces at least two major obstacles. The first is that most young people approached by members of new religious groups, even most young people attracted to their meetings, reject the overtures without getting involved.[96] Most of those who do join leave within two or three years. If the groups have such powerful techniques of persuasion, why do they not have higher rates of initial and long-term success? Of course, it is conceptually possible that most people are able to resist the methods of persuasion *and* that those who submit, possessing a lesser degree of psychological or mental strength, do not do so freely; but the modest rate of success makes it hard to demonstrate that those who are persuaded are unfree. A further difficulty for such a theory is that membership in these groups seems to serve many of the psychological and social needs of those who join.[97]

The second obstacle is that many traditional groups have employed methods of indoctrination (though perhaps not of conversion) that resemble those of the new movements. The rigors of monastic life are but one striking example. And conversion has often followed great emotional stress and led to a rejection of prior forms of life. We are told that Timothy Edwards doubted the conversion of his son Jonathan, the prominent New England theologian to be, because Jonathan had not yet been so overcome by his sinfulness that he had experienced "legal terrors" of a sort some Puritans regarded as a necessary preparatory step to truly accepting God's grace.[98]

If we ask whether the choice to join new religious groups is free or unfree, we need to confront the obvious facts that techniques of persuasion have different effects on different people and that no bright line marks the bound-

[95] See Davis, note 93 supra, at 156, summarizing the account of Margaret Singer and L. J. West. For one legal writer who strongly credits claims of psychological coercion, see Richard Delgado, "When Religious Exercise Is Not Free: Deprogramming and the Constitutional Status of Coercively Induced Relief," 37 *Vanderbilt Law Review* 1071 (1984).

[96] See James T. Richardson, "'Brainwashing' Claims and Minority Religions Outside the United States: Cultural Diffusion of a Questionable Concept in the Legal Arena," 1996 *Brigham Young University Law Review* 873, 881–82.

[97] Id. at 879–80; Davis, note 93 supra, at 161–65.

[98] George M. Marsden, *Jonathan Edwards* 58 (New Haven: Yale University Press, 2003).

ary between free and unfree choices. Rather, everyone makes decisions under varying degrees of psychological pressure. Evaluating just how much pressure any individual experiences is very difficult.

People *can* self-consciously choose to expose themselves or their children to powerful regimes of persuasion. In modern society they are most likely to do so if they seek to correct what they perceive as a serious disability, such as addiction to drugs or alcohol; but they may do so in pursuit of more positive spiritual fulfillment. Anyone who freely chooses to subject himself to the techniques of persuasion of a new religious group cannot complain about most predictable consequences.

The more typical religious recruitment may involve individuals who are not quite aware what they are letting themselves in for. Apparently, the "Heavenly Deception" that played a part in Molko's recruitment is unusual,[99] but many young people who attend meetings of fringe groups have a limited sense of the dynamics of those meetings. Nevertheless, recruitment efforts in all domains of life often play on comparative ignorance. So long as people are free to leave at any time, the proselytizing tactics of the new religious movements do not cross over the border of what is socially intolerable. Considering a claim for the infliction of emotional distress and wrongful death brought by a father whose son had committed suicide a month after dropping out of a training program of the Unification Church, a New York court concluded that the church's method of religious indoctrination was "neither extreme nor outrageous" and could not underlie recovery in tort.[100] The court correctly resolved this as a matter of law. Given the danger that jurors will react unfavorably to an unpopular religion, the question of whether indoctrination tactics are "outrageous" cannot be left mainly to them.

This leaves us with the complexity that, according to his complaint, what led Molko to open himself up to the persuasive tactics of the group was its initial deception. Had Molko been initially deceived but then been provided full information about the group and put under no pressure to join, his choice to join would not count as a result of the deception.[101] And apparently the court assumed that had Molko known from the start that the group was connected with the Unification Church, its tactics alone would not have

---

[99] See Davis, note 93 supra, at 157–58.

[100] *Meroni v. Holy Spirit Association for the Unification of World Christianity*, 506 N.Y.S.2d 174 (App. Div. 2d Dept. 1986).

[101] This would be true even if the deception was a "but for" cause of his joining. To draw an analogy, if a woman says she will not "date" anyone over fifty-five, a sixty-three-year-old man lies that he is fifty-four, he reveals the truth on their third date, and they become engaged three months later, his lie is not a "proximate cause" of the engagement even though that would never have occurred without the initial lie.

undercut the voluntariness of his choice to join. The theory is that the initial deception plus the tactics may have amounted to a form of coercive persuasion. The court understandably did not want to approve of groups concealing their actual character from potential recruits. Nonetheless, Molko joined the group well after he learned the truth. It is not clear that he would have been more likely to have suffered "brainwashing" than someone who, before the first gathering, was aware the group was religious but had no advance knowledge of how it attempts to persuade people to join. On balance, the court should not have allowed the "brainwashing" theory to be put to the jury.[102]

If courts should not declare the typical recruiting tactics of new religious movements to be intolerable, or allow that question to go to juries, it follows that deprogrammers should not be permitted to use physical coercion on adults who have chosen to join the movements.[103] Barring some extraordinary individual circumstances, deprogrammers who have kidnapped converts and kept them in isolation for days should not be able to raise a defense to criminal or civil liability that their actions were necessary to avert a greater evil.[104]

Finally, courts should not sidestep the ordinary rules by appointing parents as conservators of their adult children who have chosen to join fringe religious groups. Such assignments are proper if there is some independent basis to conclude that the children are incompetent, but membership in an unpopular group neither demonstrates incompetence nor is independent evidence of incompetence.

CLERGY MALPRACTICE: COUNSELING

In recent years, the idea of clergy malpractice—holding clerics liable in tort for failing to perform their roles properly—has gained some currency.[105] That doctors, lawyers, and accountants, among others, may be charged with practicing in an inappropriate manner is well established. Malpractice may underlie criminal charges, civil claims, revocations of licenses, or lesser sanctions of professional associations. A person injured by a doctor's incompetent performance may sue under the specific rubric of malpractice, or for

[102] *Molko*, note 88 supra, at 143–56 (dissent of Anderson, J.).
[103] Minors, over whom parents still have substantial control, are another question.
[104] See *Scott v. Ross*, 140 F.3d 1275 (9th Cir. 1998).
[105] See, e.g., Robert J. Basil, "Note, Clergy Malpractice: Taking Spiritual Counseling Conflicts Beyond Intentional Tort Analysis," 19 *Rutgers Law Journal* 419 (1988); James L. Lehman, "Note, Clergy Malpractice: A Constitutional Approach," 41 *South Carolina Law Review* 459 (1990).

another tort, such as wrongful death, with malpractice figuring in the theory of recovery.[106]

We may notice immediately three crucial, and related, differences between the clergy and other professions. First, the state neither licenses members of the clergy nor sets up standards for how the clerics should practice. Second, people disagree more widely about how those functions should be performed than they do in respect to other professions. Third, keeping dissenters free to practice according to their beliefs is an important aspect of the free exercise of religion. The state cannot determine what is spiritual harm and competent spiritual leadership.[107]

The state should not impose general standards for clerical practice. Much must be left to specific understandings among particular religions. Any recovery against clergy for harmful practice must be because they have committed independent torts or have breached duties that are not in serious question. We have already looked at a range of torts that clergy, as well as others, may commit, including defamation, invasion of privacy, and the intentional infliction of emotional distress. Here we turn to torts that depend on special roles or relationships, such as that of a professional counselor or money manager. Perhaps clergy should be liable for breaching the responsibilities of special relationships they have with those to whom they minister.

The main activity that raises this question is counseling. Should clergy who counsel parishioners be liable based on (1) bad advice, (2) a failure to refer to mental health professionals, (3) disclosure of confidential communications, and (4) sexual intimacy? Many clergy make themselves available for counseling on a regular basis; should their liability track that of psychiatrists, psychotherapists, and secular marriage counselors?

The problem of sexual intimacies is relatively straightforward. Without doubt, clergy who are counseling people occupy a role of authority and influence similar to that of secular professionals. Without doubt, the damage they can do if they take advantage of that role to engage in sexual relations

---

[106] A surgeon defendant might claim that the deceased died during a needed operation. The surviving family member would argue that the surgeon had been guilty of malpractice and was negligent in failing to exercise reasonable care.

[107] Someone might quarrel with the idea of *three* differences, claiming that everything boils down to what the state is willing to enforce. If one includes all forms of alternative medicine, people do disagree greatly about approaches to mental and bodily well-being; but the state stifles disagreement by privileging one kind of approach over others. The practical thrust of this critique is to suggest that the state may be too restrictive in its regulation of medicine, but what concerns us is the state's approach to religious practice, not medicine or law. We need not worry too much about whether the law's approach to medical practitioners and lawyers is too restrictive.

Reasons not to impose liability for clergy counseling are summarized in Esbeck, note 7 supra, at 83–84.

with their clients can be just as great. With limited qualifications, they should be liable to the same degree as secular counselors.

That religious counselors, like anyone else, can be liable for nonconsensual sex or sex with minors is obvious.[108] The issue concerns consensual sexual relations between adults, relations in which two people would generally be free to engage. Business executives and their assistants, professors and their adult students, producers and aspiring actors are allowed by the law to be intimate sexually.[109] Although many now view the conscious or unconscious use of power to achieve sexual advantage as a serious form of exploitation, an imbalance of power does not turn sexual involvement into a tort. A much greater consensus now exists that psychological counselors should not engage in sexual relations with those they counsel. Such intimacies are thought particularly likely to cause emotional harm to the more vulnerable partner. Courts are likely to find a fiduciary duty arising out of the relationship of counselor and counselee and to conclude that sexual intimacy breaches that duty.[110]

Such liability can fairly be extended to religious counselors.[111] Although unlicensed, clerics who hold themselves out as offering regular counsel (not just as giving occasional pastoral advice) undertake the role of counselor. Across a very broad spectrum, religious groups do regard sexual intimacy between clerics and those they counsel as deeply wrongful. If no one, including the counselor and the members of his religion, defends the taking of sexual advantage as justified for religious reasons, liability for undoubted intimacies does not impair religious exercise.

Of course, *any* form of liability, including fraud and theft, presents the possibility that someone will go after an unpopular religious figure with a phony claim; but if a factual inquiry need not concern competing religious claims, the risk of false complaints is tolerable.

Another possible objection is more troublesome, but it affects very few circumstances. A religious counselor might claim that sexual relations within the counseling context are positively beneficial from a spiritual and psychological

---

[108] Scandals involving Roman Catholic priests during the last few years have almost entirely concerned sexual contact with minors.

[109] However, some businesses and universities now prohibit sexual liaisons of this type. As these perceptions and forms of internal regulation become more widespread, we may see more instances of recovery in tort by the "weaker" person in the relationship.

[110] See, e.g., *Destefano v. Grabrian*, 763 P.2d 275 (Sup. Ct. Colo. 1988).

[111] See id.; *Erickson v. Christenson*, 781 P.2d 283 (Or. Ct. App. 1989). But see *Strock v. Pressnell*, 527 N.E.2d 1235 (Ohio 1988), in which a husband sued a minister for having sexual relations with his wife during a period when the couple was engaged in marriage counseling with the minister. The court ruled that the husband could not recover for intentional infliction of emotional distress, given the state's abolition of amatory actions.

point of view. The law cannot directly judge what is spiritually beneficial. The law might impose liability on the basis of what is harmful from an ordinary psychological perspective, but typical psychological damage is evaluated in the context of ordinary relationships; evidence may be scant about the harms and benefits of particular practices *for believers* within a community that standardly engages a practice that its members regard as beneficial.[112]

One might suppose that *most* religious counselors should be liable for sexual intimacies and that formulating an exemption is too difficult; but, in fact, the law could reasonably provide a limited exemption when (1) the idea that counselor-client sexual relations are beneficial is an aspect of the counselor's religion; and (2) either (*a*) the client is a member of the religion who should be aware of this practice, or (*b*) the counselor informs the client of the practice well before encouraging any sexual relations. If these narrow conditions are met, those seeking counsel should not be able to recover for sexual intimacies in which they have voluntarily engaged.[113]

If liability for sexual intimacies is generally appropriate, liability for bad advice is not. A religious counselor is mainly giving counsel and advice from a spiritual perspective. If a counselor urges a client to read the Bible and develop a sense of sin about her relations with her lover, the law should not decide that this advice is unsuitable because it contrasts with what a secular counselor would say. Given their disagreements over religious beliefs and practices, religious counselors will offer radically different advice about some subjects. We should not think of religious counselors as offering ordinary advice with religious bonus, although some clerics may view their role in just this way. Many, maybe most, will see the spiritual dimension of what they do as permeating all they say. To make clerics liable for the content of their advice falls very close to imposing liability for the expression of their religious beliefs.

Is liability for bad advice ever called for? One possibility involves encouragements to undesirable acts, such as lawbreaking or leaving one's spouse. Counselors should be able to advise clients to engage in any acts that are

[112] Given the present legal tolerance of fornication and even adultery, a state could not now reasonably ground liability on a theory that all sexual relations outside marriage are wrongful and that the counselor's role gives him primary responsibility to avoid such relations.

[113] It might be argued that an exemption administered in this way would be unfair to maverick counselors: those who dissent from the puritanical altitudes of their larger group. Why should not an individual cleric not be able to invoke the exemption if *he* believes sexual intimacies are spiritually beneficial and he has so informed his client? The problem with such an extended exemption is obvious. It creates too great an incentive to counselors strongly attracted to their clients to decide that sexual relations will have a positive effect. In few aspects of life are human capacities for rationalization and self-deceit as strong as this one. Further, one can imagine disagreements over just what a counselor said and when, if everything comes down to his providing adequate information in advance.

lawful. If a wife can lawfully leave her husband, no counselors, religious or other, should be liable for disinterested advice that a separation would be healthy. A counselor should be liable only if he gives his advice to gain a sexual or other advantage or to satisfy a malicious motive, such as personal hostility toward the husband.

So long as he offers advice that is disinterested, offered in the spirit of what is best for his client, a counselor should be free even to advise committing an illegal act. If the advice becomes instigation, however—"I urge you strongly to assassinate this public official"—then it is not protected, whether offered by a religious counselor or any ordinary acquaintance.[114] In one case, parents complained that religious counselors had indicated to their son that suicide might be preferable to continuing a life of sin.[115] In fact, the counselors were positively encouraging the son to stop sinning, not to commit suicide. But, contrary to what the court assumed, a counselor should not be liable for an honest spiritual appraisal that because a life of continuing grave sin is so horrible even suicide would be preferable. The hardest issue is when a counselor *instigates* behavior that is not criminal or tortious by itself but is against public policy. Religious counselors may insist that members separate from spouses who have fallen away or do not embrace the correct faith.[116] So long as a counselor is clear about the reason for his insistence, his liability should track that of religious leaders who urge members to shun spouses.

Instances in which religious counselors either fail to warn clients that they need professional help or positively discourage their seeking that help raise deeply troubling questions. In one well-known case, parents claimed that religious counselors had failed to refer their obviously suicidal son for appropriate psychiatric treatment.[117] In reality, the counselors had encouraged the young man to seek outside help. But let us consider the stark situation. A client is identifiable as suicidal. Religious counselors do not refer him to anyone else, they do not warn anyone else (such as his parents), and they discourage his seeking any assistance outside the bosom of the church. If the client commits suicide, should parents be able to succeed in a wrongful death action?

We need first to know how the religious counselors have represented themselves. If they have claimed, directly or by membership in a relevant professional organization, a mastery that one associates with licensed secular counselors, clients who use their services may assume that they can identify highly

---

[114] On the line between disinterested advice and active instigation, see Kent Greenawalt, *Speech, Crime and the Uses of Language* 110–23 (New York: Oxford University Press, 1989).

[115] *Nally v. Grace Community Church*, 240 Cal. Rptr. 215, 219 (Ct. App. 1987), rev'd on other grounds, 763 P.2d 948 (Cal. 1988), cert. denied, 490 U.S. 1007 (1989).

[116] See *Bradeska v. Antion*, 21 Ohio App. 2d 67, 255 N.E.2d 265 (1969); *Radecki v. Schuckardt*, 50 Ohio App. 92, 361 N.E.2d 543 (1976).

[117] *Nally*, note 115 supra. A good discussion is in Esbeck, note 7 supra, at 79–81.

dangerous inclinations and will act accordingly. In that event, the counselors should be liable for a failure to refer (or for mistaken advice not to seek further help) on the same basis as minimally qualified secular professionals.

Matters become more difficult if a religious counselor offers no such assurance. She says implicitly that she offers spiritual counsel, that she claims no expertness in psychological maladies. On one view, a counselor who does not hold herself out as an expert in psychology should be no more liable than a friend or family member who gives inept advice or fails to refer or warn.[118] A friend who offers his own opinion has no duty to be competent. Perhaps the religious counselor should be treated similarly.

A contrasting view is that the religious counselor who offers to provide regular advice implies that she is available to be *the person* who helps professionally with a client's problems. Unless the counselor says, "Well, perhaps you should see a secular professional as well as me" or, "You need to understand that I do not have all the training of a licensed psychotherapist," the client may be encouraged to put his problems into the counselor's hands, unaware of the limits of the counselor's competence. The client is not treating the counselor like any friend.

Perhaps someone representing herself as available for formal counseling relationships has a responsibility either to state very clearly the limits of her competence or to possess a minimal acquaintance with highly dangerous conditions and who should treat them. If some discrete conditions are seriously dangerous and relatively easy to identify, and experts agree widely on how these conditions should be treated (e.g., by mandatory hospitalization, psychiatric help, or medication), anyone who holds herself out as a professional counselor about life's problems and who does not explicitly indicate that her competence does not extend to such matters[119] should be liable if she fails to advise a client who plainly manifests one of these dangerous conditions that require outside help, and he is damaged as a consequence.

A final category for possible liability is divulgence of confidential information, a subject we have taken up in chapter 15.

INSTITUTIONAL LIABILITY

The discussion thus far has skirted a very important practical question: when may an organization itself, as well as any individuals who cause harm, be

---

[118] If a friend does not see that a suicidal companion needs psychiatric help, or even offers advice that such help is unnecessary, he is not liable.

[119] An alternative kind of warning would be an initial statement that as a member of a particular religious group, the counselor is highly skeptical of the premises of secular psychotherapy and will not offer advice that conforms with those premises.

liable for damages? An answer involves a mix of principles of tort law and constitutional considerations, and the right resolutions for some situations are far from certain. The answer has great practical importance because the organization is likely to have deeper pockets than individual defendants and because successful suits against it may threaten its survival.

The two fundamental theories of liability are that an individual who has wronged a victim has been acting on behalf of the organization and that the organization has failed to exercise adequate care in its hiring or supervision of its employees. Recall the claim that the Scientologists had a policy of "fair game" of ruining former adherents by fair means or foul. If a victim could show that any individual Scientologists committing crimes or torts against him were carrying out the policy of the organization itself, the Church of Scientology would be liable.[120] No one claims that the Roman Catholic Church has a policy of priests engaging in sexual relations with minors. For instances of sexual abuse by priests, the most promising theory of recovery is that the church failed to use reasonable care in placing the priests and in supervising their activities.

The theory that organizations are liable for wrongful acts committed on their behalf—by employees or other agents[121]—is well settled, and creates little constitutional difficulty. This doctrine carries the hoary name of *respondeat superior*. An employee is "acting within the scope of his employment" if he is fulfilling the directions of those responsible for organization policy (as in the claim about individuals carrying out the "fair game" policy) or if he acts negligently in performing a task set for him (as when the driver of a church bus has an accident because he was not careful). At least within most jurisdictions, an organization is not responsible if an individual who is "on the job" self-consciously deviates from what the organization wants him to do, to carry out his own purposes.[122] Thus, if the bus driver spots a personal enemy and decides to run him down, the church would not be liable. Sexual acts by priests would be viewed similarly.[123] A principle of charitable immunity used to protect religious organizations and other charities from the operation of ordinary tort liability, but in most states, that principle has been revoked or greatly eroded.

[120] See, e.g., *Wollersheim*, note 31 supra.

[121] A person who is not an employee may be an independent agent acting on someone's behalf. I pass over nuances of when a relationship is one of agency.

[122] It is sufficient for liability under the law of agency that a person appears to be acting on the authority of the organization.

[123] See Nadia de la Houssaye, "Comment, Liability of the Church for Sexual Misconduct of Church Leaders," 39 *Loyola Law Review* 313, 316–19 (1993). However, *Erickson*, note 111 supra, adopted the view that sexual misconduct committed within the time and space limits of the job was within the scope of employment.

Disagreements can arise over whether someone is acting within the scope of his employment and over whose directions and encouragement count as those of the organization. These questions could raise delicate issues about religious organizations. For example, if the rector of an Episcopalian parish positively encouraged a younger priest under her authority to engage in sexual relations with an adult that the younger priest was counseling, and both priests were aware this contravened the stated policy of the national church, might the victim recover against the local church, if not the diocese and the national church? That might be hard to say without a clear sense of the rector's authority in the local church, and of relations between that church and the national, but determining those matters might draw a judge or jury into debatable aspects of church governance, a dubious enterprise for civil courts. As the last chapter explains, the Supreme Court has said that in intra-church disputes over property, civil courts should not be resolving debatable matters of doctrine and church government. That "hands off" principle is the backdrop for perplexities about institutional tort liability.

The particular issue whether parishes and dioceses can be liable for sexual misconduct by priests reaches claims about negligence, to which we now turn, as well as ones about scope of employment. A victim of sexual abuse by a priest may claim that higher authorities irresponsibly placed the offending priest in circumstances where he could engage with minors, or irresponsibly failed to supervise his activities, or both.[124] For example, a bishop may have assigned a priest to ordinary parish duties after becoming aware that he had molested children in another parish, and the bishop may then have failed to set in place close supervision of the priest's activities.[125] The theory of negligent hiring and supervision has become well established;[126] liability under that theory for a nonreligious private school whose headmaster was irresponsible about an elementary school teacher in the manner the bishop was irresponsible about the priest would raise no constitutional difficulty. But is such liability permissible for religious organizations? That depends on whether judges or jurors can decide without improperly interfering in church governance or unacceptably assessing risk and benefit.

Because the Roman Catholic Church has settled a great many of the claims against it based on sexual abuse by priests, possible constitutional defenses have not come before courts as often as they would have had the church consistently opposed claims by victims. Courts facing the issue about church

[124] See Restatement (Second) of Agency § 213 (1958).
[125] One chilling account of instances of reckless disregard of the interests of abused children by members of the Roman Catholic Church hierarchy is in Marci A. Hamilton, *God vs. The Gavel: Religion and the Rule of Law* 13–19 (New York: Cambridge University Press, 2005).
[126] See de la Houssaye, note 123 supra, at 324–27.

governance have divided.[127] Some have said that any imposition on a church of liability would require a degree of investigation of how the church runs that would be unduly entangling.[128] Others have said that no searching inquiry of church governance is necessary, and that principles governing internal property disputes do not apply when third parties sue.[129] Each side of the argument has part of the truth. *One* reason for the "hands off" approach to property disputes is that secular courts should not be resolving internal religious disagreements; but the concern that courts should not resolve debatable matters of doctrine and governance goes further, and it is relevant when third parties sue as well. The key about governance, however, is that courts should not resolve *debatable* matters of governance. No harm to church-state relations is done if a court recognizes the undoubted facts that Catholic bishops assign priests to parishes and have general supervision over the affairs of dioceses.

As we saw in the previous chapter, some versions of the "hands off" approach *require* courts to identify a church's basic form of governance. The mere fact that a court makes some determination about church governance does not itself constitute undue interference in religious affairs. Suppose that the bishop is informed that a priest has had sexual relations with minors. The bishop requires the priest to undergo rehabilitation. After six months, the bishop assigns the priest to a parish in a different county, providing the local church no information about his past history of sexual relations and making no suggestion that he be supervised. Determining that the highest official within the diocese has made the decision about assignment and bears some responsibility for an absence of supervision is straightforward. One can conceive of a question whether the diocese should be responsible for the actions of its bishop, but probably that can be resolved as would the analogous question for a nonreligious organization.

However, one can imagine a case in which the authority of higher-ups and the relative autonomy of priests or ministers is in dispute, *and* the possible liability for the organization turns on the answer. In that circumstance, a court's resolution might require that it decide issues that were not appropriate for it.

As far as governance of a religious organization is crucial, the proper approach is this: Courts may take undisputed relations of authority into account, but if a substantial disagreement about governance arises, a court

---

[127] See id. at 313.

[128] See *Ayon v. Gourley*, 47 F. Supp. 2d 1246 (D. Colo. 1998), aff'd on other grounds, 185 F.3d 873 (10th Cir. 1999).

[129] See, e.g., *Malicki v. Doe*, 814 So. 2d 347 (Fla. 2002); *Smith v. O'Connell*, 986 F. Supp. 73 (D.R.I. 1997).

should not try to resolve it. If the court can dispose of the victim's claim without resolving the dispute, it should proceed in that way. If the disagreement is critical, the court should assume for purposes of the case the resolution that is most favorable to the religious organization. Thus, a court will avoid imposing liability on the basis of a debatable assertion about church government *and* it will avoid trying to settle matters it is ill suited to resolve. This approach may seem somewhat unfavorable for victims, but it is much less so than imposing an absolute bar to liability, and it will allow recovery in many instances.

A related point concerns liability for negligence. Perhaps it is too intrusive for courts to ascertain just what religious authorities should have known that they did not know. Negligence liability is problematic in that it can make someone liable who lacks any actual consciousness of danger. For churches and other religious organizations, courts should require that a higher-up either has known about an individual's wrongdoing or has been alerted to that possibility. (Thus, it would be sufficient if someone complained that a priest had abused a minor, and the bishop dismissed the complaint out of hand without any investigation.)[130]

The following issue about risk and benefit has yet to surface. Perhaps no church could honestly present it in light of the claimed abuses; in any event, making any radical claim about prospective benefit would be impolitic in the extreme. But suppose a bishop, or other high authority defended his actions with one or two of the following claims: (1) "Whatever statistics about rehabilitation of sex offenders may show, I take it as a matter of religious faith that one whose rehabilitation is in the bosom of the church and is accompanied by a confession of past sins *is* fully rehabilitated." (2) "As bad as sexual relations with minors may be for the victims, the status of souls matters more, and reassigning this priest to ordinary parish duties was the most promising course for his soul."[131]

These possible claims, and especially the second, raise issues about ordinary risk and spiritual benefit not unlike those about snake handling we examined in chapter 3. There we inquired whether states can assign a peculiarly low value to claimed spiritual benefits in deciding to prohibit risky actions. Here the issue is whether states *must* assign a peculiarly high value to possible religious benefits or *must* refrain from striking any balance whatsoever.

---

[130] This is close to making the standard one of recklessness, but the diocese could be liable even if the bishop foolishly thought there was no risk.

[131] In *Smith v. O'Connell*, note 129 supra, the Roman Catholic Church did claim unsuccessfully that subjecting the church to the demands of tort law would require them to deviate from church doctrine and would violate the free exercise rights of the hierarchy.

The best approach reaches neither of these conclusions. On the degree of factual risk, churches should be held to judgments that fall within a range reasonably supported by evidence other than religious faith. If studies show that the incidence of sexual abuse is high among past offenders, even those who have undergone rehabilitation, and there is no evidence that priests undergoing rehabilitation in connection with the church have a strikingly high rate of rehabilitative success, the bishop must, in respect to potential liability, judge the risk to be substantial, whatever his religious faith tells him.

The balance of risk and benefit is more complicated. Perhaps we should say that a church may treat the potential spiritual benefit as being as great as the analogous benefit for any comparable secular undertaking, but a church cannot trump any ordinary evaluation of risk and benefit by saying that the welfare of a single (priest's) soul outweighs any degree of violation and psychological harm to minors. For purposes of civil liability, the church must assess risks and benefits within a range that would be comparable for secular undertakings. This is merely a more complex application of a principle we see in some other chapters of the book, including those of dangerous activities and medical procedures and child custody, discussed in chapters 21 and 22: namely that the state should protect secular interests against harmful or extremely risky actions defended as serving overarching spiritual objectives.

CHAPTER 18

Employment Relations:
Ordinary Discrimination and Accommodation

The book's final chapters mainly concern the law's treatment of relations between private parties in respects that reach beyond the ordinary law of civil wrongs. This chapter and its successor examine laws that bar religious discrimination. These are followed by an examination of when religious bodies may discriminate on grounds that would be barred to other organizations. Chapter 21 considers privileges to refuse medical treatment and to refuse to participate in medical procedures. Chapter 22 asks how far the courts should be responsive to religious considerations in determining custody of children and the conditions under which that custody is granted.

How employers respond to religious differences is a crucial aspect of the exercise of religion within a society. Previous chapters have examined relations between the government and individuals, including constitutional rights individuals may have. Because private employers are not directly regulated by federal and state constitutions,[1] legislatures must adopt statutes if the law is to forbid private discrimination.[2] Constitutions come into play only at a second level. What the government requires of private employers may be unconstitutional. For example, if, in order to curb offenses to religious sensibilities, a statute provided that "No employer shall allow any employee to discuss religion during working hours," a worker could claim that the law violates First Amendment safeguards of free speech and the free exercise of religion.[3] Thus, we can ask what employers should do, how far legislatures should constrain their choices, and what legislative constraints overstep constitutional boundaries.

---

[1] Except for prohibiting slavery and involuntary servitude, the federal Constitution does not regulate private persons or organizations, and typical state constitutions are similar.

[2] Constraint can take the form of direct requirements or of conditioning the grant of government contracts on the meeting of certain conditions. I do not discuss separately the conditions under which government contracts should be granted.

[3] Were an employer on his own to forbid religious speech, the Constitution would not be involved, but once the government insists that employers do this, it has acted unconstitutionally.

Employment Relations, Religion, and Fairness

Before we engage these inquiries, it helps to have a sense of basic possibilities and complicating factors.[4]

The Range of Possibilities

Straightforward Possibilities

Someone may be denied a job, or not promoted, because an employer or supervisor makes a negative judgment about his religious convictions or identity. This is what I call "ordinary" discrimination on the basis of religion. Another form of discrimination involves harassment. Christian workers taunt a Muslim colleague, making her working conditions extremely unpleasant. A third straightforward circumstance involves a request for accommodation. A worker—say an Orthodox Jew who wants a Saturday off—seeks to be relieved from a standard job requirement that an employer developed without respect to religion.

Complexities: Employer Practices and Coworker Speech

An employer who wants a religious environment in his company may promote workers with congenial views or require all workers to attend religious gatherings. In that event, what hurts workers on religious grounds represents the employer's endeavor to exercise his own religion.[5] In this chapter and the next, we consider otherwise typical business enterprises whose owners see their mission as substantially religious. Chapter 20 takes up associations that are dominantly religious, such as churches and synagogues.

Harassment usually includes language that aims to offend, but listeners can also be troubled by a coworker's speech that flows from sincere religious conviction, and is not designed to humiliate. Proselytizing, with its explicit religious content, is a prime example. Other speech grounded in religious convictions may not be religious on its face. A striking illustration was a button with an antiabortion message that a woman wore at work.[6] The but-

---

[4] In this section, I do not refer to actual laws and their interpretations, but I use standard statutory categories to organize issues, and I draw some examples from cases I subsequently analyze.

[5] Religious speech also raises free speech concerns. It is a hard question, to which I shall return, whether an employer's religious speech should be privileged more than other speech.

[6] *Wilson v. U.S. West Communications*, 58 F.3d 1337 (8th Cir. 1995). Opposition to freedom of choice about abortion is so commonly based on religious grounds, one might think of such

ton had a color photograph of an eighteen- to twenty-week-old fetus. Ms. Wilson had chosen the button because she wanted to be an instrument of God and she had made a religious vow to wear the button.[7] Workers who present ideas motivated by their religious convictions have claims based on free exercise, as well as free speech, to be left free; these claims can run up against the interest in protecting coworkers from disturbing messages.[8]

Appropriate Employer Policies and Justified Government Restraint: Ordinary Discrimination

Appropriate Employer Behavior

How should employers regard what I have labeled ordinary discrimination—denying someone a job or promotion because of her religious beliefs or affiliation? When the government itself is the employer, this form of religious discrimination is plainly indefensible.[9] Governments in the United States may not discriminate on religious grounds. Our country now enjoys a broad consensus that religious discrimination by private employers is also wrongful. Any modern list of unacceptable discriminations begins with race, religion, gender, and ethnic origin, and then moves on to more novel or controversial grounds such as physical and mental disability, sexual preference, and marital status.

Yet in one aspect religious discrimination differs from other discriminations to which it is commonly linked. Some religious discrimination is what I shall call "positive," a desire to be with people like oneself rather than hostility to those who are different. Such "positive" religious discrimination may not be wrongful in itself. With race and gender, distinguishing positive from negative discrimination is usually difficult; dislike or distrust of the other mixes with the wish to be with those like oneself.[10] People frequently have a positive desire to be with co-religionists, even though they lack any

---

a button as on its face having an implicit religious message. If one includes implicit messages, the line between speech that is religious in content and nonreligious speech that is religiously motivated erodes.

[7] Id. at 1339.

[8] One person's proselytizing may be another person's blasphemy or deep religious offense. But disturbance need not be on religious grounds. People exposed to a photo of a fetus or to continual proselytizing may be disturbed for reasons unrelated to their religious convictions.

[9] As chapter 3 indicates, such discrimination denies the free exercise of members of excluded groups, and it establishes the religion of groups that are favored.

[10] Insofar as one can generalize, positive discrimination on the basis of gender is more often distinguishable from negative feelings than such discrimination on the basis of race.

negative feelings toward those outside the fold.[11] Nonetheless, much religious discrimination is not positive; it is ugly, based on bigotry and unjustified stereotypes. Employers should eschew most religious discrimination.[12]

Government Intervention

We might grant that religious discrimination in employment is generally bad, but doubt that legislators should prohibit it.[13] Even if we do not follow the few writers who, trusting in the free market, would allow every form of private sector discrimination,[14] we might wonder whether religious discrimination should be allowed. It apparently occurs much less frequently than racial and sexual discrimination,[15] and it is more random in its effects. The overwhelming preponderance of instances of employers favoring members of a race or gender involve whites and males discriminating against people of color and women. With religion, some employers may discriminate against Jews or Mormons, others in their favor. Finally, the benignness of some positive religious discrimination *might* count against government control.

What may be said to the contrary? In many parts of the country, particular religious groups have a distinct minority, and disfavored, status. After the terrorist attacks of September 11, 2001, and subsequently, many citizens view Muslims with suspicion; Jews remain a common target of discriminatory attitudes, and in some regions anti-Catholic sentiment still flourishes. We should not fool ourselves into thinking that religious discrimination will not disadvantage anyone. Much of it remains negative. Although a desire to work with co-religionists may be understandable, attitudes of exclusion and feelings of being excluded are unhealthy. Our society has developed an ethos that favors a diverse workforce. After school age, workplaces are *the primary locations* where people mix closely with others who are different. In a polity in which citizens need to recognize each other as equals, and groups

---

[11] A desire to work exclusively with co-religionists may not seem bad, and if it seems somewhat bad, it may seem less so than a desire to work exclusively with members of one's race or gender. One might build a similar argument about some ethnic and national origin discrimination—the desire of a Polish American employer to be surrounded by Polish American workers may not seem objectionable in and of itself.

[12] I reserve the discussion of positive accommodation for a later section. Harassment is taken up in the next chapter.

[13] Some subjects may be appropriate for agreements between employers and unions, though not government prohibition.

[14] Richard Epstein, *Forbidden Grounds: The Case Against Employment Discrimination Laws* (Cambridge: Harvard University Press, 1992).

[15] This is evidenced by numbers of complaints to agencies enforcing fair employment laws. Such figures, of course, do not *prove* that discrimination based on religion is less frequent. Instances might be less clear, or those who suffer might be less likely to complain.

need to coexist with a degree of harmony, diverse workforces yield social benefits.[16] That is true for religious diversity, as well as racial diversity. And full religious liberty for workers is implicated in what employers do. When employers base decisions on religious criteria, workers are thereby made susceptible to a particular form of outside pressure in deciding what religion, if any, to practice. Although the government cannot combat all the various personal and social pressures that may lead people to join religious groups, and it would be extremely unwise to try, it can reasonably minimize the degree to which the job market forces people to profess one religion or another. Governments have ample reasons to forbid religious discrimination by ordinary employers.

Whether an exception should be made for small employers or employers with a self-conceived religious mission is a more difficult question. Against laws that restrain small employers, two standard arguments are that people with a handful of employees should be able to do as they like, and that, in any event, enforcement against them is not worthwhile. One may also say that a religious employer who is involved directly in his business, such as a grocery store, may understandably want to work closely with others of the same religious persuasion; he may feel uncomfortable working daily with people whom he believes belong to the religion of the anti-Christ and are consigned to hell.[17]

A more serious practical issue involves employers who want their mundane businesses to exemplify deeper religious values of life. Should this minuscule proportion of the country's business employers be able to use religious standards to enhance their religious missions?[18] The conflict between employers who wish to engage in positive religious discrimination and the ideal of worker diversity turns out to be less irreconcilable than it first ap-

---

[16] Cynthia Estlund, *Working Together: How Workplace Bonds Strengthen a Diverse Democracy* (Oxford: Oxford University Press, 2003).

[17] This possibility of freedom for small employers has no direct relevance for the government as an employer, but an analogous argument may be made about close personal relations. Perhaps when an official hires someone who will be an alter ego, a personal assistant with whom she will have continuing contact, she should be able to discriminate on grounds that would otherwise be inappropriate. The idea is that a supervisor needs to work comfortably with her assistant, and that comfort may be determined partly by religious and ethnic background. (Of course, comfort may also be determined by race or gender, but one may reasonably believe that those correlations need to be resisted more strongly.) In fact, the grounds for choosing personal assistants are so vague and subjective, establishing discrimination will be very hard. (However, evidence can pile up over a period of many years—as with law clerks to Supreme Court justices.) Officials effectively have the ability to rely on forbidden grounds; but for legal purposes, no exceptions should be made in respect to personal assistants.

[18] If so, an evangelical Christian employer could prefer evangelical Christians to religious Jews and atheists, but not atheists to religious Jews.

pears. *If* the number of religious employers is few, their outright discrimination presents only a modest danger to a diverse working population. On the other hand, if religious employers are allowed to engage in various religious activities, perhaps they need not engage in outright discrimination.

The extent to which employers want their businesses tinctured by religious practices varies. The owner of one firm may wish the Christmas cards sent on its behalf to include a message about Christ's birth.[19] Another employer may regard her "secular" company as a vehicle to live out a deep religious understanding, in something like the way the Salvation Army considers its charitable activities as a way to embody and spread its religious understanding.

There is a substantial argument that the relatively few employers whose business understanding is deeply religious should be able to hire co-believers as supervisors and require that ordinary workers be at least sympathetic with their religious missions.[20] However, judges should not have to say which employers in the commercial marketplace are candid about their religious sentiments[21] and have developed a sense of mission powerful enough to warrant an exemption from standard rules against discrimination.[22] These problems about factual determinations and line drawing counsel against such an exemption.

Commercial employers should not be able to engage in outright religious discrimination in hiring and promotions. (Further, *the degree* of an employer's religiosity should not determine whether his religious expression is protected. Administrators and judges can inquire whether religious expressions are pretexts to harass nonbelievers, but they should not calibrate an employer's degree of privilege to his strength of religious commitment.)

The larger an enterprise, the less compelling the religious mission of individual owners becomes in comparison with the values of employment opportunity and a diverse workforce. A legal exception cast in terms of small size is much more feasible than one framed exclusively in terms of religious mission.

---

[19] In *Kentucky Comm'n on Human Rights v. Lesco Mfg. and Design Co.*, 736 S.W.2d 361 (Ky. Ct. App. 1987), the employer wanted his worker to answer the telephone during the Christmas season with "Merry Christmas." The worker was a Jehovah's Witness who believed in principle that people should not celebrate Christmas.

[20] See *State by McClure v. Sports and Health Club, Inc.*, 370 N.W.2d 844 (Minn. 1985). Thomas C. Berg has a thoughtful discussion of this possibility. "Religious Speech in the Workplace: Harassment or Protected Speech?" 22 *Harvard Journal of Law and Public Policy 959*, 1003 (1999). The law, as we will see in chapter 20, does allow religious organizations to engage in religious discrimination.

[21] One concern would be fraud; another would be that some individuals with discriminatory inclinations would develop genuine convictions about ancillary religious missions.

[22] It would presumably not be enough if an employer says that she hopes in business, as in the rest of her life, to live as a Christian.

What Is "Religious Discrimination"? Preliminaries

We have thus far proceeded as if identifying "religious discrimination" that the law should restrict is simple. It is time to introduce complexities.

First, if someone is not hired because she is Jewish, is this *religious* discrimination? If an employer refuses to hire an Orthodox Jew because he objects to that religion, the answer is obviously "yes." But most people in the culture, including most Jews, consider persons of Jewish heritage to be Jewish, even if they are not actively religious. Still, prejudice against Jews is grounded at least partly on the Jewish religion; perhaps discrimination based on the religion of one's forebears remains "religious." In any event, if discrimination against Jews is not always "religious," it is unacceptably based on ethnic origin.[23]

Further issues about the boundaries of *religious* discrimination concern the status of atheism and strongly held moral convictions. If one wants to stop discrimination based on religion, one will wish to protect atheists who suffer discrimination because they have negative views about traditional religious claims.

How to regard the strong convictions of workers that are not connected to traditional religious views is more difficult. Is an overriding concern for the environment in itself religious? In employment discrimination, that question arises mainly in relation to accommodation and harassment, and we will address it in those contexts.[24]

The edges of "discrimination" are not easy to trace. Suppose a religion requires a mode of personal appearance that offends an employer. A Sikh appears for a job interview with long hair and a turban. The employer responds: "I don't care about anyone's religious views, but it's un-American and obnoxious for men to wear such silly hats indoors. I won't hire you." Of course, the employer may be lying; but suppose he has never heard of Sikhs and has freely hired many non-Christians, including Hindus and Buddhists. This illustration exemplifies the broader problem of how far religious "discrimination" in law should require a malign motive, and how far it should be determined by an objective standard of disadvantage that attaches because of a victim's religious views and practices.[25]

The next section on legal responses addresses two other complex issues about religious discrimination. The first involves an employer whose nega-

---

[23] When religion is closely mixed with culture and ethnic origin, specifying one particular ground of discrimination is largely artificial.

[24] We have looked at the more general problems of "defining" religion in chapter 8.

[25] The problem of subjective motivation versus objective standard is partly, but not entirely, dissolved by requiring accommodations to religious practices.

tive treatment of a worker flows from a moral judgment that connects closely to his religion. The second is what exactly should constitute religious discrimination when employers or coworkers engage in religious expression.

LEGAL TREATMENT AND CONSTITUTIONALITY

This section introduces the most important statutory provision dealing with employment discrimination, considers cases interpreting it and similar provisions, and deals briefly with constitutional problems.

As one part of the Civil Rights Act of 1964, Congress adopted Title VII to restrict employment discrimination.[26] An employer cannot discriminate against anyone "because of such individual's race, color, religion, sex, or national origin"; an employer cannot segregate or classify his employees in a way that would tend to deprive someone of employment opportunities "because of . . . religion."[27] An employer may use religion (and sex and national origin but not race or color) as a criterion when that is a *"bona fide* occupational qualification."[28] Because Title VII does not directly regulate the activities of fellow workers, workplace harassment becomes a legal wrong only when the employer bears responsibility for it. By now, virtually all states have similar fair employment laws, reaching smaller employers than does the federal act.[29]

Well after passage of the act, courts accepted the theory that harassment constitutes a form of discrimination,[30] even if a worker shows no other deprivation of employment opportunities. Another post-1964 development was in the statutory language itself. After the Sixth Circuit Court of Appeals decided that an employer can meet his obligations by treating employees similarly, without respect to their religion,[31] Congress responded by providing, "[T]he term 'religion' includes all aspects of religious observance and

---

[26] §§ 701–18. The act applies to employers of twenty-five or more persons whose business affects interstate commerce, and to labor organizations.

[27] § 703(a)(1)2). Similar restrictions apply to labor unions and to training and apprenticeship programs, § 703 (c)(d).

[28] § 703 (e).

[29] N.Y. Executive Law § 292 (McKinney 2005) does not include employers with fewer than four employees; Fla. Sta. § 760.02 (2005) covers employers with more than fifteen employees.

[30] See *Meritor Savings Bank v. Vinson*, 477 U.S. 57 (1986).

[31] *Dewey v. Reynolds Metals Co.*, 429 F.2d 324 (1970). The Supreme Court affirmed by an equally divided court. 402 U.S. 689 (1971). An affirmance by an equally divided court has no precedential value. The case is discussed in Steven D. Jamar, "Accommodating Religion at Work: A Principled Approach to Title VII and Religious Freedom," 40 *New York Law School Review* 719, 741–42 (1996).

practice, as well as belief, unless an employer demonstrates that he is unable to reasonably accommodate to an employee's or a prospective employee's religious observance or practice without undue hardship on the conduct of [his] business."[32] Although confusingly suggesting that whether an observance or practice *is* religious (under the act) depends on its being able to be reasonably accommodated,[33] this language has a clear practical thrust: *unless* an employer makes a required accommodation, he has discriminated.

Early on, the Supreme Court adopted a partially objective test of what constitutes discrimination under Title VII.[34] If an employer uses a test, or other standard, for employment that disproportionately favors members of one race (or gender or religion) over another, use of the test constitutes discrimination unless the employer can show that the test is required by business necessity.

Simple Discrimination

Under Title VII, an employer cannot refuse to hire or promote a worker because of her religion, unless religion is a bona fide qualification for a job, as it would be if an employer decided to hire a Protestant chaplain for his dominantly Protestant workforce. An employer's sense of religious mission does not privilege him to make faith a qualification for his ordinary workers or supervisors.[35] Were he to claim that he has a free exercise right to engage in outright discrimination, courts would answer that the government has a compelling interest in eliminating religious discrimination.[36]

The law barring use of religion covers discrimination against Jews (whatever their individual religious views) and atheists.

---

[32] § 701 (j).

[33] This is indisputably an inadequate approach to the problem of what *counts* as religious; a practice is no less religious because the employer cannot accommodate it.

[34] *Griggs v. Duke Power Co.*, 401 U.S. 424 (1971). In 1989, the Supreme Court significantly restricted opportunities for recovery under this theory. *Wards Cove Packing Co. v. Antonic*, 490 U.S. 642 (1989). Congress then adopted a statute that brought the law back to its pre-1989 posture. 42 U.S.C. § 2000e 2(k). These developments are discussed in Jamar, note 31 supra, at 735–38. He points out that establishing a statistical imbalance is much more complicated for religion than for race and gender, because of numbers of subgroups of major religions and the presence of sects so small it is impossible to say what a natural proportion in the workforce would be. Id. at 794–95.

[35] See Jamar, note 31 supra, at 744–45.

[36] The Minnesota Supreme Court wrote in one case, "In a pluralistic and democratic society, government has a responsibility to insure that all of its citizens have equal opportunity for employment, promotion, and job retention without having to overcome the artificial and largely irrelevant barriers occurring from gender, status, or beliefs to the main decision of competence to perform the work." *McClure*, note 20 supra, at 853.

More Complex Issues about Discrimination

A more complex issue about discrimination that I mentioned earlier concerns moral judgments by employers that depend on religious convictions. This issue was raised obliquely in a case brought by a fired restaurant worker, Ms. Turic, a single woman who had become pregnant.[37] Other members of a "very Christian restaurant staff" were offended by discussions whether she should have an abortion. Concerned that gossip about the situation was disruptive, the restaurant manager and her assistant told Turic that she would be terminated if she continued to discuss her possible abortion at work. Successfully claiming that her subsequent firing violated the Pregnancy Discrimination Act of 1978, Turic also contended that management's decision to protect the staff's religious sensibilities forced their religion on her and amounted to religious discrimination. Finding inadequate evidence that the feelings of others on the staff were connected to religious doctrine, the court nonetheless remarked that Title VII would protect someone from being fired because she does not share the religious views of her employer or other workers.[38]

Whether Title VII should apply if an employer fires someone because of his own religiously informed moral sensibilities or those of his workers is troublesome. Let us imagine that Turic had behaved in a manner that was legally permitted but not protected against employer response—say, she frequently became drunk in public—and that her employer or her colleagues regarded her actions as sinful.

If the behavior of our hypothetical Turic offended the employer's own religious sentiments, he would not be firing her because of her religious beliefs, but because her behavior violated his moral sense informed by his religious understanding. Whether this is *religious* discrimination is debatable, but when we consider an employer's undoubted powers, we should conclude that it is not.

Unless the worker is protected by a union contract or some particular law, an American employer is legally free to fire her because he finds continual drunkenness away from work to be immoral or disgusting from a nonreligious point of view;[39] he should not sacrifice his ability to invoke his sense of moral

---

[37] *Turic v. Holland Hospitality, Inc.*, 849 F. Supp. 544 (W.D. Mich. 1994).

[38] Id. at 551. The court relied on *Blalock v. Metal Trades, Inc.*, 775 F.2d 703 (6th Cir. 1985), aff'd after remand, 833 F.2d 1011 (6th Cir. 1987), cert. denied, 490 U.S. 1064 (1989). In that case, plaintiff was fired partly because his religious views came to differ from those of his employer.

[39] One might well believe that employers should not fire people because of their private lives, even that the government should forbid employers from doing so. My comments assume a regime in which employers have wide freedom to fire workers on grounds they choose.

appropriateness because that sense happens to derive from his religious convictions. As Laura Underkuffler has argued powerfully, the state should not choose between employment philosophies on the basis of which happen to be religious.[40] This point is most obvious for conditions *at work*;[41] an employer who has religious reasons for insisting on cheerfulness and discipline among his workers should be no less able to fire a surly, irresponsible worker than an employer whose reasons for wanting cheerful, disciplined workers have nothing to do with religion.[42] The employer's capacity to act on religiously informed judgments should extend to outside behavior that does not directly affect job performance, so long as other employers might find the behavior morally objectionable (and a basis for dismissal) on nonreligious grounds.[43]

The conclusion that our employer may fire the worker who frequently becomes drunk finds further support from his power to fire a worker who actually agrees with his religious belief that drunkenness is deeply sinful but cannot control his urge to drink.[44] The ground for firing treats workers equally, independent of their own religious views.

If an employer can act on his own religious sentiments about moral behavior, he should be able to respond to religiously based sentiments of his workers that similarly would conform with moral judgments others would reach as nonreligious grounds.[45] If fellow workers regarded Turic's life outside work as deeply immoral, whether their moral judgments happened to be religious should not have been crucial.

The conclusion differs if a moral judgment is one that virtually no one would make *except* on religious grounds. If a strict Christian employer fires a worker for playing baseball on Sunday, that does amount to discrimination because of religion. This moral judgment operates strongly to the disadvantage of those who happen not to share the employer's religious convictions; and his reliance on it could well be a means to remove workers of faiths different from his. The employer is insisting that his religiously based, rather idiosyncratic, standards of proper behavior be followed. Thus, the right criterion for whether a reli-

---

[40] Laura S. Underkuffler, "Discrimination on the Basis of Religion: An Examination of Attempted Value Neutrality in Employment," 30 *William & Mary Law Review* 581, 588–89 (1989).

[41] The same analysis applies to behavior outside work that bears directly on how a worker performs her job.

[42] See id. at 605.

[43] I have in mind here such behavior as abusing members of one's family and continual heavy drinking or drug use. In *McCrory v. Rapides Regional Medical Center*, 635 F. Supp. 975 (W.D. La. 1986), the court allowed dismissal of employees who were committing adultery, contrary to their employer's religious beliefs.

[44] I have not addressed the situation in which the worker's practice is demanded or encouraged by her religion. That worker has a stronger argument that she is being dismissed because of her religion, or that at least she should be accommodated. See note 46, infra.

[45] See *Turic*, note 37 supra, at 551 n. 5.

giously based moral judgment underlies impermissible religious discrimination is whether, in our culture, a significant number of people would make a similar negative moral judgment on nonreligious grounds.[46]

Another difficult question of categorizing the boundaries of religious discrimination arises when an employer has a religious message she wants conveyed and does not select her audience based on their religion. The status of such employer messages is sharply posed by mandatory worship services. *Equal Employment Opportunity Commission v. Townley Engineering and Manufacturing Company*[47] involved the religious activities of employers who manufactured mining equipment. A married couple who founded the company and owned 94 percent of the stock wanted to operate "a Christian, faith-operated business."[48] All workers were required to attend weekly devotional services. Pelvas, an atheist, asked to be excused. His supervisor refused to excuse him, but said that Pelvas could sleep or read the newspaper during the services. The Equal Employment Opportunity Commission argued that having a requirement of mandatory attendance at religious services was discrimination under Title VII. The firm argued that Title VII did not cover its policy and that to do so would violate the First Amendment. Whether or not the firm had to accommodate Pelvas by excusing him, an issue we shall examine shortly, was the court of appeals right to conclude that the company did not have to end its mandatory services?[49]

---

[46] By this criterion, firing someone who drinks a slight amount of alcohol probably amounts to religious discrimination. Even though people might believe on nonreligious grounds that total abstinence is desirable, few people condemn a slight drinking of alcohol as morally abhorrent except on religious grounds. In a case treating the firing of a worker living a homosexual lifestyle as not involving religious discrimination, the court emphasized that the employer did not use the worker's religion as a basis for the decision. *Pedreira v. Kentucky Baptist Homes for Children, Inc.*, 186 F. Supp. 2d 757 (W.D. Ky. 2001). See also *Hall v. Baptist Memorial Health Care Corp.*, 215 F.3d 618 (6th Cir. 2000). According to the principle of these decisions, firing someone for taking a sip of alcohol would not be religious discrimination even if the employer's motivation was unmistakably religious.

To be clear about the scope of my view: I am not suggesting that an employer can treat a worker unfavorably because of a direct judgment about her religious observance if other employers might make a somewhat similar judgment on nonreligious grounds. To treat a worker unfavorably because she engages in particular religious practices or fails to engage in particular religious practices is to discriminate on the basis of the worker's religion, whether or not another employer might find a nonreligious basis for a similar judgment. Although this may be drawing the line too fine, an employer might fire a worker who uses peyote if he thinks all use of hallucinogenic drugs is immoral; he might fire a worker who fails to respect community practices by making noise on Sunday. He could not fire a worker for being a practicing member of the Native American Church or failing to go to church on Sunday.

[47] 859 F.2d 610 (9th Cir. 1988).

[48] Id. at 612.

[49] Because its analysis of the legality of a mandatory service was not consistently separate from its analysis of the worker's claim to be excused, the court's treatment of the requirement that workers attend the services was not entirely clear.

The judges apparently believed that mandatory services *would have* constituted religious discrimination, except for the employer's free exercise claim. However, under a compelling-interest-least-restrictive-means analysis, ending mandatory services was not necessary to accomplish the goals of Title VII.[50]

If those who object can be excused, we might initially suppose that a court's decision to permit mandatory services has little consequence, but that would be a mistake. Workers can be required to attend legally permitted mandatory services if they have no religious objection to doing so and if the services do not create a hostile environment for them. To be excused, a worker must come forward and explain that attendance is at odds with her own religion (the basis for an accommodation) or creates a hostile environment (the basis for relief from harassment). Because many workers will hesitate to offer either assertion, more workers will attend mandatory services than voluntary ones.

As some imaginary examples show, a state that forbids religious discrimination properly limits mandatory religious indoctrination. Suppose an employer with an even mix of Christian and Jewish workers requires all workers to sit through a Christian service once a day. That constitutes discrimination against Jews in the terms of employment. To sharpen this, imagine that two hours of each day are devoted to mandatory Roman Catholic services; that would be discrimination against non-Catholics. Even though some non-Catholics will not mind them, such services constitute an unfavorable condition of employment for those who do not practice Roman Catholicism, whether or not the employer is aiming to discourage non-Catholics from applying for his jobs.

If we put aside the force of the employer's own religious claims, the better view is that forcing workers to listen to one religion discriminates against those with other religious views. An employer definitely cannot insist that workers attend the Sunday services of his favorite church; the result should be the same if he sponsors in-house services during business hours.[51] Brief reflection on

[50] Therefore, the district court was mistaken in ordering the employer to end mandatory services. One might view the opinion as declaring that the First Amendment bars what Title VII here requires—the ending of mandatory services—but the opinion can better be taken to say that, read in light of the First Amendment, Title VII does not require that mandatory services be stopped.

[51] It does not matter that he is paying workers during business hours. If one conceives of a salary as paid for fulfilling a set of obligations, the employer who insists that workers attend his church on Sunday must set his salary high enough to cover that time away from business hours. Indeed, one way to perceive a difference in terms of employment is to think of the effective salary as being higher for workers who would attend the employer's church in any event. They need no extra compensation, and so are receiving a kind of windfall.

analogous illustrations regarding gender and race strengthens this conclusion. If an employer calls regular meetings at which his representative engages in persistent racist or sexist expression, that amounts to ordinary discrimination against the members of the races or gender that are "put down."[52]

Whether mandatory services are viewed as ordinary discrimination or as amounting to a form of harassment makes a difference in terms of the theory of challenge and appropriate remedy. If mandatory services constitute ordinary discrimination, a nonbeliever can object regardless of his own psychological reaction to having to attend.[53] A victim of harassment must subjectively perceive the environment as pervasively hostile,[54] and perhaps her feeling must relate to her religious identity (if the employer has not selected her on the basis of religion). The remedy for simple discrimination is to stop the practice. A remedy for a hostile environment might be to change the victim's circumstances.

In the following chapter, we shall take up the possibility that an employer's free exercise interests in providing mandatory religious services might justify what would otherwise be unacceptable ordinary discrimination against those who reject the perspective of the services.

Appropriate Policies and Justified Restraint: Accommodation

Do an employer's responsibilities reach beyond not discriminating? If he develops a reasonable work rule that has nothing to do with religion, should he make an accommodation if the rule has harsh effects for a worker's religious practices, and should the government require him to do that? A variation on

[52] Laura Underkuffler has reached a different conclusion, note 40 supra, at 613. Attacking the myth of value neutrality, she has urged that a "valid claim of religious discrimination in employment should be limited to situations in which the employee's religious status (religious affiliation or identity or lack thereof) is the reason for the employer's action." Because the Townleys wanted all employees to attend their services, they did not discriminate under the standard Underkuffler proposes. The strength of her argument is much greater for moral and business judgments that are based on religious premises than it is for mandatory explicit religious indoctrination. See notes 40–43 supra, and accompanying text.

[53] Some writers have assumed that for an atheist, prayer services are only a waste of time, not an offense to his religious views. See, e.g., David L. Gregory, "Religious Harassment in the Workplace: An Analysis of the EEOC's Proposed Guidelines," 56 *Montana Law Review* 119, 139 (1995). This misses the way in which an atheist could be offended in conscience by forced attendance at ceremonies she thinks have no ground in reality; but even the "waste of time" objection would be sufficient for challenging ordinary discrimination.

[54] According to *Harris v. Forklift Systems, Inc.*, 510 U.S. 17, 21 (1993), conduct constitutes harassment only if it creates an environment a reasonable person would find hostile or abusive and the victim subjectively perceives the working environment in that way.

the question whether people should possess free exercise rights to be relieved from some general rules and practices, the possibility of exemptions from work requirements raises fundamental questions about fairness to the worker who seeks special treatment, to her fellow workers, and to her employer.[55]

If an employer who requires Saturday work excuses an Orthodox Jew, he may be short on staff, or pay another worker overtime, or require a fellow worker with greater seniority to work on that day.[56] The concern about fairness to coworkers who do not receive the benefit given the accommodated worker is much greater than any analogous concerns about excusing conscientious objectors from military service or granting Sabbatarians unemployment compensation. A man who has earned enough seniority in a small firm to avoid Saturday work may care greatly about spending that day with his school-age children. If his boss tells him that he will continue to work on Saturday because a newly hired Orthodox Jew is not "able" to work on that day, that may not satisfy him, and it is not clear that it should.

Fairness to the employer does not involve such a direct trade-off. The employer is not deprived of the very thing that the employee gains;[57] his loss will be in cost or efficiency. When an employer happens to hire a person needing an accommodation, forcing him to carry the burden of providing it is troublesome in a competitive economy.[58] An employer will be tempted to pass over an applicant who will need a costly accommodation, whatever the rules about nondiscrimination.[59]

In respect to these issues of fairness, we can roughly categorize: (1) accommodations involving only very slight inconvenience; (2) accommodations

[55] Of course, fairness to the employer is mainly in issue only if the employer is *required* to accommodate. If he is freely choosing whether to accommodate, fairness to him comes up only in the sense of a factor he may take into account in deciding what to do. Fairness to fellow workers can be an issue whether the employer is freely choosing whether to accommodate, or is required to accommodate.

[56] The practice of allowing more senior workers not to work on Saturday may be part of a collective bargaining agreement with the union.

[57] However, if the business is very small, the employer might need to pick up the slack by working himself on Saturday.

[58] This contrasts with unemployment compensation, for which the burden is spread among employers or taxpayers generally. Insofar as the cost of accommodations is monetary expense to the employer, one possible approach would be to allow employers to recover from a fund set up to recompense employers for the costs they bear in accommodating. Such a scheme would spread the cost of accommodations more generally, as already happens when the government, as employer, "accommodates" at some financial expense.

[59] If employers refuse to hire people they would have to accommodate, the result will be much the same as if they had no duty to accommodate, because people who could not fit into ordinary work rules would not get the jobs. If employers decline to hire anyone they think they *might* have to accommodate, a requirement of accommodation could hurt some people who might otherwise get jobs. (Absent a requirement to accommodate, the employer might hire someone and wait to see if a conflict of conviction and employment responsibilities develops.)

creating inconvenience that falls between very slight and serious; (3) accommodations that require a serious cost to employers or a loss of privileges that fellow workers value highly. The crucial practical questions are when employers should make such accommodations and when the law should demand them; a related conceptual question is when a failure to accommodate should be regarded as a form of discrimination.

To begin with very slight inconvenience, suppose an employer requires all workers to take vacations in July and August, and grants each worker ten sick days per year. The only Jew on the payroll wants to be off on Yom Kippur, which never falls in those months and is the most holy day in the Jewish calendar. She is willing to count it as either a vacation or sick day. The employer can cover the day without much inconvenience and is unconcerned about similar claims by other workers. In a country of religious diversity, where work schedules largely reflect the dominant Christian religion, a failure to accommodate here would be so unfair we may comfortably label it discriminatory.[60] As the costs of accommodation rise, problems about unfairness increase, and labeling a failure to accommodate as genuine discrimination becomes more strained.

If *some* accommodations are to be made, what class of persons should benefit? An individual employer should respond flexibly to powerful demands for exemptions from ordinary rules, including ones based on strong personal needs that are not religious in any traditional sense. But a legal regime must categorize. Although for reasons given in other chapters, a worker should not have to be attached to an organized religious group to have a right to accommodation, a legal rule that employers must offer reasonable accommodations in response to personal needs is too indefinite in its coverage. Officials, for example, should not have to assess the strength of a worker's desire or need to avoid travel so he can spend more time with his family. *Most* claims for religious accommodation have no nonreligious parallel of equal strength; but a nonreligious pacifist could be deeply offended in conscience at having to produce arms. The law might sensibly limit itself to religious claims or cover all claims with a strength similar to typical religious claims.

When it is his religious speech that a worker wants accommodated, special issues arise.[61] If the speech causes religious offense, the problem involves harassment, which we shall examine in the next chapter. Speech that does

---

[60] To take another example, an employer who requires workers not to cover their heads should allow a Sikh to wear a turban, if there is no serious issue of "fit" appearance before customers.

[61] I count here speech that is explicitly religious or is motivated by religious conviction.

not offend in that way but violates an employer's work rules raises more straightforward questions about accommodation.[62]

One possible position is that an employer should not have to accommodate any speech to customers that he does not wish to sponsor. Thus, if his general rule were no speech of a personal nature with customers, he would not have to accept a cashier's remarking as she bags groceries: "We'd like to see you Sunday at the First Baptist Church." The employer undoubtedly has three legitimate concerns. The cashier should not waste time, she should not appear to represent the business in a misleading way, and she should not offend or pressure customers. But if she makes clear she is speaking on her own and she does not waste time, and the employer has no reasonable basis to suppose his customers will be offended, he should accommodate. Workers should be conceived as having some personal life during working hours. Within the boundaries of the demands of the job, they should be able to converse with fellow workers and customers they serve; employers should not have a right to scotch any messages they would not want to sponsor.[63] For purposes of accommodation, religious speech should be viewed like other religious practices if the worker so regards it.[64]

One concern about such an accommodation involves a comparison with nonreligious speech. A store owner is legally free to fire a clerk for expressing support for a Democratic candidate or for asserting that physical ailments often have psychological causes.[65] Probably legislatures *should* adopt general protections of free speech in the workplace, but short of doing so, they reasonably protect religious speech. If they want to prevent religious discrimination and encourage equal opportunity, they should insist that employers tolerate expressions of religious views that do not create workplace disturbances.[66]

---

[62] Of course, if an employer treats a worker negatively just because the worker expresses religious views of a certain kind, that constitutes simple discrimination. And if an employer bans religious speech, but not other speech, that may be discrimination against religious workers.

[63] This point is less arguable when the speech is with coworkers, not customers.

[64] For some people, speech about religious subjects outside of religious ceremonies is not itself regarded as a kind of religious practice. In respect to these people, a general privilege of accommodation to religious practice would not cover their religious speech.

[65] However, collective bargaining agreements often provide a range of protection.

[66] A distinction between religious and other speech involves a form of content discrimination, something that often requires a substantial justification if it is to pass constitutional muster. In general, principles of free speech do not permit favoring some kinds of speech over others. But if the law is to combat discrimination on grounds of religion and attempt to create equal opportunity for members of different religions, religious speech needs some protection. Part of the problem is that an employer who really dislikes a worker's religion may take the occasion of her religious speech to fire her. But even if the employer has no such view, those with conventional religious views and attitudes are unlikely to cause a stir, and religious dissidents and strident evangelists will find their speech becoming the occasion for unfavorable treatment.

Some of the most nettlesome questions about religious speech involve offense to fellow workers. If that offense is unrelated to their religious views, may the employer discharge the offending worker, or must he accommodate her religious practice?

Suppose that worker A, out of a sense of religious commitment, keeps trying to persuade worker B that abortion is a grave sin. B finds the persistent badgering to be highly annoying but not for any reason related to her religion. If B has clearly indicated her objections to such speech, an employer should be able to stop it. The religious liberty of one worker to speak is not reasonably accommodated by compelling an unwilling listener to hear.

A more complex circumstance is presented when A aims her expression at all coworkers, and a number are offended. This was the case with the antiabortion button that carried a photo of a fetus. Unless an employer forbids all controversial speech, a worker should be free to express the idea that abortion is morally wrong. But a photo of a fetus on a button is a different matter; it can offend apart from the message conveyed, as could a picture of a line of corpses on a button opposing genocide. If the button causes deep offense to fellow workers, that is a sufficient reason to forbid it in the captive environment of the workplace.

I have mentioned that one question about employment discrimination is how far courts should apply objective standards that do not require an employer's conscious discrimination. By compelling responses to powerful religious claims of workers, a requirement of accommodation introduces one kind of objective standard for employer behavior.[67]

Legal Treatment and Constitutionality: Accommodation

Title VII and Its Interpretation

A major issue in the Title VII law of religious discrimination is just how far an employer must bend, given statutory language that provides that he must "reasonably accommodate to an employee's or a prospective employee's religious observance" if he can do so "without undue hardship."[68] A related question is how far the Establishment Clause permits accommodation. For the government as employer, a further concern is how Title VII accommoda-

---

Under these circumstances, this degree of content discrimination in favor of religious speech is appropriate.

[67] The requirement is "subjective," however, in depending on the actual convictions and feelings of the worker who makes a claim for accommodation.

[68] § 701 (j). The reference to prospective employees makes clear that an employer cannot refuse to hire someone because he believes the person will require an accommodation.

tion compares with the demands of the Free Exercise Clause and the Religious Freedom Restoration Act.

The Supreme Court addressed Title VII accommodation in *Trans World Airlines v. Hardison.*[69] Hardison had converted to the Worldwide Church of God, whose members will not work on Saturday. When shifted to a new building, he lacked the seniority to avoid Saturday work. TWA encouraged the union to work out an arrangement, but the union was unwilling to deviate from the seniority system. TWA would not let Hardison work only four days, paying overtime to someone else or leaving work positions unmanned on Saturday. The Supreme Court said that TWA had taken steps to reasonably accommodate Hardison, short of incurring undue hardship. TWA could not be expected to leave a position vacant, to pay overtime, or to breach the seniority provision of its employment contract with the union, imposing hardship on fellow workers.[70] In relation to the inconvenience an employer might have to accept, the Court said undemandingly that an employer need not "bear more than a de minimis cost."

In a case after *Hardison,* the Supreme Court indicated that so long as an employer's offered accommodation is reasonable, it need not be precisely what the worker seeks. In *Ansonia Board of Educ. v. Philbrook,*[71] the worker sought to take paid days of personal leave to observe religious holy days; the employer's allowance of unpaid leave was a reasonable accommodation, whether or not Philbrook's own proposal would have involved undue hardship.

A study by Karen Engle shows that courts have generally been very resistant to claims that employers should deviate from neutral rules of general

---

[69] 432 U.S. 63 (1977).

[70] Title VII applies to unions as well as employers. If a collective bargaining agreement insisted that an employer not make a required accommodation, the agreement would be illegal in that respect. See id. at 79. Thus, the fact that an agreement forbids an accommodation cannot itself be conclusive. The Court may have supposed that maintaining standard seniority practices was of enough value so that breaching them would constitute undue hardship, even if an employer established the rules on his own. But the Court may also have concluded that an agreement between management and labor increases the importance of adhering to seniority. Relying on language in Title VII that protects seniority systems, the Court did assume that employers would never have to deviate from the "'routine application of a bona fide seniority system.'" Id. at 82. A number of courts have given great weight to what collective bargaining agreements say in concluding that an accommodation would involve undue hardship. See Mark A. Spognardi and Staci L. Ketay, "In the Lion's Den: Religious Accommodation and Harassment in the Workplace," 25 *Employee Relations Law Journal*, no. 4, pp. 7, 15 (2000). One may reasonably think that an agreement with a union could increase the degree of hardship of an accommodation at odds with the terms of the agreement. Particularly if one is thinking of what an employer should understand that he should do, as contrasted with what a court might order, one could not expect the employer to breach an agreement in instances in which it was unclear whether the agreement requires a violation of the law. See, e.g., *Getz v. Commonwealth*, 802 F.2d 72, 75 (3d Cir. 1986).

[71] 479 U.S. 60 (1986).

application.[72] The one major exception has been the sustaining of claims not to join unions, with a requirement that the equivalent of union dues be given to charity.[73] Other sorts of measures courts have sometimes required of employers have included unpaid leave for religious holidays and adjustments of work schedules that do not violate seniority arrangements and do not involve significant expense.[74] Courts have continued to employ the *Hardison* standard of undue hardship, which is lenient to employers, although when the federal government is the employer, that standard lies in tension with other, apparently more demanding, legal standards.[75]

I believe too little has been required of employers under Title VII. A more appropriate standard would be that incorporated into a bill called the Workplace Religious Freedom Act of 1999. It defined "undue hardship" as an "accommodation requiring significant difficulty or expense." Among factors to be considered would be the cost of the accommodation, the cost of lost productivity, and the cost of retraining, hiring, or transferring other employees, in relation to the employer's size and operating cost.[76] Under these standards, employers would have to undertake measures that approximate the ways they must respond to physical and emotional disabilities.[77] The stan-

[72] Karen Engle, "The Persistence of Neutrality: The Failure of the Religious Accommodation Provision to Redeem Title VII," 76 *Texas Law Review* 312, 392–406 (1997).

[73] E.g., *McDaniel v. Essex International, Inc.*, 571 F.2d 338 (6th Cir. 1978).

[74] See Spognardi and Ketay, note 70 supra, at 13–19.

[75] The most severe surface discontinuity exists with respect to the Religious Freedom Restoration Act (RFRA), 42 U.S.C. § 2000bb-1–2000bb-4 (2004), whose application to the federal government is presumably valid. The act declares that if the government imposes a substantial burden on someone's exercise of religion, it may do so only if it has a compelling interest that cannot be accomplished by less restrictive means. Its compelling interest test applies to the government as employer and appears to require more than Title VII, although legislative history suggests that RFRA was not intended to affect accommodation under Title VII. See Vikran David Amar, "State RFRAs and the Workplace," 32 *UC Davis Law Review* 513, 526 (1999). Amar, at 523–24, remarks on "the judicial carelessness that characterizes much of the religion case law." See also Sidney A. Rosenzweig, "Restoring Religious Freedom to the Workplace: Title VII, RFRA and Religious Accommodation," 144 *University of Pennsylvania Law Review* 2513, 2526–27 (1996). Rosenzweig points out that RFRA could affect an employer's use of a collective bargaining agreement or a statutory requirement as a defense to an accommodation claim, even if it does not alter the basic "de minimis" standard. Id. at 2527–28, 2533–35. A similar compelling interest test appeared to apply under the Free Exercise Clause, prior to the Supreme Court's 1990 decision of *Employment Division v. Smith*, 494 U.S. 872.

[76] See Spognardi and Ketay, note 70 supra, at 23. The bill also would have limited the extent to which a seniority system provides a defense against a claim for accommodation. Similar bills had been introduced in previous sessions of Congress.

[77] Although some relevant provisions of the ADA are similar linguistically to Title VII, for example, requiring employers to make a "reasonable accommodation" unless this imposes "undue hardship," 42 U.S.C. § 12111(10) makes the defense much harder to assert. Whereas the Supreme Court in *Hardison* equated more than a de minimis cost with undue hardship under Title VII, that approach is expressly rejected in the legislative history for the ADA. H.R. Rpt. No. 101–485, pt. 3, at 40 (1990). And the ADA itself defines "undue hardship" as actions

dards would also bring accommodation requirements more nearly in line with the language of the Religious Freedom Restoration Act, when the federal government is the employer.

Constitutional Limits

My conclusion that Title VII, as interpreted, demands too little of employers depends on judgments about the limited reach of the Establishment Clause

---

requiring "*significant difficulty and expense*" in light of several factors including, but not limited to, (1) the nature and cost of the accommodation, (2) the type of operations of the covered entity, (3) the number of employees of the entity, and, most importantly, (4) the overall financial resources of the covered entity. 42 U.S.C. § 12111(10). Accordingly, if the cost of an accommodation, although a large sum, constitutes only a small fraction of the covered entity's entire budget, the employer cannot claim undue hardship on that ground alone. H.R. Rpt. No. 101–485, pt. 3, at 41. Additionally, the history specifically rejects a proposed "safe harbor" provision that costs in excess of 10 percent of an individual's salary would, as a matter of law, constitute an undue hardship. Id. Rather, what constitutes "undue hardship" under the ADA must be determined on a "case-by-case analysis" that carefully considers the factors provided in § 12111(10). S. Rpt. No. 101–116, at 32 (1990); *Olmstead v. Zimring*, 527 U.S. 581, 606 n. 16 (1999). A court's determination of undue hardship under the ADA is not subject to hard and fast rules; nevertheless, unlike accommodation under Title VII, the clear tenor of the ADA's provisions, when read in light of the legislative history, is that an employer *may* be expected to incur more than just a de minimis cost in order to fulfill his duty under the act.

Although plaintiffs making claims under ADA often lose, nonetheless the case law, albeit sparse, indicates that employers must take more substantial steps to accommodate disabled employees than would be needed to avoid liability under Title VII. See, e.g., *Harmer v. Virginia Electric and Power Co.*, 831 F. Supp. 1300 (E.D. Va. 1993) (providing fans, smokeless ashtrays, and air purifiers, while separating smokers from nonsmokers in the workplace, for employee with pulmonary disability held "reasonable"); *Davis v. York International, Inc.*, 2 A.D. Cases (BNA) 1810 (D. Md. 1993) (installing extra phone line and computer at home, while lessening work responsibilities for employee with multiple sclerosis held "reasonable"); *Bombrys v. City of Toledo*, 849 F. Supp. 1210 (N.D. Ohio 1993) (excluding insulin-dependent diabetic from police force held "unreasonable" when providing food, glucose, and injection kit in patrol car would not be an "undue hardship"). At the other end of the spectrum, accommodation costs that are clearly disproportionate to the benefits produced, or costs that would jeopardize the financial stability of the employer, are "undue." *Borkowski v. Valley Cent. School Dist.*, 63 F.3d 131, 138 (2d Cir. 1995). See generally Lawrence P. Postal and David D. Kadue, "An Employer's Guide to the Americans with Disabilities Act: From Job Qualifications to Reasonable Accommodations," 24 *John Marshall Law Review* 693, 712–18 (1991); Samuel Issacharoff and Justin Nelson, "Discrimination with a Difference: Can Employment Discrimination Law Accommodate the Americans with Disabilities Act?" 79 *North Carolina Law Review* 307 (2000); Sue Krenek, "Note, Beyond Reasonable Accommodation: Allocating the Costs of Compliance with the Americans with Disabilities Act," 72 *Texas Law Review* 1969, 1986–88 (1993).

In *US Airways Inc. v. Robert Barnett*, 535 U.S. 391 (2002), the justices divided among four different theories about how "reasonable accommodation" related to breaches of seniority standards under ADA. A majority, with Justice O'Connor voting for an approach other than the one she most preferred, determined that a "reasonable accommodation" would typically not require a deviation from seniority, but that a complainant might show that in an individual case, such a deviation would be required for a reasonable accommodation. (Even then, an employer might be able to carry his burden of showing that the accommodation would require

and about permissible accommodation to religion under the Constitution. The *Hardison* Court left open whether even the imposition of minimal costs would violate the Establishment Clause. Although subsequent cases give us reasonable assurance that Congress can require employers to bear such costs, they do not resolve whether Congress could impose more onerous accommodations.[78] Supreme Court opinions presuming that legislatures may choose to accommodate religion have never suggested that they may impose no more than minimal costs on the government itself. Whether laws may force costs beyond minimal ones on private employers is more arguable. Some opinions suggest that an accommodation to religion is permissible only when the government lifts burdens that it has imposed.[79]

The Court struck down a Connecticut scheme that required employers to grant workers their Sabbath off,[80] but because the justices assumed that the state had imposed absolutely and unreasonably on private employers, they do not tell us whether more modest impositions would have been acceptable.

If government cannot accommodate by imposing burdens on private employers, even the minimal accommodation requirements under Title VII seem questionable. The standard response is that Title VII is an antidiscrimination law and that the government can forbid religious discrimination.[81] No doubt some failures to provide accommodations are so egregious we may easily consider them to constitute outright discrimination—an intentional, or at least irresponsible, disregard for a worker's religious faith and practice. But the language of Title VII goes beyond failures to accommodate that can easily be labeled discriminatory; it may go beyond failures to accommodate that interfere with equal opportunity; and it requires more accommodation of religious practices than it does of practices strongly connected

---

"undue hardship.") The statute's legislative history indicated that Congress intended to give less absolute deference to seniority arrangements than does Title VII.

[78] Were more costly accommodations to violate the Establishment Clause, any tension between Title VII and RFRA would be neatly resolved. RFRA allows impairment of religious exercise if the government is serving a compelling interest. Avoiding Establishment Clause violations is undoubtedly a compelling interest. If the imposition of more than minimal cost violates the Establishment Clause, RFRA does not require any accommodation that goes beyond minimal cost.

[79] See Michael McConnell, "Accommodation of Religion: An Update and a Response to Critics," 60 *George Washington Law Review* 685, 712 (1992). On this view, a legislature *could* *decide* to grant an exemption from criminal laws against using peyote, but could not require that private universities allow students to use peyote in worship services (barring some argument that public laws against peyote underlie the universities' restrictions).

[80] *Estate of Thornton v. Caldor, Inc.*, 472 U.S. 703 (1985).

[81] In the Connecticut case, Justice O'Connor commented on the implication of that decision for accommodation under Title VII. She wrote that "a statute outlawing discrimination . . . has the valid secular purpose of assuring employment opportunity to all groups in our pluralist society." Id. at 712 (O'Connor, J., concurring).

with race, gender, or national origin. Neither the accommodation language of Title VII nor its stingy application by the Supreme Court can be justified as simple antidiscrimination law.

This analysis leaves us with the stark question whether legislatures can impose at all on private citizens in requiring accommodation, beyond protecting against discrimination. I do not see why not. Many impairments of fundamental liberties can come from the private sector, and private employers enjoy the success they do from a fabric of supporting laws and government practices. So long as the federal government has jurisdiction to regulate private behavior, say under the Commerce Clause, it may permissibly protect religious liberty.[82] State legislatures, under their general police powers, may similarly regulate private enterprises. As volume 2 argues in greater depth, governments can mandate some private accommodations to religious needs without violating the Establishment Clause; they should require more than *Hardison* demands.

Illustrative Cases Involving Expression

Three interesting accommodation cases involving religious expressions give a sense of how Title VII has been and might be viewed and also offer helpful comparisons for the harassment cases we shall examine in the next chapter. The first case involves an employer's mandatory religious meetings, the second the antiabortion button with the photo of a fetus, the third a government supervisor who engaged in a variety of religious activities.

Employer Speech

The *Townley Co.* case,[83] which we have already reviewed in respect to ordinary discrimination, presented a debatable question about accommodation. The Townleys required all their workers to attend religious meetings. Pelvas, an atheist, asked to be excused.[84] His supervisor said he could read or sleep, and could wear earplugs during the services, but would not be excused. The

---

[82] I am, to be clear, not suggesting that the First or Fourteenth Amendment confers such regulatory power on the federal government; I am assuming that those amendments concern only interferences with rights that come from the government itself. However, the Free Exercise Clause could figure indirectly as a defense against a challenge that protection against private interferences with religious exercise amounts to a forbidden establishment of religion.

[83] Note 47 supra.

[84] If the meetings constituted a form of harassment creating a hostile environment, a worker would have had yet another basis to be excused. Someone might conceivably have an objection in conscience to attending without necessarily feeling that forced attendance creates a hostile environment.

accommodation issue was critical, because the court decided, mistakenly in my view, that the mandatory services themselves were permissible.

The court concluded that Townley Co. had made no effort to accommodate Pelvas's objections to the services. It acknowledged the possibility that an employer's "spiritual costs" might count, but said that these must connect to a disruption of work routine or an imposition on coworkers. By these standards, excusing Pelvas from the meetings would not cause undue hardship.[85]

John Noonan, a judge who is also a prominent scholar of the religion clauses, dissented. The supervisor's proposal that Pelvas could wear earplugs and read or sleep was an offer of a reasonable accommodation; and Townley Co. should be allowed to reject any sharp dichotomy between secular and religious activity.

All the judges agreed on a point that deserves brief repeating here. Atheists have rights to have their beliefs accommodated under Title VII.[86] An atheist's beliefs about religion may lead him to feel deep offense if he is forced to listen consistently to religious doctrines he rejects.[87] Once we recognize that, we can understand that the company did not offer a reasonable accommodation, and that excusing Pelvas would not have imposed an undue hardship on it. Pelvas found it unpalatable to sit through religious services of a faith he rejected. Earplugs and newspapers were not an adequate answer. Earplugs do not keep out all noise, and, even if they did, forced attendance could feel objectionable.

On the question of "undue hardship," it is difficult to perceive even de minimis costs if Townley Co. excused Pelvas.[88] To succeed with a claim of

[85] Because the case was decided in 1988, two years before *Employment Division v. Smith*, the court considered the employer's free exercise claim under the old approach of *Sherbert v. Verner*. It said the impact on the owner's religious practices of excusing those with religious objections would not be great, and that the government's interest in ending religious discrimination was a strong one.

[86] The statutory language requires accommodation to religious "belief" as well as "observance and practice."

[87] Thus, one should not conclude that "[f]or committed atheists, prayer is a silly waste of time." Gregory, note 53 supra, at 139. Compulsory prayer may strike an atheist as a waste of time, but it may also be offensive to his conscience.

[88] I adopt the court's supposition that the amount of business discussion carried on at these meetings was not in itself sufficient to require Pelvas's presence or to render the meetings other than worship services.

In 1992, the Supreme Judicial Court of Massachusetts considered a worker's claim that her employer had improperly conditioned her employment on continuing to attend a week-long seminar in which scriptural references were used to reinforce teachings, and a video presentation indicated that wives should be subordinate to husbands. *Kolodziej v. Smith*, 588 N.E.2d 634 (Mass. 1992). Plaintiff had failed to make a Title VII claim, so the court was limited to deciding whether the employer had interfered with her state "constitutional right to believe and profess the religious doctrine of her choice." Id. at 637. (A state statute forbade private interference with constitutional rights. The quote represents the court's paraphrase of the right

undue hardship, the employer should be able to point to a difference that the presence of someone sitting with a newspaper and earplugs will make. In common experience, having indifferent and inattentive attenders, who are seen to be so by everyone present, is much more destructive of fruitful meetings than absentees.[89] Judges could allow an employer to prefer inattentive presence to absence only if they left it completely to the employer to determine what count as spiritual costs that are sufficiently important. If courts accepted all assertions about spiritual costs that are not evidently insincere, the result would be to eliminate the accommodation requirement for any employer who offers his own competing claim of religious exercise. The court, rightly, does not go down that road.[90]

Worker Speech

In *Wilson v. U.S. West Communication*,[91] Wilson wore an antiabortion button with a color photograph of an eighteen- to twenty-week-old fetus. Although the button was not religious on its face, Wilson was a Roman Catholic who had made a religious vow to wear it "until there was an end to abortion or until [she] could no longer fight the fight."[92] She chose this particular button because she believed the Virgin Mary would have chosen it. Some coworkers found the button disturbing for personal reasons, such as infertility problems, miscarriage, and the death of a premature infant. Some threatened to walk off the job. (No workers, apparently, claimed that they

---

of free exercise.) Plaintiff argued that both the view taught at the seminar that husbands have authority over wives and her competing view were religious. Noting the difficulty of distinguishing secular from religious beliefs, the court accepted this contention of the plaintiff; it followed that she would have a right not to attend the seminar if it was a religious activity. But the court concluded that the seminar was not a religious activity. Had the court directly faced Title VII issues, it would have had to decide if her religious objection to participating in a seminar would have entitled her to an accommodation of being excused. One guesses the court would have said that the seminar, dealing with matters like interpersonal conflicts, bore sufficient relation to legitimate business concerns of the employer so he would not have had to make that accommodation.

[89] Even if the court mistakenly underrates the significance of "spiritual costs," it is difficult to see why completely inattentive presence would be better than nonattendance. If the supervisor had a rational basis for his compromise, it may have been that few employees would have the gall to be so openly disrespectful; whereas more employees might seek to be excused. Perhaps the employer just wanted to force people to be there to hear the true word, but *this* aim, if achieved, would constitute religious discrimination against those who object.

[90] I have previously suggested that employers in ordinary businesses should not have the rights to discriminate on religious grounds of religious organizations. See text accompanying notes 18–21. Nonetheless, such an approach would be preferable to acceptance of all claims about spiritual costs.

[91] Note 6 supra.

[92] Id. at 1339.

felt harassed because of their religious beliefs.) Supervisors offered Wilson the options of (1) wearing the button only in her cubicle, (2) covering the button, or (3) wearing a button with the same message but without the photograph. She refused all three options, and was dismissed. She argued that the coworkers should have been instructed to ignore or tolerate the button.

The court of appeals decided that U.S. West had offered a "reasonable accommodation." It relied partly on the district court's conclusion that Wilson's views did not require her to be a "living witness." Had this issue been resolved in favor of Wilson, her supervisors' offers might not have been ones of reasonable accommodation, since none allowed her to witness at work, outside her cubicle, with this button. The court of appeals' treatment of reasonable accommodation was flawed, but its ultimate conclusion was correct because of "undue hardship."

The behavior of the supervisors was rightly judged according to what they could fairly understand, not on the basis of Wilson's uncommunicated feelings; but an accommodation should not have been considered reasonable, if what the supervisors learned during their conversations with Wilson would have led them to see that what they offered would not resolve her religious conflict. The court of appeals disposition was unsatisfactory in emphasizing the exact content of Wilson's initial vow,[93] rather than what her conversations with supervisors disclosed.[94]

---

[93] The court's handling of the "living witness" issue was also unsatisfactory in a more technical aspect. The central question was not, as the judges suggested, whether the district court *clearly erred*, id. at 1340, but whether the district court's finding was appropriate, given the limited scope of inquiry courts should make about a complainant's religious understanding. In cases such as these, courts must be ready to make some determinations about sincerity, but they should not declare a claim to be insincere if that is in serious doubt. Wilson's understanding of her vow should have been accepted, unless that was obviously insincere. By that standard, the district court erred because it did not give Wilson the benefit of the doubt.

The parties had stipulated that Wilson was sincere, but the district court said that the stipulation did not cover the details of her vow. If Wilson had clearly indicated on other occasions that her vow did not include a particular element, a judge could decide that it lacked that element even if she claimed otherwise at the time of the suit. However, any uncertainties should have been resolved in Wilson's favor.

Both courts did refer to what Wilson had said on other occasions, but those statements did not decisively resolve whether her oath included being a living witness. See id. at 1341.

[94] Suppose that when she made her initial vow, Wilson had not focused on whether she needed merely to wear the button or to have it exposed to view. When the supervisors offered her the button-covering option, she realized that she felt compelled to keep the button exposed. If she then communicated that to her supervisors, the supervisors should have taken her religious practice as wearing this particular button, exposed, in the entire workplace. If Wilson's communications to her supervisors had been unclear, and they reasonably thought that neither her vow nor her present sentiments required an exposed button, their proposed accommodations would have been reasonable, even if her actual sentiments rendered them inadequate. But conversations between Wilson and her supervisors definitely revealed her claim that the button had to be exposed.

What should have been the central focus in *Wilson* was whether satisfying her request for an accommodation would have involved "undue hardship." If the cause of disturbance had been the *substance* of the antiabortion message, U.S. West should have had to accommodate. The need to accommodate a worker's speech should usually not depend on the congeniality of the message for coworkers.[95] But the sticking point with Wilson's button was its photograph.

Some photos are deeply disturbing. An antialcohol button might show a vomiting drunk, an antiwar button a family being burned by napalm. Work-

---

In *Chalmers v. Tulon Co.*, 101 F.3d 1012 (1996), a divided court resolved when a worker must inform an employer about the need for accommodation. Motivated by religious concerns, an evangelical Christian worker wrote to her immediate supervisor at his home suggesting that he was doing something in his life that God was not pleased with. Chalmers had in mind that LaMantia had given customers false information about the turnaround time for jobs. The supervisor's wife opened and read the letter, and concluded that her husband was committing adultery. Chalmers was subsequently fired, not because of her religious views but because the letter had caused her boss anguish and put a strain on his marriage. The court affirmed a summary judgment for the company, concluding that Chalmers had not been dismissed because of her religion, that she had no claim for an accommodation because she had not asked for one prior to sending the letter, and that, in any event, the employer could not be expected to accommodate to the sending of disturbing personal letters.

As Judge Niemeyer's dissent points out, the majority's approach on the question of notice is too rigid. Only when her letter caused such turmoil did Chalmers realize that what she was doing was at odds with what the company wanted. That was the appropriate time to see if an accommodation could be reached. Although she was moved to send the letter (and at least one other) by a religious impulse, she never indicated that she felt a religious obligation to mail letters to the homes of fellow employees. She might have limited herself to conversations and notes at work, if told to do so. The employer could have taken the occasion to warn her and to see if she would accept a reasonable accommodation that would fit with its business needs. Its firing her without exploring that option should have been regarded as a failure to accommodate.

But the case had a special feature. What Chalmers had already done had caused a very serious breach between her and her immediate supervisor. The company could not have avoided that, because it had no prior warning she would send such a letter. The company could reasonably take the view that no future course of action by Chalmers would be likely to repair the breach with her supervisor. For that reason, Chalmers was an unsuitable employee, and the employer did not need to figure out whether future religious communications by her were capable of being accommodated. The court does remark that had the company accommodated Chalmers, it might have faced religious harassment claims by employees receiving her letters. Id. at 1021. As Thomas Berg has noted, note 20 supra, at 984, it is a difficult question whether such letters could be treated as harassment, given free speech considerations, but I do not understand the employer to have relied on this rationale, and I do not think it is central to the court's decision.

[95] However, an employer should be able to say sometimes that certain kinds of messages are so fraught with controversy that speech about those subjects will not be tolerated at work. If an employer makes such a decision, banning, for example, all electoral buttons at work, he should not have to make an exception for those nonreligious electoral buttons whose wearing happens to be motivated by religious conviction. Some other messages may be so outrageous in general opinion, for example that parents should have the discretion to kill any child of theirs until the child is one year old, that an employer who bans them would not need to make an exception for a religiously motivated statement of this sort.

ers who sympathize with the basic message could be put off, even deeply troubled. We need to see such photographs from time to time, but we don't want or need constant exposure to them at work. Whatever their success in achieving it, most people seek a comfortable working environment, and they are more productive when they get it.

For the sake of his workers' serenity and productivity, an employer is justified in forbidding disturbing photographs from the common working environment. The evidence suggested that Wilson's photo was one of these, that other workers were deeply disturbed, that productivity declined, and that some workers were inclined to stay home if Wilson continued to wear the button. The possible option of counseling workers to ignore the photo disregards human psychology. People do not easily avert their eyes when a disquieting sight comes within range. And it would have been very difficult to look at Wilson without seeing the photo. The accommodation that Wilson sought did involve undue hardship, whether one uses the Supreme Court's approach of more than de minimis cost or a standard much more favorable to accommodation.[96]

Speech by a Government Supervisor

Government workers may make claims for accommodation when supervisors curtail their religious speech. Unlike private workers, federal and state employees have a general right to speak freely about matters of public concern[97] unless their interest in speech is outweighed by the government's need to promote "the efficiency of the public services."[98] To restrict religious

[96] The district court reached this conclusion. The court of appeals, having found (mistakenly in my view) that U.S. West offered a reasonable accommodation, did not have to consider the issue of undue hardship; but it remarked that "the district court did not err" in reaching its conclusion on that score. Some scholars believe *Wilson* was wrongly decided. See, e.g., Thomas Berg, note 20 supra, at 978–83; Theresa M. Beiner and John M. A. DiPippa, "Hostile Environments and the Religious Employee," 19 *University of Arkansas at Little Rock Law Journal* 577, 602–8 (1997). I am not sure how far my difference with them depends on a conflicting appraisal of the degree of unavoidable disturbance, rather than a different sense of how much cost courts should impose in the interests of accommodation.

I should note that I do not regard this as like a situation in which customers, or coworkers, are directly disturbed by a worker's race, gender, or religion. I assume that any concession to such feelings violates the statute.

[97] One particular subject about which workers can speak is how the workplace is operating.

[98] *Pickering v. Board of Educ.*, 391 U.S. 563, 568 (1968). See *Connick v. Myers*, 461 U.S. 138 (1983); *Rankin v. McPherson*, 483 U.S. 378 (1987); *Waters v. Churchill*, 511 U.S. 661, 664 (1994). In *Connick v. Myers*, rejecting a worker's claim, the Supreme Court said, "When employee expression cannot be fairly be considered as relating to any matter of political, social, or other concern to the community, government officials should enjoy wide latitude in managing their offices, without intrusive oversight by the judiciary." Could one argue that religious

speech, the government must ordinarily make at least the showing required when it restricts speech about job-related and political concerns.[99]

One might believe that Title VII or RFRA accords governmental workers more protection for their religious speech than they have for nonreligious speech. But we have seen that the Supreme Court has interpreted Title VII's accommodation section not to demand much of employers, and, despite the compelling interest test of RFRA, courts, supported to some degree by the act's legislative history, have assumed that RFRA is not more demanding than Title VII.[100] Under existing law, the religious speech of government workers apparently enjoys the same degree of protection as other speech about public concerns.

One could argue that religious speech *should* receive extra protection, that it is uniquely important or uniquely safeguarded in our constitutional scheme.[101] Much might be said about this, but I believe the Supreme Court has been right in recent decades to assume that religious speech does not enjoy a special degree of constitutional protection.

Contentions about the religious speech of government employees were sharply exhibited by *Brown v. Polk County*,[102] in which the Eighth Circuit Court of Appeals, considering the firing of a director of a county department who had been engaging in various religious activities, assumed that the First Amendment protected at least as much religious behavior as Title VII's accommodation language. The basic issue turned out to be which activities the county should have accepted, and which it reasonably had told Brown stop. Brown had properly been told not to direct his secretary to type Bible study notes and not to have employees gather in his office to say prayers before

---

speech is not of "public concern" in the sense that the Court means? The Court has not addressed this precise question, but religious speech (and other speech about general ideas) should count as being of public concern, if any such line is to be drawn. That the Free Exercise Clause protects religious expression can be taken to support this conclusion, or to underlie a judgment that the "public concern" requirement should be irrelevant for religious speech. See *Eiland v. Montgomery*, 797 F.2d 953, 956 n. 4 (11th Cir. 1986) (if speech has independent constitutional protection, it need not meet public concern test). In general, and in contrast to the Supreme Court's approach, I do not think expression about personal matters should be less protected than speech about broader concerns. See Kent Greenawalt, *Speech, Crime, and the Uses of Language* 44–46, 83–84 (New York: Oxford University Press, 1989).

[99] However, if the speech were thought to suggest a government endorsement of religion or were regarded as harassing another worker, it could be restricted even though the reason would not be well phrased as "promoting the efficiency of the public services."

[100] See note 75 supra, and accompanying text.

[101] See Betty L. Dunkum, "Where to Draw the Line: Handling Religious Harassment Issues in the Wake of the Failed EEOC Guidelines," 71 *Notre Dame Law Review* 953, 989 (1996); Kimball E. Gilner and Jeffrey M. Anderson, "Zero Tolerance for God? Religious Expression in the Workplace after Ellerth and Faragher," 42 *Howard Law Journal* 327, 344 (1999).

[102] 61 F.3d 661 (8th Cir. 1995) (en banc).

the start of the workday. However, the county had erred in forbidding Brown from having occasional prayers and references to Christianity in his office during the workday, and in directing him to remove all items with a religious connotation from his office.

The county's instruction that Brown not have his secretary type notes of Bible study involved no substantial interference with his religious exercise. As to the opening of his office for prayers, the court said that an employer need not open offices before the working day for nonworking affairs. The county could take the position that workspaces were meant for work, not the carrying on of personal business. The court's conclusion about Brown's office was highly questionable. My working experience, limited as it is but including three different jobs with the federal government, is that one can go to one's office before the working day begins and chat about trivia with coworkers. Whatever the county's formal policy, it strains credulity to suppose that it would have reacted negatively if the meetings in Brown's office had been about Little League or stamp collecting. If, in fact, the county would have accepted regular meetings on other nonwork subjects, it should not have been able to invoke a general policy of work to restrict religious meetings.

Forbidding Brown from having religious items in his office and from making occasional religious statements during the working day substantially interfered with his religious practices. Failing evidence that these practices significantly disturbed coworkers or divided the office between Christians and non-Christians, the county could have accommodated them without undue hardship. Failure to do so violated both Title VII and the Free Exercise Clause.[103]

Four dissenters to this en banc decision thought that Brown had failed to show a substantial interference with his religious exercise and further believed that in a balance of interests, the county should have prevailed, given Brown's status as a supervisor, and the likely effect of his activities on workers beneath him.

People can disagree about exactly which activities of Brown's should have been protected, but the court undertakes the right kind of inquiry, assuming that public workers should have latitude to communicate their religious opinions unless the consequence is disruption of work or disturbance of other employees.[104] It is vital, however, that if supervisors like Brown engage

[103] The court explicitly analogized the case to ones involving nonreligious speech by government employers, and saw "no essential relevant difference" between free speech and free exercise rights. Id. at 658, referring to *Pickering*, note 98 supra.

[104] A different issue is religious speech that seems to represent the government itself. That would be a critical concern for a schoolteacher or a chief executive. I am assuming that Brown was not in a position for that to be a problem.

in religious speech, they make clear that advancement in the workplace does not depend on workers "going along."

In 1997 the executive branch issued guidelines for religious speech by federal employees.[105] According to these, workers are to be free to express religious ideas unless that creates the appearance of government endorsement, intrudes on the efficient provision of public services, or "intrudes upon the legitimate rights of other employees."[106] Supervisors, as well as ordinary workers, can express personal religious views if they make clear they are personal views. Employees must refrain from expression directed at a fellow employee when the fellow employee indicates it is unwelcome.[107]

In appraising the guidelines, we need to understand that some people are particularly insistent about pressing their religious views, offering a hope of salvation to their listeners. Although such speech is very disturbing to some listeners, they may be cowed and disinclined to express their discomfort, especially if the speaker is a supervisor, even one careful to distinguish his personal views from his office responsibilities. This reality could underlie an argument for discouraging religious speech, but the guidelines' approach is preferable. Workers should be told that they need not listen to unwelcome religious speech. If they feel harassed by it, they need to say so. This balance of speaker's and listener's rights, though not perfect, is the best this subject allows.[108]

What Is Religious under Title VII?

What counts as "religious" under the accommodation provision of Title VII? The practical significance of this question was much diminished by *Hardison*, which renders an employer's burden very slight, even if a belief or practice is religious. Prior to 1980, some courts assumed that claims had to be

---

[105] Press Release, The White House Office of the Press Secretary, Guidelines on Religious Exercise and Religious Expression in the Federal Workplace (Aug. 14, 1997).

[106] Religious speech is to be treated like other speech, including ideological speech on politics, not treated unfavorably because of its content.

[107] See Section 1 (A)(3).

[108] This subject allows only a certain degree of precision, and I believe the general tenor of the guidelines is appropriate. For a criticism of the guidelines as too vague and not adequately protective of the religious speech of government workers, see Stephen S. Kao, "The President's Guidelines on Religious Harassment and Religious Expression in the Federal Workplace: A Restatement or a Reinterpretation of Law?" 8 *Public Interest Law Journal* 251 (1998). (The author also argues that the guidelines exceed the president's jurisdiction in covering employees not in the executive branch, and that their issuance improperly avoided public scrutiny of their content.)

based on institutional religion, while others drew on *United States v. Seeger*[109] and *Welsh v. United States*,[110] and ruled that sincerely held beliefs that were religious within one's own "scheme of things" were sufficient.[111]

In 1980, EEOC Guidelines on Discrimination Because of Religion decisively adopted the broader view of what counts as religious. The introduction says:

> The Guidelines do not confine the definition of religious practices to theistic concepts or to traditional religious beliefs. The definition also includes moral and ethical beliefs. Under the Guidelines, a belief is religious not because a religious group professes that belief, but because the individual sincerely holds that belief with the strength of traditional religious views.[112]

Enlightened though it may appear, this approach is extremely vague about what are qualifying moral or ethical beliefs and about how speech is to be treated. A worker with a conscientious belief that he cannot perform a particular action, such as a nonreligious pacifist who seeks a transfer because he refuses to produce arms, would hold an ethical belief with the strength of a traditional religious one. If the employer could accomplish the transfer easily, he would have to make the accommodation under the EEOC guidelines. But what of a worker's strong ethical sense that does not amount to a conscientious objection? A worker, required often to travel, feels a powerful responsibility to spend time with her family. She requests "an accommodation" of being shifted to another department whose workers need not travel. Is the statute relevant here? Virtually every request based on family needs is an ethical one in a broad sense. Treating as "religious" all requests based on a strong ethical sense would make the statute potentially applicable in too many instances and would render it very hard for officials to say when the border line of "religion" had been crossed.[113]

[109] 380 U.S. 163 (1965).

[110] 398 U.S. 333 (1970). This case and *Seeger*, involving the statutory exemption from military duty for conscientious objectors, are discussed in chapter 4.

[111] See Engle, note 72 supra, at 373–81.

[112] 45 Fed. Reg. 72, 610 (1980) (codified as revised at 29 C.F.R. § 1605 (1996)). Under this interpretation, religion in Title VII is treated as is religion under the Selective Service Act, according to the *Seeger* and *Welsh* cases. For a case applying the guideline to protect white supremacist speech (away from the job) by a follower of an arguably religious group called Creativity, see *Peterson v. Wilmur Communications, Inc.*, 205 F. Supp. 2d 1014 (E.D. Wis. 2002) The court treated the speech as an absolutely protected aspect of belief. Thus, plaintiff had to be retained in his position, although he supervised and trained a number of nonwhite workers. I have argued in chapter 3 that protection of religious expression should not be absolute if it connects closely to requisites of performance of a job.

[113] The practical effect of this breadth and uncertainty would increase greatly if the *Hardison* duty to accommodate were made more demanding.

Another troubling aspect of the guidelines concerns speech. Few workers will make demands that are nonreligious (in the traditional sense) for special conditions at work, such as having Saturdays off or keeping a beard;[114] more workers may feel, as a matter of conscience, that they should speak to co-workers on subjects of concern. If a sense of ethical compulsion to speak qualifies for accommodation under Title VII, much speech might be protected that is neither explicitly religious nor motivated by a traditional religious belief. Thus, someone without traditional religious beliefs whose overriding concern is saving the environment might have a claim to have his environmental advocacy accommodated.

This extension creates problems. If a worker wants to talk about subjects of deep personal or public concern, is statutory protection to depend on whether she feels conscientiously compelled to do so? That would be a difficult inquiry, and it would reward rigid ideologues (who are likely to feel compelled) over people with more nuanced views of life. If protection extended to all those who think their speech is highly desirable from an ethical point of view, the standard would become virtually unadministrable.

One might react positively to this development if one thought that workers should have general rights of free speech vis-à-vis private employers. A very broad notion of religious speech would constitute a giant step in that direction. But within a regime that requires accommodation of religious speech but not other speech, such an extension of religious speech is undesirable and perhaps untenable. These broad implications of a generously expansive view of religion seem not to have been recognized by the EEOC.[115]

---

[114] However, workers may want to wear particular clothes or be groomed in an unusual way out of a cultural or ethnic sense that is not religious.

[115] In *Van Kuten v. Family Health Management*, 955 F. Supp. 898, 902 (N.D. Ill. 1997), the court cited the guidelines approach approvingly, but discerned no evidence that the plaintiff had been fired because he held "Wicca" beliefs or had expressed some of them in the workplace. See also *Seshardi v. Kasrain*, 130 F.3d 798, 800 (7th Cir. 1997), in which Chief Judge Posner made clear that religious beliefs need not be orthodox, but without trying to conceptualize the outer limits of protected beliefs.

The question of what counts as religion can arise in respect to harassment and ordinary discrimination, as well as accommodation. I address the EEOC approach in connection with harassment in the chapter that follows.

CHAPTER 19

Employment Relations: Harassment

Given that ordinary discrimination is undesirable, so also is harassment. Title VII and similar state laws have been interpreted to forbid workplace harassment because of race, color, religion, sex, or national origin. Harassment is often caused by the speech of employers or fellow workers. Evaluating speech that is well intended but causes deep offense is especially perplexing.

EMPLOYER CHOICE AND APPROPRIATE LEGAL CONTROL

Quid Pro Quo and Hostile Environment

We need initially to distinguish two kinds of harassment: quid pro quo and hostile environment. Although quid pro quo harassment is most familiar in respect to sex—a male supervisor tells a woman he will fire her if she does not have sex with him—religious harassment can also take this form. A supervisor lets a worker know that her promotion depends on her attending a particular church. If employers should not engage in ordinary religious discrimination, they should not encourage or tolerate this kind of harassment.

A government that forbids religious discrimination should undoubtedly forbid quid pro quo harassment. A worker told that her job depends on her religious commitment may feel pressured to "comply," or be unwilling to do so, resigning and finding another job where her prospects are not correlated to religious faith. Because her ability to pursue employment opportunities independent of her religion has already been compromised, she has suffered discrimination well before any threat is acted upon.

Harder questions are presented when a worker is denied no specific job benefit but suffers pervasively hostile working conditions. Three of those questions are these: When does an employer become responsible for the actions of his supervisors and workers? What severity of offense makes a worker a victim of harassment? How should an employer respond if the behavior causing offense is sincere speech or religious practice?

The first two of these questions are not well cast for an employer who is considering what to do, independent of any legal regulation. He should try to create a congenial atmosphere for his workers, without stifling their liberty, as in a family, parents should aim for a supportive atmosphere, but not one devoid of all frictions. The employer should eliminate actions that cause substantial offense, whether the trigger relates to religion, sex, or race, or some personal element, such as a worker's appearance or family history.

The third question has more substance for an employer free of regulation. If what causes offense is the employer's own religious speech or the religious speech or practice of coworkers, a sensitive employer must balance the interest in free speech or religious practice against the benefit of a working environment that is not oppressive, taking into account the same kinds of factors that matter for legal regulation.

Elements of Religious Harassment

When employers (or fellow workers) perform actions that deeply offend a worker, religion may figure in one or more of three ways. An employer's practice or speech may be religious; it may be directed at a worker because of her religion;[1] it may cause her offense based on her religious convictions or identity. If the law should concentrate on a limited set of categories of discrimination,[2] including religion, we need to consider what elements are needed to constitute harassment on the basis of religion.

If the three ways in which religion might figure join together—religious speech is directed at a worker because of her religion and causes her religious offense—any harassment obviously counts as religious. If religion is not involved in any of the ways, religious harassment has not occurred. Doubts arise when religion is involved in only one or two of the ways.[3]

When an employer singles out a worker based on her religion, his behavior is undoubtedly religious discrimination combined with either of the other two factors. First, if an employer persistently proselytizes a worker because of her religion, and continues despite her expressed wish that he stop, that is religious harassment, even if her sense of disturbance does not concern her religious convictions or identity.[4] Second, if an employer focuses on a worker because of her religion, say Roman Catholicism, and she is deeply disturbed as a Catholic at what he insistently advocates, this constitutes religious harassment even though the content of his discourse—say, strong support of

---

[1] A remark is "directed" in this sense if it is made to a more general audience but with the aim of reaching those of a particular religion.

[2] Employers should not harass workers on the basis of height or eating habits, but these, along with many other possible grounds, are not made subjects of regulation.

[3] I suppose other requisites of harassment are satisfied, and I disregard the possibility that some interest in speech or religious exercise justifies what would otherwise be harassment.

[4] In this respect, a claim for accommodation differs. That depends on a religious belief or practice of the claimant.

gay marriage—is not explicitly religious.[5] Although the case is somewhat harder if the employer's attention is based on a worker's religion—she is Catholic—but neither his speech nor her grounds of offense are religious,[6] his reliance on her religion is definitely, by itself, a cause for concern if the employer's aim is to humiliate or embarrass, and it should be enough for religious harassment even if the employer's motives are benign.

As I have claimed in chapter 18, an employer can discriminate even when he has not selected his audience on religious grounds. If the employer has mandatory religious meetings that create a hostile environment for some workers because of their religious identity, the meetings can constitute religious harassment; but if any disturbance a worker experiences because of broadly disseminated religious communications has nothing to do with his own religious convictions or identity, he has not been harassed on grounds of religion.[7]

A final variation on the theme of nonselectivity involves an employer who directs *non*religious speech at all employees, and offends a worker on religious grounds. An employer urging his workers to eat pork to benefit the state's economy might distress workers who are Orthodox Jews or Muslims. Or an employer's strong advocacy of abortion rights might offend a Roman Catholic. If the employer neither aims at religiously grounded offense nor should perceive that many of his workers will experience it, he has not engaged in harassment because of religion. However, the law should regard an employer's speech as religious harassment if it would predictably cause religious offense to a large proportion of the workforce.

Employer Speech

Part of the equation for deciding what should finally count as forbidden harassment concerns the interests of employers and fellow workers who want to communicate important messages. Various factors are highly relevant to regulatory choices.

An employer expressing sincere views, religious or not, has a substantial claim to be left free; one whose aim is to humiliate or embarrass workers

[5] I mean here that the employer picks the worker out because she is Roman Catholic, not just that he wants to talk to likely opponents of gay marriage and assumes that she falls into that category because she is a Catholic.

[6] She feels serious discomfort about advocacy of homosexual rights, but she does not attach her discomfort to her religious convictions or identity.

[7] However, an argument could be made that harassment should be treated like other forms of discrimination, and these might occur even if selection and feelings of offense are not based on religion—if, for example, the employer requires a demanding religious practice of all workers and some workers object because they think it is a waste of time.

has a much weaker claim. An employer with deeply felt opinions about important social issues might print appeals to contribute to charities on his paychecks, or mount posters expressing approval of the country's involvement in a war, or urge his workers to give blood.[8] When we think about such nonreligious speech, we may be led to ask whether religious speech should be specially favored or disfavored by law.[9]

Someone might argue that religious speech should be less protected than other speech because it connects to a forbidden form of discrimination; but most religious speech differs from much racist and sexist speech.[10] *Unless* religious speech advocates religious discrimination, it is not likely to be in tension with a norm of nondiscrimination. An employer may consistently say that hiring should not be based on religious grounds, but that all people should be encouraged to accept the true religion.[11]

An employer's personal interest in engaging in religious speech might not depend on the size of his firm, on the number of other employers similarly inclined, or on administrative difficulties, but these matter for regulatory decisions. First, consider firm size. An employer might care more about expressing his views if he knows his workers well, but the crucial relevance of firm size is that an owner's control of great economic resources should not allow him to dictate the religious environment for thousands of workers.

If very few employers want to set a religious tone at work, the effect on workplace conditions overall will be much less than if many employers have the same desire. Here, regions of the country differ. Many Utah employers may prefer a Mormon atmosphere at work, but few New York employers are so inclined. Unfortunately, many antidiscrimination laws are national or statewide, not easily bent to fit local conditions.

Administrators and judges would find it hard to distinguish between employers' deep desires to establish a religious tone and more common preju-

---

[8] Some workers might object to such messages on religious grounds; a pacifist might find the approval of war objectionable on religious grounds, and a Jehovah's Witness, opposed by religious conviction to blood transfusions, might object to being forced to listen to a plea to give blood.

[9] In the examples I have chosen, the other "missions" may be more temporary than religious missions, but an employer could have a long-run aim to help the poor or protect the environment.

[10] If employers cannot practice racism or sexism, their free approval of these practices may undermine to some extent their own practice of nondiscrimination and may contribute to unhealthy attitudes, and this could happen even though an employer who believes in some form of racism or sexism accepts a norm of nondiscrimination in employment.

[11] Further, whereas most racist and sexist speech reinforces dominance of whites and males, see J. M. Balkin, "Free Speech and Hostile Environments," 99 *Columbia Law Review* 2295, 2308, 2315 (1999), much, perhaps most, religious speech does not reinforce some dominant religious perspective (if we do not count proselytizing by evangelical Christians as reflecting the dominant perspective among Christians, and we disregard narrow localities where most workplace religious speech may reinforce that community's religious view).

dice against those who do not conform. The law needs standards that can be administered. Rules about employer speech cast in terms of firm size are much more practical than assessments of the seriousness of religious missions.

We can draw some preliminary conclusions about employers and religious harassment. An employer definitely cannot *require* employees to engage in actions that affirm particular religious beliefs or commitments, such as taking communion or making creedal statements. Similarly, an employer cannot require attendance at religious meetings limited to those who do not presently affirm his faith.

An employer's religious speech should not be illegal simply because some workers fear that religion may be a factor in employment decisions. Although a worker blatantly out of step with the expressed religious inclinations of an employer may worry about his prospects, what counts are the employer's directions about job evaluation and promotion, not his religious expressions. The way an employer treats his workers is a much better test of whether he is discriminating than his public religious expressions, and curbing the expressions will not eliminate the possibility of discrimination.[12] Employers should be required to make clear that opportunities at work will not depend on conformity with their religious views.

One of the hardest issues involves meetings that mix business with religion in such a way that allowing objectors to absent themselves is not a feasible option. Workers should have to tolerate minimal religious involvements, such as being present when someone says a prayer to open a day's meeting. But what if talk about the religious mission is continually interwoven with business talk. An employer, or his representative, repeatedly emphasizes: "We are not just a business; we have a higher purpose to be God's servants, and we need to remember that when we deal with customers." This setting may be uncomfortable for workers who reject the employer's religious ideas, but accommodating their feelings would seriously undercut the religious mission as the employer sees it. The choice is not easy, but I believe, subject to two caveats, that the employer should be able to express his mission, including the interweaving of business and religion.

---

[12] What if employment decisions are made by lower supervisors or by groups of team members of equal status? The employer has religious meetings that most workers attend. Is it not possible that the attendees will develop a bond that excludes those who do not attend? Their sense that the nonattendee is an outsider may affect their evaluation; so also may their sense that the nonattendee is at odds with the employer on religious matters, even though the employer has said that employment decisions should not be made on the basis of religion. This worry is far from fanciful, but it should not be enough to shut down an employer's religious expression.

The first caveat is that the religious talk is positive. A Roman Catholic worker should not have to sit through an anti-Catholic diatribe.[13] The second caveat is that the privileging of religious (and other) speech offensive to the religious sentiments of some workers might reasonably depend on an owner's being directly involved with a significant percentage of workers. An operable legal rule might set a limit in terms of number of workers.

Coworker Speech

The speech that disturbs a worker may be that of a coworker, rather than the employer or a boss. Except in work situations in which fellow workers decide on advancement, speech by coworkers differs from employer speech in not implicitly raising the threat that employment decisions may be made on the basis of religion. Matters are simplest when one worker talks directly to another.

With such directed speech, the key is that the listener should be able to stop unwanted speech. The speaker may sincerely want to save his coworker, or he may wish to annoy her, but if the listener is deeply offended, or highly annoyed, she should be able to prevent future speech of that sort directed at her.[14] No one should be privileged to direct messages at someone who has clearly indicated she does not wish to hear them.

Nondirected employee speech present greater difficulties. A worker engages in speech that is not directed at any particular coworkers, as with the antiabortion button discussed in chapter 18, or his speech is directed at coworkers who do not object, and is overheard by other workers who do object, or the speech is directed at a group of employees, only some of whom object.[15] The troublesome situations are those in which the speaker is neither

---

[13] This approximates racist and sexist talk workers would not have to tolerate.

[14] If a worker engages in religious speech but chooses his listener for reasons other than the listener's religion, and the offense the listener feels is not connected to her religion, the speech should probably not count as religious harassment. The listener's reactions, however, retain significance, if the speaker claims that his religious speech should be accommodated. In that event, the strength of the reactions of others is relevant, as I explained in connection with the antiabortion button in the last chapter, whether or not those reactions are based on religion.

[15] Another possibility is that although the speech is general, say a button or a flyer in a general work space, the very aim of the speech is to reach people with religious views that vary from those of the speaker. And a considerable percentage of *those* recipients do object. For example, the workplace has eighty-eight Christian and twelve Jewish workers; someone posts a notice by Jews for Jesus that is directed at the twelve Jews and is offensive to most of them. Such speech is directed at that subgroup of workers, and if most of them object, it should be treated as unwelcome speech, particularly if it is feasible to reach the Jews who do not object by some other means.

Speech also counts as directed if it is made to a group, but the very aim is to irritate some individual with particular religious views. Thus, three coworkers may use crude expressions in their conversations just because they want to provoke a fourth whose religious beliefs make such speech deeply offensive to him.

seeking to cause offense nor aiming his remarks at those with particular religious views, but what he says is offensive to some who see or hear.

Workers should be able to display what they want in their own private work spaces, at least if those spaces are not areas to which others are constantly exposed; and, in general, workers should also be able to say what they want to willing listeners. If four of five workers in a telephone repair crew that travels in a van to and from jobs happen to be evangelical Christians who like to talk about their church and the need to be born again, the fifth worker, an atheist, should (usually) have to tolerate these conversations he is bound to overhear.[16]

The law may reasonably demand a standard of minimal politeness in the workplace.[17] Workers should not be able to converse with coworkers in a manner that would be heedlessly rude to feelings about religion (or race or gender) of other workers who are bound to overhear. In our example, the four conversants should not emphasize that atheists are damned. If they do so, they fail to be minimally polite and their actions could underlie a claim of harassment.

Perhaps the thorniest issues about worker speech involve common work areas. Some workers wish to speak to all who share the space in a way that offends a proportion of their fellows.

Emphasizing that workers are "captives" in their workplace, unable to avoid offending speech, some have argued that people should not be forced to endure speech they abhor. But it is also true that speakers are captives during working hours, capable of communicating only with fellow workers, and perhaps customers or clients. The general resolution of these competing considerations is that people should be allowed to communicate their sincere opinions to willing listeners (even if others will overhear), but should be restrained by conventions of polite and respectful speech—not the conventions of a highly literate class, but the conventions of those who are involved.

The general question of how objective a legal standard should be arises in connection with harassment. When a worker claims that various practices disturb her, she should ordinarily have to meet both an objective and subjective standard; she should be disturbed and a reasonable person in her position might be disturbed.[18]

---

[16] I am assuming, crucially, that their talk about being born again is not directed at him and would be the same were he not there.

[17] Officials might infer that grossly rude speakers meant to direct their comments at those the remarks offend, or they might say that a failure to satisfy minimal standards of politeness counts as directing their remarks, whatever the actual intentions of the speakers.

[18] Neither employers nor fellow workers should have to guide their behavior by what a particularly sensitive fellow employee feels; but if someone targets a worker *because* of her sensitive feelings, he should be regulated in accord with the reactions he expects.

Legal Treatment and Constitutionality

Title VII, which prohibits discriminating against anyone in employment because of his religion, has been interpreted to preclude religious harassment, which, as we have seen, could result from quid pro quo threats (or offers) that a worker's employment status will depend on her religious activities *or* from other "severe or pervasive" conduct that creates an atmosphere so hostile that one can say it alters the terms or conditions of employment.[19]

Employer Responsibility

Because the act addresses only employers and unions, the hostile actions of fellow workers become harassment covered by Title VII only when they can be attributed to the employer. If a supervisor fires a worker because she is Jewish, he is taken to act for the employer; but when coworkers make repeated offensive remarks, the employer becomes liable only when he knows, or should know, what is happening and fails to take adequate steps to stop it.

In 1998 the Supreme Court addressed the responsibility of employers for harassing behavior of supervisors that does not involve a tangible employment action, such as a firing or a demotion.[20] To oversimplify, the Court had to decide whether an employer is liable only for his own negligence or is vicariously liable for the actions of his supervisors. Drawing from the general law of agency and the policies of Title VII, the Court held that the employer is vicariously liable, but that he has an affirmative defense if he exercised reasonable care to prevent and correct harassing behavior and if the plaintiff unreasonably failed to take advantage of preventive or corrective opportunities.[21] In its approach, the Court declined to draw as sharp a distinction between quid pro quo and hostile environment harassment as earlier cases had suggested, treating unfulfilled quid pro quo threats by supervisors as raising hostile environment issues, not as constituting tangible employment actions.[22]

At an initial glance, this treatment of supervisor threats is incongruous with an employer's liability for a supervisor's discrimination. If an employer who has exerted energetic efforts to stop discrimination is liable when a supervisor fires a worker because of her religion, why should the law treat the supervisor's threats differently? As I have argued, quid pro quo threats

---

[19] *Burlington Industries v. Ellerth*, 524 U.S. 742, 754 (1998).

[20] Id.; *Faragher v. City of Boca Raton*, 524 U.S. 775 (1998).

[21] 524 U.S. at 765 (*Ellerth*), at 807 (*Faragher*).

[22] Part of the Court's concern was the difficulty of drawing the line between quid pro quo and other harassment and the incentive that line created for plaintiff's lawyers to characterize comments as quid pro quo. 524 U.S. 752–53 (*Ellerth*).

made to workers by those with power to affect their opportunities already discriminate, because they strongly encourage a worker to act in the way that will cause the discriminating result.[23] If a serious quid pro quo threat itself alters the worker's terms of employment, the same theory that attributes a supervisor's act of firing to the employer should also attribute his threat to the employer.

Despite the logic of this analysis, the Court's approach is at least defensible. Many remarks suggesting a quid pro quo may be less than explicit or not obviously serious. For administrative bodies and courts, discerning the exact content of asserted threats and their degree of seriousness is elusive. Further, workers should be encouraged to go over the heads of abusive supervisors.[24] Thus, the Court's refusal to conclude that all quid pro quo remarks by supervisors should be attributed to employers represents one reasonable approach.

Abusive Remarks

Under Title VII, abusive remarks about a worker's religious identification are like similar remarks about race or gender. A supervisor in an early case referred to a worker as "the Jew-boy," "the kike," "the Christ-killer," and the "God-damn Jew."[25] Such abusive remarks, springing from a hostile animus, are indisputably unwelcome to the listener. Treating them as the basis for a hostile environment harassment claim is straightforward.[26] The same is true if abusive speech or other conduct, while not referring to religion, is designed

---

[23] That is, if the worker submits to a sexual act or reforms her apparent religion, in order to receive a promotion she otherwise deserves, she has suffered a wrong.

[24] The Court leaves open whether a single serious threat could itself "constitute discrimination in the terms or conditions of employment." 524 U.S. at 754 (*Ellerth*). Thomas Berg, Religious "Speech in the Workplace: Harassment or Protected Speech?" 22 *Harvard Journal of Law and Public Policy* 959, 968–69 (1989), is critical of the Court's treatment of unfulfilled quid pro quo threats, but suggests that a single serious threat might be sufficient to create a hostile environment. Were the Court so to hold, the practical effect of *Ellerth* for supervisor threats might be slight, but its conceptual approach would remain less than satisfactory. To make out a hostile environment claim, a plaintiff must establish that she felt the work atmosphere was seriously hostile. One can advance a straightforward claim of discrimination without any assertion about one's subjective feelings. In theory, a worker might yield to some quid pro quo threat without feeling the work environment was seriously hostile.

[25] *Compton v. Borden, Inc.*, 424 F. Supp. 157 (S.D. Ohio 1976). For a state court's conclusion that a supervisor's anti-Catholic remarks, had they been tolerated by an employer, could have constituted impermissible harassment, see *Vaughn v. AC Processing, Inc.*, 459 N.W.2d 627 (Ia. 1990).

[26] One might have a very expansive notion of speech the First Amendment protects that would cover such remarks in the working context, but one would then object to virtually any notion of hostile environment harassment based on speech.

to offend a worker and is a response to her religious convictions. In one state case, coworkers rubbed their genitals because they knew that, as a religious person, the complaining worker found that behavior offensive.[27] In an another case, coworkers made salacious comments about a man's wife, after he had expressed a religiously based objection to their crude sexual talk.[28]

The latter case presents a slight complexity in the notion that harassment be because of someone's religion. Finnemore, a fundamentalist Christian worker, said that coworkers had made sexually explicit comments about each other's wives in his presence. He had complained that such talk was offensive to his religion. His fellows responded by making his wife the target. Reversing the trial court, which had ruled that the comments were not religious, the Maine Supreme Judicial Court said, "A test for determining whether a comment is of a religious nature is whether it occurred *because of* an individual's religious beliefs or would not have occurred *but for* the individual's religion."[29]

The decision in Finnemore's favor was clearly correct. When a worker is singled out because of his religious views and suffers remarks that disturb him deeply because of his religion, he is harassed because of religion even if the remarks themselves lack religious content. But the court's exact "test" is either imprecise or flawed. It is unclear how it would apply if a fact finder concluded that the men would have acted similarly toward Finnemore if he had objected on nonreligious grounds.[30] The employer could then argue that the coworkers' comments were not *because* of Finnemore's *religion*; he could respond that he would not have complained *but for* his religion, so the coworkers' remarks did occur because of his religion. Although the court's general test is ambiguous on this point, religious harassment took place so long as the coworkers' taunting was based on Finnemore's complaint, and they knew his complaint had a religious basis.

Communicating Serious Ideas

The main complications for Title VII harassment arise over the communication of serious ideas. One example is remarks that are highly critical of a worker's religion but are not meant to be personally abusive—"I like you a

---

[27] *Golden v. G.B. Goldman Paper Co.*, 199 WL 157385 (E.D. Pa. Aug. 8, 1991).

[28] *Finnemore v. Burger Hydro-Electric Co.*, 645 A.2d 15 (Me. 1994).

[29] It. at 17.

[30] Suppose the fact finder, hearing testimony from the coworkers, reaches the following conclusion. They knew Finnemore was offended by their remarks and they knew his offense was religious because he said so, but they thought his whole attitude was ridiculous. They felt that real men indulge in crude humor, and anyone who complains about that is a pest who deserves to be ridden until he changes his attitude or gets off the job.

lot, but I am very sorry you are a Roman Catholic. The pope is the Antichrist, and all Catholics who do not convert are doomed to Hell." Although the speaker does not mean to humiliate, the listener may perceive such comments as putting her in a second-class or inferior status.[31] A related problem involves proselytizing that is not directly critical of anyone's religion but is so persistent it becomes deeply unsettling, creating a hostile environment.

Disturbing theological assertions and insistent proselytizing raise the special perplexity that with religion, much more than with race, gender, or national origin, the speech that offends the listener is offered out of the speaker's religious concern for her welfare. Further, the speaker may himself have a statutory accommodation claim under Title VII. Thus, the listener's claim not to be harassed runs up against the speaker's claim to freely express his views. Sorting out these threads is a major challenge. Decisions interpreting the federal law and similar state laws find liability, for the most part, in the situations for which I have suggested restriction would be appropriate.

The simplest situation involves speech by the employer. In *Meltebeke v. Bureau of Labor and Statistics*[32] the sole proprietor of a small painting business continually witnessed to his Christian faith, encouraged his worker to go to church, and chastised him for sinful activities. According to regulations of the state bureau, harassment on the basis of religion includes verbal conduct of a religious nature that creates a hostile or offensive working environment. The Oregon Supreme Court determined that the rule, in general, was appropriate and that it covered the circumstances of the case; the worker's lack of religious beliefs did not deprive him of protection against discrimination. However, the regulation could be applied only if the employer was aware that his actions were having a harmful effect; that condition had not been met, since Meltebeke's worker did not tell him that the continual preaching disturbed him.[33] Requiring that an employer know, or be told (he might be told but disbelieve), that his religious proselytizing has such a negative effect is a proper condition for liability.[34]

Employer speech was also involved in *Brown Transport Corp. v. Commonwealth*.[35] A lower state court indicated that Bible verses on paychecks and Christian content in a company newsletter were sufficient to sustain a

[31] I was struck at a conference on the place of religion in public life by a Jewish writer's intense feeling that remarks that Jews cannot be saved (unless they convert) demeaned her and other Jews. Awareness that the typical theological position of those making the statements is that no one except Christians (in their sense of Christians) can be saved did not assuage her feelings.

[32] 903 P.2d 351 (Ore. 1995).

[33] The court considered the rule and its application under the provisions of the Oregon constitution dealing with free exercise.

[34] Such a requirement would not be warranted if the speech were intentionally abusive toward a worker because of her religion.

[35] 578 A.2d 555 (Pa. Cmwlth. 1990).

finding by the Human Relations Commission that the employer had harassed Soffer, a Jewish employee.[36] Soffer had testified that these religious messages led him to worry about his job security and to believe that an employee would need to be Christian to be promoted into upper management.

Stopping a Christian message is hardly the way to assure non-Christians that the employer will not discriminate in hiring and promotions. Title VII, and similar state laws, should be interpreted to demand that employers who convey religious messages assure workers that they will not discriminate, but the law should not be taken to prevent all religious messages by employers. If it were so interpreted, employers would be able to convey controversial nonreligious ideas of every kind (except racist, sexist, and xenophobic ideas) but not religious ones. The *Brown Transport* court was right to conclude that a pattern of general messages to all workers *could* amount to religious harassment, but the expressions in that case were not sufficient to cause a reasonable worker to feel that the working environment was hostile or abusive.[37]

In a case involving a government supervisor, *Venters v. Delphi*,[38] the court considered a radio dispatcher's claim that her boss had given her religious lectures, had criticized her life of sin, had said that suicide would be preferable to continuing that life, had indicated that he would "trade" her if she did not play by God's rules, and had fired her because she did not conform. Assuming that the boss behaved in the coercive way that Venters claimed, she was denied rights under the Free Exercise and Establishment clauses, despite her failure to complain.[39] The court concluded correctly that the supervisor's comments had mixed elements of quid pro quo harassment with standard hostile environment harassment.[40] The supervisor had a First Amendment right to express his religious views but could not "require his subordinate to conform her conduct and her life to his notion of 'God's rule book.'"[41]

[36] Id. at 562. One might characterize this conclusion as dictum. The court also concluded that Soffer should have been accommodated, and that he was fired as a consequence of his complaining.

[37] Perhaps Soffer should have been entitled to some accommodation, such as getting a special paycheck without the religious message, and Brown Transport may have been at fault for firing Soffer because he complained; but the finding of harassment reached too far.

By comparison, this was a much milder form of religious expression than mandatory religious meetings, which the *Townley* Co. court did not think were barred by Title VII. I suggested in chapter 18 that that conclusion was mistaken. The court there did not consider a claim of harassment, although an atheist's request for an accommodation to be excused came close to an assertion that he felt harassed.

[38] 123 F.3d 956 (7th Cir. 1997).

[39] She "had a right under the free exercise clause to work for the City of Delphi without being compelled to submit herself to the religious scrutiny of her superior." Id. at 971. That constitutional claim, of course, would not be available against a private employer.

[40] See Eileen Goldsmith, "God's House, or the Law's," 108 *Yale Law Journal* 1433 (1999).

[41] *Venters*, note 38 supra, at 977.

Four Questions

Having had a look at the basic law of harassment and some representative cases, we need to examine four general questions. (1) How exactly does it matter whether a claim is treated as one of harassment, rather than ordinary discrimination or accommodation? (2) What counts as religious for purposes of religious harassment? (3) Against a claim that it harasses, does religious speech of employers and workers fare better than other speech? (4) How should the law be understood to resolve conflicts between sincere speech and felt offense?

Harassment, Ordinary Discrimination, or Accommodation

In some instances, it may be hard to decide just what kind of claim is made or should be upheld. When an employer establishes mandatory Christian meetings, a Jewish worker might say that creates a hostile environment, or that she should be accommodated by being excused, or that the employer has engaged in ordinary discrimination against non-Christians. The difference between these three characterizations might seem like legal mumbo-jumbo; after all, is not the key question whether the worker must attend or not?

However, as the last chapter explains, there prove to be significant differences in what the worker must show and in the right remedy. She is "harassed" only if the meetings make her feel she is in a hostile environment and if a reasonable non-Christian (or a reasonable Jew) would have that reaction. To gain an accommodation, she must show that she has an objection based on her religious convictions or identity.[42] She *could* make a claim of ordinary discrimination without showing the requisites either for accommodation or for harassment. The usual remedy for ordinary discrimination is to stop a practice; for accommodation, excusing the complaining worker is sufficient; and that remedy may also be adequate if a few workers feel harassed.

What Is "Religious"?

In chapter 18, we examined the EEOC guidelines, which adopt a very expansive definition of religion,[43] treating as "religious" ethical beliefs held with the strength of traditional religious views. I argued that this concept of reli-

---

[42] She *could* have a right to an accommodation without perceiving a hostile environment, and conceivably someone might experience a hostile environment without having an objection to participation based on religious belief or practice.

[43] The introduction to the guidelines says: "The Guidelines do not confine the definition of religious practices to theistic concepts or to traditional religious beliefs. The definition also includes moral and ethical beliefs. Under the Guidelines, a belief is religious not because a

gion is too broad for purposes of typical accommodations; it is also inapt for claims of harassment.

Imagine that a recent college graduate decides to see what work in the logging industry is like. She quickly reveals to her companions that she thinks natural forests should be kept pristine. This opinion proves to be politically incorrect within the logging community, and supervisors and coworkers ridicule her for her environmental views. If the graduate complains of the abusive treatment she receives, must an employer's representative decide whether environmentalism is a cause for which she feels a religious-like commitment, and perhaps, whether coworkers should have been aware of that? The application of Title VII should not rest on such uncertain judgments. Such a very broad definition of religion is even more strikingly mistaken for harassment than it is for accommodation.

We can finally reject the EEOC approach only if we see a preferable alternative. More than one alternative is preferable; but in chapter 8, I defended a position that courts should use an analogical approach to conceptualizing religion, one that asks judges to start from the characteristics of undoubted and paradigm instances of religion and to determine how closely an arguable instance of religion resembles these.[44] Under that approach, many conscientious ethical stances and expressions do not count as religious for purposes of Title VII.[45]

Religious Speech and Other Speech

Under present law, does religious speech receive more protection than other speech and, if so, is that appropriate? This turns out to be a multipart question, aspects of which we have reviewed in the previous chapter.

One crucial distinction is between the government as employer and private employers. The government itself has no right to engage in religious speech; its doing so violates the Establishment Clause. Since the government, as the government, can take positions on most other subjects, such as the health benefits of exercise or the wisdom of protecting the environment, the government has less right to engage in religious speech than other forms of speech. However, as the president's guidelines discussed in chapter

---

religious group professes that belief, but because the individual sincerely holds that belief with the strength of traditional religious views."

[44] See also Kent Greenawalt, "The Constitutional Concept of Religion," 72 *California Law Review* 753 (1984), and "Five Questions About Religion Judges Are Afraid to Ask," in Nancy L. Rosenblum, ed., *Obligations of Citizenship and Demands of Faith* 196, 206–24 (Princeton: Princeton University Press, 2000).

[45] However, one might argue that since initial application will be by employers, a simpler approach is called for under Title VII.

18 provide, government employees should have rights of religious speech as extensive as their rights to engage in speech about (other) subjects of public concern.[46]

When we turn to private employers, we need to consider the rights of speech of employers and workers. The last chapter has proposed that employers' missions should be treated equally, that employers should have as much right to engage in religious as other speech.[47]

The rights of workers to speak present further complications. When a worker seeks an accommodation, a claim to engage in religious speech is more powerful than a claim to engage in other speech, which the employer is under no legal requirement to accommodate.[48] Such a distinction is defensible as an aspect of a statutory scheme preventing discrimination, assuring workplace equality, and protecting religious exercise.

When the employer is considering, because of Title VII, whether to stop harassing speech, the relevance of the subject of speech is crucially different. Once the law tells employers to suppress or restrict worker speech, the Constitution is involved; Congress can no more tell employers to suppress nonreligious speech than religious speech. Thus, the worker who engages in nonreligious speech that might harass on the basis of religion (or another forbidden category) is protected by general rights of free speech. When speech rights of workers are offered as a defense to harassment claims, religious speech should have the same protection as other speech.

Resolving Conflicts of Speech and Offense

My views about how conflicts of speech and felt religious offense should be resolved under Title VII largely replicate what I have suggested about desirable restrictions; but we face nuances that we have not yet addressed. As we have seen, the speech that disturbs other workers because of their religion may or may not be religious speech, and religious speech that disturbs workers may or may not do so because of their religion;[49] but a significant proportion of speech that offends because of a religion is religious speech.

---

[46] However, the employees cannot engage in religious speech when they would seem to speak for the government, and they cannot engage in religious harassment. (Nonreligious speech can generate harassment on religious grounds, but religious speech is more likely to do so).

[47] One could reasonably argue that at least large employers should have no rights of religious speech, that in order to promote religious equality in the workplace, large employers (or employers whose stock is mainly owned by the public) should be like the government. The present law draws no such distinction between large and smaller employers, and I am inclined to think it should not; but perhaps size and public ownership should be taken into account in resolving particular cases.

[48] The worker engaging in religious speech is directly protected by Title VII.

[49] Thus, in *Finnemore* the court treated crude sexual talk about a worker's wife as harassment because of his religion; and in *Wilson* the court treated a woman's religiously motivated

Dominantly abusive speech that harasses because of religion closely resembles much racist and sexist speech, and has little to recommend it. Even if some implicit theological propositions may be lurking in the background—some of those hurling epithets at Jews may suppose that God has condemned them for their role in Christ's death[50]—such speech does not deserve protection in the workplace setting,[51] if a speaker is aware that those she abuses will be among her listeners.

The difficult problems arise when the speaker sincerely expresses religious (or other) convictions in a nonabusive way. When a coworker's speech is directed at an individual, the key is that the listener should be able to stop unwanted speech.[52] The speaker may sincerely want to save her listener, but if the listener is deeply offended, or highly annoyed, she should be able to prevent future speech of that sort that is directed at her. No one has a right of free speech to direct remarks to an unwilling listener. Although some workers may hesitate to say they do not want to receive messages, especially if their supervisor is speaking, employers should not restrict sincere speech because some workers *might* be offended. For harassment law to give proper respect to free expression, the worker who feels harassed needs to say so.

Nondirected worker speech present the greatest difficulties. A worker, without seeking to offend, engages in speech that is not directed at any particular coworkers, as with Wilson's antiabortion button; or she speaks directly to coworkers who do not object, and is overheard by other workers who do object; or she directs her speech at a group of workers, only some of whom object. So long as most listeners are not offended, and the speaker observes minimal politeness, Title VII should be taken to require that members of an audience tolerate such speech.

Communications which, singly, may be constitutionally protected, but which together create a seriously hostile environment, raise a complex problem.[53] To use an illustration of Thomas Berg's, one sign that "Jesus Saves"

---

wearing of an antiabortion button as religious speech, but concluded that the reasons why other workers were disturbed did not have to do with their religious convictions.

[50] According to New Testament accounts, Jesus was put to death by the Romans, but with the encouragement of some Jewish leaders.

[51] For a contrary view by the scholar who has most powerfully defended the importance of free speech protections in the workplace, see Eugene Volokh, "Freedom of Speech and Workplace Harassment," 39 *UCLA Law Review* 1791, 1812–14 (1992).

[52] See, e.g., Kent Greenawalt, *Fighting Words* 86–91 (Princeton: Princeton University Press, 1995); Berg, note 24 supra, at 985–86; Volokh, note 51 supra, at 1863–67. I do not mean that the present law gives the worker the right to stop such speech if it is not connected to a statutory category of discrimination. I mean only that the employer may provide this protection and that if a law required the employer to do so, it would not violate the First Amendment.

[53] When comments that alone would be protected yield evidence about the significance of unprotected behavior or add to the force of a substantial amount of unprotected behavior, I

may not bother non-Christians, but if such signs are all over the workplace, their reactions may differ.[54] The position most favorable to speech is that individually protected acts cannot be cumulated into an unprotected combination,[55] but I believe that approach is mistaken. Whether acts are protected depends partly on the strength of the government's interest in restriction, and that interest can increase as the acts multiply. If the acts together have effects that are harmful enough, they may lose protection that they would otherwise have.

This point is easiest to make when an individual, or the same group of individuals, engages in repeated acts that offend. If four Christians in a van continually talk among themselves about how atheists are damned, after their colleague has explained that this bothers him, they fail to exhibit adequate respect for his feelings. What was initially insensitive has become rude and unfeeling. The character of the remarks has altered.

Cumulation of actions is more troublesome if unconnected individuals act in similar ways.[56] Nevertheless, cumulation could still be appropriate, partly because individual workers are typically aware what other workers are doing, so the nature of the acts of each is affected by his knowledge of what others do; but more importantly, because the main remedy for harassment is future restriction, not punishment. Workers whose comments cause distress are being told to stop in light of the harm it causes.

Although otherwise protected expression may become unprotected because a number of similar expressions cause serious distress, administrators and judges should be very hesitant to reach the conclusion that otherwise protected comments should be restricted. The values of free religious expression should not be lightly disregarded.

My combination of positions opens me up to the following attack.

Whatever you say about protecting expression, judges and administrators will find harassment too easily and will impose remedies that are much too sweeping. Indeed, if the harm is caused by fifteen independent comments, those fashioning a remedy will have no way to determine what to allow and what to restrict, other than restricting everything. Further, employers worried about harassment claims will comfortably forbid all expressions that *might* in combina-

---

assume they may count in a finding of a hostile environment. See Greenawalt, note 52 supra, at 95–96.

[54] Berg, note 24 supra, at 991. One cannot argue that since an employer by himself can freely restrict the speech of workers, none of these individual acts of expression warrants protection. Once the government prohibition figures in the employer's response to expression, the Constitution is involved.

[55] See Volokh, note 51 supra, at 1812–16.

[56] See Berg, note 24 supra, at 992–93, distinguishing cumulation by the same individual from that of several unconnected workers.

tion harass. The end result of your flexible approach will be a drastic overrestriction of religious speech. Therefore, the only sensible approach is the strict one of never allowing otherwise protected expressions to cumulate into violations of Title VII.[57]

This defense of a strict approach is grounded on the realities of decisions by employers, administrators, and judges, and its degree of persuasiveness depends on a close acquaintance with behavior that is not reflected in appellate opinions. Short of convincing evidence that the approach I suggest is unworkable, I would not embrace the position that when multiple instances of otherwise protected expression overwhelm those with a different religious view or identity, the victims are left without recourse.[58]

[57] These are my words, but I believe they capture part of Professor Volokh's basis for his position. See, e.g., Eugene Volokh, "What Does 'Hostile Work Environment' Harassment Law Restrict?" 85 *Georgetown Law Journal* 627, 638–46 (1997), and "Thinking Ahead About Freedom of Speech and Hostile Work Environment Harassment," 17 *Berkeley Journal of Employment and Labor Law* 305, 310–12 (1996). See also Volokh, note 51 supra, at 1809–12.

[58] My position here represents a modest shift from my previous view that "a finding of hostile working environment cannot be based exclusively or dominantly on protected remarks." Greenawalt, note 52 supra, at 95. I then did not explicitly address the possibility that remarks that might individually be protected could become unprotected in combination, but what I wrote implicitly treated such an approach as inappropriate.

CHAPTER 20

Rights of Religious Associations: Selectivity

Religious groups are not quite like others when it comes to discrimination; this chapter explores these differences. Associations that are undeniably religious, such as churches, synagogues, and mosques, may choose their members and staff on grounds that would be improper for a commercial company. Here we shall inquire how these religious associations should regard such choices and how far government should regulate them. The law on this subject includes explicit statutory treatment, limitations on statutory coverage drawn from fundamental principles, and constitutional rights. Among the questions we shall examine is how the treatment of religious associations should compare with that of "ordinary" nonreligious associations and expressive associations.

SHOULD RELIGIOUS GROUPS BE ABLE TO DISCRIMINATE?

Use of Religious Criteria for Membership and Hiring

In accepting members and hiring personnel, churches and other religious organizations may discriminate on grounds that other organizations should eschew. Matters are simplest for straightforward religious discrimination. Most religious organizations restrict membership to those who express adherence to the group's doctrines or practices. Christian churches often have confirmation classes leading up to affirmations of faith. An applicant who, with extraordinary candor, repeatedly said, "I like the social advantages of this church, but all its beliefs and practices are utter foolishness, worthless even if taken symbolically or metaphorically," would probably not be admitted to membership.[1] In most Christian churches, scrutiny is hardly rigorous. People are taken at their word, and many prospective members, as well as clergy, may not believe standard doctrines in their literal sense. But some religious standards for membership do exist.

---

[1] My sense, based partly on what my sister Ann has told me about a United Church of Christ where she served as a pastor, is that some churches would leave it up to the individual to decide whether to join; but not many churches ever deal with people who want to join *and* are so frank in their dismissal of the church's activities.

Religious organizations also have employees. We may here draw a distinction between positions of religious leadership and ordinary positions, without worrying for the moment just where this line falls.[2] For positions of leadership, all religious associations employ religious criteria, and many do so as well for ordinary jobs.

How should church members respond if someone says, "You know, religious discrimination is generally wrong; perhaps you should not be discriminating on religious grounds for ordinary jobs."? Although the members might answer that hiring their own members helps maintain the right religious atmosphere,[3] they should ask themselves whether the religious affiliations of ordinary workers really affect the atmosphere of their community. Thoughtful members of a church will ultimately evaluate the desirability of religious discrimination largely from a religious perspective, deciding what practices fit best with the religious aspirations of the organization.

The state's perspective is different. It asks whether a general policy against nondiscrimination should give way when religious organizations are concerned. No one doubts that religious organizations should be able to employ religious criteria in choosing leaders and that they may condition membership on a form of adherence to beliefs and practices. But it is a serious issue whether the government should override claims of religious groups that religious considerations support their discrimination for ordinary jobs and, if so, whether officials are capable of drawing the necessary distinctions between positions of leadership and ordinary jobs.

Use of Criteria of Race and Gender in Membership and Hiring

Various religious organizations use criteria other than religious belief, for membership and staff, that would be unacceptable for ordinary business enterprises. Notably, many Christian churches have practiced racial discrimination; Orthodox Jews, Roman Catholics, and most Muslim groups do not allow women to be clergy. Other standards of selection concern activities that a religion deems to violate God's will. More than a few Christians believe that heterosexual intercourse outside of marriage and homosexual acts

[2] Clerics and others who participate in leading church activities count as leaders. Those responsible for the orderliness of church buildings count as ordinary employees. How to classify paid members of a choir would be more arguable.

[3] They may also wish to help members by providing jobs for them. If the general principle of nondiscrimination on grounds of religion is sound, most employers should not aim to benefit members of their own faith in hiring decisions; churches should examine that particular basis for favoring members in light of the general policy against it. Members might decide that the policy itself is unsound or that churches have some special reason to benefit their own, such as encouraging adherence to the faith.

are sinful. A church may refuse to hire leaders who publicly disobey God's laws about sexual behavior. Such disapproval of particular acts however, cannot explain discrimination based on race or gender; it is not a sin to be a woman or a member of any particular race.[4] Church members who examine such discrimination thoughtfully may decide that they have perpetuated cultural stereotypes that lack any genuine religious foundation, or they may reaffirm that God does not intend women to perform the Mass or wants members of different races separated.[5]

How should the state react if religious bodies engage in racial and gender discrimination? We need to look at three possibilities: (1) the discrimination is closely connected to a group's religious beliefs and practices; (2) the discrimination does not appear to be closely connected in this way; (3) the group itself has a policy against such discrimination.

If churches are to be left free to choose as they wish, it is not because government has no interest in ending such discrimination based on race and gender. The government's interest flows from the central place churches have in many communities and from the way their understanding of roles can radiate into the rest of social life. The reason why religious bodies should have latitude to discriminate is that the government's enforcing standards for members and officers would unacceptably encroach on religious affairs. The government cannot tell the Nation of Islam ("Black Muslims") to admit whites; it cannot tell a white supremacist church to admit blacks. It cannot tell the Roman Catholic Church it must have women priests. Religious organizations should have the liberty to carry out their beliefs in decisions about membership and leaders.

Part of the problem here is practical. In ordinary circumstances, a person who is hired because the law forbids discrimination can do effective work and realize most of the job's benefits. Not too many people would wish to join a church whose members take a person like them only because the state forces them to do so; and what status would a woman priest have if few members of a church acknowledge that she possesses valid religious authority?[6] But more important than these practical impediments is the total inappropriateness of the state's dictating that religious organizations carry on their internal life against their firmly settled religious beliefs and practices.

---

[4] I put aside here any fringe groups who do regard being a member of some race as a reflection of sin.

[5] For many years, leaders of the Dutch Reformed Church in South Africa supported the practice of apartheid in that country on theological grounds.

[6] However, if the members themselves are divided, she may function effectively for those members who think she does have religious authority; and the law might, thus, strengthen the hand of some members who are not in positions of leadership.

A privilege to discriminate becomes more debatable when religious bodies self-consciously engage in forms of discrimination that seem to outsiders, even after explanation, to bear no significant relation to the group's religious beliefs and practices.[7] But having secular officials judge whether purported religious reasons suffice to sustain practices of discrimination would threaten religious liberty and separation of church and state. Thus, churches and similar bodies[8] should often be able to discriminate even when others perceive little basis for their doing so.

A religious body's right to discriminate is least strong if it has announced that it does not discriminate on certain grounds, and an individual claims that she has suffered discrimination on just those grounds. For example, if a woman asserts that a church has denied her a position as pastor because of her gender, the state could be in the position of enforcing a policy in which the church concurs.

For religious groups, however, the problem of identifying violations and enforcing nondiscrimination is complicated. In a country that accepts both free exercise and nonestablishment of religion, the state should not dictate who leads organizations whose vision and purposes are substantially transcendent. To determine whether a group has discriminated, officials must make inquiries and factual findings; they must decide (unless the discrimination involves blatant exclusion) whether an applicant would probably have been hired if standard criteria for the job had been used. How can officials be confident that a woman was not hired as a minister because she was a woman rather than because of a subtle sense that her spiritual qualities were less stellar than those of the man chosen in her place. Secular officials are not fit to decide who is most competent to provide spiritual leadership.

The best resolution of two variations in which discrimination is more transparent (or appears to be) is more arguable. In the first variation, if a local church announces that it has refused to hire a woman in contravention of the stated, and controlling, policy of its denomination,[9] courts still should not order that she be made the minister; but monetary damages might be an acceptable remedy for discrimination that unambiguously violates both the law and church policy. In a second variation, a local church continually passes over highly qualified women. Since people long habituated to male clergy might unconsciously suppose that women typically lack some central element for

---

[7] Many Christian churches in the country's history have discriminated on racial grounds even though doing so had little support from religious doctrines they accepted.

[8] This conclusion may not cover bodies like the National Council of Churches that represent many religious organizations together.

[9] I specify "controlling" because an organization might recognize substantial local autonomy; the central denomination might recommend policies that would not bind local churches.

spiritual leadership, or are unlikely to be forceful preachers,[10] officials might still have difficulty concluding that self-conscious discrimination has taken place. Because of the autonomy desirable for religious organizations, recovery of damages should not be granted for anything falling short of self-conscious discrimination.[11] Although, viewed in isolation, a legal remedy might be acceptable if a local church concedes that it is violating broader church policy or it acts too blatantly to leave any doubt, local bodies will usually not make their disregard of binding church guidelines obvious. Thus, legislatures should not bother to adopt a ban that covers only such discrimination.

In contrast with how they choose leaders, most religious groups are comparatively unselective about membership. If prospective members follow a course of study and commit themselves, no one makes a searching inquiry of their honesty or spiritual qualities.[12] If African Americans who apply for membership are rebuffed, no one can doubt that racial discrimination has transpired. At present, becoming a member in a church organization is not in itself an interest the law protects.[13] Although forcing local churches of a national denomination that has a binding policy against discrimination to take particular members would be less troublesome than forcing them to take particular clergy, the state's interference with church autonomy might still be too great,[14] and probably it is better to leave this problem in the hands of the denomination itself.

Decisions about "ordinary" employees, such as secretaries and custodians, are far further from the core of religious practice than are choices about members and leaders. We can imagine circumstances in which a standard of race or gender might seem important for such jobs. A religious group dedicated to the purity of one race might wish not to hire a member of an "inferior" race; a group with a strong conviction that women belong at home might want to hire only men.[15] However, allowing all religious groups to hire ordinary workers on any grounds they wish would give them too sweeping a

---

[10] An academic analogue is (or used to be) worry that a woman may not be an effective teacher of large classes.

[11] Even when a pattern of discrimination is clear, a court may be uncertain whether any particular woman would have been hired in its absence, but it can conclude that a woman was not fairly considered.

[12] In *this sense* of unselectivity, religions that discourage converts, as do many Jewish groups, may not differ from those that reach out to acquire new members, as do most Christian churches.

[13] However, a court could be concerned about membership if control of property or some other tangible consequence turned on whether someone was a member.

[14] Since membership, by itself, carries no economic reward, it is hard to conceive what would be appropriate money damages.

[15] For these applicants *not* to be excludable on grounds of belief (rather than race or gender), we need to suppose that the first applicant actually accepts the group's racial views and that the woman agrees she should be at home, but desperately needs to support her children.

privilege to discriminate when they would rarely have religious reasons for doing so. Were the law to forbid all but religious discrimination in respect to ordinary jobs, some religious groups would suffer interference with religiously motivated choices to discriminate by race or gender, but few religious bodies in the United States assert religious bases to discriminate on these grounds for ordinary jobs.[16] A better approach is adopting a general ban on such discrimination, but granting a privilege to religious bodies that can present a plausible connection between those kinds of discrimination and their religious beliefs and practices.

This approach does require officials to consider whether religious claims are genuine and to distinguish ordinary jobs from positions of leadership; but administrators could largely accept what groups say about their reasons to discriminate for ordinary jobs.[17] Someone might object that any such prohibition would have little point, since churches could cook up any old justification for their discrimination; but the self-examination and publicity that such an approach would demand of religious groups could have an effect. Many people who comfortably engage in racial or gender discrimination would dislike announcing that they do so and trying to explain how their religious beliefs and practices support them.

The Law of Discrimination for Religious Bodies

The law that governs discrimination by religious bodies mixes statutory prescriptions and constitutional principles.

Employment Discrimination Statutes

The basic federal law against employment discrimination, Title VII, covers religious bodies, except for an explicit exemption and an "implicit" exception courts have developed.

The statutory exemption in Title VII, initially allowing religious discrimination, by religious associations and educational institutions, only in respect to religious activities, was extended in 1972 to cover all activities.[18] This

---

[16] The interference would be more frequent if the general rule of nondiscrimination included sexual preference and marital status, because religious groups might understandably feel they should not have to hire, even for ordinary jobs, people they regard as committed to a life of sin.

[17] The approach of forbidding *all discrimination* by race and gender for ordinary jobs also requires drawing the ordinary job-leader line, if the privilege to discriminate for leaders is greater.

[18] The ordinary rules against discrimination do not apply to religious associations and educational institutions "with respect to the employment of individuals of a particular religion" to perform their work. 42 U.S.C. § 2000e-1. The relevant history is traced in Scott D. McClure,

exemption was challenged as an impermissible establishment of religion by a former building engineer, that is, a janitor, in a gymnasium run by organizations of The Church of Jesus Christ of Latter-day Saints. He had been fired because he failed to qualify for a temple recommendation certifying his good standing in the Mormon Church.[19] The Supreme Court decided that allowing religious organizations to use religious criteria for employment in their secular nonprofit activities was constitutional.[20] The majority offered the controversial, flawed, ground that the law was all right because discrimination was by the religious group, not the state.[21] All the justices united behind another rationale: because the practice of state officials deciding which nonprofit activities by employees are religious, and which are not, would interfere with the autonomy of religious organizations, granting a broad exemption for all nonprofit activities was justified.[22] Thus, the Mormons did not have to show any particular religious need to fire their janitor.

The justices by no means decided that the earlier distinction between religious and nonreligious activities was itself unconstitutional. As two concurring opinions noted, any exemption of this sort for religious groups interferes with the freedom of employees to choose their own religious commitments without fear of losing their jobs.[23] On balance, a narrower privilege limited to positions that have arguable religious significance seems the preferable policy.[24] Groups should be required to make some minimal showing that a

---

"Note, Religious Preferences in Employment Decisions: How Far May Religious Organizations Go?" 1990 *Duke Law Journal* 587, 592–93. For an educational institution to qualify, not any religious affiliation will suffice; it must have "extremely close ties to organized religions." *Siegel v. Truett-McConnell College, Inc.*, 13 F. Supp 2d 1335, 1340 (N.D. Ga. 1994). See *E.E.O.C.V. Kamehamelia School/Bishop Estate*, 990 F.2d 458, 460–64 (9th Cir. 1993).

[19] *Corporation of the Presiding Bishop of The Church of Jesus Christ of Latter-day Saints v. Amos*, 483 U.S. 327 (1987).

[20] For the suggestion that religious discrimination for some for-profit activities should be constitutionally permissible, indeed constitutionally protected under the Free Exercise Clause, see McClure, note 18 supra, at 600–606.

[21] The flaw was failing to see that the privilege to discriminate is limited to religious groups. If only some religious groups could discriminate for secular activities, that would "establish" those groups in relation to groups denied the privilege. If all religious groups, but no others, are given the privilege, that would "establish" the religious groups *unless* the government had some good reason to give them the privilege.

[22] For an argument that mandatory collective bargaining may interfere with religious practice, see Kathleen A. Brody, "Religious Organizations and Mandatory Collective Bargaining under Federal and State Labor Laws," 49 *Villanova Law Review* 77 (2004).

[23] *Amos*, note 19 supra, at 340–41 (Brennan, J., concurring), id. at 347 (O'Connor, J. concurring). John H. Garvey, "Churches and the Free Exercise of Religion," 4 *Notre Dame Journal of Law, Ethics, and Public Policy* 567 (1990), develops a general argument that freedom of church groups should be favored over freedom for individual members.

[24] Nancy L. Rosenblum, "*Amos*: Religious Autonomy and the Moral Uses of Pluralism," in Nancy L. Rosenblum, ed., *Obligations of Citizenship and Demands of Faith: Religious Accommodation in Pluralist Democracies* 165–95 (Princeton: Princeton University Press, 2000).

position has religious significance. But the Court rightly regarded the decision by Congress to create a more absolute privilege as an acceptable method to accommodate the free exercise autonomy of religious bodies.

Present antidiscrimination statutes do not provide any explicit exemption for discrimination based on gender or race. The law does allow hiring on the basis of religion or gender (but not race) if that is a bona fide qualification; but it is highly doubtful if this alone would warrant excluding women from the clergy. One cannot make gender a bona fide qualification simply by asserting a strong ideological reason to restrict a position to males. One must show more objective reasons to hire a man, as when the job is to model men's clothing or play the part of George Washington.[25]

Courts have consistently declined to apply antidiscrimination statutes to the hiring of clergy and some other leadership positions, either discovering an implicit "ministerial exception" or ruling directly that application would violate the First Amendment. Courts adopting the first approach follow the guide of the Supreme Court, which refused in 1979 to apply the National Labor Relations Act requirement of collective bargaining to parochial schools, construing the law not to apply in order to avoid the risk of infringing the Constitution.[26] The Colorado Supreme Court adopted the second approach in *Van Osdol v. Vogt*,[27] an intriguing case in which the court de-

---

[25] See *Diaz v. Pan American World Airways, Inc.*, 442 F.2d 385 (5th Cir. 1971). In *Pime v. Loyola University of Chicago*, 585 F. Supp. 435 (1984), aff'd, 803 F.2d 351 (7th Cir. 1986), the court said hiring Jesuits in preference to other candidates for tenure was reasonably necessary to the university's operations. See Robert John Araujo, S. J. "The Harvest Is Plentiful but the Laborers Are Few: Hiring Practices and Religiously Affiliated Universities," 30 *University of Richmond Law Review* 713, 733–34 (1996).

[26] *National Labor Relations Board v. Catholic Bishop of Chicago*, 440 U.S. 490 (1979). See *Equal Employment Opportunity Comm'n v. The Catholic University of America*, 83 F.3d 455 (D.C. Cir. 1996) (complaint of nun denied tenure in department of canon law); *Larsen v. Kirkham*, 499 F. Supp. 960 (D. Utah 1990) (complaint of teachers of secular subjects at religiously affiliated university); *Silo v. CHW Medical Foundation*, 27 Cal. 4th 1097 (Cal. 2002) (complaint of employee at religious-affiliated health care organization about dismissal for religious speech). For a case holding that *Employment Division v. Smith* did not eliminate the ministerial exemption of Title VII, see *Gellington v. Christian Methodist Episcopal Church, Inc.*, 203 F.3d 1299 (11th Cir. 2000). For a discussion of many of the cases and a skeptical appraisal of the "ministerial exception," see Marci A. Hamilton, *God vs. The Gavel: Religion and the Rule of Law* 189–99 (New York: Cambridge University Press, 2005). See also Janet S. Belcove-Shalin, "Ministerial Exception and Title VII Claims: Case Law Grid Analysis," 2 *Nevada Law Journal* 86 (2002). University hiring practices are considered by Robert John Araujo, S. J., note 25 supra, at 713.

[27] 908 P.2d 1172 (Colo. 1996). See also *Minker v. Baltimore Annual Conference of United Methodist Church*, 894 F.3d 1354 (D.C. Cir. 1990) (age discrimination suit by minister barred, but not contract claim); *Dayton Christian Schools, Inc. v. Ohio Civil Rights Comm'n*, 766 F.2d 932 (6th Cir. 1985) (school could fire teacher for failing to follow "Biblical Chain-of-Command"); *McClure v. The Salvation Army*, 460 F.2d 553 (1972) (sex discrimination claim by minister barred by First Amendment).

clared that applying Title VII to prevent revocation of a minister's license would violate both religion clauses. *Van Osdol* well indicates crucial issues and various alternative resolutions.

Van Osdol was granted a novitiate minister's license in the Colorado branch of the United Churches of Religious Science and was given permission to start a new church. A month later, she informed the Ecclesiastical Committee that Vogt, a prominent church leader, had abused her sexually two decades earlier when he was married to her mother, and further that he had, she believed, abused a parishioner and several employees of the organization. Vogt denied the charges, and requested a church investigation. Two months later the Ecclesiastical Committee revoked Van Osdol's license and rescinded her permission to open the church. Van Osdol made thirteen different claims, but the ones the state supreme court reviewed involved the revocation and recision. She argued that these were in retaliation for her assertions about sexual harassment by Vogt, and were therefore barred by Title VII, which prohibits retaliation for reporting illegal employment practices.[28]

The court ruled that a regular court could not try these claims consistent with the religion clauses. Choosing clergy is an ecclesiastical matter; a "church's decision of who to hire as a minister necessarily involves religious doctrine."[29] The court quoted an opinion from the U.S. Court of Appeals of the District of Columbia: "'We cannot imagine an area of inquiry less suited to a temporal court for decision; evaluation of the "gifts" and "graces" of a minister must be left to ecclesiastic institutions.'"[30] A court could not even get involved to the extent of determining whether purportedly religious reasons for a church's decision were a "pretext." Drawing from other cases, the court assumed that a hearing to determine whether purported religious reasons were really a pretext would be appropriate if a parochial school had dismissed a lay teacher, where an employee might "prove his or her claim without resort to analysis of church doctrine. This may be possible in a case involving . . . a choir director, a church secretary, an organist, or other employees of a religious organization, but it is not possible in a case involving a choice of a minister."[31]

Addressing the argument that *Employment Division v. Smith*[32] eliminated any free exercise exceptions to general laws, the court pointed out that applying an antidiscrimination law to a church just as if it were any other

[28] 42 U.S.C. § 2000e-3.

[29] *Van Osdol*, note 27 supra, at 1128.

[30] Id., quoting *Minker v. Baltimore Annual Conference of United Methodist Church*, 894 F.2d 1354, 1357 (D.C. Cir. 1990).

[31] Id. at 1129.

[32] 494 U.S. 872 (1990).

organization would involve judging the belief system of the church, just what *Smith* aimed to avoid.[33] The court found further support for its position in *Serbian Eastern Orthodox Diocese v. Milivojevich*,[34] which, as we saw in chapter 16, held that internal church decisions are immune from judicial review.[35] As that case had rejected an "arbitrariness" exception to the rule against judicial involvement, so too should courts reject any "fraud" or "collusion" exceptions to such involvement.[36]

The court's opinion regrettably detaches itself from the facts of the case. Van Osdol had made startling accusations against one of the most influential and best-known leaders of her church. If members of the Ecclesiastical Committee believed her, revocation of her license was certainly an unjust act. If they thought she was probably lying, or was confused about the truth, they understandably did not consider her a suitable person to be leading a local church.[37] To sustain a "pretext" argument, Van Osdol would have needed to show that the members thought she was probably telling the truth. None of this apparently had *anything* to do with church doctrine.[38] The real issue was not about inquiry into doctrine, but how far courts should inquire about the sincerity of church officials and the inner workings of their decision-making bodies.

A sensible approach, when a clergy position is involved, is that a plaintiff should need to present powerful evidence of "pretext" or "fraud" before any civil inquiry takes place. For instance, suppose Van Osdol had a tape of the committee meeting or correspondence among members to some such effect: "Of course, Van Osdol is telling the truth, but this is an embarrassment to the church and we need to sweep it under the rug by getting rid of her." Such evidence should allow her to go forward. If it appears that resolution would come down to assessing sincerity on an uncertain record, courts should not get involved. Had the judges been more sensitive to what civil courts could, and could not, do, they would not have placed such an absolute bar on Van Osdol's claim, though her prospects for success under a correct approach would still have been daunting.

---

[33] Id. at 1130–31.

[34] 426 U.S. 696 (1976).

[35] The court treated the case as part of an Establishment Clause analysis, id. at 1131–32, but it is relevant for both clauses.

[36] Id. at 1133.

[37] If they were uncertain where the truth lay after investigation, they *might* reasonably have given the benefit of the doubt to Vogt, their longtime associate.

[38] If the committee had said that according to their religion, no one should criticize a leader, however accurate the accusations, that stance would invoke doctrine. But a court should not assume such an unusual stance before a religious group adopts it.

Constitutional Freedom of Association

Two important decisions about the freedom of nonreligious associations to choose members can help us reflect on how constitutional freedoms of religious groups compare with those of "ordinary" associations and ideological or expressive associations. Religious groups have powerful bases for special treatment in certain respects, but many privileges they receive should also extend to nonreligious ideological associations.

Limits on Freedom of Nonreligious Associations:
Roberts v. United States Jaycees and Boy Scouts of America v. Dale

Roberts v. United States Jaycees[39] exemplifies the Supreme Court's acceptance of a legislative decision to restrain discriminatory choice. The Jaycees are a nonprofit corporation founded as the Junior Chamber of Commerce. Prior to *Roberts*, national bylaws restricted full membership to young men, although women could be associate members and participate in most activities. The Minnesota Supreme Court had determined that a state law forbidding discrimination in places of public accommodation covered the Jaycees and thus, within the state, made the exclusion of women illegal.[40] The Jaycees argued that they had a federal constitutional right, based on freedom of association, to select according to their bylaws.

Justice Brennan, writing the Court's opinion for five justices,[41] distinguished two senses in which the Supreme Court has referred to freedom of association. One line of decisions has involved protecting "intimate human relationships" from "undue intrusion by the State";[42] the other has recognized a right to associate to engage in activities protected by the First Amendment, including speech, assembly, and the exercise of religion.[43]

---

[39] *Roberts v. United States Jaycees*, 468 U.S. 609 (1984).

[40] State and federal laws that forbid discrimination in places of public accommodation are mainly directed at businesses such as hotels, theaters, and restaurants. One cannot say the Minnesota legislature had made a clear choice to restrict organizations like the Jaycees, given the awkwardness of considering them "places of public accommodation." But once the Minnesota Supreme Court interpreted the statute in that way, the U.S. Supreme Court had to accept its understanding.

[41] Chief Justice Burger and Justice Blackmun (both from Minnesota) did not participate; Justice Rehnquist concurred in the judgment.

[42] Id. at 617–18. An example is *Griswold v. Connecticut*, 381 U.S. 479 (1965), protecting the right of a married couple to use contraceptives.

[43] An example is *NAACP v. Button*, 371 U.S. 415 (1963), which held that the NAACP did not have to comply with certain state restrictions when it provided legal services to advance social objectives.

About the sanctuary of highly personal relationships, Justice Brennan indicated that they cultivate and transmit "shared ideals and beliefs; they thereby foster diversity and act as critical buffers between the individual and the power of the State. . . . Protecting these relationships . . . safeguards the ability independently to define one's identity that is central to any concept of liberty."[44] Although in reality many religious groups strongly partake of the elements of such association,[45] Justice Brennan had in mind "the personal affiliations . . . that attend the creation and sustenance of family."[46]

About First Amendment freedom of association, Justice Brennan spoke of protecting "collective effort on behalf of shared goals" to preserve "political and cultural diversity" and shield "dissident expression from suppression by the majority."[47] Interferences with the right to associate for expressive purposes are to be judged according to the compelling interest test.

Although the Jaycees had taken public positions on diverse issues, its constitutional claim failed because the state had a compelling interest in prohibiting gender discrimination in places of public accommodation.

Justice Brennan's linkage of religious activities with other expressive activities tends to suggest that the constitutional status of discrimination by religious groups is the same as that of discrimination by the Jaycees, but on reflection, religious bodies should have more latitude to choose members than Minnesota accorded the Jaycees, and that freedom should be taken as protected by the Free Exercise Clause.

Justice O'Connor agreed with the result in *Roberts*, but she challenged much of the Court's opinion. Regarding the Jaycees as essentially a commercial association, and noting that shopkeepers and labor unions can be forbidden to discriminate on grounds of gender, she thought that the state needed only to establish a rational basis (a much weaker hurdle than compelling interest) to support its legislation. For associations whose activities are "predominantly of the type protected by the First Amendment,"[48] she implied that the choice of members should be absolutely protected. Justice O'Connor's approach would give political organizations the same protection in choosing members that I have suggested religious organizations should have. *Roberts* was not a reliable indication of what a majority would decide about restrictions on membership choices of a dominantly expressive association,

---

[44] Id. at 618–19.

[45] They cultivate and transmit shared ideals and beliefs; they foster diversity and act as critical buffers between the individual and the power of the state; they provide emotional enrichment and contribute to the self-definition of members.

[46] Id. at 619.

[47] Id. at 622.

[48] Id. at 635.

for example, an association that limits its members to African Americans or women and whose overriding purpose is to promote the rights and interests of those respective groups.[49]

In the more recent case of *Boy Scouts of America v. Dale*, the Court upheld the claim of the Boy Scouts that they had an associational right to discriminate against homosexuals, overriding New Jersey's policy that such discrimination was illegal.[50] The case was notable both in accepting the dubious assertion that expressing a rejection of homosexual activity was an important aspect of the Boy Scouts[51] and in granting much more generous protection to organizational expression than had the Court in *Roberts*.[52] The Court, thus, moved substantially toward Justice O'Connor's approach, even though the Boy Scouts are hardly a "dominantly expressive association." It is not now clear that religious groups have more liberty to choose participants than do nonreligious expressive associations.

Some Variations on Associational Claims to Discriminate and the Relevance of a Religious Character

The nonreligious associations that are most closely comparable to religious groups are dominantly expressive, or ideological, associations. To test just how similar to religious groups their constitutional privileges to choose members and officers should be, we need to explore nuances about discrimination that we have previously considered.

DISCRIMINATION WITH A CLOSE RELATION TO PURPOSES

What the opinions in *Roberts* and *Dale* mainly consider is discrimination that is the announced policy of an association and has some relation to its aims. The clearest right to "discriminate" involves ideological screening; a politically active group may restrict its members or officers to people who

---

[49] For someone evaluating the two opinions in *Roberts*, the numbers are a bit misleading. Presumably Justice Brennan assigned himself the majority opinion after a vote in conference. (Since the chief justice did not participate, Brennan, as the senior justice voting with the majority, assigned the opinion.) The Jaycees were going to lose in any event; why worry too much about using a test that made their case appear stronger than it might otherwise have seemed? Justices joining the majority opinion may not have resolved all the disagreements among themselves, and they may not have been overly concerned about nuances of language that troubled Justice O'Connor but had no effect on the outcome.

[50] *Boy Scouts of America v. Dale*, 530 U.S. 640 (2000).

[51] Much of the disagreement in the Court's five-to-four split was taken up with this issue.

[52] One wonders if the justices were more sympathetic to state efforts to eliminate gender discrimination than to eliminate discrimination based on sexual preference.

subscribe to its purposes.[53] Resolution should be similar if an association requires members or officers to be part of the group on whose behalf an organization is formed. Although such restrictions are not exactly ideological,[54] organizations dedicated to the political advancement of women, men, blacks, or Native Americans should be able to restrict membership or official positions to just those persons. Most members may believe that only people who belong to the groups they benefit can be trusted, or that one critical avenue of advancement is holding positions of power, formulating and executing policies uninfluenced by outsiders. Such discrimination should be protected constitutionally.[55] Indeed, an expressive association's deliberate choice to restrict membership in a manner that relates closely to its purposes should receive absolute constitutional protection.

DISCRIMINATION WITH A REMOTE RELATION TO PURPOSES

What if outsiders can see no important relation between the discrimination and an organization's underlying purposes.[56] One possible stance is that the

---

[53] Since statutes do not forbid ideological discrimination, organizations pursuing political or social agendas do not need exceptions for that; but the privilege to select according to adherence to an organization's aims is definitely of constitutional dimension. No legislature may bar a church from using religious criteria to select members or bar a political organization from using political criteria.

However, many well-known expressive associations are ones in which policy is determined and implemented by a small core of officials. Ordinary membership amounts to the privilege of donating money and confers no genuine participation. These groups typically accept money from wherever it comes, making no inquiry about whether those making donations understand and share the association's purposes.

For discrimination that is on the basis of the message itself, *Hurley v. Irish American Gay, Lesbian, and Bisexual Group of Boston*, 515 U.S. 557 (1995), establishes that a group ordinarily has absolute control over what message it will convey. On a debatable reading of the record, the Court concluded that GLIB had been denied a place in Boston's St. Patrick's Day–Evacuation Day Parade not because of the sexual orientation of its members (they could have marched with other units), but because of its message that people of gay, lesbian, and bisexual orientation should receive unqualified social acceptance. Thus, the state's application of its public accommodations statute to require a place in the parade for GLIB violated the First Amendment rights of the parade organizers.

[54] A man may care about the advancement of women, a white about the advancement of blacks, and so on.

[55] In *New York State Clubs Association v. New York City*, 487 U.S. 1, 19 (1988), Justice O'Connor, concurring, commented that "there may well be organizations whose expressive purposes would be substantially undermined if they were unable to confine their membership to those of the same sex, race, religion, or ethnic background."

[56] *Roberts* indicates that when fulfillment of an organization's purposes will not be frustrated by ending discrimination, the state may require that. The Court says in *Roberts* "that the Jaycees' right of association depends on the organization's making a 'substantial' showing that the admission of unwelcome members will change the message communicated by the group's speech." Note 39 supra, at 632. But it was ready to sustain application of Minnesota's antidis-

government has no business interfering with any association's discrimination unless membership confers significant public and commercial opportunities,[57] but that position underrates the corrosive effects of discrimination. Suppose a golf club of three thousand members does not allow Jewish members. If the club admits atheists, and indeed makes no inquiry about religious beliefs, the club's rationale cannot be that members want to associate with persons who share their religious perspectives. And, if the club screens for "congeniality," any assertion that "our members feel they would get along less well with Jews" can only reflect a prejudice against Jews, a preference to avoid social contacts with Jews because they are Jews. Whether public and commercial opportunities are directly affected, such attitudes are unhealthy in a liberal democracy. *Even if* the members assure us that they will extend equal respect to Jews in political and commercial life, we must doubt whether most people are capable of such a sharp dichotomy between semiprivate social life and public life. If it is said that the state is powerless to change such attitudes, the answer is that bastions of social exclusion perpetuate prejudices within and across generations.

Although states may reasonably decide not to prohibit such discrimination, if a state does adopt a ban, it should survive claims of constitutional right by members of an "ordinary" association. The members have some interest in associating with whom they please, but this interest is considerably weaker than it is in very small, close-knit groups. The Supreme Court has sustained such restrictions against large New York City clubs,[58] and one would expect the same outcome even if a law's application was tied less directly to trade and business than was the city's Human Rights Law.[59]

What if a dominantly expressive group self-consciously engages in discrimination that bears no discernible relation to its purposes? Imagine that an environmental group refuses to admit any African Americans, or bars them from official positions. Although Justice O'Connor's proposal of abso-

---

crimination law even if the group's message *would be affected*: "In any event, even if enforcement of the Act causes some incidental abridgment of the Jaycees' protected speech, that effect is no greater than is necessary to accomplish the State's legitimate purposes." Id.

[57] This was the basis on which New York City successfully restricted large private clubs. *New York State Clubs Ass'n*, note 55 supra. A legislature might conclude that large clubs, in general, do affect political and business opportunities, because business is transacted there and because membership in a "leading" club confers status. Asking courts to make individualized contextual judgments about the disadvantages of being excluded from particular clubs is unwieldy, so a law might properly bar discrimination in all large clubs of this sort.

[58] See notes 55 and 57 supra. It is doubtful whether the federal government would have authority to forbid such discrimination, since there are limits to what it can do under the Commerce Clause and the Fourteenth Amendment.

[59] See also *Board of Directors of Rotary International v. Rotary Club of Duarte*, 481 U.S. 537 (1987).

lute liberty makes sense when an expressive organization produces a plausible reason why its limits on members, or officers, relate to its objectives, a
legislature might fairly attack discrimination for which no such connection
can be shown. Expressive groups, in contrast to religious groups that *claim*
that their discrimination fits with their religious vision, should not carry an
absolute constitutional privilege to engage in such discrimination.[60]

DISCRIMINATION THE ASSOCIATION FORBIDS

When a claimant contends that an organization has discriminated on
grounds that the organization itself forbids, the state's latitude to restrict
nonreligious expressive groups should also be somewhat greater than it is
for religious groups. If an applicant asserts that a local branch of a national
nonreligious expressive organization denied her membership on grounds of
race or gender, contrary to binding national organization policy, public enforcement of nondiscrimination, and deeper investigation of whether it has
occurred, would be appropriate.[61] Individual assessment whether officials
have discriminated is more acceptable for nonreligious expressive associations than for religious groups.

DISCRIMINATION IN MARGINAL ACTIVITIES

What constitutional privilege should exist for discrimination by expressive
and religious associations in respect to marginal activities such as the janitor's position at the Mormon gymnasium? Although neither federal nor state
law now forbids most ideological discrimination,[62] they could be altered to

---

[60] This approach differs from what the Court in *Roberts* suggests in the following way. The
Court assumes that a compelling interest for the government is sufficient to end discrimination
in expressive organizations even if the organization has some substantial reason to discriminate.
Under my suggestion, a compelling interest would be sufficient *only* if the reason to discriminate
is not substantially related to the purposes of the organization.

It might be objected that this proposal would encourage organizations to adopt explicit discriminatory objectives. One answer is that many organizations would hesitate to do so. People
might feel more comfortable excluding blacks than announcing that their aim was to protect
the physical environment for whites but not others. A second answer requires closer scrutiny
of what count as crucial objectives. An "objective" that is just a cover for discrimination should
not be sufficient. More importantly, an "objective" that concerns comfort in association rather
than expressive purpose should confer no greater constitutional privilege than a similar "objective" in the golf club example. For an article suggesting parallel treatment for religious and
expressive associations, see Steffan N. Johnson, "Expressive Associations and Organizational
Autonomy," 85 *Minnesota Law Review* 1639 (2001).

[61] Government should not require expressive organizations to place particular people in high
positions, but damages for discrimination in choosing officers are all right.

[62] Firing, or refusing to hire, someone because of positions about labor relations could violate
laws dealing with that subject. In some states, firing people because of political opinions might
amount to a form of unlawful discharge.

cover that. The right of expressive associations to use ideological standards to choose leading personnel should not extend to positions that are unrelated to expressive activities. The National Rifle Association need not hire a director who favors gun control, but it should have no constitutional right to put janitorial applicants through ideological screening.[63] Thus, if Congress adopted a law forbidding discrimination based on political opinion, it should not extend an exemption for all nonprofit activities of expressive organizations.[64] Any argument by the NRA and similar groups that the government should refrain from determining which activities relate to its expressive purposes would be much weaker than the analogous argument for religious organizations. Most expressive associations are less all embracing in their purposes than are religious groups, and the domain of their objectives is more comfortably assessed by public officers.

INDIRECT BENEFITS

Beyond direct restrictions on discrimination, questions arise about when the government may, and should, remove otherwise available tax exemptions because of discrimination that offends public policy. In a case involving Bob Jones University, the Supreme Court accepted an arguable reading, adopted by the Internal Revenue Service, of what the statutory word "charitable" entails:[65] namely, that a university engaging in racial discrimination is ineligible for an exemption that goes to charitable activities. Turning to the constitutional issue, the Court concluded that the government's interest in ending racial discrimination overrode the university's free exercise claim that it had a right to carry out its religious understanding about racial relations without penalty. This resolution is appropriate for independent activities carried on by religious groups; but tax exemptions given to churches *as churches* should not depend on whether such discrimination exists.[66]

---

[63] I am putting aside screening to ensure that a custodial "spy" does not steal memos thrown in wastebaskets.

[64] If it gave such a broad exemption, such an exemption should probably be treated as unconstitutional. This is a difficult question of constitutional law. Such an exemption could be defended on the grounds that the organization, not the state, discriminates and that the Free Speech Clause lacks the "no establishment" content that would preclude a privilege to discriminate conferred on just these groups. My position in the text requires rejecting the first basis for the majority's decision in *Amos*, see text accompanying note 20 supra, and discerning an antidiscrimination principle in the Free Speech and Equal Protection clauses.

[65] *Bob Jones University v. United States*, 461 U.S. 574 (1983).

[66] See also *Gay Rights Coalition of Georgetown University Law Center*, 536 A.2d 1 (D.C. App. 1987), holding that a Catholic university need not grant official recognition to gay rights groups but cannot, under the city's human rights law, deny tangible services on the basis of a group's sexual orientation.

General Reasons for Differentiation between Religious and Other Associations

What may be said in favor of the view that appropriate legislative treatment and constitutional protection of religious organizations differs to some degree from that of nonreligious expressive associations? The crucial factors boil down to these: (1) religions make claims on the whole lives of their members; (2) typically they are grounded in beliefs about transcendent or immanent reality removed from everyday human experience and ordinary political affairs; (3) forms of religious "reason" and justification differ in substantial degree from those used in ordinary affairs; (4) historically, ties between church and state have been divisive and have threatened both church and state; (5) legal support for special treatment in the United States is provided in the religion clauses. It is, of course, possible to imagine nonreligious expressive associations that exhibit some of these features, but most do not. There is good reason, as Justice O'Connor explains, for the government to keep its hands off the membership choices of genuine expressive associations; but certain government restrictions on nonreligious expressive associations might be wise and constitutionally acceptable, even though similar restrictions on religious associations would be unwise and not acceptable.

My understanding of how the fifth factor, constitutional law, relates to the other four has been suggested by earlier chapters, but here is a summary. Although the conceptions of people at the time the Bill of Rights and Fourteenth Amendment were adopted, as well as the constitutional case law, suggest that religious organizations deserve distinct treatment in some respects, were that approach seriously unjust, as some commentators believe, constitutional law should develop toward elimination of that distinctiveness. Thus, I do not claim the religion clauses somehow *require* distinctive treatment for religious groups regardless of the strength of the other factors. For American society, the other four factors support that treatment.

Someone can believe that religious groups should receive special treatment without supposing that religion is "intrinsically good." In the history of this country, most people have supposed that religion in some form (if not religion in general) is intrinsically good for human beings. A person who holds that belief, or who acknowledges that it is embedded in our culture, has some reason to support special treatment for religious groups;[67] but the four

---

[67] There is a complicating wrinkle. If one believes that the right religion is intrinsically good but others are intrinsically bad, and one acknowledges that the government may not favor one religion over other religions, one might conclude that religious groups in general should not receive special treatment.

factors I have mentioned have independent force. They should be persuasive to someone who thinks religion is a matter of indifference and who places no weight on a contrary cultural view.[68]

In thinking about situations in which religious groups may have greater rights than other associations, we need to remember that in some respects religious groups do, and should, receive less favored treatment. These matters are explored mainly in volume 2, but outright public funding of churches from tax money is impermissible, even if churches fall into some broader class of organizations that receive funding. Further, government may not publicly endorse the aims of religious groups, as it may publicly endorse the aims of the Red Cross or the Sierra Club. The same factors that point towards more favorable treatment of religious groups for some matters also suggest a distance between government and religion that produces less favorable treatment in other respects.

One crucial lesson of a careful treatment of associational rights is the need for nuanced evaluation. Any easy generalizations about how religious bodies compare with expressive associations are too simple. In some respects their basic rights should be the same; in other respects differences are justified.

---

[68] Someone who thinks religion is positively evil might well resist any favored treatment.

CHAPTER 21

Medical Procedures

Poignant issues about free exercise arise when people have religious convictions against receiving standard medical treatment for themselves or their children, or against participating in providing forms of treatment. Should the state accept decisions to decline treatment or intervene to require it? Should it protect medical personnel who object in conscience to providing treatment?

REFUSALS TO RECEIVE TREATMENT

In our examination of refusals to receive treatment, we need to recognize that some religious persons who decline ordinary medical assistance believe that an alternative form of treatment, say faith healing or meditation, will be more effective in curing their illnesses.[1] Christian Scientists, for example, do not *believe in* much standard medicine, because they conceive physical illness as based on a kind of mental illness or misperception.[2] By contrast, Jehovah's Witnesses acknowledge that blood transfusions may be needed for physical recovery, but they believe that God's will is that they not accept transfers of blood.[3]

The law may intervene over decisions about medical treatment in either of two ways. Officials may directly authorize treatment, overriding the judgment of the person who would typically choose, or the law may subject people to penalties for failures to obtain needed medical assistance. Determinations of child neglect have aspects of both approaches: they are based on past behavior; they can also lead to a loss of custody or restrictions on parental choice.

---

[1] Indeed, they typically believe that the alternative treatment alone would be at least as effective as the alternative treatment plus standard medical treatment.

[2] See Nathan A. Talbot, "The Position of the Christian Science Church," 309 New England Journal of Medicine, 1641 (1983); Jennifer L. Hartsell, "Mother May I . . . Live? Parental Refusal of Life-Sustaining Medical Treatment for Children Based on Religious Objections," 66 *Tennessee Law Review* 499 (1999).

[3] Literature of the Jehovah's Witnesses suggests many of the dangers of blood transfusions; but it implicitly acknowledges that, on occasion, transfusions have a greater promise of saving life than alternatives. Even in these situations, no one should accept a transfusion because doing

The relation between free exercise claims and general principles of autonomy is very important for this topic. People have a wide range of choice when to seek medical treatment and what form of treatment to accept or not accept. To judge whether religious claimants should have any special range of choice, we need a sense of the choices everyone does, and should, possess. Because adults now have virtually unfettered discretion to decline forms of medical treatment for themselves, the crucial practical questions about possible religious exemptions involve decisions about children.

Adults Choosing for Themselves

Under the common law and as a matter of constitutional right, adults—at least those who are not parents of a young child—can refuse to seek any medical treatment at all or decline to accept measures doctors recommend.[4] Does this wide power to decide make good sense? Because punishment after the fact is not at issue here,[5] the serious question is whether the state should ever compel treatment that the individual refuses.

A wide range of choices about medicine is now regarded as reasonable. Doctors often disagree about helpful treatments or the desirability of risking harmful side effects to achieve likely benefits. Having evolved from a culture in which doctors often made such decisions themselves, our ideal now is that patients choose after receiving full (enough) information from their doctors. The only conceivable situations in which one might reasonably think the law should intervene are when a person's choice is unreasonable from a medical point of view or her motivation is inappropriate.

Although a legal focus on motivation might initially seem attractive, it would not provide a workable legal approach. A person's medical choice is ordinarily based on an assessment of likely benefit, harmful side effects, and suffering. Because of the last two considerations, someone may choose against a treatment that best promises to preserve her life for the longest

---

so violates God's will, revealed in scripture (see Gen. 9:4, Lev. 17:14, Acts 15:19–20), and threatens one's eternal soul.

[4] See *Schloendorff v. Society of New York Hospital*, 105 N.E. 92 (N.Y. 1914) (common law); *Cruzan v. Missouri Dep't of Health*, 497 U.S. 261 (1990).

[5] If an adult dies because he has failed to receive treatment, he is not available to be punished. An adult could be punished for "harming himself" by refusing to get medical treatment, but no one has proposed this as a form of criminal liability. However, it can be criminal to injure oneself to avoid military duty; and a failure to obtain standard medical treatment in order to remain incapacitated might count as an injuring of oneself. See Lieutenant Colonel Bowe, "Confusion about Malingering and Attempted Suicide: A Self-Inflicted Wound," *Army Lawyer*, June 1992, 38.

time. A patient with incurable cancer may decide in favor of a better quality of life for the time that remains instead of suffering further radical interventions that will prolong life but cause excruciating pain and debilitation. But suppose a patient refuses medical treatment because she wants to die? If people are not legally free to commit suicide, perhaps they should not be able to bring about their deaths by refusing treatment.[6]

The ethics of declining treatment in order to die is arguable. One might think that actively committing suicide is morally wrong but that allowing illness or injury to take its natural course without medical intervention is morally permissible, even if a person's motivation is to die.[7] Or, one might think that a motivation to die makes a choice to decline treatment immoral.[8]

For our purposes here, we need not resolve the morality of declining treatment in order to die, because that is not a standard that the law could comfortably adopt. Imagine that patients A and B are offered a painful course of medical treatment that will almost surely prolong their lives. Both decline the treatment. A does not want to suffer the pain, B actually desires to die, and would refuse the treatment even if it was painless. We cannot expect doctors, hospital administrators, and courts reviewing applications to make deference to a patient's choice turn solely on whether a patient wishes to die. Such a practice would simply encourage patients to be less than honest about why they decline treatment.

A more plausible possibility would be to order medical treatment if its refusal was grossly unreasonable.[9] It is a hard question whether a citizen's autonomy should extend to refusing medical treatment, even though the highly probable consequence of doing so is avoidable death or serious bodily harm. The argument for intervention is that people's lives and bodies should be protected against their own rashness and stupidity. One argument for freedom of choice, even unreasonable choice, is that the making of such decisions should be an aspect of liberty in a free society. People who are allowed to do

---

[6] Although suicide is no longer a crime, it is not legally permitted. (I put aside Oregon's law, Or. Rev. Stat. 127.800–127.897, which, in limited circumstances, allows people who are terminally ill to choose to die.) State authorities will intervene to stop a person attempting to kill herself if they are able. And assisting suicide remains criminal in virtually every state.

[7] Of course, if one believes active suicide is itself morally acceptable, one will think that a refusal of medical treatment in similar circumstances is also acceptable.

[8] See John Finnis, "A Philosophical Case Against Euthanasia," in John Keown, ed., *Euthanasia Examined: Ethical, Clinical and Legal Perspectives* 23, 28 (New York: Cambridge University Press, 1995).

[9] We need not pause to consider exactly what the standard should be, but, roughly, if a competent doctor or a reasonable person would definitely choose in favor of medical treatment, medical personnel, backed by legal authorities, could impose the treatment against the patient's wishes. If someone refused to have a broken bone set, or to take an antidote to a poison, or to receive a lifesaving blood transfusion, the treatment would be imposed.

all sorts of dangerous things—climb high mountains, swim in shark-infested waters, bungee-jump, skydive, etc.—should be allowed to refuse medical interventions on their own bodies, even when the refusal is highly dangerous. (Although one might think that climbing high mountains is life-affirming in a way that does not apply to refusing medical treatment, the privilege to decide what is done to one's body seems at least as important as the privilege to undertake risky activities.) A second argument for freedom focuses on institutional decisions. The vast majority of people, advised by doctors, make reasonable medical decisions. Diluting the legal right of choice so it does not cover the infrequent instances of very foolish decisions would open up too many debates about the boundaries of reasonable choice, and would leave uncertain the status of too many patient wishes. Better to have an absolute right, even if the result is to give effect to a few misguided choices that, looked at in isolation, the state might override. Whether or not people should be able to make foolish medical decisions as a matter of principle, giving people an absolute choice to decline treatment is the proper approach.[10]

This principle of absolute choice does not address respective rights and duties when a provider of medical services declares he will not provide service at all unless it includes a form of treatment.[11] Suppose a doctor who is to operate says a transfusion will be necessary to keep the patient's blood supply at a minimal level; otherwise, the patient's chances of survival will be slight. I do not assume that a patient should have a legal right to compel treatment on the exact terms he wants, only that he cannot be forced to accept treatment that he does not want.

If adult citizens should not be forced to accept medical treatment they do not want, adults with religious reasons to decline medical treatment need no special privilege.[12]

Certain forms of medical intervention, such as vaccinations to prevent serious illnesses and blood tests administered prior to marriage or to determine paternity, are intended to benefit other members of society as well as those who are the object of the intervention. With such health measures,

---

[10] However, absolute choice is for competent adults, not for those who are senile or suffer serious mental illness. If people are incapable of making a thoughtful choice, close relatives or medical personnel must choose for them. (I do not assume that everyone who makes an unreasonable choice is incompetent. Some competent people may have strong aversions to forms of medical treatment or be highly resistant to sound medical advice.)

[11] Whether providers should be able to refuse to afford certain forms of ordinary treatment is taken up in the latter part of this chapter.

[12] The issue about such an exemption would arise if treatment was sometimes forced on others. A choice to refuse a blood transfusion necessary to save life that would be grossly unreasonable by ordinary standards might not seem grossly unreasonable if it was a response to a perceived prohibition issued by God.

people may reasonably be required to submit even if they choose not to. But what if they have religious reasons to refuse? Having been married twice, once in Croatia (then a part of Yugoslavia) and once in New Jersey, without undergoing a premarital blood test, I am skeptical about its necessity,[13] but a court facing the issue decided that a state did have a compelling interest in imposing these tests and that it need not make any exceptions.[14] Courts have also judged the state's interest in determining paternity to be compelling.[15]

Because most vaccination requirements apply to children, we shall look at the possibility of a religious exemption in that context.

ADULTS WITH SMALL CHILDREN

It is a serious question whether adults with young children should have the same range of choice as other adults.[16] Perhaps they should not be able to make choices that will lead almost certainly to their own deaths, especially if no other close relations will remain alive to care for their children. Courts have divided over whether mothers with very young children should be able, based on religious objections, to refuse treatment necessary to keep them alive.[17]

As a general matter, parents with young children are allowed to choose activities as dangerous as those in which other adults may engage, but that does not settle whether the state should intervene if a parent makes a choice virtually certain to result in death and the state can approve treatment that will prevent that eventuality.

If we put aside religious reasons, why might a person refuse treatment necessary to save her life? Ignorance, fear of pain, or a wish to die are possible explanations. Viewed in isolation, the state's interest in preserving the best possible environment for a child might well override the parent's claim

---

[13] Since some states require such a test and others do not, and many foreign countries do not, any state will have living within its boundaries many married couples that have not undergone such tests. Nonetheless, a state might say that such a test is required to protect each member of a couple from being deceived about the health of the other.

[14] *In re Kilpatrick*, 375 S.E.2d 794 (W. Va. 1988). Of course, under *Employment Division v. Smith*, a legislative decision to require tests generally would be conclusive.

[15] *State v. Meacham*, 93 Wash. 2d 735 (1980); *Essex County Div. of Welfare v. Harris*, 189 N.J. Super. 479 (A.D. 1983).

[16] Kristin M. Loumond, "An Adult Patient's Right to Refuse Medical Treatment for Religious Reasons: The Limitations Imposed by Parenthood," 31 *University of Louisville Journal of Family Law* 665 (1992–93).

[17] Compare *Mercy Hospital, Inc. v. Jackson*, 489 A.2d 1130 (Md. App. 1985) (parent can refuse if doing so does not threaten physical harm to child), with *Application of President and Directors of Georgetown College, Inc.*, 331 F.2d 1000, 1008 (D.C. Cir.), cert. denied, 377 U.S.

to make an autonomous choice about medical treatment.[18] The parent's claim seems decidedly stronger if she feels she has a religious obligation not to receive treatment. One might conclude that for parents with small children, religious claims to decline treatment should succeed, even though claims of autonomy should not.[19] However, considering the freedom parents generally have to create various living arrangements for their children and to put children up for adoption, all parents with young children should also be granted a freedom to make decisions about their own medical treatment as broad as that of other adults.

Choices for Children

The difficult issues about refusing medical treatment involve parents making decisions for children: should the state compel treatment, if it has the opportunity? Should it punish parents who fail to seek treatment or deprive them of custody? For these questions, the possibility of a religious exemption figures importantly.

Compelling Treatment

What should the law do if parents refuse treatment for a minor child, when, from an ordinary medical perspective, the only reasonable choice is accepting the treatment? A striking example would be a parental decision to refuse a blood transfusion for a six-year-old girl that is almost certainly necessary to save her life.

The right course is easy if the parents' choice is based on simple bad judgment, say, a belief that, despite what doctors tell them, virtually all blood used for transfusions carries HIV (the virus that causes AIDS). The same conclusion follows if the parents have a perverse attitude about child development—that any child who cannot survive without a transfusion does not deserve to live. No one argues that for these matters, parental autonomy in respect to children should be absolute. The state should not allow a child to

---

978 (1964) (parent could be compelled to take blood transfusion rather than "abandoning" small child).

[18] Barring terminal illness, a parent's wish to die would probably be regarded as a symptom of mental illness. If the parent has a terminal illness, forcing treatment would not save the parent for very long to nurture her child.

[19] However, hospital officials and judges might determine that the parent feels that she cannot consent to treatment but that no spiritual harm will be done if it is imposed against her will. Perhaps treatment then should be compelled; but doctors and judges should not assume the parent has this attitude unless she or loved ones make clear that she does.

die just because parents have exercised a patently indefensible judgment about the child's medical needs.[20] As with many other aspects of child welfare,[21] the state constrains the choices of parents to some degree; all states have laws requiring parents to assure medical treatment for their children.

What the state should do is somewhat more debatable if the parents' reason for refusal is religious—if, for example, they believe that their souls and the souls of their children will be jeopardized if the children receive a transfusion. Someone might argue that the state should defer to the parents, because no one knows what acts will endanger souls. Certainly it is better to lose one's life on this earth than to suffer eternal damnation, *if* that is the choice. But the notion that the state should not determine that the parents' choice is ill-advised has a serious flaw. Once that line of argument is accepted, it would open the door to the state's accepting every form of behavior judged by participants to be good eternally for all concerned. Members of a religion practicing child sacrifice might believe that every child sacrificed is assured of eternal happiness. The state should not abandon its determination about secular welfare in the face of such beliefs, and it properly requires medical treatment that is essential for life, even against a parental claim that the treatment is harmful religiously. Even when the parents' interest in practicing their own religion and transmitting it to their children is added to their more general interest in deciding how to raise their children, these are not sufficient to outweigh the state's concern for the lives of children. When this particular conflict reaches courts, judges have not hesitated to order treatment over the parents' wishes.[22]

Analysis become more difficult if a parent's refusal of medical treatment does not threaten a child's life or basic health, or if the advantages of treatment are more arguable, but the treatment would definitely be desired by the great majority of people. Suppose doctors propose to close a cleft palate or to treat a broken leg so that a child will not limp for the rest of his life. Or doctors recommend a highly invasive, very painful course of chemotherapy that could itself cause death and that promises only a 40 percent chance

[20] The state's interest is sometimes put as one in its own survival, dependent on healthy young people. See David E. Steinberg, "Children and Spiritual Healing: Having Faith in Free Exercise," 2000 *Notre Dame Law Review* 180, 182, 196–99. Given the infrequency in which parents, by choice or through ignorance, jeopardize the lives of their children by failing to get necessary treatment, and the ample number of citizens reaching adulthood here or immigrating to the United States, we need to see the state's main interest as preserving the lives and health of individual children, not as maintaining a sufficient number of healthy citizens.

[21] Parents cannot, for example, choose to put their young children to work. See *Prince v. Massachusetts*, 321 U.S. 158 (1944).

[22] See, e.g., *Matter of Hamilton*, 657 S.W. 425, 429 (Tenn. Ct. App. 1983); *Custody of a Minor*, 393 N.E.2d 836 (Mass. 1979).

of survival.[23] The parents refuse. Should parents be able to make a final decision, and should it matter if their reasons are religious?

I am inclined to think that when a child's life is definitely at stake, courts should feel free to intervene, even when the parents' choice to decline treatment could receive some defense apart from religion,[24] but that parents should have authority about medical measures when life and basic health are not threatened.

However, one might believe parents should not be able to make unreasonable decisions about a child's welfare. In one New York case, the court authorized a dangerous operation to partially correct the massive, "grotesque and repulsive" deformity on a boy's face caused by neurofibromatosis; and it directed that blood transfusions be given during the operation, over the objections of his mother, a Jehovah's Witness.[25] It declined to wait until the boy could make a decision for himself at the age of twenty-one, because of the physical and psychological damage caused by his disease. Were the courts to override parental choices more frequently, perhaps parents acting on religious reasons should be afforded a greater range of choice, able to decline treatment they believe is opposed God's will.[26]

Vaccinations raise a special problem. A vaccination protects the person who receives it, but it also protects others against the spread of disease. Some people have adverse effects from vaccinations. Very few people in the United States will ever acquire diseases against which the vast majority of citizens have been vaccinated. An individual making a purely selfish choice might reasonably conclude that he would risk more by being vaccinated than by refusing. Yet the effectiveness of the vaccination program may depend on near universality. Parents may oppose vaccination for their children because

---

[23] *Newmark v. Williams*, 588 A.2d 1108 (Del. 1991).

[24] I see *Newmark*, id., as such an example. One can understand a parental choice against a painful treatment not likely to save a child; but almost all doctors and parents would choose a 40 percent chance of survival against virtually certain death.

[25] *In re Sampson*, 317 N.Y.S.2d 641 (Fam. Ct. 1970), aff'd, 323 N.Y.S.2d 253 (App. Div. 1971), aff'd, 278 N.E.2d 918 (N.Y. 1972). The American Academy of Pediatrics has recommended that parents' objections be overridden "when . . . treatment is likely to prevent substantial harm or suffering or death." Committee on Bioethics, American Academy of Pediatrics, "Religious Objections to Medical Care," 99 *Pediatrics* 279 (1997).

[26] But see id. Were the privilege given to theists, I assume it would also go to other religious persons with a powerful objection to treatment. But the typical objection would be of the sort I discuss. Conceivably any privilege to decline treatment should depend on parents acting for the welfare of the child, not authorizing parents to satisfy their own spiritual welfare, as they see it, at the expense of a child; but such a limit probably does not make sense, in part because almost every parent will think a child will be better off if the parent follows God's will. Thus, parents who refuse an operation because God must have intended their child to have a cleft palate would think it better for the child to "submit" to this misfortune than to have it altered.

of a rational calculation (by ordinary standards) of what is best for them, because of nonreligious beliefs about physical and psychological health, or because of peculiar religious objections. States with requirements that children be vaccinated before entering public school have understandably not chosen to exempt all children whose parents object to their being vaccinated. But some state legislatures have created an exemption for parents with religious objections. In New York, for example, standard requirements do not apply to children whose parents "hold genuine and sincere religious beliefs" that are opposed to vaccination.[27] In applying this law, courts have not required typical theist beliefs,[28] but they have insisted that the objection be more than "medical or purely moral,"[29] and one court, after examining parents' testimony very carefully, concluded that their references to standard biblical sources did not reflect the true health-related and moral grounds of their objection to vaccination.[30]

There are two arguments against courts singling out religious claims as bases parents may use to refuse medical treatment. One is that such an approach is at odds with the spirit of *Employment Division v. Smith*. That case does not bar individualized judicial determinations about medical treatments, based as they are on common law and statutory powers, but it might be thought to count against any distinctive favoring of religious grounds that is not specified by a legislature. A second argument against favoring religious claims is that when parents have specific religious grounds to oppose medical treatment (such as scriptural passages), there is even less basis to suppose that their decision could be defended as reasonable according to ordinary secular criteria than when parents offer nonreligious grounds for judgment.

By and large, the best strategy for judicial deference to parental choice about medical procedures for their children concentrates on the kind of medical procedure involved, not the exact grounds of parental judgment, but it may be that in some instances the special strength of religious claims against treatment should make a difference.

[27] New York Public Health Law 2164 (9).
[28] See *Sherr v. Northport–East Northport Union Free School Dist.*, 672 F. Supp. 81 (E.D.N.Y. 1987).
[29] Id. at 92; *Farina v. Board of Educ. of City of New York*, 116 Supp. 2d 503 (S.D.N.Y. 2000). See also *Friedman v. Southern California Permanente Medical Group*, 125 Cal. Rptr. 2d 663 (Ct. App. 2d Dist. 2002) (rejecting claim of employment discrimination based on refusal to hire plaintiff who, as a vegan, was unwilling to be vaccinated for mumps (the vaccine was grown in chicken embryos)). The court concluded that veganism was a moral code, not a religious set of beliefs, using the analogical approach suggested by Judge Adams of the Third Circuit (discussed in chapter 8). (The *Friedman* opinion, applying a California statute, contains an explicit rejection of the EEOC approach we reviewed in chapters 18 and 19.)
[30] *Farina v. Board of Educ.*, note 29 supra.

Medical Choices and Teenagers

Questions about how far the judgments of older (mature) children will count can be especially acute when medical treatment is involved. A teenager may want treatment that the parents wish to decline, or may want to refuse treatment that the parents wish her to have, or may agree with her parents in declining treatment.[31] Of course, "teenager" is a broad category—let us focus on a minor who is sixteen or seventeen, not old enough to vote or sign contracts but approaching that age, and past the age when she would become a full member of a Christian or Jewish congregation.

The simplest situation is when the teenager seeks to decline ordinary medical treatment that the parents want—want even after they realize their daughter's wishes and have tried unsuccessfully to resolve the disagreement.[32] The state should support the parents. A teenager should not be able to refuse treatment that any doctor would recommend and that the parents want for her. Certainly a child should not be able to refuse life-saving treatment that the parents wish her to have; a sixteen-year-old has not reached a level of maturity that should permit her to make an unreasonable medical decision that will probably result in her death. Instances of future disfigurement or modest physical incapacity, such as a limp, are more troublesome,[33] but probably the parents together should have final authority to decide on medical treatment, *if* their daughter's wish, religious or not, is unreasonable according to ordinary medical standards.

How should courts react if the situation is reversed—the teenager wants treatment that doctors strongly recommend, but the parents wish to decline it? Needless to say, the treatment should be given to the teenager if the state would override the parents' wishes to refuse it for a very small child; but what if the parents' wishes would control were the child small? I have suggested that parents should have authority to decline an operation that will correct a cleft palate or prevent a future limp. As to such matters of appearance or physical capacity, a teenager who wants treatment that virtually all doctors would strongly recommend should be able to determine her own future.

A counterargument against this position is that because teenagers can exert great influence and make life miserable for parents, because few par-

[31] Yet another variation is when the parents themselves have opposing views.

[32] I am not addressing commitment to a psychiatric facility. The wisdom of commitment is often arguable, and parents may have important interests, most notably relief from strife and acute frustration, that may not correspond with what is best for the child. See, e.g., *Parham v. J. R.*, 442 U.S. 584 (1979); Lois A. Weithorn, "Mental Hospitalization of Troublesome Youth: An Analysis of Skyrocketing Admission Rates," 40 *Stanford Law Review* 773 (1988).

[33] They are more troublesome because one might think a teenager is old enough to opt for these consequences if she chooses.

ents will withstand the combined force of medical recommendations and teenage insistence, it makes sense to stick with a legal rule that parents can make final decisions about medical treatment for all minor children. However, this counterargument faces two powerful objections. First, given that parents almost always want the physical health and well-being of their children, they will be likely refuse operations that will prevent disfigurement or incapacity only if they possess strong religious convictions that the operations are wrong. With such convictions, they may not accede to what they see as their disagreeing child's erring ways. Most religions recognize by their age of confirmation that teenagers are old enough to make their own religious choices. If the child wants treatment any doctor would recommend, the parents should not be able to prevent it because they have religious values that the child now rejects.[34]

The Supreme Court's approach to abortion, which takes final decision-making power away from parents, has relevance here. Laws that would prevent minors from having abortions without parental consent are unconstitutional.[35] A young woman's right to make the choice whether or not to have an abortion has implications for ordinary medical procedures. Although one might conceive of abortion as special because the alternative is having one's body bear a fetus and then giving birth to a child, disfigurement and irreversible incapacity can involve the teenager's body for the rest of her life. If she can choose to terminate the life of the fetus, she should be able to choose to prevent long-term harm to her body, as well.

A range of delicate questions arise if child and parents disagree, and each choice is reasonable according to ordinary medical standards. One can imagine a variety of possible approaches.[36] I shall suggest that the kind of medical procedure and motivations should make a difference, but without defending that approach against various alternatives.

If a treatment involves imposing on the patient's body, as by an operation or painful course of chemotherapy, it should not be forced on a teenager whose reasonable decision is that she does not want it. In the reverse situation, when the teenager wants treatment that the parents have decided is ill advised, the outcome should depend on the parents' reasons. If parents and the child both rely on ordinary criteria for their decisions, and the parents

---

[34] It does not follow that parents should have to pay for the treatment; their objection to it should probably be sufficient for them to avoid paying.

[35] See *Planned Parenthood of Central Missouri v. Danforth*, 428 U.S. 52 (1976); *Bellotti v. Baird*, 443 U.S. 622 (1979).

[36] Parental or teenager choice could control in all circumstances, or the balance might be struck against treatment, or the nature of the medical procedure and motivations could matter. Courts could or could not evaluate the maturity of individual teenagers. Whatever standards are adopted need to be administrable, as well as yielding appropriate outcomes in theory.

conclude that a treatment is too risky, although the teenager is willing to undertake it, doctors and the state should not overcome the force of reasonable parental judgment. Matters look different if quality of life is at stake. Doctors, parents, and child agree on the likely benefits and harms of treatment. Parents think the treatment will be too painful, but the teenager wants to undertake it. Here, her choice should have more force; after all, it is her life that is at issue. A similar conclusion holds if the disagreement is over religious values. The parents make a choice that is reasonable according to ordinary medical standards, but their reason is a religious one that the child rejects. The teenager has reached a stage at which her religious sense should not be overridden by that of her parents.[37] My overall conclusion is that treatment should not be undertaken if either parents or a teenager makes a reasonable choice to refuse it, *unless* the parents' choice relies on values that the teenager should, at this stage of her life, have the autonomy to reject.[38] An interesting implication of this approach is that within the range of reasonable choices, parental decisions based on religious premises will carry less weight than their ordinary risk assessments. The reason is not a general downgrading of religious convictions, but rather a conclusion that in this domain parents should not be able to dictate to older teenage children.[39]

One might object that an approach that privileges teenage judgments and distinguishes risk assessment from quality of life will set members of families in opposition to each other and will require courts to make judgments that are too difficult. In answer, parents, teenagers, and doctors will almost always reach agreement; the law will rarely intervene. Although the line between risk

---

[37] However, if the treatment would generally be classified as "optional," such as "ordinary" plastic surgery, it is more doubtful whether doctors should proceed if the parents object. They should not be forced to pay, and perhaps for such elective measures, a child should need the consent of her parents or wait until she is an adult. It may be relevant that the state will not supply such treatment to indigents.

[38] The law of abortion provides support for aspects of this approach. The choice about abortion concerns quality of life and ethical responsibility, not ordinary risk assessment. If the teenager can choose abortion, she should probably be able to make other medical choices for which values are central.

Readers who reject the whole notion of a liberal abortion law may suspect any analogies that draw from it. But the force of the analogy does not depend on the fundamental right to abort. The main objection to permissive abortion laws is that the fetus deserves the state's protection, even if a pregnant teenager and her parents choose abortion. The crucial question about reasonable medical treatment is who can make a choice that parents and child can undoubtedly make together. Some reasons why the teenager's choice in respect to abortion should prevail over the parents' may have broader applicability, even if the underlying premise that anyone can choose abortion in ordinary circumstances (not involving rape, incest, or risk of death) is itself misconceived.

[39] Parents might substitute grounds of risk assessment to cover their religious reasons, and indeed those reasons may influence their honest risk assessments (Jehovah's Witnesses are particularly likely to think blood transfusions are dangerous); but many religious people will not wish to conceal their religious opposition.

assessment and quality of life is difficult, it best captures the domains where a parental choice to decline treatment should or should not control.

The most stark issue about the state and older children arises when a teenager joins parents in wanting to decline treatment, such as a blood transfusion, that parents could not decline for a small child. The child has now reached an age when her own religious convictions carry weight, and she makes a choice, supported by parents, that an adult could make for herself. It is one thing to conclude that a child's religious convictions should count heavily if they line up in favor of a reasonable course of medical treatment; it is quite another to say that the convictions can support what would otherwise be an unreasonable choice, especially about treatment necessary to save life. Although in past eras, teenagers may generally have accepted parental values, or at least not have explicitly rejected them, perhaps now it is fairer to assume that a sixteen-year-old who subscribes to her parents' religion has made a serious, independent choice to do so.[40] With hesitation, I incline to the view that a teenager who is sixteen or older who wants to decline even life-saving treatment for religious reasons, and is supported by her parents, should be free to do so.[41]

This privilege should not extend to a foolish choice that is not made from deep conviction. Suppose parents have ill-formed ideas about medical practice; they believe that blood transfusions usually carry HIV, despite assurances by doctors to the contrary, and they have persuaded their sixteen-year-old to their view. Although an otherwise competent adult with that opinion should be able to decline medical treatment, even life-saving treatment, doctors, with the state's support, should be able to say that such a view is mistaken and impose the transfusion over the objections of the parents and the teenager. Probably the state should also be able to override parents and a teenager if their objection is religious, in a sense, but yields a view that is demonstrably wrong as a matter of physical fact (such as the prevalence of HIV).

Judgments of Neglect and Punishment

Often, neither doctors nor officials learn of the need for medical treatment until it is too late. The child dies or suffers harm before outsiders learn of

[40] However, the critical question is not really about most teenagers, but about teenagers whose parents are in groups that have unusual views about medical treatment.

One possibility is an individualized inquiry to see if the teenager is mature enough to have made an independent judgment, but such an inquiry would be fraught with a potential for a doctor or official to conclude that no one would independently accept some "bizarre" religion.

[41] A case that reaches this conclusion about a seventeen-year-old Jehovah's Witness who objected to a blood transfusion is *In re E.G.*, 549 N.E.2d 322 (Ill. 1989).

his condition. Should the law treat parents as neglectful or abusive? As guilty of negligent homicide, if the child dies?

1. *Neglect*. A judgment of neglect could be the basis for criminal punishment or for a determination that a child is not safe in his parents' custody. If a judgment about custody exclusively concerns safety, it should matter whether a particular incident teaches anything new about the child or his parents. If the great majority of Christian Scientists will not seek medical care if their children have very high fevers, two Christian Scientist parents have relied only on prayer and Christian Science practitioners when their child has suffered a very high fever, and the child has survived, officials have learned nothing new about the parents.[42] Unless the illness suggests a higher probability of similar illness in the future than apparently existed before the incident, removal of custody cannot be based on a sense that the danger to the child is greater than it seemed in the past.[43]

2. *Punishment*. Is punishment warranted for parents whose acts, or failures to act, are based on religious convictions if those acts would constitute serious neglect by ordinary parents? This question poses issues about religion more sharply than does state intervention to compel treatment. The reason is this. With decisions about whether to decline treatment, parents have a wide range of autonomy, but it is limited. Ordinarily, parents with religious reasons to decline treatment for their children should not be treated differently from parents with other reasons to decline treatment. Thus, the range of parental autonomy depends little on whether reasons are religious or not.

The argument that religion should matter is more powerful in respect to punishment. If criminal punishment is appropriate for parental neglect of children, liability should not depend on whether parents are careless or ignorant or pigheaded. Parents A do not realize their child is developing a very high fever. Parents B are ignorant about what doctors can do to help people with high fevers. Parents C distrust doctors and refuse to use them. If a failure to consult a doctor is highly unreasonable, all three sets of parents have failed to exercise reasonable care for children.[44] If the children die, all three sets of parents are guilty of negligent homicide. Parents have no general right of autonomy to risk their children's well-being by failing to get medical treatment.

---

[42] Except that they do not fall within the class of Christian Scientists who would seek medical help in a serious emergency.

[43] However, one might defend a general presumption that the law does not intervene against parents based on propensities; it waits for manifestations of danger.

[44] No doubt, one might judge these sets of parents more or less harshly as individual details of the children's illnesses and the parents' own backgrounds were filled in.

But what should be done about parents D who have strong religious reasons not to seek treatment? Should these parents escape liability if other parents do not? A simple argument against their liability is that criminal sanctions are futile, that these parents will follow their deepest religious convictions to benefit the physical and religious health of their children. Such parents will not be deterred by the state's threat of harm if things go badly. As far as blame is concerned, parents who seek the best for their children in light of the spiritual principles in which they believe are not to be condemned. Neither deterrence nor retribution is served by imposing criminal penalties on conscientious parents who already suffer greatly if their children have died.

This forceful argument is neat, but it is too simple. Many parents who are attached to religions that disparage ordinary medical treatments agonize over what they should do. Some may be pushed over the line to consult a doctor by knowing that criminal penalties may follow a failure to do so; others may, at least, not try to conceal their ill child. Further, people deciding whether to align themselves with a religion may be affected by a highly publicized criminal conviction that follows a child's death. They may be somewhat less inclined to join a religion whose practice could endanger their children. Criminal punishment may not be wholly ineffective to affect the behavior of others.

Still, it is a large price to pay to punish those who have used their best judgment to serve the welfare of their children, relying on spiritual grounds that to some degree at least are not the business of the state. Most states have adopted statutes that exempt parents from judgments of neglect or abuse when their failure to seek medical treatment involves a practice of their religious beliefs.[45] These laws typically do not preclude a court's ordering needed medical treatments for a child. As far as I am aware, no state legislature has explicitly created an exemption from the application of all of its homicide laws.[46]

---

[45] See generally Eric W. Treene, "Prayer-Treatment Exemptions to Child Abuse and Neglect Statutes, Manslaughter Prosecutions. and Due Process of Law," 30 *Harvard Journal on Legislation* 135 (1993); Jennifer Stanfield, "Faith Healing and Religious Treatment Exemptions to Child Endangerment Laws: Should Parents Be Allowed to Refuse Necessary Medical Treatment for Their Children Based on Their Religious Beliefs?" 2000 *Hamline Journal of Public Policy* 45. The initial impetus for such laws was the Federal Child Abuse Prevention and Treatment Act of 1974, which was interpreted by the Department of Health and Human Services to condition certain federal funding relating to children on state's adopting such exemptions. See Marci A. Hamilton, *God vs. The Gavel: Religion and the Rule of Law* 314 n. 81 (New York: Cambridge University Press, 2005). In 1983, this implication was disavowed by new legislation.

[46] Hamilton, id. at 35–36 and n. 103, cites three states providing a defense to some homicide provisions.

Some critics have objected to any exemption from criminal liability on the ground that it leaves too little protection for children at risk,[47] but so long as courts can order necessary medical intervention, these children receive some degree of protection. Another complaint is that religious motivations should not be singled out specifically for an exemption.[48] This is the familiar concern we have considered at many points in this volume; here, as in a number of other instances, an exemption limited to religious claims seems appropriate, although formulations that are limited to particular named religions or favor some religious understandings over others similar in their views about ordinary medicine are not acceptable.[49]

Harder questions are raised by legislatures adopting exemptions that reach minor criminal charges and do not include manslaughter or negligent homicide. Legislators understandably do not want to appear to countenance unnecessary deaths of innocent children. But, as far as individual parents are concerned, minor penalties for failures to get medical help for children who survive might be effective in changing their behavior. Serious punishment after a child dies is too late to help that child. Moreover, punishing as serious criminals parents whose failure to get medical help has already brought them the worst misfortune most parents imagine is to inflict further pain on people who are already suffering terribly. Still, insofar as criminal penalties can affect the behavior of other parents, highly publicized instances of prosecutions for homicide may be more likely to be productive than minor penalties for neglect.

In states with religious exemptions from determinations of neglect for parents who decline medical help in favor of spiritual healing, parents do have available a twofold argument that (1) the law implicitly authorizes, and ren-

---

[47] E.g., id. at 31–39, who says, at 33, that the exemptions send a message that "the child's life is not all that valuable"; Ivy B. Dodes, "Note, 'Suffer the Little Children': Toward a Judicial Recognition of a Duty of Reasonable Care Owed Children by Religious Faith Members," 16 *Hofstra Law Review* 165, 183 (1987).

[48] See, e.g., James G. Dwyer, "The Children We Abandon: Religious Exemptions to Child Welfare and Education as Denials of Equal Protection to Children of Religious Objectors, "74 *North Carolina Law Review* 1321, 1326–28 (1996); Anne D. Lederman, "Understanding Faith: When Religious Parents Decline Conventional Medical Treatment for Their Children," 45 *Case Western Law Review* 891, 926 (1995); Ann Maclean Massie, "The Religion Clauses and Parental Health Care Decisionmaking for Children: Suggestions for a New Approach," 21 *Hastings Constitutional Law Quarterly* 725, 775 (1994).

[49] See Ariz. Rev. Stat. Ann. 8–201.01 (Wes. 1989) (covers "child who in good faith is being furnished Christian Science treatment by a duly accredited practitioner"); G. Code Ann. 15–11–2(8) (Supp. 1989) (covers children "given spiritual treatment according to the tenets of a recognized church by an accredited practitioner"). It is all right to name some particular religious groups so long as others are not excluded. The sentence on an exemption in the text does not address the possibility of distinguishing views that are opposed to plainly demonstrable physical facts from views that are not susceptible to physical demonstration.

ders unpunishable, the behavior that leads to their child's death, and (2) they have not had fair warning that their behavior is criminal. The argument that the neglect provision insulates against a prosecution for homicide has proved unavailing,[50] but some courts have been persuaded that the statutory scheme has failed to provide parents the adequate notice that due process requires.[51] In one of these cases, the court explicitly resolved that the neglect exemption did not itself insulate parents against a manslaughter prosecution, before proceeding to find notice inadequate; it did not indicate whether its own opinion on the issue of coverage would itself provide adequate notice for parents in the future.[52]

I believe there is a strong argument that parents who have conscientiously done the best they can for their children's welfare, according to their religious lights, should not be punished as criminals; but a final judgment on that score must depend on a careful evaluation of the possible benefits of criminal sanctions. At a minimum, a prosecutor should exercise her discretion sensibly, not pursuing parents who have conscientiously and thoughtfully sought what they regarded as the best treatment for their child,[53] unless persuaded that criminal punishment can accomplish something more than satisfying the sentiments of those outraged by the child's death.

A judgment that people who act on their religious convictions when they fail to seek ordinary medical treatment for their children should usually not be punished does not settle whether in jurisdictions that retain a compelling interest standard for judging claims of free exercise, parents should enjoy a free exercise right to escape criminal punishment.[54] I think not. The parents have failed to seek medical treatment that the state could have compelled if a welfare worker had become aware of the child's condition, and the state's interest in preserving the lives and health of children is a very important one. If the state can require treatment, the parents have no right to avoid it. A state's decision to punish parents for not seeking treatment is a judgment

---

[50] See, e.g., *Walker v. Superior Court*, 763 P.2d 852 (Cal. 1988), cert. denied, 491 U.S. 905 (1989). One way of viewing the situation is that the parents' behavior is permissible until it becomes extremely dangerous to the child's life. Another perspective, persuasive I think if the state can directly override the parents' choice and compel treatment, is that the exemption is better seen as an excuse than a privilege not to seek medical treatment. The excuse would not reach the penalties for homicide.

[51] *Hermanson v. State*, 604 So. 2d 775 (Fla. 1992); *State v. McKown*, 475 N.W.2d 63 (Minn. 1991), cert. denied, 502 U.S. 1036 (1992).

[52] Id.

[53] A skeptic might say no one can thoughtfully reject standard medical treatment, but we know that otherwise thoughtful and intelligent people are Christian Scientists and do reject medical treatment, and the numbers and social status of Christian Scientists testify that this is not a religion chosen by the indifferent and irresponsible.

[54] The free exercise claim could arise under a state constitution or a state RFRA.

about means within the range of what the state may do to pursue its legitimate ends.[55]

This conclusion faces a possible objection based on ideas about the least restrictive means: if the state can compel treatment, it doesn't need to punish parents criminally, so punishment is unnecessary and, therefore, unconstitutional. This objection suffers the double flaw that officials commonly do not know about the need for treatment at the outset and that the alternative to criminal punishment might be much more extensive intrusions into the homes of members of groups that disparage medical treatment. From one standpoint, rare criminal punishment may seem a less restrictive means than constant home visits by welfare workers.

Although parents should rarely be prosecuted for secular medical harms that befall children because of religiously grounded failures to seek treatment, a right to this effect should not be accorded under state constitutions and RFRAs.

REFUSALS TO PARTICIPATE IN MEDICAL PROCEDURES

Issues of religious conscience can arise for people who provide medical services, as well as for parents and children who stand to benefit from them. Doctors, nurses, orderlies, pharmacists, hospitals, and HMOs may be so opposed to a particular medical procedure that they cannot comfortably participate in providing it.[56] Among the services to which health care providers may object are abortion, sterilization, artificial insemination, medical experimentation, withdrawal of life support, withdrawal of nutrition and hydration, organ transplants, autopsies, blood transfusions, and the provision of "morning after" contraceptives. Should providers be given a legal privilege to refuse to participate in some or all of these services, and, if so, how broadly should the privilege extend?

A privilege might be limited to excusing a provider from legal consequences that would otherwise arise; it might also protect an individual from conse-

---

[55] One possible counterargument to this analysis is that the parents have a right not to be enlisted in treatment. Therefore, the state cannot punish them for failing to seek treatment. This argument seems mistaken. Parents have custody. If the state can compel an operation, it can order parents to produce the child for an operation. One should not view the parents as possessing some absolute privilege not to assist in any way.

[56] See Lynn D. Wardle, "Protecting the Rights of Conscience of Health Care Providers," 14 *Journal of Legal Medicine* 177 (1993); Kathleen M. Boozang, "Deciding the Fate of Religious Hospitals in the Emerging Health Care Market," 31 *Houston Law Review* 1429 (1995); Bryan A. Dykes, "Proposed Rights of Conscience Legislation: Expanding to Include Pharmacists and Other Health Care Providers," 36 *Georgia Law Review* 565 (2002).

quences that normally follow if he refuses to do what his employer tells him to do. Federal and state statutes and regulations set some medical standards;[57] others are established by semipublic bodies[58] or accepted norms of the medical profession,[59] with failures to perform adequately potentially constituting a basis to conclude that a doctor or hospital has been negligent. Lurking in the background is possible criminal liability. Thus, if a patient dies because a doctor in an emergency room fails to authorize a blood transfusion, the doctor could be charged with negligent, or even reckless, homicide.[60]

In other instances, the question is not one of legal liability, but whether a hospital, doctor, or drugstore can require employees to participate in services to which they object, on pain of being disciplined or dismissed.

We need to understand that more general legal norms about freedom of religion provide some protection. Under Title VII, an employer might have to "accommodate" the religious refusal of an employee to participate in a particular medical service. Under the constitutional law of free exercise that survives *Employment Division v. Smith*, were an employee to lose his job because he could not conscientiously participate, he would be eligible for unemployment compensation.[61] And when states have RFRAs or constitutions interpreted to retain a requirement that the government not impinge on religious exercise without very strong interests in doing so, providers might be protected against some legal consequences or dismissal from a government-run hospital.[62] But we have seen in chapter 18 that the accommodation requirement of Title VII has been construed to demand very little of employers. Short of a specific "right of conscience" provision, workers have little protection against being dismissed by employers in the private sector.

---

[57] See, e.g., Katherine White, "Crisis of Conscience: Reconciling Religious Health Care Providers' Beliefs and Patients' Rights," 51 *Stanford Law Review* 1703, 1704 (1999). In many instances, individual health care professionals have no legal obligation to render service, but residents, interns, nurses, and orderlies may have duties as employees of hospitals to do so. (Most physicians are independent businesspeople allowed to practice in hospitals.)

I do not discuss the interplay of federal and state power. The main trigger for federal regulation here is federal funding, for which the government can attach conditions. State legislatures have broad authority to promote the general welfare, so long as they do not violate constitutional rights or standards set by organs of the federal government.

[58] For example, the Accreditation Council for Graduate Medical Education has required that obstetrical and gynecological residents who do not object to performing abortions receive training in performing them. The council's earlier withdrawal of accreditation partly for a failure to provide such training was upheld in *St. Agnes Hospital v. Riddick*, 748 F. Supp. 319 (D. Md. 1990). The court discussed whether actions of the council amounted to state action.

[59] Coverage by HMOs and insurance companies also influences what treatments are provided.

[60] Recklessness requires that the actor be aware of an unreasonable risk; negligence requires only that the risk be unreasonable. For criminal liability, behavior must be grossly unreasonable.

[61] *Thomas v. Review Bd.*, 450 U.S. 707 (1981).

[62] Federal hospitals are subject to the federal RFRA.

A possible argument against any such protection is that no one need be a doctor, nurse, orderly, or pharmacist. If a person chooses to enter one of these vocations, the government and employers can set conditions on how she exercises it. Because a person can always pursue a different vocation, no conflict of conscience arises. The flaw in this argument is evident. There is a powerful reason not to force people to choose between offending their consciences or foregoing a major vocational option. When the rules of appropriate behavior change radically, as with the status of most abortions, one especially cannot expect people to abandon a vocation with the onset of a novel conflict between general expectations about its practice and individual moral standards. Further, ministering to the sick has been a traditional religious vocation; the government should not create conditions that force individuals and organizations long committed to that task to give it up.[63]

Standards authorizing refusals vary in the attitude they require of those who are to qualify. Statutes authorizing refusals are commonly referred to as "conscience clauses,"[64] but some laws simply provide that no one may be required to participate in a covered medical procedure.[65] Under such a law, one whose refusal was based on unpleasant memories or aesthetic distaste, rather than moral or religious conviction, would nevertheless be protected.[66] Other clauses protect refusals by those whose basis is moral or religious grounds, those who want to avoid an act against conscience, or those who have a conscientious objection.[67] These, and other, variations

[63] See Boozang, note 56 supra, at 1475–79 (1995); Angela C. Carmella, "The Religion Clauses and Acculturated Religious Conduct: Boundaries for the Regulation of Religion," in James E. Woods and Derek Davis, eds., *The Role of Government in Monitoring and Regulating Religion in Public Life* 21, 30 (Waco, Tex.: J. M. Dawson Institute of Church-State Studies, Baylor University, 1993). The sentence in the text is about forcing individuals to provide treatment; the government appropriately insists that treatment that is provided satisfy medical standards.

[64] Various standards and citations to provisions containing them are contained in Wardle, note 56 supra, at 179–202. See also White, note 57 supra, at 25–26. If the law sets limiting criteria for protected refusals, and an intern, nurse, or orderly gives appropriate notification that she is not bound to participate, hospital officials will initially have to decide whether she has adequate grounds to refuse. Were they to decide that her claim is not sufficient, a court might have to resolve the question. When a hospital itself claims an exemption against a patient or doctor who wants a procedure the hospital refuses to allow, courts must also be ready to pass on the grounds for the hospital's stance.

[65] Professor Wardle, note 56 supra, at 197, suggests that these laws presume that refusals to participate in abortions are based on a conscientious objection, but it may well be that state legislators unsympathetic with the Supreme Court's decisions about abortion want to maximize possibilities for refusal.

[66] However, I assume such laws would be interpreted to demand at least a consistent refusal to engage in a particular procedure; it would not be enough that one wished to be elsewhere for a single occasion.

[67] What is commonly referred to as the "Church Amendment" (after its sponsor), adopted by Congress in 1973, granted an exemption from participating in sterilizations and abortions based on "religious beliefs or moral convictions." See White, note 57 supra, at 1707–8.

in phraseology may carry little practical significance, but they have subtly different connotations.

"Moral grounds" is a broader category than "conscientious objection"; the notion of not committing an act against conscience probably lies closer to "conscientious objection" on this spectrum of possibilities. Consider a nurse who is convinced that elective plastic surgery represents the worst of a materialist, superficial culture, perpetuates unhealthy denials of aging, and wastes resources. She may have moral reasons not to help in such operations, but the reasons do not amount to a conscientious objection, and they might not render her assistance an act against conscience.

Sincerely held reasons that do not amount to a conscientious objection can be religious as well as nonreligious. If our nurse conceived attempts to reverse the aging process as a sin against God's creation, she might have a religious basis not to assist elective plastic surgery that was less than a conscientious objection.

Standards for exemptions raise the question just why any refusal of conscience should be allowed. Facing this question leaves little doubt why so many exemptions focus on abortion. A legislator might think that protecting conscience is so important that persons should not be made to act against conscience, however odd the basis for their judgments. But a legislator who believes that a particular procedure is seriously wrongful, and should be performed as little as possible, might approve a right of refusal independent of any special sensitivity about the conscience of those who refuse.[68]

Without doubt, legislatures can, in principle, extend a right of refusal to all those who have a conscientious claim to refuse, to all those with moral grounds to refuse, to all those who wish to refuse, or those refusers who fit within some other categorization that either makes no reference to religion or treats religious and nonreligious claims in the same way. The serious constitutional issue is whether an exemption can be given to religious claimants and no others.

We have seen, from earlier chapters, that material in Supreme Court decisions looks in both directions on this question, but, on balance, the cases indicate that exemptions limited to religious claimants are at least sometimes acceptable.[69] But that does not tell us whether exemptions limited to religious conscience are wise or constitutionally acceptable in this context or whether exemptions, cast in religious terms or not, may be excessive in their impositions on others.

---

[68] An intermediate position could be that a right of conscience should be recognized whenever society is sharply divided about the acceptability of a procedure.

[69] The crucial cases are *Wisconsin v. Yoder*, 406 U.S. 205 (1972); *Employment Division v. Smith*, 494 U.S. 872 (1990); and *Corporation of the Presiding Bishop v. Amos*, 483 U.S. 327 (1987).

The answer about impositions is fairly straightforward. Exemptions can be undesirable, or even unconstitutional, if they impose restraints that are too severe on private actors. When Connecticut tried to guarantee that all workers would be given their Sabbath off, the Supreme Court, by a wide margin, held that this amounted to an establishment of religion, because the law imposed too great a burden in its restrictions on employers.[70] This case has potential implications for victims who suffer deprivations because others refuse to participate in ordinary medical treatment.[71] The "victims" might be individual health care providers, hospitals, or people seeking medical services.

Some Catholic hospitals have a requirement that their doctors not perform abortions on their premises or on any others. If a law provides that such an institutional requirement is exempted from any negative legal consequences, a doctor could complain that her actions are excessively restricted, as were the actions of the Connecticut employer, Caldor, Inc. (However, unlike Caldor, the doctor is originally restricted by a private actor's conditions.)

A closer analogy actually involves the reverse situation. A nurse or resident relies on a conscience clause to refuse to participate in a procedure that a hospital provides. The hospital complains that the exemption imposes too severely on it. In an actual case, a nurse-anesthetist relied on a conscience statute to refuse to participate in a sterilization.[72] The district court found that the nearest substitute nurse-anesthetist was fifty-five miles away, and that continual arrangement for substitutes was costly and created scheduling difficulties and uncertainties about when sterilizations could be performed that were detrimental to patients. Although the hospital raised no constitutional argument, its complaint about impracticality was very much like Caldor's, which asserted that giving its employee his day of worship off would be expensive and would impose on other workers.

Yet a third possible victim is the private individual who fails to receive a form of medical treatment. Let us suppose that a refusal provision leaves a woman who has been raped without the possibility of getting a "morning after" pill that would prevent or terminate a pregnancy.[73] She asks for a pill

[70] *Estate of Thornton v. Caldor, Inc.*, 472 U.S. 703 (1985).

[71] The claim of right made by the "victim," whether the victim is a patient or someone who provides medical services, need not have an independent constitutional status. Caldor did not claim that a state could never impose such onerous restrictions on it; it successfully asserted that the state's preference for religious interests violated the Establishment Clause.

[72] *Swanson v. St. John's Lutheran Hospital*, 597 P.2d 702 (Sup. Ct. Mont. 1979).

[73] As Boozang explains, note 56 supra, at 1447–48, the pill may prevent fertilization or inhibit implantation on the uterine wall. On the official Roman Catholic view, the latter is a form of abortion. White, note 57 supra, at 1715–16, indicates that some rape victims live in communities in which the only local hospitals are Catholic ones, most of which will not supply

in the only emergency room in her area and is refused. (Her physical injuries are so severe that she cannot leave the hospital for three days.) Her conscience draws the line between taking such a pill, which she accepts, and having a standard abortion, which she regards as murder. She becomes pregnant. Thus, the hospital's refusal to provide the pill has led her to sustain an unwanted pregnancy. Although she was not restricted in the manner of the doctor in the Catholic hospital or the hospital told that it cannot fire a refuser, she can argue that the state has tipped the balance too far toward acceding to religious conscience and away from safeguarding her bodily health and physical integrity according to ordinary medical standards.[74]

Because people who can get treatment elsewhere and have adequate information about alternative possibilities have a much less powerful claim that refusal impinges on them to an impermissible degree, the challenge to excessiveness might be viewed as to particular, atypical applications of a refusal statute, rather than to the law as a whole. However, one serious concern about granting pharmacists a right of refusal is that it may make filling prescriptions too cumbersome in many circumstances.[75]

Concerns about impositions on innocent victims are clearly worthy of legislative attention, and they might recommend withdrawal of any refusal right for emergency situations. Excessive imposition might also violate the Establishment Clause. An exemption cast directly in religious terms is most clearly vulnerable in this respect. Were a law to justify all refusals, or all refusals based on conscience, those who benefit might contend that the statute cannot be establishing religion, because religion receives no preference. The answer is that laws mainly designed to protect religious conscience may establish religion by an excessive imposition, even if the laws also benefit some persons with nonreligious grounds. Of course, a law that privileges

---

a morning-after pill. For a case in which a court, denying recovery to a woman who did not become pregnant, suggested that a rape victim might recover if she was denied information about and access to a morning-after pill, and then became pregnant, see *Brownfield v. Daniel Freeman Marina Hospital*, 256 Cal. Rptr. 240 (Ct. App. 1989).

[74] If we imagine the totally unrealistic example of a law authorizing human sacrifice of unwilling victims, performed out of religious conscience, the victim's claim that the law impermissibly established religion would be very powerful (even assuming the law placed no requirement on the victim to submit). To descend to the slightly more plausible, suppose that a refusal statute justified not giving blood transfusions, that the only hospital close enough to save a victim of an auto accident treated him but refused to give a transfusion as a matter of religious conscience, that the victim died, and that virtually all doctors would agree that a transfusion would have saved him. The claim that the state's authorization of the refusal was excessive and amounted to an establishment of religion would be strong.

[75] See Molly Teliska, "Recent Development: Obstacles to Access: How Pharmacist Refusal Clauses Undermine the Basic Health Care Needs of Rural and Low-Income Women," 20 *Berkeley Journal of Gender Law and Justice* 229 (2005); Rob Stein, "Pharmacists' Rights at Front of New Debate," *Washington Post*, March 28, 2005, A1.

less behavior, and imposes less on others, is less subject to challenge on this ground than a law that might deprive patients and doctors of important benefits or impose substantial costs on health care facilities.

Most existing refusal statutes apply only to abortion; many fewer reach sterilization or contraception.[76] Most statutes do not require religious grounds for objection, but that may be partly because many of those who have legislated exemptions from participation in abortion are either opposed themselves to abortion or have deep doubts about its morality. Among the critical questions about a privilege to refuse are whether it should be extended to many other medical procedures and what attitude potential refusers should need in order to qualify.

There is a strong argument for extension. In principle, people should not have to render services that they believe are forbidden directly by God or are deeply immoral. However, any privilege to refuse needs to be compatible with individuals being informed about and being able to acquire standard medical services and with health care institutions not having to turn handsprings to have personnel on hand to provide those services. A legislature might expand protection procedure by procedure, after careful study of potential claims to refuse and likely imposition on victims if a privilege is granted. But I think a preferable course is extension in more general terms, with measured qualifications for situations in which recognizing the privilege would interfere too greatly with the provision of health services.

However broad a privilege is, the question arises whether it should be limited to religious conscience. In regard to individuals, a more inclusive approach is both intrinsically preferable, and more sensible politically, winning allies and softening potential opposition. If in actual administration, most medical personnel are effectively going to be allowed to refuse on their own say-so, it probably makes sense to extend the privilege to anyone who wishes to refuse.

Whether nonreligious refusals in conscience are at all frequent must depend on the particular medical procedure. Some nonreligious individuals are convinced by natural law arguments that a human life with full value begins at the moment of conception; some strongly resist any measures taken for the purpose of ending life. It is harder to imagine nonreligious objections in conscience to blood transfusions or advice about contraceptives.

Because the great majority of existing refusal laws do not single out religious conscience, because a broader law is less vulnerable to challenge, and because some nonreligious persons will have strong moral reasons not to participate in certain medical procedures, general privileges to refuse should not be limited to religious claimants.

[76] See Wardle, note 56 supra, at 76.

The issue is harder with respect to institutions. Although it is somewhat difficult to say what gives a collective entity an objection in conscience, we do understand that a hospital that is run by a religious group has a powerful reason not to allow actions on its premises that the religion regards as murder or as another serious moral wrong. Although a hospital run by a nonreligious entity could be dedicated to ideas of "holistic medicine" that condemn certain standard forms of medical treatment, my decidedly nonexpert sense is that there are now few, if any, such hospitals. But there certainly are nonreligious hospitals—public and private—in areas where many people condemn abortion. The directors of such hospitals might wish not to have abortions performed there for moral or political reasons, and their moral reasons might be religiously informed. They might wish to have hospital policy reflect their sense of what is morally acceptable practice. An extensive right of refusal based on moral grounds might reach some of these circumstances, if not all.

My view is that no special right of conscience should protect hospitals whose individual directors happen to feel strong disquiet about procedures on moral or religious grounds. (This is not to say the hospitals necessarily have to perform the procedures; there is a degree of flexibility of choice that does not depend on a legal right of refusal.) If this conclusion is sound, limiting institutional exemptions to religious organizations makes sense.[77] An Alaska case provides modest support for this course. Interpreting a state refusal law that applied to hospitals declining to offer abortions, the state supreme court ruled that the law was invalid unless limited to sectarian facilities, since the general interest in protecting conscience did not outweigh the constitutional right to abortion.[78] Even if this decision is mistaken in suggesting that a refusal law for abortions must be so limited, it offers grounds for thinking that a law may be so limited.

---

[77] See Boozang, note 56 supra, at 1505–8.
[78] *Valley Hospital Assoc. v. Mat-Su Coalition for Choice*, 948 P.2d 963 (Alaska 1997). See also *Doe v. Bridgeton Hospital Assoc.*, 366 A.2d 641 (N.J. Sup. Ct. 1976).

CHAPTER 22

Child Custody

Parental struggles over the custody of children raise thorny questions about the law's treatment of religious convictions and practices. The two main occasions for these disputes are when one divorcing parent claims that the other's religious practices constitute a reason to refuse that parent custody, and when one parent seeks to control what the other does with the child in regard to religion—for example, stopping her from taking the child to religious services or involving the child in undesirable religious practices. The basic issues of principle are similar for the two kinds of cases.

The serious controversies in both categories arise only with religious practices that are not illegal, practices in which a united married couple could involve their children. Certain religious activities—child sacrifice is an extreme example—are criminal for anyone. The law also forbids children's participation in some activities, such as ordinary work, that are fine for adults.[1] And, under general standards regarding abuse of children, state authorities would stop parents from pressing their children into harmful activities, such as a religious vigil in which participants remain awake for seventy-two hours. For these activities in which officials would restrict parents whether they acted together or alone, a member of a divorced couple can get a court's help to prevent the other from involving their child, and might even be awarded custody on that basis. We reach the debatable questions when we turn to the wide range of activities in which a united couple could legally include their child.

Contests over Custody

When divorcing parents cannot agree who will have custody of their children, the courts must achieve a resolution. The dominant standard courts

---

[1] Even parents who consider work a religious responsibility will be held to have violated child labor laws if their small children do ordinary work. See *Prince v. Commonwealth of Massachusetts*, 321 U.S. 158 (1944). In id. at 166, the Court said that "the state has a wide range of power for limiting parental freedom and authority in things affecting the child's welfare." For a case in which a court denied visitation rights until the father ceased daily marijuana use, although his use was part of his Rastafarian religious practices, see *State v. Waters*, 951 P.2d 317 (Ct. Apps. Wash. 1998).

now employ is "the best interests of the child,"[2] embodied in many state statutes.[3] When a court decides that one parent will have primary custody and the other only visitation rights,[4] it determines which of two home environments will be more conducive to a child's healthy development. What concerns us here is how far the court may take religious practice into account in determining what is best for the child.

Judges traditionally gave some "credit" to a parent who was a regular churchgoer, believing that church attendance signaled a parent's sound morality and that a life including religious practice would be better for a child. Just how much judges should credit such religious affiliation is now a substantial question.[5] Under a principle that the state should not sponsor or assist religion, judges cannot give credit for religious practice because it reflects a true view about God.[6] But they probably can take participation in religion as *one* indication that a parent cares about moral and social responsibility, and can assume that religious activity will help promote those attitudes in the child.[7]

The situation that draws our attention is rarer. One parent claims that the other's religious practices will positively harm the child, according to broad cultural standards of healthy development. Given principles of free exercise and nonestablishment, what relevance, if any, should judges assign to such religious practices? What approach reflects an appropriate neutrality among competing religious views and groups? And should any protection that religious beliefs and practices receive also be extended to nonreligious beliefs and practices?

---

[2] See, e.g., *Morris v. Morris*, 412 A.3d 139, 141 (Pa. Sup. Ct. 1979). Shauna Van Praagh has suggested that in cases in which religion plays a role, a court's inquiry should be more complicated than assessment of the child's best interest. "Religion, Custody, and a Child's Identities," 35 *Osgoode Hall Law Journal* 311 (1997).

[3] See, e.g., Ky. Rev. Stat. Ann. § 403.270 (Michie 1980). Occasionally, a formulation also refers to the interests of others, but this is a minor deviation from the emphasis on the child's interests. Arizona's statute refers to "the mental and physical health of all individuals involved." Ariz. Rev. Stat. § 25–403 (1996). If a court is seeking in part to promote the health of all individuals involved, it is possible that a resolution that seems best overall will seem less than optimal for the child where custody is being determined.

[4] Parents may, instead, agree to joint custody or have that imposed on them by a court.

[5] Some statutes actually refer to the religious or spiritual needs of the child, see, e.g., Alaska Stat. § 25.24.150 (Michie 1983); S.C. Code Ann. § 20-3-160 (Law Co-op 1996); but at least one court has indicated it could consider religion only if it could do so under a "harm" standard. *Bonjour v. Bonjour*, 542 P.2d 1233, 1237 (Alaska 1979).

[6] Probably they cannot assume that religious practice is more conducive to moral development than a nonreligious participatory association that seeks to support morality.

[7] A court would not need to, and should not, assume that religious participation would be more constructive than participation in an atheist group that seeks to develop moral and political responsibility, only that it is one avenue for such development.

The 1967 dispute of *Quiner v. Quiner* starkly posed the central issues about reliance on religious practices.[8] A California court addressed the fundamental question whether a wife's religious beliefs and practices could count negatively in the battle over custody. We can sharpen the modern relevance of the dispute by altering some features of the actual case, assuming that a court is making an initial decision about custody under a "best interests of the child" standard, and that factors other than those related to religious belief and practice tip slightly in the mother's favor.[9]

When the Quiners married, both belonged to a group called the Plymouth Brethren. Disagreement within the Brethren arose, and the group split in two, with Mr. Quiner joining a faction that did not accept the majority's move toward exclusivity and separation from society at large. Mrs. Quiner remained with the more exclusive group, which her father helped lead. Mrs. Quiner believed she had to be "separate" from her husband, who "had chosen to be out of the fellowship." She could neither eat meals nor have sexual intercourse with him. She acknowledged that she would instruct her son, John Edward, in her religious faith and that, if he accepted the faith, he would "separate" from his "spiritually unclean" father. Nevertheless, she would teach her son to love his father and to respect and obey him.

The children of the "Exclusive Brethren" were told not to eat in the school cafeteria but to eat a box lunch alone, separate from their schoolmates; the children could not affiliate with any outside organization or participate in any extracurricular activity; they could not visit and play with other children; they could not have toys or pets; they could not watch television or listen to the radio; and they were discouraged from reading anything except schoolwork and the Bible. Adult members did not vote or participate in civic or government activities, and they did not have television sets or radios in their homes.

Mrs. Quiner attended religious meetings six nights per week and three times on Sunday, and she would take her child to many of these. Women were apparently not allowed to speak at these meetings.[10] As early as the age

[8] 59 Cal. Rptr. 503.

[9] In the actual case, John Edward, the child, had already been with his father from the age of two and a half to five, in accord with the trial court's award of custody. The appellate court treated the then existing law as requiring a grant of custody of a child of tender years to a fit mother, barring truly extraordinary circumstances. That approach is now regarded as violating the Equal Protection Clause, under which women and men must be treated equally in respect to custody. See *Weinberger v. Wiesenfeld*, 420 U.S. 636 (1975). Mothers continue to receive custody of small children in the vast majority of circumstances, but courts do not invoke any nearly automatic principle. Finally, appellate courts generally defer to the discretion of trial courts that have decided on custody, accepting determinations different from those they would have made.

[10] For this proposition, the court relied, 59 Cal. Rptr. 506 n. 1, on the *Encyclopedia of Religion and Ethics*.

of six, a child might be converted to full membership. The trial court remarked that "such a schedule leaves practically no time for defendant to
spend in the normal activities of mother and child in training, recreation
and otherwise attending to her child's needs." Mr. Quiner, who also had
Protestant fundamentalist beliefs but did not live "separate" with all its limitations on ordinary life, argued that he would be the better custodial parent.

The issue posed by *Quiner* is not simple. In custody disputes, like disputes
over church property, the state does not have the option of "staying out"; a
court must decide for one parent or the other.

Four conceivable bases, all connected to religion, might be relied on by a
judge to award custody to Mr. Quiner. (1) Mrs. Quiner's separatist beliefs
are bizarre and unsound. (2) Internal aspects of the practice of that religion,
including the rule that only males speak at assembly meetings, teach implicit
lessons contrary to the ideals of democratic citizenship. (3) Mrs. Quiner's
attitudes create severe risks that her son will want to avoid contact with his
father, or will suffer emotionally from the pull of her beliefs against his father's love. (4) Separation as practiced is so severe that a child will be ill
prepared for ordinary life.

We can dispose of the first and second possible grounds fairly quickly.
Secular courts may not decide that some religious beliefs are intrinsically
more sound than others. Nor should they base decisions on judgments about
how well worship services and organizational principles comport with ideals
of liberal democracy. Although, in fact, some church practices do comport
better with social ideals of fairness and equality than others, legal institutions, as chapters 16 and 20 suggest, should not get in the business of favoring particular religious groups over others based on such judgments.
(Were a father's religion to teach that women should be subordinate in all
areas of life to men, that could aversely affect relations of a child to its [inde-
pendent] mother. A consideration of that possibility should not be blocked
by a principle that bars judgments based on the organizational practices of
religious groups.)

The third and fourth potential grounds are more promising. Mrs. Quiner's
telling her son that his father is "spiritually unclean", and should be separated from, could detrimentally affect the relationship of son and father.
Mrs. Quiner has indicated that she will raise John Edward to have minimal
contact with other students and with the external, general culture. One
might reasonably conclude that a child who does not participate in any extracurricular activities, is not exposed to television or radio, and reads little
other than school assignments and the Bible will be less well prepared for
ordinary life than a child given the more usual upbringing Mr. Quiner offers.

Of course, the child may be well prepared for life within the "Exclusive Brethren," but suppose he leaves?

For this aspect of the inquiry, the track record of the "Exclusive Brethren" might be relevant, as it was for the Amish who wanted to withdraw their children from school. If *most children* reared in this and similar groups remain within the fold, a risk of poor preparation for ordinary life might be tolerable. But if most children eventually leave such groups, the chances are high that John Edward's rearing will leave him less well prepared for the life he will finally choose.[11]

We can imagine two quite different judicial responses, each of which might be characterized as "not taking religion into account." A court might disregard all aspects of Mrs. Quiner's plans for her son that are connected to religion.[12] That approach would best protect her religious exercise against negative or hostile judgments, but it might ill serve the son's interests, as those are understood from a nonreligious point of view. A contrasting way "not to take religion into account" would be to consider Mrs. Quiner's plans with "blinders" about their religious source—for example, assessing her proposals not to have her son watch television or read outside material detached from their religious motivation. This approach would afford Mrs. Quiner minimal protection and yield an unrealistic assessment of how the various deprivations would operate in her son's life.

Instead of choosing between these stark alternatives, a court might adopt an intermediate approach, one that would not treat Mrs. Quiner's religiously based choices just like any other unusual plans, but would take them into account if their negative effects were likely to be significant. An intermediate approach is less clean conceptually than the other two; but I shall argue that it makes the best sense.

Accepting Mrs. Quiner's claim that an award of custody to her husband "penalized her for her religious beliefs,"[13] the *Quiner* court construed the federal and state constitutions to forbid any legal penalty "imposed upon a person because of any religious beliefs which are not immoral, illegal or against public policy."[14] The court would be opening a "Pandora's box" if it could "weigh the religious beliefs" of each parent to decide which is for the best interests of the child.[15] Unable to conclude that John Edward will

---

[11] However, it is troubling that a parent's right to custody might turn on general statistics about the ability of separatist groups to hold members.

[12] This approach would be qualified, of course, for any activities a court would forbid to married couples with a unified view.

[13] Id. at 510.

[14] Id. at 510–11. The court emphasized that had the Quiners stayed together, they would certainly have been free to raise their son as Mrs. Quiner planned to raise him.

[15] Id. at 517.

not grow up to be a constructive, happy, law-abiding citizen, the court commented, "Precisely because a court cannot *know* one way or another, with any degree of certainty, the proper or sure road to personal security and happiness or to religious salvation, which latter to untold millions is their primary and ultimate best interest, evaluation of religious teaching and training and its projected as distinguished from immediate effect (psychologists and psychiatrists to the contrary notwithstanding) upon the physical, mental and emotional well-being of a child, must be forcibly kept from judicial determinations."[16] A court would later be able to intervene if John Edward was taught not to love and respect his father, or if it found actual evidence that his "emotional and mental well being has been affected and jeopardized."

The dissenting judge objected to a result that will "with practical certainty . . . produce tragically harmful effects inimical to the welfare of the . . . boy."[17] Pointing out that once psychological damage is actually done, a lifetime of remedial care may not undo it, he argued that custody should be awarded on the basis of "reasonable probabilities."

A judge would undoubtedly consider the restricted social life and separation from his father that Mrs. Quiner proposed for her son, were these not tied to her religious convictions and group practice. Imagine a mother who said, without any religious basis or associational tie, that she would teach her child to withdraw from social contacts, to refrain from reading books, and to separate from his father. That would count against custody for the mother.[18]

Quiner effectively qualifies the usual best-interests-of-the-child approach. Its unexpressed rule of law is, "We will award custody according to what will probably be in the best interests of the child, except that we will not make judgments about projected plans for a child that relate to a parent's religious beliefs and practices, even when the risks of undesirable outcomes (social withdrawal and possible separation from the father) can be identified without reference to the religious beliefs and assessed according to a nonreligious cultural understanding about a healthy upbringing." So perceived, the principle of the case is debatable and raises a delicate issue about baselines.

---

[16] Id. at 516.

[17] Id. at 518 (dissenting opinion of Herndon, J.). For a dissenting opinion complaining that a district court should have considered a church's teaching that a wife should be subservient to her husband, see *In re Marriage of Wang*, 896 P.2d 450, 452–54 (Sup. Ct. Mont. 1995).

[18] Judges might decide that activities that are ordinarily undesirable can be positively valuable in a religious setting, but that is not the court's rationale in *Quiner*. If Mrs. Quiner belonged to a nonreligious expressive association with similar practices, she might argue that the state should not penalize social beliefs and the practices that follow from them; but a court would not regard itself as disqualified from assessing likely effects on the child.

If one begins from the premise that courts should take into account all factors that can be evaluated on a nonreligious basis, it would be most "neutral" to consider the likely effects of not allowing a child to read books, sit with other children during lunch at school, and so on. On this view, for judges to give some weight to such plans would not inhibit religion or entangle the state with religion, because all effects would be judged without reference to religion. If, instead, one begins from the premise that parents should have wide latitude to determine the religious activities of children, one will regard a judge's reliance on factors related to religious practice as inhibiting religious exercise. Although no one would stop the parent from practicing her religion, she would be effectively forced to choose between gaining custody and adhering to an unconventional faith that includes her children.[19] A rule that treats factors like not reading books negatively whatever their source provides an incentive to parents to choose safe religions.

Any judicial attempt to consider practices apart from their religious setting raises an independent difficulty. Either the court will make an unrealistic appraisal or it will find itself evaluating the religion. Practices imposed on a child by an isolated parent will operate quite differently from practices that are aspects of life within a close-knit religious community.[20] And a judge would be hard put to evaluate practices as they actually operate without assessing religious elements, because religious assumptions are so deeply embedded in the practices.[21]

These difficulties support the *Quiner* court's conclusion not to treat religious factors like any other factors; but its principle of disregarding factors deriving from religion, in the absence of evidence of actual harm, is not the soundest approach. A better approach is to look at such factors, but to give them weight *only* when they point strongly against custody for the parent with the unusual religious beliefs and practices.

In a case that called the approach of *Quiner* "improvident," another court held "that the requirement of a reasonable and substantial likelihood of immediate or future impairment [of the child's physical or mental well-being] best accommodates the general welfare of the child and the free exercise of

---

[19] The parent might follow a religious faith on her own, affording the child a more "normal" life; but one can see that this would be almost impossible for a member of the Exclusive Brethren, *even if* her religious principles allowed her to provide a normal life for her child.

[20] A judge might ask, 'How would these practices look in a nonreligious community?" but this is not going to be a very helpful inquiry if all the communities that actually engage in the practices are religious.

[21] One *can* evaluate how often children die because their parents refuse blood transfusions, but one cannot evaluate the effect of separation from the external community without considering the support given by an internal community.

religion of the parents."[22] This kind of intermediate approach avoids the nearly absolutist approach of *Quiner*, but regards religious practices as something more than factors to be thrown into the mix with everything else that is relevant.[23]

According to one writer, state courts have adopted three different approaches to the threshold of harm that must be crossed before they will consider factors that relate to parental religious practices.[24] Under a "temporal welfare" approach, courts consider any practices that are likely to affect a child's worldly well-being. That would certainly include much of Mrs. Quiner's plans for John Edward. Under the "threatened harm" approach, courts consider factors that threaten a child's physical or mental well-being, a narrower category than all of temporal welfare. Under an "actual harm" approach, that of the *Quiner* majority, a court considers only religious practices that have already caused physical or mental harm.

Drawing a line at "actual harm" as contrasted with "threatened harm" does not make sense if one has in mind a discrete harmful occurrence that may or may not happen. A striking example is the refusal of Jehovah's Witnesses to seek, or allow, blood transfusions for their children. Let us suppose that one parent seeking custody is a Jehovah's Witness and the other is not. Should the risk of the child's not receiving a transfusion count against custody for the Jehovah's Witness? One court said that this possible harm, a hypothetical future event, was not a sufficient basis to deny custody.[25] Suppose after custody is awarded to the Jehovah's Witness, the child needs a transfusion and his mother tries to prevent his receiving one. Should that alter a judge's appraisal of custody if the child survives?[26] Unless the incident shows an increased likelihood of a need for a future transfusion, the judgment about custody should not change since the child's need for another transfusion remains only a contingent future possibility. One transfusion incident does not tell us whether the child in the future will be safe with the Jehovah's Witness parent.

What this analysis reveals about discrete harms that occur on particular occasions is that the real issue should not be "actual" or "threatened harm,"

---

[22] *In re Marriage of Hadeen*, 619 P.2d 374, 382 (Ct. App. Wash., Div. 1 1980). See *In re Marriage of Short*, 698 P.2d 1310, 1313 (Colo. Sup. Ct. 1985); *Morris*, note 2 supra, at 144.

[23] A case that approximates this position is *Petersen v. Rogers*, 433 S.E.2d 770 (N.C. App. 1970). See also *Pater v. Pater*, 63 Ohio St. 3d 393, 588 N.E.2d 794 (1992).

[24] Gary Miller, "Balancing the Welfare of Children with the Rights of Parents; *Petersen v. Rogers* and the Role of Religion in Custody Disputes," 73 *North Carolina Law Review* 1271, 1285–86 (1995).

[25] *Garrett v. Garrett*, 527 N.W.2d 213, 220–21 (Neb. Ct. App. 1995).

[26] The child might survive despite not having received a transfusion or because a court ordered a transfusion over the parent's objection. The death of a child could have implications

but the degree of probability of future harm. If a serious harm is highly probable to occur in the future, a court should take it into account. The no-transfusion harm will arise only if (1) a child needs a transfusion, (2) the parent will stick to her guns and not consent to it,[27] and (3) hospital authorities will not be able to intervene and get a court to order the transfusion over the parent's objection. If this danger should not count, the reason is its low probability, not that it lies in an uncertain future.

Analysis of emotional harm is different. Predicting how life's events will affect people's emotional well-being is hard. One might think that judges cannot predict emotional harm with sufficient accuracy to justify their assuming that religious practices may have a negative effect.[28] But, for two reasons, a sharp distinction between actual and probable harm is too neat. Often, experts may disagree whether actual harm has occurred. A court relying on less than certain evidence may base a decision about actual harm on a probability that is no greater than is a high likelihood of future harm. Another reason to act if future harm is highly probable is the difficulty of reversing emotional harm that has already occurred. When judges estimate *both* actual emotional harm and highly probable emotional harm from religious practices, their evaluations, and those of experts, may be influenced by opinions about the religious practices; but this risk cannot be wholly avoided. Requiring a high likelihood of serious harm is a more appropriate safeguard of religious practice than responding only after harm already has occurred.

Whether a religious parent is connected to a religious group may not matter for the threshold determination of how a judge should treat factors connected to religious practice, but it will loom large in a final evaluation of those factors. In the case at hand, John Edward would grow up with the support of a like-thinking group. Imagine the emotional strain for a child who is required to separate in almost every aspect of life and has no close association with anyone other than a single reclusive parent devoted to an idiosyncratic religious path. Further, the child's chances of eventually rejecting that way of life would be much greater without the group.[29] As with other areas we have examined, the parent who is connected to a religious

---

for the custody of other children, but the danger to other children would be subject to the analysis of the text about the danger to the child not given the transfusion.

[27] An actual incident does provide a strong indication of what a parent will actually do when the need for transfusion arises.

[28] On the view of the *Quiner* court, only a finding of actual harm would be reliable enough.

[29] Another consideration, although not one a court is likely explicitly to rely upon, is that an individual who arrives at such beliefs on her own is much more likely to be viewed as emotionally unstable than someone who has participated in group life. In Mrs. Quiner's case, the leadership of her father provided a natural explanation of why she was attached to her group.

group will fare better in court than individuals who lack associational ties, or whose only associational ties are nonreligious.[30]

Child custody determinations are governed by a mix of common law, statute, and constitutional law. Courts long ago developed their own approaches to custody disputes, but the "best interests" standard is now widely prescribed by statutes. Courts deciding how to treat religious factors in light of that standard must assess statutory policy, surviving common-law understandings, and federal and state constitutional principles. In examining constitutional restrictions on what a court might otherwise be inclined to do, I shall take free exercise and establishment concerns in order.

The serious free exercise question is whether some accommodation to religious exercise is required, as the *Quiner* court assumed. If a state court uses a compelling interest test under its own constitution, custody determinations will not be allowed to impair the free exercise of religion unless the standards a court employs are necessary to serve a compelling interest that cannot be served by alternative means. A standard that treats factors derived from religion like all other factors does indeed impair the exercise of religion, and the state lacks a compelling interest in using that approach,[31] since it can adequately protect the child's important interests under a "threatened harm" standard. (Against the argument that a "threatened harm" standard is unnecessary, because a narrower, less restrictive, "actual harm" standard will do, the answer is that the difficulties of identifying and undoing actual physical or mental harm provide a state ample basis to use the threatened harm standard, if it chooses.) A state requiring a high likelihood of serious harm should succeed in arguing that that approach is necessary to serve a compelling interest.

Analysis of federal free exercise rights under prevailing doctrine is less than straightforward. *Employment Division v. Smith* says that religious claimants should be treated like all others, unless they receive a statutory exemption, fit within the *Sherbert v. Verner* class of cases, or raise a hybrid claim. A religious parent has plausible arguments that *Smith* does not apply to custody determinations. Her claim to have religious factors disregarded is far removed from unemployment compensation, but the *Smith* Court throws out the possibility that the relevant category for free exercise protection may be situations in which officials make individualized judgments about exemptions. Someone in Mrs. Quiner's situation could contend that

[30] It is hard to imagine a nonreligious association with attitudes similar to those of Mrs. Quiner. Were there one, a court could probably not assume it would have much staying power; this is one of those areas in which a court might reserve special treatment for religious groups.

[31] One might say that the state has a compelling interest in the child's welfare, but that interest can be served by a less restrictive means.

since judges make highly individualized judgments about custody, her situation resembles Sherbert's, and her religious exercise should be taken into account. However, because custody judgments do not concern exceptions from ordinary legal requirements, this argument is a stretch.

A religious parent might argue that her claim involves parental rights over the upbringing of children as well as freedom of religion, and thus falls within the embrace of *Wisconsin v. Yoder*, which *Smith* treated as a hybrid case. But a parent like Mrs. Quiner seeks to have a court disregard factors normally relevant for custody determinations; for this topic, she does not have a separate parental right apart from religious exercise.[32]

The free exercise exemptions left standing by *Smith* are so hard to justify, along with *Smith*, that one cannot sensibly determine whether the religious parent claiming custody should fit within one of the categories *Smith* does not purport to cover.[33] Since *Smith* itself is misconceived, as I argue in chapter 5 and elsewhere in this book, a broad construal of exceptions to it is desirable; its overruling would be preferable. In the meantime, state courts should use a compelling interest approach (or something similar) for their own states' free exercise provisions, and should insist that trial judges in custody disputes use a "threatened harm" for religious factors, rather than treating those factors like any other considerations.[34]

Under the threatened harm approach, religious factors are treated differently from other factors. Does this establish religion? Such approaches do "favor" religion in some ways, but there are two strong answers to those who might say that this tends toward the establishment of religion.

First, religion is not *relevantly* favored. If a judge does not take into account a factor that he otherwise would, such as not having television or

---

[32] To be more precise, she has parental rights to raise her children, but none of those bear on how factors should be considered in a contest with another parent who has the same basic parental rights.

[33] Future results will depend on whether the Court wants to push *Smith* to its logical conclusion or back away from it.

[34] There are two arguments that the temporal welfare approach, which treats religious factors that bear on temporal welfare like nonreligious factors, violates the Establishment Clause. One argument is that the approach inhibits religion by pushing parents to deny their true faith, if that religion is judged bizarre by others, and to adhere to safer religions. Under standard establishment analysis, this effect should be regarded as remote and indirect, rather than a forbidden primary effect, since the standard itself makes no reference to religion. *If* the effect is regarded as primary, the law is more conveniently seen as denying the free exercise of religion in any event, so long as any free exercise test is used other than the neutrality approach of *Smith*. The second argument that the temporal welfare approach is an establishment is that judges, and other officials, must make impermissible (entangling) judgments about religion in order to decide if practices are likely to affect a child's temporal welfare. I have suggested that the difficulties of these inquiries is a reason to avoid the temporal welfare approach, but the

radio (or a computer) in the household, that does not encourage anyone to take a particular religious view. No one will adhere to a religion as a cover for not having a television. Religion is favored *only* in the sense that what would otherwise count negatively is disregarded. Second, even if a threatened harm approach significantly favors religion, it is a permitted accommodation to free exercise.

RESTRICTING PARENTAL ACTIONS

Apart from determining custody, a court may be called to respond when one parent objects to the other's exposing their child to a faith that the former does not wish the child exposed to,[35] or seeks to compel the other to take the child to religious services, or tries to stop the child's participation in a religious practice that causes harm unrelated to religion.[36] The situations involving harm unrelated to religion resemble those we have just considered, except that, instead of requesting custody, the objecting parent wants a court to constrain the custodial parent.[37] For example, a Mr. Quiner might ask a court to require Mrs. Quiner to give John Edward access to schoolmates and to television.

Should a court feel freer to dictate such terms of custody than to deny custody to Mrs. Quiner in the first place? In one sense, the court's intervention is less troublesome, because Mrs. Quiner will be less drastically affected; she will keep John Edward subject only to some conditions. But in the initial custody battle, a judge had to decide which of two environments was preferable; he was not compelling anyone to raise a child in a certain way. A judge who tells Mrs. Quiner what she must do with John Edward interferes more directly with her life, including her religious practices.

People may differ over the weight of these two countervailing factors— less drastic consequences and greater interference—but a stringent threatened harm standard is the best approach to custodial conditions, as well as to the underlying dispute over who has custody. That is, a judge should

---

degree of entanglement may not be undue, in a constitutional sense, if judges stick scrupulously to likely effects measured in nonreligious terms.

[35] See, e.g., *Pater*, note 23 supra.

[36] In these two situations, it is typically the custodial parent who seeks to restrict the activities of the noncustodial parent.

[37] A common idea of harm is that exposure to two different religions will be disturbing. These cases are discussed below.

forbid religious practices only when they pose a high likelihood of physical or emotional harm.[38]

When one parent tries to "enforce" a particular religious upbringing for the child, a court may face issues about conflicts between religious viewpoints and about the relevance of prior agreements and established practices.

One parent (usually the one with custody) may insist that the other not take the child to the services of a different faith, fearing this will cause stress and undermine the child's religious upbringing. How harmful it is for children to be exposed to two religions? This depends greatly on parental attitudes, the child, and the two religions. Children can accommodate two religions more comfortably if they are open and inclusive rather than closed and exclusive. A child needs an unusual degree of detachment to maintain equanimity if she is regularly barraged by two religions, each of which stridently asserts that the other's members follow the anti-Christ and are doomed for eternity. In all likelihood, judges should not themselves determine on their own that exposure to two religions will be harmful, unless a child shows signs of emotional disturbance.[39]

A court's task is complicated if the complaining parent relies on an explicit agreement about the child's religious education or an established family practice. A judge adhering to either of these might regard herself as deferring to judgments about harm made by the parents themselves or as granting parental understandings the kind of enforcement she gives to other contractual undertakings. But we need to be very careful about the justification for each of these rationales.

Many of the dimensions of this problem can be developed from the facts of *Zummo v. Zummo*.[40] The parents had agreed orally before their marriage that they would raise their children as Jewish. During the marriage the family participated in the Jewish faith, and the children attended no other services. Upon divorce, the Jewish mother, Pamela, received custody. The father, David, wished to take his children to Roman Catholic services. Pamela, concerned that inconsistent religious teachings would "confuse and disorient" them, sought a prohibition against David's taking the children to non-Jewish services.

In such a case, the court faces an initial difficulty in assessing what the parental agreement was meant to cover: the circumstances of its application

---

[38] Determination of conditions of custody can connect to the decision who has custody in the following way. If a custodial parent refused to forego the practice a court has forbidden as potentially harmful, that would be a significant basis to shift custody.

[39] See *Munoz v. Munoz*, 489 P.2d 1133, 1135 (Wash. 1971) (en banc). Courts should not be delving into the details of the two religions to a degree that would enable them to say that exposure to both will be destructive.

[40] 574 A.2d 1130 (Pa. Super. 1990).

and the particular activities it required and forbade. The fundamental question about applicable circumstances is whether an agreement about the marriage was intended to survive a divorce. David may have accepted the children not being exposed to any religion other than Judaism, because he saw this as conducive to a compatible, unified family. Once the family is broken by divorce, he may feel that taking the children to Catholic services helps give them a sense of his identity and causes no harm. Pamela may rejoin that all this shows is that David now regrets what he agreed to. Often it will be far from clear whether someone understood his original oral agreement and his practice within a unified family as designed to survive divorce. And it will not be clear just what the two partners would have agreed to if they had explicitly focused their attention on a possible divorce.

This doubt about intent is overcome if the parents have a written premarital agreement that explicitly covers divorce, or if the agreement to raise the children in one faith is part of the divorce settlement itself.

Can the problem of intent be overcome in a different way—namely, by a conclusion that the parental agreement and family practice show that the parents regarded exposure to two religions as harmful and that courts can fairly rely on that judgment? Usually not. In some instances, positive evidence that the parents together had made such a judgment may be forthcoming, but I strongly suspect that is atypical. The common circumstance is that one partner feels deeply about having the children raised in his or her faith. The other partner, usually less intense about religion, accedes. A variation on this theme is one partner's membership in a church that will not recognize a marriage unless the other partner agrees to raise children in that faith. In these instances, the acceding partner does not reach a judgment that exposure to two faiths will be harmful for children. Rather, believing that his loved one will not marry him unless he agrees, or motivated by an aim to eliminate a potential source of marital tension, he accepts the strong wish of his partner about religious upbringing. Divorce nullifies these reasons. A court can rarely infer that the partners together have reached a judgment that exposure to two religions would, in conditions of divorce, be harmful for the children.[41]

When one turns from the circumstances in which it applies to the particular actions it forbids, interpreting an agreement or practice may not become easier. If a father has visitation rights one weekend a month and a child is to be "raised as a Roman Catholic," *must* he take the child to a Catholic church on his Sundays with the child? If not, may he take the child to a Presbyterian

---

[41] Of course, a divorce itself imposes a considerable emotional strain on children; but the noncustodial parent is unlikely to think that strain will be (much) increased if he is allowed to take a child to his place of worship.

church? Suppose he says he is only exposing the child to that religion, not raising him as a Presbyterian. If he should not take the child to his church, may he tell the child what he believes, including his disbelief in transubstantiation and in the authority of the pope?

The divorce in one case provided that the children were to be raised as Jewish, but the non-Jewish custodial mother had enrolled her son in a Roman Catholic school.[42] The father sought to compel her to transfer him to public school. Most married couples who practice a form of Judaism would hesitate to send their children to Roman Catholic schools, but some do so. Would one or both parents have thought their agreement to raise a child as Jewish precluded enrollment in a Catholic school? That is very hard to say.

Many agreements are imprecise about such details. Of course, agreements of all sorts are vague, and courts interpret them as best they can, but the special difficulty here is that courts may be unable to interpret imprecise agreements without trying to understand what is crucial for the religion in which the child is to be raised. In the case we have been examining, that might mean delving into the particular form of Judaism and what is taught in the Roman Catholic school to determine the degree of incompatibility.

One way out of this difficulty is to treat such agreements as nonenforceable. A better way to handle this problem is not to restrict the liberty of a parent unless the agreement definitely entails that restriction *or* a parent's aim is to undermine what she agreed to. That would mean allowing the child's enrollment in the Catholic school unless the judge were convinced that the parents meant to bar that or that the mother's aim was to combat the child's Jewish upbringing. A court in serious doubt whether an agreement limits a parent's freedom should decide against restricting that parent.

Enforcement of agreements about religious upbringing raises still more fundamental problems about the state's role. Suppose the noncustodial father in a case like *Zummo* did specifically agree that he would not take a child to Catholic services, that he would not influence the child in any way in favor of Roman Catholicism, that he would have the child raised exclusively as Jewish, *and* that this agreement would cover circumstances of divorce. For a court to regard such an agreement as legally effective, it must concern itself with intended legal effect, possible duress, and continuing constraint on religious liberty.

The most straightforward question is whether the agreement was intended for secular legal enforcement. When couples sign agreements to satisfy church authorities who will not sanction marriages to nonmembers unless

---

[42] *Gottlieb v. Gottlieb*, 31 Ill. App. 2d 120, 175 N.E.2d 619 (App. Ct. 1961).

they agree to raise children in the faith, a nonmember may subscribe to a written agreement to satisfy the church, but without intending to be legally bound. The nonmember may gain some support for his position that such an agreement is not of legal effect from the disinclination of courts generally to enforce such agreements so long as couples remain married.

Parties can assure that a court will recognize an intent to accomplish legal bindingness by saying so in the agreement itself. For this purpose, it should not matter whether the original initiative comes from a church or from one member of the marrying couple, so long as the aim for legal effect is explicit. Nonenforcement of such agreements during marriage has only peripheral relevance. Courts rightly take the position that married couples must look mainly to themselves to work out problems; for courts to intervene in the affairs of couples who remain married would tend to undermine marriage bonds. Once the marriage has broken, and courts are entwined in the divorcing couple's affairs, *this* reason not to enforce a specific agreement evaporates.

A second question is whether the agreement was the product of some kind of duress; one member of a couple may have had a strong desire or need to be married, and the other may have extracted unfair concessions. A parent seeking to enforce the agreement will have a strong response to most contentions about duress. No one has to get married. If a man wants to be married so badly that he gives up things he would otherwise want, that does not constitute duress.[43] This conclusion is supported by the enforcement of premarital agreements about property that leave a divorced spouse with many fewer assets than he or she would otherwise have received.

The most troubling issue of all is whether a person should be bound to what he has agreed to years earlier, when the agreement concerns his exercise of religion. Imagine that at the time he got married, David Zummo was an indifferent Catholic, who hardly cared about the religious identity of his children. During the marriage, he has a religious experience and becomes devout. His change in respect to religion becomes one of the sources of tension within the marriage. Should he now be restricted by what he had agreed to years earlier, or would that interfere with his exercise of religion?

Without doubt, enforcement of an agreement constitutes a limit on a parent's exercise of religion, which includes some influence over the upbringing of his children. A restricted parent, in effect, is forced to surrender that aspect

---

[43] The strongest argument for duress may occur when a woman is pregnant, wants to be married to the father when she has the baby, and must agree to unpalatable conditions to achieve that. One can also imagine a situation in which the pregnant woman is planning an abortion and the prospective father desperately wants the child to be born, perhaps because he believes abortion is a terrible sin. He may agree to conditions he does not like to achieve the child's birth.

of his exercise of religion. But it does not follow that such restricting agreements should never be enforced. Matters of degree are important, as are conflicting religious liberties.

The degree of restriction on free exercise can vary significantly. If a parent is told that he can never discuss or explain his own religious ideas when he is with his child, that constitutes a very severe restriction. If he is told only that he may not take the child to specific religious services, the restriction is less. What if he is told that during his visitation time he *must* take the child to services of a faith not his own, one he may now abhor? At first glance, forcing a parent to take a child to religious services seems more of an impingement on free religious exercise than forbidding the parent to take the child. But we need to be realistic about what "taking" a child means in context. If the parent must sit through services of an alien faith, that is a serious restriction. But all the parent may have to do is "drop off" and "pick up." That seems a modest deprivation of the parent's *religious* liberty, especially if the agreement clearly covers the child's attending services that occur during visitation times.[44]

We should not look at the religious liberty interests as all on one side, or as lacking a dimension of time. Suppose, before marrying, Pamela has firmly resolved that her children will be raised as Jewish. She regards that as a vital exercise of *her* religion. She has expected to marry a religious Jew, but she falls in love with David Zummo, a Catholic. She is torn about marriage, but she never wavers on the point that her children must be Jewish. David proposes a resolution. He will agree that the children will be Jewish whatever happens. Pamela is satisfied she can marry the man she loves and carry out her religious imperative in respect to her children. If courts refuse to enforce such agreements, they maximize the present liberty of each adult to do what he or she thinks best, but they do so at some sacrifice of the original liberty of one partner to reach an agreement that will carry forward his or her concept of a religious imperative or religiously desirable outcome.

I do not mean to suggest that the two liberties always carry the same force. In some rough sense, I think the religious liberty of people at the time they act should be given a priority over the liberty to lock in a desired outcome by an agreement. In general, people should be able to act according to their present religious understandings. But it is too simple to say, as some courts

---

[44] Otherwise, visitation days might have to be formulated so the custodial parent can ensure that the child gets to services. In *Carrico v. Blevins*, 402 S.E.2d 235, 237 (Va. App. 1991), the court said that a noncustodial mother could not be required to take her son to church during her visitation days because "the state may not require a citizen to attend any religious worship." The case did not involve any prior agreement about religious practice. See also *Lundeen v. Struminger*, 165 S.E.2d 285 (Va. 1969).

have, that religious freedom is inalienable and cannot be bargained away.[45] A weak restriction of present liberty, for example, dropping off and picking up, may fairly be imposed in order to satisfy a strong religious expectation that one partner has carried forward from an earlier time.[46]

Courts that declare they will never enforce agreements about the religious upbringing of children go too far, but formal and informal agreements, often vague in content and unspecific about their implications for divorce, are hardly the key to resolving disputes over the exposure of children to religions.[47] Some agreements, if they are specific enough about what is at issue, plainly contemplate divorce, and do not impair anyone's religious liberty to a substantial degree, deserve enforcement because that is what the parties have agreed to. Other agreements may have some bearing on how a court should evaluate harm.

Very often, however, courts will be left to evaluate the harm of exposing children to competing religious ideas and practices. As difficult as distinguishing the emotional harm of divorce from the emotional harm of exposure to conflicting religions may be, especially when parents may invest some of the negative emotional charge of the divorce into their comments about the two religions, courts should not assume exposure to different religions will be harmful *unless* there is evidence that harm is occurring.[48] There is room for mistake, and even abuse, in this approach, but it is preferable to any other.

I have not focused here directly on constitutional limits; but something like this approach to restrictions on parental activities should be viewed as required under the Free Exercise and Establishment clauses together, for reasons essentially the same as those I offered with respect to disputes over custody.

[45] *Zummo*, note 40 supra, at 1146–48. For an older case refusing to enforce a prior contract about the religious training of child, see *Stanton v. Stanton*, 100 S.E.2d 289 (Ga. 1957).

[46] A legal economist might inquire whether, if courts do not stand ready to enforce such agreements, the consequence will be that people will not enter desirable marriages, because they cannot get needed assurances. I think this scenario is fanciful. The vast majority of people entering marriage are convinced, despite dispiriting divorce statistics, that *their* marriage will survive. They rely on the good faith of their spouses. Further, given possibilities of evasion by a noncustodial parent, a person is not likely to rely heavily on civil law enforcement in any event. The legal fate of such agreements probably has little to do with whether they are reached and whether prospective marriages occur. The issue about enforcement is one of fairness, not of influencing patterns of marriage.

[47] Compare Jocelyn E. Strauber, "A Deal Is a Deal: Antenuptial Agreements Regarding the Religious Upbringing of Children Should Be Enforceable," 47 *Duke Law Journal* 971 (1998).

[48] If, on surface examination, a judge can see that two religions are so hostile to each other he cannot imagine a child comfortably being mainly reared in one and having substantial exposure to the other, perhaps that could be a basis to restrict. But the better rule is not to allow judges to rely solely on the doctrines and practices of the religions, however harshly incompatible they seem.

CHAPTER 23

Conclusion (and Introduction)

Is the free exercise of religion an important aspect of our constitutional order? Our examination of free exercise in a variety of contexts helps us to understand why answering this apparently straightforward question is not so simple.

In one sense, it is beyond doubt that the free exercise of religion is a vital constitutional principle. There it is in the First Amendment, along with freedom of speech and of the press; and anyone naming the basic liberties of our society would include religious liberty. That liberty is supported by many overlapping considerations, including the centrality of religion in the lives of many of our citizens, the widespread sense that one's religious obligations are more ultimate than those of the social order and should take priority if the two come into conflict, the desirability of avoiding conflicts between religious institutions and the government, the need to prevent the special distress people may feel if they cannot practice their religion, the value of respecting autonomous choice about religion, and the benefits to society of having religious groups operating as vital associations intermediate between individuals and government and creating a barrier to government domination of social life.[1] Although many of these considerations apply to some nonreligious activities and groups, together they constitute a strong basis to mark religion for special protection. This protection applies to individuals, but it also applies to religious groups in ways that are not always easily reducible to protections of the individuals in the groups.[2]

Doubters about the importance of protections of free exercise do not really contest the significance of freedom of religious practice. Rather they ask whether the Free Exercise Clause does anything that is not accomplished by other constitutional provisions. Given the Supreme Court's recent interpretations of that clause, this is a serious question. If the Free Exercise Clause has become redundant, providing no protection that is not to be gleaned from other constitutional provisions, one might fairly say that the Free Exercise Clause has ceased to function practically as a crucial component of our

---

[1] See generally Steven H. Shiffrin, "The Pluralistic Foundations of the Religion Clauses," 90 *Cornell Law Review* 9 (2004).

[2] See John H. Garvey, "Churches and the Free Exercise of Religion," 4 *Notre Dame Journal of Law, Ethics, and Public Policy* 567 (1990).

federal constitution. What our review of free exercise issues has shown us is that the significance of the federal Free Exercise Clause has been much diminished, but not eliminated by the Supreme Court's decision in *Employment Division v. Smith*,[3] and that the special protection of free exercise now rests substantially on federal and state statutes, on judicial interpretations of state constitutions, and, to a lesser extent, on judicial development of the common law.[4]

We have seen that the Free Exercise Clause does provide a core of undisputed protection. Neither the federal government nor states can interfere with religious belief or religious expression or with religious practice that causes no harm apart from its religious significance;[5] no government can single out a religion for adverse targeting as in the Santeria case;[6] no government can discriminate against one or some religions in relation to other religions. In considering this core of protection, we have noted some perplexing issues, such as what exactly constitutes "discrimination" and whether government may ever take religious speech into account in deciding to deny someone an official position.[7] We have also reviewed arguments that the courts should do more than they have to guard against unequal treatment, to regulate schemes that provide administrators discretion to reach arbitrary decisions, and to insist that limitations on religious activities be reasonable in terms of time and place.[8]

In respect to the importance of the Free Exercise Clause, the crucial question is whether that clause is necessary to protect any of this core, or whether the Free Speech and Free Press clauses, the Equal Protection Clause, and perhaps the Establishment Clause would provide the same coverage. I shall not undertake the detailed analysis that a full treatment of this question would require, but one illustration concerns the relation of religious speech to criminal encouragement. People are not permitted to urge each other to commit crimes, but some public arguments that particular crimes are justified are protected by the Free Speech Clause, as interpreted by the Supreme Court.[9] Some clerics of extreme Orthodox groups have suggested that assas-

---

[3] *Employment Division v. Smith*, 494 U.S. 872 (1990).

[4] The subject as to which common-law development may be most significant is the law of torts, including defamation and infliction of emotional distress, still left by legislatures mainly to judicial determination.

[5] That is, the government cannot forbid a religious practice that causes no nonreligious harm because it disapproves of the religious conceptions that lie behind the practice.

[6] *Church of the Lukumi Babalu Aye, Inc. v. City of Hialeah*, 508 U.S. 520 (1993).

[7] See chapter 3, supra.

[8] See, e.g., chapter 13, supra; Frederick Mark Gedicks, "Toward a Defensible Free Exercise Doctrine," 68 *George Washington Law Review* 925 (2000).

[9] See *Brandenburg v. Ohio*, 395 U.S. 444 (1969).

sination of Israel's prime minister might be justified on religious grounds,[10] and we have similar examples from other countries and other religions. Such comments, when made in the United States, clearly raise the difficulty of distinguishing constitutionally protected speech from impermissible criminal encouragement. I have not discussed that problem in this book because I have assumed that speakers who enjoy a position of religious leadership or who adopt a religious point of view have no special privilege in this regard via the Free Exercise Clause; rather, they fall into a broader category of speakers with ideological messages, and the Free Speech Clause is the basis for determining the degree of protection for all such speakers.[11] This is one example about which one might say that the Free Exercise Clause covers activity in a sense, but analysis of what is protected and what is unprotected takes place under another constitutional provision.

How much *Employment Division v. Smith* leaves to distinctive free exercise analysis is less than clear. That case ruled that in respect to the applications of ordinary laws, people with religious reasons to disobey have no special privilege under the Free Exercise Clause. But the precise coverage of *Smith* remains uncertain. The opinion talks of an odd hybrid category for which free exercise values may still be important; it explicitly treats the free exercise protections of unemployment compensation cases as still applicable. Together with the subsequent Santeria case, it suggests that other regulatory programs requiring individualized assessments under vague criteria—such as schemes of zoning regulation[12]—*may* not be subject to its sweeping rejection of free exercise rights. The range of this last category could prove to be narrow or broad.

Smith focuses on circumstances where a statute adopted by a legislature applies to people generally; to create a religious exemption, the Court says, would be to require courts to assess religious burdens and state interests—a task that is inappropriate if not impossible. On examination, we have seen that the very reasons *Smith* gives not to treat religion as special turn out to be reasons to treat religion as special in some other domains. If, in property disputes, for example, courts were to require religious groups to be faithful to their purposes in ways that would track what could be required of nonreligious groups, civil judges would have to examine the significance of shifts in church doctrine and practice.[13] If courts treated proposed religious up-

---

[10] See Ehud Sprinzak, *Brother Against Brother* 257 (New York: The Free Press, 1999); Mark C. Alexander, "Religiously Motivated Murder: The Rabin Assassination and Abortion Clinic Killings," 39 *Arizona Law Review* 1161, 1164 (1997).

[11] See Kent Greenawalt, *Speech, Crime, and the Uses of Language* (New York: Oxford University Press, 1989).

[12] See chapter 14, supra.

[13] See chapter 16, supra.

bringing like any other facts in custody disputes, they would have to evaluate the likely effects of competing religious approaches.[14] Assessing a claim that a religious superior has been negligent in supervision of a priest might demand discernment of respective religious responsibilities and evaluation of whether internal relationships are defensible.[15] Our survey of a variety of free exercise subjects, thus, has shown that *Smith* leaves more of free exercise rights intact than one might initially suppose. Nevertheless, despite its protestations that it is faithful to prior principles and will have little practical effect, it performs radical surgery on the scope of free exercise claims.

To a large degree, *Smith* shifts choices about whether to protect religious practices to legislatures and to state courts. In reflecting on those choices, we have paid close attention to categorization—may religious claims be treated more favorably than analogous nonreligious ones? I have assumed that such a categorization is sometimes, but not always, permissible. I have noted that the categorization question involves the Establishment Clause, but without exploring the establishment aspects in depth.

That is a topic for the companion volume. Under the Establishment Clause, as we shall see, the government is not supposed to support particular religions or, more controversially, religion in general. It should not endorse particular religious positions. *Permissible* accommodations to religious practice are typically seen as other than (relevant) support or endorsement. But some attempted accommodations cross over the line. They support and endorse religion and constitute forbidden establishments. The determination of when accommodations involve impermissible support and endorsement is one of the most complicated problems in the law of the religion clauses.[16] An aspect of the inquiry of when the constitutional line is crossed is the form of classification—a subject we touched on in respect to exemptions from performing medical procedures, such as sterilizations or abortions.[17] A classi-

---

[14] See chapter 22, supra.

[15] See chapter 17, supra.

[16] Mark Tushnet, "The Emerging Principle of Accommodation (Dubitante)," 76 *Georgetown Law Journal* 1691, 1702–3 (1988), suggests that failures to accommodate may be regarded as signals of indifference, but accommodations may be seen as messages of approval of religious excuses. Michael W. McConnell, "Accommodations of Religion," 1995 *Supreme Court Review* 1, 34–35, comments on the distinction between facilitating religious liberty and granting unwarranted benefits. Douglas Laycock, "Religious Liberty as Liberty," 7 *Journal of Contemporary Legal Issues* 313, 347 (1996), argues that exemptions may expand religious liberty, and thus fit his paradigm of substantive neutrality, if they do not encourage religious belief or practice. In "Quo Vadis: The Status and Prospects of 'Tests' under the Religion Clauses, 1995 *Supreme Court Review* 323, 385–88, I claim that in determining if accommodations to religion lift burdens or promote religions, courts can rely only up to a point on categorical analysis; some decisions will come down to matters of degree.

[17] See chapter 21, supra.

fication explicitly in terms of religion is much more likely to be seen as a support or endorsement of religion than a broader classification in terms of conscience (even if the vast majority of people with objections in conscience have religious objections).

We, thus, are not done with issues of classifications or with arguments that *any* classification explicitly favoring religious claims or religious groups violates the Establishment Clause. We have yet to examine more nuanced arguments about nonestablishment that affect this topic. The classification issues are one exemplar of our fundamental concerns about fairness and about which kinds of equality are most relevant.[18] The companion volume on nonestablishment adopts a different starting point, but a sensitive appraisal of fairness and equality in respect to religion remains at the heart of the matter.

[18] McConnell, note 16 supra, at 6, has remarked, "Virtually every controversy under the Religion Clauses can be understood as raising the special status of religion."

INDEX

abortion, 327, 335, 343, 348, 350, 406, 407n38, 413, 414n58, 415–20 passim. *See also* medical procedures

Adams, Arlin, 128–29, 138–39, 142n62, 144, 272n32, 404n29

Africa v. Commonwealth, 129, 138n52

African religions, 24

Aglikin v. Kovacheff, 282n56

Agrawal v. Briley, 220n67

Ahlstrom, Sydney E., 193n3

Allard v. Church of Scientology, 298n35

Alpine Christian Fellowship v. County Comm'rs of Pitkin County, 243n37

Alito, Samuel, 32n91, 85n64, 230n109

Alston, William, 140n56

Amar, Akhil, R., 23n47

Amar, Vikran David, 345n75

American Indian Religious Freedom Act of 1978 (AIRFA), 199–200

American Indians. *See* Native Americans

the Amish, and claims to withdraw children from school, 87–88, 90, 93–100, 208

Anderson, Jeffrey M., 354n101

animals: sacrifice of, 36–42; and special significance, 223–24

Ansonia Board of Educ. v. Philbrook, 344

Anthony, Dick, 312n93

Antioch Temple Inc. v. Parekh, 276n46

Araujo, Robert J., S. J., 384nn25 and 26

atheism, atheists, 18, 147–56, 185n4, 391; and agnosticism, 147–48, 151–52

Audi, Robert, 6n8

Australia, and legislation to protect sacred sites of Aborigines, 193n4

Ayon v. Gourley, 323n128

Baldwin, Monica, 308n77

Balkin, J. M., 362n11

bankruptcy, 224–28

Barry, Brian, 52n18, 87nn4 and 7, 88nn10 and 12, 91n31, 94n42, 95

Basil, Robert J., 315

Battin, Margaret, 255n33

Bear Lodge Multiple Use Ass'n v. Babbitt, 200n33

Bear v. Reformed Mennonite Church, 293–95

Beiner, Theresa M., 353n96

In re Belcher, 226n91

Bennett, Roger, 275n44

Bennison v. Sharp, 286n68

Bentham, Jeremy, 238, 247

Berg, Thomas C., 216n51, 228n97, 353n96, 367n24, 374–75

Berman v. United States, 51

Bible, the, 27, 40, 175

Bill of Rights, 50. *See also* First Amendment

Bishop and Diocese v. Mote, 285

Black, Hugo, 36, 62, 66, 126, 190n21

Black Hawk v. Pennsylvania, 223n83

Blackmun, Harry, 38, 76, 78n47, 162n20, 163n24, 196n13, 387n41

Blalock v. Metal Trades Inc., 335n38

Bob Jones University v. United States, 393n65

Bohner, Robert, 286n68

Boggs, Danny Julian, 106, 107n92

Bonjour v. Bonjour, 422n5

Boozang, Kathleen M., 413n56, 415n63, 417n73, 420n76

Borkowski v. Valley Cent. School Dist., 346n77

born again Christians. See evangelical Christians; Fundamentalism, Fundamentalists

Bouldin v. Alexander, 270n29

Bowen v. Roy, 195–97, 212

Boy Scouts of America v. Dale, 389

boycotting, by religious groups of outsiders, 297–98

Bradeska v. Antion, 319n116

Brady, Joel, 200n33

Brandenberg v. Ohio, 440n9

Braunfeld v. Brown, 188–91; as compared with *Sherbert v. Verner*, 190–91

Brennan, William, 30, 43–44, 45n43, 46–47, 163, 178, 180n36, 181, 190, 197–200, 203, 266n18, 270, 383n23, 387–88, 389n49

Brody, Kathleen A., 383n22

Brown v. Polk County, 354